Data Protection

Data Protection
Ensuring Data Availability

Preston de Guise

CRC Press
Taylor & Francis Group
Boca Raton London New York

CRC Press is an imprint of the
Taylor & Francis Group, an **informa** business

AN AUERBACH BOOK

[second] edition published [2020]
by CRC Press
6000 Broken Sound Parkway NW, Suite 300, Boca Raton, FL 33487-2742

and by CRC Press
2 Park Square, Milton Park, Abingdon, Oxon, OX14 4RN

© 2020 Taylor & Francis Group, LLC

CRC Press is an imprint of Taylor & Francis Group, LLC

ISBN: 978-0-367-47410-2 (hbk)
ISBN: 978-0-367-25677-7 (pbk)
ISBN: 978-0-367-46349-6 (ebk)

Typeset in Garamond
by Deanta Global Publishing Services, Chennai, India

For my husband, Daz, my father, Peter, and my mother, Lynne

Contents

Preface

We live in an information age. There has quite simply never before been so much information available to individuals at the touch of a button.

Almost everything about our lives has been digitized. Our photo albums are stored in the cloud. Bank accounts are just rows in a database. Mortgages are electronic, payslips are PDFs, and letters to grandma have been replaced by live video calls. Even a kilogram—a fundamental unit of measurement—is no longer based on a real, reference object, but determined by specific information.

Data, the building block of information, has become an essential part of our lives, both personally and professionally. Data protection has never been more important.

This expanded and revised edition of *Data Protection* goes beyond the traditional topics including deduplication, continuous availability, snapshots, replication, backup, and recovery, and explores additional considerations: legal, privacy, and ethical. A new model is presented for understanding and planning the various aspects of data protection—essential to developing holistic strategies.

Increased focus on cloud addresses the growing adoption of software and function as a service, and how to effectively plan over the lifespan of a workload: what the best mix of traditional and cloud native data protection services might be. Virtualization continues to present new challenges to data protection, and the impact of containerization is examined.

"The edge" may nowadays refer to *Internet of Things* (IoT), but within data protection there are several topics to consider at the edge: remote office, end user compute, and, of course, IoT itself. All of these present unique issues compared to datacenter-based services.

Longer-term issues are examined, in addition to how automation, machine learning, and other adaptive processes are impacting the data protection landscape, and what considerations are required when using data protection services for compliance retention.

Chapters have also been updated to include self-reflection questions to encourage the reader to consider and develop a more nuanced understanding of key discussion points throughout the book.

Acknowledgments

Every book is an amalgam of ideas and feedback, and that's before you start to consider all the long-term background learning that goes into the foundation concepts. There's also the inevitable lost time with friends and family that comes from investing so much of yourself into a long-term creative project. So inevitably there's a host of people who specifically need to be called out in gratitude and thanks for their help in bringing this book to completion.

First and foremost, I have to thank my husband, Daz Woolley, for always being there for me—not just when working on the book, but throughout my career. He's been my continuously available backup, and every other pun you can think of for data protection, for decades.

My parents put me on an IT path when I was relatively young, and actively encouraged me in my interests as I was growing up, culminating in funding university for me, letting me concentrate on my study throughout my time there. Lynne and Peter, I can never repay what you did for me all those years ago.

I remain grateful to the team at Taylor & Francis, especially John Wyzalek, for the assistance in getting this book completed.

Thanks of course go to those who were able to assist me during the review process— Ben Adamson, Peter Marelas, and Mike van der Steen. (Of course, it goes without saying that I'm still grateful for the feedback I received during the production of the first edition of the book: Berin Smithson, Brendan Sandes, Conrad Macina, Danny Elmarji, Deborah van Petegem, Geordie Korper, German Garcia, Jerry Vochteloo, Jim Ruskowsky, Michael Arnold, Michael Levit, Mike van der Steen, Nicolas Groh, Pawel Wozniak, Peta Olson, Peter Hill-Cottingham, Rajesh Goda, Russell Brown, Steve de Bode, Tony Leung, Vedad Sapcanin, and Warren PowerJones.)

I am lucky enough to work every day with spiritual brothers and sisters: people who share a passion for data protection that is so much more than just a job. That includes being guided by people in the data protection industry who've likewise spent their careers absolutely passionate about, and dedicated to successful outcomes—of these, P.K. Gupta springs most to mind.

There's another group of people who need to be called out in thanks: my customers. Over the years I've been graced with a plethora of customers from the smallest to the largest, in pretty much every industry vertical, and it's been their trust in my work and my recommendations, and their collaboration with me on data protection projects, that's given me the depth *and* breadth of experience, both technical and business, that served as the foundations of this work. Not all journeys have been smooth sailing, but every journey has been instructional and formative.

Finally, of course, I have to thank you, the reader, for having the interest in and desire to learn more about data protection: for being willing to invest your time to read what I have to say on the topic. I truly hope that if you're not actually already passionate about data protection, I'll have imparted some of my passion to you by the time you finish this updated and expanded book.

Chapter 1

Introduction

In 1799, French forces discovered the Rosetta Stone. It contained on a single piece of stone the same decree, written in ancient Egyptian hieroglyphics, Demotic, and Ancient Greek. Until the discovery of the Rosetta Stone, ancient Egyptian hieroglyphics had been a mystery. Meanings had been guessed and argued for decades, but ultimately they were just guesses. The Rosetta Stone allowed scholars to build an accurate translation mechanism by offering comparative text in other known languages. In doing so, they opened up for us a realm of understanding that might otherwise have been forever lost.

Human history is replete with examples of what happens when data is *not* adequately protected. Speculation abounds as to what information was lost with the destruction of the Library of Alexandria (pegged as happening during one of several events between AD 48 and AD 642), yet it remains indisputable that a significant amount of knowledge was, indeed, lost.

More than ever before, we are now at a crossroads in human information history: we have the capability of ensuring information is preserved, generation-to-generation, without loss.

This is data protection.

All the storage in the world will not help ensure continuity of information if adequate steps are not taken to preserve it. In a perfect world, no one would ever need Redundant Array of Independent Disks (RAID) protection, no one would ever need to recover files, and no one would need to protect against loss of a site. It is not a perfect world: mechanical failures happen, as does corruption, accidental deletion, site failures, and malicious acts. The simplest part of preserving information is to store it—the more complex task is to *protect* it.

When examined in isolation, those who work in data protection preserve information for banks, for airlines, for search engines, for telecommunications companies, for small businesses, and even for individual people, but at a collective level, data protection is the pursuit of *information preservation*.

1.1 The Value of Data

In 2017, *The Economist* declared:

> The world's most valuable resource is no longer oil, but data*

The value of data continues to increase. Traditional businesses that have operated for decades, if not centuries, have found themselves increasingly *disrupted* by newly emerging competitors who have focused on one key thing: harnessing data to greater effect. For example, hotel chains have found themselves competing with Airbnb, which is in itself little more than a data merchant: its service allows people to rent out rooms or entire houses to people who are looking for short-term accommodation. People might seek Airbnb for higher quality yet cheaper options than hotel rooms because they are more conveniently located, or they allow for a higher seeming degree of independence and flexibility than a regular hotel. The real value though is in the data: allowing people looking for accommodation to find people offering it.

---

* www.economist.com/leaders/2017/05/06/the-worlds-most-valuabl e-resource-is-no-longer-oil-but-data

Australia's largest airline, Qantas, achieves data value not only in standard flight and passenger details, but also in its frequent flyer program:

> Credit Suisse Group estimates that business is worth almost $4 billion, which is more than the Australian flag-carrier's international business and double some valuations of the loyalty unit when its sale was contemplated in 2008.[*]

Information preservation of course is not just some ephemeral goal based on the noble act of protecting data for future generations. There are immediate, tangible business benefits too. The "Data Protection Index," conducted periodically by Vanson Bourne on behalf of Dell EMC (formed after the acquisition of EMC by Dell in October 2015) has produced useful information about the impact of data loss to businesses.

The 2014 survey, polling 3,300 IT decision makers across 24 countries, found the average surveyed business had lost 2.33 TB of data, at a cost of US$1.02 million, over the prior 12 months—yet only 64% of respondents claimed that data protection was critical to the success of their organization.[†]

The 2016 version of the survey, covering 2,200 IT decision makers in 18 countries, found an average of 2.36 TB data loss per respondent over the prior 12 months, with a decrease in cost to US$900,000. However, only 18% of the surveyed companies were confident in the changing digital landscape that they had a data protection solution that would meet future as well as existing business challenges.[‡]

The 2018 survey, again covering 2,200 IT decision makers in 18 countries, found the average data loss size had dropped to 2.13 TB, but the average cost of data loss had increased to US$995,613. Businesses were increasingly likely (81%) to take data protection more seriously for more valuable data. The potential value of data was seen by 92% of businesses, with almost 40% investing in tools that would allow them to monetize data for the business.

Data is business—big business. Consider hyperscalers, such as AWS[§] and Azure. While neither provides breakdowns of their revenue streams based on compute, networking, storage, and so on, even a casual analysis of their pricing models reveals serious money to be made in their easily consumable storage, regardless of whether that's cheap object storage, or more expensive block storage servicing IaaS environments. One might even suggest an operating model in many instances of "Come for the compute, stay for the storage" for many cloud service providers.

It is in another area of cloud that we perhaps see our best possible example of the value of data to businesses: Software as a Service (SaaS). These models are predicated on the subscription service providing the entire stack, from storage and network all the way up to the actual application, with the individual subscriber effectively only supplying the data and the users. One of the drives towards SaaS is the notion that certain business functions just don't make sense being run in-house. For example, in its first fiscal quarter 2019 results, Microsoft noted that Office 365 had grown to 155 million monthly active users, yet consumer subscribers contribute only 32.5 million of that number; well over 120 million users were in fact from business.[¶] Businesses are increasingly turning to Office 365 as a means of providing comprehensive email services to their users without the headache of managing increasingly complex Microsoft Exchange environments on-premises. The value is the data and how it is used, not the technical nous required to install, configure, and maintain an email service. As businesses seek to strip out traditional IT infrastructure spend in order to enable more modern services, consolidation into SaaS is practically inevitable for some functions.

Salesforce, which defines itself as the world's number one customer relationship management (CRM) platform, is another SaaS provider that helps define the value of data to businesses: it exists as a platform to provide customer and sales data for organizations.

> Salesforce surpassed $10 billion in annual revenue in fiscal year 2018, and we reached this milestone faster than any other enterprise software company in history … In the past year, Salesforce powered nearly 2 trillion business-to-business (B2B) and business-to-consumer (B2C) transactions for our more than 150,000 customers. Our artificial intelligence technology, Salesforce Einstein, now generates more than 1 billion predictions a day.[**]

---

[*] Qantas frequent flyer program turning into airline's biggest money spinner, Angus Whitley, 12 May 2017, *Sydney Morning Herald*, www.smh.com.au/business/companies/qantas-frequent-flyer-prog ram-turning-into-airlines-biggest-money-spinner-20170512-gw3 4wq.html

[†] www.emc.com/about/news/press/2014/20141202-01.htm

[‡] www.emc.com/collateral/presentation/emc-dpi-key-findings-global. pdf

[§] Amazon Web Services.

[¶] Office 365 soars to 155 million active users, Tony Redmond, 25 October 2018, Petri, www.petri.com/office-365-soars-155-milli on-active-users

[**] Salesforce Fiscal Year 2018 Annual General Report, https://s1.q4cd n.com/454432842/files/doc_financials/2018/Salesforce-FY18-An nual-Report.pdf

The six largest companies in the world in 2018 in order of market value were Apple, Amazon, Alphabet, Microsoft, Facebook, and Alibaba:* all these companies in some form have a relentless focus on data, regardless of what other lines of business they might engage in. Certainly, they all enable consumers and businesses alike to get easier access to their data and derive value from it.

1.2 The Lay of the Land

Backup is dead.

If it seems odd to the reader of a book titled *Data Protection* that one of the earliest statements of the book is *Backup is dead*, imagine how much more surreal it is to write it as a consultant who has worked with backup technology almost exclusively for over 20 years.

Yet, this is the fundamental truth about data protection: backup is dead.

Or rather, *backup and recovery*, as a stand-alone topic, no longer has relevance in IT. As a stand-alone topic, it's been killed off by seemingly exponential growth in storage and data, by *the cloud*, and by virtualization. Each one of these alone represents a substantial assault on backup and recovery as a dedicated topic, but combined, it's insurmountable.

Originally, backup and recovery systems were a function of system administrators. Over time, those systems evolved and became a specific job function. A company could potentially have hundreds of system administrators spread across a large number of geographic locations, but it might have backup services centralized and controlled by a small number of administrators operating out of a single location.

By itself backup and recovery does not offer sufficient scope in *data protection* for the needs of the modern business. Regardless of whether those backups are executed as daily fulls, weekly fulls with daily incrementals, grandfather–father–son mixes of fulls, differentials and incrementals, or even incrementals forever and synthetic fulls, growing data and shrinking windows in service-level agreements have fundamentally altered the way organizations consider and plan data recoverability.

It used to be that saying *data protection* to someone meant *backup and recovery*. Such is the state of the business IT environment now that data protection is a considerably broader topic.

1.3 What Are You Doing Here?

You've been looking forward to your holiday for months. You spent a year saving for it, then finally purchased the round-the-world ticket, organized the accommodation, booked dozens of hotels in the United States, the United Kingdom, France, China, Japan, and Australia. You've spent seemingly countless evenings working out things to do in each city you'll be visiting and budgeting how much you can spend in each country.

Then, when you turn up at the airport, you're told that the airline doesn't have your booking. You've got a printout of your ticket, *showing* your flight details, but those seats have been allocated to someone else who has already checked in: the airline lost your data and rebooked your seat.

Of course, that doesn't happen—businesses have long known that they have to take steps to ensure the recoverability of data. Losing airline bookings, forgetting salary payments, corrupting driver's license details—none of these are acceptable. Short of the provision of the service itself, nothing is more important in IT than data protection.

Conventional backup techniques have been around for decades. The *towers of Hanoi* backup regime may no longer be directly relevant, but *full*, *incremental*, and *differential* levels remain the staple of the backup and recovery world.

As the song says, though, *the times, they are a changin'*. New approaches to service provisioning, higher volumes of data than we've ever seen before, and the commoditization of IT have demonstrated *peak scaling* in conventional techniques.

Vendors and mega IT companies—especially those at the apex of social media—are furiously rewriting the definition of a *datacenter*. Companies now have a plethora of options for their data—in-house conventional, in-house (private) cloud, hybrid cloud, colocation centers, or public cloud. That data may be substantially beyond the capabilities of conventional tools to analyze as well, regardless of where it's hosted.

With all of these options, and considering the snowball effect of virtualization in the midrange space, the conventional approaches to backup and recovery no longer economically scale to meet all options—and even when they do, the next challenge is whether or not they're even compatible with *where* your data is hosted.†

This book doesn't pretend to have all the answers—that's not possible when the questions are still being written and revised sometimes seemingly on a daily basis. Ten years ago, when midrange virtualization was still a relatively young

---

* The 100 largest companies in the world by market value in 2018, Statistica, www.statista.com/statistics/263264/top-companies-i n-the-world-by-market-value/

---

† While we're on the topic of *midrange*, it's these systems with their cheap compute and storage costs that have driven so much of the data explosion. Long gone are the days when "serious" applications and data were reserved for mainframes or supercomputers.

topic, and *cloud* was something that rained on you, such an assumption might have been made, but no more.

It's often the case that real knowledge comes not from knowing the answer to every question, but from knowing which questions you *don't* know the answer to.

1.4 What's Changed in the Datacenter?

When I first started working in backup, in 1996, the local datacenter of the company I worked for had:

- A collection of Unix hosts (primarily Solaris, HPUX, and Tru64, but with a smattering of AT&T Unix systems as well)
- A growing number of Windows NT4 servers
- A couple of Tandem FT servers
- An IBM mainframe
- Several VMS clusters
- Novell NetWare servers

In addition to that, there was the standard collection of tape drives, network switches and hubs, and a few other bits and pieces. There were even one or two systems still using reel-to-reel tapes, and someone would carry them out of the datacenter each morning, threaded onto arms like some fantastical set of technological bracelets.

Storage was all either internal or Direct Attach Storage (DAS). There were some storage options just starting to appear in the datacenter that, when coupled with Veritas Volume Manager™ (VxVM), would allow volumes to be migrated from one host to another, so long as both hosts were plugged into the same storage. *That* was cutting-edge technology.

In 1999, VMware Workstation appeared, allowing Unix system administrators to switch to a Linux desktop and still access Windows, rather than running highly problematic emulation software. VMware server products (and in particular, VMware ESX server, released in 2001), served as a significant pivot point in the midrange systems marketplace—indeed, one might arguably say that it led to the fundamental alteration of approaches to IT.

The modern datacenter looks very different. It may not be on-site, and it may not be owned by the business using it. Colocation ("colo") facilities offer physical hosting services; cloud providers offer service or platform provisioning where the *equipment* that the company runs business critical applications on may not even belong to the company. For some businesses, the on-premises server room for a business may now be tiny compared to what it was 10 years ago, acting as a mere tip of the iceberg for a much larger presence in a shared datacenter or public cloud facility. For other businesses, particularly those centered around the bourgeoning

mobile and cloud platform, there may be *no* datacenter, with all of their resources provided by a cloud service provider. Yet, public cloud is not a fait accompli; many businesses adopting a cloud model for agility are keeping their cloud private, and their datacenters are growing as they add petabytes—or even in some cases, *exabytes* of data. We are even seeing businesses that previously went into the cloud adjusting their processes and re-evaluating which workloads belong back on-premises.

1.5 What Is Data Protection?

Like so many terms in information technology, *data protection* has become significantly overloaded, and therefore it can mean very different things to different people. There are three essential activities that refer to themselves as *data protection*; while they all overlap in terms of scope and function, each operates as a reasonably self-contained field with its own specialists and domain nomenclature. The three activities are:

- Data protection as a *storage* and *recovery* activity
- Data protection as a *security* activity
- Data protection as a *privacy* activity

1.5.1 Data Protection as a Security Activity

In some senses, data protection as a security activity can almost be entirely defined as being about *access control*. Who has access to data within an environment? Of course, in both the architectural planning and practical implementation, *access control* is significantly more complex, and covers a plethora of activities including, but by no means limited to:

- *Network access control*: Who can gain access to the network, and from where:
  - Originally, network access control was almost entirely devoted to firewalls at the edge, establishing a perimeter around the business's network to prevent unauthorized electronic intruders external to the company
  - Over time, with increased threat recognition and stronger attention to more granular access, network access control has become an internal function as well—firewalls can exist in many parts of a business network, and micro-segmentation focuses on limiting not only users, but systems in what they can communicate with, and how.
- *User access control*:
  - Can Pam from engineering log onto the workgroup drive for the finance team? Can Adam from finance log onto the workgroup drive for the board of directors?

– Do user access options change as people move to different roles within the same workgroup? Do user access options change as people move to different roles within the company as a whole? Do user access options change depending on whether someone is logged onto the corporate network, or accessing externally (e.g., via a VPN, or even without a VPN)?
– To what extent can users automatically be assigned access rights to data based on their position in the corporate hierarchy? (As opposed to a horde of IT administration staff—e.g., database administrators, system administrators, storage administrators, and so on, manually receiving ticketed requests to *Give Alice access to the HR database*.)

■ *Data access control*: Just because someone has access to data does not mean they have full control over that data:

– In the simplest, this is about differentiating between *read, write, create*, and *delete* security. Bob at reception might have *read*-access to the CEO's calendar, but does this mean Bob can *change* the CEO's calendar? Aleks may be a storage administrator, but just because he *can* circumvent security to view the privileged report about financial issues presented to the CEO does not mean he is *allowed* to.
– Additionally, this covers what people can do with data beyond their own personal access to it. What are they allowed to send out of the company, acting as an agent of the company? Who are they allowed to send that to? Can Nate, for instance, send a spreadsheet containing the names, phone numbers, and email addresses of every customer his division works with to a friend at a competing company (i.e., what can be done to prevent data leakage or exfiltration)?

In each case from a security perspective, there are functions that can be performed to enable or prohibit access, and there will be extensive logging and monitoring that is also required. In fact, in some cases, security issues will be detected not by a user attempting to do something that the system blocks them from, but more from a constantly evolving understanding of what represents normal activity, thereby allowing the identification of abnormal activity. For instance:

■ Does Sam in San Jose usually log on at 3am via a VPN originating out of Chechnya?
■ On any normal day, the average salesperson in the company accesses approximately 0.05% of the CRM. Why has Jo accessed 6% of it in under an hour?
■ On the first of the month, the company has outgoing web traffic in the order of approximately 100 MB/s;

any other day of the month it's usually less than 75 MB/s. So why, in the middle of the month, has outgoing web traffic for the company spiked to 400 MB/s?

In each of these scenarios, there may be a perfectly valid explanation: Sam might be using a VPN originating out of Chechnya because he's on holiday and received an email asking him to review something that he felt compelled to look at—and 3am San Jose time is mid-afternoon in Grozny, Chechnya. Jo might have accessed 6% of the CRM database in under an hour because she's testing a new customer profiling tool her sales team has been developing—and outgoing web traffic may spike in the middle of the month because the marketing team is pushing out a major new multimedia initiative.

Or not. It could be that at 3am, Sam is sound asleep in San Jose but someone has bought a block of passwords off the dark web and it so happened that Sam used the same password and username that he used for work as he did for an online dating site. Jo might be planning to leave the company and is planning on taking a raft of confidential data with her. And it could be that the marketing department is away on a retreat and that 400 MB/s transfer is a nation-state hacker exfiltrating a significant portion of the company's intellectual property as part of a plan to enable that country to dominate the industry.

While there is a lot in security that can be set with hard and fast policies, data protection as a security function is increasingly becoming one based on pattern analysis of current activities compared to both historical trends and external data sources. Such is the value in understanding current patterns of activity that some companies may even outsource part of their security monitoring to third-party specialists who aggregate observed trends across their entire customer base in order to deliver greater protection against unknown hostile behavior.

Failures in data security can increasingly lead to serious impacts for businesses, particularly when they result in privacy breaches. The General Data Protection Regulation (GDPR) allows for significant fines to be levied against companies who fail in their regulated obligations towards consumer data privacy, and in May 2019, Moody's, an American credit rating agency, downgraded Equifax's credit rating outlook over the severity of its 2017 cyber-security breach:

> Moody's cited Equifax's recent $690 million first-quarter charge for the breach as contributing to the downgrade. The expense represents the company's estimate for settling ongoing class action cases, as well as potential federal and state regulatory fines.[*]

---

[*] Equifax just became the first company to have its outlook downgraded for a cyber attack, Kate Fazzini, 22 May 2019, *CNBC*, www.cnbc.com/2019/05/22/moodys-downgrades-equifax-outlook-to-negative-cites-cybersecurity.html

1.5.2 Data Protection as a Privacy Activity

Our society is evolving into one where data, and usable insights from that data, have the potential to deliver significant economic benefit. Large social media and web-search companies can make significant profits by using the often sensitive data they have on individuals to sell highly targeted advertising, putting emphasis on the adage, "if you're not paying for it, you're the product." Businesses overall are looking to leverage the data they have on customers to construct campaigns and sales offers that are *too good to resist*. This may not always yield the results that a company or its customers expect.

An example of this was documented in "How Companies Learn Your Secrets" (Charles Duhigg, 16 February 2012, *New York Times*), which covers an incident based on Target's data processing. Target in the United States started using data analysis to assemble value-add offers to customers. This included analyzing the sorts of products that customers purchased when they were expecting a child—particular skincare lotions, vitamin supplements, and items of specific utility. Using this information Target could predict with a reasonable degree of accuracy if a shopper might be pregnant, and send out coupons for other pregnancy-related products:

About a year after … a man walked into a Target outside Minneapolis and demanded to see the manager. He was clutching coupons that had been sent to his daughter, and he was angry, according to an employee who participated in the conversation.

"My daughter got this in the mail!" he said. "She's still in high school, and you're sending her coupons for baby clothes and cribs? Are you trying to encourage her to get pregnant?"

The manager didn't have any idea what the man was talking about. He looked at the mailer. Sure enough, it was addressed to the man's daughter and contained advertisements for maternity clothing, nursery furniture and pictures of smiling infants. The manager apologized and then called a few days later to apologize again.[*]

The above example highlights not only the ethical challenge facing data analytics today, but also a broad swathe of privacy issues as well. While governments and businesses have been collecting data about citizens and customers for

decades—centuries, in some cases—objections to intrusive use of gathered data are only now gaining traction.

The principal limitation of the reliance on paper was also its greatest strength in terms of popular acceptability. Record linkage was a cumbersome process. Basic demographic data was readily obtained from the General Register Office, but otherwise the national insurance system, in common with most official database of the era, was sufficient unto itself.[†]

The transition to electronic records during the development of the digital age has left many people increasingly uneasy about the use of records relating to themselves and their families. As data processing speed increases and more sophisticated approaches are developed to cross-reference data, building increasingly accurate models, we have seen many companies and governments explore new ways to make use of the data, without necessarily considering legal or ethical ramifications.

By 1980, half the members of the OECD had already passed or formulated data protection laws. In the context of the digital revolution, the rhetoric of privacy threatened to collide with the project of deregulation and open markets.[‡]

One might suggest that modern approaches to data monetization are inherently at odds with established beliefs regarding privacy.

While the term "data protection" has been used to represent privacy in the past, it has been more recently cemented as a definite umbrella term for privacy by the European GDPR laws. Data protection as a privacy function is focused on understanding and enforcing boundaries between data that companies collect and what can be done with that data, from the perspective of the individual from whom the data has been collected.

In addition to earlier considerations, modern data privacy regulations such as GDPR focuses on taking control of personal data out of the hands of businesses and returning it back to the individual, such as:

■ Allowing the individual to assert ownership/control over the use or retention of the data that has been collected about him or her

---

[*] How companies learn your secrets, Charles Duhigg, 16 February 2012, *New York Times*, www.nytimes.com/2012/02/19/magazine/shopping-habits.html

[†] *Privacy: A Short History*, David Vincent, Polity Books, 978-0-7456-711-30 (2016).
[‡] Ibid.

- Allowing the individual to query and be informed *what* data a business holds about him or her
- In the case of systems such as GDPR, giving the individual the *right to be forgotten*—that is, request that data pertaining to them is removed

The above functions represent an evolutionary change from what has traditionally been seen as data privacy within most businesses, that is:

- *Relevance*:
  - This relates to reducing the scope of retained data gathered and retained to only those essential details required by the company
  - Privacy functions around relevance can be reduced to a simple question for the business: *do you need this data at all?*
  - If for instance, you are completing a survey as to which backup product you use, is there any relevance to being asked your gender?
- *Anonymization of data*:
  - Does data need to be linked back to the individuals it comes from, or can be it scrubbed of all identifiable information?
  - The goal in anonymization is to turn data into content that can safely be used without the chance of identifying individuals from whom the data originated?
  - For example, a human rights group might wish to determine whether LGBTIQ individuals are paid more, the same, or less than heterosexual, cis-gendered colleagues. They may ask questions in an online survey relating to gender, sexual orientation, job title, industry vertical, and salary. To ensure anonymization, the IP address of the respondent is not noted, and the respondents are not asked for their name, contact details, etc.
  - The above example reflects anonymization at the point of gathering the data, but other processes may require data that is not anonymized to be gathered initially, for a specific purpose. The company may wish to aggregate this data into a larger data pool when the specific function has been completed, but to do so it removes any details that could be used to link an individual back to a record.
- *Understanding and tracking personally identifiable information (PII)*:
  - PII is any specific piece of data that can be used to identify an individual. The US Government Accountability Office defines PII as "(1) any information about an individual … that can be used to distinguish or trace an individual's identity, such as name, Social Security Number, date and place of birth, mother's maiden name, or biometric records; and (2) any information that is linked or linkable to an individual, such as medical, educational, financial, and employment information."*
  - There are effectively two focuses when it comes to PII—determining and limiting when it is collected in the first place, and secondly, once collected, applying a more stringent security and access profile to that information to limit the risk of a privacy or security breach that may impact those people for whom the data is held.
- *Understanding and tracking sensitive personal information (SPI)*:
  - SPI is often seen as a subset of PII, but usually engenders further security/privacy considerations
  - For instance, personal also includes specific details that can be used to cause issues for individuals—bank account numbers, social security numbers (USA), passport numbers, and so on. These may be used to either defraud or conduct identify theft against the individual, for instance
  - However, other examples of SPI can include things such as political affiliation, religious beliefs, and sexual orientation.

Privacy as a data protection function will continue to gain focus in the coming decades. Never has it been so easy for governments and businesses alike to accumulate data on individuals, and even at a time when governments are starting to act on privacy concerns when it comes to *business access* to data, many continue to seek ways to increase their gathering and analysis capability. While many people often assume a right to privacy, in practice the levels of privacy permitted to citizens (and therefore, privacy of their data) vary from country to country, and even within countries, from jurisdiction to jurisdiction. Even in countries such as the Netherlands, where privacy is enshrined in the constitution,† allowances are of course made for situations where the government may require data gathering to take place.

1.5.3 Data Protection as a Storage/Recovery Activity

Privacy and security are both relevant and important aspects of the umbrella term, "data protection," but the focus of this book will largely be about the third use of the term: the various

---

* Alternatives exist for enhancing protection of personally identifiable information, GAO Report GAO-08-536, May 2008, https://www.gao.gov/new.items/d08536.pdf
† Online Privacy Law: Netherlands, www.loc.gov/law/help/online-privacy-law/2012/netherlands.php

functions that surround ensuring that data we write to storage can be reliably retrieved, even in the event of a failure.

Even this type of data protection can mean many things to many different people. For instance, just within this field if you ask an IT worker "What is data protection?", the answer will vary substantially:

- "Backup," says a junior backup administrator
- "Recoverable backups," says a seasoned backup administrator
- "RAID," says a junior storage administrator
- "Replication and snapshots," says a seasoned storage administrator
- "Clustering," says a system administrator
- "Automated data replication," says a database administrator

About the only guarantee on this topic is that every answer will be correct, yet every answer will be *incomplete*. The reason for this is simple: data protection is *not* an IT function—it's a business function. IT may enact specific functional aspects of data protection, but the core decisions and processes should come as a result of close, strategic alignment between IT and the business.

For the purposes of this book:

> Data protection is the mix of proactive and reactive planning, technology, and activities that allow for data continuity.

This is shown in Figure 1.1.

The proactive and reactive technologies are in themselves mostly straightforward:

- *Proactive*: Attempting to avoid data loss:
  - RAID (and other forms of low-level fault tolerance)
  - Continuous availability
  - Replication
  - Snapshot
  - Backup
- *Reactive*: Responding to data loss, or situations that may lead to data loss:
  - Restoration and recovery
  - Rebuilding and reconstruction
  - Replication

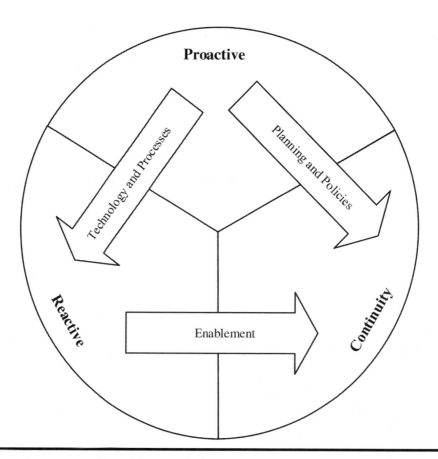

Figure 1.1   Data protection as an enabler of data continuity.

Yet, none of these components can be reliably deployed without appropriate planning and policies. *Doing* is easy. Doing it *right* is another matter. As we will see in later chapters, doing it *right* includes consideration for a variety of functions including capacity planning/management, testing (including automated testing), documentation and processes, just to name a few.

1.6 Key Challenges

1.6.1 *The Rise of Unstructured Data*

If you can recall data protection conversations businesses were having a decade or more ago, the key focus was more often than not the mission-critical database systems requiring protection. While they present their own management and data protection challenges, databases were generally *easy* data protection sources because they represented that holy grail of data protection: structured data. Structured data keeps data all in one place, collated and condensed into predictable locations and stored in such a way as to allow for high-speed streaming or transfer of it.

Databases and the other various forms of structured data still exist within the business, but unstructured data—file data, sensors, streams, and other disorganized information—has been growing rapidly for some time and shows no sign of slowing down. Unstructured data by its very nature is less predictable, less organized, less *known*, and as such more difficult to protect. An IDC whitepaper predicts the "digital universe":

> …is doubling in size every two years, and by 2020 the digital universe – the data we create and copy annually – will reach 44 zettabytes, or 44 trillion gigabytes.[*]

IDC acknowledged much of the "digital universe" they were describing would be transient:

> Most of the digital universe is transient – unsaved Netflix or Hulu movie streams, or Xbox One gamer interactions, temporary routing information in networks, sensor signals discarded when no alarms go off, etc.[†]

This data transience is a boon for data storage since data storage itself is growing at a slower rate than the digital universe. IDC added in their report that the worldwide storage capacity of 2013 could hold only 33% of the digital universe, and that by 2020 that would have shrunk to less than 15%, despite the growth in storage capacity. In updated reporting, IDC has predicted that the digital universe will be 175 zettabytes by 2025.[‡]

Estimates for the percentage of unstructured versus structured data (both now and in the future) vary from the very conservative 50% unstructured through to the highly worrying 80% or more.

Unstructured data has been making its mark in the traditional datacenter for some time and has led to the concept of *scale-out* network attached storage (NAS). NAS has been traditionally expanded by adding shelves or trays of disks until an array is at its maximum size, then deploying a new NAS to accommodate new systems. This worked for multi-terabyte storage, but as data growth continued this created excessive management and data migration headaches—and of course the staffing cost associated with managing so many storage arrays continued to balloon. Scale-out NAS works on the principle of an ever-increasing number of nodes (physical storage appliances) attached to a single addressable storage system, with the filesystem(s) presented dynamically expanding (scaling out) as nodes are added. This allows for a company to meet unstructured data growth without seeing its storage administrator staffing costs skyrocket. Scale-out NAS allows businesses to have multiple *petabytes* of storage under the control of a single administrator.

Of course, scale-out NAS isn't the only solution to unstructured data, but it helps to demonstrate how businesses are already adapting their data storage solutions (and vendors, their offerings) to deal with this onslaught of potentially disorganized data.

1.6.2 *Big Data*

Big data is often characterized by the "four Vs": volume, variety, velocity, and veracity where

- *Volume* refers to the amount of data being dealt with.
- *Velocity* refers to the speed at which data is coming in (or going past).
- *Variety* refers to the seemingly inexhaustible number of forms data may now take.
- *Veracity* refers to the measure of reliability (i.e., accuracy) of the data.

---

[*] Vernon Turner, David Reinsel, John F. Gantz, Stephen Minton, The digital universe of opportunities: Rich data and the increasing value of the internet of things, IDC, April 2014, IDC_1672.

[†] Ibid.

[‡] IDC: Expect 175 zettabytes of data worldwide by 2025, Andy Patrizio, 3 December 2018, *Network World*, www.networkworld.com/article/3325397/idc-expect-175-zettabytes-of-data-worldwide-by-2025.html

All of these *on their own* present unique challenges to data protection planning within an organization—combined, they can represent a substantial headache to coherent, reliable, and cost-effective protection solutions. Big data requires big, bold data protection strategies and relies on a very meticulous data classification program, something we'll cover more in Chapter 2.

1.6.3 Cloud

Stepping away from which particular model might be considered (private, public, hybrid, etc.), cloud computing is potentially the greatest disruptive factor to the traditional IT environment that we've ever seen, and it's being increasingly adopted. It represents the commoditization of IT functions and deployment models through self-service portals and multitiered service catalogs. Except in perhaps the smallest of businesses, it won't *end* the IT department, but it will have a profound impact on the way IT departments run and present services to the core business in almost all organizations. This can drive greater efficiency in the delivery of IT services to the business, and in some cases, might even pivot the IT department away from infrastructure functions. Rather than managing conventional infrastructure, the IT department might instead focus on development, and service brokerage for the business.

Using a simple web interface, a person untrained in IT can deploy core business IT systems such as email, CRM, and database servers with minimum effort ... but at what cost of data protection? This has led to the term *shadow IT*, which is as concerning in practice as it sounds.

Case in point: In most modern countries, a mandatory requirement to driving a car is getting formal approval from a government body to be allowed to *drive* a car: getting a driver's license. Having a driver's license verifies someone has obtained sufficient knowledge of the road rules and demonstrated a practical ability to drive a car on a road. Shadow IT is akin to anyone being able to get in a car and drive without getting a driver's license. Sure, there is nothing *technically* stopping people from doing it, but the implications can be serious—and dangerous—if the person turns out to make the wrong decisions due to a lack of formal training.

The industry abounds with stories of businesses that trusted in a single public cloud provider only to have their entire operations grind to a halt during cloud-wide disruptions. Many cloud providers provide data protection that is limited solely to protecting the base *infrastructure* only—the subscriber often remains blissfully unaware that their own data is largely unrecoverable for most situations until it is too late.

Yet still, cloud is here to stay, and both IT and business personnel must focus a high level of attention to the data protection considerations of its use or else risk the entire organization to ultimate data disaster scenarios. This is why IT departments in organizations must realign themselves to be able to *broker* cloud services; by doing so, they can vet the available cloud services, picking or designing the ones that match business requirements, ensuring they're safe and compatible with Service Level Agreements (SLAs) and/or Service Level Objectives (SLOs). Returning to our driver's license analogy: by taking control of the cloud experience, IT departments have the opportunity to ensure if someone jumps into a car without a license, they put neither themselves nor others at risk.

1.6.4 Virtualization

What was once the domain of mainframe systems only, virtualization is now a cornerstone in the IT environment for almost all businesses. It allows for high-density application and business functions through optimized use of compute, storage, and memory and introduces enhanced management functions as a result of entire hosts being nothing more than moveable data. Virtualization is expanding to encompass storage, networks, and almost everything else in the datacenter, and each item in turn raises new considerations for the data protection administrators within a business. In a little more than a decade, we've seen the rise of virtual servers, virtual storage, virtual networking, and even the *virtual datacenter*. Seemingly everything in IT now can be software defined. This provides new opportunities for highly customized control, but equally presents new challenges for ensuring we don't forget about data protection along our *software-defined* journey.

1.6.5 Containers and Functions

While virtualization is still the lynch-pin of the datacenter, and many cloud operations, emerging trends towards light-weight microservice architectures are seeing changes in how virtualization is performed. Consider the service model for products such as the VMware ESX/vSphere Hypervisor, which provides comprehensive separation between the guest and the platform: the platform presents a fully virtualized machine: networking, CPU, memory, storage, and so on. In order to make use of that virtualized machine, one must supply an operating system, application framework, data, and so on.

The emergent container-based virtualization system eschews comprehensive separation for convenience; some of the underlying OS components of the "hypervisor" (the container host) are shared by the guest. This results in efficiencies—launch time for containers can be an order of magnitude faster than launch times for virtual machines, but there are new challenges as a result.

Beyond virtualization and containers, cloud providers have launched services that might best be described as *Function as a Service* (FaaS)—"serverless" models where developers can run functions and scripts without actually having to specify what infrastructure it runs on at all. (Of course, "serverless" is a misnomer: it may seem serverless to the person running the function, but there will be some server, of some kind, that actually executes the function—it's just sufficiently abstracted as to allow the term to work.)

To a degree, the goal of containers and functions is to render *stateless* services; services that can be started anywhere, at any time, without need to reference previously worked data. In reality though, services don't *always* end up being stateless, which creates tricky requirements around protecting the data being generated.

1.6.6 Data and Systems Complexity

A business might have 10,000 virtual machines and 200 physical servers (beyond the virtual machine hypervisors) running their production environment. Running on those systems will be a plethora of databases, collaboration tools, messaging systems, document sharing services, and bespoke applications. Underpinning all of that will be a mix of different networking protocols and segments, and storage platforms—block, file, and, more recently, object.

How does a modern data protection professional decide which systems should be protected, and when? How does someone determine whether a collection of 200 virtual machines is best backed up at 17:45, or 18:03? Which volumes and systems should switch from synchronous to asynchronous replication between datacenters out of business hours? How should a 10 PB NAS server be "broken up" in such a way as to allow a once-a-month backup of each share it presents in addition to the daily snapshots that are performed?

As the amount of data and infrastructure (virtual and physical) has increased within businesses, so too has the complexity of managing that data. There is an increasing need in business to automate infrastructure as much as possible: whereas once the automated deployment of a virtual machine may have been deemed a sufficient end-goal, we are now starting to see a push towards adaptive automation: systems using machine learning to determine how to optimize the environment when the number of variables for a decision is too many and complicated for a human to process.

1.6.7 The Law

Digital data retention was once a very informal thing. Some businesses would approach it from a reasonably formal perspective of mapping old-style record retention requirements, others would retain what they could and not worry about the rest, and others would deliberately delete data as soon as possible, regardless of whether or not an impartial observer might consider it to be morally

correct. It was entirely possible to be told any of the following within an IT department:

- We keep everything because it's just safer that way.
- We only keep email for mid-level executives and higher for more than 12 months.
- We get told to delete all email older than 6 months for "capacity" reasons.
- We have no idea what retention we have to apply to data.
- The business has no idea what retention we have to apply to data.
- The business hasn't told us how long we have to keep data for, and if we don't ask, we can't be blamed.

Numerous scandals and major financial crashes have seen this ad-hoc approach to electronic data retention largely disappear. While smaller organizations may sometimes be ignorant of their data retention requirements, larger organizations, enterprises, and businesses operating in a financial or legal sphere will now be intimately aware of what sort of data they need to retain and how long they need to retain it for. This is a major realignment from the datacenters of old and has introduced new constraints on how data protection strategies need to be developed, what sort of data protection storage can be used, and how rigorous businesses need to be about ensuring data is not prematurely removed.

1.6.8 Crime

Just like the rest of IT, criminal use of IT has continued to evolve. Where once we were worried about viruses causing system crashes, worms deleting data, or denial of service attacks flooding external connectivity, we're now in an era where criminal organizations and individuals seek to inflict maximum damage or extort as much money as they can. The attack-de-jour that keeps IT managers and board members awake at night time now is cryptographic—viruses that don't *delete* data, but instead *encrypt* it. *Ransomware* packages in the hands of criminals can create a significant financial impact on businesses: "pay up or never see your data again." A single cryptographic attack within a business can result in it losing hundreds of gigabytes or more of data unless steep ransoms are paid—tens or hundreds of thousands of dollars are now being regularly paid out by businesses desperate to get their data back. We are also seeing a rise in *hactivism* and similar attacks. This is where a business is specifically targeted in a meticulously planned (or at least executed) way. There have been multiple examples already of businesses where hackers, having penetrated the network, delete backups and other forms of data protection *first*, before moving on to delete or encrypt data on original systems. (This new type of threat is already driving an evolution in data protection practices which we will cover later.)

1.7 A Brief History of Data Protection

It's worth starting this book by looking back at how data protection has evolved over the decades. We start with Figure 1.2.

As computer use grew, it became apparent that it was necessary to protect the data that was being stored on them. The starting point, for the most part, was a completely decentralized backup strategy where tape drives would be attached to each server deployed. Backups would be run nightly (sometimes less frequently), and there would be a modicum of protection available in the event of a system failure. Over time though as disk capacities increased while prices (slowly) decreased, the amount of data stored on servers grew. Likewise, the criticality of the data to the business increased, and the *tolerance* within the business to a sustained outage due to hardware failure fell. This resulted in adding RAID to server storage to allow systems to continue to operate even if a disk failed, such as that shown in Figure 1.3.

With RAID we could achieve higher levels of availability, protection, and hardware failure tolerance, but through it all we still needed backup.

As the number of servers within a business grew, the practicality of deploying tape drives on every single server for backup fell sharply. Tapes might have been comparatively cheap compared to disk, but since the amount of data on a server was traditionally tiny compared to the capacity of tapes, every tape that was sent off-site would usually be half empty—or more. Media wastage was common.

The next phase was to start centralizing backup operations, shown in Figure 1.4.

By shifting to a client/server architecture, backup protection storage—at this point still tape—could be centralized at a single host in the environment and more productive use could be made of the tape media. Tapes could be filled more regularly, and because a backup server wasn't doing business production activities, it could start to do additional data protection activities, such as duplicating backups for higher levels of redundancy during recovery.

Particularly in the midrange systems market this drove the adoption of tape libraries to further consolidate

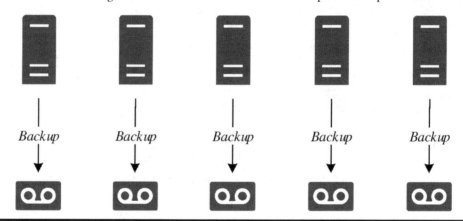

Figure 1.2   Fully decentralized backup strategy.

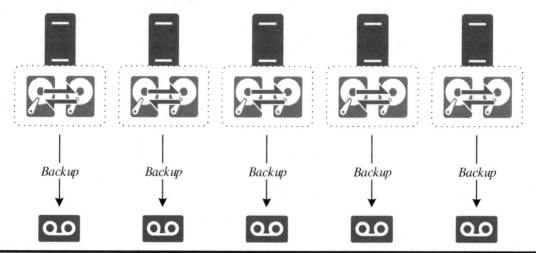

Figure 1.3   Redundant Array of Independent Disks (RAID) added a new layer of data protection for business.

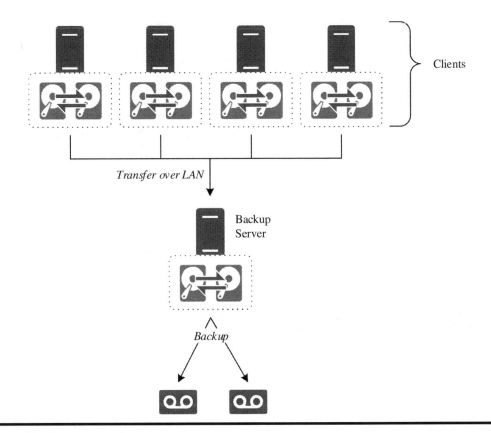

Figure 1.4   Centralized backup topology.

resources—rather than individual drives that required tapes to be manually changed, increasingly larger units could be deployed with multiple tape drives and slots for tens, hundreds, or even (over time) thousands of tapes all within the reach of a robotic arm.

Another consolidation was starting to happen in the datacenter around the same time though—centralized storage. This allowed for more efficient use of disk, easier management, and more RAID levels. It also allowed the individual servers accessing the data to have data management decoupled—the central storage server would take care of that. This ended up in a layout similar to that shown in Figure 1.5.

The advent of centralized storage systems increased online and storage-related protection activities. Whereas the previous focus had simply been around RAID to protect against individual drive failure, new options were needed both from the centralization of the storage and continually shrinking outage tolerances. Thus, snapshots and replication entered the datacenter—shown in high level in Figure 1.6.

The volume of data in the datacenter was continuing to explode, and centralized backup servers were becoming increasingly unable to handle the load. Scaling occurred by introducing secondary backup servers—"media servers" or "storage nodes" dedicated to data movement and under the direction of a backup server that may or may not still actually perform backups itself. Fiber-channel networks in

particular—originally developed for access to centralized storage systems—played a critical part in this by allowing multiple systems to access the same tape infrastructure (though often at the price of stability and reliability). Thus, the three-tier backup environment became commonplace, shown in Figure 1.7.

With the introduction of storage nodes or media servers, the 3-tier backup environment also became a 3.5-tier backup environment as that same media throughput functionality often migrated into the backup client software as well, allowing the largest systems to also connect to shared tape infrastructure to reduce the network impact and speed up their backups.

As disk capacities increased and their prices started to fall more dramatically on a $/GB ratio, the inherent limitations of tape became increasingly apparent. While the performance of tape is excellent for streaming sustained loads, it comes at the cost of easy, random access, or efficient handling of gaps and pauses in a stream. Systems were growing to have millions or tens of millions of files, and the backup process in reading from these types of systems suffered inherent limitations. Thus, we evolved to the notion of staging storage for backup—"backup to disk to tape," shown in Figure 1.8.

Data protection continued to evolve beyond this point. As will be discussed in their specific chapters, we've seen additional enhancements including:

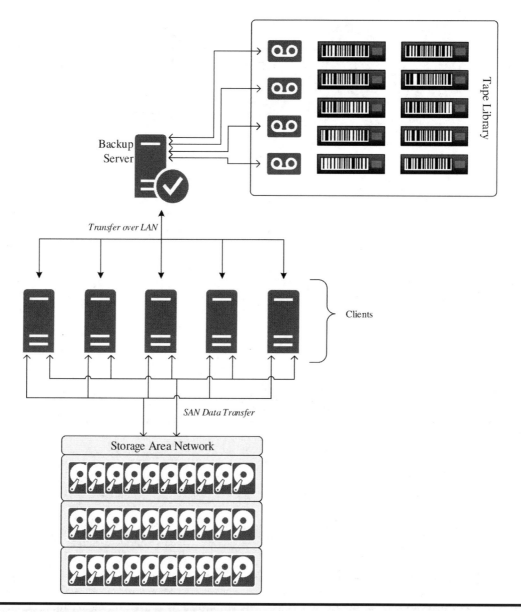

Figure 1.5   Centralized storage and centralized backups.

- Continuously available storage
- Continuous data protection—journaled, application-aware replication
- Purpose-built backup appliances—offering advanced protection options and reducing the overall backup storage footprint with deduplication
- Integrated data protection appliances—offering capability beyond just backup, integrating deeply with end-point applications and storage systems
- Advanced snapshots at the storage and virtualization layers
- Elimination of tape from backup workloads entirely for some organizations
- Protection for data moved to, or originating, in the cloud

There have been multiple points in the history of data protection where it's been declared innovation is over—or no longer required. The simple truth though is that data protection has been forced to grow and evolve as the volume and criticality of data have evolved.

1.8 The Miserly Hoarder

There's a common enough saying in the traditional backup and recovery discipline:

> It's always better to backup a little too much than not enough.

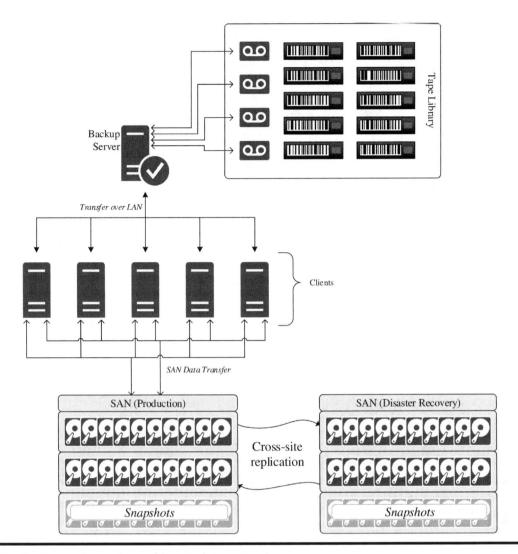

Figure 1.6   Replication and snapshots adding to data protection.

This is true of the broader topic of data protection, but newer technologies are proving that there *are* limits to this. We may want to preserve as much information as possible, but this doesn't necessarily apply to all *data*. Temporary data—cache print cache files, program "scratch" files, etc.—are data, but their value beyond the momentary executed function is arguably negligible.

Constantly increasing storage capacities have enabled businesses to keep truly staggering amounts of data online—yet, there will always be physical and logical limits to the amount of data it is practicable to hold or manage. Thus, businesses have to walk the fine line between being miserly with their storage and being data hoarders.

The Data, Information Knowledge, Wisdom (DIKW) model usually presents us with a good explanation of the need to be focused in data protection scenarios. A simple representation of this model is shown in Figure 1.9.

The DIKW model emphasizes that while data may be useful it's more of a *start* rather than *end* point. For instance, we might produce the following model:

■ *Data*:
  – The item is red.
  – The item is round.
  – The item is edible.
■ *Information*:
  – The item is a tomato.
■ *Knowledge*:
  – Tomato is a fruit.
■ *Wisdom*:
  – Tomato doesn't go in a fruit salad.

Consider a grocery store: there's potentially a lot of data to track and protect when it comes to their supplies, but it's unlikely the store would specifically need to track the number of *red* items it has in stock or the number of *round* items it has in stock. It *might* track the number of *edible* things it has in stock, and it would definitely want to track the number of tomatoes it has in stock.

This process is often distilled to the idea of eliminating "ROT"—redundant, obsolete, and trivial content. If data

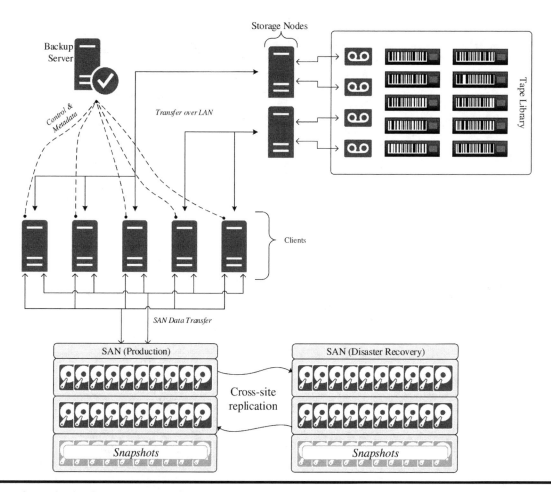

Figure 1.7 Three-tier backup environment.

has served its operational or compliance purpose, there is arguably no need to keep it. As we'll see in later chapters, the amount of data a business keeps has a significant flow-on effect on data protection. Understanding the data of the business is something we'll focus on more in Chapter 2.

1.9 Summary

We live in a digital age. The accumulation of data continues to accelerate, with seemingly no end in sight. In 2018, Domo predicted that 1.7 MB of data will be created every second for every person on the planet.* UN population reports and calculators suggest that there will be approximately 7.8 billion people on earth in 2020;† combined, these are non-trivial amounts of data: 13 PB of data generated per second, worldwide—just shy of 1,146 EB a day.

Each of us, individually, find more of our lives and memories encapsulated in some digital format. Whereas previously families might maintain photo albums generation to generation, each of us individually now have thousands or more digital photos at our fingertips via smartphones. The loss of a smartphone isn't just an inconvenience when it comes to being contactable; one might, in fact, argue that this is the least upsetting thing that can come from losing such a device. Instead, a lost or destroyed smartphone might mean losing all the photos and videos of all the holidays you've been on in the last 5 years, the final video you ever recorded of your grandmother before she passed away, the one and only time you managed to record your cat playing fetch, or any other number of events that have great personal meaning to you. Your laptop may contain the only remaining copy of the notes and research material from your university degree—thousands of hours of work. Years of scanned receipts and tax returns may exist only on your desktop computer, and that novel you secretly hope to elevate you to Tolkeinesque

---

* Data never sleeps: sixth edition, DOMO, www.domo.com/solution/data-never-sleeps-6

† UN World Population Prospects 2017, https://population.un.org/wpp/DataQuery/

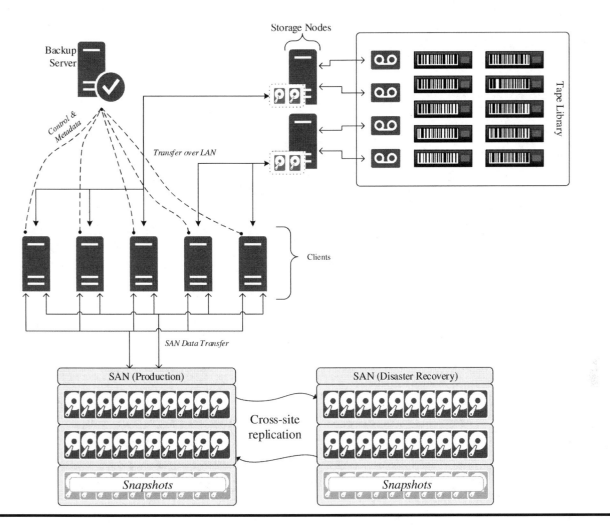

Figure 1.8   Disk-based staging of backups.

levels of fame might exist only on your tablet. Your phone, tablet, laptop, and desktop computers might all synchronize email for you, but what would happen if somehow a fault or mistake caused the email service to *delete* it?

Such is the nature of the way we interact with the modern world that we are constantly exposed to the risk of data loss, and that data loss may have a significant personal impact on us.

While this book primarily focuses on data protection as it applies to business, understanding the personal impact of data loss helps us focus on why data protection is important. After all, if your bank loses the data associated with your savings account, your airline loses your flight booking, or your power company "forgets" that it has to supply power to you, there is a direct, tangible impact that you will experience. The marketing database your employer maintains might not personally mean anything to you, but it means something to someone, and it might be a critical link in the sequence that leads to your monthly salary. Data isn't just the new oil, it's

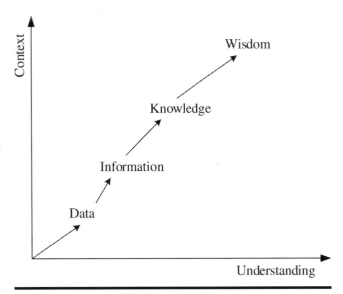

Figure 1.9   DIKW model.

the new currency. Hence, protecting it has never been more personally or professionally important.

1.10 Self-Reflection

Personal Data

Think about the number of points in your personal life where data might be generated: cellular phones, tablets, laptops, desktops, and public cloud services for a start.

For each of these, ask yourself the following questions:

1. How is the data in this device or service protected?
   a. Is the protection something I have control over?
   b. Do I know if I can actually recover data if it is lost?

2. How would this impact me, either directly, or potentially, should I lose part or all of this data? It is often useful to consider this from several time-points:
   a. Today's data
   b. Yesterday's data
   c. The most recent month's data
   d. Data older than a month, to the age of the oldest data on the device or service

3. When considering the impact above, consider it from several perspectives:
   a. Financial
   b. Reputational
   c. Emotional

It's particularly important when we consider the consequences of data loss to understand it from varying perspectives, either personally or for a company. After all, losing the last recording of your grandmother before she passed away is unlikely to have a *financial* impact on you, but emotionally it may be considerable, and if family members were relying on you sending that video to them, it could equally have a strong, personal reputational impact. By comparison, if a business loses data due to say, a ransomware attack, the reputational impact may significantly outweigh the financial impact (or perhaps more correctly: the reputational impact may cause significant flow-on financial damage).

Business Data

Having considered some personal data loss situations, now think of the top three business systems you use on a day to day basis. For each one of those, ask yourself:

1. Do you *know* if the data in that system is protected?
2. How does this impact me, personally, if data is lost? This might be in time, satisfaction, reputation, or any number of other considerations.
3. What is the impact to the business if data is lost? Is it an essential or non-essential system, for instance?

Chapter 2

Contextualizing Data Protection

2.1 Introduction

Data protection is an umbrella term that encompasses multiple information disciplines, including storage, backup, and recovery, and systems and application administration, just to name a few.

As mentioned in the introduction, there are two distinct fields of activity within data protection: *proactive* and *reactive*. Proactive activities refer to such areas as:

- *Storage*:
  - RAID (and other forms of fault tolerance)
  - Snapshots
  - Replication
  - Continuous data protection (CDP)
  - Continuous availability
- *Backup*:
  - Establishing backup and recovery systems
  - Maintaining systems and adding hosts for protection

On the other hand, reactive activities focus on:

- *Repair*:
  - Reconstruction (automatic or manual) following storage failure, or within fault-tolerant components
- *Recovery*:
  - Retrieval of information from backup systems
- *Restore*:
  - Reinstating integrity of recovered data (usually an activity relating to databases and other complex applications)*

In order to have a true data protection strategy, a business needs to focus holistically on both proactive and reactive activities, and these activities *must* be considered synergistically rather than individually. Without that approach, a business can develop storage strategies and backup/recovery strategies, but these will be silo-like in nature: lacking in both efficiency and capability.

Merging storage and backup processes is often seen as the *key* approach to developing an effective data protection strategy. While this is important, there's another step—a precursor step—that many organizations pay insufficient attention to: measurement.

One of the most central tenets of almost all processes, including project management, ITIL[†] and COBIT[‡] (just to name a few), is the simple truism:

> If you can't measure something, you can't improve it.

By *improve*, we mean not just a case of random pot luck or educated guesses, but actual tangible results, such as being able to assert an anticipated percentage improvement in return for a particular investment in terms of cost and time—and then confirm whether or not it was achieved.

The same is true of data protection—but contrary to popular belief, that doesn't start with being able to measure your backup and/or recovery speeds, or the length of time it takes a RAID-6 system to rebuild after a drive failure. Those are important metrics, and metrics that are essential to understanding service-level offerings and

---

* While the terms *recover* and *restore* may seem synonymous, they are often perceived as being quite different, particularly in the realm of database administration. This allows database and application administrators to differentiate between the act of retrieving *crash-consistent* data (recovery) and the act of applying *application consistency* (restore) to that data. We'll cover terms such as *crash consistency* and *application consistency* in later chapters.

---

† Information Technology Infrastructure Library.
‡ Control Objectives for Information and related Technologies.

capabilities within a business, but they're not the *starting* metrics; the starting point for the metrics actually derive from data classification.

Many businesses will go out of their way to avoid data classification, believing it to be too hard or too costly (or both). It's something regularly shied away from, its utility questioned, and its expense exaggerated. The negativity toward data classification invariably comes from a perception that at whatever time it's discussed there's already too much unclassified data in the business to ever allow the process to complete. As the amount of unclassified data in the business grows, this becomes a self-fulfilling prophecy. Like a proverbial ostrich with its head stuck in the sand, this approach simply means the business remains unaware of the holes and gaps in a data protection strategy that has been built on shaky foundations.

We will see in this chapter why data classification is imperative for the purposes of building a holistic and successful data protection strategy.

2.2 Data Classification

Data classification, regardless of how formally it is done within an environment, provides the baseline metrics required for data protection and ultimately assists in identifying data by five fundamental questions about data—what, where, who, when, and how:

- *What* is the data?
- *Where* is the data?
- *Who* uses the data?
- *When* is the data used?
- *How* is the data used?

In a broader scope, data classification is used within information lifecycle management (ILM) to address other management aspects of data, including access restrictions and regulatory compliance relating to the data. Thus, a fully established data classification process operating as an ongoing exercise will yield substantial benefits to a business—both at the frontline and in relation to back-end processes. The value to the business extends far beyond that of making data protection more accurate.

2.2.1 What Is the Data?

The first metric—arguably the most important metric—is to know *what* you actually *need* to protect. If you can't measure and articulate that, you're designing blind. If you can't say *what* your data is, you can't in any meaningful way argue that it's being adequately protected, regardless of operational

metrics such as the success rates of your backup/recoveries or the reliability of your storage systems.

> Case in point: You might be able to get 100% successful backups of 100% of your servers from a file-level agent, but if every one of those servers has a database on it, it is likely every single one of those backups is useless for the purposes of recovery.

For data protection to be effective, you need to not only understand what you're protecting, but what you're *not* protecting—and in both cases, this needs to be documented. While everyone understands the need to document what *is* backed up, documenting what *isn't* tends to be less understood. If we compare data protection to an insurance policy, we can immediately see why—insurance policies are *always* written with exclusions and disclaimers as to what is and isn't covered. It's just as important to know what events *aren't* covered by your home insurance policy as knowing what events are. Similarly, keeping accurate documentation as to what data *isn't* protected allows a business to gauge the level of risk it's exposed to *and* determine whether that's acceptable.

Except for particularly special environments, data isn't stagnant. The way the business uses it adapts over time, and the content can obviously change as well. This can happen in three distinct ways:

- *Seasonally*: The importance placed on data may depend on the time of the year. Educational facilities, for instance, will have maximized requirements for data protection on enrolment data for a period of months around the start of a new educational year. Financial organizations will require additional protection processes during end-of-month (EOM) and end-of-financial-year (EOFY) situations, and so on.
- *By evolution*: Some data will grow and change with the business: standard financial records, filesystem data, etc.
- *By revolution*: Few, if any, businesses work entirely in a vacuum, independent of the marketplace. Businesses may face revolutionary changes to the importance of their data as new competitors emerge, or existing competitors introduce substantially new products. In such times, the company may be forced to adopt completely different business approaches, which in turn may leverage their data and information systems in substantially alternate ways. Additionally, companies leveraging research or exploration can face major new data requirements whenever these activities pay off. For

example, a pharmaceutical company may bring a new drug onto the market or an exploration company may find and start working on mining a new gold deposit.

In short: What was unimportant last month or last year may be important in 3 months' time—but if the data was lost or forgotten about because of its *perceived* irrelevance, it's likely no one will notice that it's become important until too late.

An understanding of *what* the data is will immediately set some broad parameters on how the data will be protected. For instance, consider the following collections of data:

■ *Business-critical database*: Core business operations require this database to be up and available at all times.
■ *Corporate fileserver*: Used by a significant number of users for standard file storage.
■ *Development database*: Used by the database/application administration team to develop new functionality for the business-critical database systems.
■ *Software installation repository*: Used to hold all the various installers, packages, and stand-alone binaries deployed by the company for the build of laptops, desktops, and servers.

Each of these systems will trigger completely different data protection strategies (Table 2.1).

2.2.2 Where Is the Data?

In addition to needing to know *what* you need to protect, you equally need to know *where* it is. This serves two key purposes:

1. *Data placement*: You could have three arrays maintaining synchronous replicas of RAID-10 volumes, with each array asynchronously replicating to other arrays geographically dispersed around the world, knowing that if a single hard drive or a single array fails, there's no way you'll lose any data *as long as that data is stored*

on the arrays. If you can't be certain that the data will be *on* the arrays, then you equally can't be certain that your data protection system works.
2. *Protection options*: Many businesses refer to different *tiers* of data protection (e.g., "gold," "silver," and "bronze"). Once data has been located, it is usually the case that various forms of data protection will fall into place based on the redundancy options associated with the storage.

Consider as well both cloud services and colocation/shared datacenter facilities: as such, asking *where is the data* is potentially a significantly more complex question than even 10 years ago. Discovering data locality is no longer a case of determining if it's on a server, storage array, or laptop, but covers a multitude of options, including:

■ Is it on centralized business-owned storage?
■ Is it stored on desktops/laptops?
■ Is it stored only on mobile devices (phones, tablets)?
■ Is it stored in a colocation facility?
■ Is it stored in a cloud? If so
    – Public?
    – Private?
    – Hybrid?
    – Geographically, where in the world is the cloud?

If data is determined to be stored in a colocation facility or cloud, this raises additional questions that must be considered around the data protection services offered for those locations and can lead to alternate service-level agreements (SLAs) tiered on locality alone. For example, consider sample SLAs for recovery time objective (RTO) of data based on whether the data is stored traditionally, in a hybrid cloud, or in a fully public cloud (Table 2.2).

Note that while a hybrid cloud is effectively a cloud service that spans both a private cloud and one or more public clouds, we might differentiate between hybrid cloud and the other forms of cloud for SLAs in recognition that the

Table 2.1 Sample Data Protection Strategies Based on Data Type

Collection	RAID	Snapshots	Replication	Backup
Business-critical database	RAID-10	Hourly, 24 × 7, expiring after 48 hours	Synchronous	Nightly full, half-hourly incremental log backups
Corporate fileserver	RAID-6	Hourly from 7am to 7pm, retained for 1 week	Asynchronous	Weekly synthetic full, daily incremental from 7pm snapshot
Development database	RAID-5	None	None	Nightly full
Software installation repository	RAID-5	Weekly	Asynchronous	Quarterly full

Table 2.2 Sample Recovery Time Objective (RTO) SLAs for Data Based on Locality and Importance to the Business

	Traditional Infrastructure or Private Cloud	Hybrid Cloud	Public Cloud
Gold	1 hour	4 hours	8 hours
Silver	4 hours	8 hours	24 hours
Bronze	1 day	2 days	7 days

workload could be moved (either automatically, or manually in response to some requirement) from the private cloud infrastructure to a public cloud provider, or vice versa. This could require different planning for SLAs compared to a workload that will only exist in public cloud, or only exist on-premises. Often a key consideration will be, "is this a system of record?" That is, a focus on where the origin of the data is, rather than where copies of the data are stored.

In such scenarios, for instance, it may be that no data protection activities are taken on bronze data in a public cloud, and this would require reseeding from a private source. Alternately, while a 1-hour RTO may be *desirable* for gold cloud data, the longer RTO may recognize the potential for longer outages where the business is just one customer among many, rather than being completely in control of its own datacenter. As such, the SLAs documented may not be representative of the ideal goals of the business, but of the hard limitations of the chosen location for the data, and becomes statistical information that feeds into the decision-making process on where data will be stored.* (One mistake made by some cloud adopters, for instance, is failing to reconcile internal business SLAs with those offered by the cloud services providers for the storage and systems their data and applications reside on, or that can be achieved based on different data protection techniques available in the cloud than used on-premises.)

Seemingly a simple question, *where is the data* provides a wealth of information for data protection activities.

2.2.3 Who Uses the Data?

The importance of data, and therefore how it is to be protected, will often be measured against the user(s) accessing it. In some instances, this will be due to the number of users who access it, and in other instances, it will be due to the *roles* of the users accessing it.

This introduces a more-difficult-to-quantify consideration that still has to be factored into the data protection equation, notably *perceived* versus *actual* importance by user role. For instance, in accounting or legal firms, it's not uncommon to see considerably more attention paid to data protection for partners with a financial stake in the organization than for standard employees within the business, regardless of what those employees do. While someone in IT may not necessarily see the difference between the sets of data accessed by the different user roles, the *business* does and therefore we can say that the *perceived* importance overrides the *actual* importance. (Or to be more accurate: the perceived importance *becomes* the actual importance.)

While this may not necessarily impact the actual data protection mechanisms invoked from a technical perspective, it may impact the SLAs and operational-level agreements (OLAs) established around that protection.

2.2.4 When Is the Data Used?

Data protection activities are typically *secondary production* activities, with the actual work done by the business being *primary production* activities. A common mistake, even in the data protection industry, is to classify data protection as *non-production*. This is a fallacy: it's a secondary production activity or a production support activity. Regardless, its function is a production one.

As *secondary* production activities, however, it's critical that data protection does not unduly interfere with the actual work the company needs to do. For smaller businesses and noncritical systems in larger enterprises, that simply means backups run outside of standard business hours. However, it can fundamentally change *how* the protection takes place for those businesses with 24×7 requirements.

Data may also have different use cycles—financial account databases, for instance, require extreme availability during the day for banking institutions, but may not become immediately available for backup purposes after end of business. Such systems may instead be required for use in batch processing systems, further reducing the window of availability presented to data protection administrators. An entire subset of data protection is devoted to 24×7 use cases, that being CDP.

2.2.5 How Is the Data Used?

As much as anything this refers to the activity profile of the data and covers a variety of questions including (but not limited to):

■ How regularly is the data updated?
  – Daily?
  – Weekly?

---

* In other instances, businesses may require the same SLA for data tiers regardless of where the data lives. This still requires an understanding of data placement however, since it will alter the protection options deployed in the various possible locations of the data.

- Monthly?
- Even less frequently?

■ Is the data *transient*? Transient data is that which passes from system to system, requiring protection only in one location (usually the original source).

■ Is it immediately visible data?
  - To the public?
  - Internally only?
  - A mix?

■ Is the data directly worked on, or is it *reference* data? Meaning
  - If the data is directly worked on
    • What is the criticality of the data to the business processes it relates to?
  - What is the criticality of those business processes to the business?
  - If the data *is* reference data:
    • Is it read-only?
    • How many systems and applications reference the data?
    • How critical are *those* systems and applications?
    • How would those systems function without the data being available?

While this is often considered from the perspective of how the data is to be stored, it also directly impacts the level and frequency of data protection required.

Consider, for instance, traditional backup and recovery strategies, which see backups run once every 24 hours. If data is likely to only change at most once or twice a day, then that 24-hour data protection approach may be sufficient. If it's likely to change *hundreds* of times a day, additional strategies involving storage snapshots, replication, or CDP may also need to be taken into consideration.

2.2.6 Summarizing Data Classification

Many businesses resist engaging in comprehensive data classification. The objection is always that it can be a fiddly operation and they have a large amount of existing data. This may be true, but the corollary is that the data will only *continue* to increase, so if data classification hasn't been a management activity *yet*, the best time to do it is now: kicking the can down the road, so to speak, just makes for a bigger problem later.

Failure to conduct data classification can result in significant costs for the business, which may be:

■ *Financial*: Data classification is an essential aspect of information lifecycle management; without classification, businesses tend to continually grow their primary storage footprint (and therefore data protection footprints as well). While it might be seen as an activity that will have a financial cost to execute, there is always a cost in *not* executing it.

■ *Legal*: For many businesses, there are legal aspects to at least some of the data held and accumulated. Taxation and fiduciary requirements around retaining and securing data can directly impact how storage, retrieval, and protection operations should run. Increasingly, privacy requirements may similarly impact those activities.

■ *Reputational*: In addition to any fines that might be incurred for mishandling data, companies can suffer significant reputational impact over the failure to correctly store, secure, or protect data. A fine may represent only a minuscule portion of the annual operating revenue to a multinational company, but a concerted grass-roots boycott campaign by activists around the world could have significant long-term impact on the business.

2.3 Protection Methodology

While information lifecycle management (ILM) does have an operational context to refer to data protection, it's constructive to think of there being a sibling activity to ILM, that being information lifecycle protection (ILP).

In this sense, ILP is the recognition that data protection doesn't necessarily come from a single stream of activities or that the protection mechanism remains the same for the entire lifespan of the information. As information ages, or as its access model changes, so too might the protection mechanisms applied for it.

For example, consider a protection model that might change for a business based on the age of the information, as shown in Figure 2.1.

When data is newly captured into the environment (either received, or created), there typically exists a brief window where the only protection the data has is *online* protection: requisite fault tolerance in the form of RAID, then for a typical business, replication, and depending on the type of data, snapshots. Since most businesses will perform a backup every 24 hours, we assume this initial state of data protection will last for approximately the first 24 hours of life within the business.

After that, we transition lifecycle protection to an operational, or active state. This may vary depending on whether the information is high priority, or lower priority. Higher priority content may receive fault tolerance, replication, snapshots, and backup. Lower priority content might instead receive fault tolerance, replication, and backup. As content ages, it could move into being held *just* in the long-term retention backup cycles for the business—i.e., it is no longer on primary storage. At that point, it only has protection in the form of backups, and whatever fault tolerance is assigned to the backup environment. Alternately, it may have been removed from backups and primary storage, placed in an

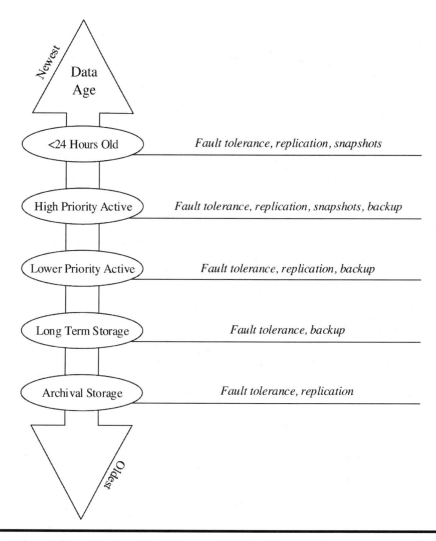

Figure 2.1 Changes to how information is protected across its lifecycle.

archival platform instead, in which case it's moved to a protection methodology based on fault tolerance and replication (with appropriate controls to prevent deletion or modification, of course).

Of course, the information protection lifecycle within a business will vary depending on the business, its industry vertical, and the importance of that information (usually categorized by its *workload* function to the business, but not always). The model described in Figure 2.1 then is a sample only, and not intended to represent the *only* way that information lifecycle protection would work.

When considering protection for a workload or its data, it's important to understand that different groups within IT or the broader business (particularly when we configure public cloud workloads) may be responsible for protection—i.e., protection is not guaranteed to be provided by the one team within the business. For instance, if we consider traditional IT infrastructure (with compute, network, virtualization, storage, and backup all being separate teams), then the storage strategy within the organization will consider RAID

levels and snapshots, as well as replication, but won't necessarily deal with backup and recovery. The backup and recovery strategy may not deal with snapshot or primary storage replication.

The importance of developing holistic data protection strategies rather than independent storage and backup/recovery strategies is simple: combined, they synergistically offer a better solution than any one strategy might in isolation.

2.4 Protection vs Regeneration

When planning protection strategies, there's one other option to consider: whether the cost of protecting the data exceeds the cost of regenerating it. In this consideration, cost can refer to any of:

■ *Time*: How long it takes to be protected
■ *Accuracy*: How accurate the regeneration is
■ *Fiscal (Protection)*: Dollar price of protecting the data

■ *Fiscal (Regeneration)*: Dollar cost of regenerating the data

For many types of conventional data and data sources, this isn't a discussion point—an airline booking system, for instance, can't possibly be recovered in the event of failure by asking customers to recreate their bookings, nor can medical records at a hospital be recreated by doctors and nurses re-entering details.

Decisions that can impact whether data will be protected or regenerated include:

■ *Original or copy?* Data that is original is more likely to require protection. Data that is a copy (e.g., a test/development copy of a production database) may not need the same level of data protection, if at all. (Transient data, merely being accessed from another source, will also likely fall into the "copy" category except for very rare circumstances.)

■ *Organic or predictable?* Random data, such as that coming from end users, standard interactions, and normal use scenarios, is more likely to require data protection. Data that can be recreated by rerunning calculations against locked or read-only data and collecting the results may require less data protection.

■ *Importance of specific content?* Data whose content itself is not immediately valuable (just the presence of it) may not necessarily need protecting. For example, random blocks of data used for performance testing, or corporate web-proxy data, may be considered sufficiently unimportant from a *specific* content perspective that they can be allowed to repopulate rather than be recovered.*

2.5 Organizational Change

It's no longer sufficient to merely have *backup policies* and *storage policies* when those policies are isolated from one another, either in their development or in their operation. A variety of factors, including data growth, data use, and data locality, mean that it's absolutely critical for businesses to focus more on *data protection* policies that encompass all aspects of data protection—storage, replication, backup/recovery, and regeneration.

By necessity, this can lead to different organizational approaches. In the late 1990s, it became popular to separate enterprise backup administration into its own team to reflect the broader centralization that was taking place. Rather than having backup administrators for Unix, for Windows, and so on, there would be a single team of administrators providing backup services to all of IT and by extension, the entire business. This entirely made sense, and businesses that followed that lead were almost invariably able to deliver far more efficient and cost-effective backup and recovery solutions than those who kept the backup strategies for each operating system or application siloed.

Centralized backup administration is still critical to a robust data protection policy, but it's no longer enough in and of itself. Instead, centralized backup administration must be combined with centralized storage administration so that fully dependable and appropriate data protection policies can be developed, implemented, and maintained.

Indeed, we're now seeing the emergence of a new breed of administrators within IT organizations, driven by hyperconvergence and the need for agility—the *infrastructure administrator*. These administrators need to have control over and input into the storage, virtualization, and data protection processes, and a data protection solution that doesn't include infrastructure administration focus is likely to be insufficient.[†]

2.6 Summary

Data protection is no longer as straightforward an activity as it was once considered. Data growth, changing locality, and increased reliance on 24×7 operations means that the more simplistic approaches for data protection developed in previous decades are now unaligned to business requirements.

Of course, that doesn't mean data protection is impossible—but just like any other evolving field, it now requires greater maturity and thought in order to successfully solve the problems faced by businesses.

Achieving adequate data protection requires a more centralized approach and a broader understanding of the classification of data within the organization. Without both of these aspects, a business is more likely to have isolated and inefficient policies covering *just* storage or *just* recovery.

Once the data is classified and understood, the next challenge becomes obvious: how to manage it in the context of data protection. This has significant overlap with the broader topic of ILM, and we'll refer to it as the *data lifecycle*, a topic to be discussed in detail in the following chapter.

---

* Alternately if it were necessary to, say, repeat performance tests on new systems, keeping that random data in order to ensure test consistency might be entirely justifiable, but requiring a substantially lower tier data protection than, say, mission critical database data.

[†] This of course doesn't reduce the need for application, database, and system administrators to be involved in the data protection process. In fact, we are seeing a new type of data protection evolve now where administrators and architects have control over the broad policies for backups and copies, as well as the protection storage, while application and database administrators maintain control over day to day data protection operations.

2.7 Self-Reflection

Consider a business that you might regularly interact with. Consider three different types of data (the *what*) that the business might maintain, and from that, the other aspects of data classification that might come into play, viz.:

- Where might the data be kept?
- Who would make use of the data?
- When would the data be used? (And would there be changes to how the data is used depending on the time of day, week, month, or year?)
- How would the data be used?

Chapter 3

Data Lifecycle

3.1 Introduction

Developing data protection policies in isolation and disconnected from any planning around data lifecycle is a serious error for any business to make. For example, a common criticism of backup and recovery in general is it's a "budget black hole"—that is, money is sunk into it without any return. Putting aside for the moment that the critical return from an adequately funded backup and recovery system is the insurance of being able to *recover data* when needed, there are two other key factors that lead to this erroneous attitude, namely:

- Unmanaged, unpredicted data growth
- Insufficient secondary use case scenarios of backup data

The second factor will be discussed later in the book, but the first often stems from a core failure to maintain an appropriate data lifecycle.

Data lifecycle management is something that should be absolutely fundamental to the IT organization within any business, yet remains randomly or haphazardly implemented in most. (Arguably, this is for the same reasons as discussed under "Data Classification" in the previous chapter.) For many organizations, data lifecycle "management" resembles a process such as that shown in Figure 3.1.

Data can appear within the digital borders of a business in one of two ways: it is either created, or it's ingested. Created data can come from a variety of sources: staff, algorithmic processes, customer interactions, and so on. Ingested data will come from sources external to the company—data that has been received elsewhere and the company receives a copy of.

Regardless of whether we've created or ingested the data, after we've used it and have no legal, operational, or functional requirement to keep it, deleting it makes sense: it removes the ongoing storage and protection requirements for that data. More commonly however, once data use is complete, it instead stagnates on primary storage, consuming space but not providing any benefit in return. One can argue that the difference between *storage* and *stagnation* is whether there is a lifecycle policy for the data.

A high-level view of an ideal data lifecycle management policy will be similar to Figure 3.2.

It's important to note that the first step in a well-defined data lifecycle should be data classification. As data is captured in the digital borders of the business, regardless of whether that's through creation or ingestion, the data should be classified. The reason for this is straightforward: data can't be assigned a lifecycle policy until it's classified. In some situations, this will be immediately evident as a result of the system the data has been created or ingested in. In other situations, it may require processes to analyze user-supplied, free-form data (for example, identifying data that includes customer credit card details, or sensitive medical information, etc.).

Data management and classification specialists often refer to the issue of "ROT," as mentioned in the introduction (redundant, obsolete, trivial). The purpose of data management and classification is effectively to eliminate the "ROT" from business storage, focusing on:

- *Redundant data*: This includes additional copies of data, or data leftover from processing where the source is irrelevant once results have been determined.
- *Obsolete (sometimes referred to as outdated) data*: Data which has no requirement to be kept any more. While this can refer to other forms of data, we would often consider compliance data which has passed a mandatory retention time to fall into the obsolete category.
- *Trivial data*: This includes temporary files and non-business data (e.g., an invite to a child's fifth birthday party, generated during a lunch break and saved to a home drive).

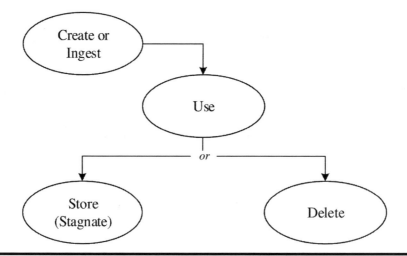

Figure 3.1 Data lifecycle "management" approach used in many organizations.

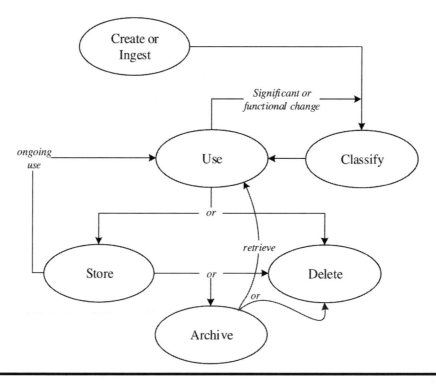

Figure 3.2 Ideal data lifecycle management flow.

One common mistake is for businesses to seek to perform data classification as part of the backup process: this is literally reminiscent of the adage, "closing the stable door after the horse has bolted"; at the point of backup, data has been residing on business systems for potentially 24 hours or more. Further, data classification as part of a backup process doesn't deal with assigning data lifecycles to the original (primary storage) copy of the data. (When we consider that some data may have resided within an organization for years before a backup product with data classification is installed, this increases the severity of the problem.)

After the data has been classified, it goes into primary operational use. Note that there is scope for the data to be *re-classified*; should the data undergo significant functional or content change, there may be a need for it to be subjected to the classification process again. (A classic case in point would be data being updated to include personally sensitive or identifying information, where it previously did not have that content.)

Data should then be stored according to a lifecycle policy; this will see data continue to be used as required, but the classification process should have identified the operational lifecycle assigned to the data. This operational lifecycle will place limits on how long the data resides on primary storage before it is archived, tiered to alternate storage, or deleted entirely. Data that is archived will either remain there until it is past its retention date, and deleted, or if it is recalled for use, will be potentially returned to the overall use cycle. Data retrieved from archive might be either accessed read-only, copied, or returned as the original, read/write enabled. While accessing read-only archive data should not change the overall assigned lifespan of the data, copying the data would result in an entirely new classification and lifecycle process. Whether the data can be retrieved as a copy or returned for read/write access should be decided by the data classification and lifecycle policies.

The important aspect of the entire data lifecycle process is that data is *under management*. Data management implies:

- Data is placed in an appropriate location based on its content and use, with the appropriate protection (all three forms: security, privacy, and storage) policies applied.
- Data is used for an "operational" period, after which it is not *forgotten about*; the lifecycle processes should be embedded into archive and aged data should be deleted as required.

In some IT departments, *data deletion* is a particularly indelicate term, but *archiving* isn't far behind it. These IT departments are guilty of *data hoarding*—they mistakenly believe that it's cheaper (in terms of expenditure and time) to keep everything on primary storage than to actively reduce it.

Data hoarding is a serious problem well entrenched in many enterprises, and with the explosive growth of data within business, the problems faced by hoarders only continue to grow. Quite simply: 1 TB of data rarely, if ever, occupies just 1 TB of storage within a business, and the longer data lifecycle management is ignored, the larger the waste-data problem becomes within a business.

Needless hoarding can also have unexpected legal or privacy implications. The business may be only legally required to retain key data for 7 years, but during a discovery process, older data that still exists is usually subject to capture and use. If data is maintained on business customers and private individuals, retaining it past its required timeframe can have consequences if found by auditors, or cause financial and reputational damage to the company if exfiltrated or otherwise accessed during a security incident.

Continuing down a path of not properly managing the data lifecycle is only going to continue to cost businesses more. Eventually, all businesses must face and tackle data lifecycle management, and the longer it is avoided the more painful it becomes to initiate.

There are three incorrect techniques that businesses can become trapped in rather than true data lifecycle management:

1. Getting stuck in the "use" cycle for all data
2. Archiving but never deleting data
3. Deleting rather than archiving data

The first is penny-wise/pound-foolish, the second is true hoarding, and the third is usually quite reckless.

3.2 Understanding Copy Proliferation

To understand the importance of implementing a data lifecycle management policy, let's consider the earlier statement: 1 TB of data rarely, if ever, occupies just 1 TB of storage within a business.

One way to understand why data classification and data lifecycle management are important is to actually expand on that 1 TB of data to see how much data exists. So let's explore a simple question: how much storage does a 1 TB database occupy within a business?

To begin with, there's likely to be RAID considerations. A 1 TB database may, for performance reasons, reside on a RAID1 volume (we will cover RAID in a later chapter), thereby actually using 2×1 TB drives to present 1 TB of usable storage with fault tolerance. So immediately, our primary copy of a 1 TB database consumes 2 TB of storage.

However, this is merely the beginning of the answer to the occupancy question. Data within a business environment—particularly mission critical data—will have a variety of data protection options assigned to them, and the amount of data consumed by the protection techniques should be factored into understanding how much storage a particular workload occupies. This becomes important when workloads are moved between on-premises locations and public or hybrid clouds and helps to demonstrate why unmanaged data growth within an organization should be discouraged.

For example, in Figure 3.3, we see that a 1 TB database will in fact have many copies, both logical and separate within the business. That 1 TB database will be replicated to an alternate location in case the primary storage/instance fails. Assume the same RAID levels are used, the 1 TB database can now be said to occupy 4 TB of actual storage; 2 TB for the primary copy, and 2 TB for the replica copy.

For rapid recovery purposes, application-consistent snapshots may be triggered hourly, gathering changes in the database and transaction logs into rollback points. If we assume that there's a 10% daily change rate for the database, and amortize these snapshots, then we'd assume that every hour, on average, 4.167 GB (or thereabouts) of change data is written. This will be written into the database, and

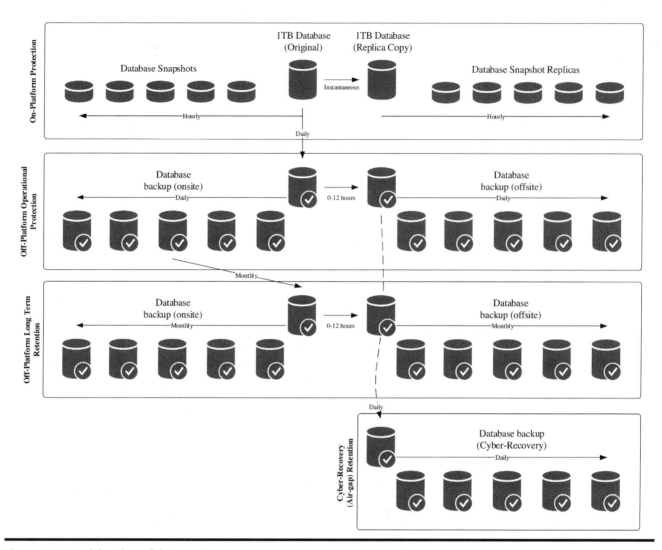

Figure 3.3　Proliferation of data copies.

also the transaction logs for the database, allowing for application controlled rollbacks, and we'd assume the transaction logs will be similarly protected. If we also assume that the transaction logs occupy no more space than the actual changed data within the database, our 4.167 GB of data per hour becomes 8.3 GB of data per hour. Again, this is before RAID is taken into consideration, so that 8.3 GB of data is 16.67 GB per hour once RAID is taken into consideration. Those 24 logical copies will potentially consume 400 GB of actual storage.

But, of course, the snapshots will also be replicated to the alternate site; again taking into account RAID on the remote site, our daily snapshots plus replication for a 1 TB database add another 800 GB of required primary storage.

So the 1 TB database isn't 1 TB of storage; it's 4.8 TB of storage at the end of 24 hours.

As we'll continue to discuss in later chapters, on-platform protection is unable to provide total protection against all forms of failure, so we must also have off-platform

protection—backups and backup copies. These will fall into two categories: the daily backups, and their copies, used for operational recovery (for instance, for up to 31 days), and the monthly, long-term retention backups (and their copies), used for long-term retention. (They may be managed from the same system, though will often have different access and storage profiles.) Therein, we have another 230 copies potentially to concern ourselves with, between 62 backups/backup copies in the operational retention window, and 168 backups/backup copies in the long-term retention window.

If backups are written entirely to tape, then we'd expect perhaps a 2:1 data reduction as a result of streaming hardware compression; this gives us another 115 TB of storage for our 1 TB database covering the short-term and long-term retention copies within the backup system.

Alternately, if we're using deduplication storage for the backup, we might be able to assume a 10:1 deduplication ratio for the short-term operational retention of the database. That would reduce the 62 copies at 1 TB logical size per copy to 6.2 TB physically occupied, but again we'd have to apply RAID on top of that. Parity based RAID systems such as RAID-6 add a percentage overhead that's lower than straight mirroring, but still has to be factored. 8 × 4 TB drives would offer 32 TB of raw storage, but in a RAID-6 configuration only 24 TB of storage is present, thereby giving the RAID protection for that specific drive/capacity combination a 25% overhead. So the 6.2 TB of deduplicated, compressed backup data in a deduplication system would still occupy 7.75 TB storage for operational (short-term) retention.

Our *long*-term retention data—84 months backup and backup copy might get a lower cumulative deduplication ratio due to drift in the data set, so let's assume that comes down to 8:1 deduplication over its lifespan. So the 168 TB of logical copies of the database backup stored for long-term retention could drop down to 21 TB, but again with a similar RAID profile, with a 25% RAID storage overhead, result in 26.25 TB of data stored.

Over the lifetime of the data (assuming the data doesn't *grow*—quite unlikely in most cases), our 1 TB database uses around 38.8 TB of storage if we're using deduplication, or almost 120 TB of data if we're using tape for backup.

In all of this, we've not discussed the concept of *hot spares*—data drives sitting idle waiting to be inserted into the system for rebuild operations should a drive fail. These too contribute to the effective used storage throughout the environment, since the number and size of hot spares are effectively decided by the amount of data storage you intend to provision for.

If the database is mission critical, then it might also be replicated into a cyber-recovery area. That may be a shorter retention—say, 14 days, but that's another 14 copies to be considered; assuming this is deduplicated with a 10:1 reduction ratio, but again with similar RAID overheads, we'd be adding another 1.75 TB of storage overall for our database, bringing our 1 TB database to using 40.55 TB of overall storage.

Over a full 7 years, that 1 TB database has also yielded 294 logical copies, all of which will consume storage. As we'll discuss in later chapters, some of those copies may be logical, and some may feature high levels of storage efficiency, however, what we do see from this are two key features:

- Being able to reduce the total volume of data within a business, even by just 1 TB, can have a radical impact on the overall storage under management, particularly data storage protection.
- Data storage efficiency—particularly deduplication, a topic for which we discuss in detail in its own chapter—can be used to significantly offset the amount of usable storage required for both on-platform and off-platform copies of data.

Don't forget, the copies discussed thus far have all referred to the *original* 1 TB database, not additional copies that might

be made for testing, development or validation purposes: each of these in turn will potentially spawn a whole new family of data protection copies too.

Per-project based capacity provisioning within modern businesses can mask the copy proliferation problem. If we assume deduplication will be used rather than tape for backup storage, then looking at the extrapolated storage requirements for a 1 TB database as part of transformation processes for that database, a net requirement across a 7-year period of having to fund back into the business 41.55 TB between primary, disaster recovery, cyber-recovery, and backup storage doesn't seem too onerous. Even if we assume an annualized 10% growth rate, the overall requirements for our 1 TB database might still seem acceptable, except, of course, that the same scenario of copy numbers and associated required protection storage will play out for *every* workload and data set within the organization. Of course, the numbers will change depending on the volume and nature of the data within each workload or data set, but there'll continue to be an impact on storage requirements following similar considerations. If the business has 100 TB of mission critical databases all with the same lifecycle requirements as our 1 TB example, the overall storage required would be 4 PB.

Comparing the individual workload consideration to the overall storage requirement for all workloads is a perfect example of what's referred to as the *creeping normality* problem, or, in lay-terms, "death by a thousand cuts." When viewed through the narrow scope of an individual workload, it's easy for a business to declare data lifecycle management too challenging or complex a task. If you were able to apply data lifecycle management to 100 TB of mission critical databases, halving the data stored, the business might consider going from 100 TB to 50 TB lacking in commercial incentive. Yet, considering the alternate perspective of reducing *overall storage requirements* from 4 PB to 2 PB should be seen as an entirely worthwhile business cost-saving exercise.

In *The Odyssey*, Homer described the fate of Sisyphus thusly:

And I saw Sisyphus at his endless task raising his prodigious stone with both his hands. With hands and feet he tried to roll it up to top of the hill, but always, just before he could roll it down on to the other side, its weight would be too much for him, and the pitiless stone would come thundering down again on the plain.

The fate of Sisyphus points to the fate of storage and IT teams in businesses that don't use a data lifecycle: they are tasked daily with the ever harder task of keeping all data generated by the company safe and secure. It ignores the obvious truth that data sizes have exploded and will continue to grow.

While companies will try to insist that "storage is cheap," there's nothing cheap about paying to store data that you don't need. There's a basic, common logic here—what do you *personally* keep, and what do you personally throw away? Do you keep every letter you've ever received, every newspaper you've ever read, every book you've ever bought, every item of clothing you've ever worn, etc.? (Few people do, and those who do are recognized as obsessive-compulsive hoarders who need help, not more storage space.)

The answer for the vast majority of people is no: there's a useful lifespan of an item, and once that useful lifespan has elapsed, we have to make a decision on whether to keep it or not. The unpleasant truth is that saying "storage is cheap" is akin to closing your eyes and hoping a freight train barreling toward you is an optical illusion. In the end, it's just going to hurt.

Ironically, ongoing advances in primary storage systems may be a blessing for businesses in terms of achieving high performance, normalized storage with seamless snapshot and instant copy functionality, but the flip-side is that they continue to masquerade the need for data lifecycle processes. Consider how solid state drives (SSD), and more recently, non-volatile memory express (NVMe) enabled storage systems, combined with advanced storage processors allow for higher data efficiency: compression reduces the footprint of data blocks, deduplication reduces the number of data blocks, and the sheer speed of the storage reduces many of the operational overheads associated with snapshots and producing secondary copies. Yet, even though deduplication and compression can solve many problems, retaining data that's past its use-by date remains an exercise that can cost a company much, and as mentioned previously even more: regardless of what the legally *required* retention period is for data, if a company is still holding onto data because that's easier than deleting it, it can be subpoenaed, audited, or stolen.

When we actually take the time to consider the nature of copy proliferation for any particular workload, it's clear that the "original copy" footprint of data within an organization can pale almost into insignificance compared to the amount of data (and certainly the number of logical copies) generated to protect it. Data lifecycle management policies should be seen as an essential activity rather than a luxury.

3.3 Archiving and Deleting

No matter how you look at it, primary storage in an enterprise isn't cheap. Enterprise grade storage area networks (SANs) and NAS systems have a higher per-TB cost than say, cheap DAS storage, but offer degrees of protection,

reliability, flexibility, and performance orders of magnitude higher than DAS storage.

Consider a sample enterprise archive arrangement whereby:

■ NAS is used for file serving.
■ Long-term inactive data is archived from NAS to single-instance write-once read-many (WORM) storage.
■ The single-instance WORM storage is replicated for redundancy and protection.

Like it or not, there is a real, tangible cost to the storage of data at each of those steps. Undoubtedly, there is some data that must be kept on primary storage, and undoubtedly, there's some data that legitimately must be kept, but can be moved to archive storage. Yet equally, siphoning off irrelevant data to archive storage—data that has no purpose, is no longer used, and has no legal/fiscal requirements for retention—"just to keep it" will still cost money.

Failing to delete data can also expose the clients of the company to all manners of risks and in doing so expose the company to litigation—not to mention, reputational damage. In 2015, for instance, an online dating company suffered substantial data theft, exposing its users, *including those users who had requested their profiles deleted.*[*]

Just as good storage isn't necessarily cheap (remember that there's a difference between *cost-effective* and *cheap*), effective and efficient archival systems that are wholly integrated into data access mechanisms also aren't cheap. Ideally, archived data should only require minimal data backup, but that means it must be replicated and highly protected. Why waste that storage by pushing irrelevant and unnecessary data on to it?

A common point of conversation you'll hear among long-term members of the backup community is *backup isn't archive*. Unfortunately, this gets discussed so regularly because for some businesses, that's *exactly* what backup becomes. In order to properly consider the recklessness of this, consider one important difference between backup operations and archive operations, namely:

> A backup is about generating an extra copy of your data in case you lose the primary copy.

* Ashley Madison database suggests paid-delete option left identifiable data intact, Alex Hern, August 20, 2015, *Guardian*, www.theguardian.com/technology/2015/aug/19/ashley-madisons-paid-delete-option-left-data-identifying-users-post-claims

Backup should never delete, alter, or move the data being protected—it is and should always be the process of taking a new copy of that data. On the other hand:

> An archive is about moving your primary data copy.

In short, archive should be about storage, and backup should be about protection. A good storage policy and a good data protection policy will both consider the other topics, but there's not a 1:1 mapping between the two. There is a mistaken belief that all compliance data can be accommodated via archive. This is not guaranteed to be entirely accurate, and as we'll see in Chapter 25 (Long-Term Retention Considerations), even archiving content can't guarantee usability of recovered compliance content.

Refusing to archive data can have one of two consequences:

1. The company continually expands its primary storage to always ensure that all data can be stored.
2. Users delete data to make room for new data.

It's very, very rare to find the decision *not* to archive coupled with unlimited primary storage budget—precisely because the decision not to archive is typically discussed as a financial one. Yet, the net result is a reckless approach to *relying* on the backup system as an extension to primary storage.

> A University in Australia instituted filesystem quotas to limit data growth. Due to their interpretation of how academic freedom of expression and communication worked, they didn't institute email quotas.
>
> At some point, an academic came up with the notion that when his home directory filled, he could create a zip file of everything in it, email it to himself, delete the contents and start afresh.
>
> As a direct consequence, primary storage within the university suffered explosive, unplanned growth.

In the scenario described here, it was the email system, not the backup system, used as an adjunct to primary storage, but the net effect was remarkably similar—a system not designed to act as primary storage (email content) was enlisted to do so, all because archiving wasn't pursued for storage systems.

Choosing to treat a backup system as a safety net or blank check for data deletion is quite a reckless thing to do. It may seem "smart" since the backup system is designed to

recover lost data, but it introduces a few vexing problems, namely:

- Requires intimate knowledge of the backup cycles
- Increases the recovery load on the backup environment
- Hides the real storage requirements, even resulting in supersaturated storage

Consider the first point—doing this requires intimate knowledge of the backup cycles. Consider a user who has heard that the quickest way to get more capacity is to delete some data, since "it can be recovered." However, if the data-generation cycle didn't match the data backup cycle, it's entirely plausible that such data might *only* exist on daily and weekly backups, not the monthly backup retention period. Thus, if the user goes to recover it in 3–4 months when it's needed again, it may have been irretrievably lost.

Assuming the user *can* recover it, what's to say that the recovery of that data won't impact other backup and recovery operations that *technically* are more important? If it's just a single user doing it, the chances of impact are going to be reasonably low—but if it becomes a common enough practice within the organization, all those additional recovery requests are going to start impacting what we'd call the *true* backup and recovery operations.

If users and/or administrators are deleting *sometime-required* data at a whim, rather than seeing it archived, this has the potential to massively hide the measurement of how much storage is actually (not just currently, but *actually*) in use. On any given day, it may *seem* that there's plenty of storage available, but that can just be a mirage. This leads to what is perhaps best described as *supersaturated storage.** Supersaturated storage resembles overprovisioned storage, but because it's something that results from a lack of lifecycle management, there's no monitoring or reporting across the storage systems that will reveal the problem to the business.

First, consider overprovisioning. If we look at virtual machines, a common storage saving technique is to allocate a maximum boundary on the storage the virtual machine will use, but allow storage to only be allocated as it's required. For instance, a Linux virtual machine might be created with a 100 GB virtual hard drive, with *thin provisioning* enabled. At the end of the operating system installation process for a server, the actual used storage might be 3 GB or less. Thus, 97 GB of storage hasn't been consumed *yet*.

Thin provisioning can lead to more storage allocated than is actually available to the operating environment. Ten

---

* If considering this simply from the perspective of storage management, the above might be termed as *overprovisioned*, but in this context, supersaturated is more appropriate. After all, *overprovisioned* implies a level of monitoring and management—neither of which applies to supersaturated storage.

virtual machines, each with the *potential* to grow to 200 GB of used data might reside cooperatively 800 GB of SSD storage still with room to spare by virtue of knowing that the overall allocated storage for each virtual machine is unlikely to be consumed. In fact, capacity management approaches within the modern IT environment will factor in allowances for a particular level of *over-subscription* of storage; it might be acceptable, for instance, for virtual machine storage volumes to host virtual machines that have a theoretical maximum capacity of two and a half times the actual storage capacity.

Such over-subscription can be handled because there are monitoring and reporting systems in place. The hypervisor management system can track the difference between *consumed* and *allocated* storage, reporting on the disparity and allowing allocation limits to be automatically enforced.

Supersaturation though is a problem usually created by end users in response to insufficient storage. A 100 GB filesystem that's filling up might have 10 GB of data deleted by a user, knowing that the data will exist in backup and can be recalled at a future point. However, with that 10 GB of data deleted, there's capacity for *more* data to be added; so the system is again filled up to 100 GB. Another 10 GB more "recoverable" data is deleted, and the storage is filled up, yet again. So while the storage administrators might believe that the users are managing their storage appropriately, the users are creating a situation where a complete recovery of the data requires 120 GB of storage, not the 100 GB which is allocated. Hence, the storage is supersaturated.

The most common objection raised by businesses to a formal archive architecture is the perceived cost of infrastructure required and the necessity to still perform data protection against the archival storage. Both of these are real costs, but they're invariably developed on the false premise of equivalence to primary storage costs.

Consider that data is archived because it falls into two key categories, namely:

1. It is old and infrequently accessed (if at all).
2. It is required for compliance reasons and will not be accessed except for a legal reason.

True archive systems however provide guaranteed WORM-level protection, compliant with a variety of legal and fiduciary requirements. This effectively means that data archived to compliant archive storage systems *cannot* be modified, even by the vendor. There are no *back-doors* to the system, no way to alter or delete content, and all of this can be continually proved via logs and algorithmic verification. (The only form of "modification" would be physical destruction.)

The net result is that when archive data is replicated to a secondary archive system for disaster recovery purposes, it no longer needs to be backed up, since it is inviolate. Returning

to our previous example of 100 TB in mission critical databases, if we could *archive* 20 TB of that, *creeping normality* would suggest it's too much effort for not enough return; however, removing it from backup cycles, we'd save 715 TB of backup and recovery storage alone over a 7-year point of view, which would significantly offset the relatively minor archive storage requirements that would be added for that data set.

3.4 Summary

Storage isn't cheap or infinite, and time is always limited. While businesses can "get lucky" at times by not having data lifecycle policies, a truly enterprise class and dependable data protection schema should fully integrate with data lifecycle policies to deliver optimal protection at optimal cost for the business.

True hoarding is a recognized psychological condition. Just as we'd be concerned for Aunt Kim and Uncle Gary having a house stuffed full to the rafters with towers of newspapers in every space not occupied by appliances or bedding, we should be concerned with a business that accumulates all data without any consideration of expunging or archiving.

3.5 Self-Reflection

Consider the data you have stored at home; this might be aggregated across all your computers and devices, or you might focus on an individual location (especially if you're using a home NAS environment).

As a thought exercise, first guess what percentage of data you have that you've actually accessed in the past month, then try to *estimate* the percentage of data that you have accessed over that time against the total amount of data stored. In particular, do you think you've accessed all of the data, or a subset, with some data accessed repeatedly?

Look for data that you have not accessed for more than 6 months, or more than a year. What sort of percentage might it represent of your overall data?

What percentage of data do you estimate you access without modification?

If you're using macOS, you'll be able to use the Finder search function: this allows you to search for files based on "Last opened date," where you can specify a *before* date. For Linux or Unix users, you would be able to use the *find* utility to search for files with a last access time that exceeds a particular threshold (e.g., +1 year). Windows users will be at a slight disadvantage here: from Windows 10, the operating system no longer updates *access time* by default when you open a file. Instead, for Windows systems, focus your search on *modified time*. While it's useful for data lifecycle management, it's not as efficient compared to access time—can you think why?

It is common to assume a larger percentage of in-use data when we're not using data classification and data lifecycle management, and it's that natural assumption that we're *actively* using more data than we really are that so often encourages businesses that there's no point in applying data lifecycle policies. (For instance, you might guess 10%—however, assuming you have 8 TB of stored data, between photos, movies, TV-series, games, general documents, etc., 10% accessed is 800 GB.)

Chapter 4

Elements of a Protection System

4.1 Introduction

It's a common misconception in IT that technology solves everything. If this were true, IT would be an entirely commoditized, cookie-cutter industry with no need for operational specialists or experts.

This is as equally true in data protection as anywhere else.

As shown in Figure 4.1, there are six distinct elements in a data protection system:

- People
- Processes and documentation
- Service level agreements (SLAs)
- Testing
- Training
- Technology

In essence, technology comprises only one-sixth of the elements—and it is by far the simplest to deal with.

Arguably some of these topics might be considered to be subsets of one another; testing, after all, is something that by rights should be handled as part of a documented process, and training is something given to people. Yet when we collapse these into umbrella terms, it's common for individual requirements to be forgotten and harder to reconcile the different roles and functions that help to ensure these topics are dealt with. In a similar way to how ITIL differentiates between those who are *responsible* and those who are *accountable*, we deal with each of the components in the previous list individually to ensure their requirements are explicitly understood.

4.2 People

There are three essential participants within data protection, regardless of how significantly it has been automated. These are:

- Designers
- Operators
- End users

4.2.1 Designers

Ultimately, it makes little point what processes are put in place, what technologies are deployed, what SLAs are established, and what training is developed if the actual system as designed can't meet those requirements.

The designers or the architects of the data protection environment have the critical responsibility of ensuring that the system as planned and subsequently implemented meets the business requirements for protecting data. This of course includes both the *proactive* and *reactive* components.

More so than any other people involved in a data protection system, it will be the designers who will need to understand the business level requirements of the system. The designers need to concentrate on a very broad set of considerations that include disaster recovery and its role in business continuity as much as individual system recoverability. This includes (but is certainly not limited to) understanding each of the following:

- What IT systems map to which business functions
- Dependencies between IT systems
- Criticality of the business functions
- The dependency between business functions
- The order in which IT systems should be recovered in the event of catastrophic loss

A protection system designed or implemented *without* these considerations is unlikely to meet the overall requirements of the business—except perhaps by sheer luck.

The designers *have* to interface with the broader business in order to steward a functional data protection solution into daily operation. IT cannot—and must not—have sole input

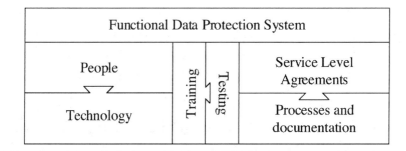

Figure 4.1 Elements of a functional data protection system.

into the requirements of a data protection solution, since the data protection solution must effectively meet the needs of the business.

You will note that we have used the term *designers* rather than *administrators* or *architects*. This is because optimum data protection solutions will draw on the collective knowledge of the administrators (the people with day to day high level oversight of the environment), the various stakeholders in the business who may provide input to the design, and of course the architects (the people with the "bigger picture" view of IT infrastructure and processes).

4.2.2 Operators

Coming from a classic datacenter environment tends to encourage thinking of *operators* and *administrators* separately. This can still be the case in many businesses today, but the differentiation is increasingly a blurred one.* Ultimately, both roles end up operating the environment, be it through maintenance, configuration, or business as usual functions.

So regardless of whether a person's job title includes *operator* or *administrator*, they're both tasked with making sure the systems, once put in place, run correctly, continue to function, and support growth.

While the system designers are responsible for making sure the data protection systems are *capable* of meeting the established SLAs, it's the job of the operators to ensure the systems *do* continually meet those SLAs. The designers focus on the theoretical, while the operators on the practical. (The most apt comparison is building a house: An architect will design the house and ensure the construction takes place as per the design. It's the people who take possession of the house afterward that have to live in it and make it a *home*.)

Similarly, once the designers have overseen the deployment of their solution, the challenge of making the environment livable for business comes down to the operators, and this necessitates a suite of activities including but not limited to

- Administration
- Operation
- Monitoring
- Reporting
- Maintenance and remediation
- Forecasting and trending

Most of those activities are understood well by the majority of those businesses. In an optimally designed and deployed environment, many of those functions should be significantly automated, too. This makes the role of the operators more focused on dealing with exceptions and projects rather than mundane activities. The lingering challenge within many organizations, however, is *forecasting and trending*. These are important for two entirely separate reasons:

- To predict ongoing conformance to SLAs or identify where they can no longer be met
- To provide detailed input into the *next* product cycle

Technology has a definite lifecycle—it's planned, tested, installed, used, and then either phased out or upgraded. It's what happens next that can be wastefully challenging. If a business has not been collating data on the data protection systems and as a result has not been producing trending information and forecasts, then the *next* acquisition cycle can be potentially just as painful or more so than the previous one.

Anecdotally, it is usually the case that businesses which fail to adequately forecast their environmental growth and/or fail to adequately classify their data are the ones who are most likely to resent whatever investment they make into data protection. (One might suggest that appreciation of functional results can only be achieved when the goals are known and the targets are measurable.)

4.2.3 End Users

Even end users have a place in a data protection system, albeit a role that is substantially removed from that of administrators or operators.

Common sense dictates that while users shouldn't have to be personally involved in data protection activities (and

---

* As we will cover in greater detail later, converged and hyperconverged environments are causing the lines to be significantly blurred between traditional infrastructure roles within an organization, also.

indeed should be able to assume that adequate steps are taken by the business to prevent data loss), they should also behave responsibly. In some organizations, users have taken advantage of data protection systems by deliberately deleting data to free up space, fully intending to request recovery of the deleted data at a later time.

Equally, users *should* be informed of situations where data protection doesn't take place, such as situations where data is refreshed from other sources as necessary, rather than being actively protected. (Test and quality assurance systems are quite typical of this.) This comes from having well-defined and documented SLAs that are mapped to business functions so they're clearly documented for and articulated to the end users in business-appropriate (rather than IT-focused) language.

Finally, users should understand how to make recovery requests—if they don't, it may be that they waste time recreating data that could otherwise be quickly retrieved from protection sources.

More recently, attention to user interaction with data protection has come from workforce transformation. Workforce transformation seeks to provide more useful tools (that are more satisfactory to use) to an often mobile or remote workforce. Particularly as newer generations of workers with different priorities enter employment, providing adequate tools is becoming essential, not only for productivity, but also for staff retention.

As businesses transform the other services of their business (e.g., traditional IT infrastructure into private or hybrid cloud, and digital transformation—next generation applications running against platform as a service (PaaS) or software as a service (SaaS) stacks), end user accessible data protection services will gain priority. For instance, users may have concerns about the transition from a traditional, desktop-application serviced email system to one which is primarily accessed through a browser or smart phone/tablet, but this could be tempered by easy access to backup and recovery services, allowing self-service retrieval of any lost items.

4.2.4 Data Protection Team

It's no longer the case that data protection options can be arranged in isolation. The traditional model that evolved from classic system administration teams saw backup, storage, and virtualization administrators all belonging to different units. Given the plethora of data protection options that may need to be deployed in a modern business:

- *Backup administrators* need to understand storage and virtualization options in use.
- *Storage administrators* need to know how and where backup will supplement replication, snapshots, and fault tolerance, and be closely aligned to virtualization for performance and protection reasons.

- *Virtualization administrators* need to know what protection, capacity, and performance options are available to them.

The best way to efficiently achieve this is to combine all three—backup, storage, and virtualization—into a single functioning team for the business. (We are already seeing businesses do this by establishing *infrastructure* administration teams, tasked with all of these.)

Increasing requirements around agility, driving the adoption of converged and hyperconverged infrastructure is making the move toward infrastructure administrators increasingly a question of *when*, not *if*, within the modern enterprise. Even if a business is large enough that combining their storage, backup, and virtualization administrators is seen as operationally impractical, the likelihood of there being at least *some* staff with oversight of administration at the infrastructure view is high.

4.3 Training

Sadly in many organizations, training of staff in relation to data protection is inadequate, which can lead to significant challenges, such as:

- Inefficient processes that do not maximize the capabilities of the technologies at hand
- Higher chance of human error via insufficient understanding of the products

Depending on who interacts with the protection systems (and in what way), a variety of training options are available to choose from. The first step will be to determine who requires certification-level training. Certainly for some staff that certification will be an important aspect of their training and development. This will particularly be the case for protection system designers and administrators. Past that, in-house-developed training courses or those offered by third-party suppliers, such as systems integrators and professional consultancy agencies, may offer more than sufficient knowledge transfer.

Of course, individual staff members themselves need backups. Having only one person trained in any particular aspect of a protection system is an undesirable concentration of knowledge that should be strongly discouraged, no matter how small the environment. Thus, at least two or more people should receive training wherever possible in the various data protection systems used within the organization. This fulfills several purposes, allowing for staff to:

- Be on leave, sick, or otherwise away without compromising the business

- Move on without fear of essential knowledge being lost
- Peer review one another's planned or implemented changes

Companies tend to experience the most problems with enterprise data protection technologies when they don't allow staff to develop skills properly or refuse to accept that daily administration of such technology is part of the IT role. There is always a direct correlation between the level of customer staff involvement in the installation, configuring, testing, and training and the quality of the experience they have in using the products. That is, untrained employees are likely to have more issues and ultimately put the ability of the business to ensure data recovery at risk.

TRAIN THE RIGHT USERS

Optimally, the people who should be trained in a product are those who will have the most daily interaction in it, with some training (usually more high level) provided to others, such as architects, capacity managers, etc. Training the wrong teams or individuals (e.g., to simply key a training quota requirement) is often counter-productive.

Sellers in the data protection space (regardless of whether they are vendors or integrators) have known for some time that a lack of customer training in their products can be a significant cause for lowered customer satisfaction. It's not uncommon for IT management to believe data protection is a 'simple' function that requires little or no training, perhaps beyond reading the documentation and watching a YouTube video clip. Increased focus on modern, browser-based interfaces that present a simplified view no doubt increase this sense of simplicity, yet like the proverbial duck on a pond, the serenity seen in a modern interface can belie the knowledge required to maximize the full potential of a solution. While a system should be designed such that someone with sufficient knowledge can approach it without fear of surprise, that doesn't mean someone with *no* knowledge of the products involved should be in charge of design or operational functions of the solution.

4.4 Documentation and Processes

One could argue that *processes* and *documentation* are two separate items, but in terms of describing a system in its design and operation, they are invariably two sides of the same coin—processes that are not documented are of little

benefit, and documentation either will exist to describe a process or should have been created *using* a process.

We can broadly break the requisite documentation for a data protection system into three categories:

- Design
- Implementation
- Operational

Andy Hertzfeld, in Mac Folklore, wrote a story about the development of the *round rect[angle]* function in QuickDraw. When Steve Jobs saw a demo of QuickDraw functionality, he asked for rectangles with rounded corners, which Bill Atkinson, the developer, objected to:

Steve suddenly got more intense. "Rectangles with rounded corners are everywhere! Just look around this room!" And sure enough, there were lots of them, like the whiteboard and some of the desks and tables. Then he pointed out the window. "And look outside, there's even more, practically everywhere you look!" He even persuaded Bill to take a quick walk around the block with him, pointing out every rectangle with rounded corners that he could find.

When Steve and Bill passed a no-parking sign with rounded corners, it did the trick. "OK, I give up," Bill pleaded.

Over the next few months, roundrects worked their way into various parts of the user interface, and soon became indispensable.*

Just like Bill Atkinson originally disagreeing with implementing round rectangles, only to discover how useful they were, it's quite regular to encounter such similar opposition to formal documentation within IT. It often gets short shrift in IT—yet we are often so demanding of it of others, both within IT and without. Someone who may studiously try to avoid writing any documentation about *how* they'd implemented a system would nevertheless rigorously complain if a critical component were left undocumented by the vendor. Equally, someone who insisted on up-to-date details about how a system has been implemented would vehemently reject the notion that the local bank staff will just try to "remember" their current bank balance after a paycheck has cleared, rather than it being recorded in the system.

Particularly in larger environments, or where the cost of implementing or altering a data protection solution is higher,

---

* Andy Hertzfeld, Mac Folklore, www.folklore.org/StoryView.py?story=Round_Rects_Are_Everywhere.txt

it is very likely there will be formal workshops taking place during the pre-purchase, design, and implementation phases. It is crucial for the long-term success of a data protection solution that these workshops be documented: that is, have minutes taken outlining the participating individuals (their roles as well as their names), which companies or parts of the business they were from, and of course the decisions and actions (and the results of the actions) from the workshop. Workshops can often play a pivotal role in determining the functional and non-functional requirements of a data protection solution, after all. Common challenges introduced by not formally documenting workshops include:

■ Individual participants each view the discussions and outcomes with different priorities—what someone perceives to be as critical, another may not.
■ Action items are regularly taken during meetings such as projects and workshops, but humans have a tendency to forget to follow up on items. Assigning responsible people to actions and following those actions through ensures that items deemed important to the success of a solution do not get forgotten.
■ People who do not attend the workshops (particularly those who will either have responsibility or accountability over functions delivered by the intended solution) will need a way of establishing a background over the key discussion criteria.
■ Workshop sponsors will want to see clear evidence that *their* goals have been met by the activities.

4.4.1 Design

Design documentation reflects architectural information about an environment and, except in the smallest of environments, should be quite formal in its structure. This is also the documentation that will refer back to business goals and requirements most, since the design itself should be premised *on* those goals and requirements.

An adequately planned data protection environment will be developed from a series of business requirements, which are typically broken into two key categories:

■ Functional requirements
■ Non-functional requirements

If these requirements *have* been outlined, then they form the absolute core of the details that should be addressed in the design documentation. For instance, consider the functional and non-functional requirements outlined in Table 4.1.

The design documentation produced, in addition to outlining the *actual* design, must cite how the solution design meets originally stated requirements *and* just as critically, where it doesn't. Wherever possible, design documentation should also

Table 4.1 Sample Functional and Non-Functional Requirements

Type	Requirement	Criticality
Functional	Shall support duplication of backups.	Mandatory
Functional	Shall support block-based backup of Windows filesystems.	Mandatory
Functional	Shall support block-based backup of Linux filesystems.	Desirable
Functional	Shall support online backup of Oracle databases.	Mandatory
Functional	Shall support online backup of PostgreSQL databases.	Desirable
Non-functional	The off-site copy of backups should always be up to date within 12 hours.	Mandatory
Non-functional	The system should support use by color-blind individuals without impairment.	Mandatory
Non-functional	The system should have a REST API.	Desirable

outline *why* the system is being designed as it is. This "show your working" approach helps future designers, operators, managers, and auditors (among others) to understand critical decision parameters that occurred within the design. For example, consider the scenario where a particular type of database could be backed up either using a daily full backup, or a weekly full backup with daily incremental backups. If the design documentation calls for this type of database to always receive full backups, the reasons behind this should be documented. By capturing this information, it helps to avoid "second guessing" and making changes later that have unanticipated flow-on effects—and it equally allows the business to re-evaluate design decisions if the variables that led to those decisions change. For example, using our database example, it might be documented, "The database server only supports the removal of transaction logs after a full backup." At a future point in time, the database developers might change this functionality, allowing the original backup design to be safely altered.

The design must be as complete as possible. Using the example of a backup and recovery system, for instance, simply stating schedules, policies, intended device configuration, and the data retention policy is insufficient—it must also outline the reports and monitoring options that will be configured, too.

4.4.2 Implementation

Once a data protection system has been designed, it has to be implemented, and documentation will be of critical importance to satisfy a service transition manager that there is sufficient explanation of the environment to enter an ongoing operational phase.

4.4.2.1 System Configuration Guide

From an individual project point of view, we often consider implementation documentation to refer to as "as-built" or "system configuration" guides. These outline (sometimes, seemingly in excruciating detail) exactly how the system is put together and exactly what the system looked like at the conclusion of the implementation. These form a *line in the sand*, so to speak. They clearly state what the system should look like and clearly outline (approved) deviations between what was designed and what was implemented.

As-built material typically falls into two categories, which for want of better terms we'd describe as *initial* and *ongoing*. The initial should be a static description of the environment at the conclusion of implementation, but since the system is likely to change over time, those changes should be reflected in updated implementation documents. Both variants are necessary.

4.4.2.2 System Map

A system map can best be described as a network diagram/map showing systems connectivity, as well as system and application dependencies. In this case when we refer to *systems*, we refer to all components that make up the system, namely,

- Hosts
- Applications
- Networking connectivity
- Data storage

The dependencies tracked in a system map are best described as *operational* dependencies and reflect the interoperability of the environment and allow the mapping and prioritization of protection and recovery.

A system map should be a core component of the IT environment documentation for all organizations but in actuality mostly exists in the minds of IT staff and then only in segments—that is, different departments in IT will usually have different views of the system map.

As the size of the environment grows, the chances of a system map being an actual diagram decrease—just the same way as the chances of it being an actual comprehensive network diagram for the business IT environment decrease. In these scenarios, it's necessary to produce the system map as a table that accompanies the network diagram or diagrams.

A basic network diagram focusing just on the core production systems for a small business might resemble Figure 4.2. While this broadly shows the key components within an environment, it doesn't provide any details on how they relate to each other and how they map to business functions. For instance, there's nothing in Figure 4.2 that indicates that the intranet server hosts a web-based call management system that interfaces with the database server, using the authentication server to ensure only those users who are allowed to access the system can retrieve data. Thus, it's fair to say the standard network diagram is incomplete for the purposes of data protection.

Without this relationship information, there is no clear mechanism to determine the criticality of systems for protection or the recovery order in the event of a catastrophic datacenter failure. A common consequence of this is that even IT staff may not fully appreciate the recovery prioritization order or the level of protection required for individual system components. For example, most environments fully rely on centralized host resolution (e.g., Domain Name System (DNS))—yet a network diagram in itself will not explain the criticality of DNS for successful business operations.

By having a system map, not only can system and application dependencies be recorded visually, but they can also be referred to during data protection planning, design, and implementation activities and during disaster recovery and business continuity scenarios. A system map might extend the network diagram from Figure 4.2 as shown in Figure 4.3.

In Figure 4.3, we have mapped dependencies as follows:

- Each piece of infrastructure is numbered.
- In addition to the infrastructure shown on the network diagram, we have introduced business functions. This is imperative: it ensures we identify not only individual systems, but the "net functions" that the business sells and relies on.
- Each system is labeled with its function and also its dependencies. For example, the figure shows that the file/authentication server (1) depends on the DNS server (5) for successful operation.

As the size of the infrastructure grows, the system map as a literal diagram can become unwieldy for successful maintenance—or reliable interpretation. At some point, it will usually become necessary to construct a system map as a table that accompanies the network diagram or diagrams. Such a table might resemble the one shown in Table 4.2.

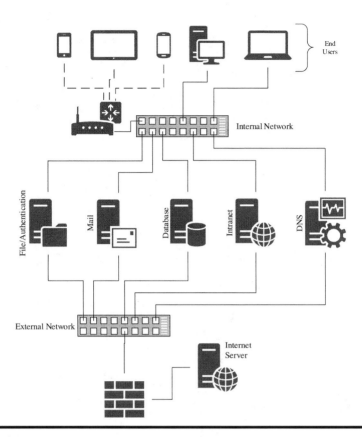

Figure 4.2 Basic network diagram.

With this in place, the level of importance can be assigned to a system not just by the *perceived* user importance but by the number of systems that depends on it. This in turn may reveal the importance (particularly from a disaster recovery perspective) of systems not previously seen as high priority.

Based on Table 4.2, we can make the following observations—particularly when considering *production* systems (though of course there may be exceptions):

■ The higher the number of dependencies, the earlier a system is likely to require recovery.
■ The smaller the number of dependencies, the more *visible* a system is likely to be to the company or end users.

Some organizations feel system maps are only required for extreme circumstances, such as if all system administrators are unavailable *and* a disaster happens. It is believed in these situations that risk mitigation (e.g., having company policies prohibiting all system administration staff from traveling together) resolves this problem. However, system maps serve a far more important business need—they help to ensure that IT activities and systems are correctly aligned to business functions, activities, and products. Without a system map, many businesses end up in situations where the data protection goals of the IT environment don't align correctly to business needs.

It should be noted that in addition to their use for determining recovery order for data protection, system maps have also developed as an essential feature of *application discovery*. As the number of applications within businesses increase, the dependencies between applications and the systems they run on become increasingly complex to map and manage. Businesses looking at moving workloads (e.g., to the public cloud, or between datacenters) or decommissioning them can make use of application discovery utilities and services to effectively map out, via network connections, which systems communicate with one another, thereby establishing threads of interconnectedness that might otherwise be missed.

4.5 Testing

Without a doubt, testing is critical for adequate assurance of data protection capabilities. It is often said, for instance, that an untested backup is a failed recovery, yet it equally applies to all aspects of data protection, including RAID, snapshots, and replication.

4.5.1 Type Testing

The statement *an untested backup is a failed recovery* may rankle some, and this is where the concept of *type testing* must

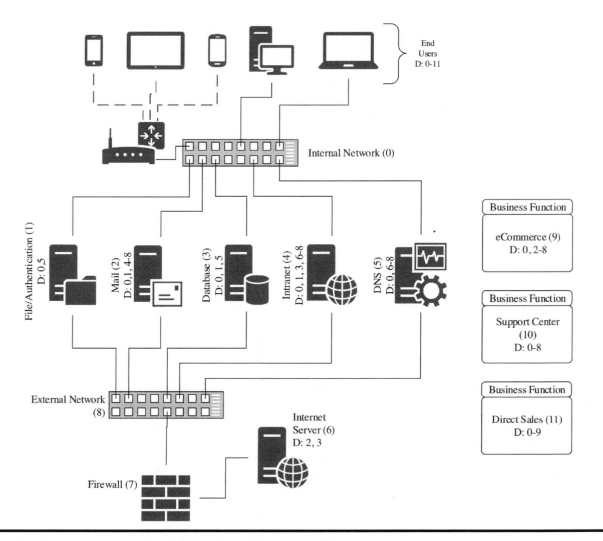

Figure 4.3   System map as an extended function of the network diagram.

come into consideration. Type testing is the means by which reasonable assurance can be provided of data recoverability without testing every single *instance* within an organization.

For instance, limiting ourselves to recoverability for the moment, consider that a heterogeneous enterprise backup and recovery system may be used to protect Solaris, Linux, Windows, AIX, HPUX, and VMware systems within an environment. A needlessly excessive test process would see comprehensive testing done on *every* Solaris server, on *every* Linux server, on *every* Windows server, and so on.

Type testing usually allows for sufficient assurance by identifying each unique *combination* of tests and randomizing the testing process against those combinations.

So, with a backup and recovery system, this would mean tests such as

- Filesystem backup for Solaris
- Filesystem recovery for Solaris
- Filesystem backup for Linux
- Filesystem recovery for Linux

- Filesystem backup for Windows
- Filesystem recovery for Windows
- Filesystem backup for AIX
- Filesystem recovery for AIX
- Filesystem backup for HPUX
- Filesystem recovery for HPUX
- Image-level backup for VMware
- Image-level recovery for VMware
- File-level recovery from image-level backup for VMware

In such scenarios, the tests are not repeated on every single instance of each platform, just one instance of each platform. In certain cases, there may be repeats—"platinum-level" systems—such as those deemed absolutely critical to the business or requiring satisfaction of particular legal/financial tests might each be tested, but overall the complete number of tests performed within the environment is significantly reduced. Type testing is most reliable in environments making use of "standard builds," or "standard operating

Table 4.2 Tracking System/Functional Dependencies in a Table

System/Function	Depends On	Number of Dependencies
Internal network	None	10
DNS	Internal network External internet server Firewall Secure network	8
File/authentication server	External network DNS	5
Mail server	Internal network File/authentication Intranet DNS External internet server Firewall External network	4
Database server	Internal network File/authentication DNS	6
Intranet server	Internal network File/authentication Database server DNS External internet server Firewall External network	1
End users	All	0
Business function: eCommerce	Internal network Database Intranet DNS External internet server Firewall External network	1
Business function: support center	Internal network Database Intranet DNS External internet server Firewall External network	0
Business function: direct sales	Internal network File/authentication Mail Database Intranet DNS External internet server Firewall External network eCommerce Function	0

environments" (SOEs), thereby providing a level of assurance that the base systems are designed and behave in an expected manner.

The previous list could be further simplified, depending on the needs of the organization. For instance, since we can assume that recovery has a dependency of a successful backup, we might instead perform type testing only on a few critical *backup* types (e.g., filesystem backup and VMware image-level backup), then move on to conduct all of the recovery type tests in the previous list. Since filesystem recovery for Linux by necessity means that a filesystem backup has been completed successfully, once backups in a new system have been shown to be successful, type testing similar backup types may no longer be required, so long as recovery testing can be completed successfully.

Of course, type testing applies to all aspects of data protection. Environments that make use of mirroring and replication will see similar type testing performed, such as:

■ Successful mount of replicated Windows filesystem
■ Successful mount of replicated Solaris filesystem
■ Successful read/write open of Oracle database on replicated Windows filesystem
■ Successful read/write open of Oracle database on replicated Solaris filesystem

Further, testing will be integrated where data protection activities are integrated. Consider an environment where, for performance reasons, production filesystems are not directly backed up, but instead, replicated tertiary mirrors are split off, mounted on another host, and backed up from there. In such situations, type testing might include:

■ Filesystem backup from replicated Solaris split
■ Filesystem backup from replicated Linux split
■ Filesystem backup from replicated Windows split
■ Successful recovery to production filesystem of data backed up from replicated Solaris split
■ Successful recovery to production filesystem of data backed up from replicated Linux split
■ Successful recovery to production filesystem of data backed up from replicated Windows split
■ Successful read/write open of Oracle database recovered to production environment from backup of replicated Windows filesystem
■ Successful read/write open of Oracle database recovered to production environment from backup of replicated Solaris filesystem

This further goes to show the importance of data protection to be approached from a holistic measure—it's not sufficient in such integrated environments that each component be tested individually, for the success of a system recovery (from the *business* perspective) can only be evaluated at the conclusion of *all* linked activities.

4.5.2 Informal vs Formal

Both informal and formal testing should be conducted. Informal testing is often considered a function of the original system implementation—that is, as technology is rolled out, those implementing it will periodically run snap tests to confirm that a particular aspect of the technology as deployed is working as intended. This could include:

■ Removing a hard drive in a newly created RAID-5 group, replacing it, and confirming the array rebuilds it successfully
■ Confirming basic file backup/recovery to disk and tape options
■ Confirming successful mount of a split, replicated filesystem on another host
■ Powering off a switch in a redundant configuration to ensure no data access operations fail (or failover successfully to the alternate data path)

During an implementation phase in particular, informal testing is typically seen as a basic "sanity" test on the system before moving on to conduct formal testing. Particularly given that formal testing typically involves multiple staff and therefore is more costly (both in terms of time and money) to perform, informal testing can in fact speed up implementation.

Beyond implementation, informal testing can be a means of conducting quick, random spot-checks, particularly for staff training or post-repair validation.

Unlike the more relaxed process of informal testing, formal testing is usually a time-intensive activity designed to meet legal or compliance requirements. Formal testing involves:

■ A test register
■ A test procedure
■ A documented evidence of completed tests
■ A signed/notarized acceptance of each conducted test by two or more people
■ A defect register

A business planning on undertaking formal testing will need to verify whether there are any regulatory requirements associated with that testing. For instance, some industries may have requirements that formal testing be conducted only by employees of the business and vetted by an external auditing agency. Other industries may be more relaxed and allow formal testing to be conducted by the company implementing the solution and so on. By verifying the regulatory requirements for formal testing ahead of conducting such tests, a business avoids both unpleasant repetition of activities *and* the risk of compliance-based fines.

4.5.2.1 Test Procedure

In formal testing, the test procedure should outline, at minimum, the following:

- The procedure version and publication date
- The author of the procedure
- The purpose of the test
- The details of who (i.e., role) should conduct the test
- The test prerequisites
- The sequence of steps to perform test (or reference to exact documentation elsewhere)
- The expected results
- Known defects or mitigations that need to be considered when conducting the test

Each test procedure forms part of the overall documentation of the environment. The test procedures are then "checked out" and used as part of the test register, which we will cover next.

4.5.2.2 Test Register

The test register is a document that outlines:

- The formal tests that have been established for the environment
- The results of those tests each time they have been performed

When performing a formal test, at minimum the following should be recorded:

- The name and version of the test conducted
- The date the test was conducted
- Actual results recorded
- Actions taken (e.g., if the results did not match the expected results)
- Whether the test was deemed successful or not
- Names and roles of those who performed/witnessed the test
- Signatures of those who performed/witnessed the test
- Defect register and risk mitigation statements

Essentially, the test procedures are templates for the tests that will be periodically conducted within the environment (both for system commissioning, and ongoing periodic operational validation); the test register is the formal record of the tests having been conducted.

4.5.2.3 Test Schedule

It matters little how rigorously defined tests are if they are not performed. As such, the purpose of the test schedule is to outline the regularity at which each specific test should be conducted.

To ensure tests aren't forgotten, the test schedule should be automated. In its most primitive form, this may be something as simple as periodic evaluation of the test schedule and creation of suitable reminders and tasks for people to conduct the tests. For instance, a management team might review the test schedule quarterly, determine which tests need to be conducted during that time, and set calendar tasks and appointments as necessary for the appropriate staff and alerts for themselves to follow up with staff to ensure the tests have been performed and the results documented. More formal test management systems may handle that automation directly. (Note that automation of the test process is somewhat difference from automating the test schedule, and is a topic we will consider later in this chapter.)

4.5.3 Performance Testing

Equally important as functional testing is performance testing. Whereas functional testing determines whether or not something can be done at all, performance testing establishes a baseline of how *long* something should take to complete.

Performance testing applies to all aspects of data protection and involves three separate activities:

- Baselines
- Standard testing
- Resampling

Baselines identify the expected amount of time activities should take in controlled situations. For example, on storage systems, baselines might be established for the rebuilding of RAID logical unit numbers (LUNs) following drive replacements where:

- The filesystems are inactive.
- The filesystems are under moderate access load.
- The filesystems are under substantial access load.

Of course, multiple RAID types might be used (particularly in conventional, hard-drive based storage arrays), so the business might also need to evaluate such performance baselines based on a variety of anticipated RAID types, since each RAID type presents a different rebuild performance profile.

Baselines relating to replication might include:

- Length of time to perform first synchronization over a specific speed link

- Length of time to resynchronize over a specific speed link after 10% change during split
- Length of time to resynchronize over a specific speed link after a 30% change during split
- Length of time to resynchronize over a specific speed link after a 10% change during split while the source system is rebuilding its RAID system
- Length of time to resynchronize when the link is unused, 25% used, 50% used, or 90% used by other data if in a shared bandwidth arrangement

Baselines relating to backup systems might include:

- Length of time to backup a 100 GB filesystem of no more than 100,000 files
- Length of time to backup a 100 GB filesystem of 1,000,000 files
- Length of time to backup a 1 TB database
- Amount of data that can be backed up in an 8 hour window
- Length of time to rescan 1 TB of backed up data without access to media indices

Equally, baselines for recoveries from the backup environment might include

- Amount of filesystem data for files between 5 KB and 1 GB that can be recovered in a 1 hour window over 1 Gbit and 10 Gbit network links
- Length of time to recover a 100 GB filesystem of no more than 100,000 files
- Length of time to recover a 100 GB filesystem of 1,000,000 files
- Length of time to recover a 1 TB database
- Length of time to recover a 500 GB database
- Length of time to recover 100 files from a virtual machine image-level backup
- Length of time to recover a 100 GB virtual machine image-level backup as a new virtual machine
- Length of time to recover a 100 GB virtual machine image-level backup leveraging change block tracking for incremental restore when 5% of the virtual machine has changed since the backup

Ultimately, the number and type of baselines established for testing will vary based on the individual needs and size of each business. Optimum establishment of baselines should see tests repeated at least three times and their results averaged. Where performance is absolutely critical, it may even be necessary to run even more tests, discarding maximum and minimum results and averaging the others, or using the median performance value rather than averaged

performance, though for practicality reasons this will be the exception rather than the rule.

Some tests may even need to be baselined at different times of the day—for example, recovery performance of a critical system at 9am, midday, 4pm, and 1am. Alternately, when load varies depending on the day of the month (particularly in relation to end-of-month processing), it may be necessary to gather baseline performance data from multiple days and times during a month.

Standard performance testing should be a mix of formal and informal testing, periodically confirming whether activities still complete within an acceptable degree of variance from the established baselines. Like standard functional tests, the formal performance tests should be scheduled and the results documented.

Where standard performance testing reveals that baselines are no longer accurate or in situations where there has been a substantial technology change or tangible data volume change, resampling will be run in order to determine new baselines. Optimally, the original baselines and new baselines established by resampling should be documented so that trending can be established throughout the lifecycle of the systems.

In an increasingly interconnected IT environment, performance testing is *at best* a decidedly complex challenge. Consider a wholly typical medium-size enterprise with

- Shared storage (a mix of fiber-channel and IP attached storage)
- Mix of virtual (80%) and physical (20%) hosts
- Virtual hosts that can reside on any one of a number of physical servers
- Shared fiber-channel networking for both standard data and backup/recovery
- Shared IP networking for standard data and backup/ recovery

At a high level, this may resemble the interrelationships shown in Figure 4.4.

In such a typical system, where networking and storage are all shared, and virtual machines also share compute and memory, the performance of an individual component (e.g., a single virtual machine) is as much, if not more, dependent on the interplay of all the other components and the workloads they are experiencing at any given time as it is on its own operating system, applications, and usage profiles. A backup performance test conducted at 10am on a Sunday may have no correlation whatsoever between a backup test conducted at 11am on a Monday and so on. While many individual components may have the ability to set performance guarantees, getting these to all align across potentially multiple levels of virtualization and resource sharing is as likely to be

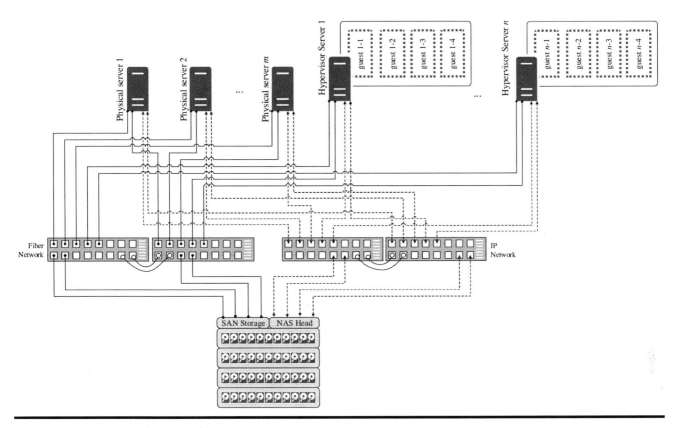

Figure 4.4   System interconnectedness.

an art form as it is a science—particularly when required for *many* business systems concurrently.

There is no simple solution to planning adequate performance testing in such an environment—and there's certainly no *cheap* solution. Indeed, it would be impossible to accurately state the performance of an individual component from a single test. (Multiple tests at specific—or perhaps even randomized times with the results averaged may even be merely a starting point.)

When approaching performance testing of the data protection environment, determining the initially required accuracy *and* measuring the overall loading of the environment become critical. Thus, it might be stated that the financial database server can be backed up at 2.5 GB/s, *when:*

- The FC network is at no more than 20% utilization.
- The IP network is at no more than 60% utilization.
- The specific virtualization server hosting the database is at no more than 60% CPU load.
- The specific virtualization server hosting the database is at no more than 50% memory utilization.
- The SAN is recording less than 100,000 concurrent IOPS.

Even this list is entirely simplistic for a truly accurate performance testing in an enterprise environment, but as such

it still demonstrates the point: performance testing is a topic often bandied about in enterprise environments, but is no longer one that can be *casually* approached with any chance of reliability.

4.5.4 Test Risks

It's easy when first approaching testing to assume that testing is about mitigating risk in the environment. This of course is true. However, if conducted incorrectly, testing can *introduce* risk into the environment, and it's therefore important to plan tests in such a way as to minimize the impact they may have on the overall environment.

In an entirely optimum scenario, IT staff will have available to them a test environment that is isolated from but, to all intent, mirrors the production environment. For many organizations, this might sound like the perfect use case scenario for disaster recovery systems, but doing so introduces additional risks that must be managed. For instance, if destructive testing is taking place in the disaster recovery environment *and* a critical fault occurs within the production environment, what challenges and delays does this introduce into switching production operations over?

Equally, test scenarios that have the potential to impact actual production systems have to be evaluated seriously; removing a spinning drive from a production SAN, for instance, in order to confirm the system appropriately rebuilds RAID units is likely to succeed, but at the cost of a performance-impacting storage rebuild. Or it might introduce additional errors into the environment—the removed drive might be pulled out too far, too quickly, while still spinning down and become damaged. Or—since it's not an effective test of disk failure anyway*—it might work but bear no relation to a real failure scenario anyway.

For some tests, it's important to consider not the immediate risk, but the potential for cascading risk. For instance, if cross-site replication is being used for critical storage and the replication is deliberately broken in such a way as to force a new, full replication to take place, consider the following:

- The immediate risk is that production traffic making use of the cross-site link may be compromised by higher utilization for replication (particularly if quality of service is not used).
- If a failure occurs in the production storage during the testing, there's the potential that the outage will be longer, requiring restoration from backup, given the online, remote replica has not completed rebuilding.

Even standard recovery testing can pose challenges—periodic testing of the recoverability of data (particularly critical data) is important, but the risk needs to be understood that human error might result in the recovery overwriting in-use data or going to the wrong location and filling a filesystem or, in secure environments, traversing an unencrypted network link and being exposed to third-party snooping.

The potential risks in testing—particularly when the test environment is not 100% isolated from the production environment—are many, and the acceptable risk level will be largely needed to be decided by individual companies in response to the financial and regulatory implications of that testing.

Another test risk is to not test *complex* scenarios. The most common example of this is disaster recovery/failover testing. For many businesses, disaster recovery testing, where workloads are transitioned from one datacenter to another ("failover"), is done as unit testing. Can the content management system (CMS) be failed over from Melbourne to Sydney? A business might conduct successful workload failover tests between their datacenters for *every* workload the business hosts within its own infrastructure, only to find in a full disaster recovery situation that the interdependencies between systems prevent successful complete datacenter cutover.

4.5.5 Automated Testing

When we discuss the potential for automated testing with data protection environments, it's worthwhile keeping in mind the song line, "You say 'tomato,' I say 'tomato.'" Automated testing has different meanings depending on whom you're talking to, and this makes discussions around such testing at times challenging.

That challenge becomes more complex depending on whether the automated testing is required to fulfill some internal SLA, or whether it's required to allow the business to demonstrably prove, for the purpose of external audit or compliance requirements, its ability to successfully recover data.

Of course, automated testing might cover more than just data recovery, but in almost any case where "automated testing" is considered relating to a data protection environment, that testing will be focused on the recoverability of the data. After all, in a modern context almost everything else can easily be automated (if it hasn't already been done so): the backup function is already automated in the vast majority of instances. Regular operations (e.g., capacity management) should be "lights out" and therefore already automated, and modernized infrastructure, where the datacenter functions more as a private cloud, should feature deep automation into data protection enablement as a provisioning function.

This is why we'll approach the topic of automated testing from a recovery perspective.

So the fundamental question is: what constitutes an *automated* test? You might think this is a straightforward question to answer, so let's consider something that should be rather simple, such as recovery testing for a VMware virtual machine backup.

In this scenario, we want an automated test that allows us to verify, without human involvement, whether or not a virtual machine can be recovered from its image-level backup, presumably to satisfy either an external compliance requirement, or internal service level agreement.

The goal of this test is to verify the virtual machine can be recovered, but what does that mean? It could be any of the following:

- The image datafiles can be recovered without a read error.
- The image datafiles can be imported onto a vSphere server via vCenter and successfully registered as a new virtual machine.
- The registered, recovered virtual machine can be booted to a login prompt on an isolated network, error-free.
- The registered, recovered virtual machine can be booted to a login prompt on an isolated network, error-free, and a port-scan reveals expected ports associated with a service are listening and accepting connections.
- The registered, recovered virtual machine can be booted to a login prompt on an isolated network,

---

* Unless there's a known risk that people will randomly remove active and working drives from enclosures.

Elements of a Protection System

error-free, logged into, and a process listing shows that the essential services provided by the virtual machine are running.

■ The registered, recovered virtual machine can be booted to a login prompt on an isolated network, error-free, logged into, a process listing shows essential services provided by the virtual machine are running *and* some additional data verification process can be executed (e.g., a database within the virtual machine can be connected to, data retrieved from, and verified as real data).

Depending on the level of compliance required and maturity of operating models within a business, any of the above might be deemed to be a fully successful automated recovery test—or even higher verification levels may be required.

To elaborate, let's review the interpretations previously given. This is outlined in Table 4.3.

In addition to any or all of the above, traditional recovery testing challenges remain, such as:

■ Avoiding recoveries from the same logical backups (e.g., it is tempting to recover only from full backups as they're most convenient)
■ Avoiding recoveries for the same data (e.g., recovering the same content for each required type, such as the same directory on a NAS share for all file-level recovery tests, and so on)

It's usually the case that in many situations, the ability to automatically run recovery tests is limited to addressing only primitive functionality, such as successfully booting a recovered virtual machine to its login prompt, or running a basic port-scan.

Does this mean that recovery testing can't be automated? No. What should be considered though is that automated recovery testing is something each business will need to consider itself. Businesses wishing to utilize automatic verification of recoveries would almost invariably be better off programmatically exploring this functionality as "custom built," in order to truly meet both internal SLAs and

Table 4.3   Functional Achievement of Automated Test Levels

Test Level	What the Test Achieves …
The image datafiles can be recovered without a read error.	This is nothing more than simple backup verification. It doesn't provide any insight into whether the recovered data is usable.
The image datafiles can be imported onto a vSphere server via vCenter and successfully registered as a new virtual machine.	This provides backup verification and tells us the virtual machine *configuration file* was successfully processed and accepted as valid by the vCenter server. It doesn't give us insight into whether the virtual machine is usable.
The registered, recovered virtual machine can be booted to a login prompt on an isolated network, error-free.	This provides backup verification, virtual machine configuration verification, and a level of validity. However, it doesn't tell us if the virtual machine can be used for anything functional beyond this point.
The registered, recovered virtual machine can be booted to a login prompt on an isolated network, error-free, and a port-scan reveals expected ports associated with a service are listening and accepting connections.	This provides backup verification, virtual machine configuration verification, and validates that expected *incoming* communication ports are listening—i.e., some aspects of tested services have started. However, there's no verification that the system will act properly on connection to those ports, or that it can communicate *outward* in the expected manner.
The registered, recovered virtual machine can be booted to a login prompt on an isolated network, error-free, logged into, and a process listing shows that the essential services provided by the virtual machine are running.	This starts to show more useful information. We have backup verification, virtual machine configuration verification, access verification and a hint that the services may be running. We don't have confirmation that the executing services can be used as would be expected in a normal production environment.
The registered, recovered virtual machine can be booted to a login prompt on an isolated network, error-free, logged into, a process listing shows essential services provided by the virtual machine are running *and* some additional data verification process can be executed.	This gives us verification at the backup level, virtual infrastructure level, and functional application level—but it doesn't provide certainty that the virtual machine will behave exactly as we would anticipate because it's not connected to the production network.

compliance requirements for verification processes. This, of course, requires making use of products that are susceptible to automation, either by conventional command line functionality, or in a more modern context, through RESTful application programming interfaces (APIs). Later chapters will continue to explore the essential nature of automation within the realm of data protection.

4.5.6 What Is a Test?

Before we finish testing, it's worth briefly considering the question: what *constitutes* a test? For instance, consider a business that has decided a complete filesystem recovery will be conducted at least monthly, on a random day for one randomly chosen Tier 1 system in the organization. If we come to the third week of the month and the test has not yet been conducted *but* a full filesystem recovery is performed for a Tier 1 system due to a production issue, *does that qualify as a test?*

From business to business there is no consensus on this question. In a business where there are no formal legal requirements for testing, it's entirely possible this *can* be designated a successful test execution. For those organizations bound by strict corporate compliance requirements, authorities (and therefore corporate legal counsel) may not agree—or they may be unbothered but the company's legal team are unsure, and so the recovery is not classified as a test, *just to be sure.* This is something that should be explored carefully and well documented in any business where reasonably formal testing processes are required.

4.6 Service Level Agreements

The SLAs are crucial to understanding the nature of the data protection and data recovery options that will be required within the environment.

For data protection, we usually consider SLAs around two key factors:

- *Recovery time objective (RTO)*: How long it takes to recover data
- *Recovery point objective (RPO)*: How much data can be "lost" in time

Table 4.4 gives several examples of possible RTO and RPO SLAs for a backup and recovery environment.

One thing that usually becomes immediately obvious from a review of RPOs and RTOs within an environment is that traditional once-a-day backup models don't always provide sufficient recovery capabilities.

This helps to highlight that data protection in the modern organization can't be met through the activities of traditional backup and recovery alone. In fact, the more

Table 4.4 Sample Recovery Point and Recovery Time Service Level Agreements

System	RPO	RTO
Corporate NAS	1 hour	8 hours
Key financial database	15 minutes	15 minutes
Archive server	1 day	5 days
User authentication	1 day	30 minutes
Standard server	1 day	8 hours
Email system	1 day	4 hours

urgent the RPOs and RTOs, the more likely it will be that a data protection design will need to meet these *without* resorting to traditional recovery mechanisms. (Consider, for instance, the corporate NAS example in Table 4.4, which is cited as having an RPO of 1 hour and an RTO of 8 hours. Clearly, in this scenario, if the maximum amount of data that can be lost, expressed in time, is just 1 hour, then a traditional backup that is performed just once every 24 hours is not suitable.)

It should of course also be noted where stated service levels are agreements (SLAs) or objectives (SLOs). Typically an SLO is a desired outcome, but not mandatory, whereas an SLA is typically seen as being a mandatory outcome.

As data protection becomes increasingly mature within businesses, additional SLAs are emerging beyond recovery point and recovery time objective. For many organizations, these have previously been seen as design goals; increasingly though, they are becoming codified as true service level agreements, just as essential as the recovery point and recovery time objectives. Examples of additional SLAs include:

- Cross-site replication should not be more than 15 minutes behind for Tier 1 workloads.
- Cross-site replication should not be more than a half hour behind for Tier 2 workloads.
- Number of copies.
- Number of off-platform copies.
- Speed at which off-site copies are generated.
- Number of off-site copies that are generated.
- Number of air-gapped copies that are generated.

Effectively, what we're seeing is a movement away from data protection SLAs almost exclusively focused on RPO and RTO. A mature business will also see SLAs around how *protected* the protection environment itself is—such SLAs are often as driven by compliance concerns or fiduciary regulations as they are by business preferences.

While business process management (BPM) defines key performance indicators (KPIs) as different from SLAs, it is also worth considering here the role of KPIs within data protection. We might say that KPIs provide a measure of whether or not we are *meeting* (or able to meet) the various SLAs that are established within the environment.

In organizations with more mature data protection processes, KPIs will be used by the business or senior IT management to help profile the overall risk exposure of the business. Examples of KPIs might include:

- Percentage of time during a month that secondary site replication was more than 15 minutes behind for Tier 1 workloads
- Percentage of time during a month that secondary site replication was more than 30 minutes behind for Tier 2 workloads
- Success rate (measured as a percentage) of backups during a month
- Success rate (measured as a percentage) of recoveries during a month
- Percentage of backups that took more than 8 hours to complete
- Percentage of off-site cloning of backups that took more than 8 hours to complete

More will be discussed relating to KPIs in Chapter 6 (Monitoring and Reporting).

4.7 Technology

Once everything else in a data protection system has been considered, we're left with the easiest components: the technology. It goes without saying that some of the technology deployed may be complex, and the implementation, maintenance, and ongoing operation of that technology requires specialist training. Yet, even taking those factors into consideration, the technology is the easiest aspect of the entire system.

There are two key considerations for technology selection in a data protection system: the technology must be fit for purpose and the technology must be adaptable to purpose.

In the first instance—the preferred instance—the technology being used is immediately applicable to the requirements at hand. In the shortest sense, this would imply that the technology being used meets *all* the functional requirements of the business and most, if not all, of the non-functional requirements as well.

Yet that is not always going to be the case—unless bespoke technology has been commissioned *and* the needs of the business are static, the technology deployed for data protection (like any other solution within the business) is unlikely to meet *all* functional requirements, let alone all non-functional requirements. This brings us to perhaps one

of the most important aspects of any technology use for data protection in an enterprise environment: it must be at minimum a *framework* technology. That is, in addition to providing its base functionality, it should be extendable, and those capabilities should be well documented.* Where possible, it should be a *modular framework*—that is, it should be built in an agile way that allows rapid insertion of new functionality. In many scenarios, this would imply at *least* one of the following:

1. There should be comprehensive command line utilities associated with the system.
2. There should be a complete administrative and operational API available for at least one or more common programming languages freely available.
3. The system should integrate all administrative and operational functions with industry standard management utilities.†
4. If *completely* graphical user interface (GUI) based, the system should offer its own automation options and *all* functions of the GUI should be susceptible to automation.

Since the requirements of most businesses change over time, it can be readily argued that this extensibility and adaptability of enterprise technical solutions via scripting, programming, or other automation methods is *equally* as critical as whether the technology can perform the initial requirements on deployment.

4.8 Summary

Except in perhaps the most esoteric of business requirements, it's usually the case that the simplest component of a data protection solution is actually the technology to be used. It's the other components—SLAs, processes and documentation, people, training, and testing—that will typically be the deciding factors in whether or not a solution is going to work. There's almost always some data protection technology that will tick more functional boxes for a business than other technology, but just because its functions logically map

---

* Indeed, the increasing pervasiveness of DevOps, REST APIs and the need for cloud-like business agility demonstrate exactly why framework technologies are so essential—and superior—to monolithic technologies in a modern business environment.
† This is often a double-edged sword. Integration with SNMP-based products, for instance, may allow monitoring and basic management functions to be performed from a third-party enterprise technology management system, but it's unlikely the third-party system will be able to manage *all* aspects of the product. In these scenarios, it's preferable that such extensibility is not the *only* form offered.

to business requirements, it will not in any way be the sole reason for whether it works or not for a business.

When choosing data protection products, price will also, always play a part. It may be that on technical scoring, one product has the highest ranking for meeting functional and non-functional requirements, but costs 20% more than another product that meets almost the same number of requirements. Of course, it's also essential that costing analysis captures not just *bill-of-material* costs (i.e., any capital expenditure), but other soft costs, such as installation and support services, ongoing maintenance fees, and operational expenditure costs, such as media and pay-per-GB storage.

Correctly determining the *right* data protection components and systems for a business is a process that has to start from above—there must be oversight, clear architectural direction, and strong guiding principles to the implementation of such solutions. These will be covered in more detail in Chapter 5.

4.9 Self-Reflection

When we think of recovery time objectives and recovery point objectives, we usually focus on either the criticality of the data, or the legal/fiduciary requirements relating to that data. However, another item for consideration can be the number of affected users. After all, *time is money*, from a business perspective, and so if a system failure affects user productivity and there is no workaround, the number of affected users will have a cumulative impact on the challenge it poses to the business.

Revisit the sample RPOs and RTOs presented in Table 4.3, and consider them from the perspective of a business with 100 employees. How might the recovery time objectives, in particular, change in each situation where there is a single employee affected, 20% of employees affected, and 100% of employees affected?

Consider a small business that has:

- One Windows fileserver with approximately 1,000,000 files in four different shares
- Seven Microsoft SQL databases on one database server
- Three Microsoft SQL databases on another database server
- A pair of Active Directory servers
- Three Linux servers: one small server that hosts the development source code and two build servers.

Assuming you have a virtualized test environment (e.g., a "sandpit"), note how might you schedule tests in that environment so that:

(a) The tests are not always run against the same type of backup.
(b) No two scheduled tests in a row are for the same system.
(c) No two scheduled tests in a row are for the same type of service.
(d) At any point it should be possible to show to the directors of the business evidence that recovery tests have been conducted for all systems within the last 6 months.

Also give consideration for how you might isolate the test environment so that you can conduct recovery tests during the day without impacting normal use of any of the systems in the environment.

Chapter 5

IT Governance and Data Protection

5.1 Introduction

In his book *An Executive's Guide to IT Governance: Improving Systems Processes with Service Management, COBIT and ITIL* (Wiley, 2013), Robert Moeller says of IT governance:

> IT governance is concerned with the strategic alignment between the goals and objectives of the business and the utilization of its IT resources to effectively achieve the desired results.

Everything done in IT for a business should align with the strategic goals of the business and fall under the aegis of IT governance. Even those businesses that may not necessarily refer to their control processes relating to IT as *governance* will eventually institute governance-like controls if they want a well-integrated IT department. (Even test and development systems and processes should fall into IT governance, albeit with different constraints and requirements compared to production processes.)

IT governance of course is a large enough topic that it would be impossible to map all its topics and considerations into data protection activities in a single chapter. Instead, this chapter will focus on the high level picture of integrating IT governance with data protection, namely:

- Architecture
- Service transition
- Change management

While there will be elements of data protection to consider in almost all aspects of IT governance, these three topics represent the key junctions where data protection must be more than merely considered: it must be a *critical* consideration.

5.2 Architecture

Every solution developed by an organization, regardless of whether it uses locally created technology, purchased components, or outsourced systems, must be developed with three essential data protection tenets in mind:

- *Integrity*: The solution as a whole must provide a *sufficient* degree of data integrity in order to minimize data loss or corruption events. "Sufficient" will vary depending on the workload, and whether we are referring to on-platform, or off-platform protection for the workload. Data integrity is about instilling confidence in the business that data is safely stored and modified only by a legitimate process.
- *Reliability*: The solution should be designed to minimize the level of downtime that users will experience, both planned and unplanned. Planned downtime refers to any required function (e.g., maintenance) that blocks or impedes the time for which the service is available. Unplanned downtime, on the other hand, speaks to the *robustness* of the solution.
- *Recoverability*: Like it or not, things will happen which cannot be solved by either integrity or reliability functions. Data will be lost, or corrupted, due to the simple nature of humans to make mistakes, and the random chance to interfere with what we do. So the solution has to include functionality to recover data that has been lost. (By necessity, this implies the system also has to include functionality to *backup* that data in the first place.)

To achieve these, you need to focus on four key protection functions, which comprise the *FARR model* of data protection.

5.2.1 The FARR Model of Data Protection

Whereas once we considered data protection solely from the perspective of the datacenter (or computer room), the evolving nature of IT and infrastructure means this is rarely the only way we have to consider data protection any more. We are seeing a shift, driven by data *volume* and data *placement* to a workload-by-workload evaluation of data protection.

In some senses, this doesn't change the fundamental considerations that we have when it comes to data protection. What it does tend to change though is with *whom* those considerations have to be discussed, and the emphasis that is placed on each.

It's vitally important to understand that these considerations don't just apply to *data protection* solutions within an organization: they must apply to *all* solutions within an organization. Consider the saying: "A chain is only as strong as its weakest link." This is our guiding principle to practical solutions architecture. If systems are designed or implemented with weak data protection principles, then the overall data protection strategy put in place within the organization will be similarly compromised.

To address this, architectural approaches in IT should incorporate data protection considerations using the FARR model, outlined as follows, and shown in Figure 5.1.

The FARR model breaks data protection down into four essential functions or considerations. These are: fault tolerance, availability, redundancy, and recoverability. While at

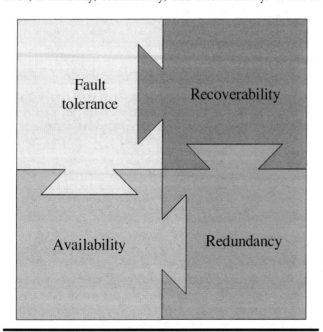

Figure 5.1 The FARR model for data protection.

the *implementation* level these functions may be split into further granularity, they broadly encompass everything involved in data protection from a storage perspective.

5.2.1.1 Fault Tolerance

At a fundamental layer, we need a level of fault tolerance in order to achieve reliable data protection. Within standard block and file storage, this is usually achieved via some form of RAID (Redundant Array of Independent Disks); in cloud object-based storage and some forms of archive storage, it could be achieved via erasure coding, effectively shifting the fault tolerance from the physical device to the individual object being stored. Regardless, the point of fault tolerance is the same: no individual component within an overall system should represent a single point of failure. A basic example of the goal of fault tolerance, via RAID, is shown in Figure 5.2.

Fault tolerance doesn't just apply to storage platforms, of course. Consider a typical enterprise server: it'll typically also use dual power supplies, have redundancy in fans, and error-correcting code (ECC) RAM. Most likely, it will have more than one network interface card (NIC) so that if a NIC fails, it can continue to function. This higher level fault tolerance overlaps with *availability*, which we'll cover in more detail next. There's always a limit to what fault tolerance can achieve, though: systems with multiple CPUs (i.e., sockets, not cores) *usually* exist for performance, rather than redundancy reasons, for instance.

When working within private infrastructure (regardless of whether that's operating in a traditional infrastructure stack, or a private/hybrid cloud), fault tolerance is something the infrastructure is expected to provide and is therefore an important design point for IT teams. When we move a workload out to public cloud, the demarcation point on responsibility for fault tolerance shifts somewhat—some of the fundamental fault tolerance we expect to see in business IT systems becomes the responsibility of the cloud provider. (However, the *responsibility* for dealing with a failure of fault tolerance still belongs to the owner of the data.)

5.2.1.2 Availability

There's an old philosophy question: *If a tree falls in the forest and no one hears it, did it really make a noise?* When it comes to data protection, one might equally ask the question: *If your data exists but it can't be accessed, does it really exist?*

Data availability refers to the challenge of making sure that data can be accessed, and dovetails neatly into some of the aspects of fault tolerance that we've already discussed. For instance, we design for data availability within the datacenter by using redundant pathing for networks, as described previously: two or more interface cards on a physical server, connecting to different switches, so that if one path goes

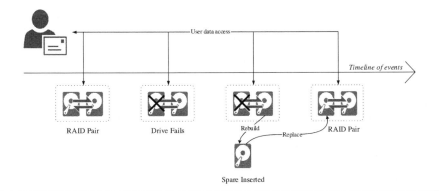

Figure 5.2 Basic fault tolerance.

down at either point, we can still access the data or network, such as shown in Figure 5.3.

(Network switches may also be linked to one another via *inter-switch links*.)

In itself, availability isn't so much a primary data protection consideration, but an architectural resilience consideration. However, what should be done if availability options *fail* can very much be a data protection consideration. For instance:

■ Software installed by customers references a database you're running on-premises. There's nothing wrong with the database, but roadworkers nearby accidentally slice through all the incoming network links to the datacenter, making the database unavailable to the customers. Do you have to wait out the network failure, or do you have an option to failover the database to an external location (e.g., public cloud)?

■ Your customer relationship management (CRM) software runs in a particular Amazon availability zone, which starts experiencing connectivity issues. Do you have a fall-back plan for continuing to access the CRM when its availability zone is unavailable?

When we build applications and workloads that reside entirely within a datacenter, availability is *almost* entirely achieved as an infrastructure function; in public cloud, there may still be some infrastructure considerations, but there'll likely also be availability considerations within the workload's application(s) as well, moving it to a shared consideration between the cloud architecture/design team, and developers writing the interfaces to the workload (even more so for workloads that might run either on-premises *or* in the public cloud). In a highly decentralized access model with potentially hundreds of thousands or more customers, you can't expect the end users to change settings in their applications to keep accessing a service, or issue an application update they all have to download, just because you've switched from say, AWS Sydney to AWS Singapore.

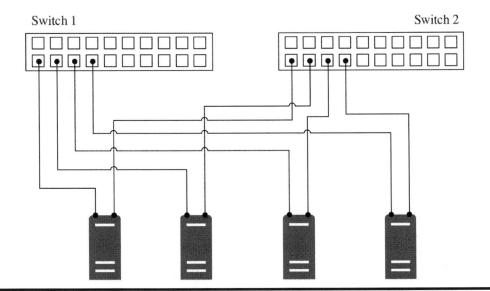

Figure 5.3 Simple network availability.

5.2.1.3 Redundancy

Traditional datacenter design has a lot of focus on redundancy, and that goes well beyond low level redundancy provided by fault tolerance. This extends to the point of considering redundancy *for* the datacenter. Some of the common models for datacenter use and redundancy are:

- *Active/failover*: All workloads run in the active datacenter, with the failover datacenter being in 'cold' or 'standby' mode. Workloads are only made active in the failover datacenter if a failure prevents them from running in the active datacenter. This is seen by many businesses now as having an undesirable cost, since equipment in the failover datacenter may run idle (other than receiving incoming replication data) for months at a time.
- *Active/active*: Workloads run in both datacenters, and both datacenters have the capacity to run either all workloads, or all essential workloads during a failover situation. This reduces the risk of equipment sitting largely idle for extended periods of time (or at least can minimize the amount of equipment in such a situation), but it carries a greater risk of interdependencies developing for services against *both* datacenters, creating higher risk of a complete datacenter failover being unsuccessful.
- *Production/non-production*: Similar to the active/active datacenter configuration, this will see test/development workloads run in one datacenter, and production in the other. Additional storage is provisioned in the non-production datacenter to hold both production and non-production data. In the event of the test/development datacenter failing, the production datacenter continues to operate. In the event of a production datacenter failure, test/development services are shut down, and those systems pivot to providing production services.
- *Tripartite datacenter configurations*: Three-site datacenter configurations can offer higher levels of redundancy by extending any of the two-site models above with a third, dedicated disaster recovery datacenter. This will often work on the basis of allowing individual workload failover between any two 'primary' datacenters, with the third datacenter only invoked/called into use in a complete disaster recovery/business continuity situation.

Whereas availability considerations cover situations where the data and its compute services are still capable of operating, but just inaccessible, redundancy considerations cover situations where data or services at a particular location have been rendered inoperable:

- A complete storage array suffers an outage.
- A power failure takes out a city block, resulting in a complete datacenter shutdown.*
- Fire breaks out in the datacenter for a public cloud provider, taking out an availability region that customer services are running in.
- All basements within 500 meters of a major river suffer flooding during torrential rain and a king tide—including the production datacenter for the business.

While datacenters are an essential aspect of redundancy considerations, redundancy also operates at a smaller scale, and involves the consideration of protecting against physical systems failure—e.g., the storage array example above, and also application/operating system failure, such as running a database within a clustered server configuration so that even if a single host fails, the database can switch over to running on another physical host. An example of clustering to provide redundancy is shown in Figure 5.4.

All in all, redundancy might be seen as a higher order form of fault tolerance; rather than providing atomic failure protection, it provides protection for a compound system or service. However, since the complexity can be significantly higher, redundancy should be approached *separately* to, rather than as, an *aspect* of fault tolerance.

5.2.1.4 Recoverability

Fault tolerance, availability, and redundancy all exist to try to *prevent* a data loss situation from happening. However, they can't guarantee you'll never encounter data loss or corruption, and in some situations, you might say they *guarantee* any data loss or corruption encountered will be successfully replicated or carried over to the redundant/failover systems.

So the final piece in the FARR model is recoverability: how to get the data back when the other forms of protection have failed. Recoverability exists for those situations where:

- The CIO has accidentally deleted all his email.
- A user in finance accidentally deletes a billing spreadsheet, and only realizes it is missing a month later, in the next billing cycle.
- Ransomware encrypts so much data on a production fileserver that snapshots are overwhelmed and unable to claw back the unencrypted data.
- The federal taxation department, having audited the tax returns of the business, requires comprehensive reports generated from sales databases covering the last

---

* Presumably either the datacenter does not have backup batteries/generators, or the primary power outage outlasts the batteries/generators.

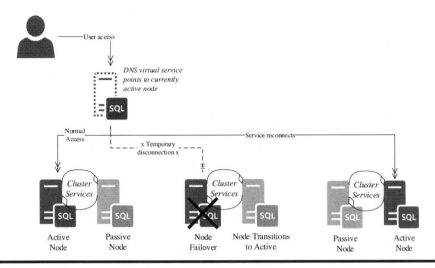

Figure 5.4   Using clustering to provide service redundancy.

7 years, and such information is retained only in long-term retention backups.

■ A RAID protected filesystem suffers a catastrophic failure when a disk fails during the reconstruction from a previous failure.

An example of a recovery scenario is shown in Figure 5.5.

Essentially, recoverability then focuses on data protection in terms of:

■ Long-term granularity
■ Failure of another protection method
■ Inability of another protection method to protect against the failure experienced

Recovery exists in a data protection model because of random chance, malicious actors, and the unpredictability of

service consumers. The other forms of protection deal with situations where there's still at least one on-platform copy of the data available, in some form or another; recovery is effectively what happens when the number of on-platform (or accessible on-platform) copies reduces to zero.

5.2.1.5 Tying the FARR Model Together

Depending on where a workload exists and how critical it is, different aspects of the FARR model will need to be considered: mission critical on-premises workloads will need all four aspects carefully dealt with. Mission critical workloads running in public cloud will typically *assume* fault tolerance exists as a function of the public cloud service provision, but will still need to deal with availability, redundancy, and recoverability. (They may in fact still need to be called on as a result of the cloud provider experiencing a failure in its fault tolerance.)

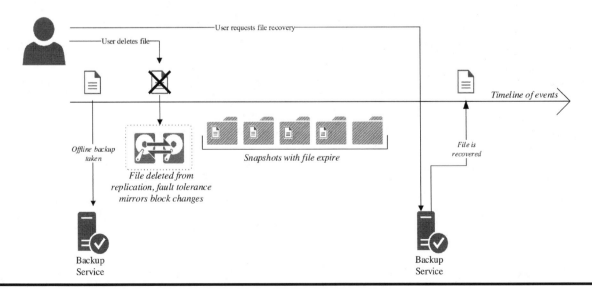

Figure 5.5   Recovery from off-platform protection when other protection methods are not usable.

Workloads that aren't mission critical—for example, test workloads—may focus on redundancy and fault tolerance, keeping recoverability and availability considerations at a minimum, regardless of where they run. Development workloads may focus on fault tolerance and availability, and *one of* redundancy or recoverability, depending on the importance of development to the business.

Ultimately what we see with the FARR model though is a mechanism by which IT can readily communicate to the business the various considerations in data storage protection, and help the business to understand that data protection is an essential activity regardless of *where* the data is.

5.2.2 Data Protection Architect (DPA)

The architecture of an environment, both the *design* and *planning* on the technical and business front, is crucial to the long-term viability of that environment. Just as there are specialist architectural roles in IT for networking, for messaging, for enterprise identification, and a plethora of other subjects, there is a clear need for specialist data protection architects. These architects will be responsible for analyzing systems and solutions architecture with a primary focus on being able to address the three tenets mentioned earlier, namely:

1. Does the system sufficiently ensure data integrity?
2. Is the system sufficiently reliable?
3. Is the system sufficiently recoverable?

More than this, the data protection architects have a role beyond the standard datacenter (or cloud); they must also think about all the areas within an enterprise where data is stored, regardless of whether it's an obvious or a nonobvious location.

The obvious locations are easy—they're the storage arrays (SAN or NAS), the individual servers, cloud object storage, cloud block storage, and the backup environments. The less and sometimes nonobvious locations relate to everywhere else in an environment, such as:

■ Network switches
■ Fiber-channel switches
■ Private automatic branch exchange (PABX) systems
■ Encryption routers, either TCP/IP network or fiber channel

All of these "black box" appliances within an organization contain data, and sometimes *business-critical* data from a communications perspective. There is little benefit in having a backup environment that can rapidly *self-restore* if the environment uses encryption keys that are only stored on an appliance whose configuration and keys were never protected (or perhaps more ignominiously, only stored once in build documentation, and never updated). If this were the sum total of where data might be stored in unconventional locations, it would likely remain manageable by the individual architectural disciplines within IT—yet the modern data landscape is so incredibly complex by comparison that it requires specialist attention. The DPA must also consider such diverse data storage as end user laptops and desktops, mobile platforms (smart phones, tablets, and even emerging technologies such as smart watches), and the cloud—particularly hybrid and public.

Locally, a data protection architect should be the sort of person who periodically walks the floor of the business and looks at every device, blinking light, or piece of technology and asks:

■ What is this used for?
■ What data does it accumulate?
■ What happens to the data?
■ What configuration does it have?
■ Where is the configuration saved?
■ What happens if it's no longer working?
  – Who fixes it, and how?
  – Has anyone tested fixing it?
    • If so, where are the results documented?
    • If not, when will it be done?
■ What is its maintenance and support process?
■ What department or functional manager is responsible for it?
■ What department or functional manager is *accountable* for it?

The mistake made in many organizations is to believe this happens only within the computer room. That's merely the *controlled* area within the IT infrastructure of an organization—it's certainly not the *only* area. The DPA will need to visit every desk, every meeting room, every storeroom in the building or buildings occupied by the company and ask the questions mentioned earlier in case no one else has. A business without a DPA is a business with an *at best* incomplete data protection strategy.

When an organization has switched to public or hybrid cloud, the task of the DPA becomes more challenging, but even more important. In these situations, the DPA must be liaising with the cloud service providers to ensure everything stored in the cloud continues to meet required service-level agreements and press the cloud service providers for the requisite evidence. Usually when this is broached with organizations, at least one of the following objections will be rolled out:

■ They don't provide specifics; we just have to rely on their stated SLAs.

■ That information requires an account manager, and our service doesn't cover that.

Neither objection is acceptable. If an organization's data is held by a third party and that third party isn't sufficiently forthcoming about the data protection and recovery mechanisms and incidents it encounters, then it's *reckless* to use that organization. *Cheap* must never come at the expense of reliability, recoverability, or integrity. This is sadly a common mistake—many businesses trust they'll have full recovery capabilities for cloud services, but a thorough review of the terms and conditions usually instead shows the service provider commits only to infrastructure availability and recoverability—not data restoration for situations necessitated by a customer fault. The obvious conclusion here is that the DPA will (among others) be responsible for determining what data protection services need to be subscribed to or deployed to protect cloud workloads.

As we see businesses transition from classic application platforms that assume resiliency and redundancy is "baked into" the infrastructure, to next generation applications built by agile processes to run on potentially a multitude of cloud platforms (either public, or hybrid/private), the responsibility to provide resiliency and other data protection functions move further up the stack—they effectively become a developer consideration.* In this, the role of the data protection architect also has to shift to cover more detailed application analysis: otherwise, businesses find themselves in the unenviable position of committing to a platform without understanding how to protect it.

In the previous edition of this book, we described this role as a data protection advocate. Yet, advocacy for the most part implies an optional or informal activity. With the growing fiscal importance of data to give a company an edge in the marketplace, it's clear that there must be a shift toward a formal, multi-disciplinary data protection architecture role in enterprise IT. In some organizations, it may even involve a team of architects who consider all three key aspects to data protection: security, privacy, and data storage.

5.3 Service Transition

While arguably service transition is just a specialist topic in change management (to be discussed next), it deserves being called out for special attention within data protection. Service transition is the *make or break* moment for a product or service within an organization. Within ITIL, service transition refers to the stage where services are either:

* Or perhaps more correctly, they become far *more* a developer consideration than previously, since applications designed for classic infrastructure still require some level of data protection awareness.

■ *Production enabled*: Moved from the development or build part of its lifecycle into full production use
■ *Substantially modified*: Beyond standard changes, such as when a central business management tool has entirely new modules implemented
■ *Decommissioned*: When the service or product is removed from active use

In all areas, service data protection must be considered. Take, for example, the lifecycle of just a single server, providing a single service, and focused *solely* on the backup and recovery considerations for that host:

1) Installation:
   a) Prior to purchase:
      i) The existing backup system should be considered in the context of the new system being purchased—that is, the existing backup infrastructure should be verified as having sufficient capacity to on-board the new system.
      ii) If the backup system needs to be expanded to accommodate the new system, the requisite components and features should be sized and purchased at this phase.
   b) Installation:
      i) New system is received and has the appropriate operating system, patching, and security options installed.
      ii) Backup software is installed on the host, and first backup is taken.
   c) Recovery testing (files):
      i) If this is the first install of this type of operating system, a complete disaster recovery test should be performed.
      ii) System has appropriate applications/software installed.
      iii) Backup is taken.
   d) Recovery testing (base applications):
      i) If this is the first install of this type of application, formal application recovery and disaster recovery testing should be performed and documented.
      ii) If this application has previously been backed up, formal checks should be executed to confirm that the setup meets backup operational requirements *or* if such checks cannot be done, formal recovery testing should take place.

2) Development cycle:
   a) Repeat:
      i) Daily development.
      ii) Daily backups, appropriate to the type of development occurring. These backups may

be different than the backups the final system may receive in production (e.g., databases might be initially backed up cold rather than hot). Where there are differences, they should be noted.

b) If the intended production backup mechanism is different to the development/test backup mechanism, the production backup mechanism must be implemented at the end of the development cycle, with suitable testing to confirm successful operations; only the production backup mechanism should be used from this time. If any expansion of the backup system was required, it should now be in place to support the new system.

c) If this is a new system or application, then during the development phase at least one total disaster recovery test should take place to ensure applications and procedures under development are indeed recoverable.

3) Test cycle:

a) End user testing with daily backups.

b) Confirmation that all of the required recovery tests have been performed successfully, with their processes clearly (and correctly) documented. These might include:

   i) Cold, offline backups.

   ii) Standard hot backups.

   iii) Disaster recovery tests.

c) An authorized manager should sign off against any decision not to conduct tests, with a valid reason given.

4) Production operations:

a) Following successful completion of steps (1) through (3), and having met the primary development and business objectives, a system can be service transitioned into production.

b) The production cycle is as follows:

   i) Daily use.

   ii) Daily backups.

   iii) Monthly/yearly/other periodic backups as required.

   iv) Periodic file, directory, and application recovery testing.

   v) Disaster recovery testing as required by company policies.

   vi) Data lifecycle operations as required.

   vii) After designated periods of time or the purchase of new backup technologies, monthly/yearly/archival backups should be migrated to new backup media or technologies, or processes

put in place for the maintenance and testing of legacy media and technologies.

   viii) After designated periods of time, older media should be destroyed if necessary.

5) Post-production:

a) System is decommissioned, with all applications shut down and no data access occurring.

b) Final copies of the system are generated through cold, complete offline backups to minimize plug-in or OS compatibility requirements during any arbitrary future recovery.

c) Documentation is generated for a recovery of the system from its final decommissioned backup and stored with the application, system, and infrastructure procedures. This documentation should include details of the backup software that needs to be used for recovery—in essence, this documentation should be written as if it were for a "green" site with no prior knowledge of the product that needs to bootstrap an implementation to recover the data.

d) For business-critical systems in particular (or those with strong legal compliance restrictions), it may also be pertinent to generate additional cold, offline backups with "common" tools such as native OS backup tools or open source backup tools, so that very long-term recovery is not dependent on a single product.

e) System is either redesigned for another purpose (potentially starting the process again) or retired.

f) Processes should be enacted to maintain, test, and as necessary destroy the long-term retention backups independent of whether the original backup product remains the primary backup tool for the organization.

Bear in mind that the description mentioned earlier covers only *one* part of the data protection spectrum—yet it serves to demonstrate just how important it is for data protection activities to be considered within the service transition process.

The above example changes somewhat as we switch to virtualized environments, cloud, and cloud-like infrastructure, where workloads are either commissioned in public cloud, or private infrastructure is deployed allowing for a highly automated, orchestrated, and service catalog access model. That's not to say it goes away, but it gets templated into the build process. For instance, rather than having to go through an exhaustive end-to-end commissioning process for a new workload, stepping through procurement, development, test, and deployment, the service consumer will be able to step through a service request form that builds and allocates the resources required to the point that the environment is ready for production data—ideally, within minutes or hours at the most. Such environments speak to the need for data protection to be *baked into* the overall solution offerings. It should be possible, for instance, to deploy a new database server within 15 minutes precisely because the data protection will be automatically deployed as part of that process, and the data protection will be reliable and known to work because the template for that service will have been developed, tested, and released into the service catalog.

5.4 Change Management

Change management sits at the heart of any professional IT organization. There are two core groups who manage change within the business—the Change Advisory Board (CAB) and the Emergency Change Advisory Board (ECAB). The first deals with regular changes to IT infrastructure and systems, while the second (usually a subset of the first) meets as required to approve highly urgent and usually unanticipated changes that occur outside of the regular change process.

If data protection is to be seriously considered within an organization, an additional board needs to be considered, one that has at least one permanent member in each of the CAB and ECAB. This additional board is the Information Protection Advisory Council (IPAC).

The IPAC will be comprised of a variety of individuals and may include such roles as:

■ *Data protection architect*: As described in the architectural component of this topic.
■ *Key users*: The people in business groups who just *know* what is done. They're the long-term or go-to people within a department.
■ *Technical owners*: While those who are accountable for a service should be involved in some level, it is the technical owners who are responsible for day to day successful operation, and as such they more appropriately sit on an IPAC.
■ *HR/finance*: If the HR and finance departments are one-in-the-same, a single representative is usually sufficient; if they are separate, there should be a representative from each department.
■ *Legal*: Somewhere, someone has to have an understanding of the legal ramifications of (a) choosing not to protect some data or (b) how long data should be kept for. This may not be a permanent role, but instead a floating role, which is invoked as required.
■ *Business unit representatives*: Where key users and/or technical owners do not cover specific key business units, those business units should have a voice within the IPAC.

To avoid becoming unwieldy, the IPAC should be comprised of both permanent and floating members—the permanent members will represent the core, while the floating members will be appointed from key user groups, technical owners, and so on, to *participate in* the group on an as-needed basis. Core members should have the authority and understanding of when and how to include interim/floating members in deliberations and decision-making processes.

The IPAC should meet independently of the change boards, and particularly for the standard change board, IPAC meetings should be scheduled such that members can evaluate proposed and upcoming changes on the basis of their potential impact to data protection capabilities within the organization. The IPAC should then determine who from the group should attend change board meetings to offer advice and guidance.

5.5 Summary

IT governance is a topic large enough that an entire book could be dedicated to covering all the aspects of integrating data protection activities into it. Instead, this chapter has been deliberately brief, focusing on the key processes at a very high level. It should, however, be a spark for much larger conversations and collaborations within an organization, with the end goal being recognition (if not already present) of the importance of data protection in *all* aspects of systems design and management.

Our next chapter, Chapter 6, will serve as an in-depth example of the degree to which data protection processes should be built into activities already performed within an organization.

5.6 Self-Reflection

Consider the FARR model for data protection, which focuses on four core activities being:

1. Fault tolerance
2. Availability
3. Redundancy
4. Recoverability

For each activity, think between 1 and 3 failure scenarios that the activity *would not* protect against. Which activities within the FARR model would protect against that type of failure?

Chapter 6

Monitoring and Reporting

6.1 Introduction

There's a simple rule in data protection: if you don't know the state of a component or an activity, *assume it failed*. That means:

- If you don't get told about the status of storage systems, assume drives are failing.
- If you don't know about the status of cross-site replication, assume it's down.
- If you don't know whether last night's backups completed without error last night, assume they all failed.

The list of potential failures could be an arm's length long and still nowhere near complete. This isn't to suggest you should be receiving constant alerts that every operation relating to data protection in an environment has finished and relating to its failure/success status. However, all of the data protection activities in an environment *should* be monitored, and you *should* receive alerts whenever an error occurs that the relevant system can't automatically correct, and you *should* receive reports of all errors, system health checks, etc. If your systems aren't sufficiently monitored, you should always be assuming the worst.

Regardless of whether it's proactive protection or reactive recovery, data protection is a critical IT function for any business, and as a critical function, it requires the appropriate level of attention, which means it must be monitored, and there must be reporting. The growing number of devices and systems to be monitored and reported on within enterprises should not be seen as an impediment or reason to avoid these activities, but instead a driving factor *to* perform them. Indeed, there is a growing industry now around automated parsing and monitoring of events at the sorts of scale experienced by large multinational organizations; millions or hundreds of millions of log entries are filtered to hundreds of thousands of events that are parsed to dozens or hundreds of

incidents that can be investigated and reviewed by an administration team within a single shift (new approaches using machine learning may see this even further refined). The two alternatives to automated monitoring are both unpalatable: linear scaling of employee numbers based on the number of log entries generated by systems or blissfully ignoring something unless it triggers a failure somewhere down the track.

Monitoring and reporting are often two sides of the same coin. It is almost impossible to build reports without having harvested useful data in the monitoring phase, and those reports allow the business to determine potential new areas to monitor. As shown in Figure 6.1, both serve the same purpose: to improve the overall data protection service.

Monitoring and reporting of data protection within an organization must be a gestalt. While each individual component (backup/recovery, storage, replication, etc.) might have their own individual monitoring and reporting options, it's important the business be able to see their health and trends as a whole. The primary reason for this, of course, is that data protection isn't an individual activity—configuring a RAID storage system doesn't guarantee against data loss on its own. Configuring a backup and recovery system doesn't guarantee perfect data recoverability, either. We define *cascading failure* to be a situation whereby two or more failures occur after one another, increasing risk of either downtime or data loss. Cascading failure must be considered at all times in understanding the true health of the data protection environment. For instance, many organizations will consider a lower-than-desirable backup success ratio acceptable as a one-off event. Trending and reporting within the backup and recovery system might indicate such one-off events are far too regular within the organization. However, trending and reporting across the *entire* data protection process might indicate a considerably higher danger level if, for instance, storage systems are encountering more drive swap-outs than normal at the same time regular backup failures are occurring. For some systems, failures are not only noted

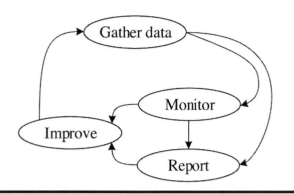

Figure 6.1 Monitoring and reporting as a feedback to systems improvement.

individually, but also cumulatively: a single backup failure for a system might be considered acceptable, but the same system failing its backup 3 days running may be considered unacceptable.

In short, an insular, silo-like approach to monitoring and reporting within individual components of data protection systems is the enemy of a healthy enterprise.

The ultimate strategy therefore of monitoring and reporting within data protection must be to have a *single source of truth*; a single platform that can reveal the entire health of the data protection environment. More so than health though, only by combining all aspects of data protection can a business understand its current risk levels, compliance levels, and operational costs. At a high level, we can envisage this *single source of truth* layer as per Figure 6.2.

The point of such a diagram is to emphasize the need to decouple the business visibility and reporting layer from the actual infrastructure and operations layer. It is common to see businesses focus too much on finding a single product that can achieve *all* of their data protection requirements; yet by the nature of the different functions, service level agreements (SLA) and operational aspects, a single tool is unviable.* Instead, the focus should be on the ability to integrate all of the *business visibility* of the discrete and individual data protection components into a single view.

With such a wide scope of data protection products and functions within the IT ecosystem, a single source of truth is rarely something that you will be able to buy off the shelf, particularly as the size and complexity of your business IT operations increase. (This is regardless of whether your infrastructure is traditional on-premises systems, private cloud, hybrid cloud, or public cloud—or any mix thereof.) For larger enterprises, some work may be required to bring data gathering from disparate systems together to build the centralized view of the data protection health of the business. In this, efficiencies can be found at times by limiting the number of vendors, but efficiencies will also be gained by ensuring there are common techniques for hooking into the inspection and alerting functions for the different data protection products used. In earlier infrastructure environments, this may have been making sure everything had a robust command line interface (CLI), and supported the simple network management protocol (SNMP). While CLIs and SNMP can still be useful, there is a growing trend toward representational state transfer application programming interfaces (REST APIs) to deliver a modern accessible process designed from the ground up for easy consumption through a web-based portal or dashboard.

6.2 Monitoring

Within data protection, monitoring is the real-time or semi real-time capture and analysis of system events and data that gives the business a clear understanding of whether the environment is *reliable* (i.e., fit for purpose).

Business Visibility

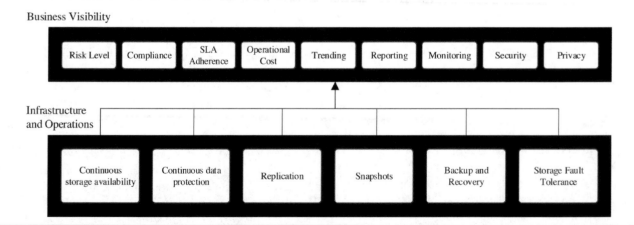

Infrastructure and Operations

Figure 6.2 Monitoring and reporting as a single source of truth.

---

* Indeed, the term "jack of all trades, master of none" is an apt description here.

There are four key focuses of monitoring in data protection:

1. Security and privacy
2. Health
3. Capacity
4. Performance

Ideally, all monitoring would be real-time—that is, an event occurs, and is immediately detected and analyzed by the business. Another approach is "semi real-time": being able to monitor events as frequently as the business needs, even if it is not actually in real-time.

However, it's essential to be pragmatic—not all software and systems will offer the same broad levels of monitoring integration, and it's (largely) unreasonable to assume that every product an organization buys or leases will immediately and seamlessly integrate with whatever monitoring product is deployed.

Monitoring should therefore be able to aggregate real-time data collection and business real-time data collection. Examples of both real-time and semi real-time data collection might cover scenarios such as:

- *Formal alerting*: SNMP is favored by many monitoring and log aggregation systems to receive information about events as they happen.
- *Text and email alerting*: Many monitoring environments are capable of receiving alerts via either email, or a custom text injection process. This allows easy adaption of alerts out of individual packages to route their data into a monitoring system.
- *Log monitoring*: Even if "events" can't be generated by a specific product, if it captures the details of events within its own logs, log monitoring or scraping can be used to detect these events and generate alerts. For systems that support sending logging information to remote hosts (e.g., the Unix/Linux syslog protocol), centralized log monitoring can reduce the effort involved.
- *Systems that do not support monitoring protocol X but do support monitoring protocol Y*: Installing or configuring an interceptor/translator should be an acceptable alternative.
- *Black box systems that perform logging only locally*: If scriptable, remote login is capable, this should be investigated to still allow for the periodic extraction of logged data and inclusion in the overall monitoring system.
- *API-based extraction*: Systems may have the capability to retrieve events via a CLI or an API. Where necessary, an adapter could be written (if not already available) to retrieve such information.
- *Web-page scraping*: Increasingly, modern GUIs are provided as web-page/HTML interfaces, thanks to the feature-rich offerings of HTML5. Automated web-page scraping may be possible to retrieve required information from dashboards or monitoring panels.
- *Systems that provide valuable data both as automated logging and executable reports*: If the executable reports generate summary information or other details not readily apparent from the automated logging, these reports should be periodically harvested if they can increase the quality of the monitoring.

In an environment that focuses on automation, logging information might also be used to automatically generate service tickets for relevant IT staff. (The open source monitoring system, Nagios, includes a basic ticketing system, and commercial systems such as ServiceNow can lean heavily into automatic service ticket creation from incoming data events.)

Of course, monitoring encompasses other areas as well. Many businesses will typically need to monitor systems for security and compliance, for instance. Any monitoring or reporting system deployed for data protection should ideally be capable of integrating into umbrella systems that provide these capabilities and whatever other options are required by the business.

6.2.1 Security and Privacy

> "It's not just that the thought a helpdesk operator might recover the CEO's email without authorization **scares** the security team," an IT architect remarked during a meeting, "it's the thought that it might go **undetected** that terrifies them."

Security and privacy teams are increasingly seeking assurance that data storage protection systems can be monitored for in real-time, or as close to real-time as possible. Some examples of events that security and privacy teams will focus on include (but are by no means limited to):

- *Data recovery*:
  - *Action stages*: Ideally, the system should be able to alert on *browsing* (looking for data to recover), recovery *initiation*, and recovery *completion*.
  - *Recovered content*: The system should be able to provide some guidance on what data was recovered, or at least what area of a system was recovered (e.g., "Recovering from *hostname:filesystem*"). Some security or privacy teams will desire even more granular recovery details, such as the full names/paths of every file recovered.
  - *Recovery target*: In addition to identifying where data is being recovered *from*, it should be possible

to identify where data is recovered *to*. Has, for instance, the CEO's email been recovered into a legal hold folder, or has it been recovered as a portable storage table (PST) file onto a USB key attached to a help desk team member's PC?

- *Operator*: Who performed the recovery? Some security teams may also want to know *where* the recovery was initiated—e.g., being able to backtrace login details to know if a recovery was initiated on-site, via a VPN, etc.

■ *Ad-hoc operations*: Beyond data recovery events, and it should be possible to capture most, if not all manual events within the data protection environment, including but not limited to:
   - Manual backup
   - Manual backup clone/replication
   - Backup deletion
   - Snapshot creation
   - Snapshot deletion
   - Change of data protection retention period (backup, snapshot, etc.)
   - Change of journaling capacity (replication, CDP, etc.)

■ *Configuration*:
   - Data protection configuration changes can have a significant ongoing impact to the business. Snapshots being disabled, backup retention being reduced, hosts being removed from backup configurations, etc., can all have a deleterious effect on the data integrity of the business.
   - Ideally from a security perspective, configuration monitoring should be able to show who has made a configuration change, and what change was made (e.g., a "before" and "after" view).

Where once there was the assumption that those with the privileges to perform an operation could, in fact, be trusted to perform it, external auditing and internal security, privacy, and risk activities all need to understand activities within data protection faster, and more accurately.

In the simplest terms, businesses should be confident they can detect and account for all data recovery operations that have taken place, and are aware of changes to the data protection configuration across their IT landscape.

6.2.2 Health

At the most basic level, monitoring for data protection health could be seen as monitoring of failures. That might include highlighting:

■ Storage components that have failed
■ Data replication functions that have failed

■ Backup and recovery failures

While this is a good starting point, it's not sufficient for truly effective monitoring of a data protection environment. Effective monitoring also has to consider data such as:

■ Mean time between failures (MTBF)
■ Mean time to repair (MTTR)
■ Predicted failures (e.g., drive S.M.A.R.T.* status)
■ Warnings

Both MTBF and MTTR offer very useful information in a data protection environment.

6.2.2.1 Drive Failures and Recovery Time

The classic use of MTBF and MTTR within data protection is of course RAID storage. While the reliability of storage systems has improved considerably over the years, they are not 100% immune to component failure.

Providing the bedrock for fault tolerance, RAID systems are a fundamental component of data protection—their entire purpose is to provide a mechanism to sustain continued access to data in the event of a component failure *and* be able to rebuild from that failure.

Consider two of the most common RAID levels:

■ *RAID-1 (mirroring)*: Whereby every block of data written to one device is written to another device. In the event of one device failing, the other device can still be read from (minimum two disks).
■ *RAID-5 (parity)*: Whereby data is written in stripes with a parity checksum written to one alternating drive in the stripe. In the event of a failure, the data can be reconstructed by the remaining data plus checksum information in each stripe (minimum three disks).

For any RAID level, we must consider that there is a cost (in time, and for that matter, energy) in re-establishing full protection after a failed component is replaced.

If a disk in a two-drive mirror fails, then the cost of reconstructing the mirror (MTTR) is in a worst-case scenario the cost of reading the entire contents of the first disk and writing that content to the replacement disk. Thus, however many blocks there are, RAID reconstruction will take double that in operations—each block will trigger a read and a write.

If a disk in a three-drive RAID-5 unit fails, then MTTR can be considerably higher than the MTTR in a two-drive RAID-1. Consider: Each stripe must be read and the data reconstructed based on the combination of available

---

* Self-Monitoring, Analysis, and Reporting Technology.

data and/or parity information, then the stripe must be adjusted in the RAID unit, either by writing the missing data/parity or rewriting the entire stripe.

Throughout the recovery time for storage, it's quite usual for storage to still be online and being used—which of course impacts the recovery time even further. (Even if the storage is used *read only*, the remaining drives will be still required to facilitate data access *while* reconstructing, and such scenarios are rare regardless.) Such an impact is of course a two-way street; while it slows down the recovery time for the RAID unit, it equally slows down day-to-day usage of the system as well. Failures that occur during critical usage periods can therefore have a substantially higher impact on operations.

Combined knowledge of (average) MTBF results and the MTTR information can yield smarter operational decisions within a data protection environment, such as:

- Understanding whether standard SLAs for data access continue to be met as the usage profile changes or the volume of data grows
- Understanding when data might be migrated between tiers or away from underperforming storage when there appears to be a higher risk of potential failure
- Predicting, based on prior recovery times, how long a recovery is likely to take in order to provide accurate performance degradation time frames to the business

6.2.2.2 Broader Uses of MTBF and MTTR

While usually considered from the perspective of disk drives and RAID units, the concept of MTBF and MTTR equally applies to other areas of data protection. Consider the different data protection scenarios outlined in Table 6.1.

Even if these aren't tracked *literally* in terms of MTTR and MTBF, it's pertinent to keep in mind that the core concepts of *time to recover* and *time between failures* are critical in the planning, implementation, and maintenance of a data protection system.

6.2.3 Capacity

While health is undoubtedly the most critical *immediate* concern for data protection monitoring, monitoring for capacity plays an important role as well.

This will likely have a significant overlap with general information lifecycle capacity monitoring, but there are particular areas that need to be focused on for data protection.

6.2.3.1 RAID/Data Storage

In a classic RAID environment where all LUNs and storage are 100% allocated on initial request, there is very little monitoring to be done within RAID or data storage for capacity as it affects data protection. That's not to say monitoring isn't required, but it falls to the broader topic of storage capacity tracking.

However, with storage systems offering increasingly advanced options relating to thin provisioning or just-in-time capacity expansion, the importance of tracking capacity and its impact on data protection *is* asserting itself.

At a most basic level, consider even home-office/small-office storage arrays from companies such as Drobo®. One of the selling points of the Drobo storage system is its ability to present a thinly provisioned filesystem constructed of multiple drive sizes and/or types while still providing data protection. A five-drive unit, for instance, might be initially populated with 5 × 2 TB drives. On the expectation that storage would *grow*, a filesystem can be presented to the end user/computer based on the *eventual* capacity of 5 × 4 TB hard drives.

Table 6.1 Broader Uses of MTBF and MTTR

Data Protection Activity	MTTR	MTBF
Backup and recovery	Time taken to recover data once it is requested *or* once the recovery commences.	How soon after data is backed up before a recovery is requested for it vs. the frequency at which the backup is performed.
Snapshots	Time taken to roll back to a point in time or retrieve data from a snapshot.	How regularly data needs to be retrieved from snapshots vs. the frequency at which the snapshots are taken.
Replication (usually cross-site)	Time taken to *either* bring the remote replica online for primary production access *or* replicate it back to repair a failed primary replica (will depend on the usage profile of the replica).	How regularly the site link fails (or perhaps more correctly—how *reliable* the site link is). The impact of the reliability of the replication link will depend considerably on the volume of data being generated and the way in which the replication system re-establishes synchronization after a failure.

Thus, the initial filesystem would be presented by around 10 TB of drives providing in the order of 7–8 TB of *protected* capacity while appearing to the operating system as being approximately 18 TB.

Obviously in this scenario, it's not possible to copy, say, 12 TB of data to the initial filesystem that's provided by just 5 × 2 TB drives. The Drobo system is designed to *monitor* and report where capacity growth is preventing adequate data protection, and thus highlight the need to replace individual drives with larger ones in order to allow for continued data growth at the requested levels of redundancy.

This is the nature of thinly provisioned storage with data protection—not only is the actual storage presented to the end user thinly provisioned, but so too is the data redundancy, hence the need to monitor such systems carefully.

Monitoring in such a scenario can and should certainly be tied to general capacity modeling/monitoring. It's no good, for instance, to know that there is sufficient room for 20% data growth if broader capacity models predict there'll be a 40% spike in data over the 3 weeks and the purchasing cycle for additional storage is 6 weeks.

6.2.3.2 Snapshots

The first implementations of snapshots within IT were closer to tertiary mirrors in RAID-1 environments where the third mirror was snapped off to allow access to a quiesced copy of the data. (Indeed, in the early days, it was more likely to be the case that it was only a dual-drive mirror and it was the secondary mirror being temporarily removed.)

Such "snapshots" presented significant performance overhead. For instance, reattaching a previously detached mirror meant recopying the *entire* contents to resynchronize the mirrors.

This slow rebuild time leads to the use of bitmaps to more rapidly reattach mirrors. The bitmap would be used to track "dirty" regions on the detached mirror; in essence, whenever a write occurred to the *actual* mirror (the one still mounted for production use), the bitmap would be updated to indicate which blocks had been written to. When the detached mirror disk was subsequently reattached, the bitmap would be referred to and only those regions marked as *dirty* would be copied back across. (Presuming, of course, the detached mirror had been used *read only*, of course.)

Most snapshots now tend to be *incomplete* copies. While many storage systems provide options for snapshots that are exact 1:1 duplicates of the original LUN, the more common scenario usually involves a variation of *copy on first write* technology. (This will be explained in more detail in Chapter 11.)

Snapshots are not pre-provisioned with storage; even a low-end enterprise storage system may support hundreds of snapshots of an individual LUN, and thousands of snapshots in total. Typically, the storage administrators will allocate a percentage of the storage array for use as a snapshot pool,

and for the purposes of data protection, this pool capacity and utilization needs to be monitored carefully. The pool utilization will be mostly dependent on the workload of the original filesystems while snapshots are active; a single LUN for which there exists a snapshot could cause the consumption of a considerable amount of snapshot pool storage if it undergoes an unanticipated volume of updates.

6.2.3.3 Replication

Replication capacity considerations fall into three main categories:

- Target capacity
- Link bandwidth
- Backlog

Link bandwidth refers to whether the connection between the source and destination replication target is sufficient to allow the throughput of the data that must be sent. The speed of the link should have been considered long before replication is turned on, as it will directly affect considerations such as whether or not replication occurs synchronously or asynchronously. (Other factors, such as physical distance and latency, will also come into play here.)

For data protection scenarios, used link bandwidth must be continuously monitored and compared to data growth and (for asynchronous scenarios) data *backlog*—how far "behind" updates the replication target is from the source. More advanced replication technologies may employ compression and other bandwidth-saving techniques, yet the efficacy of such techniques is likely to be dependent on the type of data being replicated and the frequency at which it is updated.

Additionally, replication isn't always a 1:1 ratio. A business may deploy a 500 TB SAN in their primary site, but only deploy a 200 TB SAN in the disaster recovery site, with the intention to only replicate primary production data. However, it's easy to envisage scenarios in such a configuration where the data designated as "primary production" grows to exceed the capacity of the replication target. Alternately, replication can be many-to-one—a single replication target might receive data from multiple replication sources. If one or more of those replication sources grows in capacity, the cascading effect can equally result in a failure condition. In situations where there are sources replicating in from geographically disperse areas, having to "re-seed" the replication target can be problematic and time-consuming. This scenario in itself demonstrates the need for a global view approach to capacity monitoring; storage administrators at individual sites may very well be monitoring and managing data growth for their individual systems entirely reasonably, but the cumulative effect on the capacity requirements on the replication target needs to be considered *in light* of the capacity growth on the individual systems, not apart from them.

Particularly in scenarios covering asynchronous replication (which will be covered further in Chapter 10, Continuous Availability, Replication, and CDP), the business should also be able to monitor how far *behind* replication is. With synchronous replication, this should be zero, but the entire purpose of asynchronous replication is to allow for differences in the source and target. This might be expressed in terms of maximum data backlog (e.g., "the replica target should be no more than 50 megabytes behind the replica source"), or time backlog ("the replica target should be no more than 15 minutes behind the replica source"). In either case, monitoring the backlog to alert if it no longer adheres to the configured backlog allowances can give a direct view of the risk exposure of the business in failover situations.

6.2.3.4 Backup and Recovery

The backup capacity requirement in a traditional storage model is relatively easy to understand. Let's consider a production environment that has 10 TB of data requiring backup and assume there's a 7% incremental change, day on day. Taking a fairly classic model approach, we'll assume the following backup cycles:

- Weekly full backups retained for 5 weeks
- Daily incremental backups retained for 5 weeks
- Monthly full backups retained for 7 years

For the daily/weekly backup cycle of 5 weeks, the storage requirements will be:

- 5 [weeks] × 10 TB (fulls) = 50 TB
- 5 [weeks] × 6 [days] × (7% of 10 TB) = 5 × 6 × 0.7 TB = 21 TB

For the monthly full backups retained for 7 years, the storage requirements will be:

- 7 [years] × 12 [months] × 10 TB = 840 TB

(Of course, this all assumes zero growth, which is fairly rare within a data environment.)

From these calculations, we see that a traditional backup model for 10 TB could result in storage requirements of 911 TB. Even if we shrink the requirements by dropping weekly fulls and moving to a monthly full backup cycle, the storage requirements stay reasonably high:

- (Average) 30 [days] × (7% of 10 TB) = 21 TB
- 7 [years] × 12 [months] × 10 TB = 840 TB

This gives a reduced total of approximately 861 TB—yet the ratios remain significantly high. Assuming even the better scenario of just doing monthly fulls, the ratio stands at 1:86.1—for every 1 TB of production data used, we're using 86.1 TB for the backups of that data over the lifespan of the data.

We'll cover storage requirements for data later, particularly in light of the impact deduplication is having on this footprint problem; in the meantime, the examples mentioned earlier serve well to demonstrate the profound requirement for backup capacity monitoring within an environment. Increasing the data backup requirements by a single terabyte can have significant flow-on effects to backup storage utilization, and traditionally this has been an area that businesses have paid little attention to. Tape in particular made this a hidden problem—a box of tapes here, a box of tapes there, and before they knew it businesses had *thousands* or *tens of thousands* of tapes in vaulted storage with backups on them that *may* never be recovered from.

Backup system capacity monitoring falls into two essential categories:

- *Knowing the "on-boarding" capacity of the backup environment*: In its current configuration, what is the capacity it offers for taking *new* systems in, and what is the capacity impact of doing so?
- Feeding into reporting, what does the capacity utilization growth of the backup system say about the long-term growth of the environment—that is, when will expansion be required?

Capacity also needs to be monitored for recovery situations as well, but this will be largely dependent on the products used for backup/recovery and the recovery scenarios the business requires. For example:

- Some deduplication products, for instance, may require recoveries to be staged *through* the appliance.
- If image-level backups are being taken of virtual machines but file-level recovery is not supported, it implies recovering an entire virtual machine, even if only a single file needs to be recovered from within that virtual machine.
- Database or application administrators may insist that backups be generated as dump files to disk and backed up as part of a normal filesystem backup operation. In a recovery scenario, it may be necessary to provide recovery capacity not only for the destination database, but also the dump file to restore from.*

---

* In this case, you'll note I've used the words *recover* and *restore*. Typically in database circles, a recovery refers to retrieving the files and data from the backup storage, and a *restoration* refers to either rebuilding the database from those recovered files or reinstating database consistency using those recovered files.

Recovery capacity requirements demonstrate the need for reasonably tight integration between production and backup/recovery systems capacity monitoring. It is not unheard of for recoveries to be delayed or even canceled when there's insufficient storage space for the recovery to be facilitated.

6.2.4 Performance

Having already dealt with monitoring for security, health, and capacity, performance monitoring is the simplest variable to consider, given that the performance of a data protection environment is affected and governed most by:

- *The health of the components*: Failing components or components in recovery mode will have different performance characteristics from normal.
- *Capacity*: Growth in capacity will have a direct impact on the performance of the data protection activities.

In this, performance monitoring is the most straightforward:

- *RAID and data storage*: How long it takes to rebuild
- *Backup*: Speed of backups versus backup windows

- *Recoveries*: Speed of recoveries versus the recovery SLAs required
- *Snapshots*: Whether or not snapshots adversely affect (or are adversely affected by) production storage load, and vice versa
- *Replication*: Speed at which data is either replicated from the source to the target or in the event of a significant failure from the target back to the source

6.2.5 Notifications versus Dashboards

Most, if not all data protection products, support the concept of *notifications*. Most backup products, for instance, at least support the SNMP and the simple mail transfer protocol (SMTP).

In the 1990s and early 2000s, it was an entirely normal part of backup operations to consider that the first duty of a backup administrator of a morning was to read the overnight emails detailing the results of overnight backup operations, and take, or at least schedule, the appropriate follow-up activities. For example, a backup email notification from one product, Dell EMC NetWorker®, looks like the following:

```
--- Traditional Backup Action report ---
Policy name:Platinum
Workflow name:Servers
Action name:backup
Action status:succeeded
Action start time:04/21/19 23:00:00
Action duration:0 hours 3 minutes 24 seconds
Total 4 client(s), 0 Succeeded with warning(s), 4 Succeeded, 0 Failed.
    ---Successful backups---
    abydos.turbamentis.int:/, level=incr, size 79 MB, duration 0 hours 0 minutes 7
seconds, 131 files
    krell.turbamentis.int:/, level=incr, size 28 KB, duration 0 hours 0 minutes 7
seconds, 15 files
    krell.turbamentis.int:/var, level=incr, size 228 MB, duration 0 hours 0 minutes 10
seconds, 163 files
    oa.turbamentis.int:/, level=incr, size 73 MB, duration 0 hours 0 minutes 2
seconds, 151 files
    orilla.turbamentis.int:/, level=incr, size 343 MB, duration 0 hours 0 minutes 12
seconds, 4825 files
    orilla.turbamentis.int:/nsr, level=incr, size 160 MB, duration 0 hours 0 minutes
11 seconds, 281 files
    ---Successful backups with warnings---
    none
    ---Failed backups---
    none
```

Clearly such notifications contain significant useful information, but as businesses grow in terms of data, systems, and complexity, and their data protection activities increase to accommodate that growth, there needs to be a recognition

that *monitoring via notifications does not scale*. While checking 20 emails of a morning to review notifications of 20 different scheduled backup operations from the previous evening might not be an onerous use of an administrator's time, that process does not scale when there might be 200, or 2,000 different scheduled backups for 5,000, 10,000 or more systems within the environment. Even with email filters potentially filing failed backups into a different folder to successful backups, conducting a backup-by-backup review of the overnight operations doesn't scale. Here, we've referred only to backup operations, yet there'll also potentially arise notifications from snapshots, replication, fault tolerance, and so on, which just increases the scaling problem.

Yet, in the introduction, we noted that if you don't check whether a backup ran successfully overnight, you should assume it failed.

The solution to the scaling problem is to make use of dashboards: rather than relying on an event-by-event inspection of activities. Figure 6.3 shows a sample backup dashboard with three views:

- *Asset backup results*: The results of backups for assets (e.g., clients of the backup system). In the simplest form (as shown), this might provide a breakdown of successful and failed backups, or might also include details of jobs still running, jobs queued but not yet started, and jobs that completed with warnings.
- *Backup replication jobs*: The results of backup replication jobs. Like the backup results, this might simply show success/failure, or show additional breakdowns of job status if they occur.
- *Asset three strikes summary*: The number of assets that have experienced a backup failure once, two times in a row, or three times in a row.

Dashboards will usually offer the option to view the status of operations based on a variety of timeframes; in the example dashboard both are showing results for the last 24 hours, but conceivably this could be optionally switched between 24 hours, 7 days, a month or all available history, each offering a different view of the information to the user.

Usually dashboards will also support *drill-through*; i.e., clicking on the "failed" portion of the donut graph in the *Asset Backup Results* in our sample dashboard might bring up a list of all the clients whose backup failed, with options to view the logs from the backup, and restart its backup job.

Of course, the utility of dashboards usually goes beyond the three sample views provided in Figure 6.3. Additional information you might expect to see provided in a dashboard could include:

- Data protection storage capacity
- General system errors and warnings
- Trend views of success ratios
- Detected but unprotected assets

The advantage of dashboards over notification-based monitoring should be immediately obvious: monitoring changes from being event-based to exception based, with *at-a-glance* views providing immediate visual clues as to whether anything needs further inspection.

This is not to say notifications don't need to be configured to be sent when dashboards are in use; however, dashboards generally do allow for notifications to be used as a means of feeding into broader health monitoring in the environment, rather than the primary mechanism for observing system health at any individual moment.

6.3 Reporting

Reporting is at its most useful for the business when there has been time taken to understand the KPIs for the overall data protection environment. While reporting can also provide a simple summary of monitoring events (which will be discussed shortly), reporting comes into its own as a health assessment of the environment if it is designed with specific measurements in place.

Backup Dashboard

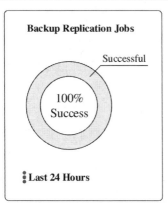
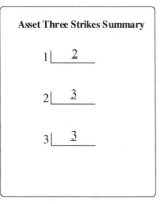

Figure 6.3 Sample backup dashboard.

Within data protection, we usually think of SLAs focused on two key areas: recovery point objective (RPO) and recovery time objective (RTO). The former covers how much data can be lost when an event occurs, and the latter how much time it takes to recover from the failure. Yet, two SLAs only do not make a data protection system; the ability to meet the core SLAs depends on the integrity and reliability of the overall system, which we can measure via key performance indicators.

Examples of data protection KPIs might include the list below, which depending on the specific metric, might be tracked daily, weekly, monthly, or on even longer cycles—and often across many.

- Backup and recovery:
  - Backup success rate
  - Reliability of backups for individual systems ("strike rates"—detailing systems that had 2, 3, 4, etc., failures in a row)
  - Recovery success rate
  - Number of backups taken for particular systems (e.g., "databases shall have 31 online backup copies at all time")
  - Storage efficiency (particularly when deduplication is used)
- Replication:
  - Percentage adherence to asynchronous replication targets
  - Percentage or number of replication pairs that were broken
  - Whether the required number of replication copies were retained
- Snapshots:
  - Percentage of taken snapshots that were used
  - Number of snapshots taken, or adherence to snapshot policies (e.g., "fileservers shall have hourly snapshots retained for 24 hours, 6-hourly snapshots retained for 3 days, half-daily snapshots retained for 7 days, and daily snapshots retained for 14 days")
- Continuous data protection:
  - Amount of rollback time provided (based on journal size and number of IOs)
  - Number of application consistent bookmarks maintained

6.3.1 Reporting via Aggregation of Monitoring

In the simplest scenario, reporting represents the aggregated data collected by the various monitoring systems in the environment. Such reporting can represent some of the KPIs established by or for the business, but it does not necessarily have to *only* be about KPIs.

Reports based purely on data collected by monitoring may focus on "dashboard" functionality—for example, the status of backup operations may be shown color coded like traffic lights—red, amber, or green depending on whether there are serious issues, warnings, or entirely successful operations, respectively.* This would allow an administrator to view the health of backup operations at a glance and only require drill down to investigate serious issues or warnings.

Aggregation of monitoring allows for at-a-glance views of overall data protection health, such as:

- Were there storage drive failures during the month?
- What capacity of the snapshot storage pool was used each day during the quarter?
- Did replication fall behind at any point during the week?
- What was the percentage of successful backups each day?
- Did any recoveries fail?

Once data protection monitoring is being aggregated into these simple reports, the business can start looking at trending.

6.3.2 Reporting for Trending and Predictive Planning

Reporting on trends is a crucial step in understanding how an environment is changing. A backup system, for instance, may be deployed on the expectation that data is only growing at 9% year on year, but month-by-month monitoring of backup utilization may quickly demonstrate an *actual* growth rate of 15% or more.

Equally, trending may determine that the bandwidth allocated for replication will be exhausted in 6 months based on data growth, not 18 as originally budgeted for when the link was installed.

Referring again to the DIKW model presented in the introduction (Figure 1.9), we can say:

- Base data is collected by monitoring.
- Information is the collection of the individual units of data into a picture of system health, capacity, or performance.
- Aggregated monitoring information presented as reports provides the business *knowledge*, be it in the form of dashboards, traditional reports, or drill-down details.

---

* A more considerate user interface may display the same information, but in a way which will work for color-blind users, as well.

■ Wisdom comes from using all the accumulated data, information, and knowledge to provide trends on utilization and predictions on system exhaustion.

Predictive planning comes from applying situational understanding from trending information or smoothing out details in order to see trends past individual spikes or troughs. In particular, many businesses have periodic or seasonal variations in their data protection utilization, which can, if not understood, play havoc with determining growth rates within environments.

Consider for instance:

■ Universities and other educational facilities typically have to provide higher guarantees of data protection during peak enrolment periods; this will potentially result in more snapshots and backups during this time.
■ Postal/logistics companies will see significantly higher volumes (sometimes orders of magnitude higher) of mail and parcel traffic during holiday seasons.
■ Banks and other finance companies will have higher service requirements for end-of-month processing in addition to additional reporting workloads at the end of each financial year.
■ Accounting firms will have higher workloads for periods around the new financial year.

Across almost all businesses, there will also be peaks and troughs in data protection requirements as a result of project work, too. Large-scale transformational systems being commissioned and brought online, with workloads either developed or migrated to them, will generate the need for substantially higher data protection requirements; engineering/construction companies will have "lumpy" data protection based on the size, scope, and duration of each project, and media companies will also see peaks in data protection while projects are active.

Considering seasonal and project variances in data protection requirements, businesses should at minimum ensure trending is more than just a simple month-by-month analysis. Rolling averages can be helpful to ease out seasonal peaks and troughs, but those peaks still have to be accommodated in growth projections and capacity requirements.

Where understanding the peaks and troughs can be particularly is in spotting *unanticipated* growth. For instance, consider a business with approximately 200 TB of front-end data being protected, with an average annual growth rate of 12%, which equals a monthly growth rate (on average) of 0.95%, where there are annualized spikes of up to 30% from mid-November to mid-January. With this trending information known, the business could more easily detect an irregular spike in April when the monthly growth in data backed up is 5% compared to the average of 0.95%. Such trending analysis allows for faster detection of unanticipated capacity utilization before it becomes an issue that can compromise the system.

6.3.3 *Automated Reporting*

It's a well-known fact within the backup and recovery realm that a backup that is not automated is not done. Or rather, while it may be sporadically performed, it hardly represents a reliable process deserving of the appellation of *system*.

One might argue the same for reports—while there will always be situations where it is necessary to manually run a report (either as an out-of-band execution of a standard report or an entirely new report), wherever possible reports should be developed to be executed and distributed automatically.

However, a report that isn't read may as well not be executed, so automated reports don't solve the perennial problem of being *used*, they just make it easier for people to use them.

As such, once the system reaches the point where there is monitoring in place, reports generated from aggregated monitoring data, and reports based on trends and predictive analysis, it becomes a *process* problem to ensure that the reports are dealt with.

As covered in Chapter 4—the technology is the easy part. The human and process aspects are the more challenging. Yet a business must be prepared to tackle these problems if it is to have any chance of reliably understanding the state or direction of its data protection environment.

Like dashboards, as discussed earlier in this chapter, automated reporting can reduce the overall effort required to understand the health and trends of the environment. Rather than being seen as "onerous to set up," making the investment in terms of time (and if necessary, money) to get reports automated is a key step to ensuring data protection professionals within the business are focused on exceptions and projects, rather than repetitive mundanity.

6.4 Summary

There's an old philosophical thought exercise:

> If a tree falls in a forest and nobody is there to hear it, does it make a sound?

In a nutshell the question is about perceived versus actual reality. This is perhaps the heart of the requirement around monitoring and reporting—if something fails but its failure is not recorded, not noted, not *noticed*, then how do we know it has failed? An environment is only as reliable as its components, and if we're not actively aware of the health of the individual components, we can't truly be aware of the health of the environment itself.

Monitoring and reporting within a data protection environment shouldn't be seen solely as a means of tracking and reporting failures or issues. While those functions are critical, monitoring and reporting make charge-back processes simple *and* accurate. Similarly, they enable the management and administrators of the environment to justify resources, budget, and attainment of key performance indicators. In compliance-dominated businesses, these details become *essential* to allowing the business to pass mandatory external audits of its infrastructure. Individually inspecting a month's worth of backup results, for instance, to calculate the average success rate experienced in the business can be done, of course, but it will be a time-consuming process potentially subject to human error. Statistics automatically published by monitoring systems every day providing the same formatted information make the auditing process simple and the justification of the data protection environment substantially easier.

Arguably you could well state that a data protection environment that doesn't include comprehensive monitoring and reporting is merely a loose assemblage of components. Indeed, far too much focus is given in most businesses toward the notion of a single unified management interface that can administer *every* layer of data protection from backup through snapshots and replication all the way through to continuous storage availability and continuous data protection. While such interfaces are likely to evolve as a result of hyperconverged infrastructure, a real data protection *environment* can be created *already* by focusing instead on a unified and integrated approach to monitoring and reporting. Having both layers available will undoubtedly further hone data protection integration, but the unified monitoring and reporting layer will *always* remain critical.

6.5 Self-Reflection

Think of backup jobs for:

■ Databases
■ Filesystems
■ Virtual Machines

For each type of backup job, note the sorts of details you would expect to see in a summary notification regarding the status of the job. Be mindful that this will include both job identification details, and more specific information about each backup executed within the job.

Next, think how this information might be aggregated into a dashboard view so that as the scale of the environment grows, health information can be seen *at a glance*.

Chapter 7

Business Continuity

7.1 Introduction

The first mistake usually made in IT relating to business continuity, particularly among the more technical or more junior staff, is an assumption that the terms *disaster recovery* and *business continuity* are synonymous. In simple terms, this would be akin to believing that a regular schedule for changing the oil in a car is the same as a complete servicing plan for it.

Business continuity is *not* an IT function at all. Or rather, it's not a function that's driven by IT. Indeed, any business that *makes* it an IT-driven function has made a critical mistake. The purpose of business continuity, as its name suggests, revolves around keeping the business running, or in the event of a significant disruption, allowing the business to recommence operations. Without a doubt, IT will play a function in this for all except the most esoteric of businesses. Yet IT can't be the driving consideration (even if the business is an IT company). The focus must always be the actual functions provided by the business to its consumers: its customers and clients, both external and internal.[*]

While business continuity does have a much broader scope, our focus in this chapter will be constrained only to those topics overlapping with data protection.

7.2 Business versus IT Functions

One of the most essential activities in working on business continuity is to conduct all planning around *business functions* rather than *IT functions*. Business continuity in and of itself is not concerned with *email* or *DNS* or *intranets*, but instead with the services and functions the business offers to perform revenue generation. Business continuity therefore concerns itself wholly with those business functions. These will inevitably vary from business to business in detail and priority, but a few common functions for many businesses might include such areas as:

- Billing
- Customer order fulfillment
- Stock control
- Payroll

While the continuity plan for any business function will very likely include IT-related disaster recovery plans, even for seemingly entirely IT-centric business functions, the IT disaster recovery plan will rarely be the *only* part of the business continuity plan.

In the same way that IT disaster recovery plans should be built around reliance on or importance of individual components via system dependency maps and tables, business continuity plans will also need to be built around the criticality of individual business functions being protected. This will typically result in business functions being broken down into categories such as the following:

- *Business (or mission) critical:* The business will fail to operate meaningfully at all if the function is not performed.
- *Critical:* The business will incur substantial costs if unable to perform the function or may be at risk of failure if multiple critical functions fail.
- *Essential:* The function is important to the business, but an outage can be sustained without *risk* to the business.
- *Non-essential:* The interruption to the function does not cost or impair the ability of the business to operate.

Such classification of business functions will itself be a *business* process, and the IT department will typically *at most*

---

[*] Think of our system maps and system dependency tables outlined in Chapter 4, for instance. The final diagram and table both made clear mention of the *business functions* as well as any supporting IT functions.

provide input as a standard business unit to such a classification process.

7.3 Risk versus Cost

Much of what we do in data protection is a *risk versus cost* decision. What is the *risk* of an event happening? What is the *cost* of protecting against it, and what is the *cost* of not protecting against it? Note that the cost to the business is not necessarily a simple number. It can refer to hard costs ("For each hour the system is down, the business will be fined $60,000"), and a mix of hard and soft costs such as wages paid for inactive staff, potential sales losses, and reputational costs—whether the business will lose standing in the marketplace that can have potentially long lasting impact.

When evaluating risk versus cost decisions for business continuity, the business should be prepared to evaluate four potentially different approaches, namely:

1. *Continuity:* where business processes must continue to run with as little (or no) interruption or alteration as possible (i.e., continuous availability)
2. *Restoration:* where an interruption is acknowledged, with deadlines established for the restoration of services
3. *Triage:* where an interruption is acknowledged, with plans for *workarounds* to be put in place before restoration can be achieved at a later point
4. *Ignore:* where the loss of the service for the duration of the incident is deemed acceptable

While such approaches *might* be determined on a company-wide scale, it will more usually be the case that they'll be determined on a business-function-by-business-function basis and will be related directly to the criticality of the business function, as discussed in the previous section. Consider an airport, for instance:

■ Air traffic control systems will require *continuity.*
■ *Restoration* plans and systems might be deemed sufficient for shared network and computing systems for individual airline help desks.
■ A failure in the scheduling systems for airport parking allocation and shuttle busses might be handled through procedural *triage* until such time as a solution is determined.
■ Loss of systems connectivity for *gift shops* within the airport can be ignored during an incident (i.e., in a significant outage, gift shops within the airport might simply be instructed to close).

While continuity and restoration approaches to handling failures will typically also include some form of triage, the difference will be that business functions will be severely impeded *without* primary restoration or ongoing operations, whereas lower priority systems might be kept running without risk or substantial business impact on an ongoing basis via triage alone.

No business, regardless of size, financial backing, employee knowledge, or geographic distribution, can entirely eliminate risk from their IT environment. For instance, with the human race effectively planet bound, even the most risk-averse company in the world is unlikely to develop strategies for dealing with scenarios such as:

■ Planet-killer asteroid hitting Earth
■ Runaway nanotechnology experiment destroying all matter
■ Rogue state destroying the moon and showering the world with debris

Business continuity therefore is *always* a risk versus cost elimination process. While a planet-killer asteroid striking the Earth would indeed represent a considerable business disruption, the cost of developing and implementing a strategy to overcome such a scenario would likely *not* be considered as something that should be invested in.

Extreme examples may sound silly, but they do serve to highlight the decision-making and planning process that goes into business continuity. A business will evaluate specific failure models or event scenarios and determine:

■ The risk of it happening
■ The risk to the business if it happens
■ The cost of protecting against and recovering from the event
■ The cost of *not* recovering from the event

After these have been determined, the business can more reasonably assess an approach to each potential scenario. It is here we start to see where business continuity strategies and considerations exceed those for disaster recovery. The IT approach or focus on a site loss will invariably deal with the infrastructure aspects of recovery—getting desktops and laptops available, enabling network infrastructure, getting servers and storage up and running, and restoration of data and activation of applications. For the business, this will be just a subset of the considerations. Other areas of focus will include plans for the number of staff that need to have access to the alternate site (and how many would be directed to work from home), physical security arrangements, general facilities management, and so on. In short: business continuity isn't specific to IT systems failures and, in addition to any specific considerations relating directly to IT systems failures, will encompass broader risks such as:

- Human resource risks
- Competitive risks
- Environmental risks
- Legal and regulatory risks

Therefore, from the perspective of the IT department, a disaster recovery plan might be titled "Restarting Production Systems at the Disaster Recovery Site," but this might be called by any of a number of business continuity plans including:

- Physical destruction of primary datacenter
- Systems search and seizure in primary (colocation) datacenter
- Natural disaster
- Ongoing city grid power outage

While undoubtedly the IT disaster recovery plan relating to the restart of production systems at the disaster recovery site will play a valuable part in each of these scenarios, it won't be the only part. Other aspects considered by the business continuity plan might include:

- Staff relocation processes
- Staff work from home policies
- Activation of crisis management teams
- Activation of fiduciary or compliance countdowns (a business, for instance, might have regulatory requirements stating it can only run without a disaster recovery (DR) site for 48 hours before it has to report to a government body)
- Changed business metrics (a plan, for instance, might work based on only providing 75% of standard business responsiveness)

While IT staff may have to change their work location in such a situation and senior IT may form part of the crisis management teams, the core business will be responsible for countdowns, changed metrics, and ownership of the crisis management process.

7.4 Planning Data Protection Strategies and Service Level Agreements

An important aspect to the IT considerations in business continuity is to have a thorough understanding of (and agreement with the business over) the impact of a disaster recovery or business continuity situation on data protection requirements.

Consider, for instance, a scenario where a business has a NAS array at their production site with a series of volumes. In addition to standard snapshots taken periodically for rapid data protection, the business also replicates *all* volumes to

another NAS array at their disaster recovery site so that if the primary site or primary array is lost, the data is still immediately accessible. This might resemble something along the lines of Figure 7.1.

This immediately makes the mirrored NAS considerably more useful to the business. Whereas before it had effectively been sitting "idle" other than to receive mirrored data in anticipation of a disaster that may not occur, it has now been incorporated more deeply into the business data protection environment by serving as the source for backups of NAS hosted data. Such a configuration is shown in Figure 7.2.

It is here that the *risk* versus *cost* component of business continuity and disaster recovery comes into play again. At this point, *in isolation to the components shown*, the business is arguably protected from the following scenarios:

- Loss of data at production site
- Loss of NAS array at production site
- Loss of production site

However, the business is *not* protected from a failure in the backup storage as historical backups will conceivably be lost. So the business must consider replication strategies for the backup storage as well. The first option might be something along the lines of that shown in Figure 7.3, where the backup storage is replicated at the disaster recovery site to a secondary copy of the backup storage.

While this protects the business against loss of backup storage, it does not protect the business from the loss of the disaster recovery site. At that point, there's no access to the backups that have been taken. To protect the business against a loss of the disaster recovery site while still theoretically allowing for data recovery from backup, a configuration such as that shown in Figure 7.4 will be required. In this configuration, the backup data is replicated across to the production site after it has been written at the disaster recovery site. (Or alternately, a third site entirely.)

In here, a business might think that it has resolved all data protection problems relating to the NAS data, but there's still another potential scenario to be considered, that being the loss of the production site *and* the failure of the backup storage. To counter this, a business would need a solution such as that shown in Figure 7.5.

The end state configuration shown in Figure 7.5 will not, of course, be a guaranteed state for any business with production and disaster recovery sites. Much of the determination of what data protection service level objectives (SLOs) will exist in a disaster recovery situation will depend on the external and internal requirements of the business. A mid-size company with little to no legal compliance considerations may feel entirely at ease with the configuration shown in Figure 7.3 or 7.4. A smaller company again might feel no need to go beyond the configuration shown in Figure 7.2. A multinational finance

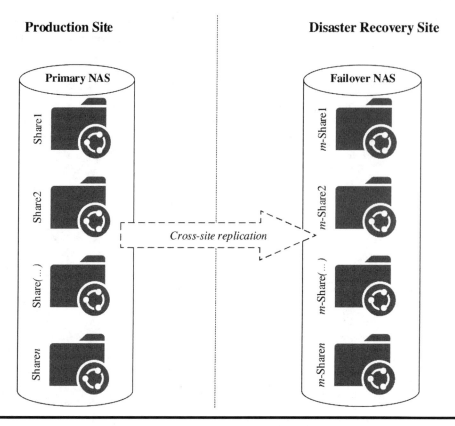

Figure 7.1   Production NAS mirrored to DR site.

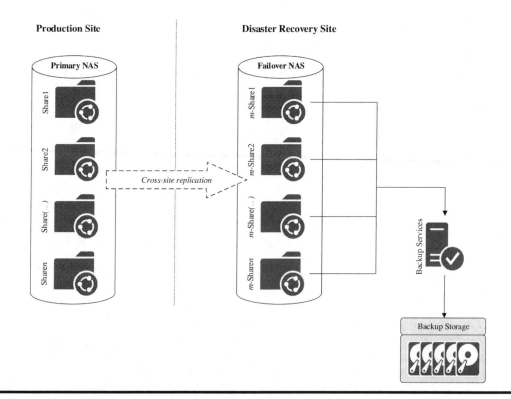

Figure 7.2   Using disaster recovery NAS replica as backup source.

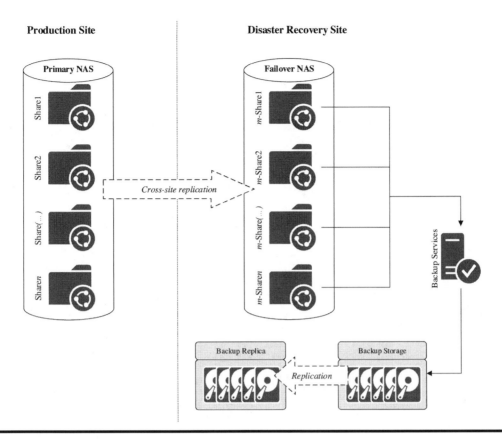

Figure 7.3   Replicating backups to provide redundancy.

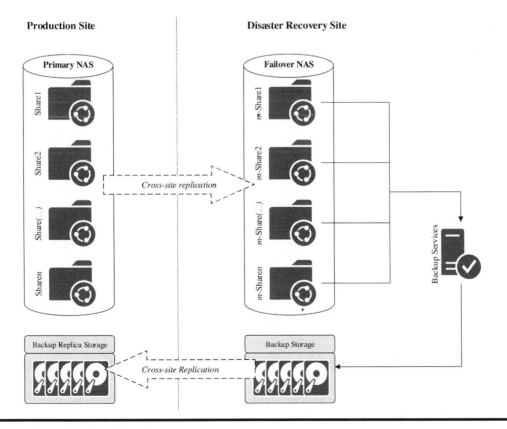

Figure 7.4   Cross-site replication of backups.

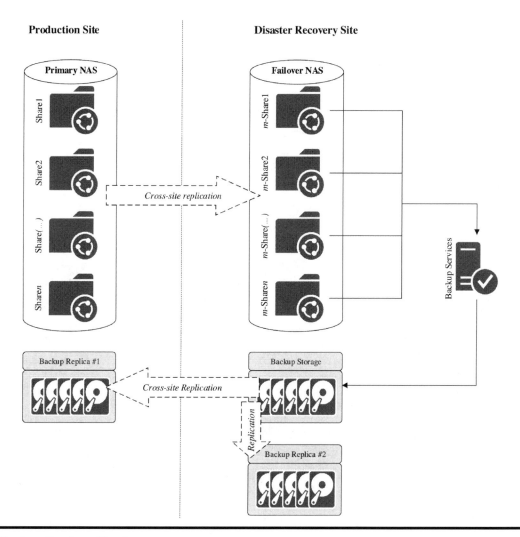

Figure 7.5   Dual replication of backups.

firm however may find that only the configuration shown in Figure 7.5 meets both their internal recovery requirements *and* their externally imposed compliance requirements.

The lesson herein is that business continuity and disaster recovery scenarios must be accounted for in planning SLOs for data protection. Part of the planning for business continuity and data protection is a series of "… but what if?" questions relating to cascading failures or scenarios, with solutions determined for each, until such time as the business decides any further risk mitigation is unwarranted compared to the cost of the protection. Contingencies and recovery scenarios need to also be mindful of not just post-recovery, but day 2, day 3, day 30, etc., after the recovery. After all, the simplest recovery solutions may allow you to restore operational services, but if the business has compliance requirements around historical data, having business continuity and disaster recovery for operational services *isn't enough*. Each contingency determined should include details of the enacted solution *as well as* changes to various targets and timings such as RPOs and RTOs—again with respect to both internally and externally imposed requirements. (This might mean that in the event of a total site loss, the RTOs and RPOs for standard recoveries are doubled, but the RPOs and RTOs for compliance-required recoveries are maintained.)

7.5 Summary

The scope of holistic business continuity planning is considerably beyond that of data protection systems. While data protection systems and policies can play a substantial part in either continuous systems availability or service restoration, they will be a subsidiary aspect to the overall process. Organizations wishing to perform adequate business continuity planning will need to be aware of a variety of factors, including but not limited to:

■ Business functions
■ Criticality of business functions
■ Legal compliance requirements (for availability and restoration)

■ Risk versus cost planning
■ Human resource considerations

Businesses wishing to engage more formally in continuity planning will need to consult legal counsel in addition to considering moral and human imperatives as well as recognized standards such as ISO-22301 ("Societal security—Preparedness and Continuity Management Systems—Requirements").

As such, the scope of business continuity is well beyond the scope of data protection systems and could occupy an entire book (or series of books) in itself, but it is now impossible for a modern company to consider business continuity *without* an adequately planned and implemented data protection system.

7.6 Self-Reflection

In Section 7.2, we introduced the concept of categorizing business functions by their importance to the business, namely:

■ Business/mission critical
■ Critical
■ Essential
■ Non-essential

In Section 7.3 we used the example of an airport to categorize functions into the above breakdowns. Think of a business that you're familiar with, and note down a few functions or services the business performs, and how they might fall into each of the above categories.

Next, consider *risk versus cost*, discussed in Section 7.3. For each of the services you previously noted, consider which approach might be taken for the service in a business continuity situation, i.e.:

1. Continuity
2. Restoration
3. Triage
4. Ignore

Chapter 8

Data Discovery

8.1 Introduction

Imagine for a moment receiving a completely sealed shipping container with no manifest or description of its contents and being told you have to protect it and its contents. With no understanding of the content, coming up with a protection scenario is going to be challenging. Do you assume it's just full of non-perishable goods? Do you assume it's full of fragile filigree? Do you assume it's full of highly explosive and sensitive bombs? Or perhaps you simply assume that it's in fact empty? Now imagine being presented with a dockyard *full* of shipping containers and not knowing *which* shipping container you're meant to protect—you're just told you have to protect *the* shipping container the company cares about. Any reasonable person would quite rightly believe this to be a task that can only ever be achieved in one of two ways based on the dearth of necessary information. The first is the easiest and cheapest, but also the least likely to succeed—pure chance. Just do an "OK" job and hope it yields sufficient results. The second is the "overkill" approach—imagine the content is everything that would be difficult to protect, imagine every possible "failure" scenario, and then do everything necessary to achieve the goal. (A good way to waste money *and* still no guarantee of success.)

You can't protect what you don't know about. This is the core message of *discovery*. If you don't take the time to discover the data and information within your environment, it's entirely possible that a significant amount of what you do for data protection is either a waste of time or a waste of money. Ideally, data discovery fits into data protection as a precursor to data classification, as shown in Figure 8.1.

We've already touched on some aspects of discovery within the introduction to the book. Section 2.2 encouraged answering the following five core questions:

- What is the data?
- Where is the data?
- Who uses the data?
- When is the data used?
- How is the data used?

Some of those topics will be partly revisited in this section for expansion, and we'll introduce some new considerations to the discovery process as well.

This chapter is not meant to be a comprehensive analysis of data discovery—that's a topic deserving of its own book. Instead, the focus will be on providing a sufficient overview to understand the importance of a rigorous data discovery process as a precursor to developing an adequately comprehensive data protection strategy.

8.2 What Will Be Protected?

Consider a public library: most people who think of libraries think of rows upon rows of shelves filled with books, magazines, and periodicals, and these days, electronic media as well. Taking a few more moments of reflection though, we know that isn't the sum total of the library content. There'll be books, media, and other material that has been acquired but not yet cataloged and added to the system. Similarly, there will be content that has been temporarily "retired" due to space considerations and stored in archival areas. There'll also be books, media, and other material that *is* in the system but is currently sitting somewhere within the library being used by a patron. Of course, there'll also be books, media, and other material owned by the library but which is out on loan. This is *still* not *all* of the library—we also have to include the metadata: catalogs of content and loan information. Then we need to also consider the personnel, not to mention all the operational data, such as finances, purchase orders, employee pay records, planning, and so on. A public library is far more than just "books."

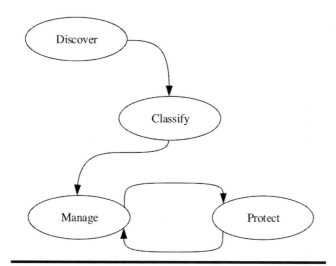

Figure 8.1   Role of data discovery in data protection.

So while the rows and rows of bookshelves in the library form an important part of the content of the library from the end users' perspective, it's not by any means the *whole* content of the library.

This in essence demonstrates a common enough mistake made in IT wherein it's assumed the servers and storage systems in the datacenters of the company are the sum total (or near enough to) of all data that needs to be protected.

Even within the datacenters, this isn't likely to be the case. Talk to just a few people in the storage industry and you'll hear horror stories where even large organizations have had their operations knocked out (or transferred to secondary sites) due to a core switch being rebooted, but essential changes made months before were never committed beyond the active state and so were lost on reboot.

Datacenters never were solely used for servers and storage systems. This should reinforce the need for data protection architects—people whose primary focus is not the management of the data but the protection of it, regardless of where it is or what it may be. These are the people who should be able to walk around a datacenter and point at every appliance and ask a multitude of questions such as:

- What is this?
- Does it have any configuration?
- Does it have any data?
- What business functions rely on it working?
- What IT systems rely on it working?
- What happens if it fails?
- Is it protected?
- How is it protected?
- Who is responsible for the protection?
- Who vetted the protection plans?
- Is the protection tested?
- What is the disaster recovery plan?
- When was the disaster recovery plan last tested?

While the average organization will these days be far more likely to have good answers to all of these questions for any server or storage array in the datacenter, network switches (be they IP or fiber channel), PABX systems, environmental systems, and so on can still yield inconsistent responses—ironically because when we consider dependency maps, these systems are often highly critical for business function continuity.

The ongoing move to *software defined* and *public cloud* muddies the discovery process more; whereas previously data discovery was about physical observation of systems, modern discovery has to take into account increasingly disparate and virtualized systems. As businesses engage more in software as a service (SaaS) products to meet specialized needs, this spread of data will continue to increase discovery challenges. Yet, the challenge does not negate the need to perform the activity.

Remember in all this there are three different aspects to data protection:

- Protecting against loss of data
- Recoverability of data if it is lost
- Protecting against loss of *access* to data

While data loss is a serious problem, loss of access to data can be just as serious from a legislative or financial perspective. In most countries, banks and other financial organizations, for instance, have rigorous compliance obligations relating just to the availability of data, and regardless of those obligations, a company that can't access data required for transactions or customer interaction will be just as helpless as a company that has lost the data entirely. It is for this reason that protection needs to focus on *all* components of systems rather than just data. What would be worse for an organization? A single server failing requiring recovery or an outage caused by a core switch being rebooted with uncommitted configuration changes? While "worse" could be quantified, it's indisputable that *both* represent an outage and both represent data loss (configuration data after all is still data). Recall the FARR model: fault tolerance, availability, redundancy, and recoverability. To implement any combination of these, you first need to *find* the data.

Just as it's foolish to imagine the only things in a datacenter requiring protection are the servers and storage, it's equally foolish to believe the only *data* requiring protection is to be found in datacenters. Even before *cloud* became a ubiquitous IT term, this was not the case: laptops, desktops, mobile phones, and other removable storage either owned by the company or by employees of the company are all potential sources of *unique* data within the organization.

Another challenge for businesses and their IT departments is posed by that double-edged sword, bring your own device (BYOD). BYOD policies have existed in a variety of businesses and forms for some time—for instance, in some countries businesses have offered novated leases on technology as well as vehicles, allowing staff to choose their own laptops outright and pay for it out of their gross/pretax earnings, with the machine belonging to the staff rather than the business. More recently, businesses have taken to encouraging users to provide their own cellular telephones and expensing the business portion of their usage rather than supplying a phone outright as part of the salary package. Similarly, many businesses now allow for users to make use of their own laptops at work, seeing every device purchased out of an employee's home budget as a potential saving.

Such savings are not without their own risks, however. Risks such as data security, application licensing, and network security are relatively well understood, but data protection is another of those risks that must be considered in such scenarios. If the device is *owned* by the user, how does the business enforce adequate protection of data on the device? Security policies might prohibit the use of local storage while connected to the network, but will be less effective when staff are disconnected, and users retaining administrative control over their own devices may very well disable any data protection mechanisms put in place. Alternatively, a blanket rule to include employee-funded devices into corporate data protection policies may leave a business exposed to copyright violations in this modern age of torrenting and pirating movies, TV, and music. Cumulatively, data protection, security, and licensing have made BYOD a Pandora's Box for many organizations, resulting in frequent and radical policy changes.

8.3 Data Gravity

In 2010, Dave McCrory came up with the term, *data gravity*, noting:

> As Data accumulates (builds mass) there is a greater likelihood that additional Services and Applications will be attracted to this data.*

The notion of data gravity is simple—the more data there is in a particular location, the more chance there is of additional services or applications making use of the data. Data protection is a good example of this theory in effect: as the use of deduplication has increased for backup and recovery storage, keeping greater amounts of data online, businesses have increasingly sought to make use of that data,

and investigated secondary use cases. In some situations, the secondary use cases have mirrored older, tape-based backups: simply being used to repopulate research, development, and test databases from production backups. More recently, other functions have become popular: conducting disaster recovery testing from live-mounted backups, eschewing the need for additional primary storage space, using backup as a means of repopulating data warehousing and data lakes, and providing a mechanism for deep search/discovery within previously protected material.

Data gravity acts as a cautionary consideration for *why* data discovery is important, particularly when we think of *shadow IT*. Shadow IT has existed for decades, but has become popularized by public cloud: business groups eschewing traditional IT services and striking out on their own, spinning up services that they directly manage. In the past, it was done as servers (and sometimes, simple desktops) stashed in a corner, or under a desk, that turns out on inspection to be running a task deemed to have importance by the business. While that can still happen, these days it will just as likely be data and services accumulating in the public cloud as it will be under someone's desk.

Particularly when we consider it from the perspective of shadow IT, data gravity poses true risk to the business: what if, for instance, undiscovered data includes personally sensitive information or PCI data? The implications of the discovery (not to mention how and when it is discovered) could have real legal implications to the business.

If we accept that data gravity is real (and it is certainly a concept that resonates with many in IT), then it helps to reinforce the importance of a constant data discovery process—that is, the flow outlined in Figure 8.1 is not just a once-off, but something which is an ongoing, iterative process.

8.4 Shades of Data

Traditionally, *dark* data is considered to be data that hasn't been classified or associated with an analytical tool or use. For example, log files that are generated but never processed might in the simplest way be considered a form of dark data.

A more comprehensive definition of dark data however expands to cover all the *unknown* data within an organization. This is the data generated by individual users on unconnected or uncataloged systems that may be sitting outside of standard storage management and protection systems. In this sense, it's not only data that is not classified or associated with analytical functions, but it's also data the business may fundamentally be unaware of.

Dealing with dark data requires three distinct disciplines within an organization: acceptance, anticipation, and discovery. Acceptance refers to an understanding that dark data *will* appear within the organization. At bare minimum,

---

* Data gravity—in the clouds, Dave McCrory, 7 December 2010, https://blog.mccrory.me/2010/12/07/data-gravity-in-the-clouds/

systems will be periodically deployed where data accumulates without monitoring and *some* users will invariably find ways around security policies that prohibit localized storage. Accepting that dark data can appear or accumulate within the organization allows the business and IT processes to *discuss* the issue with staff and develop policies for its discovery. Anticipation implies responsibility—someone (or, more correctly, some *role*) must have primary responsibility for thinking about where dark data might appear within an organization, both architecturally and operationally. The role most suited for this is the DPA, initially discussed in Chapter 5.

Following acceptance and anticipation, a business can properly discover dark data, a process that will include both manual and automated activities. The automated activities will come from the appliances and software tasked with searching, indexing, or analyzing content, and the manual processes will be where dark data is dealt with architecturally and operationally. Architecturally in examining new or revised systems, applications or business functions to determine all the areas where data might be created, and operationally in reviewing those systems, applications or business functions already *deployed* to determine what's being missed.

Once dark data has been discovered, it doesn't automatically transition to being *data*. At this point, you might consider it to be *gray* data. This is identified data outside of either storage, protection, or both management policies and requires decisions to be made on its type, function, and usefulness to the organization. In an ideal scenario, the vast amount of classification done here should be automated, but there will on occasion be a requirement for human intervention to determine the nature of the data. Such classification will be the same as discussed in Chapter 2, namely:

■ What is the data?
■ Where is the data?
■ Who uses the data?
■ When is the data used?
■ How is the data used?

Part of the discovery process may very well alter the answers to some or all of those questions. Discovered data that has real business use might be moved to centralized, protected storage and its usage profile substantially increased. Regardless of where it is moved to, we should aim to ensure all discovered data is placed under *management*—protection, lifecycle, and functional.

8.5 Indexing

For the most part, indexing is more a function of information lifecycle management (ILM) rather than information lifecycle protection (ILP). However, as a function of the discovery process, data indexing within an organization does have the potential to substantially increase the accuracy of data protection activities. Indeed, indexing can provide several data protection benefits including:

■ *Locating data that needs to be protected*: During the initial discovery phase, indexing can help to show where data exists within the business, thereby reducing the amount of dark or gray data within the company.
■ *Locating data that has been protected*: As unstructured data in particular grows within an organization, the chances of users *losing* data will also grow, but there are two types of *losing*. The conventional is accidental data deletion or corruption, but equally as vexing is users simply forgetting *where* they've saved data to. A comprehensive and accessible indexing system can reduce the data recovery requirements for an organization by allowing users to readily locate documents they've saved but subsequently lost sight of.
■ *Tracking data that gets moved*: Not all data archival is performed via hierarchical storage management (HSM) techniques. Some companies, either as a result of budget, perceived cost, or even business function, prefer to literally *move* data during the archive process rather than leaving stubs behind for seamless access. Industrial or graphic design agencies might move entire projects off primary storage a certain length of time after work has been completed, recalling media if and only if a repeat run of the project is required. Educational organizations and medical companies equally may be required from a compliance perspective to maintain their data about students and patients, respectively, but see no need to keep it stubbed from primary to archive storage once a particular period of time has passed. Indexing becomes critical in this situation to allow accurate location of data once it's been moved.

Like archive, many businesses resist data indexing technologies out of a perceived up-front cost, failing to understand the cumulative impact of reducing the accessibility and discoverability of their data. If data is not *known* about within an organization, it can't in any way be considered to be adequately protected (or for that matter, managed). Indexing is therefore not an overhead cost, but an essential part of the prerequisite discovery process for building a comprehensive data protection solution.

More often than not, choosing to avoid indexing (or the discovery of dark data) because there's "too much" exercise in kicking the can down the road. If it's "too much" effort now when the business has, say, 500 TB of data, it's not going to be any easier when the business grows to 510 TB,

550 TB, 600 TB, and so on. Just as data sizes rarely shrink over time, delaying management activities about data doesn't make future activities any easier.

8.6 Summary

Data discovery is by itself a large and complex topic that exists almost entirely within the realm of information lifecycle management. Its connection to information lifecycle protection is simple yet profound: any data protection solution developed without discovery will be blinkered and focused solely on what individual *people* within the organization *think* about data location and criticality. This is likely to be accurate only in very small or very focused businesses, and that accuracy will decrease rapidly as the business grows or its data becomes more distributed. Alternatively, a business will spend increasingly larger sums of money on data protection "hoping" they have an effective solution but really have no way of proving it. This almost inevitably leads to the business resenting data protection costs, when the real problem is a root data management one.

Some would argue that data discovery is unimportant for data protection in well-architected environments, but this assumes systems will grow in an ordered and expected way at all times. Such assumptions are almost always proven wrong; except in the most static of businesses, data growth and capture will regularly come from unexpected sources. New projects, mergers and acquisitions, changes in product focus, and a myriad of other activities will disrupt orderly plans for data growth. Businesses, for instance, will often seek to procure data protection solutions based on 3 or 5 years of linear growth patterns ("10% annual growth," "20% annual growth"), yet in practice it's rare for any predicted growth pattern beyond 3 years to have high accuracy. In fact, as businesses increasingly move workloads in and out of public cloud, the notion of a predictable linear annual growth rate seems increasingly out of reach.

8.7 Self-Reflection

While it is reasonably straightforward to contemplate data residing on datacenter servers, storage arrays, and user laptop/desktops, as discussed in this chapter there can be a plethora of appliances used in a business that don't run traditionally accessible operating systems, which alters how we can perform data protection.

Pick an IP or fiber-channel switch vendor where you can access their technical documentation, and search for ways you might ensure that device configuration can be protected. Consider options such as:

- Command line interfaces
- APIs (e.g., REST APIs)
- Whether they have formal "backup" and "recovery" options in their documentation

Assuming you can determine a way to automate the backup of the switch configuration, how might you *automate* it, so that it is performed regularly?

Chapter 9

Security, Privacy, Ethical, and Legal Considerations

9.1 Introduction

In Chapter 4, the elements of a data functional data protection system were outlined as being:

- People
- Technology
- Training
- Testing
- Service level agreements
- Processes and documentation

A data protection system however does not sit in isolation; it interacts with the systems around it, it provides a service for people, and it has the capability of affecting other systems.

As we noted in Chapter 1, *data protection* is an umbrella term in information technology that encompasses three discrete disciplines being:

- Data storage protection (the focus of this book)
- Data security
- Data privacy

Since both data security and data privacy can extend to all aspects of data handling within business and IT, it falls to reason that data protection as a storage function also must consider security and privacy; overlooking those considerations in fact can cause significant challenges to a business.

If you're to believe any western TV show or movie featuring doctors and surgeons, you'd think that every medical practitioner in the world swears by the *Hippocratic* oath, which starts with:

> I swear by Apollo the physician, and Asclepius, and Hygieia and Panacea and all the gods and goddesses as my witnesses, that, according to my ability and judgement, I will keep this Oath and this contract.*

Yet, modern medical practitioners rarely swear an oath to Apollo, Asclepius, Hygieia, and Panacea any more. While aspects of the Hippocratic oath may be appropriated into modern guidelines for ethical conduct of medical practitioners, the literal text is not used so much anymore.

It's also worthwhile keeping in mind that one of the key guiding tenets *assumed* to be in the Hippocratic oath is the phrase *First, [to] do no harm*. Yet this is actually not part of the oath at all. (The *closest* the oath comes to that phrase is to have one swear "to abstain from doing harm.") Instead "first, to do no harm," or the Latin form, *primum non nocere*, seems to have been introduced into medical and research parlance much later than Hippocrates.

In Australia, national health practitioner boards can develop/approve codes of conduct and guidelines, and when an individual applies for registration, they must sign

---

* "Greek Medicine," on the USA National Library of Medicine Website, www.nlm.nih.gov/hmd/greek/greek_oath.html

a declaration that they undertake to comply with all relevant legislation, in addition to the registration standards, guidelines, and codes of the specific board. It is therefore up to an individual health practitioner board how their specific code of conduct and operational guidelines are written, despite what television programs would have us believe.

While health is perhaps the most prominent industry where we expect someone to take an oath relating to acceptable standards of behavior, it is not alone. However, for many other industries, codes of conduct are voluntary. They might be required to be a member of a particular organization, but membership of the organization is not required to be part of the overall profession. For example, the League of Professional System Administrators (LOPSA) publishes a Code of Ethics* covering a variety of topics including professionalism, privacy, communication, personal integrity. and system integrity. However, despite LOPSA referring to itself as a worldwide organization, membership of LOPSA and sworn adherence to its code of conduct is not a mandatory requirement for all people seeking employment as IT system administrators.

9.2 Security and Privacy

It was noted in the introduction that the term *data protection* is, in itself, an umbrella term that can refer to data storage protection (i.e., the focus of this book), yet elsewhere in the IT industry, can refer to data security activities, and also data privacy activities.

As alluded to in Chapter 6 (Monitoring and Reporting), there are understandably data security and privacy considerations that need to be applied when working with data protection as a storage function.

Although data protection systems are designed to reduce the risk exposure of a business, for security and privacy teams, if misused, they can represent a significant threat vector to the business.

While unauthorized data recovery is perhaps the most obvious concern from both a security and privacy perspective, a user or administrator with sufficient knowledge and access privilege can use data protection systems for a variety of malicious reasons, including:

- Data destruction
- Denial of service
- Data exfiltration
- Sabotage
- Privacy breaches

Accidental or unintended misuse by an authorized administrator can cause significant challenges as well. A still-sleepy storage administrator responding to an on-call event might intend to delete an errant snapshot causing problems, and instead delete the wrong one. Or worse: encrypting and/or data destructive malware that's accidentally executed by someone with sufficient privileges in response to a phishing attack may be designed, among other activities, to also seek out backups for specific backup products and erase them.

A backup system, deliberately misused (either by an administrator or a malware attack) could cause significant challenges for a business. Consider the potential, for instance, of "redirected recoveries," where a recovery is pushed out from say, the backup server, to specific clients within the organization. Recovering aged authentication credentials back out to login services for instance might result in a large number of users finding themselves locked out of their accounts, and help desks overwhelmed with password reset requests (assuming they are also not affected). Local hosts' files for name resolution are frequently used to resolve connectivity where formal DNS entries can't be created— backing up a corrupt hosts file, then recovering it to random clients may result in chaos across multiple types of operating systems. Databases could be deliberately overwritten with the oldest online copy available, potentially causing downtime as they are recovered back to a more recent copy, and so on. None of the situations described here are guaranteed to cause *permanent* destruction, but they will inconvenience a business and cause downtime.

The portmanteau term *hactivism* (*hacking* and *activism*) represents a serious security concern for some organizations: the idea that someone working within the company might deliberately engage in destructive activities as a result of some activist ideal—e.g., an anti-coal activist might gain employment with an energy company with the deliberate goal of causing problems at some future date. These insider-attacks have been known to strike at backup services first: deleting all online backups and their catalogs prior to then moving on to attack primary servers, knowing that their data will not be recoverable (or at least, not readily recoverable).

Data exfiltration is a serious concern for any business— the idea of intellectual property or customer data being transferred, unauthorized, outside of the company where it might dull a competitive edge, cause significant embarrassment to the business, result in litigation, or a variety of other issues. As mentioned previously, the notion that a standard help desk operator, with access permissions into the email backup environment in order to facilitate end user data recovery, might recover the CEO's mailbox to a portable storage device and provide it to someone outside the company can be a real concern for businesses, and represents just the tip of

---

* https://lopsa.org/CodeOfEthics

the iceberg for the classic problem of how IT administrators and operators can be trusted.

A business in the import market had a significant number of sales people who all maintained their contacts and pre-deal information locally, on their desktops and laptops. While they were encouraged to maintain details centrally, it only became essential at the time of an order being placed to ensure sufficient data was logged into key ordering and customer databases. Given the importance of the data, the business also mandated that all business-related data be stored in the Documents folder of a user's login account, and backup agents were used to ensure that data was protected. One sales person, intent on leaving and taking his relationships to a competitor, deliberately quit the backup agent as it launched at login each day for three months, the retention time for desktop/laptop backups, before resigning, thus preventing the business from finalising any in-progress deals he was working on before leaving.

While privacy breaches often occur from poor security controls on the primary copy of the data in the first place, they have also been known to happen in relation to data protection, too. Businesses have been embarrassed to find themselves subject to a privacy breach not because of a security failure within their primary systems, but because someone placed a backup file in an alternate location that was improperly secured and discovered later—by the wrong person.

Data protection logically touches most, if not all, of the data within a business (or at least one copy of all the data within a business); as such, it represents a huge wealth of information about the business and warrants the same level of security and privacy considerations as the most mission critical systems within the business do.

9.2.1 Logging

As noted in the *Monitoring* section of Chapter 6, logging of events, and monitoring of those logs, is crucial not only in providing adequate security and adherence to privacy protocols into a data protection environment, but also in providing *proof* of that.

Where possible to satisfy security and privacy concerns, logging within data protection products should be real-time, or it should be possible to work around situations where logging is not real-time. This allows the detection of issues that may compromise the business as soon as possible

to the event taking place, and preferably *while* the event is taking place.

An increasing number of jurisdictions have enacted mandatory breach notification legislation targeting both external and internal sources of a breach. (We will cover this further in the Legal Considerations section, later.) This increases the risk profile posed by a data protection system if adequate logging is either not available, or available, but not monitored.

9.2.2 Encryption

With data protection, we usually consider two different areas of encryption:

- In-flight encryption
- At-rest encryption

In-flight encryption refers to the process of ensuring data sent from the source to the target in a data protection operation is appropriately secured from eavesdropping. Logically for a backup, this would resemble the process shown in Figure 9.1: as data is read during a backup operation, it is encrypted in-memory on the host being backed up, then transmitted to the data protection storage (either directly, or indirectly, which will be discussed further in the chapters on backup, architecture, and deduplication). In-flight encryption does not only apply to backup, of course: it can in theory be used in any situation where data must traverse a network (e.g., it might be used for transmission of journal information for continuous data protection, or writes for standard replication).

At-rest encryption on the other hand is focused on ensuring the data written to protection storage is encrypted, which gives protection against unauthorized reading of data in the event that the storage is stolen. In its most basic form, at-rest encryption for backup data will follow a process such as shown in Figure 9.2.

For higher levels of security, a data protection environment might combine in-flight *and* at-rest encryption. In situations where the same (and compatible) encryption algorithm/process is used at both ends, this can resemble the flow shown in Figure 9.3. If the same or a compatible algorithm is not used to mesh in-flight and at-rest encryption, the process will instead be one where data is read, encrypted, transmitted, decrypted, re-encrypted then written, which effectively doubles the handling of data within the environment, and should be avoided wherever possible. In fact, usually such a process will necessitate the insertion of a proxy server to receive the encrypted data, decrypt it, re-encrypt it, then transmit it to the data protection storage, which adds to the architectural overhead of a data protection solution. (Or it may occur in situations where the storage medium changes, such as storing encrypted data on tape.)

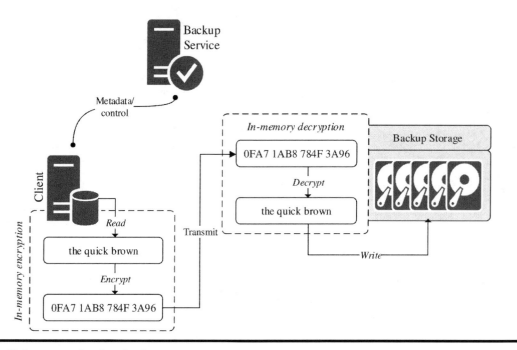

Figure 9.1   In-flight encryption in a backup process.

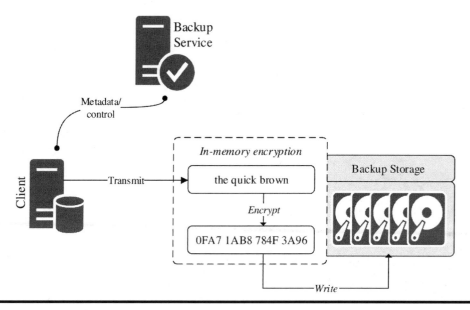

Figure 9.2   At-rest encryption of backup data.

In some cases, in-flight or at-rest encryption might be handled by specialized TCP/IP or fiber-channel switches. This has an advantage of "hiding" the encryption process from the data protection service, but with advances in CPU and memory capability, dedicated CPU instruction sets to assist with encryption, and off-loading cards (network, fiber-channel, or even encryption specifically), higher speed encryption performance can generally be achieved in a data protection environment by distributing the encryption functionality to each host being protected, rather than trying to centralize it within switches.

9.2.3 Access Controls

9.2.3.1 Multi-tenancy

Multi-tenancy refers to the process of running a centralized service which services multiple, disparate customers (these might be internal, external, or a mix of both) in such a way that the service owner has complete administrative control, each *tenant* has control over the sections they are using, and each tenancy is securely isolated from one another, preventing data leakage or theft. Conceptually, this is shown in Figure 9.4.

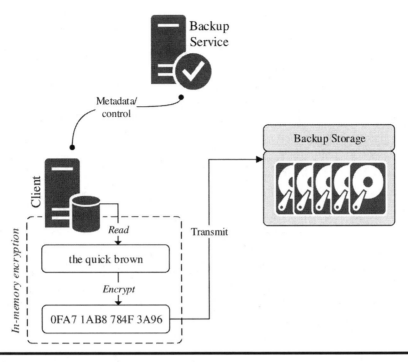

Figure 9.3 In-flight and at-rest encryption using a compatible algorithm.

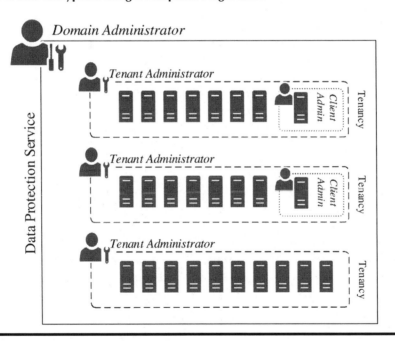

Figure 9.4 Conceptual view of a multi-tenanted data protection service.

Multi-tenancy usually results in at least three classes of users, although this can vary, service to service. Examples of the user categories are:

■ *Domain administrator*: Someone with "super-user" privilege over the entire environment. They are an administrator of the core service. Depending on the security controls within the service, they may be able to see or control aspects of a tenancy. They will also be able to create and destroy tenancies, and appoint tenant administrators.

■ *Tenant administrator*: Someone with near to super-user privilege over a tenancy. This would enable them to create new data protection policies, add or remove systems from data protection policies, create the next class of user (if needed), and so on, but they may not have the privilege to, say, completely remove the tenancy from the data protection system.

- Either/or:
    - *Client administrator*: Someone who had administrative controls over a subset of the tenancy—e.g., a single host, or a collection of hosts.
    - *Tenant operator*: Someone who has privilege to perform data protection operations (e.g., backup/recovery) within the tenancy, but cannot affect the configuration of the tenancy.

Depending on the service, there may be different aspects to multi-tenancy. For instance, back-end data protection storage might fully support multi-tenancy, but data protection products built around legacy architectures might need one instance of a product stood up per tenant, with only the back-end storage shared.

While the notion of multi-tenancy has existed for some time (in reality, operating systems such as UNIX and Windows server are built around some level of multi-tenancy) it has often been an afterthought in data protection, or only added well into a product lifespan. Newer data protection products, particularly those built around cloud models are more likely to be built from the ground up as a multi-tenanted system, rather than having multi-tenancy enabled after the fact.

Like virtualization, multi-tenancy is based on the desire to do more with less. Consider for instance, an IT provider offering backup services to its customers. Without multi-tenancy, the IT provider might need to provision (either virtually, physically, or some combination of the two) dedicated backup server(s) and backup storage for *each* subscriber to its service. However, if the products intended for use are multi-tenancy enabled, the service provider could instead focus on simply providing enough spare capacity in a system to support onboarding additional customers.

Multi-tenancy is useful even in single-business environments. Two groups within the company might compete for the same customers, or the business might operate in an environment where *ethical* or *isolation* walls are required, which could extend down to the data protection services. Alternately, the business may simply wish to segregate production and non-production services for a variety of security reasons.

Sometimes however, multi-tenancy is not enough. Military grade systems may require full air-gapped separation of systems with disparate levels of information (e.g., secret vs top-secret systems), but they are far from the only systems where physical separation may be required. Many businesses that operate key utilities or services or produce materials via hazardous operations may require similar separation for public and worker safety. Fuel plants (gasoline/petrol) and power generation will typically require the control systems for those activities to run on physically isolated networks compared to, say, the corporate database

and file-shares, and this can necessitate similar separation of data protection resources to prevent a security breach.* Similarly, companies that, say, melt down iron ore to create steel may keep the control and data protection systems for their blast furnaces completely isolated from other systems within the environment.

9.2.3.2 General User Controls

Beyond multi-tenancy situations, there is a more general realm of user access controls that we typically think of with data protection processes. Usually you would expect to see separation of duties at least between:

- *Administrators*: —People who can configure the system
- *Operators*: —People who can run the system without necessarily changing the configuration
- *Users*: —People who can retrieve content from a data protection copy

Two key aspects of general user controls sought after in enterprise data protection products are:

- Access limiting
- Identity/authorization integration

The first refers to controlling what an individual user, or class of users can do within the system. For instance, it might be desirable to define a class of users called "Oracle DBAs" within the data protection product: these can trigger new data protection operations (e.g., backups, or snapshots), manage data protection sets (e.g., expire them), and conduct recoveries from data protection copies, *but only* for Oracle backups on hosts tagged within the data protection environment as Oracle systems.

The second refers to ensuring that each data protection environment is not an island in terms of access: rather than having to define each class of user, and each user within the data protection system, it's highly desirable to integrate the data protection product with whatever enterprise identity/authorization system in use within the business. Thus, anyone who belongs in the "Backup Administrators" active directory group could be granted automatic access to a backup and recovery service, preferably with single sign-on capability, rather than having to remember a mix of different passwords, one per system.

---

* For example, if a consolidated data protection product is used for both the corporate systems and say, fuel refinery systems, it increases risk, as a malicious administrator operating out of the corporate environment may have sufficient privilege to break systems in the refinery via a destructive recovery.

9.2.3.3 Security Officers versus Service Administrator

In some cases, it may be necessary to differentiate between the role of general administrator for a data protection product, and security administrator, usually referred to as a security *officer*.

You might notionally think of this as enabling *two-factor approval* for certain operations within an environment. A regular administrator for a data protection product may be allowed to make any standard configuration change and operate the product, but may require additional approval from a "security administrator" designated user to do any of the following:

- Create or delete users (or, alter mappings between product users and enterprise authenticated users)
- Deactivate a security officer role
- Change logging details
- Prematurely age or delete protection copies
- Alter the number of protection copies that are made

(The above list is by no means comprehensive, and the details will change depending on the type of product.)

When the role is enabled, a security officer may become responsible for enabling access to the product for the administrators and operators, also.

Conversely, while the security officer can authorize "security" related changes that the service administrator has requested, they cannot adjust general configuration within the product, and there may still be limits to what they can do—e.g., if data protection storage is being used in *compliance* mode (i.e., compliant to fiduciary or judicial legislation to prevent premature erasure), even the security officer may be unable to authorize, say, the deletion of copies that have been generated with a particular assigned lifespan.

9.2.3.4 Do You Trust Trusted Access?

It's a question that has gnawed at many a business: privileged IT administrators often have complete access control over systems that hold data their job description does not entitle them to access. A storage administrator has ultimate control over a NAS platform that has a share only the board of directors is meant to see. A Unix system administrator can access the underlying filesystem for a Wiki that is otherwise locked down so only human resources people can log into it. An email administrator theoretically has the capability of peering into the CEO's mailbox.

Do you trust that people who have trusted access to the system will not abuse that trust? The same challenge applies to data protection systems as to primary production systems within an environment: is the backup administrator, or a backup operator, trusted to not use the data protection environment to access data they would not otherwise have access to? This goes slightly beyond the conventional trust problem in a primary system—either someone is, or is not a "super-user" administrator of a system. However, a data protection administrator will often be responsible for protecting data on systems he or she otherwise *does not* have access to at all, let alone have administrative access to.

Some data protection products do allow for this differentiation, effectively allowing the business to designate someone as an administrator who cannot recover data. Even if this functionality is not available, real-time logging of data recovery operations can alleviate most concerns: if a recovery can be detected as it is happening, and cross referenced against appropriate ticketing systems for instance, intervention can happen if there is no obvious sign that the recovery has been suitably authorized.

9.2.4 Standard Security Controls

9.2.4.1 Hardening Protocols

Within security environments, *hardening* refers to following best practices to reduce the potential surface area of an attack. This might include options such as:

- Deactivating insecure protocols (e.g., allowing https, but not http)
- Forcing adequate password controls:
  - Minimum time between password changes
  - Maximum time between password changes
  - Number of passwords "remembered" to prevent re-use too soon
  - Ensuring suitably complex passwords (length and number of non-alphanumeric characters)
  - Whether fragments of passwords can be reused (e.g., stopping the classic "Opensesame1," "Opensesame2," "Opensesame3," style password iterations)
- Enabling, where possible, two-factor authentication for user access
- Requiring identification by certificate
- Requiring identification by authenticated certificate
- Inactivity timeouts on login

The above represents just a brief glimpse of some of the configuration aspects that may come into play when security teams discuss *hardening*. Ideally, data protection products should come with documentation that details hardening and other best practice security approaches for using the product.

9.2.4.2 Secure Physical Access

In addition to maintaining appropriate electronic security protocols, physical security also comes into play with data protection. Like other mission critical systems within the business, data protection servers should have appropriate physical access controls; if someone must have a specially authorized key pass in order to enter a computer room because of the sensitive data owned by the company, then the backup services should have the same physical security controls.

In some instances, physical security for data protection services should operate at a heightened level compared to regular production services within the business. This might involve data protection services running within a secure cage within a secure computer room, rather than just any accessible rack. In addition to the risk of data theft should backup services or storage be physically stolen from the business, the risk of a lengthy unplanned outage caused by the data protection service no longer being available can have cascade impacts on the integrity of the overall environment.

9.2.4.3 Physical Data transport

In some data protection environments, there exists the potential for physical transport of records or protection copies. Backup tapes are a classic example of this—removable media designed to be carried from location to location. Tape storage companies usually use high degrees of caution while moving media from one place to another, but accidents do happen, and not all data protection media is moved by dedicated resources.

> The Commonwealth Bank has admitted a supplier lost two magnetic tapes in 2016 containing backup data on almost 20 million customers.
>
> …
>
> The tapes were meant to be destroyed; however, the bank admitted it had been "unable to confirm the scheduled destruction" and ordered a forensic investigation[*]

Sometimes businesses will also undertake "seeding" operations. A backup service for instance may be intended for operation in a remote environment with poor bandwidth links back to the primary datacenter that it will replicate to.

---

[*] CBA lost backup tapes with 20m customers' details, Ry Crozier, 3 May 2018, *ITNews Australia*

Rather than conducting the first replication over the WAN, a business might determine that it will be faster to:

- Ship the backup storage to the remote site
- Take the first backup
- Ship the backup storage to the replication target datacenter for high speed LAN-based replication
- Ship the backup storage back to the remote site
- Commence daily backups with incremental replication

Wherever possible, when data is being physically shipped from one location to another, adequate precautions should be taken (e.g., via encryption, strong passwords) to ensure that should the data go missing in transit, it cannot be accessed. In some cases, this may require suitably authorized officers traveling with the components housing the data, never letting those components out of their sight.

9.2.5 Secure Erasure

In the late 1990s, a journalist working for a small, local newspaper was dismissed. In a pique of rage at his sacking, he exclaimed that his in-progress work would be finished by no-one else and with a flourish dragged his documents to his computer's desktop trashcan before leaving the building. After he left, the IT staff opened the trashcan, retrieved the stories, and someone else finished them.

Secure erasure is more than simply dragging documents to the trash on a modern computer; indeed, it is more than dragging documents to the trash and then *emptying* the trash.

Secure erasure refers to deletion of data in such a way that it cannot be recovered. Consider for instance how most memory cards for cameras and smart phones either come with software, or include details of how to download trial software, that can be used to *recover deleted or corrupted data*. The US Department of Defense, for instance, requires in its basic form three data overwrites: one pass of the storage writing all 1s, one pass writing all 0s, and one pass writing a random bit. There's also a seven pass write: one pass writing all 1s, one pass writing all 0s, two random bit passes in a row, then another 0 pass, another 1 pass, and finally another random bit pass. Both overwrite options require a verification pass to confirm everything on a drive has been overwritten.

(While we usually think of secure erasure as a process that takes place at the end of the usable lifespan of some storage element, it's worth also noting that secure erasure can apply to the process of securely deleting content on storage and systems that will continue to be used: e.g., performing multiple overwrites so that if the system is stolen, deleted data cannot be retrieved.)

Returning to the data destruction aspect, secure erasure is preferred in many situations over degaussing simply because by nature, degaussing a hard drive leaves the drive unusable in future; secure erasure means the drive can be re-used by someone else without risk of data recovery.

As one can imagine, secure erasure takes time. So much so that some organizations (private, public, or government) can instead require storage drives to be *shredded*—literally passed through an industrial shredder capable of tearing a hard drive into scrap in the same way that a paper shredder might reduce documents to confetti. (Some businesses in fact will first pass hard drives through a degausser before shredding them.)

The risk of either personally or commercially sensitive data being accessed after systems have been disposed of has been known for some time.

In 2009, *The Guardian* noted:

> The only surefire way to stop criminals stealing data from secondhand computers is to destroy the hard drive, a study by Which? Computing magazine has warned.
>
> Even though people think they have wiped data from machines before they sell them on auction sites or put them onto rubbish tips, the files remain on the hard drives—and can contain vital information such as bank details and other personal data sufficient for identity theft. They can be recovered using specialist software that is widely available.*

In 2016, SC Media UK noted:

> Hard drives are not getting wiped of data at major firms, according to new research. Moreover, those hard drives contain corporate information as well as data that could identify people.
>
> Blancco Technology Group bought a random sample of 200 hard drives on eBay and Craigslist. Investigating further, researchers found around 67 per cent of the used drives contained personally identifiable information and 11 per cent held sensitive corporate data, including company emails, CRM records, and spreadsheets containing sales projections and product inventories.†

A challenge often posed for secure erasure is the time it takes to perform that erasure. ZDNet noted in 2017 that during an updated test of discarded/sold hard drives and SSDs by Kroll Ontrack:

> The company bought 64 drives on eBay: 27 SSDs and 37 HDDs. It found that "over half of the HDD drives contained traces of data while only a third of the SSD drives did."
>
> "Though SSD drives were by no means immune to identity risk, they tended to facilitate more successful data wipes," said Kroll Ontrack. The "SSDs have several functions that affect the state of the stored data, such as FTL (Flash Translation Layer function), which controls the mapping of files, as well as wear levelling, Trim, Garbage Collection and always-on encryption, all of which influence the recoverability of deleted or discarded data."‡

For the most part, businesses should apply the same considerations for secure erasure against data protection storage as they do to primary systems storage. It might be noted that individual drives within data protection storage which has utilized RAID, deduplication, and at-rest encryption might represent a low threat profile; deduplication (usually accompanied by compression) eliminates much of the repetitive information that makes data logically useful, encryption masquerades the data, and RAID sees data striped across multiple drives. However, even with these factors in mind, many businesses will still require secure erasure to meet internal or external requirements, and this should be understood and stated as a requirement during any purchase process for data protection storage.

Coming back briefly to the notion of drive *shredding*, businesses that wish to retain failed drives while still performing warranty operations on them should ensure they have discussed this in advance of any purchase with their vendors, so that the appropriate warranty processes are in place. The customer retaining failed components for shredding is not part of *standard* warranty agreements, and if not incorporated into the support and maintenance agreement up-front may result in substantial excess fees at the time of an event.

9.2.6 Privacy Considerations

Many privacy considerations within data protection come either as extensions of security considerations, or (more

---

* Before you sell your computer, smash the hard drive, says Which? Charles Arthur, 8 January 2009, *Guardian*, www.theguardian.com/ technology/2009/jan/08/hard-drive-security-which
† Two-thirds of used hard drives hold personally identifiable data, Rene Millman, 29 June 2016, *SC Magazine UK*, www.scmagazineu k.com/two-thirds-used-hard-drives-hold-personally-identifiable-da ta/article/1478199

‡ You can still buy hard drives full of other people's data, but SSDs are less risky, Jack Schofield, 30 November 2017, *ZDNet*, www.zdnet. com/article/you-can-still-buy-hard-drives-full-of-other-peoples-d ata-but-ssds-are-less-risky/

recently) as a result of changes to legislation, such as GDPR, which we will discuss later in the chapter.

There is certainly scope for mischievous or malicious misuse of data protection systems in terms of privacy; consider, for instance, an issue that periodically raises its head: law enforcement officers who conduct illegal searches of official police databases on behalf of friends (or criminal gangs) to find someone who does not wish to be found. A data protection officer within a business, having heard some gossip about another employee, could recover his or her email and search through it to discover what might be happening in that person's life, or substantiate the gossip that has been heard.

When not directly related to actual privacy legislation, privacy related concerns in data protection will usually be addressed by:

- *Secure erasure*: By ensuring any failed components are securely wiped, or physically destroyed, personal and sensitive information stored by the environment should not fall into the wrong hands even after those components have been thrown out.
- *Security of data protection*: If data protection environments are not suitably secured, people may be able to gain access to data they are not authorized to access, which could jeopardize personal security.
- *Multi-tenancy*: A subset of general data protection security, consider a situation where a backup service provider is engaged by multiple medical facilities. If multi-tenancy is not configured correctly, allowing someone to recover data from another business's backups by guessing a host name (for example), might result in a serious privacy violation.
- *Security of protection copies*: Protection copies lost in transit can potentially result in significant privacy breaches—consider, for instance, the earlier example of two backup tapes being lost when sent for destruction: had somehow those tapes been found and accessed by someone with knowledge (and not encrypted), they could have resulted in a privacy breach for a significant percentage of the Australian adult population. Such situations can occur electronically as well: there have been instances where subscribers to cloud services have generated a backup copy of marketing databases, failed to follow security practices, and left them publicly accessible.

The other challenge of data privacy that needs to be considered in data storage protection is the concept of *data re-use*. Data protection systems can represent a considerable investment, and it is increasingly common to see businesses looking for ways to generate secondary use cases for data held in data protection systems. The primary use case of course will always be service or data restoration, but in an ideal situation the business hopes to only rarely need to use data protection

services in that way (in the same way that people purchase insurance policies, but *hope not to use them*).

In short, this challenge can be summarized as: just because you *can* do something, doesn't mean you *should*. For instance, consider the famous Target case where data analysis allowed the store to predict if a shopper was pregnant, then mail coupons and discounts for other products. It's that *extra service* coming from mining disparate data which increases revenue streams—and in the Target case, revealed a teenage girl's pregnancy to her family.[*] While that occurred via deep analysis of primary data, it is by no means inconceivable that a process designed to mine and compare historical copies of databases held in online backups against current data could draw correlations that impact personal privacy.

9.3 Ethical Considerations

The next section will deal with legal considerations relating to data protection, but in this scenario, we will focus on the ethical.

> Morality differs from legality. Legally it is permissible to protect your property from someone desperate for shelter—to own second homes usually left empty, while others are homeless—yet we may doubt the morality. Something that is legal is not thereby morally acceptable. Further, that which is illegal may yet be the right thing to do; for example, opposing immoral laws that oppress racial minorities or an impoverished majority. The legal and the moral can overlap: both morality and law usually maintain that killing innocents is wrong.[†]

There is, to some, a subtle yet important difference between *ethics* and *morals*, though Cave uses the terms interchangeably for much of the introductory section of his book. In particular, those who make the distinction usually see ethics as a formal framework, or views held by a society, whereas morality is more confined to the behavior of an individual. For the purposes of our discussion, we will consider the terms synonymous.

So, the question we need to consider is: if you work in data protection, are you ethically obliged to do your utmost to protect data? We will evaluate three potential reasons that can be given for an ethical approach to performing data

---

[*] How Companies Learn Your Secrets, Charles Duhigg, 16 February 2012, *New York Times*, www.nytimes.com/2012/02/19/magazine/shopping-habits.html

[†] *Ethics*, Peter Cave, One World Publications, 978-1-7807-457-63 (2015).

protection. These are by no means the only conceivable ethical approaches that one might take to data protection, but serve as a starting point to evaluate the topic.

Note in the following that the word *ought* will be used: this reflects the approach taken in philosophy whereby *should* is treated as a subjective opinion ("I think you should buy that new car you've been talking about") whereas *ought* is treated as an objective opinion ("I think you ought to park your car only where it is legal to do so").

9.3.1 Performance of Duties

When you apply for or start a new job, there is usually a *duties statement* as part of the role description.

For example, following is a list of duties associated with a job ad placed for "Backup and Recovery Engineer" in Melbourne, February 2019* (with slight modifications):

Work with <Product Name>.

Performs leadership role in the design and administration of backup policies.

Support IT teams developing and maintaining Disaster Recovery Plans, Business Continuity Plans and other related data protection plans.

Provide technical leadership in the Backup and Recovery and Data Protection areas, investigate new technologies and develop the cost-benefit analysis for new solutions.

Data Protection technology leadership for cloud solutions including SaaS, PaaS, and IaaS

Identify issues, devise solutions and present to governance teams for resolution.

Manage prioritization and demand management of existing capabilities.

Monitors daily batch job processing for success and takes necessary actions to resolve failures.

Responsible for software product support and for interfacing with vendors, application and systems programming in troubleshooting, applying fixing and installing new releases.

Perform complex second level troubleshooting of operations incidents with Job Scheduling, Enterprise Backup, Change Management and batch job processing.

Develop detailed solutions through analysis of problems and utilizes supplied software solution.

When necessary leads projects to resolve operational issues.

---

* Seek job ads are only available for 30 days after applications have closed, hence a link cannot be provided.

One of the simplest arguments that might be made toward an ethical obligation relating to data protection is whether you are employed in a role where data protection is a job function. In such instances, it might be argued that:

> You ought to ensure data is adequately protected because that is some (or all) of the reason for which you are employed.

While an employer cannot write into the responsibilities of the job something which is clearly illegal (e.g., "if you catch someone hacking into the corporate network you are to slay them"), by signing on to a role when there are responsibilities relating to data protection in that role, you are explicitly agreeing to perform those responsibilities. Likewise, if the role you are hired into changes to include data protection responsibilities and you remain in the role, you've implicitly agreed to perform those functions.

In short, *if* it can be said that employees are ethically obliged to perform the functions for which they are employed, *then* people employed as data protection professionals ought to take all reasonable steps to protect the data they are tasked to.

9.3.2 Custodians of Data

In a typical work environment that doesn't lean heavily toward *bring your own device* (BYOD) policies, there's a fair chance that some of the equipment you'll use, as an end user, will be owned by the company. That might include:

- Monitor/keyboard/mouse when at a desk
- Laptop or desktop computer
- Mobile/cellular phone

In that sense, you are a custodian of those specific items, rather than the owner. Your employer has entrusted you to use those items to perform your job, but has not *given* them to you. Instead, you're *entrusted* to look after them, too. Smashing the monitor in frustration would be frowned upon, and selling the laptop to someone else may see you unemployed (if not criminally prosecuted).

In this, the custodian comparison extends beyond being a work function. If you borrow a book from a friend, you are acting as a custodian of the book while it is in your possession. The *general* belief in such situations is that you are obligated to take care of the things that you are holding (borrowing or otherwise) for other people. Thus, we might say:

> When you are in possession of data, as the custodian of that data, you ought to ensure it is adequately protected.

In this, it doesn't matter whether you are actually the *owner* of the data, or whether your employer is the *owner* of the data. We would argue that if the data is valuable to someone and you are in any way acting as a custodian for that data, you ought to protect it.

9.3.3 Implications of Non-Protection

Another way to consider whether we are ethically obliged to protect data is to consider the implications if we *don't*. That is, is *inaction* harmful or otherwise unethical?

It is not uncommon to think of obligations in terms of the implications of inaction; the entire process of whistleblowing, for instance (alerting authorities to an abuse of power or breaking of the law) is an example of people making an ethical choice between taking an action to address an issue, or, by omission of action, allowing a wrongdoing to continue to occur. While a legal consideration, many jurisdictions do not extend doctor/patient confidentiality to that of serious crimes. For example, if a patient confesses to his psychologist that he wants to kill someone, and the psychologist believes it to be a credible concern, they are obligated to report their concern to the authorities. In such situations, societies have recognized that there are some situations where *harm* arises from the *omission of action*.

The first thing we must consider here is that inaction is not, in itself, going to immediately cause data to be lost. If we think back to the FARR model, data protection exists to provide:

- Fault tolerance
- Availability
- Redundancy
- Recoverability

Each of the above relates to a particular category of failure situation, viz.:

- *Fault tolerance*: Individual component failure (e.g., hard drive)
- *Availability*: Communications failure (data still exists but you can't access it)
- *Redundancy*: Complex unit failure (e.g., server, or datacenter)
- *Recoverability*: Data loss beyond the capability of the above three to protect against

One might argue that if you don't perform the data protection functions that you are employed to do, there's more than likely no first level effect. However, there is significant potential for a secondary level effect—as soon as a component that *should* be protected *fails*. Thus, the ethical consideration here might be stated as:

> You ought to ensure data is adequately protected because if you do not act, the data could be compromised or lost.

The implications of non-protection can serve as an ethical impetus even more so when coupled with either of our previous considerations (i.e., you ought to take action, rather than omitting it, because you're employed to do so, or you're the custodian), but for some the implications of non-action will be sufficient primary reason to engage in data protection.

9.3.4 Why Do We Care about Ethical Obligations?

One might conclude the review of potential ethical obligations by asking *why* we need to consider them in the first place.

To understand why this is relevant, let's return to the medical profession. What happens if, when you visit your doctor, your doctor is having a *bad* day? You're a middle-of-the-day patient, and before you visited, the doctor got no sleep the night before, had two patients who were addicted to painkillers trying to scam prescriptions for opioids, dealt with multiple screaming children, and had to lance an abscess. So when you sit down and describe how you have a sore throat, are feeling feverish, have a headache and muscles are aching everywhere, the doctor waspishly tells you to go home and take an aspirin rather than putting everything together and realizing you are coming down with influenza?

When we see medical practitioners, we don't want them to be people who just turn up to get a wage, we want them to be people who genuinely *care*. Simply put, it's the feeling of an ethical obligation that turns a job into a genuine vocation.

We might consider the same ideal to be a valid one when it comes to data protection: when you work in data protection, you ought not just *do your job*, but do your *best* job. It is the sense of ethical obligation—regardless of how you ground that obligation, that can create the difference between data protection being a job, and being a vocation.

9.4 Legal Considerations

While ethics may inform you what you *ought* to do, legal considerations cover what you *must* do.

This section covers examples of legal aspects of data protection you should consider, and investigate, based on your local region. As always, any data protection policy you establish should be based on an informed understanding of legal and fiduciary requirements for the jurisdictions you operate in.

When it comes to legal considerations, the usual caveat stands: for the most part, ignorance of the law is no excuse for disobeying it. It's imperative that businesses and their IT departments understand the legal framework in which they have to deal with data protection copies, because "we didn't know" is rarely an adequate excuse.

In data protection solutions, vendors, suppliers, and staff making a recommendation are often challenged to prove the return on investment (ROI). Legal considerations are where ROI can pivot to mean *risk of incarceration* if the wrong decisions are made.

9.4.1 Knowing Your Retention Requirements

9.4.1.1 Overview

A recurring challenge in many businesses is a lack of communication between the core business units and IT concerning retention requirements for data protection. This often leads to assumptions governing data retention, such as:

■ Not keeping data protection copies longer than 90 days unless the business explicitly states a requirement to
■ Keeping all monthly backups for all systems, indefinitely
■ Keeping all monthly backups for all systems for 7 years

There is no single answer to data retention periods. It will change, jurisdiction to jurisdiction, industry to industry, and even company to company. Probably the most common scenario is to keep (at least) production monthly backups for 7 years, based on taxation legislation, but even this differs from country to country.

The story of Goldilocks and the Three Bears is the story of data protection retention: being dissatisfied with porridge that is too cold, burning yourself with porridge that is too hot, then finding the porridge that's *just right*.

For the most part, businesses tend to err on the side of caution: retaining more data protection copies than are required, because it's challenging to determine exactly what should be kept, and for how long. (If this sounds familiar, it should be: the root of this problem, from an IT side at least, comes from a lack of data discovery, classification, and lifecycle management.) This can significantly impact the cost of data protection though. Consider, for instance, protecting 200 TB of production data via a daily backup cycle comprising 5×(1 weekly full+6 daily incrementals), and 7 years (84) monthly full backups retained. Disregarding annual growth, and assuming a 3% daily change rate to size the incremental backups, the daily cycle will result in 1,180 TB of data generated for the 5-week daily backup cycle, but 16,800 TB of data generated over the 7 years for the monthly backup cycle. Over 90% of the backup data under management will be from monthly backups.

So what if the business only legally needs to retain 13 monthlies, and just 7 yearlies instead? That would bring long-term backup retention down from 16,800 TB of data to 4,000 TB of data. One would imagine that a potential saving of 12.8 petabytes of data storage and management might represent good reason to investigate exactly what retention policies are required.

Returning to our Goldilocks analogy, businesses can find themselves in trouble, legally, for either retaining data

protection copies for too short a period of time, or too long a period of time:

1. *Too short*: If the business is obligated to, say, retain data associated with sharemarket or tax office reporting for 7 years, but only keeps backup data for 1 year, an audit may result in fines or imprisonment.
2. *Too long*: Many jurisdictions allow for legal discovery to extend to all data available, not just within the retention time. For instance, if legally you're only required to keep email backups for 6 months, but you keep them for 7 years, legal discovery can potentially retrieve and analyze all 7 years of backups, rather than just the 6 months you're obligated to keep.

It is not unheard of for businesses to establish records retention policies that are deliberately too short, in the hopes of avoiding data discovery at a future point in time. However, various jurisdictions have caught onto this and:

> There is some danger in drafting document retention policies that are too short, as courts may find that the policy was created in bad faith as a means of limiting liability or damage exposure. It may be presumptively unreasonable to have a document retention policy which calls for the swift eradication of categories of documents which have historically proven to be requested or utilized in lawsuits. Purposefully destroying key documents as a matter of "policy" can backfire on your company and cause far more harm than the policy prevents.[*]

While data protection retention requirements for existing data and workloads within an environment can be vexing to back-trace and establish, it should be obvious that a good starting point for refining data protection retention models comes from any new project within the organization. For instance, if the business decides to transform its customer relationship management databases from Oracle to PostgreSQL, there will be a program of works to achieve this, rather than just simply performing an SQL dump of the Oracle database on Friday night, adjusting parameters and running an SQL import into PostgreSQL on Sunday morning. Part of that program of works—part of every program of works, should be to classify the data that will be generated and/or used by the workloads and functions within the program, and determine the retention requirements for that

---

[*] Effective document retention in the construction industry, Charles B. Jimerson, Esq., 11 August 2016, www.jimersonfirm.com/blog /2016/08/effective-document-retention-construction-industry/

data. While IT staff might ask the question, it is not for them to answer it. There must be someone within the business who knows the answer, and if not, the business should logically have a framework where it can pose the question to legal or accounting practices to determine the needs.

9.4.1.2 Sarbanes–Oxley Act 2002

It's common to hear businesses aiming to meet backup and disaster recovery requirements relating to the Sarbanes–Oxley Act (SOX) of 2002. Arising from financial scandals such as Enron, SOX actually doesn't directly focus on backup and recovery or data protection. What it *does* focus on is having processes, having those processes audited, having the processes followed (by people who are not the auditors), and reporting on compliance to those requirements.

The "mandatory data protection" aspect of SOX therefore primarily originates in the need to prove that the business has been following mandatory process requirements. Clearly in order to prove this, you need to be able to show evidence, and to show evidence you need to demonstrate details to the appropriate auditing team.

Whereas previously it might have been possible to use the "dog ate my homework" excuse of "we don't have any backups that cover that time period," SOX effectively mandates that you are able to show the work you've done. There's no statement that you must keep data protection copies in a particular format, or on/off platform, but the implicit requirement is that you won't get away with saying you don't have that data.

> § 210.2-06 Retention of audit and review records.
>
> (a) For a period of seven years after an accountant concludes an audit or review of an issuer's financial statements to which section 10A(a) of the Securities Exchange Act of 1934 (15 U.S.C. 78j-1(a)) applies, or of the financial statements of any investment company registered under section 8 of the Investment Company Act of 1940 (15 U.S.C. 80a-8), the accountant shall retain records relevant to the audit or review, including workpapers and other documents that form the basis of the audit or review, and memoranda, correspondence, communications, other documents, and records (including electronic records), which:
>
> (1) Are created, sent or received in connection with the audit or review, and
> (2) Contain conclusions, opinions, analyses, or financial data related to the audit or review.*

SOX serves to highlight an important aspect of how legislation affects data protection requirements for business: it's often a *peripheral* impact. While there will be some industry streams that actually mandate particular types of data protection (e.g., "you must have an off-platform copy," or "you must have an air-gapped copy"), the data protection requirements are often still left to the individual business to interpret as a flow-on effect of the primary legal obligations the company has to deal with.

9.4.1.3 Mandatory Records Retention

Sarbanes–Oxley is by no means the only records retention legislation in the United States. Section 17a-4 of the US Securities Exchange Act requires transaction records, financial statements, and other types of communication relating to the business to be retained:

> for a period of not less than six years, the first two years in an easily accessible place[†]

The US Health Insurance Portability and Accountability (HIPAA) Act defines a minimum retention period of 6 years for HIPAA-related documentation, though this does not extend to actual medical records, which are instead covered by specific state legislation: this results in somewhat varying records retention requirements not only state to state, but also profession to profession—for instance:

> In Florida, physicians must maintain medical records for five years after the last patient contact, whereas hospitals must retain them for seven years.[‡]

Medical records retention is a good example of how the requirements can fluctuate and change significantly even within a single industry, and not just in the United States. In some jurisdictions, medical research records must be retained for the life of the research subject. In vitro fertilization (IVF) can trigger particularly length record retention times:

---

* Cornell Law School, Legal Information Institute, www.law.cornell.edu/cfr/text/17/210.2-06

† Cornell Law School, Legal Information Institute, www.law.cornell.edu/cfr/text/17/240.17a-4

‡ Clarifying the HIPAA Retention Requirements, 15 January 2018, *HIPAA Journal*, www.hipaajournal.com/hipaa-retention-requirements/

To ensure we comply with regulatory requirements, we retain records relating to the use of donated gametes or embryos (including the identity of the donor, the recipient and any offspring born as a result of the donation) for a period of 50 years.

It is our policy to retain other medical records for a period of 25 years from the date of last treatment or the date of birth of any child born as a result of the treatment, whichever is the later.*

To a degree, financial records are usually the easiest to find records retention policies for; yet many businesses beyond medical operate in sectors of the market that require longer retention times. Within construction in the United States, for instance, it is generally recommended to retain records for a minimum of 3 years beyond the "statute of repose" for building works (effectively, the period of liability), where the statutory retention period starts at the point where construction work has been completed. Since in the United States, the statute of repose changes from state to state, again we see the potential for significant variation in records retention requirements even within a single industry vertical.

Another area that mandatory records retention can come into play relates to guaranteeing that data protection copies, once written, cannot be overwritten, deleted, or altered. While "WORM" storage (write once, read many) was initially seen as a function of archival platforms, it is becoming increasingly popular in data protection storage, particularly backup storage. Two reasons why this is so is that:

- *Risk of cyber-attacks*: By using fully compliant WORM storage, the business can write backup data with a designated retention period (e.g., 31 days for daily backups, 7 years for compliance backups) and be guaranteed that even if malware detects the backup product and issues delete commands, the storage will reject the deletion request.
- *Use of backup long-term retention for compliance purposes*: When backup is used in lieu of archive to provide long-term retention for legal compliance purposes, using WORM compliant storage helps guarantee that stored records are exact and unmodified.

In that sense, mandatory records retention legislation will not only drive consideration toward data retention periods and what degree of data protection will be configured for a specific workload, but it may also add some requirements, particularly for businesses operating in sensitive sectors (finance, government, military, and so on) for the features of a data protection storage platform, too.

Businesses seeking strong assurance that WORM type storage is sufficiently secure will typically seek out storage that offers modes guaranteed to meet requirements such as SEC 17a-4, SOX, and so on. To achieve this, a storage system must:

Preserve the records exclusively in a non-rewritable, non-erasable format. Specifically, as defined in the [SEC 17a-4] Rule itself, this requirement "is designed to ensure that electronic records are capable of being accurately reproduced for later reference by maintaining the records in unalterable form."

Verify automatically the quality and accuracy of the storage media recording process

Serialize the original, and if applicable, duplicate units of storage media, and the time-date for the required retention period for information placed on such electronic storage media

Store separately from the original a duplicate copy of the record stored on any medium acceptable under 240.17a-4 for the time required.†

9.4.2 *European Union GDPR*

The EU GDPR represents a comprehensive suite of legislation that came into effect 25 May 2018, and is designed to reinforce data ownership: while businesses may hold data pertaining to customers, GDPR enshrines the notion that those individual customers still effectively own data that pertains to them. The subject of the data becomes the owner, and the company holding the data becomes a *data controller* or *processor*.

While GDPR primarily enforces requirements around privacy and security, it does have storage data protection implications as well. On the outset, personal data processors must disclose to those impacted that it is undertaking data collection, and outline:

- The legal basis by which the data is being collected
- The purpose for which the data will be processed
- Whether the data is being shared with any third parties (regardless of whether they're in, or outside of the EU)
- How long the data will be retained for

---

* IVF Australia Privacy Policy, www.ivf.com.au/privacy-policy

† Dell EMC Data Domain retention lock software, August 2017, Dell EMC Whitepaper, www.emc.com/collateral/hardware/white-papers/h10666-data-domain-retention-lock-wp.pdf

GDPR includes mandatory breach notification with tangible fines associated with violations of user privacy. (The upper maximum currently for a GDPR violation is €20,000,000, or 4% of the previous year's annual worldwide turnover—whichever of the two is the *larger*.) Government authorities and companies whose business focus is the collection and processing of personal data are also required to employ a data protection officer (DPO) who manages compliance to the GDPR.

Subjects of data collection—people about whom data has been collected and held—under the EU have the right to:

■ Request details of what data is being held
■ Request a copy of the data in an accessible format
■ Request the data be erased

Data erasure isn't a guaranteed activity; someone with an active bank loan, for instance, can't request their bank loan details be erased, and there will still be areas where businesses are required to retain data based on fiduciary or other tax requirements. However, the right to "be forgotten," as it were, creates unique challenges in the realm of data protection. Let's say that an EU citizen, Peter Brian, finds out he's on a customer contact database for marketing. This may result in him receiving multiple calls a week, none of which he wants, so he uses GDPR to request his details be erased. The calls stop for 3 weeks, but after that, they start again. Why? A database corruption error resulted in an older version of the marketing contacts database being restored, and the company again has records for Peter Brian in their database.

Herein lies where data storage protection must be focused in GDPR situations. In the event a data erasure is requested, either this erasure event may need to retrospectively apply to data protection copies, or specific protocols must be put in place so that should content be recovered from data protection copies, Peter Brian's details are automatically deleted, or blocked from restoration.

One might note that the impact of GDPR on data storage protection is only just beginning to filter through and will undoubtedly result in product and data handling changes for some time to come. As GDPR becomes cemented as a routine regulation in the EU, you should expect to see increasing focus from data storage protection on:

■ Relationships with data indexing and classification products or vendors
■ Higher focus on searching data protection copies
■ Options to mask data on data protection retrieval
■ Processes around *staging* recoveries—isolating recovered data so that it can be combed through for data that was deleted under GDPR for removal, prior to the data being ingested back into production systems

9.4.3 PCI DSS

The Payment Card Industry Data Security Standard (PCI DSS) focuses on ensuring appropriate protection (primarily security based) is applied to payment data—data relating to credit and debit card activities. It is not uncommon for businesses to assume that compliance to PCI DSS is technology focused, yet even for the PCI Security Standards body, technology is just one aspect of PCI DSS compliance. The body defines three essential components:

> **People:** Hire qualified and trusted partners and train your staff to understand payment data security essentials.
> **Process:** Put the right policies and practices in place to make payment security a priority every day.
> **Technology:** Make sure you are using the right technology and implementing it correctly to get the best security and business benefits.[*]

In Chapter 4, it was noted that technology is just one component (and usually the simplest component) in a data protection system. The same might be said of PCI DSS compliance. The technology decisions around PCI compliance are usually quite simple, most notably around in-flight ("point to point") and at-rest encryption, so that should data be either intercepted or stolen, it is sufficiently protected from misuse.

While there can be a little more complexity to PCI DSS, for the most part so long as technology in use performs end-to-end encryption, it will achieve what's required for PCI DSS, so long as the people and processes within the environment deliver everything else that's required for PCI DSS compliance.

PCI DSS often serves as a good example that there's a lot more to legal compliance than simply having the right technology: without appropriate staff training, developed processes and adherence to those processes, the best technology will not allow the business to pass a PCI DSS compliance audit.

9.4.4 US Sheltered Harbor

While not a legally binding initiative, it is pertinent to briefly consider the US *Sheltered Harbor* initiative. The driving goal of Sheltered Harbor is the recognition that a

---

[*] PCI Security Standards Council, www.pcisecuritystandards.org/merchants/

single bank or financial institution failing due to a cyber-attack can have disastrous flow-on effects in the finance industry, due to the interdependent way the market operates. Therefore:

> Institutions back up critical customer account data each night in the Sheltered Harbor standard format, either managing their own vault or using a participating service provider. The data vault is encrypted, unchangeable, and completely separated from the institution's infrastructure, including all backups.
>
> …
>
> Institutions prepare the business and technical processes and key decision arrangements to be activated in the case of a Sheltered Harbor event; where all other options to restore critical systems—including backups—have failed.
>
> They also designate a restoration partner so that if the Sheltered Harbor Resiliency Plan is activated, the partner can restore critical customer data as quickly as possible.*

While larger institutions may very well make use of their own datacenters for such a vault, one of the goals of Sheltered Harbor is to cooperatively provide vaulted disaster recovery facilities for essential services; Credit Union A might store its vault in Credit Union B's secondary datacenter, and vice versa, thus saving them both on having to stand up a third datacenter each.

While not something subscribed to by all American financial institutions, Sheltered Harbor is a good example of an industry vertical responding to specific data protection threats in a cooperate manner, and it would seem likely other industries will adopt similar policies over time.

9.4.5 Data Separation

Data separation can be a tricky subject when it comes to data protection; just because there is a requirement to keep data separate when it comes to the primary copy does not mean businesses will automatically separate the same data for protection copies. This is something that needs to be considered carefully, since data separation:

- Can be required to keep control/management services separate; combining the data at the data protection layer may introduce a security risk or legal gray area.
- May result in unpleasantness in legal search or data seizure situations: if backup storage, for instance, contains the backups for five different businesses, and a legal search and seizure warrant is issued for one of those businesses, what methods can be employed to handover backup copies for *just* that affected business, if it is even legally permitted?

Legally, separating data that has been stored together can also be problematic. If PCI data, for instance, has been written to a storage area where it shouldn't have been, and that area subsequently backed up, it can have flow-on effects relating to *how* that backed up data must be retained and protected. (For instance, if that backup data is written to non-encrypted storage, or transferred across the network without encryption, it has already resulted in a PCI DSS compliance violation.) As you might imagine, this again brings us back to data classification and lifecycle management: content should be identified and classified up-front, before it is protected, rather than trying to classify it after it has been stored.

9.4.6 In-Flight and At-Rest Encryption

In the earlier section on security we have already discussed in-flight and at-rest encryption, but it is worth reiterating that the decision to perform either of these operations is not always one that is governed by the business itself. Further, the requirement for one form of encryption may not necessitate or mandate the other form of encryption: for instance, some countries may mandate in-flight encryption for data being transmitted but make allowances for at-rest data being stored without encryption.

Requirements for data encryption will often be governed by legislation or fiduciary requirements for specific areas of operation. For example, rather than a country legislating "all at-rest data shall be encrypted" for businesses, it is more likely that there will be legislation on a per-industry basis: finance, health, education, research, etc.

9.4.7 Mandatory Breach Reporting

Since self-regulation usually results in lackadaisical reporting of events that might prove embarrassing for businesses, we are seeing increasing numbers of governments enact mandatory breach reporting legislation. (This even forms part of GDPR.) Australia, for instance, introduced the Notifiable Data Breaches (NDB) scheme in February 2018:

---

* Sheltered harbor: how it works, www.shelteredharbor.org/how-it-works

---

Agencies and organisations regulated under the Australian Privacy Act 1988 (Privacy Act) are required to notify affected individuals and the Office of the Australian Information Commissioner (OAIC) when a data breach is likely to result in serious harm to individuals whose personal information is involved in the breach.

...

The scheme includes an obligation to notify individuals whose personal information is involved in a data breach that is likely to result in serious harm. The notification must include recommendations about the steps individuals should take in response to the breach. The Australian Information Commissioner (Commissioner) must also be notified of eligible data breaches.

Agencies and organisations must be prepared to conduct a quick assessment of a suspected data breach to determine whether it is likely to result in serious harm, and as a result require notification.*

Like mandatory breach notifications in other legislative jurisdictions, the Australian NDB scheme makes no differentiation between whether a breach occurred against a primary copy of data or a data protection copy, and nor should it: both can cause a substantial privacy breach for customers. Previously we've discussed the importance of real-time (or as close to real-time as possible) log capturing from data protection systems, and the growing trend toward mandatory data breach notifications serves as a good example of why this is important: not only will it help identify a security breach in progress (potentially allowing the business to intervene and block further damage), it will also allow businesses to determine the likely level of reporting needed in a data breach situation.

9.5 Summary

In Chapter 4 we noted that a functional, comprehensive data protection system comprises six key components, viz.:

- People
- Processes and documentation
- Service level agreements
- Testing
- Training
- Technology

---

* Notifiable Data Breaches scheme, Australian Government Office of the Australian Information Commissioner, www.oaic.gov.au/privacy-law/privacy-act/notifiable-data-breaches-scheme

This chapter should serve to highlight why technology represents only one-sixth of the building blocks of a data protection system. Regardless of whether a data protection solution is built from the ground up as a new solution, or being modified, many of the decisions that must be made focus on things other than "does product X backup database Y?". Many of the fundamental processes that ensure data protection is functionally sufficient for the needs of the organization will be driven by security considerations, which are driven by a combination of best practice approaches and legal requirements.

Yet those processes alone will provide zero benefit to the business unless they are documented such that they can be carried out in a repeatable way, they can be verified to work, and people are trained and motivated to ensure they're followed.

Data protection—regardless of whether it's misconfigured, misused or breached—can represent a significant risk profile to a business and its customers (or more generally, anyone it holds data on); in this, it can also be said there is value in encouraging employees and professionals who work in the data protection space to think beyond their work being "a job," and to find a *cause*, or even a *raison d'être*, in their work, in the same way that medical professionals so often do. The salary may be what brings the data protection professional to do their job each day, but grounding data protection in ethics could very well be what encourages them to do their *best* job, which is essential for the business, its customers, and the market it operates in.

9.6 Self-Reflection

Medical Systems Inc. is a healthcare provider focusing on:

- Imaging (X-Rays, CT Scans, Ultrasounds, MRIs, etc.)
- Same-day "outpatient" surgical procedures performed by local specialists needing an operating theater
- Pathology testing (bloods, urine, stool, etc.)

Medical Systems Inc. pride themselves on their attention to patient needs. "The patient is first" is their operating motto. You have just been hired as the team leader of their systems infrastructure team, handling both on-premises and any in-cloud services. The systems team handles all systems, from the front-of-office administration machines through to centralized patient databases and imaging/pathology results.

Take some time to consider each of the topics we have discussed in this chapter in light of your position: security, privacy, ethical, and legal considerations. How might each of those need to be considered when planning data protection services for the business?

In particular, research what considerations Medical Systems Inc. might need to consider for data protection copy retention if they were operating in your neighborhood.

Chapter 10

Continuous Availability, Replication, and CDP

10.1 Introduction

10.1.1 What's a Few Nines between Friends?

Since almost the inception of the computer industry—at least its adoption in business—an ever-increasing goal has been high availability. The more a system is available, the more the business functions that *rely* on that system can operate. As the criticality of those business functions increases, so does system availability become increasingly crucial for business operations. Further, with the globalization of commerce, more businesses find themselves having to provide $24 \times 7 \times 365$ operations in order to remain competitive.

System availability is typically measured as a percentage, and so for many businesses the most *desirable* availability is 100%. Depending on the size, location, geographic dispersal, and profitability of the business—and the nature of the IT systems—100% availability may be unachievable, and so the next best thing is "high nines" availability.

If you consider the figures in Table 10.1, you can see the differences between several common availability percentages.

While a business might be content with 98% or even 95% availability for non-production systems, it's typical that the lowest acceptable availability level for a production system is around the "2 nines," or 99% point. (Most enterprises tend to aim for somewhere around 99.99% or 99.999% availability unless regulated otherwise.) It's also worth noting that there is considerable operational difference between having a storage array that provides, say, "5 × Nines" availability (99.999%), and having a *service* utilizing the storage achieving the same availability.

Establishing percentage availability targets is not as simple as picking a number. The business also needs to determine what the availability is measured against.

In the first instance, a business needs to understand whether the availability is being measured against the *total* time in the sample time period or against the *planned availability* time in the sample time period. Depending on the business, compliance requirements, or system type, businesses might use availability periods such as:

- All times
- 00:00:01 to 23:59:59 Monday to Friday
- All days except 8am to 8pm on the first Sunday of every month

In each instance, scheduled downtime should *not* be factored into the availability statistics. Thus, a system that is available all day every day from Monday to Friday but is unavailable most weekends would still achieve 100% availability based on the second availability target cited in the previous list. This is not by any means a "cop-out," but a deliberate focus only on the availability *needs* of the business when determining achieved availability statistics.

It's also important to consider the differences between *reliability*, *availability*, and *uptime*. A common enough mistake in IT is to assume a 1:1 mapping between these—in fact, the relationship will more resemble that shown in Figure 10.1.

We define *uptime* as the period the system is actually up. If you are measuring uptime for a Windows server for instance, you would start the clock ticking from the moment it boots to a login prompt. Availability refers to the period of time the system is reachable, or contactable. If you're measuring availability for a Windows server and the system remains up, but a configuration error takes it off the network for half an hour until repaired, that outage technically doesn't count against the uptime, but does count against the availability time.

Table 10.1   Percentage Availability and Allowed Downtime

Percentage	Maximum Permitted Downtime	
	During a 30-Day Period	During a Year
99	7 hours 12 minutes	15 hours 36 minutes
99.9	43 minutes 12 seconds	8 hours 43 minutes 36 seconds
99.99	4 minutes 19 seconds	52 minutes 33 seconds
99.999	25.92 seconds	5 minutes 15.36 seconds
99.9999	2.592 seconds	31.536 seconds

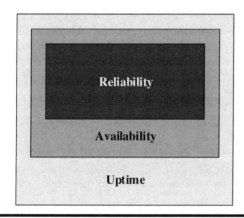

Figure 10.1   Comparing uptime, availability, and reliability.

Finally, there's the reliability time, which is a measure of the length of time the system can perform its intended function. Depending on the nature of the business, this might be sufficiently defined as to be objectively measurable ("system should present the form for inputting timesheet information in under 0.5 seconds"), or it might be more subjectively measured ("the users say the system is running too slow"). Ideally, measurements should be determined during the implementation or templating of the environment such that reliability can be just as readily measured as availability and uptime.

Use of tangible objectives for accessibility and response times allows the business to measure not only whether a system is available, but also whether it's reliably available, and provide a measure between whether the system is functioning well, or degraded, based on the potential impact on user productivity. For example, returning to our timesheet example, the business might establish measurements such as those in Table 10.2.

Accounting for different usage profiles, different access locations, and different usage periods makes measuring availability even more challenging. The timesheet example used in

Table 10.2, for instance, might have different response times required for Fridays if timesheets are due at the end of the business week and/or the final business day of the month if timesheets must be reconciled by then. If a business has staff in a dozen different offices, there might equally need to be allowances for variations in response times based on the link speed between each office and the central timesheet server location. Finally, finance teams using timesheets for processing salaries and project management teams using timesheets for client billing could have entirely different response time requirements (or at least, response times measured against other functions) to an end user wishing to update his or her timesheets.

10.1.2 Data Protection and Reliability

If you recall the FARR model from Chapter 5, it's comprised of:

■ Fault tolerance
■ Availability
■ Redundancy
■ Recoverability

When working in data protection it's important to understand there's not a guaranteed 1:1 relationship between data protection and systems reliability, though data protection can play a significant part in providing systems availability, beyond just whether something is up or down. Examples of where data protection and availability can intersect or not include:

1. A system might be considered *unavailable* due to reasons beyond the scope of a data protection system (e.g., the network between the timesheet server and the end users is down).
2. A system might *become* unavailable in the event that its active data protection processes are insufficient for the required levels of availability or those processes fail (e.g., a clustered system without any equivalent protection for the storage it utilizes).
3. A system might be considered *unavailable* due to requiring the intervention of the data protection system (e.g., a recovery).
4. A system might be considered *unavailable* due to the *impact* of data protection activities (e.g., the system uses a copy-on-write snapshot scheme and over the course of the day performance degrades due to lower speed disks being in the snapshot pool).

So while data protection alone cannot *guarantee* systems availability, the presence or absence of data protection can substantially contribute to the level of availability offered.

Table 10.2 Sample Service Measurement Times

Activity	Response Time (Seconds)		
	Reliable	Degraded	Unavailable
Load web-page	≤2	2.1–5.9	6+
Login completes	≤2.5	2.6–7.9	8+
List last 7 days of timesheet entries	≤5	5.1–12	12.1+
Load new timesheet entry form	≤3	3.1–7.9	8+
Load project code in timesheet entry	≤1	1.1–4	4.1+
Save timesheet entries	≤4	4.1–9.9	10+

10.2 Continuous Availability

Many businesses have now evolved to a point where either based on a worldwide presence (either directly, or via an internet connected, global customer base) or due to government compliance requirements they have to keep systems available continuously, and active data protection techniques can play a significant factor in ensuring such a high level of availability.

10.2.1 Clustering

Consider Figure 10.2, which shows a typical clustered application configuration—in this case, a SQL database server. In

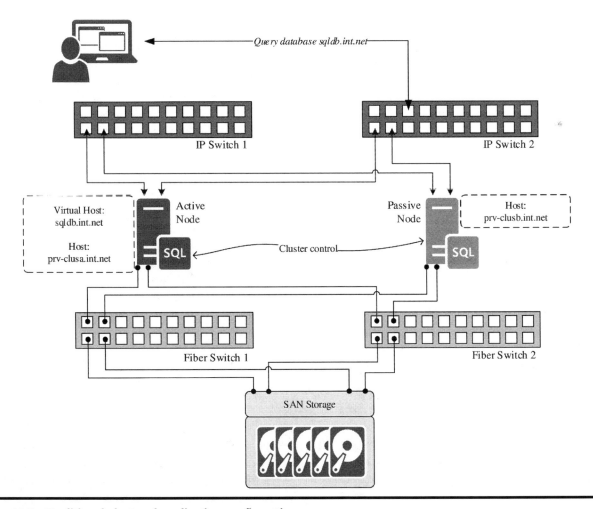

Figure 10.2 Traditional clustered application configuration.

such a configuration, two or more cluster nodes will be configured to present a virtual clustered application, database, or other service. Users and user applications do not reference the individual cluster nodes, but instead reference a virtual clustered database.

In our example, we have two physical nodes in the cluster, with it running in an active/passive configuration: that is, all services are running on the active node, and no user accessible services are currently running on the passive node. In the event of the active node failing (or administrators initiating a failover), the public facing services presented by the cluster will switch over to running on the passive node. This usually results in a small interruption for the end user services, but can be resolved by the end user services reconnecting.

In a two-node cluster such as our example, we would expect to see three hostnames and IP addresses defined:

- The private hostname and IP address of the first node in the cluster
- The private hostname and IP address of the second node in the cluster
- The public hostname and IP address of the service presented by the cluster (in this case, a SQL database)

Whichever node in the cluster is designated active will (in addition to running the requisite services) also assign itself the public hostname/IP address of the service, so that when a user attempts to connect to the clustered database, they always reach the correct node, regardless of what node is currently running the database. (This same principle will also work for backup operations: backup agents will be installed on both nodes in the cluster, and there'll be a public and private backup. The private backup will deal with the private resources—e.g., the operating system etc., on each standalone cluster node. The public backup should always be executed against the publicly accessible cluster resource so that operators and administrators do not have to remember, day to day, what host in the cluster a database or application was running on in order to recover the service.)

(Depending on the architecture, the fiber-channel switches themselves may also be linked together.)

In addition to the simple active/passive clusters, you can also have active/active clusters and n-active/m-passive clusters, where either all nodes in the cluster are actively presenting some clustered service, or *n* nodes are presenting some clustered service and *m* are passive. Where multiple (or all) nodes in a cluster are active, you would usually expect to see a specific public resource (hostname and IP address) for each clustered service—e.g., if the cluster is presenting five different databases, each database would have a public cluster service resource. This allows individual databases or services to failover between cluster nodes.

With the rise of centralized storage systems, a typical cluster will see the physical cluster nodes connecting to a fiber-channel network (or fabric), which will also have a SAN attached. Storage arrays usually employ a multitude of availability and protection features, such as:

- Redundant power supplies and cooling
- Redundant storage processor units
- Redundant data paths between storage processor units and disk trays
- RAID protection to guard against disk failure
- Hot spare disks allowing RAID system rebuilds to start immediately after a disk failure
- Multiple fabric paths to the SAN

Similarly, in a high availability environment, cluster nodes will use a form of dynamic multipathing to allow multiple connections into the SAN fabric, protecting against the failure of a single cable or perhaps even a single host bus adapter (HBA). Multipathing will also exist for the IP networking components—e.g., each node having two IP connections, with each connection going to a different switch.

In Figure 10.2 we also see a link between the two cluster nodes called "cluster control." This reflects the communications that take place between nodes in a cluster for them to be able to determine *which* node in the cluster should be the active node. After all, for a system to provide relatively high-speed redundancy/failover, the human element of deciding what to do should, wherever possible, be eliminated. Clusters typically do this via one or more of three different methods:

- *Watcher*: An independent node monitors the health of all nodes in the cluster, and initiates cluster failover when warranted. (This does pose a secondary problem: what happens if the watcher node goes down? The answer may be a heuristic decision between the remaining cluster nodes based on cluster architecture, or reversion to one of the other options below.)
- *IP heartbeat*: Cluster nodes maintain a dedicated IP link between one another, sometimes even on a dedicated switching network, or direct connections, with direct connections most likely seen in two-node clusters. If an active node stops responding to the heartbeat, the passive/other nodes in the cluster can theoretically intervene and bring up the cluster services elsewhere
- *Quorum disk*: Particularly useful when there is shared storage such as network-attached storage (NAS) and SAN systems, the quorum disk is storage accessible to every node in the cluster. Effectively providing heartbeat mechanisms through IOs instead of TCP/IP traffic, the quorum disk is used to determine whether an

active node is still active, and choosing which node should have services failed over to it in the event of an active node no longer operating.

Cluster service continuity can be more problematic than the simple descriptions above. In particular, cluster/service administrators have to ensure that the solution is architected in such a way that *split-brain* does not occur. In clustering, *split-brain* is the term used to describe the situation that can occur if more than one node believes it should be presenting the cluster service. In its simplest form, split-brain simply results in confused or failing connections to the cluster from the end users; in more severe forms (particularly when shared storage is in use), split-brain can result in data corruption. For this reason, some clustering services will use more than one detection method, and many will have a fall-back position of no node in the cluster taking up a service if the selection criteria indicate it is too dangerous to assume the service can be safely started elsewhere. That is, while clustering is designed to be as robust and autonomous as possible, there are still situations where a cluster architecture may call for a decision from a human as to what should happen.

Clustering had been the de facto standard for some time within IT for providing *high availability*. Yet such a configuration does not provide full guarantee of continuous availability—there are still single points of failure within the configuration, most notably the SAN itself. While a SAN will offer an extremely high degree of reliability, a single SAN (or NAS) is still a single point of failure and therefore an inhibitor to continuous availability. Any engineered

clustering solution employing a single point of failure will be unable to meet a continuous availability target.

10.2.2 Continuous Availability as a Virtualization Function

As they matured, virtualization environments supplanted many (but not all) of the common use cases for clusters. With multiple logically separated hosts/operating systems running on a single physical server, and the ability to transition a virtual host from one physical server to another, clustering use cases to do with hardware failure or load balancing became less pressing.

In Figure 10.3 we see an example of achieving a level of high availability via virtualization. In a virtual environment with multiple virtual machine servers (or *hypervisors*) operating in a clustered resource pool, a virtual machine experiencing performance issues might be moved from one physical host to another without any form of interruption to the users of that system. In a modern virtualization environment, this allows entire virtual machine hypervisors to be taken offline for maintenance or replacement without service interruption to the individual applications or hosts running on it.

While continuous availability and site failover mechanisms for virtual machines have reduced the use of clustering technology in many organizations, they don't entirely eliminate the requirements. If corruption occurs within a virtual machine image held at the primary site and the image at the disaster recovery site is being kept in sync, then

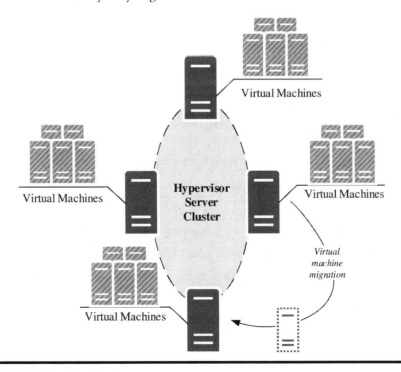

Figure 10.3 High availability via virtualization.

the corruption will become part of the failover image being maintained. With private application and operating system regions, and a shared database, a true cluster is likely to be more resilient to at least *some* forms of corruption.

Businesses in need of more comprehensive continuous availability will then combine clustering with synchronized virtual machine images, allowing for greater resilience to a wide range of failure scenarios. Virtual machine/affinity preferences can be used here to prohibit both virtual machines in a cluster from running on the same hypervisor on either site, thereby providing suitable protection against ad hoc hardware failure or maintenance.

We will revisit virtual machine availability later in the chapter when we discuss continuous data protection.

10.2.3 Continuous Availability as a Storage Function

While clustering and virtual machine high availability can both provide a reasonable degree of protection against downtime, both availability mechanisms will be dependent on the level of availability that can be offered by the storage systems in use.

Even though enterprise storage arrays often offer very high availability capability, this may not always be sufficient for regulatory requirements or mission critical systems for the largest of enterprises.

In such situations, it becomes necessary to employ overlay virtualization systems for storage, integrating two or more storage arrays (perhaps even from different vendors). Such integration allows a volume or unit of storage to be defined at the storage virtualization layer by the storage administrator (or even by an automated process in self-service environments), and mirroring of data written to the virtual volume handled between the arrays that comprise the system.

Such a system might resemble that shown in Figure 10.4.

Storage virtualization systems offering effective continuous data availability should not be confused with synchronous replication (which will be covered in a later topic in this chapter). While synchronous replication mirrors many of the features of continuously available virtualized storage, there is usually an assumption of an (even brief) outage in the event of the primary storage target experiencing a failure. Storage virtualization in this scenario *completely* masks such a failure from the hosts and applications accessing the system.

In such a virtualized storage environment the volumes presented from each array will themselves typically have a degree of data protection configured. An example of this is shown in Figure 10.5. In this example, each physical array has presented a five-disk RAID-5 volume (4 + 1) to the storage virtualization system. The storage virtualization system in turn mirrors writes between these two volumes, presenting a classic mirrored volume to the accessing hosts and applications of the storage.

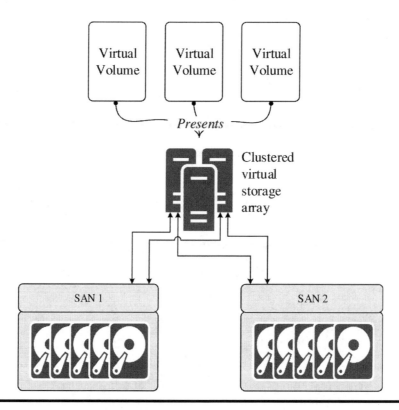

Figure 10.4   High level view of storage virtualization.

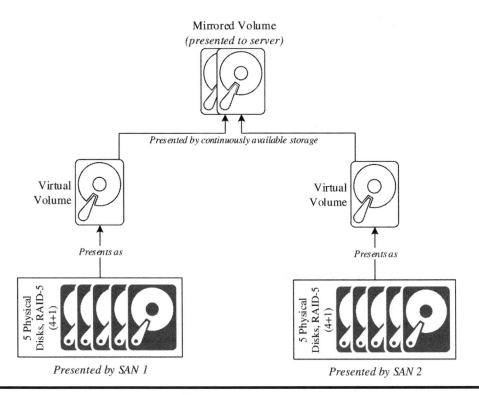

Figure 10.5 Virtual storage volume composition.

The level of data protection offered by such a configuration is quite high and allows a business to present a highly fault-tolerant storage system to mission critical applications. Just as importantly, it allows for high availability to be achieved *while* maintenance windows are still provided to the individual components. One of the storage arrays in the virtual storage system could be fully shut down for core component upgrades or datacenter power upgrades, without interrupting system availability.* This is why the individual physical logical unit numbers (LUNs) presented by the independent storage arrays will have their own data protection configured—it allows data protection functionality to continue even in the event of a storage array outage or maintenance.

10.2.4 A Combined Approach to Continuous Availability

Realistically, neither clustering, virtual machine continuous availability, nor storage continuous availability is sufficient to provide continuous availability for the most mission critical enterprise systems. In such environments where there are extreme compliance, regulatory, or fiscal requirements, the only way to provide a high guarantee of continuous

availability is to combine *all* the individual continuous availability mechanisms. In such environments, it is not uncommon to see active/active clustered virtual machines residing on clustered hypervisor environments utilizing volumes presented by continuously available virtual storage infrastructure. All of these of course also rely on fault-tolerant TCP/IP and storage networks.

10.3 Replication

Replication exists at a service level below continuous availability, but offers many shared characteristics. Replicated data storage systems are extremely important as providing the first level of data recoverability and availability in the event of an actual outage in high availability systems. Replication can be used to supplement continuous availability: a mission critical system might reside on continuously available storage systems in one datacenter, with content replicated to another array, or even another continuously available storage system in another datacenter for service continuity in the event of a site loss.

Depending on the functionality of the storage system under consideration, replication might have a variety of uses beyond simple data protection and might be available for original volumes as well as their snapshots.

Consider, for instance, a business that wants to offload as much as possible the IO impact of traditional backup

---

* Though clearly this would cause an issue in the event of a failure in the remaining array, which may introduce enough risk for some businesses to require *three-way* virtualization of storage systems.

activities on mission critical data sets. One very common approach in this configuration is to take a point in time snapshot of a replication *target* and backup that snapshot. In such a configuration, the chances of performance degradation on the primary copy of the data are substantially reduced during backup activities. (Furthermore, such backups are immediately off-site, providing a higher level of protection against site failures.)

Other businesses might choose to make use of replication target volumes for testing major changes to their production environment—in such situations, the replication might be temporarily suspended and the replication target made read/write for local operations and testing.

In any situation where a replication target is broken or suspended, modern replication offerings will typically include some form of "fast reattach" capability to reduce the amount of IO involved in getting a replication source and target back in synch. (This might even be used in certain situations where the source volume in a replication pair suffers damage and needs to be reconstructed.)

The lazy approach to reattaching a replication pair is to simply copy all of the blocks in the source volume across to the target volume. For small replication pairs, this may even be acceptable, particularly for systems that do not have extremely high availability requirements or extremely small performance impact tolerances. For larger replication pairs or any environment where the resynchronization is either time- or bandwidth-sensitive, such an approach will not be viewed as efficient or acceptable.

One way of speeding up the replication resynchronization is to maintain a dirty bitmap or write-intent bitmap region. In such a configuration, each block or a set of blocks on a volume correlates to a single element in the bitmap. In the event of a replication process being suspended, each time an update is written to the active volume, the bitmap regions associated with the blocks changed on the primary volume are also updated. When it becomes time to resynchronize the pairs, the bitmap region is used as a quick reference to determine which blocks on the source volume have to be copied to the target volume, rather than blindly copying everything.

In Figure 10.6, we see an example replication pair where the replication is maintaining a consistent copy between the source and target volume.

If the replication system supports fast resynchronization, then when the replication is broken or suspended, a bitmap region for the source LUN will be created. As blocks are updated on the source LUN, the bitmap region is updated to reflect the blocks that have changed. Note that the bitmap region *does not* need to actually contain the data that has been updated, just a space-efficient map of the data that has changed. This is shown in Figure 10.7.

When the replication is re-established between the source and the target volume, it is no longer necessary to copy the entire contents of the source volume back across to the target volume in order to have a consistent copy; instead, the bitmap region is referred to and only the blocks that changed on the source volume after the creation of the bitmap region/replication break need to be copied across, as shown in Figure 10.8.

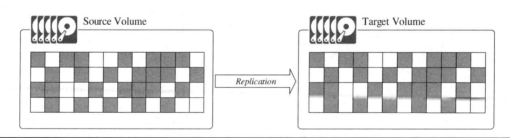

Figure 10.6   Sample replication pair.

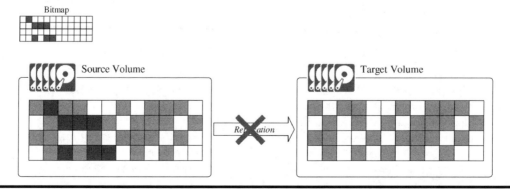

Figure 10.7   Active bitmap region to keep track of changes to the source volume when replication is broken.

Even if the target volume is made read/write during the replication suspension, bitmap regions can still be used to achieve fast resynchronization. In such situations, a bitmap region might be maintained not only by the source volume, but also the target volume. The source volume bitmap will work as described earlier, and the target volume bitmap will also be updated to indicate any blocks that are changed on it. Replication resynchronization is achieved by merging the two bitmap regions and replicating *all* changed blocks from source to target, regardless of whether the block was changed on the source or the target volume.

10.3.1 Synchronous Replication

Synchronous replication, typically available only within the datacenter, across campus, or over relatively short distances (e.g., within a metropolitan region), is a form of data protection whereby writes to one storage system are automatically written to another storage system. This effectively allows for zero lag between the content of the primary and the secondary volume.

To ensure there is no lag between the two source and target volumes, the write process in a synchronous replication pair works as follows:

1. Host sends a write instruction to the primary array.
2. Primary array sends the write instruction to the secondary array and concurrently performs the write.
3. Secondary array performs its write and sends back a write acknowledgment to the primary array.
4. Source array sends a write acknowledgment to the host.

This sequence is shown in Figure 10.9.

What is critical in this configuration is that the primary array used by the host *does not* send a write acknowledgment until such time as it has received a write acknowledgment from the secondary array. (The only way the write can be

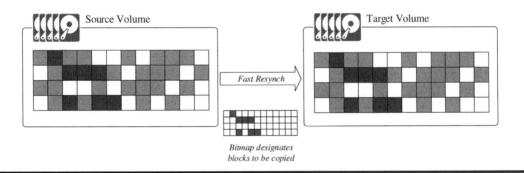

Figure 10.8   Fast resynchronization using bitmap as reference for changed blocks.

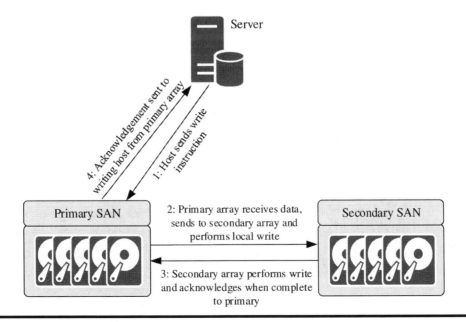

Figure 10.9   Synchronous replication processing flow.

acknowledged to the host without it being acknowledged by the secondary array is when the replication pair is broken—either by the replication system or a storage administrator—or has failed.)

Synchronous replication allows businesses to keep a consistent copy of one or more mission critical volumes at an alternate location or in an alternate array, but this will impose limits on the maximum bandwidth between sites based on any or all of the following:

1. IO requirements (specifically write IO requirements) of the systems accessing the volume being replicated
2. Distance between source and target volumes
3. Cost of bandwidth
4. Reliability of bandwidth

The distance between the source and target volumes affects not only the cost and reliability of the bandwidth that can be provisioned, but it also affects the "return trip" time for acknowledgments. For example, if fiber-optic cabling is used, we effectively have to consider the speed of light for data transmission. Consider: it is approximately 2,727 km from Melbourne to Perth. This implies a delay of *at least* 9 ms in transmitting data from Melbourne to Perth; in reality however, cabling is not done in a straight, continuous line. Signals will also typically be repeated: multi-mode fiber connections usually have a maximum distance of around 2 km, whereas single-mode might achieve 200 km, though it is common to see shorter distances used. Each time the signal needs to go beyond that, a repeater has to be inserted, which adds time to the signal. Therefore, a Melbourne/Perth link might have latency of anywhere between 25 and 50 ms or more, depending on the carrier. This latency acts as a hard barrier on the speed of an IO being committed regardless of how fast the data is transmitted—if the latency if 25 ms then committing any write takes a minimum of 50 ms (transmitting the data, then receiving the acknowledgment).

Such low level communications considerations become critical in planning for synchronous replication between sites; initially it might have only been done between two arrays in neighboring campuses (e.g., less than 1 km between sites); eventually, technology improved to allow "metro" distances; beyond that, achieving synchronous replication across vast distances is effectively limited by physics.

10.3.2 Asynchronous Replication

Asynchronous replication is the process whereby a pair of volumes is kept synchronized, but there is no guarantee that the content of the target volume exactly matches the content of the source volume at any given point in time. Asynchronous replication allows a business to achieve a still reasonably high level of synchronization between a source

and target volume, and might be used for any or all of the following considerations:

1. Budget does not allow for the dedicated bandwidth required for synchronous replication.
2. Compliance or regulatory requirements require a reasonably up-to-date copy but do not impose the need for a perfectly up-to-date copy.
3. Disaster recovery requirements for the business are adequately met with asynchronous replication.
4. Distance between sites makes it physically impossible to achieve a fully synchronous replication configuration.

Typically, asynchronous replication will be configured based on a maximum allowable gap between the source and target volumes. This might be expressed in terms of seconds, minutes, megabytes, or number of write operations, or some combination thereof—though the exact configuration options available or used will be entirely dependent on the replication software and the storage arrays involved—and of course, distance, bandwidth, and latency.

Figure 10.10 shows a high level view of the write process in an asynchronous replication pair. When a write operation occurs with an asynchronous replication pair, the sequence is usually as follows:

1. The host sends a write instruction to the source (primary) volume it is accessing.
2. The primary array writes the data and sends a write acknowledgment immediately back to the source host.
3. The primary array then seeds the details of the write to a replication journal. This will be an actual copy of the data that was written to the source volume.
4. At a suitable time (based on workload, filled buffers, etc.), the replication system will send the batched blocks in the replication journal across to the target array to be written.

Specifically in relation to point (3), it is important to understand the replication journal holds a copy of the data written, not pointers to blocks on the source volume that have been written to. This is for both performance, and consistency considerations:

■ *Performance*: By writing a copy of the data to an alternate location, replication runs against that alternate location, avoiding the need for non-workload related reads against the primary volume.
■ *Consistency*: If only pointers are used, blocks queued for replication may be modified out of sequence (e.g., due to multiple updates in short succession) from the replication process, corrupting the data on the target volume when it is eventually replicated.

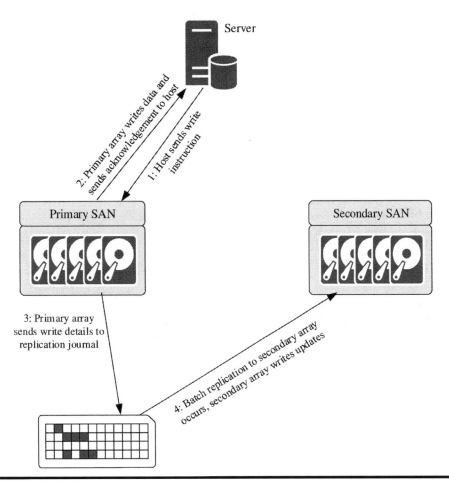

Figure 10.10 Data flow for writes with asynchronous replication.

A key consideration when designing and configuring asynchronous replication will be the capacity of the replication journal. If this journal fills, it can trigger a fault condition. The source volume may stop accepting writes, or (depending on the arrays, replication software, and/or configuration) the replication is suspended but requires a complete reseeding. Such an event becomes one to be avoided as much as possible and will usually trigger intervention by a storage administrator.

10.4 Continuous Data Protection

Continuous data protection (CDP) is an evolutionary growth beyond replication (and primarily, asynchronous replication). Whereas the purpose of replication is to get the secondary copy "up to date" either immediately or eventually, CDP provides a functionality more akin to a digital video recorder: providing a copy, but also allowing you to rewind seconds, minutes, or even longer to an earlier version of the replicated content. While CDP can be used for a variety of test and secondary copy cases, one of the key data protection aspects of CDP is a recognition that standard replication copies mistakes and corruption as readily as it does real data.

Like the journaling process for asynchronous replication, CDP provides write order fidelity—that way, if you create a new block of data and update the block of data, there will be two distinct replication events: one for the create, and one for the update, *in that order*.

Consider the diagram shown in Figure 10.11. In the diagram, we see a timeline running from 13:01:00 through to 13:06:15, broken into 15 second periods, and we are using CDP to protect a data set.

1. At 13:03:45, a corruption occurs to the data set. This is not immediately noticed.
2. At 13:06:15, the administrator has become aware of the corruption and the need to recover. If we had merely been replicating, then the corruption also would have been replicated. CDP will replicate the corruption, but allows us to "rewind."
3. The administrator rewinds the data set to 13:05:00 and determines the data set is still corrupt.
4. The administrator then rewinds the data set to 13:03:15, determines it is not corrupt, and re-enables it for write/use as of that time.

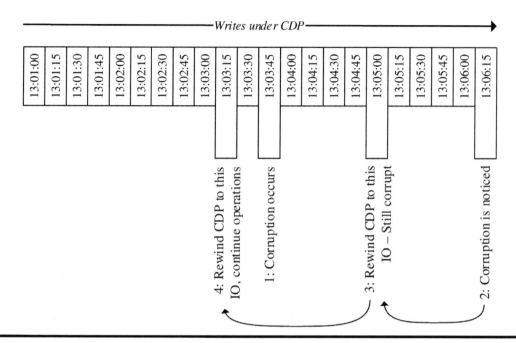

Figure 10.11   High level overview of using CDP to recover data.

It is the "rewind" capability of CDP that offers such a powerful use case for data protection operations: we still get replication (which may be synchronous or asynchronous, depending on the implementation), but the journal maintains older writes, in order, so that we can restore to a previous point in time when required.

There are two key components of CDP required to achieve the functionality it provides:

1. *The journal*: This holds write IOs that have been performed against the source copy of the data set. This covers all write IOs—creates, updates, and deletes. The journal holds these writes in the order in which they are performed, and has sufficient storage to hold hours or days of IOs.
2. *The write splitter*: In order to be effective, writes need to be sequestered as soon as they are performed, and sent to both the primary data set *and* the journal. The write splitter will sit at the logically appropriate location within the data flow and receive writes from the host. These writes will then be simultaneously written to the data set and the journal.

You'll note the write splitter is said to sit at the "logically appropriate location" within the data flow. This is effectively determined by the nature of the CDP functionality. If CDP is being provided by a storage array, the write splitter may very well exist as a function within the storage array's controllers. Alternately, if the CDP solution is a software-only package, the write splitter may be installed on each host that requires CDP, operating as an operating system or kernel extension.

Depending on the specific product, CDP can potentially also integrate with the application layer for a data set that's being protected. If we consider a database, for instance, standard byte-level data copying will result in a "crash-consistent" copy of the database. That is, if you had to roll back the CDP copy by say, 2 minutes to recover from a table being erroneously deleted, without additional logic the version of the database you instantiate from the CDP copy would be logically similar to a situation where the host has suddenly lost power and been restarted. Instead of relying from a crash-consistent restart, the CDP solution might instead integrate with the online protection capabilities of the database periodically; while IOs would be copied as they occur, an application-consistent "bookmark" might be taken every 5 minutes, allowing a rollback at any point, or a rollback of 5 minutes in such a way that the database integrity is guaranteed. (For Microsoft SQL databases, for instance, this would be achieved by periodic synchronization through the Volume Shadow copy service—VSS.)

In some cases, CDP can coordinate the write order consistency we've mentioned not only for individual data sets, but for multiple data sets. (This might be referred to as a "consistency group.") Such coordination can be particularly useful when multiple discrete systems have to be kept in synch—a database server and an application server may require logged events from the application server to be consistent with stored data on the database server. A consistency group established across both systems can ensure journal replays/rewinds for the two servers are done in parallel to the same IO/timestamp.

The most significant limiting factor to the amount of data protection provided by CDP is the size of the journal. Since the journal has to receive all writes performed by the source data set(s), the more IOs likely to take place, the larger that journal needs to be. For instance, if a 10 TB database has 5% daily change, then holding 5 days of CDP IO information is likely to require a journal in the order of 2.5 TB. Keeping 31 days of CDP IO information for such a database is likely to consume 15.5 TB—more than the actual size of the database itself. (Data efficiency might be performed against the journal, enabling either compression or deletion, but this has to be balanced against any performance impacts.)

Capacity planning for CDP is essential—as is understanding what happens if the journal fills up. Are writes to the primary data set blocked, or do the CDP copies under management go offline, requiring a complete re-initialization? Since the journals need to consume storage capacity, this also limits the utility of CDP to protect against particular types of failure. For instance, if a 1 TB CDP journal is used to store 10 days of CDP IO information at just under 10% daily change for a 10 TB fileserver, this journal would be overwhelmed if say, crypto-locker ransomware were to strike the fileserver on a Friday afternoon and encrypt all the content of the fileserver, unnoticed, over a weekend.

A common mistake with CDP is to assume that it should be used as a replacement to backup and recovery services. As is often the case with data protection, we seek to use a variety of services synergistically, since using only a single data protection service invariably creates cost and compromises, either immediately or later. While CDP can be immeasurably useful in recovering from recent issues, its utility is limited by the required size of the journal used to hold updates.

10.4.1 CDP as a Storage Function

Figure 10.12 provides a high level overview of CDP when it operates as a storage function. In this diagram we have not specifically differentiated where the write splitter sits. It may, as alluded to previously, operate as a function within the storage array controllers—however, many storage arrays also provide host drivers which can be used for multipathing (and even active/active paths with failover), and in those instances, the write splitter may be embedded into the host drivers. Alternately, third-party CDP software might be in use, which installs a proprietary driver on each host using CDP, with that driver including a write splitter. It's worthwhile noting however that when CDP is closely tied to the storage array (e.g., managed by the array's controllers, the more likely CDP will be a function at an entire volume level—in array terms, usually described as a LUN. Depending on the size of the volumes provisioned from the

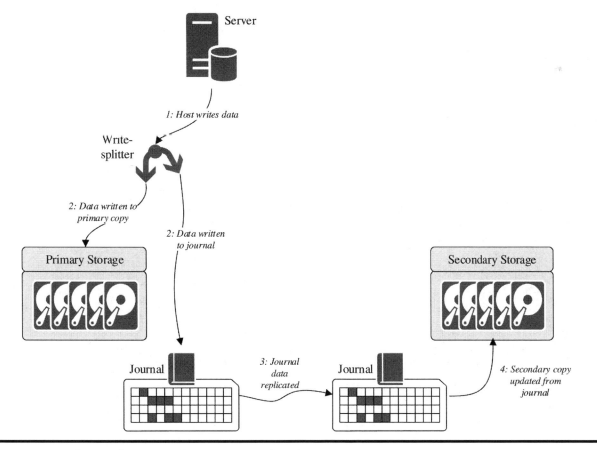

Figure 10.12 Continuous data protection as a storage function.

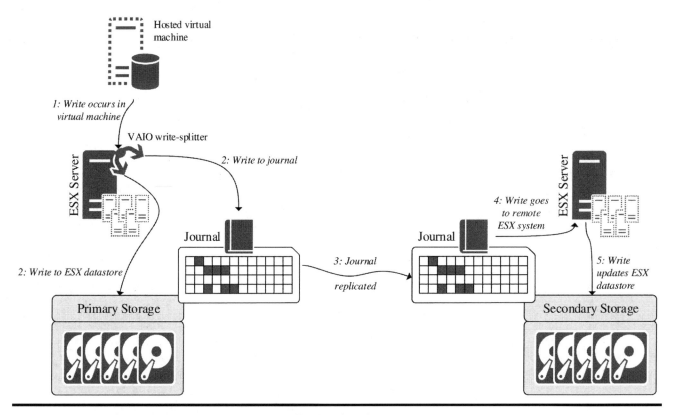

Figure 10.13   Continuous data protection as a virtualization function.

array, this can result in reduced ability to fine-tune *what* gets continuously protected.

Regardless of where the write splitter runs, the diagram outlines the high level process, being:

1. The host writes the data, which is received by the write splitter.
2. Simultaneously:
   a. The write splitter sends the data to the primary copy of the data set, *and*
   b. The write splitter sends the data to the journal (usually local).
3. The journal will then replicate data to any location that is required. (CDP can, in fact, be used as a local function only, without replication.)
4. If the journaled data is written to another journal, once received by that journal, the journal "replays" the writes into the secondary copy of the data set that it manages.

As mentioned, CDP does not have to be used as a remote protection mechanism. In some cases, the CDP environment may exist to provide local replay functionality, without necessarily shipping journaled information to an alternate site. It is not unusual to see CDP products support the maintenance of multiple copies—e.g., a local copy

via the local journal, and one or more remote copies via replicated journals.

10.4.2 CDP as a Virtualization Function

While there are a variety of virtualization systems, we will approach this from the perspective of the leading virtualization system, VMware's ESX (vSphere) environment.

Figure 10.13 shows a high level view of how CDP can operate within a virtualization environment. VMware provides a hypervisor kernel API for IO filtering (referred to as the VAIO API). To quote VMware developer documentation:

> VAIO is a Framework that enables third parties (Partners) to develop filters that run in ESXi and can intercept any IO requests from a guest operating system to a virtual disk. An IO will not be issued or committed to disk without being processed by IO Filters created by 3rd parties.*

---

* vSphere APIs for I/O Filtering (VAIO) Program, https://code.vm ware.com/programs/vsphere-apis-for-io-filtering

By using a write splitter enabled at the VAIO level, CDP can be performed at a per-virtual machine level. Per the sequence in Figure 10.13:

1. A write is performed within a targeted virtual machine.
2. A VAIO integrated write splitter on the ESX server simultaneously:
    a. Performs the write against the storage that has been presented to the ESX server for that particular virtual machine (the "datastore"), and
    b. Appends to the journal the details of the write.
3. The journal content is then replicated as required to other journal(s) (recalling the previous notes that CDP does not necessarily imply remote copying at all times).
4. The replicated journal content is received in some way into the ESX layer for the remote replica.
5. The remote content is written to the appropriate ESX datastore at the remote site.

As you would expect in a solution designed for use within a virtualization environment, this can provide benefits over standard storage-based CDP, in that:

■ The solution should be storage agnostic, allowing for different technologies to be used for each replica, from the original—this may mean different storage array vendors, or even different hardware types (e.g., a SAN at the primary, and direct attached storage at the secondary).
■ The solution can be highly granular; rather than CDP being performed against an entire volume/LUN, it can be limited to specific virtual machines, and in some cases, even specific virtual disks for virtual machines.

When architected properly, such a solution does not need to rely on VMware snapshot activities (which have limits on the frequency with which you can generate them, the number of snapshots, and challenges if there are a large number of writes being performed).

Consistency groups, likewise, might be used in a virtualized CDP environment so that multiple virtual machines are kept on synch with one another—e.g., a Microsoft SharePoint farm might have all servers in the farm collected into a single consistency group for disaster recovery purposes.

10.4.3 File Versioning

Before closing out CDP, it's worthwhile considering a variant of CDP for file storage—that being, file versioning.

File versioning is not new; OpenVMS supported the concept of storing a new version of a file with each save of the file. Thus, if you created a text document called "mynotes.txt," at the filesystem layer you would actually create "mynotes.txt;1." A subsequent update to the file would see the creation of "mynotes.txt;2," preserving "mynotes. txt;1," and so on. Such versioning provided a simple way of undoing changes.

In Figure 10.14 we see a basic high level view of file versioning—initially, the user creates a file called "myfile.doc." At a later point in time, the user makes changes to the file and saves the updated version. Rather than simply deleting the old version of the file, a versioning storage system will copy the old version of the file to either an alternate location, or simply give it a different name in the same directory (such as the OpenVMS example), before writing the new version of the file. At a later point in time, the user realizes the older version is required and uses the system-appropriate

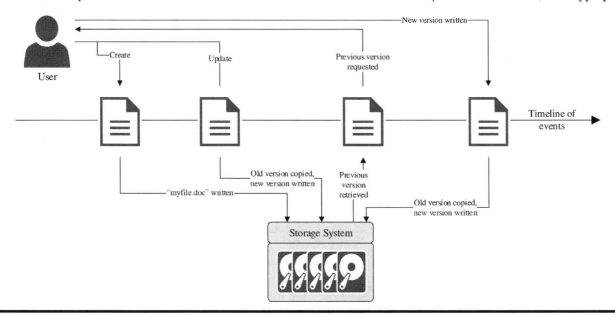

Figure 10.14   High level view of file versioning.

versioning tool to retrieve the older version. Finally, a new version of the file is written after further updates are made.

Various NAS platforms support enabling file versioning; in some cases, this can be versions accessible from snapshots, and in other situations it can literally be multiple versions retained for each file written to a share. In such situations, it is desirable to only enable versioning for systems and data that is suitable—e.g., general workgroup/file data. Enabling versioning on, say, a database hosted from NAS would be undesirable from a performance and capacity perspective.

More recently, file versioning is appearing within consumer-accessible systems as well; including consumer-grade home-NAS appliances, and operating systems such as Microsoft Windows and Mac OS X (though your mileage may vary, so to speak, depending on the application being used).

When planning a data protection strategy that involves end user data and their devices, there is certainly merit in considering what options are available for file versioning for the end users, particularly since (once trained), this allows for user self-service for simple data recovery operations.

10.5 Summary

Both continuous availability solutions and replication solutions (regardless of whether they are synchronous or asynchronous) usually provide a much higher and more granular form of data protection than be offered by traditional backup and recovery products. These become critical for any organization requiring very small RTOs and RPOs. A traditional backup and recovery system, for instance, will usually provide an RPO of 24 hours—back to the time of the previous backup. The systems and techniques discussed in this chapter may allow for an RPO as small as zero (for the most important systems) or more commonly within minutes rather than hours or days. Similarly, the recovery time might be measured in seconds, minutes, or hours instead of hours or days depending on the amount of data loss.

CDP fills a role that sits somewhere between replication and snapshots (the topic of the next chapter), while offering potentially a very fine granularity in data set recoverability, for short periods of time. While continuous storage availability can provide zero downtime in the event of a storage array or storage volume failure (so long as the other array or other storage volume is active), and replication can provide near-zero data loss situations in the event of a primary copy failure, both continuous availability and replication will fail in the event of data corruption or deletion—the nature of their operation sees corruption and deletion similarly carried across to the secondary copy. While CDP carries that corruption or deletion across faithfully, it also provides the option to rewind. While technically not normally considered to be CDP, file versioning does provide a similar style of protection when applied to regular document file-shares.

In the next chapter, we'll discuss another data protection designed to provide better RPOs and RTOs than backup and recovery software—snapshots.

10.6 Self-Reflection

Consider a business or industry vertical that you are familiar with, and some of the services that business/industry provides. From there, consider a few of the different IT functions that would be needed to provide those services (e.g., databases, file-shares, email servers).

Which services would require what level of protection discussed in this chapter?

For example, consider some of the functions of a university:

- *Student records*: Database server with front-end web-servers for accessing the data.
- *Campus facilities management*: File-share for documents and email for contacting students, academics, and staff.
- *Student file storage*: A 500 GB file-share for each student of the university. Students are encouraged to make this their primary assessment and data storage area.
- *Research storage systems*: For holding data associated with various research being conducted by professors and post-graduate students.

Chapter 11

Snapshots

11.1 Introduction

Snapshots have become an almost ubiquitous feature within data protection services, regardless of whether they occur at the operating system, hypervisor, or storage layer. Such is the utility of snapshots that they also represent the fundamental "native" data protection mechanism offered by hyperscalers in public cloud environments.

There are a variety of snapshot techniques, but most are bound by the reliance they place (be it permanent or short term) on the *presence* of the storage (or at the very least, storage *platform*) they are protecting. In this, they offer less robust protection against hardware failure than full replication, but offer potentially better RPOs and RTOs than backup and recovery software (depending on the nature of a failure experienced by a business) while still providing reasonably space-efficient point in time copies.

We typically refer to snapshots as representing *on-platform* protection. This refers to the concept that the platform being protected is providing the protection mechanism itself. Particularly when we consider traditional storage platforms (SAN and NAS), snapshots are used often to provide protection within the same storage system—a NAS home drive share, for instance, may have many snapshots on the same storage system providing granular recovery for several days. However, since there is no interoperability standard for snapshots between storage vendors, we also equally define *replicated snapshots* as being *on-platform* as well: they will be for logically similar storage, either from a storage virtualization perspective, or as two storage arrays from the same vendor. These are defined as on-platform still because the control process for the snapshots is still tied to the data being protected: the control mechanism is on the *same* platform.

Contrary to some beliefs, snapshots are not the be-all and end-all of data protection: a data protection "solution" entirely built on snapshots is not a solution at all except in perhaps the most niche of scenarios. However, it can be equally argued that a data protection "solution" that doesn't use snapshots *anywhere* may very well be suboptimal in what it offers to a business.

There are a variety of snapshot techniques that can be used in data protection, and in this chapter, we will review several of the more common techniques and their applicability.

11.2 Snapshot Techniques

11.2.1 Copy on First Write

The copy on first write (CoFW) snapshot technique is designed to minimize the amount of storage capacity required to take a snapshot of a filesystem. When a CoFW snapshot is taken, the snapshot image does not actually contain any data, but instead a series of pointers back to the original data, as shown in Figure 11.1.

The snapshot is presented as being a separate filesystem to the filesystem it is protecting, effectively seen as an independent entity even though the actual data is shared between the source and the snapshot. If an attempt is made to access data on the snapshot, the read is redirected back to the equivalent region on the source filesystem. (We should note that CoFW snapshots can equally apply to block storage, i.e., at a layer below filesystems. For the purposes of simplicity we are focusing on a filesystem example.)

Keeping in mind the goal of a snapshot is to present a point in time copy of data, and that the source data should continue to be available for whatever operation is required (and specifically, for *writing*), CoFW snapshots earn their name whenever an attempt is made to write data to the original filesystem.

Considering the snapshot depicted in Figure 11.1 again, let us step through the process that occurs when an attempt is made to write new data to the first block in the filesystem. This will resemble the following sequence:

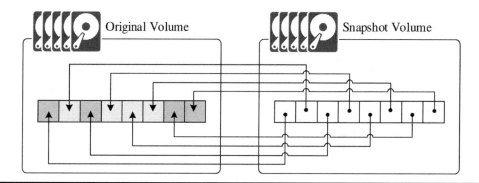

Figure 11.1 Copy on first write snapshot after initialization.

1. The accessing host attempts to write to the block of data protected by a CoFW snapshot, but this write is deferred (Figure 11.2).
2. The storage system intercepts the write: before the write can be performed, the snapshot protected content must be preserved, so it copies the original content of the block across to the equivalent empty block in the snapshot (Figure 11.3).
3. With the data copied across to the snapshot, the pointer for that block is removed (Figure 11.4).
4. The new data is then written to the block on the original filesystem, updating its content (Figure 11.5).

While CoFW is a highly space-efficient snapshot technique, you may have already noticed the performance side effects, that being every time an attempt is made to write to the original volume, an additional read and write is triggered to copy the original data to the snapshot region. Due to this overhead, it's usually recommended that CoFW snapshots only be performed against volumes that will have only a very small number of changes while the snapshot is active.

Equally, this creates the requirement that the storage pool used for snapshots has high enough IO performance as to minimize the impact of the additional write operations; performing snapshots of filesystems running on 15,000 RPM or even 10,000 RPM disk drives (let alone flash) to storage pools serviced by 7,200 RPM or 5,400 RPM drives can result in serious performance degradations even with minimal write loads on the source filesystem.

Beyond performance considerations, the sizing of the snapshot storage pool plays an important factor in the reliability of CoFW snapshots. If the storage pool that provides space for the snapshots fills, this will result *at least* in corruption within the snapshot(s), and possibly even the suspension

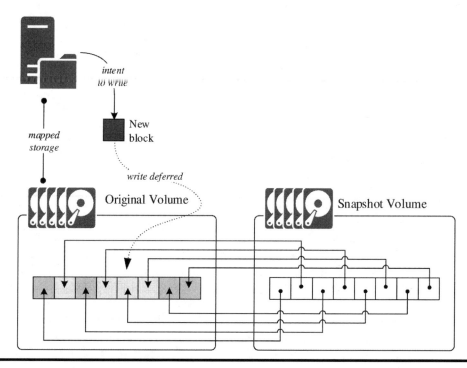

Figure 11.2 Intent to write to CoFW protected block.

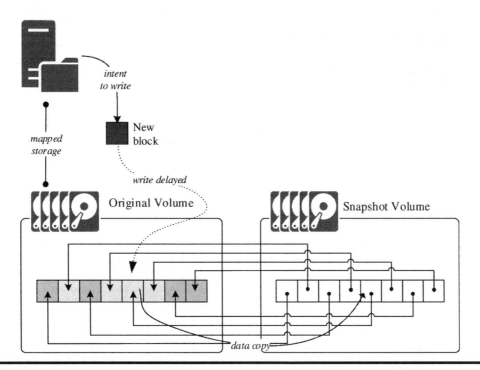

Figure 11.3   Data is copied from the original storage to the snapshot.

of write operations to the primary filesystem, depending on how the snapshot system is designed. To minimize the risk of performance and/or capacity impacts, differing storage systems may offer options such as:

■ Multiple snapshot pools differentiated by capacity and/ or performance profiles
■ Dedicated snapshot storage for individual volumes

Of course, both approaches only *isolate* the impact caused should one of the above scenarios occur, rather than entirely eliminating the potential for it to occur. Nevertheless, both options can be highly useful in a data protection configuration. Snapshot storage pools based on performance characteristics allows a business to limit the amount of snapshot storage space allocated to each performance tier (rather than the alternative of allocating all snapshot storage space from

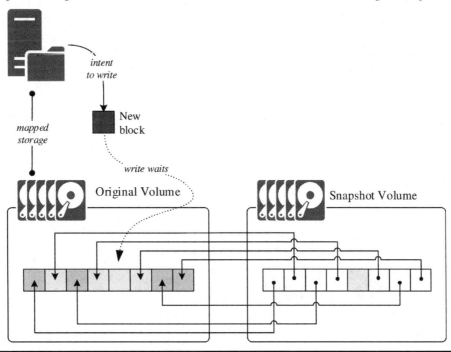

Figure 11.4   Block copied into snapshot and snapshot pointer removed.

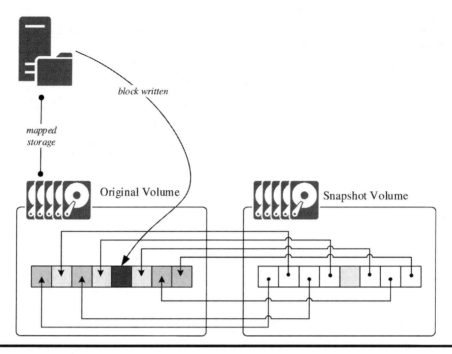

Figure 11.5   New block written.

the highest required performance tier). Equally, when a business has key storage volumes that have a very high degree of criticality and/or performance requirements, dedicated snapshot storage substantially reduces the risk of disruption from other snapshot storage areas, even on the same storage system.

11.2.2 Copy on First Access

Copy on First Access (CoFA) is a snapshot process typically associated with generating clones of data, typically at the volume/LUN level. These initially look quite similar to a CoFW snapshot, in that the snapshot copy starts as a set of pointers back to the original content that was snapshot. This is illustrated in Figure 11.6.

A CoFA snapshot starts as a series of pointers, but unlike a CoFW snapshot where the aim is storage efficiency, the goal of a CoFA snapshot is a complete duplication of the original volume.

A CoFA snapshot will see data copied progressively from the original volume to the snapshot volume as (effectively) a sequential operation—however, whenever a host process attempts to read data from the original volume, or write data to the original volume, the affected blocks on that original volume are pushed to the head of the copy queue—hence the naming of the snapshot methodology.

In Figure 11.7 we see a CoFA snapshot just after initialization, where the sequential copy of the original to the snapshot has already commenced as a background operation.

In Figure 11.8, the host attached to the storage volume attempts to read a block found elsewhere on the volume protected by a CoFA snapshot. As the block is read and returned to the accessing host, it is simultaneously copied to the appropriate location within the snapshot. The same process

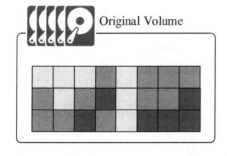

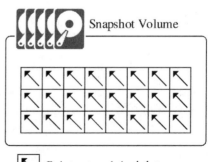

Figure 11.6   Copy on first access snapshot at initialization.

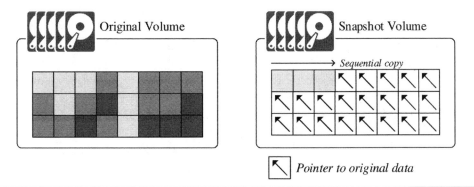

Figure 11.7 CoFA snapshot with sequential copy in progress.

occurs during a write operation—and that process is logically identical to a write operation under a CoFW snapshot.

Over time, the CoFA snapshot volume will eventually become a byte-for-byte clone of the original volume at the time the snapshot was initiated, generated through any required mix of the sequential copy, copy-on-read, or copy-on-write. The resulting duplicate volume is shown in Figure 11.9.

While a CoFA snapshot will eventually consume the same amount of storage as the original volume it was taken from, it will represent an independent copy of the original data; through pointer technology the copy is accessible immediately upon creation (avoiding the need for a potentially long wait for a full up-front copy operation), with the snapshot *eventually* being a complete clone. (While Amazon does not provide in-depth information on their snapshot creation process, the first snapshot in Amazon Web Services of an Elastic Block Store volume is described as a complete clone of the volume—particularly necessary, since snapshots are written to object rather than block storage—and so we might presume it may very well leverage techniques similar to CoFA.)

11.2.3 Redirect on Write

Virtualization hypervisors such as those developed by VMware also make use of snapshot technology. This can be handled at a hypervisor/software level above a conventional filesystem thanks to the encapsulation of a guest filesystem as a single, large file, or several smaller files, rather than each individual file that has been written on the virtual machine (e.g., a 100 GB C:\drive for a Windows virtual machine might literally exist as a single 100 GB container file on the hypervisor, or it might be broken up into say, 50×2 GB container files on the hypervisor).

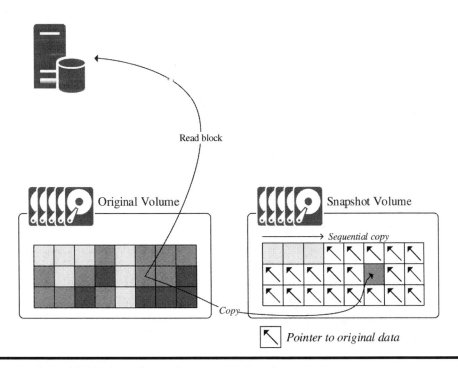

Figure 11.8 CoFA snapshot with block read out of sequence triggering copy.

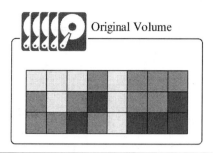 Original Volume   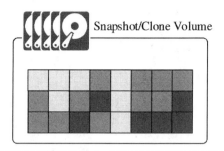 Snapshot/Clone Volume

Figure 11.9   CoFA Snapshot with cloning complete.

With snapshot functions integrated into hypervisor technology, virtual machines can be protected prior to potentially destructive changes, substantially reducing the likelihood of data loss. For instance, an administrator might snapshot a virtual machine before performing an operating system upgrade within it. If for some reason the upgrade fails, the administrator can just roll back to the pre-snapshot state to attempt the operation again at a later point in time. Snapshots are also used in backup processes to capture at least a crash-consistent copy of the virtual machine.

While the snapshot is active, any writes performed within the virtual machine are written to an alternate storage file rather than the virtual disk container files. This snapshot method also allows for the primary virtual disks associated with a virtual machine to be rendered consistent during a backup operation; once the snapshot of the virtual machine disk files has been initiated, those disk files are "static" and can be safely copied for backup and recovery purposes. An active Redirect on Write (RoW) snapshot, with data being written to the virtual machine, is shown in Figure 11.10.

In Figure 11.10 we can see that after the snapshot was initiated, a new block of data had been written. Since the original content is effectively treated as read only, the block of data was written to an alternate data file. At this point, the system will need to start maintaining a bitmap associating "changed" original blocks with the position in the snapshot data, since the content in the snapshot data file is currently the logically "correct" copy. Thus with an RoW snapshot there will also be redirected reads to access any data that has changed since the snapshot was initiated (while that snapshot is active).

As the original content continues to be used while the snapshot exists, the snapshot will grow in size—with any updates to the original (either changed, or new blocks of data) being redirected to the snapshot data file, as shown in Figure 11.11.

While filesystem snapshots are often executed on the basis of later being entirely dropped without having been accessed, or perhaps mounted independently to copy required data back, RoW snapshots such as used in virtual machines are as often as not performed with the expectation that the snapshot state will be merged *back* into the original storage state.

In the event of the snapshot being released without a state merger, the release process from this form of snapshot is fast—the original data was not changed, so there's little more to do than simply delete the snapshot data file(s). If we consider the state shown in Figure 11.11, for instance, we can see the original content is exactly as it was at the start of the

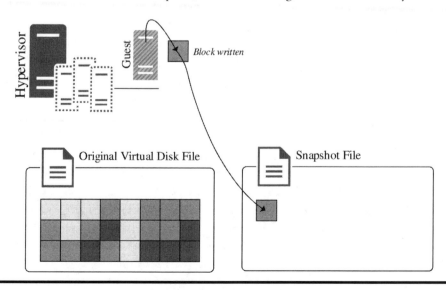

Figure 11.10   Redirect on write snapshot receiving writes from a virtual machine.

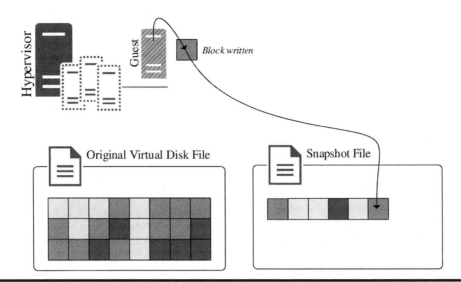

Figure 11.11 RoW snapshot with multiple writes.

snapshot process, and dropping the snapshot simply requires the deletion of the snapshot data and turning off any write-redirect process that had previously been enabled.

In the event of the snapshot being *kept*, a merge operation has to be performed; the blocks written to the snapshot file must be replicated back against the appropriate blocks within the original file, as shown in Figure 11.12.

As the snapshot merger features ongoing IO operations to the current state of the entity *and* increased IO operations to copy the content of the snapshot data across into the original data source, these snapshot mergers can cause a performance hit on the entity that had been snapshot under heavy load operations, particularly if a large number of writes/updates occurred during the lifetime of the snapshot.

It's worth noting RoW snapshots are not exclusive to hypervisors; some storage systems make use of it to provide snapshot functionality as well. As mentioned for hypervisors, merging the original content and an RoW snapshot together can create a high burst of write activity, and if not managed correctly this can cause IO interruptions for systems sitting on top of RoW. One technique to avoid this write load during snapshot merger is to simply avoid doing a merger at all; instead, a pointer system (or some variant thereof) for the

"correct" blocks can be maintained. Snapshot merger simply creates a new map to the storage system based on the correct combination of the original blocks and the snapshot blocks. However, this is not without its limitations: this can result in maintaining the snapshot(s) within the same storage pool as the original LUNs or volumes being snapped. For example, a 5 TB storage pool may be configured with 4 TB of active space and 1 TB of snapshot space, all sharing the same disks. Other snapshot methodologies such as CoFW and CoFA can better split the original storage pool and the snapshot storage pool into entirely separate collections of LUNs/volumes, thereby allowing primary volume capacity and snapshot volume capacity to be managed independently of one another.

11.3 Crash-Consistent versus Application-Consistent Snapshots

Consider again the RoW snapshot: as mentioned at the time, this is most typically used in virtualization environments, and is particularly useful in a situation where one wishes to take a backup of a virtual machine. Since the original content does not change during the backup process, it can be

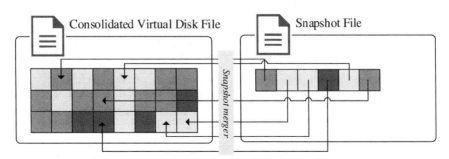

Figure 11.12 RoW snapshot merger.

safely copied into the backup storage environment for later recovery in the event of a failure. (The later chapter on virtualization will cover this in more detail.)

When we think of snapshots, we must consider whether they are *crash consistent* or *application consistent*. Crash consistent implies a state upon restoration that might closely resemble a system that has unexpectedly crashed and rebooted. When a snapshot is taken of a virtual machine, there are likely to be open files within the virtual machine, not to mention active communication states between the virtual machine and the broader IT infrastructure. If the virtual machine is restored from this snapshot, it will, to all intents and purposes, appear to the operating system within the virtual machine that it had unexpectedly restarted.

Application-consistent snapshots are a slightly different matter, however. They imply the hypervisor snapshot system interacting to a higher degree with virtualization software running within the virtual machine to suitably quiesce (at the start of the snapshot process) whatever databases may be running within the system. While the virtual machine might still, following recovery, behave as if it had unexpectedly crashed, the application/database running *within* the virtual machine would have been prepared for the "crash" state in such a way that it can be reliably restarted and used immediately, rather than requiring a separate database restore.

In effect, this crash- versus application-consistent snapshot question is one that applies to each type of snapshot technology, since a multitude of different applications or systems might be running and making use of storage that is snapshot. Virtualization systems may be the most obvious, but they are not unique in this scenario. Particularly, as 10 Gbit networking becomes ubiquitous within a datacenter, we are increasingly seeing many businesses placing application and database workloads (not to mention virtualization workloads themselves) on standard NAS. How these application layers and hypervisor layers react to a sudden reversion of a snapshot in the event of a major failure can define the difference between a successful data protection strategy and waste of money.

This yet again returns us to the fundamental data classification questions posed in Chapter 2, being:

1. What is the data?
2. Where is the data?
3. Who uses the data?
4. When is it used?
5. How is it used?

While NAS systems in particular represent easily configurable mass shared storage for a large number of users and/or systems within an IT infrastructure, the fact they provide snapshots is not sufficient demonstration of an adequate data protection strategy if insufficient consideration is made

regarding the accessibility of data residing on filesystems following a snapshot rollback/restoration activity.

This also often differentiates "workgroup" laissez-faire approach to data protections and truly enterprise understanding of the complexity of data protection. All too often new entrants to the data protection market might blithely claim that it is perfectly acceptable to perform crash-consistent backups of virtual machines running database software, using supposed "logic" such as the following:

> It **should** work, so long as the database isn't too busy, and **if** the storage system responds fast enough, and **if** the hypervisor isn't too busy doing other activities, and **if**…

Data protection promises premised on "if," "maybe," and "hopefully" are not *promises* at all—and can place business data in considerable danger. Data protection architects, in particular within an organization, must be mindful as to whether any deployed snapshot technology merely offers crash-consistent snapshots or application-consistent snapshots—and inevitably, if they're application-consistent snapshots, what applications are supported and whether there are any caveats around that support.

11.4 Read-Only Versus Read/Write Snapshots

Another consideration relating to snapshots is what utility they can offer beyond providing a reasonably high level of granularity for recovery time objective (RTO) and recovery point objective (RPO).

The level of utility that can be achieved with snapshots largely depends on whether the snapshots are made available read only or whether they are made available read/write. By its nature, an RoW snapshot is a read/write snapshot: the writes are *made* to the snapshot region. However, neither CoFA nor CoFW snapshots necessarily *have* to be provisioned as read-only.

As mentioned in RoW snapshots, an advantage of permitting read/write access to a snapshot is that a potentially destructive activity can be undertaken, and if it fails, we can rollback to a pre-snapshot state and avoid a prolonged outage or data loss situation. Along these lines, read/write snapshots of filesystems hosting databases might be used by database administrators to test major upgrades to the database software *against* production data, but without putting the "real" production data at risk (i.e., the test is made against a reasonably up-to-date replica of the production data, rather than a manual copy of the data *or* just a collection of test data).

While RoW is explicitly designed for this technique, it is equally arguable that the primary operational purpose of both a CoFW and a CoFA snapshot is to provide a "pristine," unalterable copy of the data as of the time the snapshot was executed. While logically a CoFA snapshot, once background cloning completes, could allow for an administrator to easily access the snapshot data for writing as well as reading, no such capability is inherent in the CoFW snapshot previously described. Further, in such situations, allowing users to *modify* that data is counter-intuitive: for certain, this may allow destructive testing of particular scenarios to take place, but for the duration of that testing the system doesn't have a copy of the data that can be used for restoration purposes—and this is almost always the *primary* purpose of the snapshot.

The solution for read/write snapshots is almost always provided by snapshot technology itself. If we consider a CoFW or a CoFA snapshot, we can effectively create a read/write instance of the snapshot by employing an RoW snapshot against it (or something similar). In this scenario the original snapshot data is left preserved, but a virtual copy of the data is made available to the required processes or personnel via the RoW snapshot technique.

Figure 11.13 shows a combination of CoFW and RoW snapshots being used to effectively generate an indirect read/write snapshot of the original volume. (Note that alternate terminology, such as *journaling*, might be used to describe the technical process of write-enabling a snapshot that would otherwise be read only.)

Such a combination of snapshot techniques achieves both the original data protection consideration of the snapshot *and* provides additional utility to the business by allowing potentially destructive testing to be performed against a copy of the original data.

11.5 Integration Points in Holistic Data Protection

A single snapshot by itself provides a single point in time of data protection, but snapshots become particularly more useful when we consider the speed at which they can be generated and how space-efficient they are (depending on how active the original entity being snapshot is).

This allows storage administrators (particularly when we focus on NAS environments) to offer considerably tighter and more business compatible SLAs regarding RPO and RTO than a traditional backup strategy. If a business requires no more than an hour of data loss from the filesystems presented by a NAS server, this might be achieved by taking hourly snapshots, as shown in Figure 11.14.

Many NAS vendors feature client operating system integration points with their snapshot technology that allows individual end users to perform self-service recoveries. By this, users are able to execute read-only mounts through operating system hooks (e.g., integration into Microsoft Windows Explorer) of prior snapshots of a filesystem and simply copy the files they wish to retrieve from the snapshot. This allows for easy retrieval of data without requiring a formal recovery process to be initiated, and is often seen as a major time saving advantage over traditional daily backup processes.

While this provides a high level of granularity for recovery and allows a business to meet tight RPO objectives, we must keep in mind the *potential* performance impact it can create. If volumes being protected by frequent snapshots are regularly updated, there will be a greater number of IO operations associated with writes as blocks need to be copied, or metadata/journal information must be updated to allow

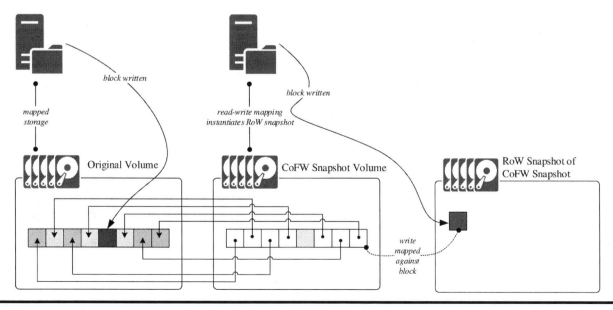

Figure 11.13   Read/write snapshot of a CoFW snapshot.

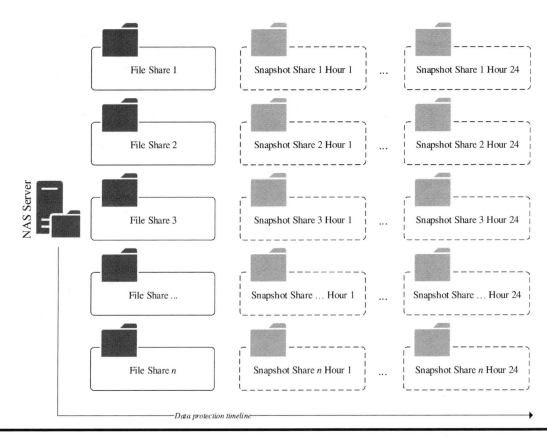

Figure 11.14 Achieving a 1-hour RPO via hourly snapshots.

changes to the original volume without affecting the point in time view of each snapshot. Higher speed storage, such as solid state devices, and more recently, NVMe systems can effectively mask this performance impact, though the management complexity (within the storage array) is largely undiminished regardless of the storage performance.

11.6 Operational versus Long-Term Retention for Snapshots

Snapshots represent an excellent on-platform technique for data protection, and the use of snapshots can result in quicker recoveries with less data loss. Their utility when it comes to medium- and long-term retention however is more questionable, particularly when it ties recoverability of compliance data to the primary storage platform it originated from. Some vendors may choose to position snapshots as the only data protection required—in reality this is more an exercise in achieving vendor lock-in than it is a recommendation around real best practices approaches to data protection.

Consider, for a moment, a business that chooses a storage platform which manages to efficiently manage metadata around snapshots such that it is possible to retain long-term retention snapshots to the point of eschewing traditional backups. This might establish a protection policy of:

- Hourly snapshots retained for 24 hours
- Daily snapshots retained for 35 days
- Weekly snapshots retained for 3 months
- Monthly snapshots retained for 7 years

Such storage technology might be effectively used for 3 or 5 years before the business decides to refresh its storage platform. At this point, an alternate vendor may offer better pricing and features, *but* since snapshots are not portable between different storage vendors, compliance retention maintained in snapshots on the existing platform create a considerable challenge. Does the business:

- Eschew the preferred features to remain on a snapshot-compatible platform from the existing vendor?
- Move to a new platform and retain the old platform to age old compliance snapshots?
- Move to a new platform and migrate the snapshots into another system (e.g., mounting month after month of compliance snapshots and generating backups)?

More often than not, the first option will be chosen because it is the "cheapest" and the path of least resistance. Furthermore, keeping long-term retention within snapshots effectively sees compliance retention stored solely within an on-platform copy, which introduces tangible risk to the business.

Unless there are exceptional reasons otherwise, long-term retention of snapshots should be frowned on, as their true function is to create a vendor lock-in situation.

11.7 Summary

Snapshots frequently offer a very efficient mechanism of achieving low recovery time objectives. In certain disaster recovery situations, a volume or virtual machine that has been snapshot can be "rolled back" considerably faster than, say, complete restoration from a traditional backup. Equally in many circumstances a snapshot can be quickly accessed to retrieve data from it rather than executing a more formal recovery process from a traditional backup system.

Also, as the amount of data to be protected grows, snapshots allow for point in time copies to be generated very quickly with potentially very little in the way of storage requirements (compared to the original data set), thus allowing a business to meet reasonably short recovery point objectives.

Snapshots do not come without their risks or limitations, however. While many storage systems theoretically support thousands or more snapshots, the performance impact from this many snapshots can make the entire exercise pointless—well-protected storage that has become unresponsive due to excessive snapshot updates is not useful to any business. Similarly, a large number of snapshots will see snapshot storage requirements continue to grow in a way that may not offer the most space-efficient form of data protection for an environment. Finally, for the majority of snapshot techniques, we must keep in mind that the original data is effectively being used to protect itself. Both CoFW and RoW, for example, can be used to protect against a large number of potential failure scenarios, but *both* become effectively useless against, say, the underlying storage suffering a catastrophic disk failure beyond the ability of the volume's RAID system to correct. Equally, CoFA only provides protection against a catastrophic failure in the source storage system *after* full cloning has been completed, and is as vulnerable to such failures while cloning is in progress as CoFW snapshots are. The incomplete nature of the copy is not an issue when we want to recover from individual file deletion or even some forms of corruption, but it doesn't protect against situations where the original data is irretrievably destroyed at a layer below the filesystem, and so should serve as a constant caution against focusing all of the data protection resources into snapshots only. An infinite number of snapshots provide zero data protection in a situation where they reside on the same array as the original storage, require the original storage to exist, and that original storage is lost.

The on-platform nature of snapshots introduces additional risk into the data protection environment; destructive software attacks are becoming more sophisticated, and it is not unreasonable to assume viruses could be readily established to seek out control software for storage arrays (particularly from popular vendors) and abuse that software, creating the potential for significant data loss. Even more likely: storage platforms are administered, at least at some level, by humans, and humans are susceptible to making mistakes. A lack of sleep caused by illness, a new-born baby or a wild night out on the town could leave a storage administrator fuzzy headed enough to make a terrible mistake—and the history of the IT industry is replete with examples of either malicious employees, or vengeful employees deliberately destroying data. On-platform protection is fast, but by itself can never be considered bullet-proof.

Later in the book we will review further the process of holistic data protection solutions, where a variety of protection functions are employed to absolutely minimize data loss risks.

11.8 Self-Reflection

In Section 11.5 it was noted that as you increase the number of active snapshots against a volume, there will be a corresponding increase in IO/metadata operations as content change on the original volume.

Consider a volume which has had a CoFW snapshot taken at 11am, with some changes subsequently made to the original volume, necessitating original data being copied into the snapshot volume. Now, while the 11am snapshot is still active, a new snapshot is taken at 1pm.

Map the sequence of operations that would be required after the 1pm CoFW snapshot is taken to successfully update content within the original volume without impacting the integrity of either snapshot.

Consider a snapshot policy on a fileserver that sees snapshots taken and kept as follows:

■ Hourly snapshots for 24 hours
■ Daily snapshots for 7 days
■ Weekly snapshots for 4 weeks

What is the maximum number of snapshots that would be present? Assuming an average 2% daily change rate and original storage size of 50 TB allocated, how much storage capacity would need to be reserved for CoFW snapshots to accommodate the change rate and snapshot schedule?

Chapter 12

Backup and Recovery

12.1 Introduction

There was a time where *data protection* was practically synonymous with *backup and recovery*. Still critical in a holistic data protection environment, recovery from backups is increasingly being seen as an action of last resort, particularly for mission critical applications and systems. Like all data protection mechanisms, the usefulness of backup and recovery systems is directly tied to the level of service level agreement (SLA) they can be used to meet. While previous chapters have talked about continuous availability, replication, and snapshots, all of which offer RPOs of zero through to minutes or at most, hours, backup and recovery systems are more likely to offer RPOs of potentially a day or more. However, while these other systems are mainly deployed for short-term retention purposes (measured in periods of "none," and seconds to days), backup and recovery services both short-term retention (in some environments as short as a day) and longer retention periods that may be measured in months, years, or even decades.

In Chapter 5, we introduced the concept of the *FARR Model* for data protection, comprising of:

- Fault tolerance
- Availability
- Redundancy
- Recoverability

While each of fault tolerance, availability, and redundancy are focused on preventing a situation where data is lost, backup and recovery more so than any other data protection technology is primarily focused on the *recoverability* requirement in the FARR model—i.e., the purpose of a backup and recovery system is, in fact, to deal with situations where the original data *has* been lost.

For the average business, a backup and recovery system represents the most pervasive data protection option that will

be deployed. Replication, snapshots, and continuous availability are typically focused on mission critical or business-essential systems (or compliance regulated systems), while backup and recovery systems might interact with as much as 100% of the systems in an environment—far more systems than end users might be aware of.

Many businesses make the mistake of assuming that because they've purchased and deployed enterprise backup software that they have a *recovery system*. Yet, as touched on earlier, data protection isn't solely about technology, it's about people, processes, documentation, and training. Software may allow a company to make the journey, but its installation is only the first step toward a backup and recovery *system*.

Before we go too far with backup, we have to stop to consider what a backup actually *is*. We will use the following definition:

> *A backup is a copy of data that can be used to recover or otherwise reconstruct the data as required.*

Note the key word there is *copy*, which differentiates backup completely from an archive. The process of archiving refers to *moving* an instance of data from one location to another. Backup revolves around making one or more additional copies of the data so that we can get the data back if necessary—further proof of its purpose as a *reactive* form of data protection.

12.2 Backup and Recovery Concepts

Backup and recovery have evolved substantially since it was first thought of in IT. As technologies, infrastructure approaches, and data localities have changed, so too has backup and recovery needed to evolve. Understanding the key concepts within backup and recovery is fundamental to understanding how backup and recovery fits into a data protection strategy.

12.2.1 Host Nomenclature

When describing a backup environment, the following terms are used to describe the hosts within it:

> *Server*: The backup server or *master** server, which is responsible for the scheduling of backups, coordination of recoveries, management of media, processing of indices, and being the repository of the backup configuration and/or service catalogs.
>
> *Client*: Any host protected by the backup server. This will usually include many or even all of the machines that would be referred to as *servers* in normal infrastructure classifications such as fileservers, mail servers, database servers, and so on.
>
> *Media server or storage node*: A host that exists between the client and the server to offload some of the processing, but still under the control and direction of the backup server. It may perform backup and recovery operations solely for itself *or* for a variety of clients.

Additionally, we should consider two more host types that have become increasingly prevalent in backup and recovery systems:

> *Purpose-built backup appliance (PBBA)*: A "black box" appliance directly targeted at providing backup storage. This will have some array-like characteristics, but also other options that are highly suited to backup, such as deduplication or back-end tape-out functionality. While many arrays can be used for backup purposes, PBBAs will be systems that are designed from the ground up for backup and recovery workloads, not primary data storage or access.
>
> *Integrated data protection appliance (IDPA)*: This will be a PBBA with additional features that allow it to operate more effectively within a data protection environment, extending backup and recovery functionality beyond traditional enterprise systems.

Such a system might offer plugins that allow specific workloads to interact with it (e.g., databases and virtual machine hypervisors) without need for backup software, or may offer an entire backup/recovery software stack as part of the overall appliance. As this is a relatively new extension to the PBBA, we should expect to see more functions evolve over time into these enhanced appliances.

There is benefit in briefly considering *what makes an appliance*? For some, an appliance is a single enclosed unit with a single software stack running from the operating system all the way up to and including the application layer. However, this is a somewhat limited definition when considering more complex functionality such as backup and recovery. After all, few "appliances" are released where the vendor has actually produced the entire software stack: i.e., the *operating system* as well as the application layer. Arguably therefore, an "appliance" that does not come with a purpose-built operating system is no different from an "appliance" that starts with a hypervisor.

In this, we look to converged, and hyperconverged infrastructure for more details. These systems are designed to provide an "infrastructure appliance" experience: minimal setup, high integration, and seamless upgrade processes. A business investing in hyperconverged systems does not worry about patching the network cards in a hyperconverged server; instead, the *entire* server is patched as a consolidated activity: system firmware, hypervisor and management software, all as a consolidated entity.

As such as we can consider backup appliances similarly; if the system is designed for a specific function (backup and recovery) and treated as an atomic unit for the purpose of management and maintenance, it *is* an appliance. Thus, there is no difference between say, a single two rack units (2RU) server running a base operating system (e.g., Linux) with a software stack on it, and a 2RU server running a hypervisor with guest systems when they are both patched and upgraded atomically.

12.2.2 Backup Topology

12.2.2.1 Decentralized

A decentralized backup environment is one where each host backs up its own data to backup devices that are directly attached to it. If a commercial backup product is involved, then typically each host within the environment is its own backup server, being entirely self-contained for operations and management. This is a backup model more commonly found in small businesses that have grown from 1 or 2 servers to maybe 10 to 20 at most, and usually all physical. In these environments,

---

* Though use of *master/slave* terminology in IT should be discouraged, wherever possible.

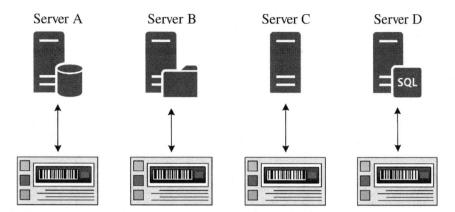

Server A   Server B   Server C   Server D

Figure 12.1 Decentralized backup topology.

backups are usually considered as an afterthought following system purchase, resulting in the perceived need for stand-alone backup storage for each system. A decentralized backup system might resemble that shown in Figure 12.1.

While smaller IT environments may see decentralized backups as having the benefit of reducing the number of dependencies each host has for recovery, their disadvantages quickly stack up, and they are unable to scale as the number of hosts and applications within an environment increases. Key disadvantages of a decentralized backup environment include the following:

- *Cost*: Unless backup and recovery software being used is free, it will invariably be the case that a single server license and multiple client licenses will be cheaper than a multitude of stand-alone server licenses. (Similarly, centralizing whatever protection storage is used will inevitably create cost optimizations.)
- *Storage inefficiency*: Attaching dedicated backup storage to each host will result in backup storage inefficiency. Consider, for instance, if tape is used as the backup medium: the backup of five servers concurrently will require the use of at least five tapes, when in actual fact under a centralized model all five servers might comfortably fit onto a single tape.
- *Reporting*: Any reporting will be on a per-host basis, making it very difficult for a business to readily understand its data protection status.
- *Configuration complexity*: While a single product protecting a single server may sound less complex to configure than an enterprise backup product, this only lasts until configuration changes across many servers have to be implemented. With enterprise backup software, changing the backup time for, say, 20 hosts could be as simple as changing one field in one resource. For a decentralized backup environment, this would involve in accessing the backup configuration on 20 hosts one after the other and making the same change. This will

not only be time-consuming, but will also introduce greater risk of configuration mismatches.
- *Media handling*: As the amount of media increases within an environment, the handling and storing costs (both human and physical) will also increase. (In fact, if media handling is not seen as an issue, it can be because the backup media is never replaced.)
- *Virtualization*: Such a topology does not lend itself well to working in virtualized environments, particularly if any form of removable media is to be used.

12.2.2.2 Centralized

A centralized backup topology, as shown in Figure 12.2, reduces infrastructure requirements, configuration requirements, operational management, and costs by having multiple hosts backup via a dedicated backup server. (We will discuss various aspects of traffic control and architectural tiers in coming sections.) The key aspect of a centralized backup topology is the logical separation between metadata and control traffic, and the actual backup/recovery traffic. Backup traffic could flow over a variety of channels, including TCP/IP, fiber, and even via direct connections. This separation of control-related communications and backup data allows for a flexible, distributed arrangement of hosts and systems to be protected, while still being centrally controlled. Note that in the diagram a single PBBA has been shown as the backup target, but this is not essential in a centralized backup topology: the key defining requirement is that a single backup server coordinates and controls the backup and recovery operations for anywhere from a few to potentially thousands of systems.

Some of the advantages of centralized backup topologies include:

- *Infrastructure efficiency*: In an enterprise environment, backup storage requirements can quickly grow to outpace the capacity of the systems they are

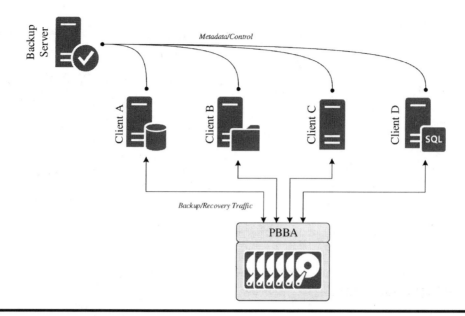

Figure 12.2 Centralized backup topology.

protecting as a number of historical copies are kept. Centralizing backup storage into fewer locations (or even a single one) allows for greater storage efficiencies. Larger storage pools allow for better deduplication rates, reducing storage footprints while still protecting the same amount of backups (and often more). If removable media is still used, management becomes easier, and it will cost less to increase capacity compared to using removable media in a decentralized model.

■ *Workforce consolidation*: Regardless of whether administrators for a backup environment are dedicated solely to that or to a mix of data protection and other infrastructure, a centralized approach to backup allows for more efficient staffing and greater levels of knowledge among the staff responsible for backup and recovery systems.

■ *More flexible recovery models*: With centralized systems, more recoveries can be facilitated from online media (disk or tape), allowing a broader spread of employees to participate in the recovery process. Thus, instead of being an activity only performed by a backup administrator, recoveries could more readily be executed by system and virtualization administrators, application administrators, help desk staff, or even end users. With cloud-based approaches to IT requiring greater attention to "self-service" models, flexible recoveries are becoming increasingly important. (In a large-scale disaster recovery operation, eliminating bottleneck of a single employee performing all recoveries is a critical design requirement.) Additionally, centralized backup services typically increase the ease at which data from one host may be recovered to another.

■ *Ease of configuration*: Since all configurations are controlled from a single source, it becomes easier for data protection administrators to adjust and review that configuration, and configuration changes become more efficient at scale by reducing the amount of effort required to alter the backup characteristics of larger numbers of hosts.

■ *Reporting*: A single centralized system can give more advanced reports and statistics on data growth over the entire environment with less need for manual collation or merger of reports generated from a multitude of individual, decentralized systems.

12.2.2.3 Hybrid/Modular Topology

Mission critical applications can introduce a challenge in enterprise backup and recovery. Businesses want the application backups to be integrated into a centralized system, but equally recognize the importance of keeping control of the backup process within the applications and/or separate enterprise job scheduling systems that can accommodate arbitrary job dependency processing.

The "classic" solution to this dichotomy has been to provision additional storage for application administrators so that they can control their application backups and write them to system storage (directly attached or mapped from a SAN/NAS), with those backups then swept up by standard filesystem backup agents. Such a model is easy, but not cheap—the storage provisioned is usually expensive primary tier storage similar to the performance characteristics of the databases, and administrators will usually request sufficient storage to hold multiple full backups of their applications. (If not given this space, database administrators (DBAs) may instead compress their backups on disk, either during or after the backup. If compressed during the backup, this will slow the backup process down, and if compressed *after,* this may compromise system performance. Additionally, large compressed files may cause flow-on challenges within the backup environment, particularly if deduplication storage systems are used.

This is usually due to the lack of integration between the application backups and the system backups—application administrators will want at least a few of the most recent backups online and accessible to meet tight RPO/RTO SLAs rather than having to resort to a two-stage recovery where application backup files are first retrieved from the backup storage and then recovered into the application. Thus, a 1 TB database might require up to 10 TB of similar storage attached to the database server for fast recovery from online backups.

Advanced PBBAs with independent software options, and full IDPAs have allowed for an efficient hybridization of the centralized/decentralized topologies while allowing both data protection administrators and application administrators to retain control over their respective processes. Figure 12.3 shows an example of a hybrid model using an IDPA.

In such a model, the data protection storage becomes a centralization locus. The backup and recovery system should still be a largely centralized environment (with even the application and database servers performing filesystem and OS layer backups to the system), which allows for continued efficient management of much of the data protection strategy for the environment. In addition, the key application and/or database servers can work closely with an integrated backup appliance via plug-ins to their native backup and recovery tools, directly controlling and administering the backup process while sharing data protection storage with the rest of the backup and recovery environment. This can substantially reduce storage costs for mission critical systems by eliminating high-tier/primary storage directly attached to the application and database servers just for the purpose of backup, while still ensuring the applications receive the highly granular backup controls required by the business. Where source-based deduplication (a topic we will discuss in Chapter 13) is used, this can also result in significant bandwidth savings compared to a "dump to disk" approach, either during the initial dump (e.g., to a NAS system), or during the subsequent backup.

Modular backup topologies are similar to hybrid approaches—a mix of centralized and decentralized controls—but allow for lifecycle protection SLAs to be established, even for those decentralized elements. For instance, DBAs might be given full autonomy over the execution of their backups, allowing them to schedule them from within their own control systems. However, to ensure that backups are compliant to the business operational and legal requirements, data protection administrators might establish policies such as:

- At all times there are to be 30 online backups, all with copies, for all systems tagged "silver," "gold," and "platinum."
- Backups may not be run more than four times a day, unless a system is tagged as a "gold" or "platinum" system.
- Backups for systems tagged "test" and "dev" must be automatically expired at no older than 14 days.
- New systems may register with the service if they meet certain criteria.
- Capacity quotas may be established. These allow the administrators of the protection storage to set limits on the amount of backup data that can be sent in say, a 24-hour period, or even in total for the accessing environment. Quotas might be "soft" (e.g., simply triggering an alert, but allowing writes to continue), or "hard" (generating a write failure).

While the goal of data protection systems design was originally oriented toward the centralized model, both hybrid and

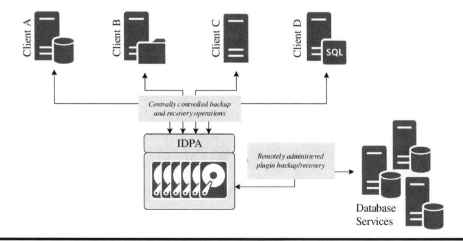

Figure 12.3 Hybrid backup topology.

modular topologies suit the ongoing growth of data within most organizations. Perhaps most importantly, the nature of these models allow subject matter experts (SMEs) (e.g., virtualization administrators and DBAs) to exert high levels of control if required over backup and recovery services for their workloads, without compromising infrastructural efficiency and compliance for the business. More so, in order to properly function as a modular or hybrid topology, a solution will ensure those SMEs can interface with the backup and recovery system from their own native tools, rather than having to learn additional products. (For example, VMware administrators might access backup and recovery functionality directly from the vSphere Web Interface, Oracle administrators would access via RMAN*, SQL Server administrators from T-SQL/SQL Server Management Studio, etc.)

12.2.2.4 Embedded Topology

This is an extension of the hybrid approach and will leverage service portal design. In such an environment, while SMEs may interact with some operations via native interfaces (e.g., performing a Microsoft SQL database recovery through SQL Server Management Studio), the goal will be to encapsulate as many configuration and operational functions *after* the initial setup within the control portals. This is sometimes referred to as "day-2 use," referring to actions performed by users of the portal, rather than "day-1 activities," referring to actions taken by infrastructure administrators to configure, then integrate systems into a portal.

This type of topology can result in configurations, for instance, where someone uses a private cloud interface to provision a new virtual machine and backup and recovery services are automatically added, or in even more integrated solutions, ticketing/management portals such as ServiceNow could see actions initiated as soon as they're requested or authorized within a service request system.

12.2.3 Backup Levels

Each time a backup is performed, data is transferred from the client storage to the data protection storage. Exactly how much data is transferred is first and foremost determined by the backup *level*. While a backup will also have some type of content selection associated with it (e.g., "all local filesystems" or "database named PROD"), the level will determine how much of the selected data set is backed up as part of any operation.

12.2.3.1 Full Backups

Full backups transfer all of the selected data set from the source to the data protection storage, regardless of how

recently it has been backed up. Particularly if tape is used, full backups undoubtedly provide the simplest recovery mechanism for businesses, as a recovery operation is a single consolidated read from the backup storage, without the need to use multiple sources generated at different dates or times.

A key requirement of a full backup is that the backup window needs to be large enough to accommodate a complete read of all data on a system for every backup. While this may be acceptable to smaller organizations, it will likely represent a burdensome requirement for many larger enterprises or businesses where data growth is occurring. Indeed, since data growth has continued at a rapid pace for most businesses while backup windows have *shrunk*, it is becoming increasingly common to see businesses try to reduce the number of full backups they need to do.

Advantages of full backups are usually as follows:

- Recovery from a full backup involves a single consolidated read from one backup "set."
- Full backups typically do not have dependencies on one another. That is, the loss of a full backup taken on day 1 will not impact the recoverability of a full backup taken on day 2.

Disadvantages however include the following:

- Without mitigating activities such as snapshots or source-side deduplication, the backup window is the largest for all types of backup levels.
- Without deduplication (source or target), a full backup will use the maximum amount of media possible for the data set per backup—and will have the most cost.

It should be noted that backup products that perform true source-side deduplication, where only unique, never-before-seen data is sent from the client to the server, may have the option of performing full backups daily without the client-side impact typically associated with daily full backups. By utilizing local databases of previously encountered data segments and integrating with operating system tracking for changed files, a source-side deduplication product can scan and process the changed content on a host far faster than a traditional full backup. We will cover such options in Chapter 13, Deduplication.

12.2.3.2 Incremental Backups

An incremental-level backup targets only those files or items that have changed since the last backup (regardless of what level it was).† This often results in considerably smaller

---

* Recovery Manager.

† Some backup products refer to incremental backups as *differential incremental*—i.e., an incremental that consists of the *differences* since the last backup.

backups and can usually be accommodated within a much smaller backup window—though the amount of data backed up may not always have a 1:1 relationship with the elapsed time.

At a filesystem level, incremental backups look for files that have changed or been added since the last backup. However, they do not apply just to filesystem backups: databases, complex applications, virtual machines, and so on all leverage some form of incremental backup technology. A 50 TB database, for instance, may have only a 2–5% change rate during the course of a day, and in the same spirit as filesystem backups, incremental database backups will allow these changes to be captured and backed up, then integrated with a prior full backup for restoration purposes if required.

Introducing incrementals into a backup strategy will often result in a backup configuration such as that shown in Tables 12.1 and 12.2.

It's worth noting that a common configuration "default" in many organizations using fulls and incrementals is to run the full backup for *everything* on the same day. Unless source-side deduplication is used, this can result in a significant peak

in terms of the amount of backup traffic generated in a single 24-hour period. (Bear in mind that the incremental backup for any individual system will quite often be 5% or less of the total data volume for that system.)

Figure 12.4 shows a change chart for different backup levels and their relationship to one another. In this case, a weekly full with daily incrementals is shown.

In Figure 12.4, the full backup is a vertical line stretching the height of the diagram. The horizontal axis represents time—the days on which the backups are executed. Each incremental backup is shown pointing *back* to the backup taken on the day before it, which indicates it only processes the data that has changed since the last backup.

Some companies subscribe to a 5×9-operations-style backup methodology where backups are not executed on the weekend—the rationale being that users are not typically making modifications to systems. This is almost invariably a false economy, and even more so unaligned to an increasingly 24 × 7 environment. Systems may automatically patch on weekends, and backups should definitely be taken before and after these. Mobile users are more likely than ever before to be checking and sending emails on the weekend,

Table 12.1 Weekly Full Backups with Daily Incrementals

Saturday	Sunday	Monday	Tuesday	Wednesday	Thursday	Friday
Full	Incr	Incr	Incr	Incr	Incr	Incr

Table 12.2 Monthly Full Backups with Daily Incrementals

Saturday	Sunday	Monday	Tuesday	Wednesday	Thursday	Friday
1/Full	2/Incr	3/Incr	4/Incr	5/Incr	6/Incr	7/Incr
8/Incr	9/Incr	10/Incr	11/Incr	12/Incr	13/Incr	14/Incr
15/Incr	16/Incr	17/Incr	18/Incr	19/Incr	20/Incr	21/Incr
22/Incr	23/Incr	24/Incr	25/Incr	26/Incr	27/Incr	28/Incr
29/Incr	30/Incr	31/Incr				

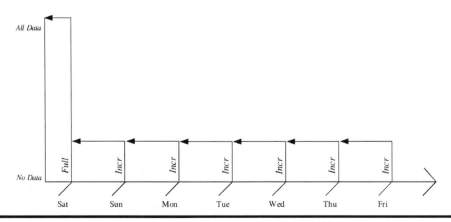

Figure 12.4 Backup change chart for a weekly full/daily incremental cycle.

and even if no users *are* accessing a system over a weekend, backups can still be used to provide recoverability in the event of corruption or data deletion by rogue processes or applications. This leads us to an essential rule of backup and recovery:

> *It is always better to backup a little more than is needed than not enough.*

The advantages of incremental backups include the following:

■ Less backup media or storage is used per backup job as only content that has changed since the last backup is copied. By implication, a backup regime combining full and incremental backups will use considerably less media than a backup regime where only full backups are performed over the same period of time.
■ The backup window can be considerably shorter than a full backup. In the (now reasonably) rare event of an outage being needed as part of the backup process, this equally can reduce the length of the outage window.

The disadvantages of incremental backups include the following:

■ Recoveries from a mixed full and incremental regime can require more media changes depending on how many incremental backups have been done since the last full backup (when removable media such as tape is used).
■ Complete recoveries have dependencies—that is, a complete system recovery cannot be done without the full backups and all incremental backups between the full and the failure. If any of these backups are lost or otherwise fail to be read from, the recovery cannot be 100% completed.[*]

12.2.3.3 Differential-Level Backups

A differential backup is one where a series of changes are backed up, possibly covering several days' worth of changes. This "rolls up" multiple changes into a single backup job.[†]

---

[*] It should be noted that some so-called enterprise backup products do not perform adequate dependency checking, and can actually delete full backups—by design—that incrementals still rely on for complete system recoverability.

[†] Some backup products will refer to differential backups as *cumulative incrementals*—i.e., an "incremental" that is the accumulation of all changes since the last full backup.

Arguably differential-level backups are now less frequently used—while they are particularly effective when tape is the primary backup target as a means of reducing the amount of media required for a recovery while still allowing for faster backups, their usefulness in environments that focus on backup-to-disk is quite limited. (This is because in a backup-to-disk environment, particularly one with deduplication used, we would expect to see sufficient backup storage capacity for an entire backup cycle—e.g., full and all contingent incrementals. Since a differential will include content saved in previously performed incremental backups, it will needlessly consume storage in a traditional disk backup environment. While the storage consumption is somewhat mitigated in a deduplication environment, it will still consume additional run-time compared to a standard incremental backup.)

While a differential backup effectively means the same thing for any standard filesystem backup, the meaning can vary quite considerably when differential backups are applied to databases and applications. A database vendor, for instance, might declare a differential backup to be one where all transaction logs since the last backup are backed up and then deleted. Another database vendor might consider a differential backup to be a backup of the appropriate data *and* the transaction logs. In short, when considering differential backups for anything other than a filesystem, read the documentation provided by both the database/application vendor *and* the backup vendor to understand how such a backup will execute and *what* will be backed up.

There are actually two types of differential backups that products might use: simple and multilevel. We will provide an overview of both.

A simple differential backup merely backs up all the changes that have occurred since the most recent full, regardless of what backups have occurred in between. Consider, for instance, a weekly backup regime such as that shown in Table 12.3.

In the backup regime under consideration, a full backup is performed on the Saturday, with incrementals performed Sunday–Tuesday. A differential backup is performed on Wednesday, with incremental backups subsequently performed on Thursday and Friday. We can show this in a backup change graph as per Figure 12.5.

In Figure 12.5 we can see that the first three incrementals simply capture the changes that have occurred since the previous day. The differential backup invoked on the Wednesday however will back up all changes that have occurred since the first full backup.

Sometimes, differentials would be used to replace incremental backups entirely. Thus, at any given day, the only backups required for recovery of a system would be the full backup and the most recent differential. This would resemble a configuration such as that shown in Figure 12.6. In such a configuration, the backups would work as follows:

Table 12.3 Sample Schedule with Weekly Full, Mid-week Differential, and Daily Incremental

Saturday	Sunday	Monday	Tuesday	Wednesday	Thursday	Friday
Full	Incr	Incr	Incr	Diff	Incr	Incr

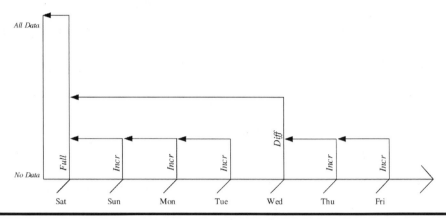

Figure 12.5 Backup change graph for a simple differential level.

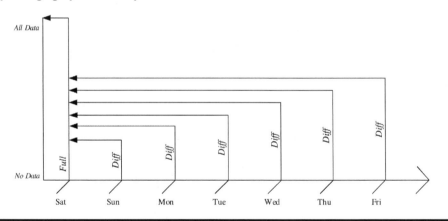

Figure 12.6 Backup change graph for weekly full with daily differentials.

- The full backup on Saturday captures all content.
- The differential on Sunday captures all content changed since the Saturday.
- The differential on Monday captures all content changed since the Saturday.
- The differential on Tuesday captures all content changed since the Saturday.
- *And so on*.

Historically, differential backups were usually integrated into monthly backup cycles—where a full backup is performed only once a month. Such a backup configuration might resemble that shown in Table 12.4.

Such schedules had two key goals:

1. Ensure daily backups take as little time as possible
2. Minimize the number of backup sets/amount of media required for system recovery

To perform a complete system recovery from such a backup configuration, the full backup, the most recent differential backup, and any incremental backups performed since that differential would be required for recovery. For instance, to recover the system on the 27th, *after* its backup, you would need to use

- The full backup taken on the first
- The differential backup taken on the 22nd
- The incremental backups taken on the 23rd through to the 27th inclusive

In addition to simple differential backup levels, some backup products may offer multilevel differentials, allowing additional options. Multilevel differential backups inherit their methodology from old UNIX tools such as "dump" and "restore." Using such methodology, rather than a single "diff" or "differential" backup level, the backup levels available become

Table 12.4   Monthly Backup Schedule with Fulls, Incrementals, and Differentials

Saturday	Sunday	Monday	Tuesday	Wednesday	Thursday	Friday
1/Full	2/Incr	3/Incr	4/Incr	5/Incr	6/Incr	7/Incr
8/Diff	9/Incr	10/Incr	11/Incr	12/Incr	13/Incr	14/Incr
15/Diff	16/Incr	17/Incr	18/Incr	19/Incr	20/Incr	21/Incr
22/Diff	23/Incr	24/Incr	25/Incr	26/Incr	27/Incr	28/Incr
29/Diff	30/Incr	31/Incr				

Table 12.5   Weekly Backup Schedule with Multiple Differential Levels

Saturday	Sunday	Monday	Tuesday	Wednesday	Thursday	Friday
Full	Incr	Diff-5	Incr	Diff-7	Incr	Diff-3

Table 12.6   Quarterly Backup Schedule, Month 1

Saturday	Sunday	Monday	Tuesday	Wednesday	Thursday	Friday
1/Full	2/Incr	3/Incr	4/Incr	5/Incr	6/Incr	7/Incr
8/5	9/Incr	10/Incr	11/Incr	12/Incr	13/Incr	14/Incr
15/5	16/Incr	17/Incr	18/Incr	19/Incr	20/Incr	21/Incr
22/5	23/Incr	24/Incr	25/Incr	26/Incr	27/Incr	28/Incr
29/5	30/Incr	31/Incr				

- Full
- Incremental
- Differential levels 1…9

In this approach, any differential-level *x* backs up all files that have changed since the last full or last lower/equal numbered differential level (whichever was more recent).

In Table 12.5, we see a schedule using three different differential levels. Note that the specific numbers used in the schedule are not as important as their relationship to one another. In the schedule described in Table 12.5, the backups would work as follows:

- A full backup is performed on Saturday.
- An incremental backup is performed on Sunday, backing up all content that has changed since the Saturday full.
- A differential level 5 is performed on Monday, backing up all content that has changed since the Saturday full.
- An incremental backup is performed on Tuesday, backing up all content that has changed since the Monday differential level 5.
- A differential level 7 is performed on Wednesday, backing up all content that has changed since the Monday differential level 5.

- An incremental backup is performed on Thursday, backing up all files and content that has changed since the Wednesday differential level 7.
- A differential level 3 is performed on Friday, backing up all content that has changed since the Saturday full.

Mainly when tape was a primary backup target, multilevel differential backups were seen as quite useful for stretching out the amount of time between full backups (particularly for larger filesystems with a very low change rate) while still attempting to minimize the number of backup sets required to facilitate a complete system recovery. For instance, a multilevel differential backup strategy might be considered for an ad-hoc archive fileserver where full backups are only performed quarterly. Such a strategy might resemble that shown in Tables 12.6 through 12.8.

In such a configuration, a full backup is taken on the first Saturday of the quarter. Incremental backups are done on all weekdays other than Saturdays. On all remaining Saturdays in the month, a level 5 backup is taken. This ensures that on any given day during the first month the only backup sets required for complete system recovery are the full, the most recent level 5 (assuming one has been done), and the

Table 12.7   Quarterly Backup Schedule, Month 2

Saturday	Sunday	Monday	Tuesday	Wednesday	Thursday	Friday
			1/Incr	2/Incr	3/Incr	4/Incr
5/3	6/Incr	7/Incr	8/Incr	9/Incr	10/Incr	11/Incr
12/5	13/Incr	14/Incr	15/Incr	16/Incr	17/Incr	18/Incr
19/5	20/Incr	21/Incr	22/Incr	23/Incr	24/Incr	25/Incr
26/5	27/Incr	28/Incr	29/Incr	30/Incr		

Table 12.8   Quarterly Backup Schedule, Month 3

Saturday	Sunday	Monday	Tuesday	Wednesday	Thursday	Friday
					1/Incr	2/Incr
3/3	4/Incr	5/Incr	6/Incr	7/Incr	8/Incr	9/Incr
10/5	11/Incr	12/Incr	13/Incr	14/Incr	15/Incr	16/Incr
17/5	18/Incr	19/Incr	20/Incr	21/Incr	22/Incr	23/Incr
24/5	25/Incr	26/Incr	27/Incr	28/Incr	29/Incr	30/Incr
31/5						

incrementals done in that given week. On the first Saturday of the second month in the quarter, a level 3 backup is performed. This backs up all content that has changed since the full done at the start of the quarter. Incrementals still occur for all days other than Saturdays, and the remaining Saturdays in the second month all revert to level 5 backups. Thus, at most a complete system recovery in the second month will only be required:

- The full backup
- The level 3 backup
- The most recent level 5 backup
- Any incremental backups that have been performed since the level 5

The third month of the quarter is a repeat of the second month for scheduling. It is only on the first Saturday of the *next* quarter (month 4) that we would see a new full backup generated.

The advantages of differentials are as follows:

- Reduces the number of backup sets that need to be referred to for complete recovery (typically not relevant unless backing up to tape).
- In a tape environment, differentials can *reduce* the risk that a failed tape will prevent complete recoverability (if content has remained static on multiple days, it will appear in multiple differential backups).

The disadvantages of differentials are as follows:

- For filesystem backups in particular, their utility when performing backup-to-disk is limited and may result in unnecessary media consumption (particularly when backing up to disk that does not deduplicate).
- Variably interpreted by database/application vendors.
- Systems where the change rate is large and the content that changes each day may generate very large differential backups by the end of a backup regime.

Multiple-level differentials are decreasing substantially in use (and even availability) as businesses are increasingly shifting toward the disk as a primary backup target. The advantages offered by differentials are mitigated when backups are available at disk speed access levels.

12.2.3.4 Synthetic Full Backups

A common problem in data protection is the amount of time it takes to perform a full backup, not to mention the potential impact to the client from performing a complete read of all its data.

A synthetic full backup approach takes the processing of a full backup away from the client and performs the work wholly within the backup infrastructure. This is achieved by synthesizing a new full backup from a previous full backup and all the incrementals that have been done since that point in time. If we consider a weekly schedule, expressed

Table 12.9 Backup Schedule using Synthetic Fulls

Saturday	Sunday	Monday	Tuesday	Wednesday	Thursday	Friday
Full	Incr	Incr	Incr	Incr	Incr	Incr
Synth	Incr	Incr	Incr	Incr	Incr	Incr
Synth	Incr	Incr	Incr	Incr	Incr	Incr

over multiple weeks, synthetic fulls could be integrated to either eliminate, or reduce the number of actual full backups required, as shown in Table 12.9.

Effectively after the first full backup, subsequent full backups are constructed (synthesized) by simultaneously reading the previous full backup and incremental backups taken since that full backup, and writing a new full backup. This new full backup then becomes the anchor point for the next synthetic full operation.

Many backup products offering synthetic full backups will provide guidance as to whether the synthetic fulls can be carried on indefinitely or whether they should be periodically supplemented with standard full backups—users of synthetic fulls should be certain to follow this guidance to avoid recoverability issues.

The advantages of synthetic full backups include the following:

- Eliminates or at least substantially reduces the need to perform multiple full backups over the lifespan of the system
- Allows for recovery from a recent full regardless of how long it has been since an actual full backup has been performed
- Useful for backing up remote offices over slow links to a central location (providing the first full backup can be performed centrally *or* a trickle* first full backup can be performed)

The disadvantages of synthetic full backups include the following:

- Usually very limited support for databases and complex applications.
- Not supported by all backup products.
- Some backup products will require periodic standard full backups after a certain number of synthetic full backups have been completed.

---

* A "trickle" full backup is where the complete data is slowly copied over a longer cycle than would normally be acceptable for a full backup. This might be as simple as the first full backup taking a week or more to complete (depending on bandwidth), or it might be through a "rolling full," whereby the first full is completed over a series of phased full backups of subsets of the data.

- While synthetic full backups might be executed to provide backups for remote offices over slow links, they do not address the potential recovery slowness that occurs over such a link.

12.2.3.5 Virtual Synthetic Fulls

This is a relatively new backup concept and refers to the capabilities offered by integrated data protection appliances, and advanced deduplicating backup appliances that offer strong levels of integration with particular backup products. In this scenario, the creation of a synthetic full is actually *offloaded* to the data protection storage—the backup service will instruct the protection storage to assemble a new full backup by combining previous backups executed and stored on the system, but will not actually do the data movement itself. Particularly when deduplication storage is used, this allows for high-speed construction of synthetic full backups without needing to *rehydrate* the data during the process.†

Virtual synthetic fulls offer all the advantages of standard synthetic full backups, but with the added advantages of avoiding data rehydration and offloading the data processing from the backup servers or media servers/storage nodes. The disadvantages of virtual synthetic fulls remain the same as the disadvantages for standard synthetic fulls.

12.2.3.6 Manual Backups

Although not technically a backup level, it's often worth differentiating whether a backup product supports manual backups. These are ad-hoc backups initiated by an administrator or end user rather than scheduled from within the backup software.

Manual backups offer an additional level of protection and allow for user extension to the backup product, catering for applications and scenarios the backup vendor was either unable to anticipate or willing to support directly. If manual backups are supported, they should be used carefully since they represent a resource utilization the backup server/services cannot anticipate. For instance, while a backup server might be sized to provide backup and recovery services for, say, 2,000 clients, this might be load balanced in such a way

---

† Data rehydration will be covered in more detail in the chapter on deduplication.

that no more than 200 clients are backed up at any given time. If individual administrators execute too many manual backups concurrently while planned backup jobs are already being executed, this could result in resource exhaustion in the backup server.

The following are the advantages of manual backups:

- Allows for ad-hoc backups to be run on as required, without scheduling
- Allows for extension of the backup system beyond the design of the original backup vendor

The following are the disadvantages of manual backups:

- If misused, may result in resource contention or even exhaustion on the backup server
- May create administrative overheads or maintenance delays if used regularly

12.2.3.7 Skipping Backups

While preventing a backup from running is also not really a backup level, it does play an important part in enterprise backup regimes. This allows administrators to deliberately prevent backups from running at predetermined times/dates. The purpose of such a feature is to avoid a scenario where backups have to be turned off and on manually. For instance, consider a business that wants

- Daily incremental/weekly full backups kept for 6 weeks
- Monthly full backups kept for 13 months

In such a scenario, it wouldn't necessarily make sense to run a full backup in the "daily" sequence on the same day (or even in the same week) as the full backup in the "monthly" sequence. Sensible backup scheduling will allow the daily sequence full to be skipped while the monthly backup full executes, without manual administrative intervention. (Indeed, in backup-to-disk environments, it may even simply be that the same backup is tagged as daily, weekly, and monthly, and it is kept for the longest required retention period.) Being able to facilitate backup skipping is actually an important feature in a backup product—without it, there is increased risk of human error and a requirement for manual intervention.

There are typically two specific approaches to "skip" backup operations:

- The skip option defined as a level, so that it can be inserted into the backup schedule as appropriate
- The skip option defined as a window during which backups cannot run (either globally or on a per backup-set basis)

The advantages of skip backup levels/windows include the following:

- Allows backup schedules to be completely automated, requiring less manual administrator intervention
- Allows non-regular backup downtimes to be scheduled in advance

The disadvantages of skip backup levels/windows include the following:

- The use of skip levels/windows should be documented and understood to prevent risk of data loss in the event of backups not running and a subsequent failure occurring.
- Backup vendors have to make a choice between reporting a skip backup as the last successful backup, or not. There are usually conflicting opinions on how skipped backups should be reported, and administrators should ensure they educate themselves for any specific product how the reporting is handled.

Another potential challenge created by skip levels is when they need to be manually defined for each date versus perpetually recurring options. For instance, while some products might support definitions such as "skip last Friday every month," more ad-hoc skip requirements (e.g., skipping each Easter Sunday) or backup skipping for products that don't support perpetual options can result in administrators bulk-setting these levels for 1 or more years in advance. If these aren't revisited regularly and updated, these may result in unexpected backup behavior.

12.2.3.8 Full Once, Incrementals Forever

While more an overall backup function, this is intimately tied to backup levels and warrants consideration at this point. Defined as a time saving function, a single full backup is generated during the first backup, but following that, all backups are incremental. This is different to synthetic full backups in that no full backup synthesis ever occurs. Instead, products featuring this technology will typically perform some form of media consolidation, whereby expired backups (either in terms of number of versions of data or the time since the backup) are expunged. For tape, this necessitates copying off current/required backups once the percentage of expired backups has reached a particular threshold. For instance, a product might be configured to keep 10 versions of a file. Once the number of files on a tape that are version 11 or higher reaches, say, 35%, the files on the tape that are still current/active are migrated to another tape so that the tape can be recycled.

In a tape-only environment, this can represent a staggering number of units of media being required for full system recovery. For instance—consider a 1 TB fileserver—some files on the fileserver may rarely, if ever, change. If we assume there are enough servers overall within an environment that 1 tape per day is used to perform backups, there will be 365 tapes after a year. Even assuming a relatively high change rate (allowing for 11+ versions to be achieved on 65% of the files), it may be that only a 5:1 media reduction occurs over the course of a year. Therefore, at the end of a year, up to 73 tapes might be required for a complete fileserver restoration.

Particularly in tape-only environments, these backup strategies typically bet on never needing to perform total system restoration, with another data protection or high availability system to perform that function. Consider, for instance, the previous example of 73 tapes (after media consolidation) being required for a complete filesystem restoration. If we assume 3 minutes of load/unload time added to the recovery for each piece of media and another 5 minutes of tape seek time added to the recovery for each piece of media, such a recovery strategy might require an additional 9.7 hours of media handling operations *outside of actual data reading.*

The advantages of an incrementals forever strategy include the following:

- After the first full backup, the backup window will be substantially smaller for all future backups.
- If a deployed backup product doesn't support synthetic full backups, but supports this model, it may allow for a smaller backup window indefinitely, albeit at a price.

The disadvantages of an incrementals forever strategy include the following:

- Even if the model supports databases, database administrators may be extremely reluctant to embrace it, requiring a two-phased backup approach.
- Complete system or complete filesystem recoveries may need to make use of a large number of backup volumes.
- Allowing for media aggregation without disrupting regular backup and recovery operations will require many additional backup devices, and this will continue to increase as the amount of data being protected by the system increases.
- Physical wear and tear on media and devices during larger-scale recoveries may be excessive.

12.2.4 Data Availability

Depending on the type of backup performed, the availability of the data to end users may be affected—or rather, the level of data availability required by the organization will make a profound impact on the type of backup operations that can be performed.

12.2.4.1 Offline Backups

An offline backup is where the data or system that is backed up is unavailable for other uses for the duration of the backup. In database circles, these types of backups are referred to as cold backups.

As is implied by its name, this results in an outage on the data and application(s) using that data and will take as long as the backup takes to complete. This presents obvious disadvantages for 24×7 businesses that cannot be denied. However, in applications or businesses where 24×7 availability is not required, there are some advantages to offline backups, most typically where there are no dedicated IT staff to perform more complex recoveries that may arise from other forms of backup.

Such backups can be cheaper, too. For some enterprise products, database backups will be a licensed feature:* businesses may enact a policy whereby hot/online backups are performed for production databases, but development and test databases requiring backup are instead shutdown.

Offline backups may actually cause performance problems *outside* of the backup window. Many modern enterprise applications, particularly databases, use sophisticated caching techniques to reduce the number of IO operations required, with SAP and Oracle being two such applications. As soon as an application is shut down, any cache it may have been maintaining is typically lost. Indeed, some vendors will strongly recommend against frequent restarts of their applications for cache performance reasons.

The advantages of offline backups include the following:

- Recovery is typically trivial.
- For even complex environments, recoveries can be performed by staff who might otherwise not be application or system administrators when following well-tested instructions.†
- When combined with snapshots, volume replication, and/or clustering, this technique might allow for

---

* For many enterprise backup products, capacity-based licensing is increasingly supplanting feature-based licensing. This allows for more adaptive deployment models where a business is entitled to use most, if not all available functionality of a product, but pays for licenses based on (approximately) the amount of data being protected. Capacity licensing might be calculated on front-end capacity (the size of a full backup of the protected environment) or back-end capacity (the total capacity of all backups that can be stored under the license). Front-end capacity licensing is usually more desirable. Alternately, socket-based licensing is becoming increasingly common in backup software.
† However, it should also be noted that when offline backups are taken of complex applications or databases, there is little flexibility in the recovery options—usually it is limited to just a complete recovery of all data. This effectively limits the practicality of offline backups for many environments.

simpler backups with minimal application downtime by performing the backup against a temporarily shut down and static copy or node.

The disadvantages of offline backups include the following:

- Without snapshots or other expensive techniques, applications that rely on data are unavailable for the duration of the backup.
- Care has to be taken to ensure that all components of the data are unused during backup. (For example, if data resides on multiple filesystems, there must be no changes to *any* of those filesystems during backup for the purposes of consistency.)
- For databases in particular, incremental offline backups are usually not supported—that is, an offline backup will force a new full backup. If the database is only a few gigabytes in size, this may be OK—however, it quickly becomes impractical as the size of the database increases.
- Over time, this model is unlikely to work as the amount of data to be backed up and the business systems availability requirements increase.

12.2.4.2 Online Backups

In an online backup, the data or systems being backed up remain completely available for the duration of the backup. Database administrators will know this form of backup as a *hot* backup.

Online backups can create an impact on the applications or systems they are protecting—the systems will remain available to the users, but will have a performance hit as a result of needing to service regular user functions as well as backup reads. Whether this is noticed by end users will depend on the design of the system, the design of the backup system, the performance characteristics of the system, the amount of processing being performed by the system during backup, and the amount of data to be backed up.

As you may expect, the goal of a well-designed database environment is to be able to perform online backups in such a way that the performance impact of the backup can be absorbed without impacting the operational requirements of the database.

Regular filesystem backups (say, of an operating system disk, user accounts) can be taken in two ways. Feature-rich operating systems with tight backup integration points may offer the ability to perform filesystem snapshots, presenting the snapshots as quiesced point in time copies to the backup application. Other operating systems may offer no such integration, and the backup becomes a risk-based approach: the backup is run at a time when the system is used least frequently. Files that are changed during backup are (ideally)

reported on by the backup application and appropriate steps can be performed to ensure the data is still protected.[*]

Some applications, filesystems, or operating systems may implement exclusive file locking for data being accessed, which can result in files being missed entirely during the backup process, and administrators should understand what options there are to avoid this situation—for example, such systems may get around the problem by offering a read-only point in time snapshot of the filesystem or data to the backup application, as discussed earlier.

Equally requiring understanding are those applications and operating systems that *don't* implement exclusive file locking. While technically these may allow entire databases to be read and backed up while they are open and being actively used, without appropriate consistency restoration processes, the data backed is likely useless for the purposes of recovery.

As even the most basic of systems become required for 24×7 availability, online backups have been becoming the *only* option for many companies. Such organizations can no longer afford to shut an application down for hours for a backup if it means an end customer will refuse to wait or a vital business process is paused for the duration.[†]

The unfortunate relationship between offline and online backups is that while an offline backup possibly represents a significant interruption to service delivery, it represents an extremely streamlined recovery. In particular, depending on the database or application being backed up, online database backups designed for no interruptions to users may require a longer or more complex recovery procedure. (Conversely, it should be noted that granular recovery options from database/application backups usually require the backup to have been done as an online operation.)

The following are the advantages of online backups:

- No outage to end users or customers during the backup process.
- Complex granular recovery for applications and databases typically require an online/hot backup having been done.

The following are the disadvantages of online backups:

- May be more complex to configure and administer.
- For databases, a trained administrator may be more likely to be required as recoveries will not be simple filesystem restores.

---

[*] In such a situation, the most common form of file that changes during a backup will be log files and temporary files. Most system, application, and backup administrators will accept changes occurring during backup to these files, particularly if they can still recover *some* of the file content.

[†] Reporting "the system is currently unavailable" to a customer is usually acknowledged as an informal way of saying "please buy this product or service from one of our competitors."

12.2.4.3 Snapshot Backups

Alluded to previously, a snapshot backup is a point in time backup that allows immediate recovery of a system to the exact time that the backup was initiated. The difference between this and a regular backup is that the snapshot provides the same point in time backup for *all* files, regardless of what time the files are backed up, whereas a conventional hot/online backup will allow the backup of different files at varying times. For example, a backup might see files copied with the following time frames:

- C:\Data\File1.dat—backed up at 22:30
- C:\Data\File2.dat—backed up at 22:32
- C:\Data\File3.dat—backed up at 22:45

The difference between a snapshot backup and a regular online/hot backup is whether or not the files can change during the backup process. In a regular hot/online backup, there is nothing to prevent "File2.dat" from changing during the backup of "File1.dat," or "File1.dat" from changing after it has been backed up but before the backup of the other files have been completed. Indeed, there is nothing potentially stopping "File1.dat" from changing *while* it is being backed up.

In a snapshot backup however, the filesystem instance being backed up is read only and cannot be updated by any processes. This means that *multifile* consistency (indeed, entire filesystem or system consistency) is guaranteed. None of the files in the example will change during the backup process.

The advantages of snapshot backups include the following:

- Allows the easy acquisition of point in time copies of the system for backup purposes.
- Can allow for faster recoveries—mount the snapshot and copy the required files (for individual file recovery) or roll the snapshot back to perform a complete filesystem recovery.
- Depending on the snapshot technology, consider the following:
  - Multiple snapshots can be performed over a short period of time, allowing systems to meet SLAs for minimal data loss that may be otherwise unachievable using standard daily backups.
  - Snapshots might be able to be mounted on alternate hosts, further reducing the load on the client during the backup process.

The disadvantages of snapshot backups include the following:

- Typically require additional volume management software or intelligent disk arrays.

- Require additional disk space (though rarely equal to the disk space being protected, thanks to modern snapshot functionality).
- Snapshot storage has to be the same speed as original disks to minimize the performance impact.
- Coordinating snapshots across multiple hosts (e.g., for clustered services or multi-host database/application servers) can be complicated, and potentially carries a higher risk of successful operation.

12.2.5 Data Selection Types

Backup products fall into two main categories—inclusive or exclusive backups. This refers to how data is selected for backup by the backup agent. Ultimately, remembering the rule that it is always better to backup a little more than not enough, exclusive backup selection models should *always* be favored over inclusive selection models.

12.2.5.1 Inclusive Backups

An inclusive backup is one where a list is populated by the administrator of the data or filesystems that require backup and *only* those items that are explicitly listed will be included in the backup process. For traditional filesystem backups, this might refer to a simple list of the attached filesystems:

- Unix/Linux:
  - /
  - /boot
  - /var
  - /home
- Windows:
  - C:\
  - D:\
  - E:\

Some organizations prefer this type of backup system under the belief that it provides them greater control regarding what data gets backed up. This is a misguided belief founded on false economies: time and time again across almost every company that uses the system this policy incurs data loss.

Most commonly, organizations using this model declare reasoning such as "we won't backup the operating system because it can be reinstalled and the settings reapplied." In most cases, this is not properly thought through. Take an average UNIX environment, for instance. The sequence might include:

- Reinstalling the operating system
- Customizing groups and users who can access the system or reintegrate the host into a global authentication system

- Making amendments to such items as the mail delivery system to suit the organization
- Recreating any printers
- Reinstalling any third-party system administration tools that reside on the operating system area
- Performing any additional security hardening required
- Installing any security certificates, joining corporate domain services, etc.

Depending on the use of the system, the level of customization may be more or less than this list, but there will invariably be some activities that are required on the host after the base operating system has been installed. This level of customization usually exceeds a "short" period of time, even for a well-documented system. Windows systems are not exempt and will have their own issues that sometimes overlap the list mentioned earlier. For example, some backup products perform special backups of key Windows components such as the registry; rather than backing up those base files that comprise the Windows registry, it is necessary to export or snapshot them properly first. These files may therefore not be backed up as part of a "C:\" backup at all, requiring additional special options enabled. A common mistake with inclusive backup policies is to forget about these special components and therefore be unable to perform host disaster recoveries.

As soon as the amount of time taken to customize a machine post-recovery exceeds a very short period of time (e.g., 10 minutes) and has non-automated processes, any perceived advantages of not backing up the operating system are lost.

Consider a situation where the operating system of the machine might represent, say, 4 GB. As the operating system region changes very infrequently, the incremental backups on such a system will have almost no impact on media requirements. It would be reasonable to assume that such an operating system region will have less than 100 MB of changes per day, excepting times where large vendor patches are issued. Plotting a 6-week daily retention backup period, with fulls once per week, we could assume this would require 6×4 GB for full backups and 36×100 MB for incremental backups. This equates to approximately 28 GB (rounded) of additional backup capacity required over a 6-week cycle. If that same system has 200 GB of production data storage requiring backups, with a 5% change rate, the data component of the backup over the same schedule will be 1.52 TB in size. Particularly when considering the growing likelihood of backing up to deduplication storage, the capacity savings of failing to backup operating system and application regions are negligible when compared to the time taken to manually recreate settings (and the risk of forgetting one or more settings).

What this example should show is that in the best case, inclusive backups represent a false economy. Saving a few dollars here and there on backup storage capacity might improve the bottom line negligibly when no recoveries are needed,

but such savings will quickly be forgotten by the business when systems cannot be accessed by even a handful of users.

Inclusive backups, however, represent a considerably worse threat than these—the potential for data loss due to human error. Inclusive backups typically end up in situations where data is stored on filesystems other than what is being backed up or an explicit list of files and filesystems to backup will miss a particular file that is required for easy (or worse, *successful*) recovery. A common mistake in inclusive backups is where an administrator adds a new filesystem to a host and then fails to update the backup criteria for the machine.

> *Inclusive backups invite human error:* A company once had an SAP system whose nightly cold backups had been manually managed via inclusive backups. That is, each filesystem to be backed up was explicitly listed. During a review, it was determined that they had added an additional 2×30 GB filesystems containing SAP database files to the host without including those filesystems in the backup regime.
>
> This error was picked up several *weeks* after the filesystems were added. Although no failure had occurred in that time, the potential for failure was high—the production operations of the *entire* company had been geared around a total dependency on SAP; thus, the complete loss of the SAP system would have resulted in significant productivity outages or perhaps even the failure of the company. Even after being corrected, this left the company exposed to a window of retention where their systems could not be recovered—a potential compliance issue.
>
> What was worse in this situation was the backup product being used normally worked via an *exclusive* file selection model but had been deliberately circumvented to be used as an inclusive backup model.

Inclusive backup policies and products should be strongly discouraged. Further, products that *only* offer inclusive backup strategies should be discarded from any consideration when evaluating enterprise backup software due to data loss potential *built into* the product.

The following is an advantage of inclusive backups:

- None. There are no features of an inclusive backup system that cannot be provided by an appropriately managed exclusive backup system.

The following are the disadvantages of inclusive backups:

- Require manual intervention into the backup configuration any time the host or application configuration changes, making it entirely unable to scale.

■ Data loss can occur, resulting in anything from additional work being required, to job loss or even the collapse of a company dependent on a critical application or system whose backups were wholly inadequate.

12.2.5.2 Exclusive Backups

These are the exact opposite of inclusive backups. Rather than explicitly specifying what should be backed up, only what should *not* be backed up is explicitly defined. The automated selection of what is to be backed up is normally achieved through specifying a special "global" backup selection parameter, such as "All" or "ALL_LOCAL_DRIVES" for "All filesystems." While the parameter will inevitably vary depending on the backup product, the net result is the same—rather than manually specifying individual filesystems to be backed up and adjusting settings whenever more filesystems are added, the one parameter will act as a catch-all.

An exclusive backup product will automatically protect all filesystems attached to a client. Usually this is restricted to filesystems that are "locally" attached to the system—that is, network attached filesystems are not normally included. (As SAN storage is seen as locally attached storage to any applications, they would normally be included automatically by exclusive backup strategies.) If necessary, network attached filesystems could be explicitly added to the backup policy.

Exclusive backup systems are designed using the axiom "better to backup more than not enough" and should be favored at all times over inclusive backup systems. In this sense, exclusive backup products have been clearly designed to maximize data protection, whereas inclusive backup products have been designed to save a few dollars (while introducing massive risk of data loss). A key benefit that exclusive backup systems grant is the reduction in risk for human error when filesystems are added or otherwise changed. The backup system should automatically detect any new filesystems on hosts configured for exclusive backups in the environment and automatically protect them as part of the next backup.*

Users of backup software that works on an inclusive model will usually object to exclusive backups on the grounds "there are things I just don't want to backup." If referring to operating system or application configuration, this can usually be discounted immediately as incorrect. In other examples, there may legitimately be a requirement to avoid some content. An organization might, for instance, want to perform fileserver backups but skip any MP3 file in

a user home directory because of the risk of copyright violation. In such cases, exclusive backups offer a better mechanism than inclusive backups: rather than having to specify everything *other* than the multimedia files to be backed up, as one would have to do in an inclusive system, the exclusive system will allow for specific actions (such as skipping files or directories) to be configured against specific subdirectory locations or known file names/extensions.

The following are the advantages of exclusive backups:

■ Maximizes the potential for the backup environment to provide recoverability of data and systems
■ Reduces the risk of human error or forgetfulness resulting in data loss

The following are the disadvantages of exclusive backups:
■ May require analysis of systems to confirm what, if anything, can safely be excluded from the backup (It should be noted that this would be considered by many to be a standard system administration function regardless.)

12.2.6 Backup Retention Strategies

The way in which a backup product handles the retention of backups directly affects how recoveries work and for how long recoveries can be performed. Because we have stated from the outset that the purpose of a backup is to allow recoveries to be performed if and when required, retention strategies have a direct impact on the quality of the backup product.

There are two broad categories for types of retention strategies within backups: the simple model and the dependency-based model. Although it is the more complex one, the dependency model is the most appropriate to present first, since an appreciation of what it provides goes to demonstrate just how poor and inappropriate the simple model is in a backup environment.

12.2.6.1 Dependency-Based Retention

This model takes the approach that a specified retention period creates dependencies among the individual backups taken for true data protection. For example, consider a schedule with weekly full backups followed by daily incremental backups, and a 6-week retention period. This implies that after a backup is 42 days old, it is no longer required, and we can show the retention periods in relation to the backups in a dependency diagram such as that shown in Figure 12.7.

Dependency-based backup retention models are designed on the principle that one individual backup may provide recoverability for the files and data contained specifically within that backup, but complete restoration of a filesystem

---

* You will note most of the discussion around inclusive versus exclusive backups center on filesystem backups. The ability to detect and automatically protect specific databases will be tied almost exclusively to the APIs offered by database vendors.

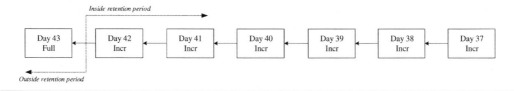

Figure 12.7   Backup dependency chain.

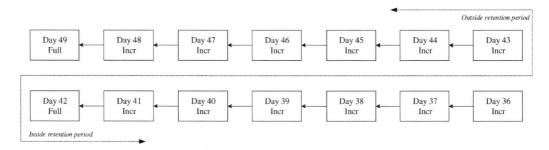

Figure 12.8   Two dependency chains.

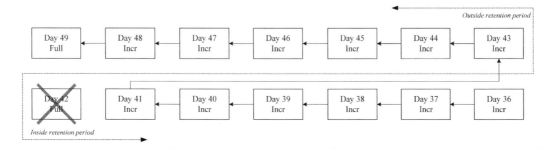

Figure 12.9   Unbroken dependency chain due to failed/unexecuted full backup.

or data will potentially require other backups that *depend* on the backup. Figure 12.7 shows a full backup that is outside the 6-week retention period. The incremental that was taken immediately following the full backup *depends* on the full backup in order to offer complete restoration capabilities. The incremental taken after the *first* incremental requires the first incremental (which in turn requires the full backup) in order to provide complete restoration capabilities.

In such models, even if a backup is *outside* its stated retention policy, it will not become eligible for removal until such time as all backups that *depend on it* for system restoration are equally outside of *their* retention policy. This will usually happen when additional full* backups are generated, breaking dependency chains. An example of this is shown in Figure 12.8.

Thus, we typically consider, in a dependency-based backup retention model, it is not the case that individual backups become eligible for removal, but rather, entire

backup *chains* become eligible for removal once all their links (i.e., individual backups) have exceeded their retention.

Another way to think of this form of retention is that it offers "complete recovery protection"—the backup product is designed to not only allow any individual backup instance to be recovered from but on the basis that the worst-case scenario (complete system restoration) also needs to be achievable right through to the complete configured retention time. If backups must be preserved for legal or auditing reasons, it may mean that dependency-based retention models are the only legally acceptable option in an environment.

Although full backups are *always* important, they become even more important in a dependency-based retention system as they start new dependency chains and allow older ones to become eligible for removal. If a full backup—or for that matter, any backup that would otherwise terminate a dependency chain—fails to execute successfully, then the existing dependency chain must continue to grow. This might in turn result in a dependency chain such as shown in Figure 12.9. In short, if a full backup fails to execute, the backup product must extend the span of the previous full and intervening incremental backups to force the integrity of the backup period set by the administrator. Note that in this instance

---

* Complex dependency chains with partial content removal can be built using differential backup models, but an examination of these is not necessary to understand dependency chains.

we're referring only to a failed full or a full backup that did not run—rather than a backup that successfully ran but was subsequently erased or the media on which it resided failed.

The advantages of dependency-based retention include the following:

- Backups that are outside their retention time are only removed when the system is certain there are no backups still within the retention period that depend on them for complete system recovery.
- Complete system recovery (barring user intervention or media failure) is guaranteed for the entire retention period specified for the backups.

The disadvantage of dependency-based retention includes the following:

- May require more backup media/storage than a simple retention model

12.2.6.2 Simple Retention Model

This is (unfortunately) still a common enough model of how backup retention is handled in some products. In this situation, the retention time specified for backups is viewed only on the basis of recovery from an individual backup.

Take, for instance, the 6-week retention time we've been using in our examples so far. This equates to 42 days of backups. Viewing the backups via the retention window allows us to see what happens to backups that move outside their retention time. In the model shown in Table 12.10, all italicized backups would be immediately considered as available for removal.

This is a retention strategy based solely on false economies. If the full system backup from day 43 is expunged, it means the system as a whole cannot be recovered for a full 6 weeks' worth of backups. Instead, only 5 weeks' (assuming all full backups succeed) worth of backups can be recovered using the full system recover model. Although the incremental backups from days 37 to 42 could still be used to recover individual files, the entire filesystem they provide backups for could not be successfully recovered. This approach in essence hedges its bets on only needing to perform a complete filesystem recovery for the most recent full backups. However, there is a plethora of recovery scenarios that this fails to address.

One of the most common and illogical manifestations of this model is the encouragement for a user to see a separation between the full backup that occurs periodically and the incremental backup that occurs nearly every day. For example, in these types of backup products, users may refer to their "weekly backups" and "daily backups" as being two distinctly different sets. This for the most part tricks the users into believing there is no relationship between, say, a weekly full backup and the daily incrementals. When considering complete system protection, such an idea is farcical.

The following is an advantage of simplistic backup retention:

- None. The perceived media saving is irrelevant when compared to the risk of not being able to recover systems.

The following are disadvantages of simplistic backup retention:

- Does not guarantee full system recovery for the entire retention period specified by the backup administrator
- Often encourages an artificial separation between full and incremental backups at the cost of system recoverability

12.2.6.3 Manual Backups, Revisited

Previously when outlining the various backup levels that might be offered by backup products, we discussed the notion of a manual or ad-hoc backup. For the most part, backup products that calculate retention dependency will avoid factoring manual backups into the dependency chain at all—that is, the dependency chain is typically built on scheduled backups only due to the likelihood of manual backups being for only a subset of a normal, automated backup.

If planning to work with manual backups, be sure to consider the impact this may have on dependencies within the backup system. This should be documented or if not readily discoverable by asking the vendor.

12.3 Recovery Approaches

There are several broad categories in which backup products will offer the means to accomplish recoveries. Not all products will support each strategy, so if looking for a new product, it will be necessary to determine which strategies are

Table 12.10 Removable Backups in a Simple Retention Model

Day 48	Day 47	Day 46	Day 45	Day 44	Day 43	Day 42	Day 41	Day 40	Day 39	Day 38	Day 37
Incr	*Incr*	*Incr*	*Incr*	*Incr*	*Full*	*Incr*	*Incr*	*Incr*	*Incr*	*Incr*	*Incr*

required the most and confirm from backup and recovery vendors which strategies are supported by their products.

12.3.1 Recovery Types

Recovery type refers to how the backup product facilitates recoveries—how files and data that have been backed up may be selected for recovery or recovered without selection. While examples here will be focused on filesystem backups, similar types exist for other forms of backups (e.g., databases). Some variances can exist for virtual machine backups, which will be reviewed in the chapter on Virtualization.

Although multiple recovery types are presented here, there are three that should be considered mandatory for a backup product:

1. *Last filesystem view recovery*: This presents a view of the filesystem as it was as of the last backup.
2. *Point in time recovery*: Although the last filesystem view is arguably the most common recovery that administrators and users will require, for many companies a substantial portion of recoveries will need to be of data that was backed up *prior* to the most recent backup. This option allows a user to step back through previous versions or views of the filesystem, allowing not only the selection of *what* to recover but *when*.
3. *Non-index recovery*: Being able to perform a recovery from an index of files backed up is an obvious requirement, but less obvious is the need to be able to still perform a recovery even if that index has been lost. This allows for emergency recoveries to be initiated immediately rather than having to recover an index first *before* starting the actual recovery.

12.3.1.1 Aggregated Filesystem View

The aggregated filesystem view is almost the logical opposite of the last filesystem recovery view. Not only does the aggregated filesystem view show the filesystem contents as of the last backup, it includes into the view all files from backups between the most recent full backup and the last run backup.

To understand an aggregated filesystem view, let's imagine a backup schedule where the full backup happens on a Friday evening and incremental backups are run Saturday through Thursday evenings. Now consider the following scenario:

■ Full backup occurs on Friday.
■ On Sunday, the directory "/Users/pmdg/Archives/Oldest" is deleted by a scheduled job.
■ On Monday, the file "/Users/pmdg/Desktop/expenses.xls" is created.
■ On Tuesday, the file "/Users/pmdg/Desktop/expenses.xls" is deleted.
■ On Tuesday, the file "/Users/pmdg/Desktop/Letter.pages" is created.
■ On Wednesday, the "/Users" directory is accidentally deleted and needs to be recovered.

If a recovery agent using an aggregated filesystem view is used to recover on Wednesday morning, it will show both the "/Users/pmdg/Archives/Oldest" directory and the "/Users/pmdg/Desktop/expenses.xls" files, even though neither of these existed as of the most recent backup performed.

Although this model may initially appear to provide a good recovery mechanism, its advantages are outweighed by its disadvantages.

The advantages of an aggregated filesystem view include the following:

■ Presents all files backed up since the last full (typically). This reduces the need to alter the point in time the recovery is browsed for.
■ Provides an easy mechanism to recover from successive days' worth of accidental or malicious data deletion.

The disadvantages of an aggregated filesystem recovery view include the following:

■ May cause a security or compliance incident. If a deletion was intentional due to security or legal considerations, the recovery operator will have no visibility over this needing to be repeated following the recovery or to exclude the file(s) from recovery.
■ Depending on the amount of data deleted intentionally, this model can result in a situation where the recovery fills up the target filesystem as older, intentionally deleted data is restored.
■ Following from the above, such recoveries may even cause compliance issues, by making it easier to restore data that had been deleted due to privacy, fiduciary or legal reasons.
■ Results in "messy" filesystems at the end of the recovery process.
■ Users may be confused by previous versions of files and directories appearing—this may even result in data loss situations by users or administrators deleting newer content accidentally in favor of older content.
■ If between successive backups files and directories have been moved around, this may result in data duplication following a recovery.

12.3.1.2 Last Filesystem View

This recovery variant only shows the files and directory structure that was present as of the last backup. That is, it assumes that deletions performed *between* backups are actually intentional and the desire is to return the filesystem as close as possible to what it was at the time of the failure.

In our previous example, we considered the following scenario:

- Full backup occurs on Friday.
- On Sunday, the directory "/Users/pmdg/Archives/ Oldest" is deleted by a scheduled job.
- On Monday, the file "/Users/pmdg/Desktop/expenses. xls" is created.
- On Tuesday, the file "/Users/pmdg/Desktop/expenses. xls" is deleted.
- On Tuesday, the file "/Users/pmdg/Desktop/Letter. pages" is created.
- On Wednesday, the "/Users" directory is accidentally deleted and needs to be recovered.

As discussed previously, the aggregated filesystem view would show those files that had been deleted prior to the Tuesday night backup on Wednesday morning, potentially allowing an operator to recover a logically inconsistent filesystem or even an overfull one.

For the last filesystem view, we literally only see the files/ directories present on the filesystem as of the last backup. Assuming a Tuesday night backup from our previous example, we would not see "/Users/pmdg/Archives/Oldest" (deleted on Sunday) and "/Users/pmdg/Desktop/expenses. xls" (deleted on Tuesday).

The advantages of the last filesystem recovery view include the following:

- Shows the filesystem as of the last backup performed. This allows recovery operators to very quickly retrieve the system state as of the last backup.
- When attempting to return a filesystem to its most recent state, it provides the most logically consistent view.

The disadvantages of the last filesystem recovery view include the following:

- Effectively requires point in time recoveries (see the following texts) in order to recover data that was deleted *prior* to the most recent backup
- May require multiple recoveries, or at least, simultaneous recoveries from multiple backup sets if data loss has been gradual

While disadvantages are mentioned earlier, it should be noted that these are *entirely* outweighed by the utility and practicality of the advantages.

12.3.1.3 Point in Time Recoveries

Point in time recoveries extend the notion of a "last filesystem view" recovery model to show a view of the filesystem as of a backup taken at a specific point in time. Examples of the usefulness of this model include the following:

- Over a series of days, a user makes a significant number of changes to a document that will be too difficult to back out of; hence, referring to the most recent backup or backups will not be useful for recovery purposes— the user will require document recovery from one or more backups past.
- Taxation lawyers request a copy of the company banking database from the closure of the previous financial year.
- A user working on a document leaves their terminal session logged on with the application running while on vacation for a few days. Unfortunately, during this time, the application crashed, leaving the document automatically saved with 0 bytes on disk. When the user returns from vacation and discovers the document "empty," a recovery from several days prior is required.
- Database administrator requests a copy of the database from a month ago to be recovered onto another server to complete last month's reporting.

In all of these examples, the goal is not to recover the most recent data backed up, but data that was backed up at some point in the past.

Point in time recoveries prove the need for backup duplication. In a later topic, we'll discuss backup duplication, which refers to generating a "backup of the backup." Some organizations insist they do not need to perform backup duplication if they backup to a remote site (e.g., protection storage in the disaster recovery site attached via high-speed networking). Point in time recoveries clearly show this to be a false statement: in the event of a loss of the disaster recovery site, although the current production data is undamaged, all file history has (conceivably) been lost.

Point in time recoveries prove that snapshots are not backups. Some will try to insist that implementing snapshots into an environment means customers never need to run another backup. However, it is neither technically nor financially feasible for almost any business to retain a sufficient number of snapshots to provide point in time recovery capabilities over the entire expected lifespan of a backup. For instance, most financial data needs to be kept for at least 7 years. The performance implications and financial cost of sufficient storage to maintain 7 years' worth of regularly executed snapshots will be very large compared to a comprehensive data protection solution. (In addition to the level of vendor lock-in this causes.)

The advantages of point in time recoveries are as follows:

- They allow prior system or data states to be recovered at any point a backup was done within the retention period rather than the most recent backup only.
- They facilitate audits and legal/tax obligations in many companies through the recovery of older records.
- They allow previously executed processing (or missed processing) to be rerun by recovering older data to alternate systems for replay without impacting or overwriting current live production data.

There are no disadvantages in a backup product supporting point in time recoveries; they are an essential aspect of data protection functionality.

12.3.1.4 Destructive Recoveries

Although a destructive recovery may sound like a contradiction in terms, what it refers to is completely replacing the contents of a filesystem, entire host, or database with that which is being recovered, thereby deleting files or data that were not present at the time of the backup. (Destructive recoveries may also be referred to as *overwrite* recoveries.)

There are two types of destructive recovery. The first is where, on a file-by-file basis, files or data that were not present at the time of the backup are deleted as the recovery progresses. The second type leverages restoration from block- or image-level backups rather than file-level backups to overwrite the filesystem completely. (We'll discuss block-level backups at a later point.)

The advantages of destructive recoveries are as follows:

- If an external agent has introduced corruption to a system, a destructive recovery may be seen as an appropriate mechanism to bring the system back to a usable state.
- If a block-level backup has been performed due to filesystem density, this may allow a recovery to be performed orders of magnitude faster than a conventional file-by-file recovery.
- When combined with a point in time recovery, a destructive recovery may provide increased coherence in the recovered system by removing files from a more recent time to the recovery.

The only effective disadvantage of destructive recoveries is as follows:

As implied by its name, a destructive recovery could result in significant data loss if not used correctly.

12.3.1.5 Non-Indexed Recovery

So far we've primarily discussed recoveries that are performed via a "browse" of the filesystem or data to be recovered.

Across almost all backup products, the indices that must be maintained for a per-file view of the backup can grow to a very large size. Additionally, indices may become corrupt or get accidentally deleted. Further, in the event of a disaster, it may be necessary to initiate a data recovery immediately due to SLA reasons, even *before* the index is available. (Additionally, some backups might even be generated with the index information deliberately turned off—for example, a "closure" backup of a fileserver used explicitly for a project might not have indices generated if it is determined individual file recovery will never be required.)

Most backup products therefore offer the ability to perform a recovery of an entire backup without the need to refer to indices. (Although for the most part this will refer to per-filesystem backups, it may encompass a larger target depending on the circumstances or the product.) That is, everything that was stored as part of an individual backup is recovered, regardless of whether the backup can be browsed on a per-file basis.

Sometimes, administrators may even choose to perform such a recovery even when the indices are available. This is typically chosen when the most recent backup is a full, and the "cost" of selecting all the files in the index for recovery is high. This cost can be perceived as high when there are a very large number of files on a filesystem as the backup product may need to enumerate the file selection process if in an interactive mode. In index-based recoveries, the index must be searched for relevant entries and those entries must be "tagged" for recovery. This requires time, and a tangible data structure must be built and maintained in memory for holding the details of the files to be recovered. This may not seem terribly relevant if waiting less than 10 seconds for file selection to complete, but if tens of millions of files (or more) need to be recovered, this may have a significant impact on the recovery time.

Depending on the backup product, non-index recoveries can also be used where there is physical damage to the backup media (especially for tape), so as to get the backup product to retrieve "as much as possible" of the backup.

The advantages of non-index recoveries include the following:

- Can allow for the recovery of data even if the backup product is itself experiencing data loss or corruption.
- Depending on the product, this may facilitate faster recoveries when there are large numbers (e.g., millions) of files to be recovered.
- Depending on the product, this may facilitate recovering data from faulty media, skipping past soft errors.

The disadvantages of non-index recoveries include the following:

- May result in additional data being recovered than intended, if not filtered correctly.

■ Typically does not "merge" multiple backups (e.g., a full and multiple incrementals) for a complete recovery; instead, each backup that requires recovery needs to be selected and recovered individually. (This may even result in the equivalent of an "aggregate view" recovery being performed.)

12.3.1.6 Incremental Recovery

This refers to a process whereby the backup product incrementally executes the recoveries from the last full to the currently selected backup, including all intervening incremental backups, whether the data is required or not.

While this may appear to be no different from a "last filesystem view" recovery, where this differs is that it performs the recovery without any intelligent mapping to expected directory contents or data that may have changed. For instance, imagine a situation where in 7 days of backups, a 2 GB file has changed each day and is backed up each day. For a last filesystem recovery, point in time recovery or aggregated recovery, recovering the filesystem will result in only the most recent (or most appropriate for point in time recoveries) copy of the file being recovered. For an incremental recovery process, *each* version of the 2 GB file would be recovered, incrementally, starting at the full backup (or the first time it appeared on the filesystem, whichever was more recent). Each copy of the file would be recovered on top of the previous copy of the file until the required version had been recovered. Thus, when recovering a filesystem from a full backup 7 days ago with six incrementals, 14 GB of data would be recovered for a single 2 GB file.

There are no advantages to a backup product offering an incremental recovery strategy, and it should be avoided if present in a product or the product avoided entirely if it defaults to this model.

12.3.2 Recovery Locality

We refer to recovery locality as where recoveries are initiated from, with respect to the backup server, and the host that owns the data being recovered. Depending on the product in use, there may be several locality options available, and this may in turn increase the level of services that can be offered.

12.3.2.1 Local Recovery

A local recovery is one where the client the data was backed up from initiates the recovery, regardless of its network location and where the data it requires may have been backed up to. This could be considered to be a "pull" recovery—the client "pulls" the files and data from backup storage.

This is the simplest form of recovery and allows for end users or system administrators of individual hosts to have control over the recovery process with minimum involvement

from the backup administrators or operators (particularly when recovering from disk).

Note that to support a local recovery strategy properly within the environment—particularly if the end users are not privy to the entire backup system—it will be necessary to configure the hardware and storage capacity of the backup environment to have enough backups online for the majority of recovery requests and automatically notify backup administrators/operators of the need to locate and load offline media to facilitate the recovery if required. This option works best in backup-to-disk environments where media load times and media contention are not architectural concerns.

12.3.2.2 Server-Initiated Recovery

A server-initiated recovery is where the backup server can be used to start a recovery, with the data either being recovered locally to the backup server or pushed out to the client. For that reason, some products will refer to this recovery model as a "push" recovery.

This offers a convenient mechanism for some recoveries, and when it exists as just one among many recovery locality options, it should be seen as a benefit in a backup product. However, products that *only* offer server-initiated recoveries may not scale well for larger environments.

12.3.2.3 Directed Recovery

Directed or remote recoveries are where the administrator or user (if appropriately authorized) can initiate a recovery on one host and recover the data to another host, which in turn may not be the host that the data was originally backed up from. A directed recovery features three different types of clients, which may or may not be the same:

1. *Control client*: The host the recovery program/process is being run from
2. *Source client*: The host whose data is being recovered
3. *Destination client*: The host that will receive the recovered data

(When a backup product supports directed recoveries, it will also typically support local recoveries in that the source, destination, and control clients can all be the same host.)

Directed recoveries allow for considerable flexibility in how recoveries are performed but do require additional security considerations to ensure that the facility isn't abused and data misappropriated. They are particularly useful as the scale of the environment grows—it allows recovery operations to be performed by help desk staff or other non-administrative IT users, and it is actually a fundamental aspect in allowing the backup and recovery system to provide additional functionality into the environment. For instance, a directed recovery could allow a data scientist to recover a production database into a big data environment for processing via a directed recovery, without in any way impacting the performance of the original production database or the workflow of the production database administrators.

An additional form of directed recovery is a *cross-platform* directed recovery. This is where files or data backed up on one type of operating system (e.g., Linux) is recovered onto another operating system (e.g., Windows). Depending on the product and its security model, this may have limited functionality within an environment—while the data itself may be retrievable, access controls, ownership, and so on will not necessarily translate between operating system platforms, even if integrated authentication is used. (Indeed, this may be considered a security flaw in some organizations.)

12.4 Client Impact

Backup products and techniques can also be differentiated based on the level of impact they have on the performance of the client being backed up, which for the purposes of this section we'll refer to as the owner-host—that is, the machine that "owns" the data being backed up. This allows us to separate data ownership from backup ownership since depending on the model used the machine that *owns* the data may not be the machine that *hosts* the data for the purposes of the backup.

12.4.1 Server-Based Backups

In backup parlance, "server-based backups" refer to backups where data is read directly from the owner-host. This is the most common form of backup used in organizations where agent-based backups are deployed. During the process, the owner-host client is responsible for reading its own data and transferring it to the backup server, to an intermediary server or directly to backup media if it has been instructed to do so. Backups of this kind have the strongest impact on the owner-host—in addition to whatever other processing requirements it has during the backup period, it must also read the data and transfer it to the appropriate host or media.

The conceptual view of data flow within a server-based backup process is shown in Figure 12.10. In the figure, we see a metadata/control connection between the client and the backup server. There is a backup agent installed on the client, which the backup server communicates to, and will be responsible for transmitting data to the protection storage (in this case, a PBBA). When a backup request is initiated, the backup agent will coordinate with the appropriate filesystem and/or application processes on the client to request data be read from storage. This data, once read, is received into memory for the backup agent, then sent to the backup storage.

This is the traditional backup model for decentralized- and centralized-via-network backups. For many organizations, server-based backups will be entirely acceptable, though virtualization may require alternate backup techniques, as can environments requiring high-performance guarantees at all times and days.

Server-based backups typically create two additional types of load on an owner-host: (1) CPU and network bandwidth for transfer of data from the owner-host to the backup media/host, and (2) disk IO from reading the data. While server-based backups were the process du jour in largely physical environments, as much of the IT infrastructure of companies has

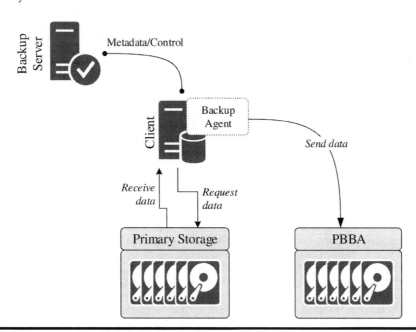

Figure 12.10 Conceptual data flow in a server-based backup process.

moved toward virtualization, the performance impact of such a backup arrangement may not be acceptable. After all: virtualization is about shared access to hardware resources on the basis that each individual system hosted by a hypervisor will only use a small subset of the performance capabilities of the hypervisor. Server-based backups are designed to transfer data from A to B as fast as possible in order to meet SLAs—a hypervisor hosting, say, 10 virtual machines, may have its required workload increased by orders of magnitude if each individual virtual machine starts doing a full backup. (The chapter on virtualization will cover alternatives to this in more detail.)

The advantages of server-based backups are as follows:

■ Simplest backup method—easy to understand. There's a 1:1 mapping between the host that owns the data and the host that transfers the data for backup, making the location of data for recovery simple.
■ Typically, no extra installation or configuration steps are required other than a basic backup agent install and setup to run this type of backup.

The disadvantages of server-based backups are as follows:

■ Backup directly impedes the performance of the host that owns the data.
■ Any outage required for the backup directly impacts the availability of the data being protected.
■ Particularly in virtualized environments, server-based backups may introduce a strain on the virtualization hypervisors beyond their limit and negatively impact the performance of a large number of hosts in the environment.

12.4.2 Serverless Backups

When discussing server-based backups, we introduced the term *owner-host*, which referred to as the machine considered to own the data being backed up. For serverless backups, we must also introduce the term *data-provider*, which refers to the machine that provides storage for data. In a directly attached storage environment, the owner-host and the data-provider will be the same. However, this is increasingly rare in enterprise environments. When virtualization, SAN and NAS are added to the picture, the data-provider may be an entirely different machine or device.

In a traditional backup environment, the owner-host is responsible for the backup of its data. This works for most situations but sometimes isn't appropriate, such as the following:

■ Where the data-provider presents data to multiple operating systems, it may not be possible (or safe) for any one operating system to take responsibility of the data backups—particularly so for NAS systems.

■ Where the owner-host has strict processing availability requirements, it may not be allowed to suffer reduced processing capacity to provide data to the backup process.
■ The owner-host may not be able to provide sufficient performance for the backup process (regardless of its production workload), whereas the data-provider can.
■ The network linked to the owner-host may not be sufficient for a high-speed backup.

We can therefore state that a serverless backup is one where the owner-host suffers minimal impact during the backup process. Note that we don't say such backups are guaranteed to eliminate *all* impact of the backup from the owner-host—in all but the most exceptionally high-performance architected environments, there will still be some impact to the owner-host either before, during, or after the backup.

Several techniques can be used to achieve serverless backups, including but not limited to the following:

■ For NAS devices, one might use the network data management protocol (NDMP), an industry standard backup and data protection protocol developed for systems where conventional operating system agents cannot be installed.
■ For SAN systems, a clone of a volume (or a snapshot of a clone volume, sometimes referred to as a shadow copy—thereby allowing replication to continue to occur) might be mounted on another host for backup processing. Depending on the proximity of the backup media, this may also result in a LAN-free backup. Similar techniques can likewise be used for NAS systems, though NDMP should still be used for the backup process.
■ When IDPAs are used within an environment, this may allow for even more advanced serverless backup techniques where, say, a database backup agent on the owner-host simply *starts* the backup, but then the transfer of data is handled directly between the primary storage and the IDPA. This effectively offloads the entire workload from the data owner. In situations where deduplication and change block tracking are used, this can massively accelerate a backup process.

Depending on the storage technology, backup product, and applications in use, serverless backups may even deliver application-/database-consistent backups through use of journaling and/or continuous data protection techniques.

In Figure 12.11 we see a conceptual data flow of a serverless backup process. (This is effectively a serverless variant of the configuration we had in Figure 12.10.) There is no longer a backup agent installed on the host we are protecting (now labeled *owner-host*). Instead, we have a proxy client

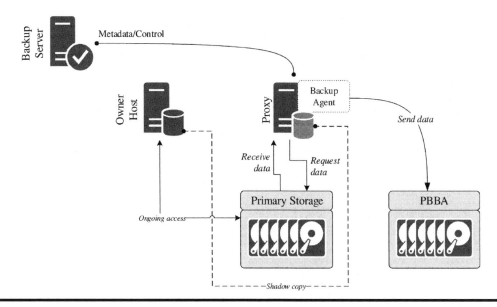

Figure 12.11 Conceptual data flow in a serverless backup process.

with the backup agent software installed on it. When the backup server initiates a backup via the metadata/control connections to the proxy's agent, the proxy mounts a shadow copy of the owner-host data. The reading of the data and transmitting to the PBBA is now performed by the proxy, removing the backup load from the owner-host. (In such a situation where, based on the diagram, we would expect the protected data to be a database, the shadow-copy/mount operation would also invoke appropriate commands to quiesce or ready the database on the primary server for backup, so that the content protected via the proxy can be restored to a consistent state later.)

The advantages of serverless backups include the following:

■ Offloads most of the impact of the backup process from the owner-host (to the point where remaining impact is deemed negligible), which is particularly critical in high-performance environments
■ May deliver higher performance during the backup process
■ Can also be used to achieve LAN-free backups

The disadvantages of serverless backups include the following:

■ Usually more complicated than a traditional server-based backup approach.
■ May require additional recovery steps or processing.
■ If volumes are mounted on alternate hosts for backup purposes, it may require additional documentation in the environment to ensure administrators are aware of *where* they need to look in order to find the data for recovery purposes.

■ May not integrate fully with all applications and/or databases used within an organization.

12.4.3 Convergent Data Protection

While serverless backups effectively require manual integration of the process that leads to a proxy gaining access to a data owner's storage, convergent data protection is an evolution that allows the complete removal of hosts from the data path, regardless of whether they are the data owner or a proxy.

Effectively, convergent data protection requires tight integration between primary and protection storage platforms. In its simplest form, it creates a data flow such as that seen in Figure 12.12.

Convergent data protection is often focused on database systems—simply because they often represent the largest single point data sets that need to be treated atomically within a backup environment. (Databases in the order of tens or even hundreds of terabytes are becoming more common, and even multi-petabyte databases can now be found.) However, convergent data protection can be used for other situations, including protection of extremely dense filesystems, and virtual machines. For the purposes of our discussion, we'll consider a database protection scenario. The process for such a backup may work as follows:

1. Host to be protected initiates a backup.
2. Backup places the database in hot backup mode, or otherwise readies it for a backup.
3. The storage array the database volume(s) are stored on takes a snapshot of the volume(s).
4. The backup finishes from the perspective of the host.

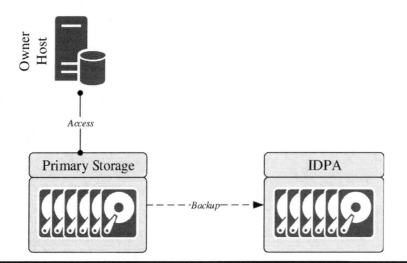

Figure 12.12 Data flow with convergent data protection.

5. At the back-end, on the storage array, for each of the snapshots of volume(s) that provide database storage:
    a. The changed blocks since the last backup are identified.
    b. The blocks are transmitted directly to the protection storage appliance.
    c. The snapshot is released.

In both server-based and serverless backups, the data must flow through a traditional host (e.g., a Linux, Windows, or Unix server), which contributes to the overall amount of time the backup must take.

With convergent data protection however, the backup communication takes place directly between the primary storage on which the data to be protected lives, and the protection storage platform—usually a deduplication appliance. Particularly when a deduplication appliance is used, further efficiency can be gained by leveraging source-based deduplication and changed block tracking to transmit from the primary storage *only* those blocks in the volumes that have changed since the last backup. The deduplication appliance then coordinates the process of converting an incremental block-based backup into a virtual synthetic full of each entire volume that has been backed up.

Such backup mechanisms can also lend themselves to faster recoveries: depending on how the data is stored, it may be possible for the protection storage to present back into the primary storage platform a read/write snapshot of the backup as virtual volumes, allowing a database administrator to mount a copy of the database for testing, copying, or review almost instantaneously, rather than having to recover a large volume of data to spare primary storage.

The advantages of convergent data protection include:

■ Allows for the backup of extremely large data sets that otherwise may be problematic or impossible to provide off-platform protection for

■ Extremely low-impact to server resources
■ Results in a high-performance backup—particularly when combined with source-based deduplication and virtual synthetic fulls

The disadvantages of convergent data protection include:

■ Typically requires primary and protection storage to come from the same vendor (and even then requires confirmation of compatibility).
■ May require additional cache, CPU or memory resources in the primary storage system to handle the backup process.
■ As a niche function, it is not suitable for all data set sizes, and will usually require additional operational processes.
■ Recovery may require the same type of storage platform as the backup was taken from.

12.5 Database Backups

Our earlier discussions on online and offline backups already introduced the concept of hot and cold database backups, respectively. We'll now discuss a few of the additional considerations associated with database backups that businesses and administrators need to take into consideration.

12.5.1 Cold Database Backups

A cold backup is the most primitive database backup that can be performed. Prior to the backup, the database and its associated processes are shut down to ensure no updates take place. The backup system then performs a simple filesystem backup of the client (i.e., database server), which encompasses all the database files.

While this sounds simple enough, we must consider that the process will require some scripting to ensure the database is shut down prior to starting the backup and then restarted immediately following the backup completing. For maximum certainty of backup success, the backup product should shut down the database using a "pre-backup" script and should also restart the database following completion. (In such configurations, it is not uncommon to have a monitoring process that can abort the backup if it takes too long so that users may access the system by a specified time.)

If the shut down and startup sequences are not handled properly and the database is shut down after the backup starts or is restarted while the backup is still running, one of the following may occur:

- *A useless backup may be generated*: Where the filesystems in use don't support exclusive file locking, the backup may continue but the data being backed up will be inconsistent and not be useful for recovery purposes.
- *The database may be corrupted, requiring recovery*: Where filesystems in use perform exclusive file locking, it's entirely possible the backup may have open handles on database files when the database is started. This can result in creating inconsistencies between files as the database processes those files on startup. Typically, such inconsistencies can only be resolved through recovery.

The advantages of cold database backups include the following:

- Complete disaster recovery or total database recovery is very easy and does not normally require intervention from an application or database administrator.
- Results in minimum software and licensing investment and may be particularly cost-effective for the backup of non-production databases where longer outages are deemed acceptable by the business.
- If a database does not support any other backup method without access to snapshot technology (either array or filesystem based), this may be the only way to achieve a backup.

The disadvantages of cold database backups include the following:

- Database is unavailable for the duration of the backup.
- For most databases, using cold backups does not allow for incremental recoveries or point in time recoveries of the database.
- If the startup and shut down sequence for the database is handled incorrectly, it may result in unusable backups or database corruption.

- If the backup repeatedly overruns the required window and is aborted each time, recoverability and any compliance requirements will be impacted.
- Databases frequently perform data caching to improve performance over time. If the database is shut down every night for backups, the benefit of that caching is lost every day.
- Uses the maximum possible protection storage capacity/media as incremental cold backups will always be full backups of the entire database.

12.5.2 Hot and Online Backups

A hot backup refers to keeping a database up and running while the backup is performed. As previously discussed, it's the equivalent of an online backup for filesystems. When a backup product supports a particular database, it usually means it has a module or plug-in agent that allows the database to be backed up while staying available to end users.

There is a subtle difference between the types of hot backups that can be performed. We refer to hot backups as those backups where the database must, in some form, be readied for the backup process. This might set markers in datafiles, or change the way logging is performed. However, not all databases require this, and can be backed up while they're online by virtue of their architecture and the overall setup of the database (though this will not mitigate the requirement to restore consistency to recovered database files). Regardless, the key factor is that the database does not need to be inactive to allow a backup to take place.

If a backup module or plug-in performs the hot backup, the process will typically be as follows:

- Regular filesystem backups occur for the client as per normal but skips over database data files.
- Backup server initiates a special database backup, using an alternate backup command on the database server.
- The command on the database server runs a hot backup, passing data back to the backup server for inclusion with standard backups to disk or tape.

The advantages of hot database backups include the following:

- Database remains online and accessible for duration of the backup.
- Recovery is typically straightforward, as it can be controlled via either the recovery utilities provided by the backup software or the recovery utilities provided by the database vendor. This may even allow recoveries to be performed without an application or database administrator being available if there are suitable "wizards" or automation processes built into the utilities.

- Usually facilitates granular recoveries—for example, for mail servers this may allow the recovery of individual mail items or user mail folders, and for databases this may allow granularity down to the individual table or row.

The disadvantages include the following:

- Depending on the backup product, this may require additional licensing.
- Initial configuration is usually more complex than cold backups—though the benefit usually outweighs such considerations.

An alternate scenario might be database plug-ins that interact with an IDPA, allowing hot backups directly to centralized protection storage while DBAs retain control of the backup process.

12.5.3 Database Export Backup

A database export is typically a series of plain-text commands that can be used to recreate the database content and permissions. For example, the following is a section of a database export from a PostgreSQL database:

```
CREATE TABLE anywebdb_saved_query (id integer DEFAULT nextval('anywebdb_saved_querie
s'::regclass) NOT NULL,
    name character varying(75) NOT NULL,
    "object" character varying(175) NOT NULL,
    username character varying(16) NOT NULL,
    private character(1) NOT NULL,
    query text NOT NULL,
    max_results integer,
    sort_field character varying(32),
    order_by character(1));
    ALTER TABLE public.anywebdb_saved_query OWNER TO pmdg;
```

Unless explicitly stated by the database vendor, you should note the database export may not actually be consistent if the database is being accessed or updated at the time of the export. Before using this backup option, it's important to confirm the database supports hot exports. If they aren't supported, cold backups or cold snapshot backups should be favored instead.

The following are advantages of database export backups:

- If exports are supported while the database is being accessed and there are no other hot backup methods available, this will present a better availability strategy than cold backups.
- This may allow a backup of a database on one operating system (e.g., Windows), with a restore on another platform (e.g., Linux).
- In particular for platform as a service databases running in public cloud, this may be the only way to extract the database in a form that allows it to be copied to an alternate cloud provider, or back on-premises.

The disadvantages of database export backups include the following:

- If hot exports are not supported, exports generated while the database is active may be inconsistent and potentially cause recovery issues.
- An export may take up even more disk space than the original database as an export contains more than

just the content of the database but also the commands required to recreate the database structure. Compressing the export as it is generated may result in significant space savings, but at a cost of high CPU load during the backup, and impact protection media compression or deduplication efficiencies.
- Typically, the export does not contain the instructions to recreate the database itself, merely its internal structure and data. The complexity/time of this task needs to be factored when planning recovery times.
- The export should be scheduled carefully in the same way as cold backups to ensure the resulting export file is properly backed up.
- An export of the database may take longer than a simple copy of the files associated with the database depending on the amount of data in the database.
- Some database vendors have additional requirements to achieve exports where binary large objects are involved.
- The export may not recreate the metadata surrounding the database. For instance, user accounts and passwords might not be exported, requiring these to be manually established prior to any import operation.

12.6 Backup Initiation Methods

Traditionally, there are two primary methods of backup initiation—server and client. While server-initiated backups are a goal for almost all enterprise backup systems, there are some situations where client-initiated backups may be required.

Server-initiated backups refer to the backup server that starts the backups itself for one or more hosts at a designated time. Almost all backup software contains backup scheduling capabilities that allow backups to be started at nominated times. The advantages of server-initiated backups cannot be overstated: they give the backup administrator control over the timings of backups, which directly affects the resources available to the backup server to provide those services. When a backup server initiates the backup process, it should have an accurate understanding of what resources will need to be allocated to allow the backup to complete and an understanding of what resources are *available* based on other activities executing at the time. Furthermore, centralized timing and scheduling of backups are critical in reducing administrative overhead in the backup environment.

Within a traditional backup and recovery architecture, client-initiated backups refer to individual machines running their own backup processes as required—either manually or via automated jobs scheduled to start at particular times from the client side. Having jobs controlled and executed on a per-client basis is a non-scalable solution and will result in resource contention on most backup servers—not to mention making it almost impossible for backup administrators to schedule maintenance activities.

Almost all backup administrators will agree on one thing about backups:

> *If you rely on users to start the backups, the backups won't run.*

For this reason, client-initiated backups should mostly be considered to be a *utility* function only—something useful for situations where administrators need to perform ad-hoc backups, but they should not generally be central to the backup process.

One partial exception to this is in multi-tenant environments with multiple network segments, virtual private networks (VPNs), and/or firewalls. These scenarios may create a situation where the client *must* connect in to the server rather than the server being able to reliably connect *out* to the client. In such a situation, scheduling will still be ideally performed by the backup server—but rather than immediately starting a backup job, the backup server would create a work order. A connecting client will check to see if it has any work orders assigned to it and initiate the required activities. An alternate approach to this is laptop backups where a backup agent automatically looks for the backup server whenever it is connected to a network and performs a backup if it is able to

reach the server. Critical to this is ensuring the user does not need to participate in the backup initiation process.

An alternate methodology for backup initiation is if an organization has batch control processes requiring initiation via a dedicated job scheduling system. In these situations, the job scheduling system should integrate with the backup product sufficiently to trigger backup jobs rather than executing manual backups from individual clients. This can be particularly useful in database backup environments where there are strict conditions placed on when and how a backup is started, making it problematic, if not impossible, for the scheduling to happen solely under the direction of the backup software. For instance, business processes may require that the backup is taken immediately following the completion of overnight batch processing activities, but depending on the data involved, this may take anywhere between 1/2 hour and 3 or 4 hours. Or it may be that the backup for a system can only be initiated after a set of several conditions have been met, each one with dependencies. Such complex scheduling operations are not normally part of the job control capabilities of a backup product and usually require consideration outside of pure data protection activities. When considering externally scheduled backup jobs, it's important to ensure the system workload and resource utilization is balanced in such a way as to allow these externally scheduled jobs to execute without causing instability in the overall data protection environment.

More recently, the development of modular, distributed backup systems that focus on centralized storage with decentralized control by SMEs has disrupted the traditional client- versus server-initiated backup model. These models exist to facilitate remotely initiated backups, but provide a framework to ensure appropriate compliance controls are met, such as:

- *Comprehensive reporting*: There is still a single source of truth for the environment that shows backup and recovery health, statistics, and adherence to compliance.
- *Copy enforcement*: While SMEs control the run-time of the backup, broader policies prevent premature deletion of backups, or enforce a specific number of backups to exist at all times on required protection storage platforms.
- *Storage quotas*: Enforceable limits prevent specific teams from consuming more storage than they should be (e.g., by running more backups than normal, without prior consultation).
- *Mandatory registration*: Rather than allowing SMEs to conduct backup and recovery activities against any particular type of storage, the business may mandate the use of centralized storage, which requires registration. This does not prevent self-service, but rather, ensures the business is aware of protected data.

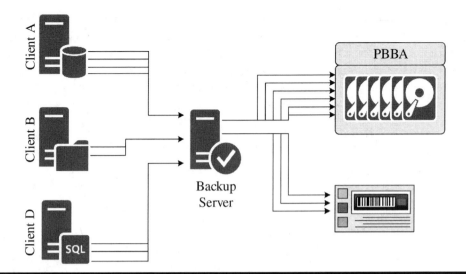

Figure 12.13   High level overview of job concurrency options.

Modular architectural approaches will also quarantine operational versus administrative functionality. SMEs for databases, hypervisors, and other applications will be able to operate their own backup and recoveries, but will not be able to impact backup and recovery operations for other systems (effectively, a form of multi-tenancy, or role-based access controls), and nor will they be able to exert control over broader backup policy, which will be maintained by the actual backup administrators and data protection architects within the organization.

12.7 Job Concurrency

While there are some backup products (most notably in the workgroup/free arena and with niche workload targets) that process all backup jobs one after the other, one of the most common features for enterprise backup technology is the ability to run multiple jobs concurrently. (This may be referred to as *multiplexing, multi streaming, parallelism,* or *concurrency,* among other terms.)

While different products may offer the option to set additional concurrency limits within particular areas of their configuration, the three most common places you can find job concurrency within a backup configuration are:

1. *Server concurrency*: The number of concurrent backup jobs the server will execute or allow to be executing
2. *Client concurrency*: The number of concurrent backup jobs an individual client can send
3. *Device concurrency*: The number of concurrent backup jobs that can be written to an individual backup device.*

Depending on the backup product, server and client concurrency *may* refer to the total number of jobs *or* the total number of backup jobs.†

Figure 12.13 shows these three primary job concurrency options—client A is sending four jobs simultaneously to the backup server, client B is sending two jobs, and client C is sending three jobs to the server. The server is accepting all nine jobs and sending six of the jobs concurrently to a PBBA, while another three jobs are going directly to a tape drive.

Note that this is not representative of what may be the *total* number of concurrent jobs that is configured at any individual point in the environment.

12.7.1 Server Concurrency

Most backup products will support a high level of server concurrency. (It is not unusual, for instance, to see backup servers in enterprise environments designed to accept *thousands* of concurrent jobs.) Due to the scale-out nature of backup environments as a result of either storage nodes/media servers and/or jobs sent directly from clients to IDPAs, server concurrency these days refers more often as not to the number of jobs being *controlled* rather than *passed through* the backup server.

Server concurrency will be primarily dependent on the following three factors:

1. The number of concurrent jobs *all* backup devices in the environment can accept. If the server concurrency is set too low, backup devices may run suboptimally.

---

* Note that device concurrency may also be tied to media multiplexing when using tape. This will be covered in more detail in the chapter on tape.

† Some products will allow recovery sessions to start regardless of the job concurrency limits—an acknowledgment of the primacy of recovery operations. Others will actually reserve a certain number or percentage of the number of concurrent jobs for recovery purposes to ensure recoveries can always be executed.

Conversely, if server concurrency is set too high, the backup server may become overloaded (depending on its processing capabilities) or jobs may become queued for long periods of time waiting for available backup devices.

2. CPU speed and amount of memory available to the backup server. In addition to the CPU/memory requirements for handling the scheduling and execution of jobs and job reports, any data being transferred through the server will require CPU and memory resources as well.
3. Network bandwidth available to the server. Particularly in situations where the backup server is also receiving backup jobs for streaming to devices, the incoming network bandwidth for the backup server will directly impact the number of concurrent jobs it can handle.

In situations where storage nodes/media servers are in use, the same potential limits on concurrency for the backup server will apply to those individual hosts, with the exception that the device concurrency limitation cited earlier will be limited to the devices directly attached to or controlled by the storage node/media server.

12.7.2 *Client Concurrency*

Client job concurrency refers to an individual host being configured to send more than one stream of data to the backup environment at the same time. Typically, by "stream" we refer to filesystems, but this could be different depending on the type of backup being performed. For instance, for database backups this may refer to the number of databases simultaneously backed up or for even larger database environments the number of database data files backed up concurrently *per* database. As you may imagine, client job concurrency is used so that the backup of a single host can be completed sooner.

The following factors must be considered when determining client job concurrency:[*]

1. Other processing activities occurring, their priority compared to the backup job(s), and the limit to which the backup job(s) may impact those activities
2. CPU/RAM capabilities of the client
3. Underlying disk subsystem or filesystem performance

4. Whether the client is performing any encryption or compression of the data prior to sending it to the backup environment[†]
5. Whether another agent (e.g., antivirus software) is scanning the data the client sends to the backup environment
6. Network link between the client and the backup environment

To a lesser degree, client job concurrency will also be dependent on the speed of the backup devices, but it is rare in modern backup and recovery devices for device streaming performance to be *lower* than individual client streaming performance, and the other considerations on this will be covered in the chapter on tape.

The performance of the underlying disk subsystem or the filesystem is a key factor in client performance that often takes people by surprise when evaluating job concurrency options for individual clients. When systems are being used for random file access, many design or layout issues (either at the operating system or at the system implementation level) may not be readily apparent—but during largely sustained sequential reads of the filesystems, previously unnoticed issues may be highlighted.

When clients are using DAS, job concurrency should (at most) not be set higher than the number of physical disks providing storage to the client. Note that we say *at most*; if there are more filesystems defined than there are physical disks, then defining a higher level of job concurrency from the client than the number of disks will likely just result in drive thrashing as large sequential reads are executed simultaneously from two different locations on a drive (though flash and solid state storage systems can reduce this concern).

RAID systems do not immediately guarantee a higher level of job concurrency being acceptable for a client. Particularly in DAS/internal RAID structures, basic hardware or even software RAID controllers may yield suboptimal performance compared to SAN-level storage systems and offer no benefit compared to lower job concurrency levels—especially if in a degraded RAID state.

While SAN storage may ideally offer the best possible performance for client job concurrency, once shared storage systems are included in the backup environment, backup and storage administrators should work together closely to ensure that mass backup operations do not overload the performance capabilities of SAN (and even more so, NAS). For

---

[*] An additional consideration will be whether the client is a physical host, or is a virtual machine (guest) in a hypervisor environment. We will discuss considerations around virtual machine backup and recovery in the chapter on virtualization.

[†] Traditionally client-side compression or encryption, performed via software, has been seen as very resource intensive. Some modern CPUs have incorporated special instruction sets and operational modes to speed up compression or encryption, and if backup software can leverage these instructions, it can result in minimizing the impact of these functions during backup operations.

instance, when evaluating optimum client job concurrency settings for clients using SAN volumes, it's necessary to evaluate the IO load placed on SAN volumes when *all* attached clients are backed up simultaneously and balance individual client job concurrency appropriately.

Flash storage, including solid state disk drives (SSDs) and non-volatile memory express (NVMe) do alter the dynamic for backup concurrency on individual clients given their high-performance characteristics, particularly for read operations. Multiple filesystems hosted on even a single SSD or NVMe system could be concurrently read significantly faster than even multiple filesystems with a 1:1 mapping between filesystem and conventional hard drive. When SSD and NVMe platforms underpin client data storage, client backup job concurrency may be more limited by factors such as the filesystem architecture and density, and the network configuration of the client.

While it is important for a backup environment to be configured such that the network links between the clients and the backup targets are not underutilized, it's equally important to avoid swamping the network—especially if the network is being simultaneously used for production activities.* When evaluating job concurrency options for clients in relation to the network, administrators are well advised to keep in mind that TCP/IP communications streams include *more* than just the data being sent—each packet sent will include metadata identifying the stream itself and the packet's position in the data stream. If a single job from a client can saturate the client's network interface, adding a second stream is unlikely to make any performance improvement and may even reduce the performance by doubling the amount of packet metadata at the expense of the actual data.

12.7.3 Device Concurrency

The number of jobs a backup device can simultaneously handle will be largely dependent on the type of device it is and its own performance characteristics. Some high-end PBBAs and IDPAs are now capable of handling a thousand or more concurrent backup jobs, and since these write data to disk, this does not impact the recoverability of the data. Tape drives, on the other hand, should be optimized to have as few concurrent streams going to them as possible or else full recovery performance for larger backups may be impacted.

When using disk-based backup devices, the job concurrency should be set in accordance to the vendor's guidance on maximum simultaneous stream counts, or if simple disk/RAID systems are being used, this will need to be

tuned per the performance characteristics of the devices. Considerations for tape-based backup devices will be discussed in more detail in the chapter devoted to tape.

12.8 Network Data Management Protocol

NDMP was developed to facilitate the backup of network appliances (i.e., NAS hosts). While these hosts include operating systems that may be *similar* to, or even based on other operating systems supported by backup products, access to the operating system for installation of third-party software is usually prohibited by the NAS vendor to ensure maximized performance and stability.

NAS systems have taken over file serving functions in most enterprises due to their ease of use and configuration, in addition to their ability to integrate into enterprise authentication systems. In particular, they allow storage administrators to easily

- Add a new share
- Allow multiple hosts to concurrently read and write to a share
- Allow multiple operating system types to concurrently read/write a share

They also provide a variety of data protection management functions, including replication and snapshots, for meeting RPO and RTO deadlines that may not be met using backup and recovery, though these are all *on-platform* protection mechanisms.

All of this typically occurs without any outage being required, even if the host has not previously accessed the NAS appliance. In comparison, adding a new host to a SAN will require zoning changes, potentially an outage to add fiber host bus adapters, and drive installation and SAN-level configuration to grant access to allocated volumes—as well as possibly additional host reboots to allow the newly presented volumes to be visible. While such configuration complexity is deemed acceptable for servers, it is impractical and expensive for direct end user desktop/laptop access.

Returning to NAS systems, there's no such thing as a free lunch. The day to day management simplicity offered by NAS comes at a price, and this price is felt during backup and recovery operations. (With scale-out NAS now allowing organizations to grow a single logical filesystem to dozens of petabytes or more in size, optimized NAS backups are a huge consideration for enterprises.)

To understand the importance of NDMP in an enterprise environment, first consider how a backup must be executed for NAS storage *without* NDMP. For this, refer to Figure 12.14.

---

* Both dedicated backup networks and source-based deduplication can be used to minimize the impact of distributed backups on production networks.

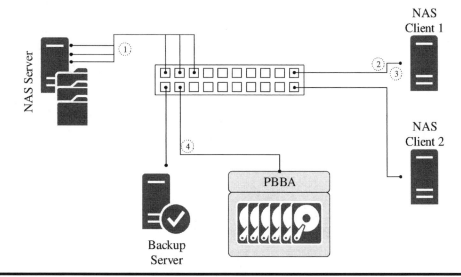

Figure 12.14 Overview of NAS backups without NDMP.

Without NDMP, there is no direct way for the backup server to communicate with the NAS system (since it is runs a closed operating system and backup agents cannot be installed), and therefore its data must be backed up through one or more of the hosts that have shares mapped from the NAS system. When it is time for a backup to be initiated, the data will stream as follows:

1. The data for a given share will be read from the NAS server across the TCP/IP network to one of the NAS clients or a specifically configured backup proxy.
2. The backup agent on the NAS client/proxy will read the data coming in from the NAS server as if it were a local filesystem.
3. The backup agent on the NAS client/proxy will then send the data back across the TCP/IP network to the designated backup target.
4. If the backup target is a network-connected PBBA or IDPA, the data will be subsequently streamed *back* across the TCP/IP network to the designated target (alternatively if going to tape, this might be sent directly from the client in question, but at the risk of introducing shoe-shining and other tape-centric inefficiencies).

Such a configuration sees the totality of the data to be backed up transmitted at least twice—the NAS client has to read the data from the NAS server, and then it has to transmit it across to the storage system (in this case, a PBBA). In situations where a three-tier backup architecture is used (server, media server, and client), the NAS client will transmit the data to the media server, which in turn will need to send it to the PBBA or other protection storage, seeing the data sent *three* times.

In addition to multiple reads/transmits of the data, such backups aren't even necessarily guaranteed to provide a comprehensive backup—if a NAS share is being accessed by multiple operating systems, such a backup will *only* protect access control lists/permissions associated with the operating system of the NAS host used to perform the backup. For example, if a Windows host was used for the backup/recovery using this mechanism but the share is accessed by Linux hosts as well, any Linux-specific access file permissions are extremely unlikely to be backed up or recovered as part of the operation. This could in fact result in security issues—recovered data might not even have access permissions correctly re-established.

The other factor to consider in non-NDMP backups of NAS systems is whether files that are currently in use on other NAS clients will even be backed up at all. It is more than usual in an NDMP backup for the NAS appliance to read from a temporary snapshot of the filesystem being protected; this circumvents the problem of files being opened and locked by a single system in the environment.

NDMP neatly bypasses the backup configuration mentioned earlier by allowing the NAS server to stream its data directly to a designated NDMP-compatible device. Depending on the version of NDMP supported by the NAS system and the options available in the backup product, this may be any one of the following:

▪ Tape drives/library directly connected and dedicated to the NAS system via SCSI or fiber channel
▪ Tape library simultaneously connected to the NAS system and other backup hosts via fiber channel, allowing shared access to tape drives
▪ Virtual tape library presented by a PBBA or IDPA
▪ NDMP service on a backup server, storage node, or proxy/accelerator

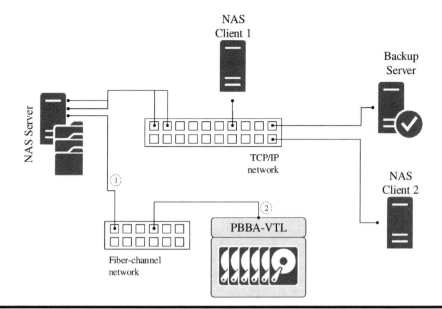

Figure 12.15 NAS backup via NDMP.

Since NDMP does not *natively* support backing up to any-thing other than a tape drive, the fourth option is the only way a backup environment can be configured to send NAS backups to anything other than physical or virtual tape. In such an environment, the NDMP service running on the backup server or storage node/media server *masquerades* as an NDMP target and then encapsulates the NDMP data into a standard backup stream. This then allows the backup product to exert more control over the NDMP data stream and introduces options such as

- Backup to a PBBA or IDPA in disk rather than VTL mode
- Multiplexing of the backup stream (not supported by NDMP natively)
- Mixing NDMP and non-NDMP backups onto the same backup volumes (not supported by NDMP natively)

Figure 12.15 demonstrates how an NDMP backup might look when writing in VTL mode to a PBBA. In this con-figuration, the NAS system has a fiber-channel connection to the VTL mode functionality within the PBBA. When the backup server instructs the NAS system to backup, the data is streamed directly over the fiber channel to emulated tape drives on the PBBA, bypassing the IP network entirely. (Further, the data is transmitted only once.)

As NAS capacities continue to grow, their backups increasingly need strong architectural attention within a business to ensure data can be adequately protected within required timeframes and will almost *always* require backup/recovery operations to be supplemental to primary protec-tion methods such as snapshots and replication.

Despite the benefits of NDMP, there are some significant limitations. The protocol has gone through several iterations:

NDMP v4 was first drafted in April 2003,* a time when tape was the primary backup mechanism used in enterprise envi-ronments. (While the NDMP specification refers to v5, it has not been widely adopted, and may never have left draft status.)

Perhaps the largest impediment to the ongoing success of NDMP is that it is not a seamlessly compatible standard. NDMP implementations and functionality can, and do, vary from vendor to vendor within storage systems. This leaves developers of backup products with the unenviable task of needing to certify that their NDMP library/functionality is compatible with the NDMP functionality embedded in stor-age systems. The net result is that there is no guarantee that just because NAS vendor A and backup vendor B both sup-port NDMP they will in fact support one another.

Between minimal maintenance of the standard, and evolving data protection options, most of the innovation seen in more recent years around NDMP has come from either tight partnerships between storage and backup vendors, or vendors that offer both storage and backup software.

The Storage Networking Institute Association (SNIA), which is now the ostensible home to NDMP states on its website:

> NOTICE: The NDMP specifications were developed independently of the Storage Networking Industry Association, but are being hosted here as a courtesy for developers and end users. Future development of NDMP is not expected at this time[†].

---

* https://tools.ietf.org/html/draft-skardal-ndmpv4-04
† Network Data Management Protocol (NDMP) page at SNIAhttps://www.snia.org/ndmp

Some backup products are now eschewing NDMP entirely, in favor of the mount-based backup approach previously discussed. In some cases, the NAS data is backed up via a share mounted to a traditional host with the standard backup agent software installed. In others, the NAS system is mounted directly by a backup appliance.

A mount-approach for backup cannot by itself resolve the challenges posed by mixed-OS access permissions, though this can be significantly mitigated by using a single authority service within the organization. For example, this may mean that a Windows Active Directory service could serve as the single point of reference for all logins: Windows, Linux, and traditional Unix platforms. In such situations, there should be reduced risks of recovered security permissions issues posed in mixed-OS access environments.

The remaining issue then is protecting open files on the NAS share. To avoid this, it becomes necessary to mount a *snapshot* of a share from the NAS server, rather than a share itself. That way, all the files in the share can be accessed without locking within the snapshot.

Ironically, this creates a situation that is no more elegant than traditional NDMP. NDMP at least has some standards relating to it, meaning vendors who wish to qualify NDMP support at least have a starting point to work from. There is no "snapshot standard" however in the industry, and each vendor implements snapshots how it wishes to do so, providing whatever APIs or CLIs they wish for remote control and management. This protection approach will require development of hooks by backup vendors; a snapshot backup function might offer integration via a process such as:

- Invoke custom command that prepares the share for backup (including snapshot and mount)
- Perform the backup
- Invoke custom command to dismount the share and release the snapshot

Such an option would allow any business with a modicum of scripting skills to ensure integration of their desired NAS with a backup product, or even allow NAS vendors to release simple instructions on performing the integration steps.

NDMP is not dead yet. Where it is used, it is still a time saving protocol; more so, a variety of NAS systems have implemented extensions to the NDMP protocol to allow for tighter integration, particularly in situations where a single vendor produces both NAS and backup products. Furthermore, where NDMP is supported by both the NAS system and backup product in use, it makes sense to use NDMP due to the seamless way it deals with the backup process. However, unless a serious rescue effort is mounted for the standard, it is likely to eventually lapse into obscurity.

12.9 Miscellaneous Enterprise Features

There is a collection of features that do not in themselves warrant entire categories but can be pooled together to form what we would still describe as enterprise features—that is, facilities that should be found in any enterprise backup and recovery product. In this section, we will give an overview of some of those features.

12.9.1 Pre- and Post-Processing

Pre- and post-processing refers to the ability of the backup product to execute arbitrary scripts or commands on backup clients before and after the backup. Examples of where pre- and post-processing might include any of the following:

- Prior to backup, a database is put into hot backup mode, and immediately following the backup, the database is brought out of hot backup mode.
- Prior to filesystem backup, a hot export is performed for a database.
- Prior to monthly backups, an application is shut down for a cold backup rather than its regular hot backup, and following the backup, the application is restarted.
- Following a successful backup completion on Friday nights, a client might be rebooted automatically to allow system updates to take effect.
- Prior to starting backups, a map might be built of a particular dense filesystem and the configuration for the client automatically adjusted to support massively concurrent backups of the dense filesystem in order to improve performance.

Pre- and post-processing allows for a backup system to be extended considerably beyond the original design considerations from the vendor and ensures the product can be tightly integrated into the processes of a business. A few key considerations when evaluating pre- and post-processing include the following:

- Is there a set timeout period for the commands or can the administrator define an arbitrary command timeout?
- Is it necessary to establish a command execution environment prior to running a pre- or post-command?
- Are pre- and post-processing commands done for each filesystem or unique backup set, or before and after all backups?
- For applications with more than one host, is it possible to schedule pre- and post-processing across multiple clients using dependencies?
- Is security provided to prevent the execution of arbitrary commands?

- Does the backup agent run under a user account that will have the authority to execute the commands to be run? If not, can the user account be changed?
- What control options are there in the event of the pre- or post-command failing?
- Who owns the scripts in terms of support and/or maintenance? The system administrator, application administrator, client owner? This can become contentious in situations where a supplier (e.g., system integrator, or even vendor) installed the solution. Some suppliers may mandate that staff are not to create such scripts at all, others may require the customer to acknowledge that ongoing support of the script is a customer requirement. (After all, there is no guarantee that the person who performed the install will be person who answers the phone when a support call is made.)

12.9.2 Arbitrary Command Execution

Arbitrary backup command execution means being able to replace the native backup mechanism with a custom backup tool for particular machines so as to be able to process data that the backup vendor did not anticipate (or feel sufficient commercial need to support). For instance, companies have been known to use arbitrary backup command execution to perform hot backups for databases that do not have an agent or to simulate such a backup by detecting and reacting differently to database files. In other cases, it may be possible for a company to retain its long-term backup product even if it adopts a new hypervisor that is not supported by that backup product by using arbitrary command execution to integrate with third-party hypervisor snapshot software.

Although it may be rare that companies would need to extend a backup product to this level, some backup products use arbitrary backup command execution as their mechanism for providing database and special application backup capabilities—that is, this is the facility they use to enable plug-ins or modules.

12.9.3 Cluster Support

For a cluster to be effective, the end users of the cluster should not need to know or care which node in the cluster is currently being accessed. They certainly shouldn't be in a situation where they need to reconfigure their access manually when a cluster node failover occurs.

At the other end of the service spectrum, backup administrators equally should not need to keep track of cluster failover manually—the backup software itself should be able to do this, either automatically or as a result of an initial configuration where the cluster hosts are identified as such.

In any *n* node cluster providing *y* virtual services, a typical configuration might be:

- *n* client instances for the physical cluster nodes, used to backup their private data and OS configuration.
- *y* client instances, one per virtual cluster service, used to back up the shared/presented data and applications.

For active/passive clusters, the goal of cluster recognition is to avoid situations where the recovery operator needs to know which node of the cluster was hosting the data backed up that now needs recovering. For active/active cluster configurations, the goal will be to avoid multiple backups of the cluster presented data, one per node.

12.9.4 Client Collections

At the most primitive, a "collection" of clients is a set of clients whose backups start at the same time. This can be handled in two ways:

1. Each client has a start time/schedule associated with it and starts independently of all other clients.
2. The backup product provides a collection configuration resource that allows the logical grouping of similar clients to force a common start time (and possibly even a common backup schedule).

Various names exist for these collections, with "group," "policy," and "class" being the three common variants. When a backup product allows such groups, the administrative overhead becomes considerably simplified. For instance, assume 50 Windows clients normally get backed up at 21:35. If it is decided these machines should instead start their backups at the new time of 22:55, it is far more convenient to adjust the start time in a single group containing all 50 clients than it is to edit the configuration for all 50 clients.

12.9.5 Backup Segregation

This refers to specifying what data can be sent to which collection of backup media. Such groupings of backup media are usually referred to as "pools." The following are some examples of backup segregation requirements:

- *Off-site versus on-site media*: Ensures that copies of backups generated to be sent off-site are not stored on the same media as copies that will remain on-site.
- *Data separation*: In some instances, it may be legally or contractually required to store backups for different divisions or companies on different media.
- *Backup retention periods*: Particularly when tape is used, backups of differing retention periods (e.g., 6 weeks for daily backups, 7 years for monthly) should be placed on different media so that media aging and recycling can occur as required.

■ *Deduplicatability*: If using deduplication appliances, there may be some data within the environment that does not deduplicate (e.g., compressed or encrypted data). Backup segregation allows for sending this type of data directly to alternate backup media, thereby avoiding capacity impact on deduplication storage.

Primitive backup products will provide segregation solely on simple and unreliable mechanisms such as

■ Which media is currently in a stand-alone device?
■ What slot number backup media is placed into in a tape library?
■ What label has been assigned to media?

In other words, the segregation in these instances is done by the backup administrator or operators as the media is provisioned. This becomes a manual process that does not scale well.

Automated data segregation however provides for splitting of backups to different media based on a variety of considerations such as:

■ Originating client collection
■ Originating client
■ Whether the backup is an original or a copy
■ Intended retention period for the backup
■ Backup level

By offering segregation based on these options, a backup product can provide automated data separation sufficient to meet the needs of most organizations and can scale with the backup requirements of the business.

12.9.6 Granular Backup Control

This refers to the alteration of the backup process for a particular host based on one or more criteria being met. One form has already been touched on in the context of data selection methods. Exclusive backup products work by automatically backing up everything on a host *except* for what has been excluded from the backup process. This in itself is a form of backup control. For instance, it may be necessary to configure granular backup control such that even though all filesystems are backed up on a particular host, any file with a ".mp3" extension is excluded.

There is, however, much more to granular backup control than merely excluding multimedia files. The following are examples of other types of granular backup control:

■ Forcing software-based client-side encryption or compression for particular files or types of files

■ Preventing database files from being backed up as part of the filesystem backup when they are protected by a database module
■ Forcing the inclusion of additional filesystems that are not picked up as part of an automated probe of filesystems (e.g., a network filesystem presented by a host running an operating system not supported by the backup software)
■ Suppression of error or warning messages about active files for system logs, etc., which don't need to be backed up or quiesced
■ Forcing an exclusive lock to be taken out on a file being backed up so it can't be modified during the process

With fine-grained control of the backup process for individual hosts, the backup system can be modified to work with systems that the backup software designers had not necessarily anticipated.

12.9.7 Backup Schedule Overrides

All backup products will support scheduling of some sort—and we've already discussed the levels associated with scheduling. A common schedule, for instance, is "daily incrementals with full backups on Friday night."

To reduce administrative overheads however, it's important the backup product offers some mechanism to set overrides to the schedules that have been established. For instance, the schedule works well if *only* daily backups are performed. If monthly backups are performed as well, it will be necessary to override the daily schedule once per month to skip the Friday full, which will instead be performed by the monthly schedule. Equally, if a company is planning on a computer room shut down for maintenance purposes, it would be desirable to be able to temporarily skip all the backups associated with machines in that computer room for the weekend only rather than manually disabling all the backups and then manually re-enabling them at a later point.

Overrides are essential in order to maximize the automation of a backup environment and grow even more essential as the size of the environment grows.

12.9.8 Security

There are two aspects to backup security that are not necessarily complementary:

■ To backup everything on a system, the backup software needs reasonably complete access to the system.
■ Due to this, if backup security is breached, the potential for data theft or destruction is severe.

With these in mind, it's imperative that organizations maintain tight, secure control over the backup environment and that the backup product supports this. Ideally, this will include having the backup software able to integrate with enterprise class authentication systems such as a centralized LDAP/Active Directory system. At bare minimum, the backup product must also be able to support defining

- Who can administer the backup server?
- Who can interact with backup media and devices?
- Who can recover data on a per-client basis?

Additionally, the backup software should provide reports, logs, and details as required on activities performed within the backup environment.

A common security flaw introduced into many backup environments is allowing too many users access to the backup administration role. Like all other aspects of IT, security via obfuscation is not sufficient, and a security breach on the backup server should be seen as an extremely risky scenario for any organization. After all, if the security for the backup server has been breached, all data protected by the backup server is potentially compromised.

12.9.9 Duplication and Migration

While this topic will be covered in more detail later, we can summarize for now that backup duplication is the method by which the IT environment (and by extension, the company) is protected from a failure occurring within any single backup. Ideally, all backups produced—at least all production and system of record backups produced—should have a duplicate copy so that in the event of the primary copy failing, another copy can be used to recover data required.

Backup migration, on the other hand, refers to moving a backup from one piece of media to another. Examples of where backup migration are used include the following:

- Moving backups written to disk across to tape or a cloud storage provider for long-term storage.
- Evacuating readable backups from failing media.
- Transferring long-term and archival backups from a decommissioned media type to a new media type.
- Media consolidation—If backup segregation by retention time was not performed, it may be necessary to move long retention backups to new media to allow media to be reclaimed when short retention backups have expired.
- Legal requirements—If ordered to destroy particular data, it may be necessary to migrate required data on the same media to alternate volumes prior to destroying

the original. Alternately, it may be necessary to handover copies of data to a departing customer or as part of a legal discovery process.

12.9.10 Alerts

Running a graphical user interface (GUI) against a backup server and observing the current state is one thing, but not all organizations employ 24×7 staff, and even when they do, staff may not react fast enough to issues if there are other activities to be performed.

With this in mind, it's important that a backup product have alternate methods of alerting users, operators, or administrators of events that require attention rather than simply expecting someone to notice output in a GUI when the event happens.

Some within the industry get obsessed over whether a product supports a particular alerting method (e.g., SNMP, mobile phone SMS). However, thinking outside the square, as long as a backup product offers custom alerts (i.e., arbitrary command execution in response to a particular event), any form of required alert can be accommodated with a little scripting or data massaging. Therefore, if the preferred alerting mechanism for a company is not directly supported by a backup product, using custom alerts, it can still be integrated. (Those seeking to *control* backup and recovery functionality via SNMP extensions would be far better off focusing instead on newer approaches such as leveraging REST APIs.)

As businesses grow and acquire other businesses, it also becomes more likely that multiple backup products may end up being in use within an organization. If all the backup products support third-party alerting, it allows for a holistic view of the data protection environment to be built up, with reporting performed at a global level rather than per product.

12.9.11 Command Line Interface and REST APIs

Although it might be said that a picture is worth a thousand words, a GUI is not necessarily worth a thousand command line options. GUIs fulfill a particular function—they simplify interaction with a computer program or operating system so as to make the system more accessible to users. This in itself is as admirable as it is required. Certainly in backup products, GUIs often allow users to get a better view of the "big picture" of the configuration of the backup server and allow for simpler control of the configuration, operation, and recoveries within the business. However, GUIs typically have limits such as the following:

- Cannot be easily automated
- Don't allow for much extensibility

- May be slower to display information across sub-LAN speed links
- Don't provide all the functionality of every single aspect of the backup system or replication of every option of every function
- May not provide the same level of error/log messages as command line options
- May not sufficiently mask data and operational information for multi-tenant environments

Command line access to a backup product can also be instrumental in remote support, monitoring, backup, and recovery operations. Many backup administrators who do not use the command line for anything in the office may find themselves making use of the command line when connecting via VPN from home.

More importantly, by their very presence, command line interfaces support ongoing extensibility of a product. This promotes integration and long-term maintenance of the product and often allows a product that cannot natively perform a particular function to be extended with minimum scripting to provide it.

As we move into environments that increasingly need to deal with multi-tenant situations, command line options (and also RESTful APIs) provide direct capabilities required by DevOps teams to integrate data protection processes into custom service portals.

An increasing focus on automation (driven from public cloud, and from IT infrastructure where the business demands increasingly more agile processes from fewer employees) has more recently seen a high emphasis on the availability of REST APIs. Whereas traditional CLIs often require some degree of interaction, and more importantly, shell level access to a system, REST APIs allow for stateless interaction between a custom built service and the infrastructure, usually over HTTP/HTTPS. This readily facilitates the integration of backup and recovery services into private and hybrid cloud portals—some vendors in fact will even supply "data protection extensions" for common private cloud services (e.g., VMware's vRealize Automation and vRealize Orchestration), allowing backup and recovery services to be readily incorporated into service templates and operations.

12.9.12 Backup Catalogs

All backup systems need to provide a backup catalog. A catalog provides a mechanism to track backups that have previously been executed, allowing for rapid retrieval of data during a recovery operation. Without a backup catalog, an administrator would have to approach recoveries as follows:

- User wants to recover file(s) or data.
- Administrator or user must determine when the files were lost.
- Administrator must retrieve the media generated on or before that date.
- Administrator must read the media to search for the file(s) or data required.

Such a "solution" doesn't scale and violates the principle that we backup to recover. As such, catalogs facilitate rapid recoveries by allowing a process that resembles the following:

- User initiates a backup search for the required file(s) or data *or* browses the backup filesystem view to a particular date and time.
- User selects file(s)/data for recovery and initiates the recovery.
- Backup software automatically recovers the data if media is online or initiates a recall operation for media that is not online but required.

At bare minimum, the backup catalog should

- Track media in use by the system.
- Track backups that are on each piece of media.
- Track backup copies.
- Prompt users/administrators for the required media when recoveries are initiated and the media is not already online.

Preferably a backup catalog should also contain features such as the following:

- For tape, sufficient indexing to allow fast-forwarding through media to the location of the backup rather than having to read through the entire tape
- For disk, sufficient indexing to know where in a backup file the data required for recovery can be located
- Searching for files and directories that users would like recovered but can't recall where they were located originally
- Media usage information—how often a piece of media has been labeled/rewritten, how many times it was mounted, when it was originally added, etc.
- Online, hot backup and maintenance of catalog data
- Automated and manual checking of catalog consistency
- Recovery of catalog data at a minimum granularity of per-client or per-volume and preferably on a per-backup basis
- Regeneration of catalog data by reading or scanning backup media

12.10 Conflicting SLAs for Backup Systems Design

A challenging conundrum that exists for backup architects is the tug-of-war that exists between the shared use of a backup and recovery system. It is entirely common to see backup and recovery systems within an organization leveraged for all three of the following activities:

- Operational recovery
- Disaster recovery*
- Long-term recovery

The conundrum that this causes is that each of the above activities has different requirements for SLAs and indeed, cost constraints. Operational recovery must be fast, and nearline. Disaster recovery, on the other hand, has a high focus on protection from local site failure scenarios. Long-term recoveries do not need to be fast at all, but the media they need to be stored on must be cost-efficient, since over a longer-term period of interest (e.g., 7 years for taxation purposes in many countries), operational recoveries will consume the vast bulk of data that resides in the backup and recovery service.

The net effect of this is that businesses invariably need to ensure adequate consideration is made of all three recovery types when planning backup and recovery services, and particularly, the storage that is used. Businesses that elect to store all backup data on Tier 1 backup storage may believe they've made the best decision in terms of simplified management, but as the amount of long-term retention data grows, they may find themselves facing uncomfortable and expensive capacity management issues.

Generally speaking, we see at least three requirements come out of the mixed SLAs:

- Short-term recovery needs to be facilitated by high-speed storage services.
- Disaster recovery mandates off-site storage services.
- Long-term recovery mandates cheap storage services.

This in turn drives various architectural considerations: tiering of aging backup data, and the ability to duplicate backups. While there can be more complexity, these two requirements serve as an important baseline to managing the

competing SLAs of operational recovery, disaster recovery, and long-term recovery. We will discuss some of these challenges in greater detail in Chapter 25, Long-Term Retention Considerations.

12.11 Summary

As the amount of data businesses deal with continues to grow, so too do the backup requirements for the business. There was a time once when it was sufficient to treat backup and recovery solely as an insurance policy within the business—it existed to facilitate data recovery should *bad things* happen. With increasing data growth, the investment required to adequately provide backup and recovery services also increases, and many businesses are looking at getting additional utility from their backup and recovery investment.

While the primary purpose for a backup and recovery system *must* still be data recovery, business processes can be extended to make use of the backup and recovery system beyond just a data recovery service.

Various businesses have had this utility approach to backups for some time. For instance, it has not been uncommon for years, if not decades, for development and test databases to be refreshed by recovering the production backups into the dev/test areas. This eliminates the need to place additional workload on the production database that would naturally occur in a direct production to development copy.

Big data is accelerating this utility approach to backups—drawing all the data required for data science activities and large-scale data analysis directly from their production sources can be time-consuming, resource intensive, and impactful toward core business functions, yet the importance of interrogating and analyzing this data for future business decisions and new market insights is indisputable. By extending the old "recover prod into development" approach pioneered so many years ago, businesses can pull the required data from their backup system into the big data environments. Yet this is even only the beginning. If we consider the growing trend toward highly IDPAs, we can already see situations where data is not actually recovered out of the backup environment for processing but is instead read *directly from it* for analysis or accessed via read/write snapshots when testing is required but the cost in time of performing a recovery first is too much.

Beyond big data usage, backup and recovery systems can provide long-term visibility over protected content. Network search appliances may be able to provide a mechanism to rapidly find data and files that currently exist within an organization, but search capabilities included in backup software allows deep version searches across *all* protected content, no matter when it was backed up. This can serve more than

---

* Except in the smallest of organizations, it's unlikely that a backup and recovery system will provide *only* disaster recovery services. Usually there will be a requirement for fast recovery from a more recent instance of the data than can be serviced through backups. Regardless of that however, it is still common to see backup services form some part of disaster recovery, if only for Tier 3 and 4 functions for the business—and of course, backup and recovery services must have disaster recovery protection, themselves.

just time saving functions for users or administrators—it could also be used during a legal discovery process to rapidly respond to searches in a fraction of the time or effort, saving companies considerable amounts of time or money.

As we move into an IT era dominated by the impact of cloud and of cloud service delivery models and particularly the notion of a service catalog, backup systems when integrated into enterprise reporting and monitoring can play a vital role in determining not only what *is* being protected but what is *not* being protected. Similarly, since backup and recovery systems are deeply integrated into the IT infrastructure of many businesses to a degree matched usually only by actual networking infrastructure itself, the capture and analysis of backup activities and faults may very well provide a company with significant insight into the reliability and stability of its infrastructure.

This is an aspect of backup and recovery that is still being developed and will continue to change in line with data growth and the need for business agility. It is therefore vital that infrastructure architects and business analysts cease thinking of backup as something used *only* for recovery and to seriously evaluate how and where an investment into backup and recovery systems can be leveraged to save the company time and money.

As the introduction suggested, backup as a stand-alone topic is now dead within IT, and we are just starting to see the business benefits of a more integrated approach to data protection.

12.12 Self-Reflection

Review the backup schedule outlined in Table 12.5, and draw the backup schedule via a backup change diagram.

Consider a backup client whose storage is provided by directly attached hard drives (not flash/NVMe). It has a two-drive mirror that provides the C:\filesystem, and a three-drive RAID-5 group that provides the D:\filesystem. What would be a likely level of job concurrency on the client that would not result in more IO requests than the drive layout could handle? Now repeat the consideration, but where there are three filesystems provided by the RAID-5 group. What would be a safe job concurrency level for that configuration?

Evaluate the backup storage requirements (without deduplication) of a backup and recovery solution that must protect 500 TB of data. For all examples, assume 10% annual growth, and a flat daily change rate of 2%. For a 3-year period of interest, calculate the minimum backup storage requirements at the end of three years, based on each of the following scenarios:

- Scenario one:
  - Weekly full backups with daily incrementals, retained for 5 weeks
  - Monthly full backups retained for 7 years (this would be reduced to 36 months in a 3-year review)
- Scenario two:
  - Daily incremental backups retained for 5 weeks
  - Weekly full backups retained for 12 weeks
  - Monthly full backups retained for 13 months
  - Yearly full backups retained for 7 years
- Scenario three:
  - Daily incremental backups retained for 14 days
  - Weekly full backups retained for 6 weeks
  - Monthly full backups retained for 7 years

Which scenario will require the most storage? What is the percentage difference, in each scenario, between the amount of storage required for operational retention, and for long-term retention?

Chapter 13

Deduplication

13.1 Introduction

Deduplication, particularly within backup and recovery environments, has very much become a mainstream technology. As the name suggests, deduplication is oriented toward eliminating duplicate data, thereby reducing the footprint occupied by data storage systems. Since duplicate data may occur across a large number of data sets spaced over a considerable amount of time, reconstructing ("rehydrating") those data in a usable timeframe relies on high-speed random access unavailable in tape.

Deduplication is a logical extension of two existing technologies—single-instance storage (used quite successfully in systems such as archival products and many mail servers in order to reduce storage requirements) and traditional file/data compression technology. In fact, deduplication can even sometimes be described as "global compression." By this, consider a directory with 100 files in it. If you create 10 compressed files (e.g., zip files), with each one containing only 10 files in it, the compression is achieved only in each case against the 10 files that have been included. Yet there may be compression matches in the other files—these will only be evaluated when they are compressed. Likewise for tape drives that provide compression, they work by having a data buffer; as data is received into the buffer, it is compressed and written out—so if the buffer is, say, 1 GB, the compression which is achieved at any given point in time will only be against that 1 GB buffer size. Deduplication achieves considerably more optimized storage savings by considering incoming data against *previously* compressed data;[*] hence "global compression" is an appropriate description.

To understand deduplication, consider a corporate presentation consisting of 10 slides that are initially developed by Lynne before being distributed to Daz, Laura, and Peter

for feedback. Daz makes changes to diagrams in four of the slides. Laura adds two new slides, while Peter removes one and adds one. This would resemble Figure 13.1.

In each case, the percentage variances between the original slide pack and the three copies are reasonably minor. If each file was stored in its entirety, there'd be a total of 42 slides across the four files.

If, however, we deduplicated at the *slide* level, linking identical slides back to the slides in the original file, we might see a space saving, which is shown in Figure 13.2.

In total, the slide level deduplication yields a considerable reduction in the amount of storage required, bringing it down from 42 to 17—a saving of more than 2:1. This occupied space reduction is the benefit of deduplication, but it happens at a more fundamental level in the storage environment than at the slide or page level of documents.

Before we can understand the benefits and impacts of data deduplication in data protection, we first need to drill down a little deeper on how it typically works in real-world scenarios.

13.2 Key Architectural Aspects of Deduplication

To say all deduplication is the same is to say all computers are the same. To be sure, after the calculator application has loaded, a $200 Celeron-based laptop with 2 GB of RAM and a 500 GB hard drive will allow you to calculate the square root of 42 with at most an imperceptible difference in performance compared to say, a $5,000 workstation with Xeon processors, 64 GB of RAM and 2 TB NVMe. When we consider the basic tasks, both systems can be broadly categorized as "computers" that do similar things. However, once more complicated or demanding tasks are required—e.g., editing 4K video in real-time, the differences will become rather apparent.

---

[*] The amount of data that incoming data is evaluated against depends on the individual deduplication product's architecture.

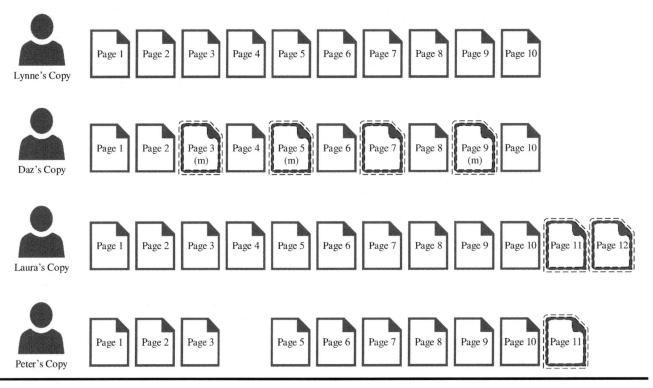

Figure 13.1   Document copies updated by several people.

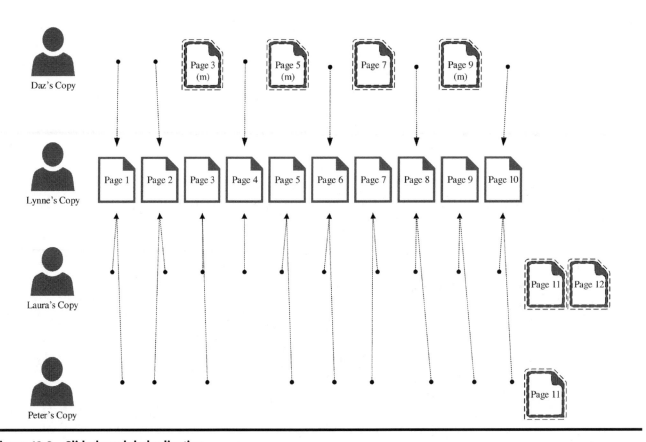

Figure 13.2   Slide-based deduplication.

In much the same way as "a computer is a computer is a computer" could be demonstrated to be syntactically correct yet depending on the task semantically inaccurate, so too is the statement used by some that "deduplication is deduplication is deduplication."

In this section we will examine five key architectural aspects of deduplication that radically set the efficiency and power of the process.

13.2.1 Inline versus Post-Processing

There are two broad processing *times* for deduplication, *inline* and *post-processing*. These refer to *when* the deduplication activity takes place. Inline deduplication is the most efficient, but comes at the expense of a higher CPU and memory load during data ingestion. In this method, as data is received by the deduplication storage system, it's immediately segmented, processed for duplicate data, usually compressed, and then written to the storage system in deduplicated format—it is never written in the original, non-deduplicated format. Such storage systems deliver optimal deduplication, but it's critical for RAM to be large enough to hold as much (if not all) of the hashing tables used to compare checksums for deduplication analysis.* (The purpose of the checksums will be explained in Section 13.2.2.)

Post-processing deduplication works quite differently to inline processing. For post-processing, the storage is effectively broken into two discrete segments: a landing/staging area, and a deduplication area. Data is initially ingested in its original format and is written to the landing area unmodified. At a later point in time (usually at most once a day due to the performance impact), the storage system sweeps the landing area and performs deduplication processing against all the data in it. As data is processed in the landing area, relevant pointers and unique data are added to the deduplication pool, and the processed data removed from the landing area. All this is *supposedly* transparent to the systems using the storage. We say "supposedly" because unless large blackout windows are observed where the system is not used, or solid state storage is used, the additional IO load from such an intensive operation almost invariably has a noticeable impact on the system performance.

The use of solid state storage to try to circumvent the IO performance requirements for subsequent deduplication is often "sold" as a benefit: supposedly allowing for faster recovery for data still in the landing area, or faster landing of data in the first place. Yet invariably where solid state storage is used as the landing area, the landing area is quite small compared to the rest of the storage footprint, requiring rapid

processing—so the chances of actually executing a recovery against data in the landing zone before it is staged out is relatively small.† As we will see in Section 13.2.3, there is also architecturally a much better way of landing data quickly than relying on SSD as a temporary cache, too.

For the most part, inline deduplication represents a considerably more efficient processing time than post-processing, particularly when we consider the sorts of disks often used in deduplication for data protection storage: SATA or NL-SAS.‡ While highly efficient at delivering dense storage, neither NL-SAS nor SATA exactly win speed races, and depending on the purpose of the deduplication storage, a landing zone may get tens or even hundreds of terabytes added to it each day for processing. As mentioned previously, this usually makes the deduplication processing *very* IO bound, which in turn becomes very difficult to optimize for performance without adding many spindles, or using faster drives.

There are also some storage arrays that support a hybrid model of inline *and* post-processing, whereby the normal approach is to perform inline processing, but in situations where the incoming IO load is extreme, they fall back to post-processing. (An alternative is deduplication storage that has a non-deduplication tier attached to it to handle data that doesn't deduplicate well—that is, a conventional storage region that is never reviewed for deduplicatability.)

13.2.2 Variable versus Fixed Block Size Deduplication

Moving beyond inline deduplication, post-processing, or even hybrid models, the analysis mechanisms tend to be either variable- or fixed-block segmentation processing. (A third theoretical model, file-level deduplication, yields minimal benefits in the real-world and is not typically considered—as mentioned previously, this is typically more associated with single-instance storage found in archive products.)

Regardless of whether we use fixed- or variable-block deduplication, the overall analysis works in the following way:

■ Segment data into blocks.
■ For each data block:
  – Calculate the checksum of the block.
  – Compare the checksum calculated against the hash/database of previously stored blocks.

---

* Larger deduplication appliances capable of addressing a petabyte or more of actual physical storage may come with upward of 384–512 GB of RAM.

† Indeed, it's fair to say that the most likely time this would happen would be during a proof-of-concept demonstration, not during production use for most businesses.
‡ NL-SAS refers to "near line serial attached SCSI," an evolution of SCSI that allows SATA drives to be connected into storage arrays more efficiently.

- If the block is unique:
  - Compress the data (for some systems).
  - Store the block and the new checksum.
- If the block is not unique:
  - Store a pointer to the block and discard the duplicate data.

The data stream being processed is therefore stored as a series of pointers to blocks within the deduplication storage, and those pointers will be to either newly stored unique data or existing data. It then becomes the responsibility of the data deduplication storage system to ensure no common data is deleted before *all* references to it are deleted and equally to clean up that orphaned data that is no longer referenced by anything. (That processing is typically referred to as *garbage collection*.) This data stream segment processing is shown in Figure 13.3.

Fixed-block segmentation, as you might imagine from the name, is where all data being processed is split into segments of exactly the same size, regardless of the type of the data or the amount of it. Spreadsheets, documents, presentations, databases, multimedia files, or virtual machine images are all split into the same size blocks, and segmentation processing (as described previously) is done against each of these blocks.

While fixed-block segmentation allows for fast *segmentation* of data being processed, it's not necessarily optimal for *any* of the data being processed. A larger block size may yield better deduplication statistics for databases or virtual machine images, but may result in almost no analysis of smaller files such as word processing files and spreadsheets. Additionally, small *inserts* of data into blocks that have otherwise previously been backed up can result in a somewhat inefficient subsequent backup due to changed block boundaries.

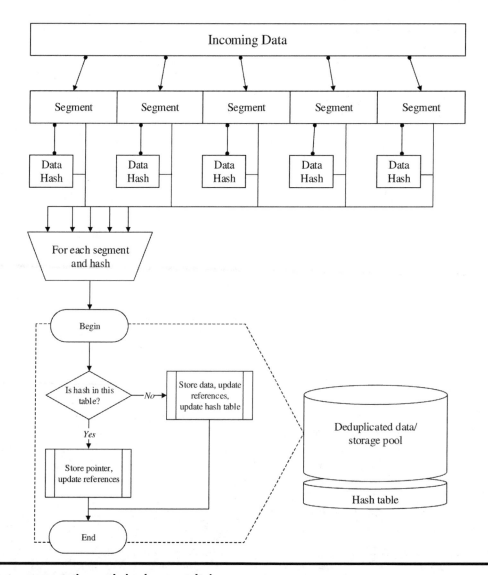

Figure 13.3   Data segmentation and checksum analysis.

For variable-block segmentation, the deduplication system will perform a preliminary analysis on the data to determine its type, and subsequently pick a segment size likely to yield the best deduplication results. Word processing documents and spreadsheets might be allocated a much smaller block size than the incoming data stream from, say, a database. Consider again the data-insertion point made earlier: in variable block-sized deduplication, the system can logically isolate the new data into relatively small blocks, keeping overall deduplication at a much higher level—something we will review in closer detail in Section 13.2.3.

Generally speaking, variable block-based deduplication may require slightly more processing time for preliminary data segmentation but can yield more optimized deduplication, particularly when the data being received for deduplication is a broad mix, or data that is still under active use and is regularly modified.

13.2.3 Segment Size

Within reason, the smaller the segment size, the higher the deduplication ratios that will be achieved. We say "within reason," because every time there is a deduplication match, there is a requirement for additional metadata storage. Thus, there is a trade-off between the amount of data stored, and the amount of data *about the data* stored. For example: in theory any deduplication appliance could store a single 0, and a single 1, which would match any incoming data bit on a conventional computer, and then just store metadata maps to the sequence of 0 and 1 required to reconstruct the data—but at this point the metadata would consume as much space as the original data would have.

To understand the impact segment size has, let us consider two different segment sizes—128 KB and 8 KB. In both instances, we'll look at the first and second backup of 128 KB of data using such a segment size, with the second backup happening after a 4 KB modification to the data.

Figure 13.4 shows the first and second backups using a 128 KB segment size. In the first backup, the entire 128 KB segment is seen as new data, so after evaluation it is compressed and stored. We assume a 2:1 compression ratio, so our 128 KB of data uses 64 KB of space in the deduplication storage pool.

In our second backup of the 128 KB data, 4 KB has changed. But because we using a 128 KB segment size, the atomic checksum against the entire 128 KB segment will differ from the checksum taken at the first backup, so the entire 128 KB of data is seen as a new, unique segment—it is compressed, again assuming 2:1 compression and written to the deduplication storage pool. The net effect being that after backing up 2×128 KB, we have stored 2×64 KB, or 128 KB.

Figure 13.5 shows the first and second backups using an 8 KB segment size. In the first backup, we assume that each of the 16×8 KB segments in the 128 KB data is unique to one another, so when each is stored with a 2:1 compression ratio, we still write 64 KB of data to the deduplication storage pool, as we did for our first backup of 128 KB using a 128 KB segment size. (In fact, when using smaller segment sizes, there is an increased likelihood that even relatively small amounts of newly encountered data may also have duplicate content—but we have assumed a worst-case scenario for this example.)

In our second backup of the 128 KB data, 4 KB has changed, and we assume as a "worst case" that the 4 KB write straddled 2×8 KB segments. Here we see the difference though in storage efficiency based on segment size—the checksums for 14 of the 8 KB segments will be identical to the previous backup. Only two of the 8 KB segments will have differing checksums, hence only two will need to be compressed and stored. The net effect then is after backing up 128 KB of data twice using 8 KB segment sizes, we have stored just 72 KB of data compared to 128 KB using our larger segment size.

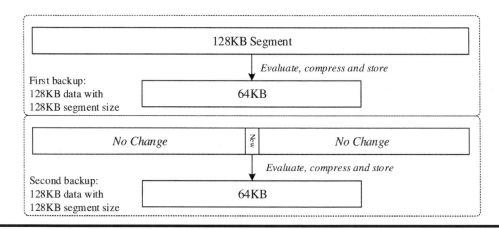

Figure 13.4 First and second backups with 128 KB segment size.

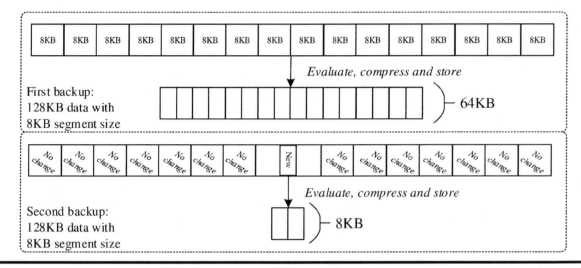

Figure 13.5 First and second backups with 8 KB segment size.

While the example effectively covers a fixed segment size, deduplication systems using variable segment sizes will *tend* to average around a particular size; it is not unusual to see products focus on speed using both fixed *and* large segmentation, whereas handled efficiently, variable and small segment sizes can still yield high speed while also drastically reducing the overall amount of storage required.

13.2.4 Source versus Target Deduplication

Particularly when we consider deduplication systems for backup and recovery, another factor for consideration is whether deduplication happens at the *source, target*, or even a mixed model. This refers to which machine or system is responsible for performing some or all of the deduplication function. Since this is largely applicable only in backup and recovery environments, it will be covered in greater detail later in this chapter.

13.2.5 Deduplication Pool Size

The size of the deduplication pool directly impacts the overall level of benefit one gets from deduplication. The larger the comparison base of data for deduplication, the more likely duplicate content will be found and data reduction will be achieved.

While this seems to create an obvious need for deduplication pool size to be kept as large as possible, the pool size can vary wildly between the implementations performed by various vendors in the marketplace. Leading technologies will typically perform deduplication across an entire storage array, where *all* data ingested for deduplication is typically compared and evaluated. Less-effective implementations may limit deduplication storage pools to arbitrary sizes (e.g., 64 or 128 TB), or individual shelves of disk drives, incoming data types or collections of stream counts, or even something

as basic as individual virtual tapes or clusters of virtual tapes within a virtual tape library.

The simplest lesson here is that the effectiveness of deduplication and return on investment from it will be limited by the size of the deduplication comparison pool, so this should be as large as possible.

13.3 What Does and Doesn't Deduplicate?

Not all data is created equally, and the less equal data is, the less likely will it yield to deduplication techniques. Deduplication ultimately depends on finding common data patterns that are identical—regardless of whether that's within the same files or across an entire data stream. Multimedia files (image, audio, or photos) tend to deduplicate poorly for instance due to space-efficient encoding algorithms used to save these files.

There are two other very good examples of data that typically yield little to no deduplication—compressed files and encrypted files. Considering compressed files first, think about what compression does—it eliminates duplicate data. Therefore, if you compress a file and it drops from 1 GB to 200 MB, deduplication on the remaining 200 MB will yield no savings. Similarly, the best encryption techniques work by removing patterns that might yield an attacker a vector to decrypt the data. For example, the very basic Caesar ("ROT13") cipher, where letters have their position rotated by 13 characters in the alphabet, can be trivially compromised by a frequency analysis of letters. While "e" is the most common letter in the English language, with the ROT13 cipher applied, "r" will become the most common letter in English language text. To avoid such compromises, modern encryption techniques highly *randomize* the data and usually even compress it before encryption to further confuse attempted analysis by ensuring pre- and post-encrypted data are of different sizes. In such situations, encrypted data sent to a deduplication system will typically be stored with no space saving at all.

While this may not seem much of an issue for, say, a single file, such scenarios are not typically encountered in isolation. Databases configured to generate compressed/ encrypted backups each day would make a substantially undesirable impact on deduplication storage.

Of course, compressed and encrypted data are just two examples of where deduplication will struggle. Other areas include video and audio files, and even photos. For instance, remembering the prior point about multimedia files, a medical diagnostics company that generates and stores magnetic resonance images (MRIs) and ultrasounds may find deduplication a poor choice, either for primary storage or backup and recovery storage.

Depending on the use case for the deduplication, some savings can still be achieved in backing up data that doesn't readily deduplicate. In particular, a 100 GB file that doesn't deduplicate sent to deduplication storage as part of a one-off backup obviously won't yield any real savings—the same file copied during the *second* backup cycle will deduplicate against the first, and so on. While this is still less than ideal, it does help to demonstrate the intended workload of the deduplication storage, which can impact what sort of level of deduplication is achieved against it over time. This variance can usually be considered in terms of *recent* deduplication versus *global* deduplication. The 100 GB file when first backed up would get a very poor recent deduplication statistic (say, 1.01:1), but cumulatively over a series of weeks if the data truly is static, it could yield much better global deduplication statistics. Returning to our previous MRI example, we can see that while the initial backup will yield little to no deduplication, subsequent backups of the same unchanging data should deduplicate well. (However, this arguably points to a better strategy of writing such data to highly protected archive storage instead and excluding it from backup cycles.)

Clearly then the deduplicatability of data within an environment will depend on multiple overlapping factors. For this reason, most vendors and integrators will be eager to perform deduplication assessments against intended workloads. This can avoid the dissatisfaction of spending potentially large amounts of money on deduplication only to find a reduction of just say, 1.5–1.

13.4 Cost Considerations

Comparing X TB of deduplication storage to X TB of conventional storage is not in any way a meaningful process. It is, to use the vernacular, comparing apples to oranges.

When comparing costs for these two storage types, there should be an estimate (based on a deduplication assessment) of what sort of deduplication ratios are likely to be achieved given the real data in the environment. Thus, if a deduplication system of 50 TB has been priced and will cost $X, it should *not* be compared to 50 TB of conventional storage (which would likely cost considerably lesser than $X). Instead, if an assessment yields an understanding that the 50 TB of deduplication storage will *actually* store 500 TB of data, then that cost should be compared against 500 TB ($\pm10\%$) of the conventional storage. This is a fundamental mistake often made when comparing costs of deduplicated versus conventional storage.

Further, and particularly when dealing with more than just a few TB of deduplication storage, the other obvious cost consideration that will need to be applied will be power, cooling, and the physical footprint of the unit. For example, considering just the physical footprint, consider a deduplication system offering 50 TB of raw storage. To reach this using, say, 4 TB hard drives, this would potentially require:

- 13 drives (12.5) for the raw storage, *or*
- 15 drives for RAID-6 across the entire drive set, *or*
- 16 drives for RAID-6 across the entire drive set *and* a hot spare, *or*
- $2 \times (9$ drives in RAID-6$) + 2$ hot spares, yielding 20 drives

While the first option is sheer folly, any of the other options would be possible depending on the potential use of the storage and the acceptable performance impact of rebuild time.

If we assume that this will successfully store up to 500 TB of data prior to deduplication, we'd compare the drive footprint not against a 50 TB conventional array, but a 500 TB conventional array.

Even without any RAID or redundancy, 500 TB of conventional storage will immediately require 125 hard drives. If we use sets of nine drives in RAID-6, with just two global hot spares, there'd be 17.8 RAID groups in the storage pool—so 18×9 drives plus another two hot spares—162 drives in total.

This is where the real comparison starts for deduplicated versus non-deduplicated storage: Using 15-drive shelves, it's entirely plausible to fit 20 drives in six rack units (RUs) of occupied space. Assuming a similar density for the conventional storage you'd instead require 33RU for conventional storage—almost an entire full-height rack (42RU). By the time you add the storage controller/head, the deduplication storage might be sitting comfortably in 8RU, but the conventional storage will have filled an entire rack or maybe even overflowed into a second rack.

When companies with datacenters employ people to ruthlessly monitor the number of rack squares occupied in the datacenter, as well as the cooling costs and power requirements for the datacenter, you can immediately understand why this footprint reduction is so desired—particularly as data continues to explosively grow in many organizations.

13.5 Deduplication Considerations for Data Protection in Primary Storage

When considering deduplication for primary storage, the key considerations typically fall into one of the two following categories:

1. Reliability
2. Performance

While we should *always* be concerned about the reliability of a primary storage system, the risk of individual component failure causing a more serious data disruption does indisputably increase when deduplication is in place, as evidenced by the cautionary statement, "Don't put all your eggs in the one basket." (In this sense, consider deduplicated storage to be a bit like fruit juice concentrate: the loss of 1 L of regular fruit juice means just 1 L of juice lost; the loss of 1 L of fruit juice concentrate might result in 10 or 20 L of reconstituted juice being lost.)

In a similar vein to how current snapshot techniques just capture the *changed* blocks between the original and a snapshot, deduplication can be considered to be extremely dense storage. Reverting to our introductory example of a 50 TB deduplication storage system providing 500 TB of actual capacity based on a 10:1 reduction ratio, the loss of even 1 GB of data will have a considerably more devastating impact. A single 1 GB "chunk" on the deduplication store may be referred to dozens or even hundreds of times,[*] and so if (somehow) that chunk of deduplicated storage were to be either unexpectedly deleted or corrupted, it would have a much higher impact on the failure of a single LUN providing storage for a single host or virtualization server.

(In reality, since deduplication within primary storage *must* always be balanced with ongoing access performance, it is more usual to see lower deduplication ratios in primary storage than we do in data protection storage. For example, primary storage systems might aim for deduplication ratios in the order of 5:1.)

Performance plays a factor at all times, but we'll consider the cost of *rehydrating* data. This refers to reconstructing the original data out of deduplicated storage. A 100 GB virtual machine image may have deduplicated down to 12 GB of storage, but if we need to replicate that virtual machine image, will the replication be done against the original data or the deduplicated data? Deduplication is *not* an industry standard. Each vendor will implement deduplication differently, so the only way to perform fully deduplicated replication is to use deduplication storage systems from the *same* vendor for both source and target.[†] Considering the need to rigorously protect deduplication storage will create a fundamental requirement to replicate, which means the previous example of a 50 TB deduplication storage system will usually end up being 2×50 TB deduplication systems with replication in all but the most specific of examples. Otherwise, regardless of whether conventional storage is selected for the replication target *or* another vendor deduplication storage system is selected as a replication target, the data replicated between the sites will be fully rehydrated as part of the process.

The other protection-related performance consideration for deduplication in primary storage relates to what is commonly referred to as garbage collection. The nature of deduplication is that data deleted from an individual host accessing the deduplication storage cannot be immediately deleted from the deduplication storage. Regardless of whether the deduplication storage pool is global, compartmentalized to multiple systems, or even evaluated only against a single accessing system, a single file on a host will not in any way be guaranteed to have a 1:1 correlation to a single chunk or block of data on the deduplication system. Therefore, when a system that is using deduplication storage *deletes* content, this will typically trigger only a pointer erasure on the storage. The deduplication storage will report that the data is deleted, but processing the deletion beyond a simple pointer removal may not occur for hours if not days.

Garbage collection therefore is the process whereby deduplication storage will complete a number of clean-up steps, typically including at least the following:

■ Removing chunks of data that are unique and not referred to by *any* pointers on the storage system
■ Performing consistency checks against the data that remains

Depending on the type of system and how it's used, additional checks relating to aging of time-locked data, rebalancing of stored data across drives, maintenance of hash tables, cross-referencing of checksum hash tables against stored data, and even moving infrequently used data to alternate

---

[*] Consider, for instance, primary flash-based deduplication storage for virtual machines or virtual desktops. If the operating system between all virtual machines is the same, and there are hundreds of virtual machines on the deduplication storage, there will be very densely utilized deduplication blocks relating to the operating systems regardless of any other common data.

[†] Depending on the maturity of the storage vendor, your mileage may still vary considerably even with a common storage vendor.

storage tiers may all be performed during garbage collection activities.

These activities, as you may well imagine, can potentially be IO and/or CPU/RAM intensive on the deduplication storage. To mitigate or even avoid this, deduplication storage systems may have one or more of the following garbage collection control algorithms assigned:

1. *Garbage collect only runs during certain windows*: In this scenario, a specific window (time of day, day of week, or even both) might be assigned to garbage collection tasks. If the tasks do not complete within this time, they may be either aborted without finalized processing taking place or aborted at the point they reached and continued the next day.
2. *Garbage collect aborts if system load grows too high*: In this scenario, garbage collection will be scheduled to run at a time when it is expected system load will be low enough that it will not be impacted by collection. If the system load grows too high, the garbage collection might be aborted, and an alert generated.
3. *Garbage collect has a performance ceiling assigned to it*: In this scenario, the garbage collection will be configured such that it cannot exceed a particular percentage of system resources (e.g., 40%), and its progress slowed or shaped accordingly. This works in much the same way that many RAID systems allow for performance inhibitors to be placed on RAID reconstruction.

Garbage collection is an essential task in deduplication storage—if it's not performed routinely enough, the utilized target storage may grow until it becomes full. This can even become a vicious cycle—garbage collection aborted because it takes too long to run and will only *increase* the amount of storage to be considered on the next garbage collection run. For this reason, it's not unheard of to encounter organizations that have mismanaged their deduplication storage *and* their garbage collection cycles and ended up in a position where they've had to suspend use of the deduplication system for *days* to allow complete garbage collection operations to take place.

13.6 Deduplication Considerations for Data Protection in Backup and Recovery Systems

13.6.1 The Case for Deduplication

While deduplication storage systems are growing in popularity for primary storage (particularly all-flash arrays), they've usually offered some of the highest cost savings and efficiency gains in backup and recovery environments.

Consider a typical backup and recovery environment circa 2001: this was the period where tape libraries still ruled the earth. Much like their dinosaur ancestors, mammoth tape libraries were potentially huge beasts occupying a large datacenter footprint. Robot heads would swing to and fro at times seemingly constantly to feed tapes into tape drives, and operators would approach tape exchange ports with sometimes buckets full of fresh tapes or to take away the accumulated media from the previous night.

Despite their speed and capacity, tapes have largely fallen out of favor as a direct backup target for many organizations for several reasons, notably as follows:

■ Contention
  – *Media*: Tapes are physical items occupying physical space, and a tape drive cannot use more than one tape at a single time. Thus, the ability to facilitate a recovery request is directly impacted by the number of free tape drives available to load tapes.
  – *Host*: Massive data growth within organizations has often led to large pools of data being concentrated in particular locations, and sending all this data across busy LAN links may not always be an option (particularly in pre-10 Gbit ethernet environments); tape drives shared via fiber channel among multiple hosts can still only be accessed by a single host at any one time, and the overall environment reliability can be greatly impacted in such environments.
■ *Access (seek) time*: No matter how fast tape gets, it will remain considerably slower than disk for both the initial access time, and any random data seek operations. The amount of time it takes to start reading from a tape will typically be measured in tens of seconds assuming that the tape has to be loaded and then a seek operation performed; for disk, the time will be at most usually a few milliseconds.
■ *Service times*: Tape or tape drive failures are notorious for causing lengthy timeout delays in environments. A malfunctioning tape may take half an hour or more to successfully timeout, re-spool, and eject from a tape drive, and during that time, the drive (and backup/recovery bandwidth) will remain unavailable to the backup and recovery system. In an environment with *shared* tape access between multiple hosts via, say, fiber channel, a single tape drive fault may impact multiple hosts and even primary production hosts, necessitating reboots or lengthy pauses on backup/recovery functionality.
■ *Sequential access*: The sequential access nature of tape leaves it limited in its usefulness that it's highly efficient for high-speed writes and reads of large amounts of data is indisputable, but for newer enterprise backup

techniques such as instantly accessing and booting a virtual machine from protection storage, this is no longer sufficient.

- *Streaming speed*: While it's indisputable that tape *can* be of high-speed, that speed suffers a sharp drop-off when the incoming data speed drops; this is nonlinear based on tape drives having minimum or step-based ideal speeds. A tape drive capable of writing at, say, 160 MB/s may not seamlessly accommodate an incoming data stream of 100 MB/s, and instead may need to step down to just 80 MB/s, and so on.
- *Cost of operators*: Like it or not, we live in a time where cost-efficiency is a golden goose for most organizations and shareholders. Employees cost a business more than just their salaries, so it's often quite cost-prohibitive to achieve true lights-out operations with tape libraries. As soon as someone needs to load or unload media, that becomes an ongoing cost to the business.
- *Reliability*: Tapes are by their very nature relatively fragile—if not in use then in transport and storage. Like disk drives, tapes may not readily survive being dropped, but unlike disk drives, tapes are also *more likely* to be physically transported. During the transport, tapes are more likely to be exposed to environmental changes (e.g., temperature and humidity) that may impact the physical reliability. Finally, tapes are actually only one-half of the equation—tape drives are equally highly mechanical devices, and a single malfunctioning tape drive may cause damage to multiple tapes.

Except in the largest of "big data" situations, tape therefore has been relegated in most organizations to one of the following functions:

- Allegedly cheap off-siting
- Allegedly cheap archive
- Allegedly cheap expansion

In each case you'll note we referred to it as "allegedly cheap." This is because few businesses actually handle tapes correctly and therefore the perceived low cost as often as anything comes from using them in a way which is not best practice. (The management processes that are often not performed are discussed in our chapter on tape.)

As disk decreased in price, tape started to be eclipsed. The starting point was using disk storage as staging or landing areas for backup. This was "B2D2T"—backup to disk (transfer) to tape. A business might deploy a 5 TB LUN of SATA disk where all overnight backups would be written. During the day, the backups would be staged out to tape for longer-term storage and the disk space freed up for the next night's backup (where required). Over time, it became obvious that

recoveries requested from data still on disk could typically be facilitated much faster, but it was still acknowledged that buying sufficient disk to house even a relatively small backup cycle (say, a weekly full and subsequent incrementals) could be cost-prohibitive.

It was here that deduplication entered into its own. With deduplication applied, that 5 TB landing zone could suddenly hold 20, 30, or 50 TB of backups, and it became *considerably* more useful.

Data growth has not necessarily been accompanied by data uniqueness. With virtualization in the midrange now practically the norm, *data* often includes the operating system and application images installed on hosts. In particular, the use of traditional backup agents installed within virtualized guests has continued to decline with increased functionality for virtual image backups. (This will be covered in detail in Chapter 15.)

More generally, however, consider typical backup lifecycles. An organization might use the following schedules for backup:

- Daily
  - Full backup on either a Friday evening, Saturday, or Sunday
  - Incremental backups for the rest of the days in the week
  - These backups would be retained for 5 weeks
- Monthly
  - Full backup once a week to be retained for 13 months
- Yearly
  - Full backup once or twice a year to be retained for 7–10 years

While the nature of an incremental backup is "that which has changed," it's fair to say the majority of the data in each of the full backups in a cycle such as that mentioned earlier will remain relatively static for *most* systems. A database for instance may experience 5% growth month-on-month, but much of the content *in* the database, once ingested, will remain the same. This could equally be said of most fileservers as well.

Assume then a 4 TB fileserver where on a month-to-month basis, there is only a 5% change in data content. On the cycle mentioned earlier, there'll be, say, 17 full backups of the system performed every year—the 12 monthly backups, 1–2 yearly backups, and 5 weekly backups.*

If this system were being backed up to either tape or conventional disk, it would require 68 TB of storage. (A 2%

---

* A typical backup strategy will see the weekly full skipped when it's time to run a monthly full, and the monthly/weekly full skipped when it's time to run a yearly full.

daily change* would add another 2.4 TB of storage requirements—so just for a year's worth of backups, 70.4 TB of storage would be used to protect just 4 TB.)

Deduplication, however, would yield a considerably more economical result. A basic analysis would suggest even with a 5% month-on-month change that the full backups might conceivably achieve ratios of, say,

- 4 TB for first full
- (5% of 4 TB) × 16 additional fulls

This would yield 7.2 TB of occupied actual storage. While the incrementals aren't counted in that, that's outweighed by the rather obvious point that there's been no deduplication applied to the first full backup, either. If that achieved even a 4:1 deduplication ratio (which is reasonably conservative for fileserver data), then instead of 68 TB used for conventional storage to hold the full backups from 4 TB, we might actually squeak in at under lesser than 2 TB:

- 1 TB occupied space for first full backup
- 5% of 1 TB × 16 additional fulls

There is a substantially reduced data footprint using deduplication; in this example, we can see 4 TB being protected in just 2 TB of occupied space versus 68 TB using non-deduplicating storage. Even if we add a second deduplication system for replication between sites, we still yield a considerably better storage efficiency than conventional storage would.

The benefits of deduplication continue to grow (unless a particularly limited version of deduplication is used): most deduplication will have a broader analysis pool than the individual systems being backed up. So cumulatively, the deduplication benefits will considerably scale. It is not unusual, for instance, for organizations to deploy even relatively small deduplication systems with the intent of keeping 6–10 weeks of data online only to discover savings that allow for 6–9 *months* of data being kept online.

These types of savings and efficiencies have seen a very high adoption rate of deduplication in the otherwise reasonably conservative technical field of backup and recovery. The Data Protection Hub,† for instance, up until 2018 conducted yearly surveys of how and where organizations are using EMC NetWorker® within their environment and since 2010 has been asking respondents for information on their deduplication take-up:

- 2010—32% respondents using deduplication
- 2011—36% respondents using deduplication
- 2012—63% respondents using deduplication
- 2013—73% respondents using deduplication
- 2014—78% respondents using deduplication
- 2015—76% respondents using deduplication
- 2016—87% respondents using deduplication
- 2018—88% respondents using deduplication

In less than a decade of polling, deduplication went from practically bleeding edge to mainstream. While this represents only a single product, it's particularly worth considering that natively NetWorker does *not* perform deduplication: instead, it leverages external deduplication technology via specific integration points, and therefore businesses using NetWorker *and* deduplication have made a purposeful choice (rather than it just being a default feature).

Deduplication neatly solves (for many businesses and data types) one of the biggest core problems with backup and recovery—handling explosive data growth and retention requirements.

In short, for a great many businesses, it's no longer a question of *why are you using deduplication* but rather, *why aren't you using deduplication?*

13.6.2 Revisiting Source versus Target Deduplication

Source versus *target* deduplication was briefly mentioned in the introduction to deduplication. This refers to *where* some or all of the processing for deduplication occurs. To understand the implications, we'll consider a backup and recovery system with three hosts using deduplication storage as the destination for backups.

For a target-based deduplication system, this will mean each time any of the hosts need to backup, they transfer their data in their original format to the deduplication storage system. The deduplication system then deduplicates the data (either inline, or as part of post-processing activities), thus performing all the "heavy lifting" for the deduplication. This is shown in Figure 13.6. In our diagram, we have three systems backing up over the network to a deduplication purpose-built backup appliance; the first system has 100 GB of data, the second, 3 TB, and the third, 250 GB. If we assume a 10:1 deduplication ratio, only 335 GB of data is actually stored on the PBBA, but we have still seen 3.35 TB of data *sent* to the PBBA, with 3,015 GB discarded as unnecessary.

For deduplication occurring at the source, plug-ins or software of some variety will be installed on each of the hosts to be backed up, and these plug-ins will integrate with the backup process. While an individual host will not have a full understanding of all the deduplicated data stored on a deduplication system, it will be able to *at least* perform the basic

---

* A 2% daily change and a 5% month-on-month change can readily be reconciled by remembering files or data may be repeatedly revised as they are worked on.

† https://nsrd.info/blog—this site is published and maintained by the author, Preston de Guise.

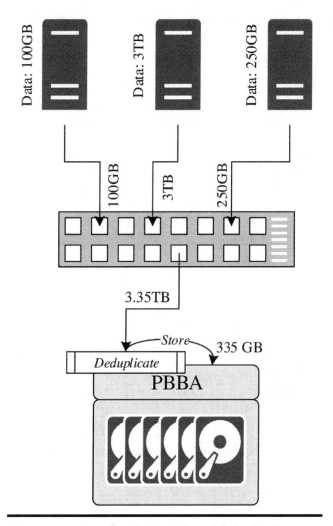

we might expect the above backup scenario to net the transmission of 50 GB + 188 MB (compressed data plus checksums)—still considerably less than 100 GB.

As mentioned, some backup and recovery deduplication systems will actually store local copies of the individual host's hashing/segment checksum information to further optimize the backup process, and this can make a tangible improvement on backup efficiency—checksums can tell us, for instance, that new data matches existing data that's already been stored for the client, so rather than sending that data, we only have to send a reference to it being used in another location and backup on the client.

Assume local hash tables were used and only 5% of the data on the system had changed (5 GB). Therefore, only checksums for approximately 5 GB of data would need to be sent to the deduplication system for global deduplication analysis. We could calculate the checksum data size for this as follows:

- 5 GB is 5,000,000 KB.
- This would generate 312,500 × 16 KB segments.
- Checksums for 312,500 segments would occupy 9,375,000 bytes at 30 byte checksums per segment.
- Total checksum data would be 9 MB.

In fact, if some of the new data on the client has checksums that match checksums already in the local cache, there'd be a further reduction in the amount of overall network traffic during the backup, as the remote checksum comparison could be skipped and the data just flagged as required for this particular backup. Using source-based hash tables for initial segment analysis, the amount of checksum data sent between the source and the deduplication appliance has decreased by *more than* an order of magnitude in our earlier example. Such savings can represent a considerable efficiency increase over WAN or even 1 Gbit link speeds and have been known to eliminate the need for businesses to deploy separated, high-speed backup networks in LAN backup scenarios.

A conceptual diagram of source-based deduplication is shown in Figure 13.7.

A key advantage of source-based deduplication is it can lead to significantly smaller amounts of data being sent across the network during a backup operation, albeit with a trade-off that the CPU and memory load on the host sending the data is sometimes significantly higher than a standard transfer. Some deduplication systems may offset this by using an *incrementals forever* approach; rather than periodically reprocessing *all* the data on a backup client, sufficient backup metadata will be maintained to only ever necessitate the processing of new or changed data. This means only the first backup will represent a significantly higher potential load on the backup clients—all subsequent backups, while still involving higher CPU load, will run for a significantly

Figure 13.6   Data flow in target-based deduplication.

block segmentation and communicate with the deduplication storage to determine whether or not individual segments need to be stored on the target or simply associated with the backup based on the hashing/checksums performed against the segments. For instance, assume a deduplication system checksums all data segments using a 30 byte checksum. If no local hash table is maintained, *all* checksums must be sent to the deduplication appliance. Assuming 100 GB of data on the source side and the data is segmented on average into 16 KB blocks, we could calculate the checksum data size as follows:

- 100 GB is 100,000,000 KB.
- This would generate 6,250,000 × 16 KB segments.
- Checksums for 6,250,000 segments would occupy 187,500,000 bytes at 30-byte checksums per segment.
- Total checksum data would be 188 MB.

If we have to send all the checksums *and* any unique data, and we assume unique data is compressed before being transmitted (a common approach for source-based deduplication),

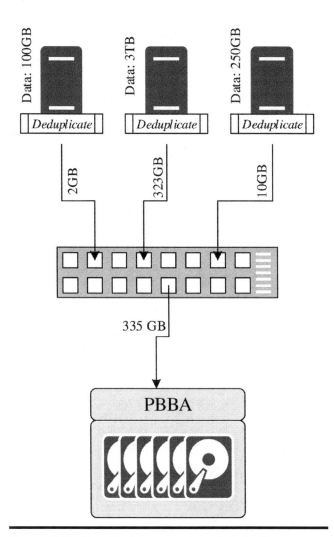

Figure 13.7 Data flow in source-based deduplication.

order to still reduce the amount of data being sent across the network.

13.6.3 Advanced Deduplication Features

By its very nature, deduplication is not the type of operation that can be performed by a "dumb" appliance. Regardless of whether the operation is performed inline or via post-processing, deduplication requires intense data analysis. As such, deduplication systems have the potential to provide more than just a "big bucket" of storage: they can provide a very intelligent big bucket.

This intelligent operation is beginning to unfold in numerous additional integration points. Some deduplication appliances for instance offer *virtual synthetic full backups*. We may recall that a synthetic full backup is one where the backup and recovery software processes previously completed full and incremental backups, combining them into a new full backup without any processing being performed on the actual backup client. The term *virtual synthetic full* therefore refers to the virtual construction of a synthetic full backup.

Synthetic full backups offer at least one, if not two, distinct advantages depending on the environment:

■ For larger systems where a standard full backup will take too much time or create too much a processing load on the client, the processing is off-loaded to the backup server (or another nominated host).
■ For remote systems where a standard full backup will take too long to traverse the network, a full backup can still be periodically generated without needing to send all the data to the backup environment again.

shorter period of time.* When we consider the CPU load associated with sustained data transfer over the network for a full, non-deduplicated backup, the net impact not only is considerably smaller but also lasts a considerably shorter period of time.

There is additionally a hybrid approach to source/target deduplication processing, whereby both the individual hosts backing up *and* the backup destination will support deduplication. This serves to significantly scale out deduplication operations: systems that do *not* support deduplication (e.g., NAS hosts being backed up via NDMP) can still send data in a standard format across the deduplication system for processing, but more conventional operating systems where agents can be installed can perform a subset of deduplication tasks in coordination with the deduplication system, in

In either case, the actual processing load for the synthetic full falls to the backup environment—typically the backup server. Depending on the size or number of data sets to be evaluated, this can considerably impact the performance of a backup server, particularly if a large number of systems are configured for synthetic full backups.

Virtual synthetic full backups therefore take advantage of the intelligence of the deduplication system and its inherent use of pointers to reference data. After all, a full backup on a deduplication system is merely a collection pointer referring to actual unique data objects required to reconstruct the data. Rather than requiring rehydration of data to construct a synthetic full backup, a deduplication system supporting virtual synthetic fulls can merely construct a new reference set of data pointers equivalent to a full backup from the full and incremental backups previously stored. This not only removes the synthetic full processing time from the backup server but also can substantially reduce the entire processing time for the activity. Constructing a new full backup from 1×4 TB backup and 30×100 GB backups (in the case of

_____

* While the logical data processed may be an "incremental," intelligent deduplication systems can in fact use the combination of new and existing metadata to map a new full from the incremental read—without the need for "synthetic full" backups.

monthly fulls with daily incrementals) may require up to 15 TB or more of backup data sets to be processed to create a new, say, 4.5 TB full backup. Collating and collecting a new series of pointers referring to data already on disk without needing to actually *read* the data, on the other hand, might be an order of magnitude faster.

Deduplication systems that tightly integrate with backup products for generating *registered* backup copies can represent a considerable time saving. Consider the replication of deduplicated backups. This similarly plays a role in backup and recovery use of the technology. When the backup system itself natively uses deduplication, or is aware of the underlying deduplication platform it uses, one would expect that two systems deployed in different sites would be able to replicate deduplicated backups between each other, thereby eliminating the requirement to rehydrate data or send data between sites if it is already present at the target.

Not all backup and recovery systems are natively deduplication systems as well, and it's equally common to see backup systems deployed using deduplication appliances as targets. In this case, even if identical or otherwise compatible deduplication systems are used at the primary and secondary backup sites, efficient replication of deduplicated data may not be guaranteed. In particular, one of the following scenarios will take place:

1. The backup replication will be initiated and executed entirely at the backup server level, resulting in a complete rehydration of data from the source for transmission to the target, with deduplication taking place at the target again.
2. The backup replication will be initiated and executed entirely at the deduplication appliance level, without any reference to or awareness of the processing by the backup system. Thus, the replicated data will be "unknown" to the backup system and may even cause issues if it becomes unexpectedly available to it.
3. The backup system will integrate with the deduplication system such that the backup system will *instruct* the deduplication system to replicate the data. The data will be replicated in deduplicated format, but the backup system will register the replicated data as an independent copy.

In the first option, the downside is a rather serious one: whatever the *original* size of the backup is, it will be the same amount of data that will be replicated. What's more, the data will be read from the source deduplication system, rehydrated for transit, sent across a link potentially slower than the normal LAN speed, and then deduplicated for storage on the target system.

The second option may reduce the data being replicated between sites, but at a cost: the backup system will

be unaware of the replicated data. This in itself will yield two different scenarios: either that data will need to be cataloged prior to its use or it will appear *entirely* identical to the backup system, making it critical for the backup administrator to prevent the data being simultaneously available at both sites. (For instance, consider replicated virtual tape media: backup products do not typically accept the notion of the same *tape* being in two different tape libraries, virtual or otherwise.) Thus, the saving in data replication time might be entirely undone by the additional management overhead of either cataloging data the backup system should already be aware of, or solving errors created by identical data appearing in multiple locations.

Backup-integrated replication, however, represents the Goldilocks scenario—the data is replicated in its deduplicated format, without any rehydration or reconstruction having taken place, *and* the backup system is fully aware of and able to use the backup copy.

Another advantage that can be offered by at least some deduplication appliances is to leverage the processing capabilities to speed up recoveries. While deduplication considerably eliminates the bandwidth requirements for *backup*, recovery by its very nature requires data to be rehydrated and sent across the network. However, by leveraging the CPU and memory within a deduplication appliance, the rehydrated data can be compressed before sending back across the network; we might assume that average recoveries in this sense could achieve a 2:1 compression ratio, and recoveries of sparsely populated datasets, pre-allocated databases, or data sources with repeated data may yield compression in the order of 4:1 or potentially higher.

An example of a compressed recovery is shown in Figure 13.8: a 1 TB database is recovered from a deduplicating appliance; as it is read and rehydrated, the data stream is compressed before it is sent over the network to the database server—in this case at a 4:1 compression ratio. As the database server receives the data stream, it decompresses it and writes the full 1 TB database to storage.

While compressed recoveries by their very nature will place additional CPU load on the recovery target, the focus in this case is a faster recovery—a modern system should be able to receive an incoming 250 GB data stream and decompress it to 1 TB faster than it would simply receive a 1 TB incoming data stream.

Other advanced functionality available in deduplication systems will be covered in Chapter 15. It's important to note this is still very much a young and evolving field: storage and data protection vendors are increasingly keen to increase the return on investment on backup and recovery systems, and the way to do this is to increase their utility. What was once a huge bucket where backups went to but were infrequently retrieved from is losing what limited appeal it did have. Intelligent storage systems integrated tightly into the

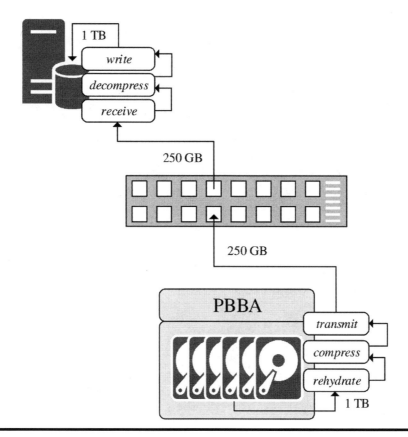

Figure 13.8   Compressed recovery from a deduplication appliance.

backup and recovery system are allowing backup to evolve from *merely* a corporate insurance system to something more practically useful on a day to day basis.

13.7 Deduplication Capacity Management

Like thin provisioning in virtual environments and modern primary storage systems, deduplication poses interesting challenges in terms of capacity management in that there is not a 1:1 correlation between the amount of data received by a deduplication system and the amount of data written. Equally, there is not an immediate correlation between data being deleted by the accessing system, and capacity being freed on the deduplication system. Finally, there is also not a 1:1 correlation between the amount of data deleted by the accessing system and the capacity that is *eventually* freed on the deduplication system.

The net result is that capacity management programs for deduplication storage—particularly in terms of our focus, deduplication appliances for backup, need to take into consideration longer-term patterns.

An initial simple rule is that 80% is the new 100%. This is not to say that deduplication appliances stop working

when they reach 80% utilization, but rather, when a deduplication appliance hits 80%, there needs to be an appropriate process in place where the business can answer the following questions:

- Is this normal growth?
- If there's unexpected growth:
  - Is it temporary and can it be expected to be deleted before it causes a capacity problem?
- Will a capacity expansion be required?

Since there is a level of unpredictability in deduplication storage, the key reason behind the "80% is the new 100%" rule is to avoid a situation where you realize too late that additional capacity *will* be required and it cannot be procured and installed as an expansion into the system prior to becoming full.

As noted previously, deduplication systems will go through a garbage collection or filesystem cleaning operation periodically; while some may do this daily, others will do it weekly. The more data that is on a system, the more data has to be evaluated during a cleaning operation and therefore the longer a cleaning operation will take. The other side of "80% is the new 100%" therefore is that if a system has a usable capacity of 500 TB, 400 TB (80%) takes less time to process for cleaning than say, 475 TB (95%), and there's more risk involved that there'll be a sudden influx of data while cleaning is still being processed.

Ideally with deduplication systems there may reach a point in time defined as *steady state*, that being when the amount of expired data that is removed from the system during its periodic cleaning cycle is significantly close to the amount of new, unique data that enters the system. This process allows for a certain amount of front-end data growth (front-end being the amount of data being protected), but with the expectation that there'll be sufficient commonality in that data and existing data that the back-end storage requirements are notionally static, or at least, growing at a very small rate.

Alternately, when data growth is still occurring, the goal will be a "saw-tooth" capacity utilization. If we consider deduplication appliances that perform weekly filesystem cleaning operations, what we would expect to see in a well-functioning system is a situation where the used capacity within the system grows at a reasonably linear rate during the week, then drops off to a value very close to the used capacity at the start of the week after the cleaning operation has completed. This might be graphed similar to the example shown in Figure 13.9.

While the glib statement around capacity management is that it must be done properly regardless of whether a storage platform is using deduplication or not, it is important to understand that with deduplication the 1:1 mapping between written and used, or deleted and freed storage is broken; this requires more diligent attention to detail and a better understanding of capacity *trends* than traditional storage platforms.

13.8 Cleaning Operations

As mentioned previously, and focusing on deduplication storage for backup and recovery services, when a backup application deletes a backup that resides on deduplication storage, the storage capacity is not immediately freed. Nor, when the delete is eventually processed, is there a guaranteed commensurate storage capacity returned to the size of the deleted backup. The reason for this of course is that the very nature of deduplication means that multiple backups may have relied on the same data.

Regardless of the data structure used, we can think of each backup as comprising of two distinct aspects when written to a deduplication platform, that being:

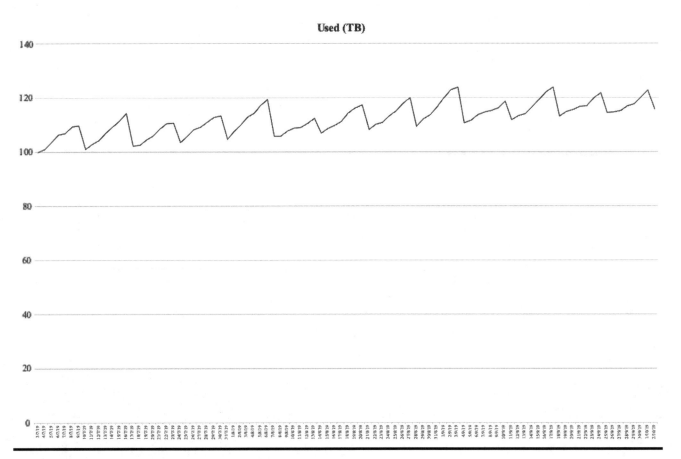

Figure 13.9 Saw-tooth capacity utilization growth.

- The pointers (and the sequence they are maintained in) to compressed data blocks, *and*
- The compressed data blocks which, when uncompressed and combined in the sequence described by the pointers, represent the original data protected.

While it is convenient to think of these pointers as a linked list, the actual data structures used are often considerably more complex—usually in the form of advanced tree-based structures, which allow for faster traversal to any individual segment of data, and describing "sets" of data which are written (e.g., a starting hash might describe the entire backup of a system, with subsequent hashes used for smaller units, until eventually individual leaves in the tree represent atomic segments of data).

Let's assume that we have two backups of the same chunk of data set, with modifications to the data between backups. We might consider these to be backup-X (bX) and backup-Y (bY), respectively, and we'll number each consecutive segment in the pointer structure starting with 1 and incrementing by 1. We'll consider a deduplication storage pool that has blocks of data written to it and labeled as ds-*N*, where *N* is an incrementing number. Assuming each backup can be reconstructed by reading eight blocks of data, this might mean there are pointer systems such as the following:

- Backup bX
  - bX-1 > ds-8
  - bX-2 > *ds-4*
  - bX-3 > ds-12
  - bX-4 > ds-9
  - bX-5 > *ds-13*
  - bX-6 > *ds-17*

    bX 7 > *ds-14*
  - bX-8 > ds-3
- Backup bY
  - bY-1 > ds-8
  - bY-2 > *ds-4*
  - bY-3 > *ds-17*
  - bY-4 > ds-9
  - bY-5 > ds-6
  - bY-6 > ds-22
  - bY-7 > *ds-14*
  - bY-8 > ds-3

Where a deduplication storage (ds) block is shown in italics, other backups we are not evaluating are also pointing to those blocks.

If the backup software deletes the file "bX," then this delete process is initially represented on the deduplication appliance by deleting the data structure for the *metadata* associated with that particular backup. Thus, the pointer sequence bX-1 through to bX-8 would be removed. However, reverse-mapping all of the existing used blocks on the deduplication data store to particular backups to see if anything else depends on those blocks will be a time-consuming process, so we only run a filesystem cleaning operation every week.

If we assume only backup bX has been deleted at the time a filesystem cleaning operation occurs, the filesystem cleaning operation will discover that only block ds-12 is actually eligible for deletion. Blocks ds-3, ds-8, ds-9 were also shared with backup bY, and blocks ds-4, ds-13, ds-14, and ds-17 were shared with both backup bY and *other* backups on the system, so cannot be removed.

If at the *next* filesystem cleaning operation, no other backups have been added and bY has been removed, we would be able to reclaim blocks ds-3, ds-8, and ds-9. However, blocks ds-4, ds-13, ds-14, and ds-17 will still be required by other backups on the system, so even though backup bY has been removed, those blocks cannot be removed.

13.9 Summary

Deduplication has now become a mainstay feature in data protection systems for many companies, and is starting to see wider adoption in primary storage systems as a means of mitigating storage costs either via reducing the amount of enterprise flash required or via automatically reducing the storage footprint required for infrequently accessed data.

Deduplication has the potential to introduce considerable savings and benefits to organizations when deployed correctly but does require careful architectural considerations to match functionality to business needs, ensure data deduplicatability, and anticipate maintenance windows associated with deduplication. The most critical consideration, as we've mentioned before, is the impact of data rehydration. A WAN-based source-side deduplication backup solution may very well meet or exceed *all* SLAs for backup *and* replication, but at recovery time still need to send data from the backup system to the recovering client in rehydrated format, thereby failing to meet the most critical SLA—recoverability. Of course, a conventional backup system will struggle on recovery (as well as the backup and replication SLAs), but this does serve to highlight despite its utility, deduplication is not a silver bullet that obviates the need for appropriate data protection architecture.

Companies that fail to plan deduplication appropriately will not achieve the high benefits already secured by so many businesses that have already successfully deployed this technology.

13.10 Self-Reflection

Source versus target deduplication can make a significant impact on the network requirements within a datacenter. Consider a situation where the weekly full backup for a large system is 100 TB: this can be backed up using source-side deduplication, or target-based deduplication. Assume in either scenario that only 5% of data is deemed new and needs to be stored.

- ■ How long would it take to send the backup to a *target-based* deduplication appliance via:
  - – 1 Gbit networking
  - – 10 Gbit networking
- ■ How long would it take to send the backup with source-based deduplication enabled, via:
  - – 1 Gbit networking
  - – 10 Gbit networking

Consider the need to store backups for 2 PB of data. There are two options available for storing the data:

- ■ A deduplication appliance
- ■ A traditional hard drive based storage array that does not deduplicate or compress

The deduplication appliance uses 3RU disk shelves that comprise 15×4 TB drives where 1 drive is a hot spare, and the remaining 14 drives are in a RAID-6 configuration (i.e., the capacity of 2 drives is used for parity). Assume a 5% capacity overhead from both the filesystem format and any metadata storage required—i.e., 95% of the presented capacity can be used for backup storage. Finally, assume a 15:1 deduplication ratio.

The traditional hard drive based storage array also uses 3RU disk shelves which comprise 15×4 TB drives where 1 drive is a hot spare, and the remaining 14 drives are in a RAID-5 configuration (i.e., the capacity of 1 drive is used for parity). As this is traditional storage, there is no deduplication ratio—1 MB of data written requires 1 MB of data stored. Likewise, there will be a 5% capacity overhead from the filesystem format once the combined storage LUN is presented to the backup server. (Do not be concerned with maximum filesystem sizes for this exercise—i.e., assume all shelves of storage can be presented as a "mega-LUN" to the backup server.)

Calculate how many shelves of storage is required by the deduplication appliance to hold the 2 PB of backups at a 15:1 deduplication ratio, and to compare, calculate how many shelves of storage is required by the traditional storage array to hold the same 2 PB of backups.

Which represents a smaller storage footprint for a datacenter?

Chapter 14

The Cloud

14.1 Introduction

Like its environmental namesake, cloud computing can be a somewhat nebulous topic, but there's no disputing it's becoming increasingly pervasive as businesses take advantage of a new utility approach to IT infrastructure (either purchased or leased). Cloud computing has seen a substantial shift toward OpEx models over previous CapEx models, allowing many organizations to take advantage of infrastructure they previously could never have afforded to purchase and deploy, let alone manage, before. (While some companies are still rushing forward with a cloud *first* policy, more mature companies have been refining this approach, instead shifting to cloud *fit*.)

The U.S. National Institute of Standards and Technology (NIST) defines five essential characteristics of cloud computing*:

1. *On-demand self-service:* The consumer should be able to select compute options and have the system automatically provision those without any human intervention.
2. *Broad network access:* Provisioned services should be available from a wide variety of client platforms, both traditional and mobile.
3. *Resource pooling:* Infrastructure will be multi-tenanted and the location of the infrastructure will have no bearing on service delivery or features available.
4. *Rapid elasticity:* Infrastructure can grow (and shrink) on demand without consumer impact.
5. *Measured service:* Resource usage should be monitored, controlled, and reported in order for complete pricing transparency for both the users and the service provider.

Broadly, the three types of cloud models available are as follows:

- *Public:* Cloud infrastructure is provided by a third party in a pure utility model, having hundreds, thousands, or more customers sharing access to multi-tenanted infrastructure.
- *Private:* Cloud infrastructure is housed entirely within the business using it. This is deployed with the same guiding characteristics of cloud computing, but the business maintains complete control and privacy over its data and compute resources.
- *Hybrid:* Private cloud that can *scale-out* to make use of public cloud as required. This typically allows a business to make use of higher levels of infrastructure than it could typically afford but still maintain a high degree of control over the placement of data and resources, their security, management, and protection.

(A pseudo-fourth type of cloud is referred to as "community" or "shared" cloud; this refers to trusted infrastructure shared by many businesses. These may be connected businesses—e.g., all sub-companies of a holding company, or just businesses that have decided to pool resourcing. While multi-tenanted, the actual infrastructure will typically be jointly owned by all the businesses cohabitating systems on the cloud service.)

The cloud model should not be confused with older data location models such as "on premises" (or "on prem") and "off premises" (or "off prem"). While it might be said that a *public* cloud definitely represents *off premises* data, off-premises does not have to mean *in-cloud*, and nor does *on-premises* mean private cloud. Equally, a business might choose to maintain a private cloud in a datacenter it does not actually own, thereby having a private, "off-premises" cloud.

Regardless of the actual cloud model used, there are a variety of service models that might be offered or available

---

* "The NIST definition of cloud computing" (Peter Mell, Timothy Grance), September 2011, Special publication 800-145, online at http://csrc.nist.gov/publications/nistpubs/800-145/SP800-145.pdf

to customers. These service models are typically defined as "X-as-a-Service," or *XaaS*, to use the common abbreviation. The three most accepted types of service models are as follows:

- *Software as a Service (SaaS)*: This refers to a software package operating in multi-tenanted fashion, providing access to a potentially large number of businesses. Businesses such as *Salesforce* represent the high end of SaaS cloud computing.
- *Platform as a Service (PaaS)*: Typically PaaS sits on top of an IaaS-like environment (managed by the cloud provider themselves), offering an extensible, high level programmable platform with specific functionality and allowing for subscriber extension without needing to manage virtual machines, operating systems, etc., which are leveraged by the service. PaaS includes services such as databases, cloud-based big data analysis systems, and frameworks for rapid cloud-based application development and/or deployment.
- *Infrastructure as a Service (IaaS)*: This allows the consumer to run (reasonably) arbitrary operating systems and applications on provisioned storage, compute, and networking infrastructure. From a pre-cloud mentality, this is a "virtual datacenter," with some limitations.

The *aaS* definition is regularly extended as cloud service models continue to grow and now includes additions such as the following:

- *IT as a Service (ITaaS)*: This is effectively a mix of outsourcing *and* IaaS, PaaS, or SaaS as required.
- *Storage as a Service (STaaS)*: This provides large-scale object-based access to storage for use in archive or other applications and may in turn be leveraged by other cloud providers for their SaaS, PaaS, BaaS, or AaaS offerings.
- *Backup as a Service (BaaS)*: Backup and recovery services provided via the cloud utility model.
- *Disaster Recovery as a Service (DRaaS)*: Typically sees service providers offering a replication target for a customer's own backup and recovery environment. In the event of a major issue, the company can recover from the replica data. This may even be leveraged with the option for the DRaaS provider to provision a limited amount of compute and storage resources to the business in the event of a disaster so they can start some operations in the cloud.
- *Archive as a Service (AaaS)*: Growing in popularity as a means of allowing businesses to forego tape entirely, archive as a service allows for large-scale storage of long-term archival or compliance data without needing to manage the storage.

- *Function as a Service (FaaS)*: This defines the "serverless" movement—developers executing functions or stored procedures without reference to the compute resources that may run them.

With all these different models and services available, it is becoming increasingly obvious that a strong focus on data protection needs to be applied to cloud computing to avoid the risk of significant or even catastrophic data loss. This focus is also important to avoid *decreasing* the level of data protection available when moving workloads into the cloud when compared to what had been used within a traditional datacenter.

14.2 Data Protection Risks in the Public Cloud

To correctly determine data protection requirements in the public cloud it is first necessary to consider the various types of risks for those operations.

14.2.1 Should the Workload Be There?

The first risk to consider with public cloud is: should the workload (i.e., the data) be present there in the first place? This comes down to two essential points:

1. Does the availability latency/bandwidth to public cloud support the workload?
2. Is the data stored in a place that the company is allowed to store it?

The first question starts as a usability focus. If a workload is primarily accessed by users within the business (rather than say, external customers), then those users may either depend on, or expect, a certain level of performance. If it's a highly interactive workload, users will care little that the compute and storage performance in the public cloud is no different (or even better) than it was on-premises if the latency goes from 2 ms to 50 ms because the workload is now hosted hundreds or thousands of kilometers away. Usability requirements therefore will drive the business to ensure that a workload which is developed or placed in public cloud is actually *usable*. Beyond usable in its normal state however, data protection does become a consideration in the broader picture of thinking about failover, availability, and redundancy. Virtual desktop services for applications with frequent user interaction hosted out of the Azure Australian South East region may offer perfectly acceptable performance for Melbourne-based office workers. However, if the service is failed over to Azure Australia East, approximately 870 km of distance will be added to the connections—a minimum latency increase of approximately 12 ms.

(Of course, if a workload is going to be used by general consumers that might be anywhere in the world, the latency and bandwidth question elevates to an overall application design consideration, rather than a general performance question for a specific geographic region.)

Beyond workload usability in public cloud, the other obvious question is: can the data be there? Various countries have legislative requirements over where data relating to citizens or government activities can be stored—this *sovereignty* question is one that businesses must resolve early in the process of public cloud consideration. It matters not if a public cloud provider has exactly what service the business needs (either primary service, or data protection service) if the data has to be hosted in a location that the company is legally unable to copy or move the data to. Various public cloud providers maintain government approved versions of their cloud services (e.g., AWS has a GovCloud service for the United States) which allows government agencies and businesses who do work for those agencies to still engage public cloud services for data meeting particular sensitivity and security requirements. More broadly, a variety of countries and legislative regions require high control over the location of private data. For example, Singapore outlines obligations of companies that collect personal data in its Personal Data Protection Act (PDPA):

> Section 26 of the PDPA limits the ability of an organization to transfer personal data outside Singapore. In particular, section 26(1) provides that an organization must not transfer any personal data outside Singapore except where it can ensure that a comparable standard of protection, as provided for under the PDPA, will be maintained over any personal data that is transferred[*]

Sovereignty can be more complex than "can this go in the public cloud?" Some businesses may be required to keep a local copy of data, regardless of where the data normally resides or is operated on. It is therefore important to map where data can and can't go so that both primary and data protection processes can be planned accordingly.

14.2.2 Is the Workload Secured?

AWS perhaps outlines subscriber responsibility to data security most effectively in its shared responsibility model,[†] which it summarizes as:

- AWS has "responsibility for security 'of' the cloud."
- The customer has "responsibility for security 'in' the cloud."

While a cloud provider is obligated to keep the overall infrastructure secured, it is up to the subscribing business to actually apply appropriate access and other security controls to the data and workloads they place in the cloud. The industry is replete with examples of businesses failing to appropriately secure workloads they place in public cloud, resulting in data breaches or data destruction. Often such breaches are caused by failing to change default passwords (or not creating passwords in the first place), not modifying access permissions, or even placing private passwords and keys within open source software hosted on public repositories.

Security of the data protection environment for any cloud workload is just as important, if not more important than the security for the workload itself. As we established in Chapter 9, improper access to the data protection environment could expose not only the current workload but also historical versions of data,[‡] and allow significant data destruction activities to be performed with ease. These considerations do not disappear just because a workload and its data are in a public cloud rather than a private datacenter.

14.2.3 Is the Workload Protected?

The short answer of course is that your public cloud workload is not protected unless you take the appropriate steps to protect it, yourself.

While cloud providers are responsible for ensuring their infrastructure is up and available for you within the availability limits they are contractually obligated to provide, if data is lost as a result of a failure, there is rarely a contractual onus on them to provide recovery services. Here we should be particularly mindful of the difference in responsibility between providing *fault tolerance*—e.g., ensuring data is not lost if a single drive in a storage unit fails and *recoverability*.

While most of us have been trained out of reviewing the terms and conditions thanks to excessively long end user license agreements (EULAs) presented by smart phones and a plethora of modern software, failure to understand the service provided in a cloud has a potentially more significant impact than not reading the terms and conditions of Instagram before embarking on a career as an "Influencer."

DigitalOcean, a cloud provider that competes with the giant hyperscalers such as AWS, Azure, and Google cloud platform (GCP), has perhaps the most succinct statement regarding data protection within its terms and conditions:

---

[*] The Personal Data Protection Framework in Singapore, Paul Lanois, 2 October 2014, International Association of Privacy Professionals (IAPP), https://iapp.org/news/a/the-personal-data-protection-framework-in-singapore/

[†] https://aws.amazon.com/compliance/shared-responsibility-model/

[‡] Remembering considerations such as the European GDPR, unauthorised access to historical data protection content may result in a significant privacy breach if data is recovered for individuals who had exercised their right to be forgotten.

9. Backup

9.1 Subscriber is solely responsible for the preservation of Subscriber's data which Subscriber saves onto its virtual server (the "Data"). EVEN WITH RESPECT TO DATA AS TO WHICH SUBSCRIBER CONTRACTS FOR BACKUP SERVICES PROVIDED BY DIGITALOCEAN, TO THE EXTENT PERMITTED BY APPLICABLE LAW, DIGITALOCEAN SHALL HAVE NO RESPONSIBILITY TO PRESERVE DATA. DIGITALOCEAN SHALL HAVE NO LIABILITY FOR ANY DATA THAT MAY BE LOST, OR UNRECOVERABLE, BY REASON OF SUBSCRIBER'S FAILURE TO BACKUP ITS DATA OR FOR ANY OTHER REASON.

In other words, we trust that you'll be responsible and back up your own data. Things happen![*]

Azure eschews all-capitals to advise:

Security. We maintain appropriate technical and organizational measures, internal controls, and data security routines intended to protect Customer Data against accidental loss or change, unauthorized disclosure or access, or unlawful destruction. Current information about our security practices can be found within the Trust Center. You are wholly responsible for configuring your Customer Solution to ensure adequate security, protection, and backup of Customer Data[†].

In general: unless a cloud service explicitly states that they will provide backup and recovery, or more broadly, data protection services, you should work under the basis that it is your responsibility to do so. This applies regardless of the sort of service being subscribed to, including the common options such as IaaS, PaaS, and SaaS.

14.2.4 What Is the Exit Strategy?

It's one thing to place a workload in a cloud, but what happens when it becomes necessary to remove the workload from the cloud?

In June 2019, Joyent announced the upcoming closure of their public cloud, providing 5 months' warning[‡] that their customers would need to find new cloud providers. Verizon, in February 2016 gave its customers just 2 months' notice to find another provider,[§] and HP announced in October 2015 that it would close its Helion Public Cloud in January 2016.[¶] Yet these timeframes pale in comparison to:

being told that your sole cloud provider is going into administration and that you have 24 to 48 hours to get your business' data and systems out and into a new environment.

The Australian Prudential Regulation Authority (APRA) supervises banking, insurance, and superannuation companies operating in Australia, and has established a variety of guidelines on cloud usage requirements over time either in response to, or working in conjunction with, financial institutions keen to offer new services. In 2018, they noted in relation to cloud usage:

APRA expects that an APRA-regulated entity would continue to meet its obligations regardless of disruptions resulting from a failure of technology, people, processes, or cloud provider[**].

It would be advisable for businesses when moving a workload to, or creating a workload in a cloud service, to have at least some contingency plan for repatriating it to a datacenter, or moving it to another cloud. Such an action might be needed for a variety of reasons, including but not limited to:

■ Cloud provider changes cost model, resulting in the workload being too expensive to continue to run with that provider
■ Change of legislation or business operational requirements that necessitates moving the workload
■ Failure of public cloud provider
■ Decision by public cloud provider to close down a datacenter
■ Alternate cloud provider offering incentives or discounts sufficient to justify relocating the service.

[*] Terms of Service Condition, DigitalOcean, 8 April 2019, www.digitalocean.com/legal/terms-of-service-agreement/

[†] Microsoft Azure Agreement, https://azure.microsoft.com/en-au/support/legal/subscription-agreement-nov-2014/

[‡] "Upcoming Changes to Our Cloud Business," Steve Tuck, 6 June 2019, Joyent, www.joyent.com/blog/joyent-announces-strategic-change-to-their-public-cloud-business

[§] "Verizon Shutting Down Public Cloud, Gives Two Months to Move Data", Yevgeniy Sverdilik, 12 February 2016, Data Center Knowledge, www.datacenterknowledge.com/archives/2016/02/12/verizon-shutting-down-public-cloud-gives-users-one-month-to-move-data

[¶] "A new model to deliver public cloud," Stephen Spector, 21 October 2015, HP, https://community.hpe.com/t5/Shifting-to-Software-Defined/A-new-model-to-deliver-public-cloud/ba-p/6804409

[**] Cloud control: APRA evolves its stance on shared computing services, Insight Issue 3 2018, Australian Prudential Regulation Authority, www.apra.gov.au/insight-issue-3-2018-cloud-control www.apra.gov.au/insight-issue-3-2018-cloud-control

The value in planning ahead—either fully, or at least in broad brush-strokes, is that exit strategies might be accommodated in a cost- and operations-compatible way via data protection options.

14.3 The Rise of Shadow IT

The term *shadow IT* has been increasingly used to define scenarios where cloud-based IT resources are procured and organized *outside* of the IT department—by managers, pseudo-technical staff, or power users within other areas of the business. Shadow IT occurs when a group within the business requires certain IT functions but are unable or unwilling to access them through conventional IT channels. Rather than waiting until the resources can be made available, they seek them through public cloud services. Thus, islands of IT the business may rely on that are outside of the watchful eye of IT departments spring up within the organization.

It can be argued that the existence of shadow IT within business points to a communication problem between the business and the IT department, and with the communication problem comes the inevitable problems of ensuring data integrity, recoverability, and availability.

Despite the potential short-term advantages presented by using shadow IT, managers within a business should be particularly cognizant of the risks posed by shadow IT: business functions might be deployed on systems that do not meet business needs for recoverability, records retention, data availability, security, privacy, or data integrity. This does not mean cloud services should be avoided, but it does show the need for increased collaboration, maturity, and communication in IT service management regardless of where the service is being delivered from.

14.4 Public Clouds and Availability

14.4.1 What's a Few Nines between Friends (Redux)?

For years the enterprise IT industry has had a particular focus on "high nines" availability, referring to the percentage a system is operational. This was discussed in the introduction of Chapter 10 (Continuous Availability, Replication, and CDP).

In the context of cloud, it's pertinent to briefly revisit high nines availability as a reminder that businesses must understand the advertised *and* achieved availability levels of cloud providers if they wish to move workloads out into a public or community cloud space.

While many public cloud providers will make strong promises relating to availability, those promises of availability do not always relate to protection—and may not even correlate to actual delivered availability. Others may simply make no promises whatsoever—which is hardly reassuring. Many public cloud providers fail to offer detailed information about their availability status, leading to the rise of third-party analysts or consultants who aggregate and present this information. For instance, CloudHarmony[*] (now owned by Gartner) states on its "About" page:

> CloudHarmony was founded in late 2009. At that time, we recognized a need for objective performance analysis to compare cloud services. Our intent is to be an impartial and reliable source for objective cloud performance analysis.

Businesses evaluating public cloud services do well to research availability of those services before becoming locked into agreements. While these figures undoubtedly reference up/accessible time, operational responsiveness of most cloud services will be almost always more determined by the link speed a business has between itself and a cloud service provider than the actual individual component responsiveness *within* the cloud.

While CloudHarmony now only present availability times in windows of up to a month, they previously would provide statistics for 365 days. On 4 July 2015, the CloudHarmony aggregated 365-day availability statistics of Amazon, Microsoft Azure, and Google are shown in Table 14.1. These range between mere minutes and *days*.

Data provided by CloudHarmony to The Information[†] listed downtime in minutes for the three primary hyperscalers in 2015, 2016, and 2017[‡] as shown in Table 14.2.

Unless a business has built high resiliency into its cloud service offerings via adoption of a multi-cloud approach with workload failover, the outages shown in Tables 14.1 and 14.2 for a business don't necessarily just represent *single system* outages but *entire datacenter* outages. That is, in each case it's entirely possible that an outage is not just a single workload but *all* workloads that have been moved into that cloud service provider. Without careful planning and architectural mitigation, the decision to move workloads to public cloud has the potential to significantly, detrimentally impact a business.

---

[*] https://cloudharmony.com/about
[†] "How AWS Stacks Up Against Rivals on Downtime," Kevin McLaughlin and Mike Sullivan, 7 March 2017, The Information, www.theinformation.com/articles/how-aws-stacks-up-against-ri vals-on-downtime
[‡] As the article was published in March 2017 it presumably only covered the first two months of that month.

Table 14.1 Example Downtimes on Three Noteworthy Public Cloud Providers

Provider	% Available	# Outages	Total Downtime
Amazon EC2	99.9984	17	1.35 hours
Amazon S3	99.9962	33	3.03 hours
Google Cloud Storage	99.9998	14	12.42 minutes
Google Compute Engine	99.9639	106	9.49 hours
Microsoft Azure Object Storage	99.9902	142	11.02 hours
Microsoft Azure Virtual Machines	99.9613	118	46.58 hours

Table 14.2 Total Time Lost in Minutes, 2015–2017 for Amazon, Azure, and Google Cloud Customers

Provider	2015	2016	2017
Amazon	135	108	205
Azure	642	270	740
Google	421	74	11

14.4.2 Data Loss versus Accessibility Loss

Particularly when we consider public cloud, data protection considerations will need to take into account both data *loss* scenarios and data *accessibility* loss scenarios.

Within the traditional infrastructure space, it's become standard practice for businesses with any operational dependency on their IT infrastructure to maintain at least two physically separate datacenters, with either datacenter capable of running *at least* the mission critical applications and functions.

The dual or multi-datacenter approach for many businesses has the primary purpose of disaster recovery and business continuity—in the event of a datacenter being unavailable, operations should be able to continue at the other datacenter. This accounts for a variety of faults, including

- Physical server failures
- Storage system failures
- Power failures
- Internet access failures
- Internal networking failures
- Physical site inaccessibility
- Physical site destruction

Such considerations should not immediately disappear for a business just because it no longer owns the infrastructure being used. Businesses must still look at the operational risk of losing access to a cloud service provider. While the rest of this chapter focuses on data loss, accessibility loss (particularly prolonged accessibility loss) can have just as negative an impact on a business as data loss itself.

> Amazon Web Services suffered database problems in its Sydney region, which had a flow-on impact on big customers including MYOB ... who reported having 40 of its services down and just two up[*].

Even the largest of public cloud service providers suffer outages. If mission critical workloads are placed in a public cloud, part of that placement must include a risk assessment not only of data loss but also of accessibility loss—and appropriate architectural and operational planning to keep the business functions going. This might be a reduced private infrastructure capability to deliver the service, emergency co-location service arrangements, or for truly mission critical systems, the same service replicated between and available from two or more public cloud providers serviced out of entirely different geographies. While some larger cloud providers may offer services that can span or failover between geographies, subscribers may be unable to leverage this if they have data sovereignty constraints. Further, all of the subscriber services are still within the same cloud provider and might still be susceptible to a truly global provider network or security issue.

This is nothing new, of course. Standard datacenter design practice will include much of the considerations that need to be dealt with in the public cloud model as well. A few rules normally considered for datacenter practice include the following:

- Datacenters should not rely on the same part of the power grid (or at least be serviced by different grid blocks).

---

[*] MYOB floored by AWS Sydney database outage, Ry Crozier, 14 February 2019, IT News Australia, www.itnews.com.au/news/myob-floored-by-aws-sydney-database-outage-519312

■ Datacenters should have redundant links from alternate network/internet providers.

■ There should be sufficient physical distance between datacenters to reduce the likelihood of the same disaster affecting both the primary and secondary datacenters.

■ Datacenters should not be susceptible to the *same* physical disaster situations (e.g., don't have two physically isolated datacenters in basements if both regions they're in happen to be susceptible to flooding).

None of these considerations go away in public cloud, and while the aim will be to ensure SLAs with the service provider cover scenarios such as protection from physical destruction, a fault in a cloud service provider's networking that impacts its infrastructure regardless of geographic location is *not* unheard of.

In essence, this is dealt with by treating public cloud providers like conventional utility providers (power, water, internet service providers), and making the same utility-like decisions to ensure the business is adequately protected from similar service losses.

14.4.3 Objectives and Agreements

When evaluating contracts or stated availability/accessibility levels of public cloud providers, potential subscribers must be particularly mindful of noticing whether levels are stated as *agreements* or *objectives*. While legal definitions may change (or be challenged) between geographies, it's usually accepted in IT circles that an SLA and an SLO have a critical difference.

We usually accept an SLA to be one that is backed by legal or financial incentives. That is, the notion of an agreement creates a contractual obligation of fulfillment, and if that fulfillment for some reason fails to take place, pecuniary penalties can be extracted by the party who has contracted the service. Depending on the severity of the failure, this may result in a refund, a credit, or perhaps even a fee-less termination of contract. In some contracts, it may even be associated with fines.

On the other hand, an SLO is seen to be one where the supplier makes no binding commitment to achieve the stated levels of service. It has an *objective* to achieve the service levels, but it doesn't as such commit to meeting them and therefore doesn't agree to be held liable if it fails to do so.

A business that moves workloads (particularly production ones) from internal IT services with fixed SLAs to external IT services offering mere SLOs is effectively *gambling* its ability to offer the business functions reliant on those IT workloads (and dangerously so if those workloads are business-critical or have externally imposed SLAs upon them). Just as Icarus fell after flying too close to the sun and having his wax-attached wings fall off, a business that *trusts*

everything will be OK could find itself plummeting through the cloud with no means of arresting its fall.

In short, the difference between an SLA and an SLO is effectively the difference between a written contract and a handshake agreement, something that reflects upon the operational maturity of a business. A business that does not allow vendor or supplier service contracts to be based on unwritten handshake agreements should be extremely leery of relying on SLOs for business systems availability, unless appropriate contingencies can be developed. The tendency for users of technology to skim over and blithely accept EULAs and the accessibility of public cloud services to even non-IT staff make the risks of placing a business workload into an insufficiently protected environment much higher than we would like to see. That is, while an IT manager engaging a new service might have the terms and conditions for that service reviewed carefully, a developer or innovator in a department standing that service up as a "test" may not. Often these "test" services get transitioned to production when they become useful to the business. In such situations, it may be that due diligence on service levels has never been performed.

14.4.4 Cascaded Providers

Another availability factor that must be considered by a business when evaluating service providers is: *who are their service providers?* While some public cloud service providers will run their own infrastructure and datacenters, cloud-consolidation is a frequent occurrence within the services marketplace. For instance, a SaaS provider offering CRM systems may in fact host its CRM systems on the IaaS or PaaS offerings of another provider, irrespective of how large they are. (For instance, a small SaaS provider might choose to run on another public service provider's platform to avoid the cost of building infrastructure that may never be used. On the other hand, a large SaaS provider might recognize that the cost of running and maintaining the level of infrastructure required for the number of customers they have is too high and choose instead to utilize a service provider to limit infrastructure costs directly based on customer numbers and workloads.)

Thus, the reliability and availability of the services being engaged is not *just* measured against the primary service provider availability, but *also* the availability of *their* primary service provider and the level of resilience they have architected into their services. Unfortunately, there is no standard for the publication of this sort of usage data, and in fact many businesses consider it to be practically an *operational secret* so as to limit their exposure. In this sense, obfuscating service providers is no different to businesses not advertising the location of their business continuity site (even to the point of having no information on buildings, being rented through an agent, acquired through a management company, etc.), though this can be cold comfort to subscribers needing to make an informed decision as to the reliability of the services they intent to engage.

14.4.5 Cloud as Another Datacenter

"There is no cloud, it's just someone else's computer" goes the cheeky rebuttal to cloud computing. It's true, and it's not. There's more to cloud than "here's a bunch of computers," but it's also undeniably true that the core of cloud is computing and storage infrastructure; it may be packaged and consumed differently to "traditional" infrastructure, but it *is* infrastructure. There's intelligent software and automation wrapping around it, to be sure, but the cloud is comprised of computers, and even serverless still uses servers.

In this sense, there is merit to considering cloud as being another form of datacenter. Again, there's more to it than that, if you want to consider a cloud service provider potentially providing services out of multiple datacenters, being able to move workloads between regions and availability zones and so on, but just like an on-premises workload will reside on one or more servers in a specific physical location, so too will in-cloud workloads reside in specific datacenters, regardless of how mobile that workload is.

14.4.6 The FARR Model Applies to Cloud

The expertise that has been developed for traditional infrastructure is not made redundant by moving workloads into public cloud. Recall that the FARR model (Section 5.2.1) of data protection encompasses:

- Fault tolerance
- Availability
- Redundancy
- Recoverability

While much of the low-level fault tolerance is delivered by the service provider in a cloud environment, it is still the responsibility of the subscriber to have adequate protection mechanisms and processes in place to deal with a situation where that fault tolerance fails. Availability, redundancy, and recoverability must all be organized by the subscriber, either as a paid enhancement to the cloud subscription, or an overlay function into the subscription.

As we will see in coming sections, applying the FARR model to workload design in public cloud applies regardless of whether one makes use of cloud native protection, traditional protection, or a mixture of both.

14.5 Cloud Native Protection

Cloud native protection is an umbrella term used to describe the practice of making use of the native protection mechanisms provided by public cloud services. Almost invariably this comes down to snapshot functionality. (While Azure provides a basic subscription backup service in the traditional sense, Microsoft has never been a "backup" company and the service can be somewhat rudimentary and limited. Likewise, the recent AWS backup service is a rudimentary approach designed to tick check-boxes rather than offer the types of feature-rich service an enterprise would be used to from traditional infrastructure services.)

14.5.1 Cloud Snapshots

For many cloud providers, snapshots work a little differently than they do on conventional storage arrays. On-premises snapshots are usually stored with the original volume (or as snapshot replicas with a replica of the original volume); it is more common than not to see snapshots in public cloud environments as data copied from block to object storage, per Figure 14.1.

When the data is being copied to an alternate storage platform, such as object, it is not particularly safe to use space-saving mechanisms such as copy-on-write snapshots. Instead, cloud providers typically introduce the concepts of

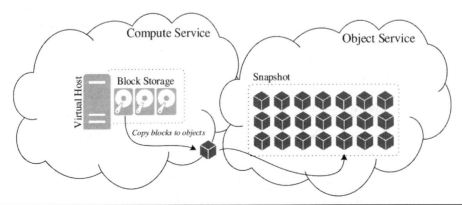

Figure 14.1 Snapshots in a public cloud environment.

full and incremental snapshots: a full snapshot is a complete copy of block storage into object storage, and an incremental is the copy of just the changed blocks since the last snapshot. (It is advisable to confirm that a cloud service supports incremental snapshots—this is not always the case, and without incrementals, all snapshots will be full snapshots.)

While in our example we have referred to taking snapshots of block storage volumes, *snapshots* are often used as the generic term for protection against other types of services in public cloud environments as well. For instance, within PaaS environments, snapshot services will be offered against a variety of databases, such as Oracle, Microsoft SQL Server, and others. Your mileage may vary, as the saying goes, on how "snapshot" as a traditionally understood function, relates to a PaaS database.

As is always the case in cloud service models, it is critical to understand the potential costs of using cloud snapshots. A common mistake is to assume that there'll be a comparable pricing structure between snapshot storage requirements and plain object storage requirements, but this is not guaranteed to be the case.

For instance, using Amazon's Cost Estimator* service, 1 TB of general purpose SSD storage in June 2019 in the Asia Pacific/Sydney region would cost US$120. With daily snapshots enabled having a 3% daily change rate, the storage cost rises to $200.99—$80.99 being EBS snapshot storage.

If we assumed even a full block to object copy including empty blocks, then the 3% daily change over a full 31-day month, 1,930 GB of S3 in the same region, by comparison, would cost $48.12—though it is noted this is has been calculated without factoring in any PUTS, GETS, or other operations that can also incur costs against object storage.

EBS snapshots do not copy empty blocks, and presumably for the average subscriber the entire 1 TB volume would not be copied completely in the first full snapshot; we can see from the comparison that snapshot storage might come at a premium, even when the cloud provider also offers cheap object storage. Since EBS (and other AWS-provided) snapshots represent a point in time copy of the volume as of the time the snapshot was initiated, regardless of how long it takes to populate the object storage copy, one might assume that some of the additional overhead in cost comes from additional block storage layers required to create that crash-consistent point in time copy.

A challenge with snapshots is ensuring you understand the level of consistency they offer. For true consistency it may be recommended to dismount a volume before taking a snapshot of it: when that volume is the operating system/boot volume for a virtual machine for instance, that implies it is necessary to shut down the virtual machine first to guarantee consistency. Usually this is not performed, resulting

in a "crash-consistent" snapshot—the recovered volume will appear as if the system using the volume had crashed. Equally it is important to understand, for systems hosting multiple block volumes, whether the snapshot is only atomic for each individual virtual disk, or whether it can be atomically consistent to all virtual disks simultaneously (important if a service being run spans and writes to multiple virtual disks).

Most cloud systems will support snapshot recovery either back to the original volume/database, or to an alternate location. The recovery functionality that is available is very much specific to each cloud provider though and should be researched carefully as part of the overall planning process.

The advantage of snapshots is that they are practically ubiquitous within cloud services; the disadvantage is that management of those snapshots is often an afterthought. While developers in particular will readily take snapshots of systems as they work, they may not exercise appropriate levels of governance in expiring the snapshots. This tends to lead to "storage creep," where additional charges are incurred monthly for storage services relating to snapshots that are no longer required. AWS themselves in a whitepaper called "AWS Storage Optimization"[†] reference a blog post by RightScale[‡] that found:

> unused cloud storage (including unattached volumes and old snapshots) represented 7 percent of cloud spend[§].

It is not uncommon to see businesses develop their own scripts and service portals to automate snapshot creation across a larger number of systems within their cloud environment, but in much the same way that traditional infrastructure has eschewed backup via manual scripting for decades, one might question the utility of such an activity: is this really the best use of developer and administrator time? While automation is essential, it can be said that services which provide the automation at a cost-effective price have merit, in the same way that enterprise backup and recovery software replaced "tar," "cpio," and "zip" decades ago.

Some cloud service systems may provide a level of automation themselves for snapshot management. AWS eventually released a backup service in January 2019, though this is backup in name only, since it relies on snapshots. When introduced, it was also a per-region process—and

* https://calculator.s3.amazonaws.com/index.html

[†] https://d1.awsstatic.com/whitepapers/cost-optimization-storage-optimization.pdf

[‡] RightScale were acquired by Flexera in 2018.

[§] AWS costs: how much are you wasting? Kim Weins, 15 November 2016, Flexera, ttps://blogs.flexera.com/cloud/cloud-cost-analysis/aws-costs-how-much-are-you-wasting/

of course, it is entirely focused on automating activities within AWS itself. Businesses seeking multi-cloud solutions may be better off reviewing options for third-party cloud snapshot management services, which may run independently of any individual cloud service provider, but allow the establishment of policies, reporting, and governance to protect instances across multiple cloud services from a single cloud. Conceptually, this resembles the process shown in Figure 14.2.

In the figure, an administrator controls the cloud snapshot management policy engine via a web browser, having logged into the snapshot management portal. Policies can be established with a variety of criteria including frequency, retention, and selection mechanism—in the example shown, a tag-based selection mechanism has been used, allowing for dynamic inclusion of new resources each time the policy runs.

Cloud snapshot management portals do not seek to reinvent the wheel when it comes to the actual taking of the snapshot; they do not aim to replace the native cloud snapshot functionality within an individual provider, but instead provide an appropriate layer of automation, governance, and reporting one would expect to see in enterprise data protection software. (We might expect to see variants however, that eventually support copying snapshots not just between regions within the same cloud provider, but also between cloud providers. This, of course, assumes the content held by the snapshot is portable, and can be instantiated as or used for a workload elsewhere.)

14.5.2 Holistic Data Protection Services

Snapshot versus backup; a perennial challenge in data protection is based on the false premise that "snapshot vs backup" is an exclusive either/or discussion. There are problems that snapshots cannot solve without introducing cost, complexity, and vendor lock-in. There are problems that backups cannot solve based on the frequency with which they are run. While the two functions can overlap, when used correctly they are complimentary, and they allow a business to achieve the appropriate mix of disaster recovery, operational recovery, and compliance recovery requirements in a highly efficient and cost-appropriate way.

As we'll see in more detail later in this chapter, many of the advances in backup and recovery services in the past decade or more have come from infrastructure being increasingly software-defined. Virtualization in particular has allowed us significant innovation by efficiently backing up the virtual disks, as opposed to needing an agent installed on every host in the environment we want to protect.

Many of those efficiencies disappear of course when we're working in the public cloud—in native public cloud. When working with technologies such as VMware in AWS (and announced in 2019, VMware in Azure), there is again access to the hypervisor, but particularly when working in native cloud hypervisor environments, individual subscribers do not get access to the hypervisor, even in an IaaS environment. Access starts at the operating system. The net result is a requirement to revert to agent-based backups—the lowest level of access for backup is the operating system, so the

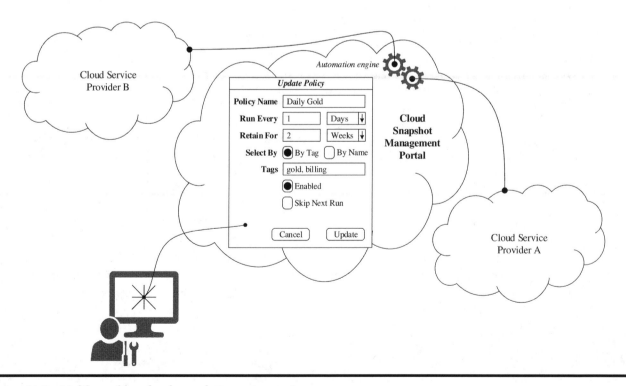

Figure 14.2 Multi-provider cloud snapshot management.

classic model of deploying an agent on each host you want to protect comes back into play.

On this front it is easy to dismiss backup out of hand in a public cloud environment as not being efficient, yet thanks to other innovations in the backup sphere (most notably, deduplication), backup and recovery services can offer a cost-effective protection solution that compliments cloud native snapshot functionality. This can result in the same sort of data protection processes running in public cloud as have been run in traditional, on-premises infrastructure: snapshots for fast, short-term retention primarily focused around disaster recovery and taking a quick copy of a system for testing/development, and backup/recovery services for granular retention that stretches from days into months and years.

For instance, consider a situation where 1 TB of data has to be protected with monthly compliance copies. (1 TB used, not 1 TB allocated.) The first snapshot would require 1 TB of storage. If we assume an 8% monthly change (not growth) rate, each "monthly" designated incremental snapshot will consume at least 80 GB of storage. Over the course of 7 years, those compliance copies might add up to 7,640 GB ($1 \times 1,000$ GB and 83×80 GB), or 7.64 TB.

However, if using a backup system with well architected deduplication software, we might reasonably expect to get 15:1 deduplication, averaged across the first and all subsequent backups for simplicity. Unlike snapshots, we would treat each monthly compliance backup as a full backup, so the logical amount of data backed up over 7 years would be 84×1000 GB = 84,000 GB. This might seem that snapshots are the winning approach—however, once we translate logical backups to used storage via the 15:1 deduplication ratio, the required storage over 7 years comes down to just 5,600 GB, a saving of over 2 TB. Assuming the deduplication software writes to object storage, we have already observed that snapshot storage for block storage systems can be more expensive than standard object storage—and if the deduplication software can write to "cooler" object storage,* this results in a better cost saving again over time. (We have not factored in yearly growth here, but it would have a comparable impact on both scenarios.)

The other advantage of using traditional backup and services in the public cloud is that they can *span* public clouds. Multinational organizations have been amalgamating backup and recovery services for decades, administering global data protection functions from a single console—why should cloud be any different? Using a common backup and recovery service that spans multiple clouds and on-premises infrastructure can yield operational and automation benefits, providing a higher degree of data and workload mobility. In essence, such approaches allow IT to "do more with less" for the business.

14.5.3 Converting Snapshots to Backups

There is a perception that if the goal is to have both snapshots and backups, then the logical requirement is to be able to have a product orchestrate the conversion of any given snapshot into a backup. This goal is rooted in on-premises data protection techniques. Products such as Dell EMC NetWorker for instance can have protection policies which run regular snapshot activities on NAS systems, with the option to "roll-over" snapshots to backup storage for operational and/or long-term retention. For instance, this might result in a configuration where hourly snapshots are executed against a corporate file-server; the 6pm snapshot though is then automatically written as an NDMP backup. This allows the snapshots and required backups of the snapshots to be controlled by the same system.

It is understandable with on-premises options such as this that there is a desire to do a similar process in public cloud. The goal in public cloud would be that virtual machine snapshots should be automatically backed up by a backup product that can address independent storage—e.g., an object bucket unrelated to snapshot storage. (This has some benefits: there is no API option for instance to take a snapshot in AWS and replicate it to Azure or GCP. Recall, too, the previous discussion about storage efficiency differences between snapshots and deduplicating backups.)

There is, however, a scalability problem with this approach based on *how* snapshots are instantiated for recovery purposes. The only way a snapshot can be converted into a backup is to:

1. Execute a snapshot recovery into a block storage volume.
2. Mount the block storage volume into a running, compatible virtual machine instance.
3. Backup the block storage volume.

First let us consider how snapshots are instantiated back to block storage volumes. From the AWS documentation:

> New volumes created from existing EBS snapshots load lazily in the background. This means that after a volume is created from a snapshot, there is no need to wait for all of the data to transfer from Amazon S3 to your EBS volume before your attached instance can start accessing the volume and all its data. If your instance accesses data that hasn't yet been loaded, the volume immediately downloads the requested data from Amazon S3, and then continues loading the rest of the volume data in the background[†].

---

* In terms of AWS, we are referring here to AWS S3 Infrequent-Access, as opposed to Glacier. Glacier's access mechanisms are not particularly compatible with interactively accessed deduplication.

† Restoring an Amazon EBS volume from a snapshot, https://docs.aw s.amazon.com/AWSEC2/latest/UserGuide/ebs-restoring-volume.html

Note the description of the data retrieval process: "…load lazily…." While AWS do not publish in-depth technical descriptions of the process, the description and the behavior matches how some on-premises storage arrays perform "instant access" of clone volumes—a logical volume is presented and a background copy is initiated against that volume. (That is, we are describing what is effectively a "copy on first access" snapshot recovery, used to instantiate a new block volume.) The volume is technically immediately accessible, and if an attempt is made to read a block that hasn't yet been retrieved from the snapshot storage pool, the block(s) associated with that request is bumped to the front of the read queue, bringing it back sooner. Yet from a performance perspective, there is still a copy operation that must be performed.

So let's reconsider the process of converting a snapshot to a backup under say, AWS, with the above information in mind:

1. Execute a snapshot recovery into a block storage volume
   - The EBS volume is available immediately, but it will be populated via a lazy-copy operation.
2. Mount the block storage volume into a running, compatible virtual machine instance—this has logistical considerations which will be discussed below.
3. Backup the block storage volume
   - The backup process will start reading the filesystem content as quickly as possible.
   - This will trigger an ongoing, sustained re-queuing of the background copy operation.
   - Rather than "backing up an EBS volume," there may be significant portions of the backup process that resembles the sequence of: "(a) read block X from EBS … (b) block X is not on EBS yet … (c) block X is pulled to the front of the read queue and is read from object storage … (d) block X is written to the EBS volume … (e) block X is returned to the backup product."

While a backup of a conventional running EBS volume will be direct reads from block storage and therefore reasonably IO efficient, an immediate backup executed from a snapshot recovery such as the above will result in sustained double-reads—the backup will not be performance bound by the speed of the EBS volume but *by the speed of the copy-to-block from object storage*. While immediately instantiated logical volumes are efficient for getting services back up and running, it doesn't guarantee full performance of those volumes.

Now let's consider the virtual machine instance aspect of this (item 2 in the sequence): what will be the relationship between the virtual machine that's backed up, and the

original virtual machine? There are a few different approaches that may be used here:

1. The virtual machine that's backed up is a multi-host proxy. For instance, a Linux virtual machine might be permanently configured as a backup proxy. Each instance that is snapshot and converted to backup might have its volumes mounted within the virtual machine (e.g., "/snapshots/vm-192.168.78.78/home," "/snapshots/vm-192.168.78.79/home," etc.) Operators needing to perform restores would need to know which virtual machines get backed up via which proxies.
2. A new virtual machine might be instantiated for each virtual machine getting a snapshot-backup operation. They might be named in such a way that the backup virtual machine can be logically mapped via tags or virtual machine names (e.g., using the same virtual machine name, but with a "-backup" at the end), so that an operator can find the backups later.
3. The backup software may allow hostname masquerading. This is often used in cluster backup configurations; rather than an operator needing to know whether the cluster services were running on cluster node A or cluster node B for instance, the backup of clustered services will always be done on the machine running the service, but saved against a client instance named after the logical cluster name. The same technique might be extended for use in this backup scenario.

Each of the above scenarios has its own challenges and benefits. The first option may be more efficient but may be unsatisfactory from a compliance perspective for auditors—and does require a mapping from original host to proxy. This might work well in situations where there are a limited number of proxies, but as the number of proxies has to increase, it will become more problematic to find the right proxy to recover from. The second and third will require more network addressing ranges for the business within the public cloud—and all three obviously consume more resources than just backing up the original virtual machine in the first place, since secondary copies of the resources are actually being created in order to back them up.

What does this mean? The result is that while this seems like a good process, it doesn't scale: it may present well in a proof-of-concept or demo situation where a small virtual machine is used (after all, no-one wants to watch a 1 TB backup run during a demo), but if a business is running hundreds or thousands of IaaS instances and wants to convert snapshots to backups this way, the performance may be quite undesirable.

An alternate solution which *does* scale may require a little more automation intervention from the developers within the business, but the net benefit is a cleaner solution. The key requirement usually is that the backup "matches" the snapshot from a timestamp perspective. This can likely be resolved in two ways:

1. By having the backup agent initiate a snapshot as part of a "pre backup" command. (This will require the installation of the cloud snapshot management tools on each client, but this usually requires very little space.)
2. The reverse of the above—if the snapshot management system being used allows for a pre- or post-command to be executed on the host at the time of the snapshot, an API call might be made to the backup product to initiate the backup for the client at the same time as the snapshot is taken.

In either scenario, the result is that the snapshot is logically taken at the same time as the backup runs. More importantly, given you pay for everything in the cloud, the resources required for both snapshot and backup are minimized.

14.5.4 Long-Term Retention and Cloud Native

Recall in Chapter 11 (Snapshots), we discussed in section 11.6 the challenges posed by using snapshot technology to provide long-term retention in additional to disaster recovery and/or operational recovery. Key challenges included:

- Vendor lock-in (easier to stay on the same platform due to the cost of migrating long-term retention)
- Cost of change (having to migrate long-term retention data, or maintain two sets of technology as long-term retention data on a previous platform ages out)
- Risk of platform failure (loss of not only operational retention, but also potentially years of compliance records).

None of these issues change when storing long-term retention data in cloud-native protection mechanisms such as snapshots. Vendor lock-in can happen just as readily in the public cloud as it does in traditional infrastructure—though one might go so far as to suggest that when there's a cost-per-kilobyte for data egress, it could equally be likened to becoming a *data hostage*.

Consider recovery of snapshots of EBS on AWS. A volume must be created from the required snapshot, and then read from. The volume is made available immediately and populated in the background with the content from the snapshot; attempts to read data that has not been retrieved will bump that read to the front of the recovery queue. Yet is still a full read required to reconstruct the entire volume.

Returning to our example in the previous section: providing monthly compliance copies of a 1 TB workload, either via snapshots or backup and recovery services. If at the end of 7 years that workload needs to be evacuated from its existing public cloud host, and transferred either on-premises or to another public cloud provider, then with deduplicating backup and recovery services, we would need to transfer 5,600 GB from the existing public cloud host to the intended target—that is, transfer the deduplicated storage, without rehydration. On the other hand, if we have retained the data in snapshots, the only way to move that data out is to extract a volume from each snapshot; this will lead to the construction of $84 \times 1,000$ GB volumes and transfer—84 *TB* of data. (Of course, optimizations might be used to shrink the data again before moving it, but there's an effective order of magnitude difference between the amount of data that needs to be moved out, between backup/recovery and snapshots.)

Keeping cloud-native protection for long-term retention/compliance copies of data should be viewed with trepidation at least. It makes exiting a cloud provider more challenging (consider for instance what might occur should the cloud provider give only a few months warning that it intends to shutdown).[*] It is also not by any means guaranteed to be the most cost-efficient data storage mechanism, which can result in escalating costs that will pose considerable financial cost to the business: for instance, retaining monthly snapshots for 7 years when there are persistent annual growth rates that can see storage costs only go in one direction.

14.6 Protecting SaaS Systems

Many of the most common major SaaS cloud providers might be said to take an almost customer-hostile approach to data protection. It is quite common, for instance, to see such providers take stringent steps to ensure data is kept available and is recoverable *for them*, but not include this in SLAs with their users. That is, their data protection strategies resolve entirely around service availability and preventing mass data loss situations, but they are not geared toward individual unit recovery.[†]

Some examples of recovery "services" offered by prominent SaaS providers include the following:

---

[*] It's worth noting, of course, that if a cloud provider advises its users that it will be closing "soon," there could very well be a mass-exodus attempt, resulting in contention and poor performance extracting data within the required timeframe, too.

[†] Given such providers are offering software or specific applications as a service, they don't, after all, have any way of distinguishing the difference between a valid data deletion or change, and an invalid one. But it's what they do *after* the data is deleted that becomes important for data protection.

- Providing a "trash" can option for documents and emails; content is automatically expired and expunged after a certain time period and can usually be expunged on user demands. Once trashed content is expunged or expired, it cannot be recovered.
- Providing a "grace" period on account deletion; account contents are automatically expired and expunged after a certain time once an administrator has nominated them for deletion. Content cannot be recovered once it has been expunged/expired.
- Offering data recoverability at extremely high unit cost and extremely slow turnaround (amounts of US$10,000 or more with 1–2 weeks resolution time have been observed).

None of these are truly effective or sufficient for data protection services for a business. In the first two instances, SaaS cloud providers might claim the "trash" or "grace" options are sufficient backup, but this is absurd. More aptly stated, such providers are implicitly or otherwise informing their users, "if you delete it, you can never get it back." Equally, a recovery service that is so costly and so tardy for data that might be deemed business-critical is clearly designed to discourage use.

Like SaaS, PaaS environments are usually far more focused on *service availability* than they are on *data protection* for individual subscribers. Typically, subscribers will be faced with ensuring they keep a copy of their data or applications outside of the PaaS environment. In the case of big data systems, where content will be replicated into the cloud from a local source, the protection will often take place in the subscriber datacenter via the local copy. For application frameworks, this may require building automation around options in the provider for exporting data and application definitions.

As such, it's important that businesses take control of the data protection process for *their* data that resides in the cloud. Several companies are now offering products for protecting data housed on SaaS and PaaS systems—"born in the cloud" data, so to speak. These products typically integrate with the tenant-wide administrator-level permissions assigned to a consumer either to allow an on-premises appliance/product to retrieve a copy of the data or to copy the data to a storage system defined in *another* cloud.

Conceptually, a SaaS provider and its customers might be represented as shown in Figure 14.3.

Any individual customer that wishes to construct an adequate and business-appropriate data protection solution to their SaaS data will be focused solely on *their* data; the solution deployed will only be applicable to their tenancy in the SaaS provider. Conceptually, this may resemble Figure 14.4.

Drilling down to a single client of the SaaS provider, *Customer 1* deploys an in-cloud backup system to provide

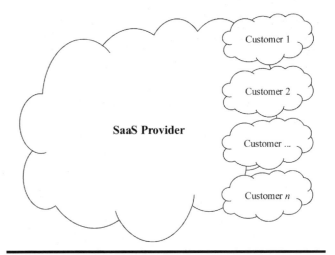

Figure 14.3 Conceptual representation of SaaS cloud provider and customers.

reasonable and appropriate data protection against the data its users generate, above and beyond the basic "datacenter protection" offered by the SaaS provider. Assuming the SaaS offering is a document system (e.g., spreadsheets, word-processor documents, presentation files), the goal of such a system will be to provide backup of documents as they are changed by the users and the option to recover documents to a specific version over the number of revisions or days/months backup copies maintained by the backup service. The backup will be written to an alternate location—usually another cloud provider. It may be that IaaS infrastructure is deployed running a traditional application to extract the data and send it to the backup destination, or it might be another SaaS service is used—this one focused on providing the complete backup service, including storage, as a simple subscription.

The net result of such a system is a far more holistic and business-centric approach to data protection for SaaS and PaaS data. Typically, such services will be charged on a flexible utility-based model per standard cloud systems—for example, a flat dollar cost per user per month, per year, or a combination of the per-user/per-period rate and a $/GB rate for the amount of backup data being generated.

This leverages data protection at two specific points:

1. Relying on data protection employed by the SaaS/PaaS provider for operational availability of the overall system being utilized
2. Relying on an external provider or service to protect the actual content/data in a suitably granular way that exists independently of the state of the service being subscribed to for compliance and retention purposes

While such a system increases the cost of utilizing cloud systems, it allows a business to adequately protect and ensure the recoverability of potentially mission critical data.

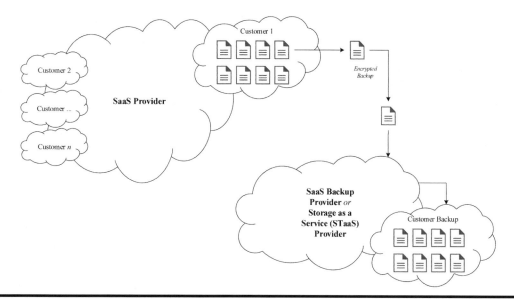

Figure 14.4 Conceptual view of a SaaS backup solution.

A particular challenge for protecting SaaS environments is that there are simply so many of them. While there are several "key" SaaS environments for many businesses (e.g., Office 365 and Salesforce are high use examples), SaaS is often seen as the ultimate architectural goal of moving workloads into public cloud—why build anything when you can just subscribe?

Yet there are no standards within the SaaS platform world. There is no common API for instance for "extract_user_data(username)" or "insert_user_data(username)"; this is partly because there is no real incentive to provide data mobility (after all, data mobility in a SaaS environment means that customers can *extract* their data and *leave* the service), and perhaps also because data protection is consistently an afterthought within much of the IT industry.

What this means is that data protection services for SaaS systems must be developed on a case-by-case basis. Just because a product supports Office365 for instance does not mean that it will support Google Mail, and being able to protect DropBox subscriptions does not automatically mean you can protect Microsoft OneDrive subscriptions.

This places a heavy onus on subscribers to SaaS solutions to investigate, in advance, how they can protect their data once it is in the service. The choice between two SaaS providers that offer similar products should as much be determined by the ability to protect the data as it is on the individual functions: after all, we might say that a service that meets 95% of the business requirements and includes a backup/recovery function in actual fact meets *more* business requirements than one that seems to meet 100% of the business requirements but has no mechanism to perform backup/recovery at all.

14.7 PaaS Protection

PaaS platforms often present similar challenges as SaaS platforms when it comes to data protection. While PaaS comes in many types, we'll limit consideration here to PaaS database services.

For the most part, PaaS databases tend to be protected via snapshot functions, since like SaaS, there is no underlying access to the operating system that the PaaS environment is running on. However, as we've discussed in 14.5, "Cloud Native Protection," snapshots have a tendency to create lock-in: if you create a snapshot of a Microsoft SQL database running in AWS, you cannot copy that snapshot across into Azure to import the database into the Azure database PaaS service.

Depending on the PaaS service, there may be options for creating true data backup exports in the sense that we would normally expect to see in traditional datacenter infrastructure, and these should be investigated when workloads are to be placed or developed in PaaS environments.

Where such options are not available, there is merit in falling back to older data protection mechanisms—exports and imports. This provides a layer of protection outside of the original cloud provider and also provides a source of data mobility, which can be important in situations where a business needs to either keep an on-premises copy, or demonstrate (to the point of meeting auditor inspection) its ability to comply to ensuring critical data is protected against cloud service failure up to and including the actual cloud service provider failing. Such a solution might resemble Figure 14.5.

Key to achieving backup and/or mobility in a cost-effective manner is leveraging deduplication technology at the IaaS layer. Even if Cloud Provider A provides a mechanism to generate a true backup of the database that can be copied across to Cloud Provider B, this backup will be *at most* compressed.

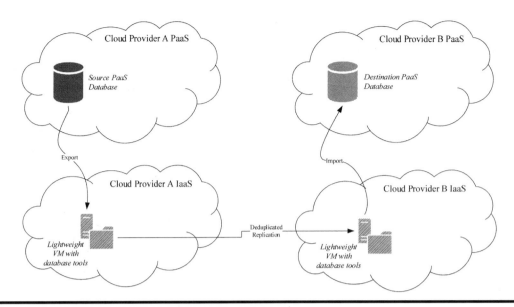

Figure 14.5   Providing PaaS protection and mobility with IaaS.

So we might assume that a 10 TB database would require the transmission of at least 5 TB (at 2:1 compression ratios). By comparison, if the export data can be deduplicated at a 15:1 deduplication ratio, considerably less data would be transmitted, even on a daily basis with incremental changes. If we assume we could somehow perpetually do incremental backups from the source PaaS database and copy those across, at a 5% daily change rate, this would equate to 500 GB needing to be transmitted per day. If that can be done compressed at 2:1 compression, it would result in 250 GB per day being transmitted. *However,* leveraging IaaS with deduplication storage at 15:1 deduplication, the daily incremental change might come down to approximately 33.3 GB after storage efficiencies. (Ideally, and particularly with smaller PaaS databases, the business would even run a cost comparison between doing a simple export and cross-cloud copy, and the resources required for deduplicated replication. In some instances with smaller data sets, a simple compressed copy may be more justifiable.)

While day to day protection within a single public cloud provider can be achieved with native tools, data protection and cloud architects considering the long-term view of compliance, cloud mobility, and multi-cloud scenarios should strongly evaluate the potential synergies offered to protection and mobility options via incorporation of backup and recovery services into even PaaS protection.

14.8 Data Protection for FaaS

Function as a Service, or FaaS, refers to *serverless* activities within the public cloud, but in a different way to *serverless* from say, a backup context (discussed in section 12.4.2).

In the context of cloud, *serverless* refers to being able to run functions without actually having to spin up the infrastructure you'd typically associate with running any form of application. A developer might use a portal to run functions to probe Internet of things (IoT) devices, initiate snapshots of virtual machines and databases, or significantly more complex activities.

This type of service is growing in popularity because billing typically only happens during process execution time, and developers do not need to worry about spinning up or configuring servers—that side of the process is fully handled by the cloud provider.

There are two aspects of data protection then for FaaS—protecting the functions, and protecting any data generated as a result of the functions.

Protecting these functions is almost entirely the responsibility of the developer at this point in time. For instance, the AWS Lambda service allows developers to use a console to manually type in (or copy/paste) functions for execution, but for repeated execution and more complex functions, developers are encouraged to submit *deployment packages*. For other serverless systems, developers are encouraged to use source-code repository systems, much as they would in normal software development frameworks.

Likewise at this point in time, protecting data generated from function execution will be a developer responsibility—this might mean writing any non-transient data to an object bucket for later retrieval, or storing the data in a persistently available database. Using these two options as an example, we would expect to see data protection options used such as:

■ Versioning, snapshot, or backup functions executed against the object storage bucket (depending on cloud provider and data protection vendor options)
■ PaaS style protection (as discussed previously) for any databases used.

This, as you may imagine, will require developers working in FaaS environments to work closely with the assigned data protection specialists for the public cloud environment to avoid business intellectual property or data from being at risk.

14.9 Data Protection for IaaS

When we move beyond SaaS and PaaS and return to IaaS, we enter more familiar territory. IaaS is essentially a cloud-based extension to the virtual datacenter, something most IT departments, CIOs, and CFOs will, by now, be extremely familiar with.

There are two distinct approaches that can be taken with an IaaS cloud environment: built-in or self-service. (A combination of the two might also be used depending on data criticality, costs, and retention requirements.)

14.9.1 *Built-in Approach*

The built-in approach will leverage an IaaS provider's own data protection offerings. Depending on the provider, this may include features and options such as

- Virtual datacenter replication (allowing high availability and protection from a datacenter failure within the IaaS provider)
- Regular snapshots of virtual infrastructure (virtual machines and/or virtual data volumes)
- Traditional backup and recovery agents and/or policies for operating systems and databases/applications

Additionally, for snapshots and traditional backup/recovery options, a variety of retention timeframes *may* be offered, such as

- Daily backups retained for 30 days
- Daily backups retained for 60 days
- Monthly backups retained for 12 months
- Monthly backups retained for 3 years
- Monthly backups retained for 7 years

Such retention will typically be charged on a cents-per-GB model, though for some providers the longevity of retention may impact the per-GB cost. (For instance, monthly backups retained for 12 months may cost less per GB than monthly backups retained for 7 years.)

Subscribers also need to anticipate that the data protection options offered by the service provider will cease at the moment the service ceases. While this may seem entirely common-sense, it has the potential to create significant impact on an organization that must retain particular key data for compliance purposes (i.e., even if a subscriber no longer wishes to use the particular service, legal compliance reasons may require backups to be retained for longer, and thus the service kept active). Alternately, this can sometimes result in a "never delete" approach for IaaS subscribers—if a database is backed up every day for a month, but no content is ever deleted from the database, then arguably the backup from any single day represents a longer retention time. While logically this *may* be true, it may not satisfy either an external auditor or a regulatory body unless suitable, government-approved approaches that are demonstrable and documented are used to prevent arbitrary data deletion. Any subscriber choosing to go down this path should engage legal teams and independent auditors from the design stage through to post-implementation to ensure a completed solution will not earn the ire of a judicial authority or government body at a later point in time.

Another additional cost factor that may be introduced into data protection services by cloud providers (IaaS, BaaS, or even STaaS) relates to the deduplicatibility of the data being protected, or the daily change rate thereof. A service provider may for instance build its internal cost model for provisioning of backups to subscribers on the assumption that the daily growth in *unique* data is never more than say, 1%. When this is regularly exceeded (e.g., on average for more days in a month than not), an overhead fee may automatically be charged to the subscriber's account to allow the provider to compensate against unplanned storage or data protection costs. Thus, a subscriber must examine not only the base service catalog offerings, but also the exclusions and any cascading costs that they might incur based on the workload or data to be stored in the system. It also allows a service provider to discourage subscribers from say, deploying databases but choosing to generate compressed dumps of them rather than electing to have appropriate data protection agents deployed as a "cost-saving" mechanism.

The service catalog offerings for data protection will usually be on top of any base data protection enacted by the service provider to ensure service continuity, but the level chosen by the subscriber will directly affect and limit the recoverability of their environment. IaaS providers will explicitly excuse themselves from data loss situations not covered by the actual service catalog options chosen by the subscriber, and subscriber agreement to this will be contingent on service provisioning. For example, a smaller IaaS subscriber may choose only a low service level (say, daily backups) from the IaaS catalog. This could allow them to recover data or databases for a defined period of time (e.g., 30 days), but in the event of a datacenter failure for the IaaS provider, the low-SLA subscriber services would *not* be available for restart on a migrated datacenter. In such a situation, they would be dependent on the IaaS provider getting the original datacenter back up and running without data loss before their service could resume.

Particularly in light of the number of businesses planning to shift even *some* of their workloads to public cloud, it is not surprising that there is a burgeoning consultancy field to assist organizations:

■ To understand the nuances and costs associated with cloud provider and service catalog selection
■ To accurately identify and classify their data and workloads to determine cloud-readiness
■ To understand the suitability of service catalog offerings for data protection to the business requirements and any gaps

14.9.2 Self-Service Approach

While the service catalog approach is usually simpler and requires less local IT resources for a business, it does open the business to several distinct risks, viz.:

■ Service catalog options may be retrograde compared to existing on-premises capabilities.
■ Longer-term retention is entirely dependent on retaining a contract with the service provider (effectively creating lock-in with an IaaS provider).
■ The subscriber will usually be exposed to the risk of total IaaS failure regardless of what individual data protection catalog options are chosen.

For these reasons and others relating to accountability and compliance, some businesses will choose to forego service catalog options offered by the IaaS provider(s) they're subscribing to and build their own data protection environment directly into the cloud environment.

Such data protection schemes will need to be very carefully planned and provisioned to avoid obvious pitfalls relating to backup data placement. For instance, consider the scenario shown in Figure 14.6.

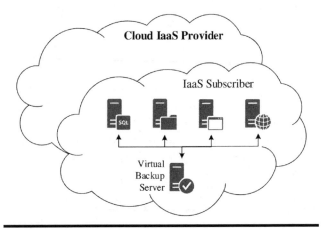

Figure 14.6 Backup in an IaaS environment with protection against local service failure

In such a configuration, an IaaS customer has deployed a virtualized backup server within their infrastructure subscription/virtual datacenter. This virtual backup server co-exists with the IaaS email, database, file, and generic servers. While this will provide localized backup/recovery services, thereby allowing recovery from individual file, email, or database loss, it still relies on the overall physical datacenter and infrastructure protection offered by the IaaS provider.

Figure 14.7 shows a more robust approach to IaaS backup, where a backup service has been provisioned within the local IaaS subscription, but the backups are replicated to another IaaS provider. (The diagram shows an alternate IaaS provider, but it could also be another region within the same IaaS provider, providing regional separation of backup and backup replicas. It might even be a case that the secondary copy is back to on-premises systems for the business.)

The cost-effectiveness of such systems will largely be driven by a few key architectural requirements:

1. The backup system should require as little infrastructure as possible—infrastructure costs money in the public cloud, so having to deploy a classic "three-tier" architecture (backup server and media server to support the clients) and protection storage will likely render the solution expensive to run. Instead, the solution should support backup data flowing with as few hops as possible to the selected protection storage.
2. Protection copies should be written to object storage—object storage is orders of magnitude cheaper than block storage in public cloud environments.
3. Efficient deduplication should be used—source-based deduplication to eliminate the amount of data that needs to be sent in the first place (critical when the network throughput available to a virtual machine in IaaS is often throttled depending on the other resources such as compute and memory assigned to the virtual machine). That deduplication should also utilize smaller segments (to minimize the amount of existing data seen as new when small blocks change) and those segments should be variable rather than fixed.

When a backup solution has been deployed within IaaS that meets the above three architectural requirements, it can serve multiple purposes, including but not limited to:

■ Efficient local granular recoveries for operational retention windows
■ Bandwidth-efficient data mobility for workloads and compliance copies
■ Bandwidth-efficient replication to meet externally or internally imposed compliance requirements around fault tolerance within data protection itself

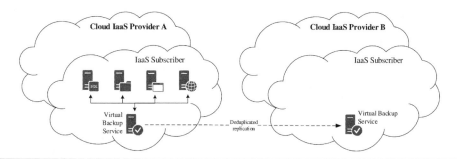

Figure 14.7 IaaS backup spanning clouds.

- A means of "trickling" daily copies of systems out of, or between clouds
- A singular point of control, assuming the same solution is used between on-premises and in-cloud solutions
- A multi-cloud data protection service that is not dependent on or locked to the features and functions of a single cloud provider

14.10 Private and Hybrid Clouds

We group private and hybrid clouds together for the simple reason that they both start *in the datacenter*. (For the purposes of our topic, that's regardless of whether it's a datacenter owned by the business, or a datacenter in which the business rents floor-space but has its own infrastructure installed therein.)

14.10.1 Private Clouds

When the term *private cloud* started to be used, it was often misunderstood as being a cunning marketing trick aimed at sticking a "cloud" badge on the same equipment businesses had previously been buying and selling at an inflated price.

What has become increasingly obvious is that businesses are looking at the fundamental aspects of cloud (in particular aspects such as rapid elasticity, on-demand self-service, and accurate measurement of service provision) and expecting their IT departments adapt to be as flexible. IT departments can choose to build the private cloud experience themselves, either completely from the ground up as an entirely custom activity, or using a reference architecture. These "build" approaches suit the needs of IT groups that still wish to exert total customization control over the individual components of infrastructure purchased.

Yet unless a business delivers managed services and private clouds to customers, its core business profits are unlikely to be derived from building infrastructure—recognizing this, some companies instead will focus on *Converged Infrastructure* (CI). At its heart, CI helps to provide a highly virtualized datacenter that centralizes compute, storage, and network and features high levels of automation for

provisioning and management thanks to a robust software overlay. Equally as importantly as the day to day management, the goal of converged infrastructure is to make sure that upgrades and patching deliver seamless compatibility up the entire stack.

For the infrastructure groups within the IT department, CI will resemble the view shown in Figure 14.8.

From within a single administrative interface, IT staff will be able to establish policies, and monitor and update the entire infrastructure stack. (Note that data protection is often an add-on to converged infrastructure, since there is usually a strong likelihood that businesses purchasing converged infrastructure already have a data protection solution—hence the diagram shows data protection separate to the core stack.)

For the end users (the consumers of the service, not necessarily the end users of the provisioned services), the view will be quite different. Their experience will be that of a web portal (or similar) that allows them to provision services—something that may resemble that shown in Figure 14.9. Through one or more portal dialogs, they'll be prompted to select the type of infrastructure they need to provision, and (usually) provide a cost center the new infrastructure is to be charged against. Other options might include inputs such as selecting the performance options for the provisioned service, and the length of time the service is to be kept for.

(In some cases, the infrastructure consumers won't even get access to the infrastructure portal; instead, it may be automatically provisioned via hooks into a fully integrated service delivery and ticketing system such as ServiceNow.)

For private cloud to work effectively within an organization, it needs to not only offer all the key cloud features users and the business is looking for, but it also needs to integrate with the process control elements of the business such as change management, service desk requests, and access control. This is typically where the infrastructure management layer will need to come into play or else the self-service web portal becomes nothing more than a simplified request layer. (In short, if a system isn't provisioned *automatically* within a predetermined period of time following the user request, it's a private cloud for marketing purposes only.)

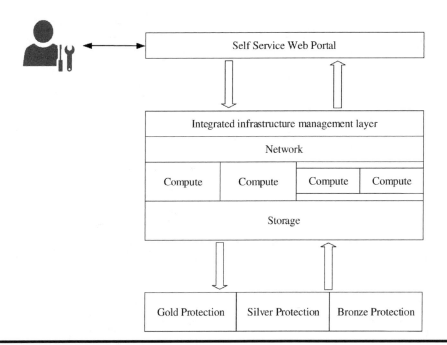

Figure 14.8   A logical view of converged infrastructure

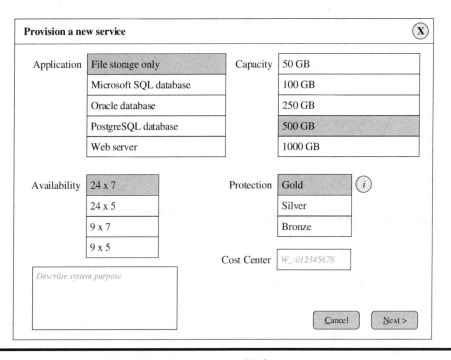

Figure 14.9   End user/consumer portal for self-service converged infrastructure

An absolute advantage for businesses pursuing the private cloud datacenter is the automated provisioning of services *and* the requisite data protection models required. For instance, if we consider the provisioning dialog from Figure 14.9, there are actually two aspects of data protection cited:

1. Protection—Gold, silver, or bronze
2. Availability—24×7, 24×5, 9×7 or 9×5

You'll note the protection levels cited align to what you'd expect to see as titles in service catalogs rather than comprehensive descriptions. A goal of cloud provisioning in general is to simplify the selection model and allow the subscriber to get on with what they *need* the components for. In this sense, IT and the business will have previously agreed on what each of *gold*, *silver*, and *bronze* protection models equate to. (As suggested by the *(i)* information button beside the protection

Table 14.3   Determining Service and Infrastructure Implications of Availability and Protection Selections in a Self-Service Portal

Availability	Protection	Service and Infrastructure Implications
24×7	Gold	*Mission Critical.* It may require continuous replication of storage and virtual machines between two sites to allow immediate transition from one datacenter to the other without visible service interruption to subscribers. While traditional backups will be taken daily, application-aware snapshots will be taken every half an hour with log shipping for applications, allowing for highly granular recoveries with very small RPOs and RTOs.
9×5	Gold	*Business function critical.* Requires continuous replication of storage and virtual machines between two sites to allow immediate transition from one datacenter to the other without visible interruption to subscribers *during business hours*, but with asynchronous replication and lag permitted out of hours. Application-aware snapshots will be taken hourly during business hours, with the final snapshot of the day "rolled over" into the daily backup for system.
24×5	Silver	*Development system.* Snapshots three times a day, with asynchronous replication having up to a half hour lag, and nightly backup.
24×7	Bronze	*Non-critical yet important service.* This may be indicative of a service that the business wants to see operational at all times, but an outage can in theory be sustained. For instance, the front-facing web services (so long as they don't include eCommerce) may be designated 24×7 to reflect a global market. This would require clustered availability rather than continuous replication between sites, and standard daily backups would likely be more than sufficient to meet RPOs and RTOs.

options in the diagram, a full portal for self-provisioning will likely include help links that provide further details about the service levels, exclusions, permitted outage times, and so on for particular options available.)

The options for availability equally provide guidance to the infrastructure requirements of the provisioned services, particularly when coupled with the protection options. Table 14.3 provides some examples of this. Provisioning portals that ask additional questions relating to system performance or encryption requirements would likely yield further automated policy granularity regarding overall data protection requirements.

An implication of such service provisioning for private cloud within organizations is a much tighter coupling of the two arms of data protection (proactive and reactive). To achieve this, data protection options within the business have to be the following:

- *Policy driven:* Administrators will define broad policies instead of pin-point per-system configuration.
- *Integrated:* The higher the service level required, the greater the integration that will be necessary between the compute layer, the data protection activities in the traditional system storage, and the backup and recovery systems.[*]

- *Compatible:* Integration implies compatibility, and compatibility will be best achieved through a narrowing of the number of vendors used to source infrastructure from *and/or* as a result of highly robust scripting from a local DevOps team.

Since the cloud model requires automated provisioning as a result of the self-service approach, storage, virtualization, and backup administrators do not have the luxury of receiving service tickets for configuring either the primary service or the associated data protection. Instead, their roles shift to a combined function of

- *Policy definition:* Creating the core policies and workflows associated with service-catalog-defined data protection
- *Service intervention:* Resolving issues that may occur with services

The end goal is that once data protection policies and the workflows required to meet those policies are defined, the management software layer driving the infrastructure should automatically add provisioned storage, virtual machines, and applications to the various workflows and policies without human intervention.

An example policy with associated workflows may resemble that shown in Figure 14.10. By developing the protection policy as a workflow, it becomes very easy to see that the configuration

---

[*] For instance, automated copying of snapshots from primary storage to backup and recovery storage, orchestrated and addressable by the backup software. To be *useful*, such snapshots would need to be entirely integrated with any applications or virtual systems stored on them.

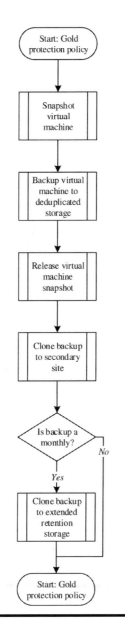

Figure 14.10 Example data protection policy with associated workflows.

process should be automatable. Rather than the backup administrator needing to launch a console, add the clients, and select groups, schedules, and retention periods, the software management layer should do all this automatically. Where data protection configuration has limits (e.g., the administrator or vendor might state that "the backup software should not have more than 150 client systems executing backups simultaneously"), the management layer should take this into account, adding schedules, groups, and containers as appropriate.

14.11 Hybrid Cloud

Many businesses will be perfectly content with private cloud arrangements only, as these will provide a level of agility,

efficiency, and cost accuracy well beyond that experienced in traditional datacenter approaches to infrastructure.

Hybrid cloud comes in for those businesses that require a level of elasticity for compute and storage beyond that which is practical for the business to acquire directly.

Automation however remains critical for the successful functioning of a hybrid cloud—workloads should shift or extend into a public cloud without requiring subscriber intervention. So long as the performance requirements of the subscriber have been met, it should make no difference where the workload is running.*

More so, the data protection policies defined and provisioned should continue to function under the aegis of the private cloud definition regardless of the location. This *may* result in some modification of the service levels. Recall Table 2.2 ("Sample RTO SLAs for data types based on locality of data"), it was suggested service levels may be altered based on whether data exist within the datacenter, in a hybrid cloud or in a public cloud. For example, the "gold" service level had RTOs of

- Traditional/private infrastructure[†]—1 hour
- Hybrid infrastructure—4 hours
- Public cloud—8 hours

As part of the provisioning and control mechanisms in a *hybrid* cloud environment, it will typically be possible to place constraints on *where* the service can exist. Mission critical systems with compliance requirements for on-premise data might be functionally locked from ever being migrated to a public cloud service. Less critical infrastructure, or infrastructure that requires the ability to say triple compute resources beyond the capability of the entire private cloud during peak loading might be acknowledged as being a hybrid deployment and therefore delivered *only* with the *hybrid infrastructure* service levels and protection options.

In all cases though, the goal will be to ensure the data protection policies defined by the IT teams and aligned to the provisioned services can be met regardless of whether those services are currently on- or off-premises.

When combined with appropriate development and service provisioning, such flexibility typically grants a business *cloud independence*. By controlling the policies within the private cloud infrastructure, the business can cease to be beholden to variable/limited-liability approaches to data protection offered by public cloud providers and automate any number of data

---

* Other factors, such as regulatory compliance around data locality, will of course be a factor in whether or not a workload is shifted into the public cloud and should be handled by the orchestration management software.
† This might equally refer to private cloud for the purposes of our discussion.

protection deployment operations automatically as workloads are moved into or stretched into public clouds.

Consider the previous workflow for the *Gold* data protection policy from Figure 14.10. Such a workflow can be mapped as equally to a private cloud environment as it can be to a public cloud environment if we make use of in-cloud IaaS backup services. A service might start in the private cloud and receive its snapshots, backup and backup cloning operations serviced from infrastructure in the business datacenter. Over time if the service requirements change, the workload might be shifted to the public cloud, but a compatible backup service in a second cloud be used to provide data recovery services. If long-term monthly style compliance backups are still required for the service, that IaaS backup in the second public cloud might subsequently be replicated *back into* the private cloud infrastructure for guaranteed long-term storage.

One particular challenge of hybrid cloud where workloads may be subject to movement back and forth between private infrastructure and the public cloud of course is— what happens to backup copies that have been generated? For instance, consider a workload that may get daily backups retained for 4 weeks, and monthly backups retained for 7 years. In a simplistic architectural model, we might assume that data protection services will run in the same location for the workload at all times. This means that if the workload is shifted from public cloud to private cloud, it is "adopted" by the on-premises backup service, and vice versa.

While it would be fair to assume that in this switch, any daily backups would simply be "aged out" from the *other* backup service, what would happen to the long-term retention backups? Over the lifespan of a workload, the amount of data held in the long-term retention backups versus the operational retention backups can be *significant*. Simply moving this data back and forth may incur significant fees—and *not* moving the data may result in operators needing to make multiple recovery attempts until they find the backup service holding the long-term retention data required. Alternately, knowing that a workload is likely to be mobile between private and public resources, it may be assigned a "fixed" backup location.

There is no right answer as to how or if the workload's backups should move when the workload is moved, but if the workload *is* going to be moved, the business needs to have a clear architectural decision on what will take place with any backups—particularly the long-term retention ones.

14.12 Extending Data Protection into the Cloud

A topic getting increasing attraction is the option of expanding traditional data protection services into the public cloud as a means of providing minimized costs for longer-term compliance backups or archives. In essence, this takes advantage of the relatively cheap per-GB costs of object-based storage in cloud storage providers, particularly if there are no strong SLAs on access speed and acceptable cost implications based on projected retrieval frequency and amount.

Such a solution might resemble that shown in Figure 14.11.

This tiering process is quite similar in principle to how businesses have tiered backup data from an online copy to tape—traditionally, daily and weekly backups, and even some monthly backups, will be stored entirely on disk (usually in a deduplicated format). The design principle is that all short-term and many medium-term recoveries will be serviced from disk, allowing for fast retrieval unimpeded by device contention or media recall requirements. Traditionally, the backups requiring *really* long-term retention (e.g., those held for 7 years for legal/financial reasons, or perhaps even several decades for medical or manufacturing purposes) have been pushed out to tape, with the tape being stored in a secure, off-site facility. (For redundancy purposes, at least two tape copies should always be generated.)

While tape will continue to exist in many organizations for some time to come (if only to service legacy access requirements), other organizations are seeing cloud object storage as a means of extricating themselves from handling large volumes of physical media, and there are several good reasons to consider this, such as the following:

- *Storage costs:* Off-site tape storage vendors typically charge per unit of media stored, in addition to monthly service fees and/or transport fees. Particularly when in-cloud object storage is written in a deduplicated manner, long-term cloud storage may represent a similar economic scale.
- *Media and equipment costs:* In addition to the actual storage costs, businesses utilizing tape for long-term storage must purchase the tapes that are written to and maintain the tape libraries and devices used to write to those tapes. Off-site tape storage usually features a higher level of media "wastage" than on-site tapes due to the requirement to ship data off-site in a relatively short period of time after it's written. That is, most tape shipped off-site for long-term storage will not have been written to their full capacity.
- *Media testing:* As they are only being infrequently accessed (if at all), it is impossible to tell whether tape has degraded while it is sitting on a shelf in a storage facility. The only way to be sure is to periodically recall media (or at least batches of media) to confirm the data on it can still be read. This takes time and resources to perform (in addition to incurring recall and new off-site shipping fees).[*]

---

[*] In reality, few businesses seem to invest the resources into this type of testing, which is a significant oversight that can result in considerable data loss.

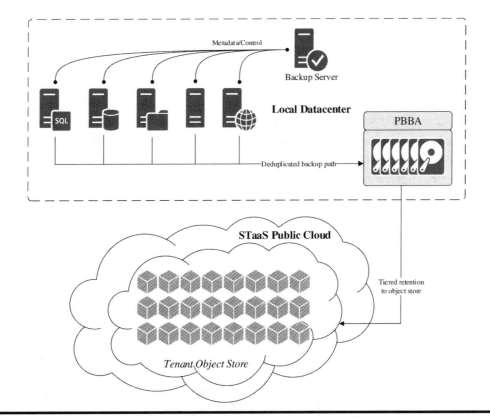

Figure 14.11 Using object storage to extend data protection services.

■ *Media refresh cycles:* A tape written 5 or 10 years prior may not be compatible with tape drives in use now. A backup requiring long-term retention on tape will need to be periodically recalled and migrated to newer tape as refresh cycles occur. (The alternative, of keeping older tape drives available for recovery purposes, rarely works out either from a reliability or maintenance cost perspective).*

■ *Availability:* While the streaming performance of a tape may arguably be higher than many cloud storage options (particularly based on available bandwidth), if the majority of retrievals are projected to be smaller units of data, this may not be a major impediment to a business, particularly when we consider the ongoing trend of cheaper *and* faster internet access. A slower retrieval from cloud storage may be mitigated by being able to start the data transfer immediately, rather than issuing a media recall notice, waiting for media to be recalled, waiting for a tape drive to be available, and then initiating the recovery.

■ *Discovery:* While there are risks associated with protection data being online,† having data online and susceptible to more convenient discovery processes (either for

metadata alone or entire content) can potentially save a business a considerable amount of time and money during litigation or compliance verification exercises. Data sitting on tape in off-site storage on the other hand will not be discoverable beyond whatever metadata was recorded at the time the tape was written.

While tape media is often rated as having a shelf life of 30 or more years in ideal circumstances, this conveniently ignores the fact that any particular tape media format becomes obsolete as soon as tape drives are no longer being produced that can read the media. The Linear Tape-Open (LTO) consortium for instance is now up to generation 8 of the format (as of 2019). LTO-2 was capable of reading and writing LTO-1 media, and LTO generations 3 through 7 have been capable of reading media 2 generations prior, and writing media 1 generation prior. However, LTO-8 has broken this, and is only able to read from LTO-7, rather than 7 and LTO-6:

In an effort to push the innovation boundaries of tape technology going forward, the current LTO format required a recording technology transition that supports capacity growth for future LTO generations. To address this technological shift and maintain affordability in times of extreme data growth, the latest LTO generation

---

* It is actually quite common to encounter businesses still storing tapes of a particular format where they've actually not had *any* tape drives capable of reading them for five or more years.

† Which, it should be noted, can be mitigated by keeping multiple copies, applying appropriate access controls and even using WORM-style locks.

8 specifications are intended to be only backwards compatible with LTO generation 7 cartridges[*].

The release years of the various LTO generations have been as follows:

- LTO-1: 2000
- LTO-2: 2003
- LTO-3: 2005
- LTO-4: 2007
- LTO-5: 2010
- LTO-6: 2012
- LTO-7: 2015
- LTO-8: 2017

With new formats being released, on average, every two and a half years, the idea of a tape shelf life of 30 + years entirely fails to take into account any needs to *read* from the media after such a length of time.

Steven Anastasi, vice president of global media archives and preservation services at Warner Bros., therefore puts the practical lifetime of an LTO cartridge at approximately 7 years. Before that time elapses, you must migrate to a newer generation of LTO because, of course, it takes time to move the data from one format to the next. While LTO data capacities have been steadily doubling, tape speeds have not kept up. The first generation, LTO-1, had a maximum transfer rate of 20 megabytes per second; LTO-7's top rate is 750 MB/s. Then you need technicians to operate and troubleshoot the equipment and ensure that the migrated data is error-free. Migrating a petabyte (a thousand terabytes) of data can take several months, says Anastasi[†].

While Hollywood movie studios may have strong media handling standards for long-term retention, it is surprisingly uncommon across the overall business landscape. It's worth noting that tape handling, particularly for long-term retention (e.g., 7 years or more), is often poor. It is reasonably common to encounter any or all of the following scenarios in a business using tape for long-term retention:

- Once sent off-site, tapes are never recalled for testing; the only time they are recalled are when they are required for a recovery.
- If a tape fails during a recovery process, even for long-term retention and the secondary copy is used, then that secondary copy is not *re*-copied before sending it back off-site.
- When new tape drive technologies are purchased within the organization, tapes in the old format are not converted into the new format.
- When long-term retention tape backups have expired, they are not purged/destroyed (or re-used).[‡]
- When new backup products are implemented, tapes in the old format are not converted or otherwise cataloged for easy access.

Failure to do any of these can result in significant issues in the event of a recovery requirement: a compliance recovery may be requested 6 years after a backup was performed only to have the business discover it doesn't even have a tape drive that can read the data. Or worse, it finds a second-hand tape drive to read the data and that drive *destroys* the tape. And worse again, it turns out the second copy of the long-term data had been lost 4 years prior when an earlier recovery was performed against the same data.

By shifting long-term storage of backups (or archives) from tape to cloud-based storage, businesses can achieve the benefits of disk-based storage for their entire data protection cycle while taking advantage of the economy of scale available to cloud providers or even private object storage. This is especially so if the cost of the long-term retention to the cloud is balanced accurately and fairly against the *true* cost of managing long-term tape retention (regardless of whether the business currently does this or not).

It should also be noted that on-premises object storage is a significantly growing area. These provide dense storage (e.g., multiple petabytes in a single rack, *before* deduplication efficiencies are taken into consideration) utilizing cloud-like access protocols. Such storage can enable a business to use private cloud storage for their long-term retention, eliminating tape and storing larger amounts of data at a lower cost than public cloud providers.

While it is indisputable that predicting data volume growth rates over extended periods of time is somewhat imprecise, when making a decision about which type of object storage should be used (public cloud or private), a view should be formed over the estimated growth rate and the period of time long-term retention backups must be kept for.

---

[*] LTO program outlines generation 8 specifications and extends technology roadmap to 12th generation. 17 October 2017, LTO Consortium, www.lto.org/2017/10/lto-program-outlines-generation-8-specifications-extends-technology-roadmap-12th-generation/

[†] The lost picture show: Hollywood archivists can't outpace obsolescence, Marty Perlmutter, 28 April 2017, IEEE Spectrum, https://spectrum.ieee.org/computing/it/the-lost-picture-show-hollywood-archivists-cant-outpace-obsolescence

---

[‡] One Australian enterprise for instance conducted an audit of their long-term retention tapes, and despite a mandated requirement to hold 7 years only of monthly backups, found a large number of tapes that were in excess of 14 years old still being held and incurring storage fees.

Table 14.4 Monthly Data Added to Compliance Retention

Year	M1	M2	M3	M4	M5	M6	M7	M7	M9	M10	M11	M12
1	504.0	508.0	512.1	516.1	520.3	524.4	528.6	532.8	537.0	541.3	545.6	550.0
2	554.4	558.8	563.3	567.8	572.3	576.8	581.4	586.1	590.8	595.5	600.2	605.0
3	609.8	614.7	619.6	624.5	629.5	634.5	639.6	644.7	649.8	655.0	660.2	665.5
4	670.8	676.2	681.5	687.0	692.5	698.0	703.5	709.2	714.8	720.5	726.3	732.0
5	737.9	743.8	749.7	755.7	761.7	767.8	773.9	780.1	786.3	792.6	798.9	805.2
6	811.7	818.1	824.7	831.2	837.9	844.6	851.3	858.1	864.9	871.8	878.8	885.8
7	892.8	900.0	907.1	914.4	921.7	929.0	936.4	943.9	951.4	959.0	966.6	974.3

Whereas public cloud vendors will often focus on a total cost of ownership (TCO) comparison between rented consumption of their services and the investment in private infrastructure for relatively short periods of interest (e.g., 6–12 months), long-term retention does not fit into such a model. Keep in mind that:

- Unlike compute-based workloads, long-term retention is not particularly elastic—it will continue to grow for the retention time, then plateau to a slower growth cycle as the oldest (and smallest) data sets age out (meanwhile, larger data sets will continue to be added monthly).
- The volume of data that will eventually be held in a long-term retention model *can* be quite significant, even from relatively low starting points, as compliance style retention is usually in the years, if not decades.

For instance, consider a business with a 1 PB data footprint. The business determines that 50% of their data falls into a compliance retention requirement, so they have to store long-term retention backups for 500 TB. Those long-term retention backups are retained for 7 years for financial/tax reasons, and the business elects to store monthly backups for the full 7 years.

As stated previously, predicting data growth rates over longer periods of time is somewhat imprecise.* However, we will assume a reasonably standard, modest data growth rate of 10% per annum across all data, including that which has to be retained for compliance purposes. While the actual shape of data growth rates over the course of a year varies, business by business, we'll assume that it follows a linear trend—so a 10% per annum growth rate will be modeled as a 0.7974% monthly growth rate. Using our starting size of 500 TB and calculating the volume of data to be pushed to long-term retention at the end of each month, we start

with an initial data push of 504 TB for the end of month 1, and end with a data push of 974.3 TB for the end of month 84. (Of course, it is important to understand that we do not "end" long-term retention at the end of month 84, we just merely reach the first point at which we can start removing data.) Table 14.4 shows the end-of-month values over the full 7 years for our model, with monthly sizes in TB.

While Table 14.4 shows the amount of data *added* to long-term retention storage at the end of each month, what we have to keep in mind when evaluating public cloud versus private infrastructure costing is that we pay for data stored, month-by-month. Thus, while the month-by-month data volume never exceeds 1 PB, the *cumulative* volume of data being held over the 7-year period is 59.96 PB.

At this point, we'll assume that we consistently achieve a 10:1 deduplication ratio across our long-term retention data, so our monthly long-term retention *storage* values are shown in Table 14.5.

However, Table 14.6 shows the *cumulative* amount of data that will be used in long-term retention storage, month-by-month, over the 7-year period, assuming the 10:1 deduplication ratio holds over our 7-year period of interest.

It is essential we consider the cumulative cost of this storage here. Using the Amazon Simple Monthly Calculator[†] for US East (N. Virginia) 16 June 2019 using the S3 Infrequent Access tier, the storage fee for 50.4 TB in month 1, year 1 will be $645.12, increasing to $82,422.59 per month for 5,996.1 TB in month 12, year 7, with a 7-year cumulative storage cost of US$3,132,598 (rounded down). Note that this costing does not include any meta-costs (e.g., PUTS, GETS, actual data egress from recoveries, etc.). When conducting a comparison between in-cloud and on-premises infrastructure costs, it is worth keeping in mind the following:

- If the PUT/GET, etc., and data egress fees are not estimated/calculated, it is not unreasonable to assume they "cancel out" in a cost comparison with the datacenter

---

* A good rule of thumb is that unless the business data cycles are very well understood, the accuracy of a predicted growth rate is likely to halve over a three to four year period.

[†] https://calculator.s3.amazonaws.com/index.html

Table 14.5 Per-Month Data Storage Requirements After 10:1 Deduplication

Year	M1	M2	M3	M4	M5	M6	M7	M7	M9	M10	M11	M12
1	50.4	50.8	51.2	51.6	52.0	52.4	52.9	53.3	53.7	54.1	54.6	55.0
2	55.4	55.9	56.3	56.8	57.2	57.7	58.1	58.6	59.1	59.5	60.0	60.5
3	61.0	61.5	62.0	62.5	63.0	63.5	64.0	64.5	65.0	65.5	66.0	66.5
4	67.1	67.6	68.2	68.7	69.2	69.8	70.4	70.9	71.5	72.1	72.6	73.2
5	73.8	74.4	75.0	75.6	76.2	76.8	77.4	78.0	78.6	79.3	79.9	80.5
6	81.2	81.8	82.5	83.1	83.8	84.5	85.1	85.8	86.5	87.2	87.9	88.6
7	89.3	90.0	90.7	91.4	92.2	92.9	93.6	94.4	95.1	95.9	96.7	97.4

fees (e.g., cooling, rack space, etc.) for any on-premises equipment to provide similar object storage—at least, for initial ballpark comparisons.

■ When moving data to public cloud, the block size will have a significant impact over the "meta" costs associated with PUTS and GETS. For example, moving 100 GB of data out in 64 KB segments, with each segment triggering a new PUT, would consume significantly more operations than the same amount of data moved out in 1 MB segments.

■ It is common to consider public cloud versus private infrastructure as an OpEx vs CapEx comparison; however, most vendors do support a variety of financial models including leases and utility consumption models to allow for OpEx consumption of on-premises systems.

■ Object storage can be used for more than just long-term retention. While long-term retention from backup platforms is often seen as an "anchor" use-case for object storage, businesses deploying it may find it useful for other functions, including archive, image storage, hierarchical storage management, and even in-house storage for mobile and other applications traditionally seen as "cloud native."

You will note our cost comparison has been performed against S3-Infrequent Access cost models, rather than Amazon Glacier cost models. This is because we have assumed an interactive deduplication process where the long-term retention is treated as a nearline extension of the primary storage. Glacier's data access model (which often sees long wait times to list or retrieve data stored there) is not compatible with an interactive deduplication engine.*

---

* In order to use Glacier, a deduplication engine would need to be able to "seal off" deduplication containers and store/retrieve them atomically with little to no reference to other containers—regardless of whether those containers are also in Glacier or more accessible forms of object or even block storage. This would likely increase the amount of data needed to be placed into Glacier.

14.13 Backup as a Service

BaaS is a burgeoning service designed to complement business offerings from cloud service providers who target the mid-market and enterprise service space. More often than not, these are to be found not from the full hyperscalers such as Amazon or Google, but from smaller cloud providers, especially those who have developed a service catalog around IaaS.

BaaS is born of the recognition that many of the SLAs for data retention and systems availability within the cloud space are expressly targeted at limiting the liability of the service provider. While this potentially provides a high level of service uptime for subscribers, it provides little or no self-controlled recovery capabilities for the service subscribers.

By offering a robust BaaS catalog for their subscribers, cloud, and service providers are recognizing that data protection is an important value addition for many businesses—and where long-term retention for backups is offered, is a "hook" to keep customers for lengthy periods of time.

It is therefore increasingly common to see providers publish compatible BaaS options for their subscribers. These are often quite economical due to a combination of buying power and strategic relationships with key vendors. (Vendors may even introduce incentives for their own sales teams for pointing businesses at a strategic BaaS provider.)

Businesses looking to use their cloud provider for BaaS functions *might* receive favorable pricing based on multiple services, or if nothing else, the convenience of limiting the number of IT utility providers they need to subscribe to. Such services should be carefully examined to ensure the business can confirm adequate separation of primary data and protection data/services for disaster and network failure situations. Additionally, businesses with long-term compliance retention requirements may still need to consider maintaining responsibility for part of their data protection activities based on service catalog options or pricing—or a desire to not be locked down indefinitely to a specific BaaS provider.

Table 14.6 Cumulative Long-Term Retention Storage Requirements, Month-by-Month

Year	M1	M2	M3	M4	M5	M6	M7	M7	M9	M10	M11	M12
1	50.4	101.2	152.4	204.0	256.0	308.5	361.3	414.6	468.3	522.5	577.0	632.0
2	687.5	743.3	799.7	856.4	913.7	971.4	1029.5	1088.1	1147.2	1206.7	1266.8	1327.3
3	1388.2	1449.7	1511.7	1574.1	1637.1	1700.5	1764.5	1828.9	1893.9	1959.4	2025.5	2092.0
4	2159.1	2226.7	2294.9	2363.6	2432.8	2502.6	2572.9	2643.9	2715.3	2787.4	2860.0	2933.2
5	3007.0	3081.4	3156.4	3231.9	3308.1	3384.9	3462.3	3540.3	3618.9	3698.2	3778.0	3858.6
6	3939.7	4021.6	4104.0	4187.1	4270.9	4355.4	4440.5	4526.3	4612.8	4700.0	4787.9	4876.4
7	4965.7	5055.7	5146.4	5237.9	5330.0	5422.9	5516.6	5611.0	5706.1	5802.0	5898.7	5996.1

Some businesses may move to BaaS regardless of whether they have content in a cloud or not. This may allow them to leverage backup technology they don't want to or otherwise unable to invest in themselves, particularly if backup is seen as a "utility" function beyond the core work requirements of the business. (You might think of this as the next evolution of managed services.) Moving to BaaS is also becoming popular for businesses switching to a maximized OpEx model over CapEx.

14.14 Disaster Recovery as a Service

"Do more with less" is the often the catch-cry of business to their IT division. IT services are expected to be more agile—indeed, more cloud-like—either without an increase to budget and staffing, or even while lowering budget and having fewer staff.

Consider now the approach that many businesses take toward disaster recovery. There will either be a dedicated disaster recovery datacenter for the business, or there will be rented rack space in a co-location facility with equipment maintained for the purposes of facilitating a disaster recovery operation.

Yet, unless the business is large enough that it can effectively run an "active/active" datacenter configuration where each datacenter is able to run *at least* the full production workload of the business, the disaster recovery environments for smaller businesses often sit idle for months on end. In a co-location facility, rack space is usually charged with power-consumption, cooling, and other charges as well as the actual space occupied, so there makes little or no difference in the

monthly fee if the equipment is powered on, or powered off. Likewise, a datacenter will have a myriad of running costs regardless of whether systems within it are being used or not.

It is here therefore we see a call for disaster recovery as a service. Instead of paying for ongoing access to rack space in a co-location facility, or a datacenter, *and* all the equipment therein required to provide disaster recovery services, businesses can choose to use public cloud as for short-term disaster recovery hosting.

Two potential ways in which DRaaS could be leveraged are shown in Figure 14.12.

In the simplest method, some form of replication service may be deployed within the datacenter. Selected virtual systems would have their state replicated, either periodically or continuously, out to the public cloud service, usually into object storage. Within the public cloud service, there will be a virtual appliance for disaster recovery orchestration; this system will be used to coordinate the reconstruction of virtual machine image data from object storage into appropriate disk files for the cloud service provider, and create the appropriate virtual machine instances in public cloud. Ideally, it will also be able to convert a system that had been failed over into the public cloud *back* to the on-premises infrastructure. Depending on the service used, virtual machine image data received may be stored only in object until such time as a disaster recovery is invoked (a "cold" recovery), or the latest copy may be automatically converted into block storage for faster use (a "warm" recovery).

The method described fits with the "Replication Service" in Figure 14.12 being directly hooked into the on-premises virtualization environment.

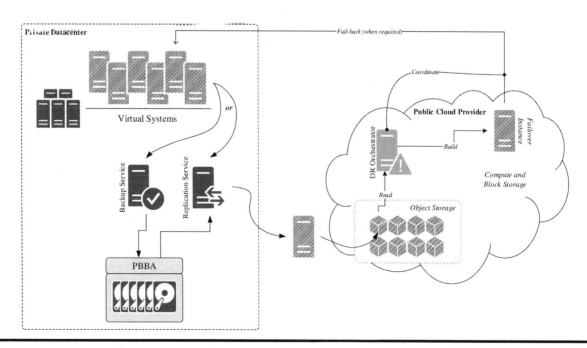

Figure 14.12 Two potential dataflows for achieving DRaaS.

The alternate method, also shown in Figure 14.12, still uses some form of replication service, but the replication is done from backup images taken within the environment. The replicator service reads from the backup data and the rest of the process runs largely the same as previously described.

An alternate method, not shown in the diagram, would have virtualized backup infrastructure running in the cloud service provider, with the on-premises backup data replicating to the cloud-hosted backup environment. Since on-premises hypervisors are almost invariably different to in-cloud hypervisors, there would still be a service run in the cloud which would orchestrate the conversion of virtual machine images to a cloud-service compatible virtual machine.

In any scenario, the DR orchestration appliance should also handle the post-failover and post-failback tasks, such as reconfiguring virtual network interfaces, setting IP address and hostname details, etc., as required.*

The "warm" and "cold" DR preparedness each have their own advantages. While the warm method will allow a workload where failover has been initiated to start faster (as there will be no read from object storage), block storage in public cloud does cost significantly more, as a general rule, compared to object storage. (For example, 10 TB of S3 standard for Amazon US East (North Virginia) as of 22 June 2019 would cost $235.40 per month to hold. By comparison the same storage in "Throughput Optimized HDD" for block would be $450 per month (assuming no snapshot storage), or $977 per month for "General Purpose SSD.")

You might typically expect a service restart time from cold DR storage of 1–4 hours (or perhaps more, depending on the size of the service to be converted), whereas the warm method might allow a service restart time in the order of 5–30 minutes, depending on when the warm instance has been populated.

In previous chapters we've discussed a variety of methods that can render a zero or near-zero failover time between the production and disaster recovery workload. Continuously available storage can prevent outage time at all if the outage is confined to the storage platform; clustering, replication, and continuous data protection may allow for failover in the order of seconds, and snapshots combined with replication may allow for failover within a few minutes. It is obvious that DRaaS does not as yet provide that level of service protection, and should not be used for that purpose. While DRaaS has its best fit for mid-sized and smaller businesses, it will often be marketed toward larger enterprises as being a valid use case for "Tier 3" and "Tier 4" workloads, rather than the

mission critical and business-critical workloads, which will still be protected via traditional high availability options.

14.15 Architectural Considerations for Cloud Service Providers

For cloud service providers, one of the biggest challenges for data protection services relates to multi-tenancy. While this technically affects a business running a private or hybrid cloud, multi-tenancy considerations to data protection become especially critical for public cloud providers.

It's one thing for instance to be able to offer a service catalog for data protection utilizing an enterprise class backup and recovery product, but if it isn't architected from the ground up for multi-tenancy (either by the vendor, or by the provider), the potential security implications from information leakage is extreme.

This is essentially no different from standard security considerations in multi-tenanted environments, but data protection by its very nature has potential to expose an *entire* business to information theft or data destruction. Whereas a private or hybrid cloud service provider might be able to leave multi-tenancy considerations as a lower order priority compared to recoverability, it's arguable a public cloud provider must make it the highest priority in design considerations. This is represented as a high level view in Figure 14.13.

At bare minimum, a service provider will need to maintain two separate zones within their networking infrastructure; the private or internal zone will be entirely invisible and inaccessible to any cloud tenants. There will additionally be a shared zone that contains systems and infrastructure providing services to tenants. There will likely be a significant networking gap (either physical or firewalled) between the shared services zone and the private service provider infrastructure. (For instance, jump boxes may be required to reach from the private to shared services zone, with no connections permitted from the shared services zone into the private zone.)

While each tenant zone will be able to connect to the shared services zone, security will need to be established to ensure that no tenant can "peer over the fence" at another tenant.

Returning to our example of backup and recovery software, information leakage might happen in one of two different ways if not controlled:

1. *Visibility:* If a tenant can "view" monitoring information or reports that reveals hostnames or operational status[†] of other tenant zones or the shared services

---

* We would also expect the network configuration between the cloud and the on-premises environment to be sufficiently compatible that clients of the workload being failed over would not need to be reconfigured, even if the networking configuration for the workload itself must be adjusted.

† We could refer to this as *metadata* leakage.

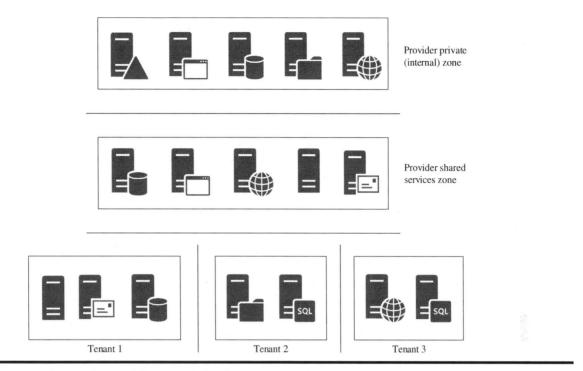

Provider private
(internal) zone

Provider shared
services zone

Tenant 1   Tenant 2   Tenant 3

Figure 14.13   Separated zones in a multi-tenanted cloud service provider.

zone, this information might be used as part of social engineering or even to provide information usable in a direct hack attempt.

2. *Access:* Allowing one tenant to recover data backed up by another tenant would make irrelevant any security steps taken against *primary* tenant data and zones.

Multi-tenancy considerations will apply to more than just the risk of data leakage however. They will also directly impact the efficiency and cost-effectiveness of the services offered by

the cloud provider. For example, consider the implications of multi-tenancy on system or service replication. Figure 14.14 shows a basic view of virtual machines on shared storage, both at the primary and disaster recovery site.

From a standard storage consideration, it does not matter whether the virtual hosts sitting on a datastore presented for virtualization storage belong to a single tenant, or a mix of tenants. However, depending on the service levels offered by the cloud provider to tenants for data protection and recoverability, the layout of virtual machines and storage *will* be significant. Consider for instance a

Function	Bronze	Silver	Gold
Failure protection	In the event of storage failure, system will be restarted with no more than 24 hours data loss.	In the event of storage failure, system will be restarted on alternate storage in the same datacenter with no more than 15 minutes data loss.	In the event of storage failure, system will be automatically transitioned to alternate storage in the datacenter with no interruption to services or data loss.
Availability	System will not automatically transition to an alternate datacenter in the event of site failure. System will remain unavailable until hosting site is operational again.	System will automatically transition to alternate datacenter in the event of a site failure. System will reboot and up to 30 minutes of data loss may occur.	System will automatically transition to alternate datacenter in the event of a site failure without interruption or data loss.

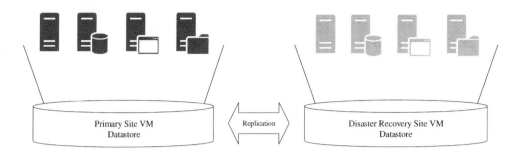

Figure 14.14   Basic view of virtual machines on shared storage.

basic service catalog for data protection and availability* as shown in Table 14.6.

Each of these service offerings requires distinctly different storage and availability options:

■ Bronze
  - *Failure protection*: Snapshot replication performed on a 24-hour basis
  - *Availability*: None
■ Silver
  - *Failure protection*: Asynchronous in-datacenter replication with a maximum 15-minute lag
  - *Availability*: Cross-site asynchronous replication with a maximum 30-minute lag
■ Gold
  - *Failure protection*: Synchronously mirrored storage systems continuously available and managed as a single unit to the virtualization layer
  - *Availability*: Metro or similar synchronous system mirroring

Such a disparate service catalog requires the service provider to ensure systems are provisioned on storage that matches the offerings the customer has chosen. At the physical storage layer this might require three distinctly different storage systems, or a management layer on top of fewer storage systems that allows for a high level of granularity and control over provisioning and protection systems. Consider for instance that each of the protection and availability models will have both a cost to customer *and* a provisioning cost to the cloud services provider. Even if the services can be managed such that say, a bronze-level customer can have data or systems residing on gold-level infrastructure but only get the *appearance* of bronze-level service, this will have a negative impact on the cost model for the services provider, since bronze-level pricing will undoubtedly be developed against being delivered from bronze-level infrastructure.

Thus, our service and storage model at a high level view instead of resembling that shown in Figure 14.14 might instead more resemble a view such as that shown in Figure 14.15.

---

* Backup and recovery services that might be offered as part of the data protection plans are not shown, for brevity.

While initially this model may require additional provisioning cost for the service provider, the end result in a more tightly controlled cost model that allows for appropriate allocation of tenant subscription options to the most efficient and appropriate infrastructure.

14.16 Summary

Despite the relative popularity of cloud in the IT operations for many businesses, this new OpEx/Utility model for infrastructure and IT services is still young compared to traditional IT infrastructure in terms of data protection maturity. There is undoubtedly considerable scope for businesses to achieve agility and cost control orders of magnitude more impressive than available with traditional approaches to infrastructure management, but it can come at a savage cost if not approached carefully. Cloud services are akin to the "wild west:" there's a fortune to be had, but it's not without risks and challenges. Businesses that move workloads into that space without taking adequate steps to protect their data may find themselves in a precarious, if not critical condition.

For service providers themselves, the multi-tenancy nature of cloud adds a considerable layer of complexity in managing and delivering efficient, secure, and cost-effective data protection options to subscribers. Immature service providers that don't sufficiently plan ahead and reconcile service catalogs to infrastructure capability may find their offerings unprofitable at best, and at worst, decidedly insecure for themselves and their tenants.

Ultimately, "the cloud" is an operating model as opposed to a particular destination. This means that private cloud infrastructure is just as valid for a business to consume as public cloud infrastructure—and it would seem that as businesses refresh their on-premises infrastructure, we truly are seeing an emphasis on delivering a cloud-like experience, at least in terms of automation and service provisioning. Elasticity is perhaps more challenging to achieve in private infrastructure, although it can sometimes be accomplished with utility consumption from private infrastructure

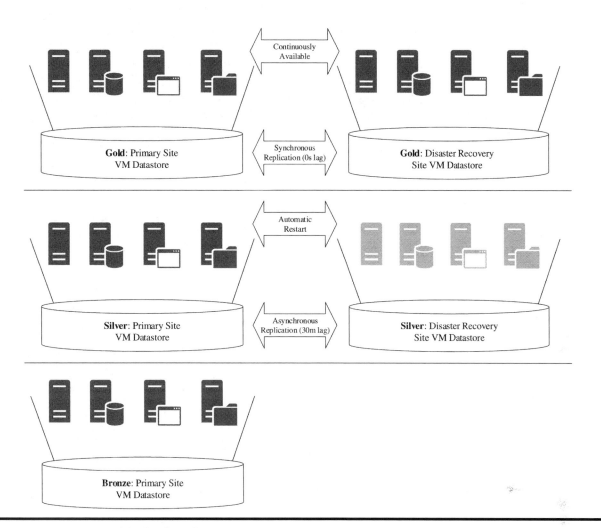

Figure 14.15   Storage provisioning based on service catalog options.

vendors.* More comprehensively, it is hybrid cloud that helps to deliver elasticity: being able to "burst" workloads out into a public cloud when there are higher resource requirements.

Perhaps the simplest way to consider data protection in relation to the cloud is this: it matters naught where a workload is if it is unprotected. While public cloud service models in particular have a "shared responsibility matrix," the FARR model should always be followed to address fault tolerance, availability, redundancy, and recoverability requirements that the cloud service provider does not provide.

_____

* A vendor for instance may deliver on-site double the storage requirements under a utility model. Just as in public cloud where resource reservation leads to cheaper prices, the business might "rent" a base capacity of 50% of the storage. When additional storage is temporarily required, the business can burst into the spare storage capacity and pay additional fees for the duration of the use. Similar options may be available for compute, as well.

14.17 Self-Reflection

Perform a few web searches for "data breach," "cloud security," "cloud data loss," "data leak," "privacy failure," and note examples of where businesses have hosted data in public cloud but encountered failure situations. Reflecting on guidance such as the Amazon Shared Responsibility Model, do you think the failure in the incidents you've found lay with the cloud provider, or the user of the cloud?

Pick an industry vertical in your country (e.g., engineering, medical, government, education, etc.), and search for information about whether there are any restrictions on that industry in relation to what data it can or can't host in public clouds. In particular, be certain to note whether:

■ Data can be stored in public cloud at all
■ Data can leave the country
■ Data must be stored or transmitted encrypted

Revisit the 7-year AWS long-term retention cost model discussed (see Tables 14.4 through 14.6). Re-calculate it for the AWS region closest to your location, and note:

- What will be the year 8 and year 9 storage requirements, month-by-month, given that the year 1 and year 2 storage will be purgeable during this time period?

- What is the change to storage requirements if monthly backups are only retained for 13 months, and 2 × yearly backups are instead retained for 7 years? (For the purposes of your calculation, assume the yearly backups retained are taken at the end of month 6, and the end of month 12.)

Chapter 15

Protecting Virtual Infrastructure

15.1 Introduction

Virtualization has become absolute mainstream in most organizations. What was once the preserve of mainframe environments only has become so pervasive that a *lack* of virtualization is more likely to elicit surprise than the implementation thereof.

Virtualization tackles key IT problems for many businesses, including but not limited to:

- Deployment speed
- Hardware compatibility
- Manageability
- Cost-efficiency
- Power efficiency
- System reliability
- High availability

Ironically, as previously dedicated workloads have been consolidated onto virtual infrastructure and allowed for innovative solutions to the issues mentioned earlier, virtualization introduced a mixed bag of benefits and challenges in the data protection space. These are best addressed by tackling each relevant data protection activity in its own right.

15.2 Snapshots

Our earlier chapter focusing on snapshots introduced many of the considerations, advantages, and disadvantages that come from using snapshot technology within data protection, and those carry through to the use of snapshots within virtual infrastructure.

Snapshots play such a large part in virtual infrastructure protection that you could arguably say a full machine snapshot is the holy grail of system administration. While volume management systems (e.g., Veritas Volume Manager, Logical Volume Manager (LVM), Microsoft VSS) have offered snapshot capabilities for some time, and snapshots are also readily available at the SAN and NAS level, these have usually had one substantial frustration: being divorced from the operational or configured state of the host they're associated with.

Consider for instance a Linux host using LVM: at any point a system administrator could issue a snapshot command against individual filesystems on the host, thereby creating a point in time copy of filesystem state. Yet it is rare for all content of a system to be on a single filesystem, so administrators taking a snapshot of just the data region on a server might offer protection for it, but at a cost of consistency when compared to other filesystems if it is to be rolled back.

Figure 15.1 shows this scenario: a host might have three distinct filesystems, one for the operating system, one for the data region, and one for the application/log region. In this example, we have two different snapshots taken of the "Data" filesystem. At any point the system administrator might choose to roll back to either of those snapshots and it would be perfectly valid to do so—but application logs and operating system logs stored on the other filesystems will no longer be consistent with the state of the data region. So while protection had been provided for the data region, it hadn't necessarily been provided in a sufficiently consistent way.

One obvious solution to this would be to simultaneously create a snapshot of all three filesystems—operating system, application/log, and data. Thus, the overall state of the system could be rolled back at any point. However, not all operating systems support running on filesystems that can be snapped for the OS or boot region, and since the OS must be running to support a snapshot being taken, the overall state of the host might be a little unreliable if snapshots are rolled back.

Equally, disk or LUN level snapshots executed at a storage layer might not offer application-consistent states and at best offer crash-consistent protection. There is also the question of filesystem-to-filesystem consistency: if a snapshot is

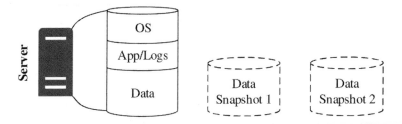

Figure 15.1 Software controlled snapshots on physical servers.

created for the data volume and takes 3 seconds to return with a "success" flag, then subsequently a snapshot is taken for the "logs" filesystem, is there risk that changes to the two filesystems during this period are enough to create consistency issues if both filesystems are later reverted to the snapshot copy?

Virtualization therefore can allow for considerably easier whole-system snapshot scenarios, as shown in Figure 15.2. In such a situation, so long as all the storage devices on the virtual machine can have a snapshot taken, the snapshot becomes a purely binary operation. In particular if the virtual machine has been shut down before the snapshot has been taken, then even if it is rolled back to a particular snapshot, it should be entirely consistent on restart.

This introduces considerable efficiency improvements for many organizations: reliable and cross-filesystem consistent snapshots can be taken for an entire virtual machine practically at the click of a button before a critical maintenance activity is attempted. This applies not only to production servers but also to development, lab, or training servers. (For instance, it is quite common to see virtual machine snapshots used in short-term training and lab environments to allow a baseline setup of a virtual machine to be reset at the conclusion of training.)

Even if a virtual machine has not been shut down before the snapshot, the snapshot remains considerably more useful

than a conventional per-filesystem snapshot or per-LUN snapshot, particularly when coupled with modern backup techniques. This is something we'll go into greater detail in the backup topic later in this chapter.

It is however important to note that *some* storage presented to virtual hosts may not be susceptible for snapshot operations. For instance, virtualization environments usually offer some form of *independent* and *raw* disks. An independent disk is one that is explicitly excluded from any snapshot operations taken. This might be for performance reasons or because snapshots aren't supported for the type of data to be housed on that disk. Equally, a raw disk is one where storage is presented directly to the virtual host without any virtualization layer involved, and is typically done so for specific performance requirements. Finally, and particularly in support of virtualizing systems that require clustering, virtualization systems can also support *shared* disks, where a virtual disk is presented to multiple virtual servers simultaneously.

The use of such storage with virtual machines (regardless of the nomenclature of any particular virtualization system) can represent a considerable roadblock for administrators, given either of the following:

- Prevent a virtual machine from being snapshot at all, reducing the data protection options available.

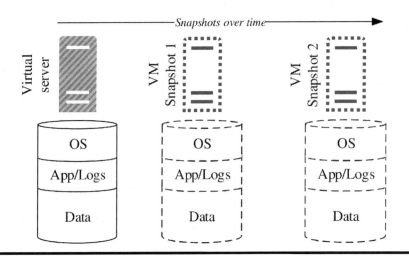

Figure 15.2 Virtual machine snapshots.

■ Silently skip the disks that *can't* be snapshot during a snapshot operation, allowing for the creation of a snapshot as inconsistent as if it had been done at the operating system layer in a traditional approach.

In such situations it becomes important that the data protection patterns established for virtual machines take into account those systems that cannot be protected by snapshot activities. This is particularly important to understand because during a virtual machine *image-based backup*, it is more typical than not to see a snapshot temporarily established for the entire virtual machine so that a consistent backup may be taken.

15.3 Replication

Traditionally, there have been two reasons why clustering has been used within IT—for performance scaling and for high availability. While both remain valid considerations, virtual machine replication has significantly reduced the need for many organizations to consider clustering at the operating system level for high availability.

There are a variety of ways in which virtual machine replication can take place.

Hypervisor controlled replication is where the virtualization servers themselves are responsible for the replication of virtual machines between two locations. (For example, VMware's Site Recovery Manager (SRM) can be used to orchestrate failover of services between sites where virtual machine replication is performed.) In this scenario, the virtualization hypervisors involved in presenting virtual machines handle the replication of changes in virtual machines from one site to the other, updating blocks within virtual machine files as appropriate. While an advantage of this is that replication happens at a layer quite close to the virtual machines, it can create a higher workload on the virtualization servers as they manage both standard virtualization tasks and data replication—particularly as the number of virtual machines to be replicated between sites grows.

The second approach is to use storage level replication. In this scenario, volumes presented to virtualization systems at the production site are replicated to an alternate site via the storage systems, thereby offloading the data processing requirement of replication between sites. This comes at the potential cost of replicating entire LUNs, and so requires careful planning between virtualization and storage administrators to ensure there is no mixing of virtual machines that require replication and virtual machines that don't require replication on the same LUNs. The benefit this technique brings is to offload the replication functionality from the hypervisors, and can scale better as the number of systems to be replicated increase. To be safely performed however it still

usually requires storage arrays and hypervisors to be "aware" of each other's functionality.

However, while this may offload the replication performance from the hypervisors, it can equally create challenges. Most seriously, unless appropriate integration is provided between the virtualization environment and the storage infrastructure, the replication may not be *consistent*; that is, a virtual machine that is started from its replicated copy in the event of a failure will likely to be at *best* crash consistent, and perhaps worse, if in-guest database/application quiescing is not performed as part of the replication process, may run the risk of not being usable if the virtual machine services are unable to start. As you might also expect, this method is really only applicable when external storage systems (SAN and NAS) are in use. Hyperconverged technology, which virtualizes and abstracts the storage layer (e.g., VMware vVOL and vSAN) will not support volume/LUN level replication as we've described.

Of course, replication is not a perfect replacement for clustering. A key feature of clustering n systems is to allow some number m to fail (where $m < n$) without impeding the delivery of services. Virtual machine replication will replicate all aspects of a virtual machine—corrupt and noncorrupt (or, at least, to specific replication checkpoints). Therefore, virtual machine replication isn't a like-for-like replacement of clustering, but more a means of rapidly standing up a disaster recovery instance of a machine after site loss (regardless of whether that's permanent or transient).

So a third approach is to use integrated continuous data protection (CDP). Recall from Figure 10.13 (Continuous data protection for virtualization) that this approach integrates IO splitters into the hypervisors, and leverages journaling technology to ensure write-order-consistent replication of data between sites, or even locally. Using CDP approaches instead of traditional replication can offer more advanced recovery options, including:

■ Consistency groups for multiple virtual machines (e.g., ensuring all virtual machines in a Sharepoint farm are consistent)
■ Local *and* remote protection options
■ Cloud disaster recovery options (where a virtual machine replica can be failed over into a cloud service provider, then failed back when required)
■ Virtual machine rollback—not just providing an up-to-the-second copy of a machine, but also allowing a machine to be rolled back to any point in the replication journal

Organizations can either choose to wear this risk or deploy forms of CDP where the virtual machines are replicated with periodic checkpoints. Thus, if a virtual machine becomes corrupt, the replica of the virtual machine from, say, 60

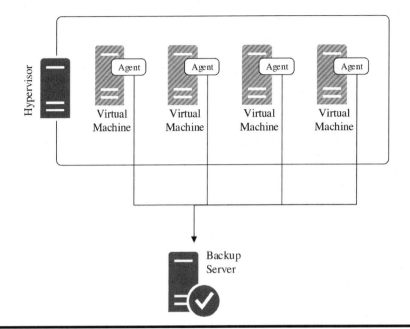

Figure 15.3   Agent-based virtual machine backups.

minutes ago, prior to the corruption having occurred, can be activated at the alternate site (or even the local site).

15.4 Backup and Recovery

15.4.1 Image-Level versus In-Guest Backup

There are two distinctly different techniques virtual machines may be backed up: guest and image. Guest-based backup sees a traditional backup agent or client installed in the individual virtual machines, and the backup system treats each virtual machine as a standard client. This is often considered to be a *legacy* backup option, and is shown in Figure 15.3.

This backup technique allows for maximum granularity of control over the backup process. Backup systems supporting fine-grained control over what files or data on a client are or are not backed up will perform no differently with client software installed within a virtual machine as they would within a physical host. When virtualization was still within its infancy, this was definitely the preferred backup option. However, as virtualization has expanded and subsumed an extremely high percentage of the IT infrastructure within most businesses, this method has not scaled. To understand the *why* of this, we need to come back to one of the fundamental gains of virtualization: better resource utilization. As CPU speed and memory capacity has increased, virtualization has offered considerable cost savings by recognizing that many systems run at much lower resource utilizations than the hardware offers. A DNS server, for instance, provisioned on a dual-core system with even just a modest 4 GB of RAM and dual-core CPUs, may on average never consume more

than 10% of those resources. Virtualization offers a neat way around that—multiple guest systems running on a single piece of hardware with the hypervisor directing cooperative use of system resources.

This works neatly until you encounter individual systems that are resource hogs. High-performance systems (be they raw compute, data manipulation, or databases) can still be found deployed on physical hardware not only to provide dedicated resources, but also to ensure those high demand hosts don't strip resources from other virtualized systems that are resident on the same hypervisors.*

To put it mildly, backup software—particularly *traditional* backup software—is always designed to be a resource hog. A fundamental purpose of backup software is to generate a protected copy of data as quickly as possible (or likewise, recover from that copy as quickly as possible). It is not uncommon to see poorly designed backup environments using in-guest agents to saturate many, if not all, resources within hypervisors: storage IO, network bandwidth, and CPU utilization. This of course violates a fundamental requirement of a backup and recovery system: to not unduly interfere with core operations in order to perform data protection.

Reducing load on hypervisors during backup operations is challenging when using traditional agent software installed within the individual guest operating systems. A

---

* Most virtualization systems allow for resource limiting in terms of CPU and RAM, which covers initial allocation (e.g., two CPUs) and maximum slices of CPU time (e.g., no more than 6,000 MHz), both for individual virtual machines and *pools* of particular virtual machines. However, resource limitations work only so long as you have no systems that require *maximum* resources.

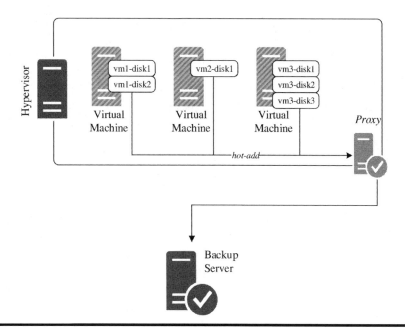

Figure 15.4 Image-based backup of virtual machines.

backup administrator might carefully assemble backup policies, grouping virtual machines in such a way as to prevent any one hypervisor from becoming overloaded during the backup process, but if either virtualization administrators or the virtualization management software can migrate virtual machines between hypervisors, this work could be undone at any point. Further, since in-guest backup processes will align to standard backup processes, standard operating system backup challenges will remain—for instance, virtual clients with dense filesystems will still take longer to backup than desirable.

The second backup method for virtual machines is an *image*-level backup, as depicted in Figure 15.4. This relies on the obvious fact that each virtual machine is actually at some level a distinct collection of data files. For the purposes of simplification in Figure 15.4 only the "virtual disks" have been cited, but accompanying the virtual disks for virtual machines will typically be a number of other small files representing the current configuration and other state files.* This method is seen as considerably more scalable and is generally preferred in most environments.

There are several distinct advantages of image-level backups. These include the following:

■ When integrated with snapshots, they allow for a reasonably consistent backup.
■ They do not suffer *dense filesystem* issues an in-guest backup process would.

■ They can be executed in a more controlled manner to reduce hypervisor and virtual environment loading.

A typical concern with image-level backups of virtual machines is the fact that very little data within the virtual machine may change between backups, yet the virtual machine image file to be backed up may be quite large. Consider a "full Saturday, incrementals Sunday–Friday" backup schedule: if that schedule were applied to an in-guest traditional operating system agent, then only the files *in* the virtual machine that have changed will need to be backed up. On the other hand, given virtual machine disks are usually represented by flat, large files within the hypervisor, an incremental backup is effectively meaningless at a hypervisor file level.

One way of resolving this is sometimes referred to as *changed block tracking*. Rather than actually backing up the entire virtual machine disk file from the hypervisor, the backup product queries the hypervisor to find what *blocks* within the file have changed since the previous backup, and only backs up those blocks.

The other key method to mitigate this problem is via a previously discussed topic—deduplication. Consider a virtual machine that has 50 GB of space allocated on the hypervisor for its virtual disks. A full backup will, by necessity, be of the entire 50 GB, but once deduplication comes into play, this will very likely be substantially reduced in size.[†]

---

* Recall in Chapter 12 we discussed block-based backups. Image-level backups of virtual machines closely mirror the advantages of block-based backups.

[†] Further, if virtual machines have been deployed with thick provisioning enabled (where the entire size of a virtual drive is allocated on creation), this may mean they contain a large amount of empty space.

Subsequent backups (either as incrementals or fulls) will continue to make use of this functionality. Indeed, it is not unusual to see 20, 30, or 50:1 deduplication ratios achieved over repeated backups of virtual machines. However, image-level backups to conventional, non-deduplicating storage might be seen as extremely wasteful, consuming large amounts of space.

In short, organizations do not need to fear image-level backups of virtual machines as being a space hog so long as the appropriate infrastructure and technology is used.

There are several different methods an image-level backup can be accommodated, and most backup products will support more than one method. In the simplest scenario, agent software might be installed on the individual hypervisors, in much the same way that agent software can be installed on any physical host. However, this typically relies on the hypervisor running a complete operating system. So-called bare metal hypervisors that maintain at most a minimal operating system, used *just* to provide the virtualization services, are typically not compatible with agent installation. For instance, the Linux Kernel-based Virtual Machine (KVM) system sees virtual machines (guests) deployed on top of a traditional Linux server (e.g., RedHat or CentOS). In such a configuration, it is possible to deploy the Linux backup agent on the hypervisor server (or servers, since virtual machines will usually be run from a cluster of physical servers), and use that agent to perform image-based, virtual machine backups. However, in such a scenario it is not merely sufficient to have a traditional filesystem agent backup the virtual machine files—appropriate care must be taken to snapshot virtual machines and redirect writes while the backup is running or else the virtual machine will be unrecoverable.

When we move to more sophisticated, bare metal hypervisors such as VMware's vSphere/ESX server, the option to deploy an agent drops away—the operating system for the hypervisor is considered as untouchable as the operating system for a NAS server. At this point, we rely on backup integration options provided by the hypervisor provider. For instance, staying with the example of VMware, virtual machines hosted by vSphere can typically be protected via one of three different *transport* methods:

■ SAN transport
■ Hot-add (pictured in Figure 15.4)
■ LAN transport (network block device transfer—NBD)

The SAN transport methodology, as you might intuit from its name, is an option focused on SAN presented storage to a virtual machine environment. In this scenario, the various storage volumes that are presented to a cluster of VMware vSphere servers are also mapped via standard SAN techniques to an external, physical server (usually Windows or Linux). The backup agent is installed on that external server.

This server would often be referred to as a proxy. When the backup starts on the proxy, the backup agent has sufficient integration with VMware libraries that the virtual disks can be cleanly backed up as a filesystem backup. (This will usually still coordinate snapshots of the virtual machines in the background during the backup process.)

While this allows for a backup that offloads processing requirements for the backup from the hypervisors, it is not without challenges. For instance:

■ Various flavors of Windows previously would automatically prompt to write disk signatures to newly encountered disks. It was not uncommon to hear of "horror" stories where a SAN transport proxy was being initially configured and an administrator would accidentally click "yes" to such a prompt—rendering the disks corrupt from VMware's perspective.
■ The volumes do have to be presented read/write (to facilitate restores); even if the above mistake was never made, a physical proxy operating like this represents a security challenge to the environment: it has permanent access to all the volumes presented to VMware, and could either be accidentally or deliberately used to cause significant disruption to the virtual infrastructure.*
■ This method only works when SAN storage is being presented.

It is perhaps the final challenge that places the most significant limitation on the SAN transport methodology—it will not "carry forward" into the software defined storage model used in hyperconverged technologies and the software defined datacenter. (For example, SAN transport cannot be used with VMware vVOL or vSAN.) It would be fair to describe SAN transport as "dead-end" technology: it can still be used where the underlying storage *and* backup software supports it, but it does not necessarily offer a continued data protection path as businesses renew their hardware and move toward private cloud experiences.

LAN or NBD-based backups see the hypervisor running any individual virtual machine transmit the entire virtual machine across the network (this may have software-encryption enabled at a higher-performance penalty). This is a "fallback" backup transport methodology that is usually considered unscaleable; since the hypervisors don't include deduplication technology, when the backup is run the entire virtual machine must be read and transmitted across to a

---

* A "SAN transport" proxy running a traditional operating system such as Windows, infected by crypto-locker style ransomware would represent a nightmare scenario to any business, for instance, since it could rapidly corrupt an entire virtual machine farm.

designated agent or proxy within the environment.* Thus, while it may be acceptable for NBD processes to be used in particular edge cases (e.g., a single hypervisor running remotely to the rest of the environment), or as a fallback if a higher-performance proxy method fails, the best practice view of VMware backup deems this method to be unscaleable as the number of virtual machines grows into the many hundreds, or thousands.

In response to the scaling limitations of NBD processes, and the technology dead-end that is SAN transport, VMware developed *hot-add*, which might be considered a *safe,* virtualized version of SAN transport. The hot-add approach allows for virtual proxies to get temporary mapping to the settings and disk files associated with the virtual machines being protected. In its simplest form, this might be seen as no better than a LAN transport process—however, the strength of this comes from allowing any system to act as a virtual proxy. This allows backup vendors to provide (usually light-weight) proxies that run within the virtual environment with say, deduplication functionality. Thus, backups will go through an ethernet connection, the amount of data sent daily could be trivial compared to a SAN transport or traditional LAN backups. Ideally, these virtual proxies will be stateless, so that they can be redeployed, destroyed, and moved as required to suit the overall distribution of virtual machines that require protection.

While physical proxies for SAN transport backups will often need to be high-performance systems (a common configuration would use 8 CPU cores, 32 GB of RAM and multiple high-performance fiber-channel and/or ethernet links), proxies making use of deduplication can afford to be much smaller. Dell EMC Avamar for instance, uses proxies with just 4 GB of RAM, 4 vCPU and less than 30 GB of storage. Virtual proxies will also usually run completely idle unless a backup or recovery is performed, representing little overhead to a virtualization environment. (Likewise, when backups *are* being performed, proxies may be busy, but will ideally compensate by substantially reducing the amount of data that needs to be sent.)

15.4.2 Virtualized Database Backups

It's worth noting the techniques described in the previous section primarily refer to decision points relating to virtualized *systems* that do not guaranteeably include database applications (e.g., Oracle, Microsoft SQL Server, Microsoft Exchange Server).

While image-level backups of virtualized systems are becoming increasingly popular, increased in-guest complexity, typically through the introduction of a database, reduces

the likelihood of the method being appropriate. The "holy grail" for backup systems covering virtualized infrastructure is to perform an image-level backup of an entire database server and do a recovery of a single table or other "atomic unit" of the database from that backup.

As discussed in Chapter 11, snapshots come in two broad categories: crash consistent and application consistent. This becomes particularly important when we consider virtual machine backups where a database or database-like application resides within the virtual machine. A crash-consistent backup will allow the operating system to be restored successfully, as if it had suffered an unexpected power loss. However, without particularly tight integration between the hypervisor, backup software, database, and/or virtual machine tools, backups may not be application consistent. Without application-level consistency, a snapshot style image-level backup of a virtual machine hosting a database may be recoverable, but not restorable within the application, leading to a corrupted database after recovery.

There is growing capability on this front for many backup vendors. For instance, it is becoming increasingly common to be able to use Microsoft Volume Shadow Service (VSS) hooks called from within the guest tools (e.g., VMware Tools) for SQL and other application services—this allows an image-based backup to be taken where the database is in a consistent and recoverable state.

More complex database services and configurations can yet still require an agent-based approach. For instance, some database configurations may require consistency between multiple hosts within an environment, and unsurprisingly, some database vendors may not support their product being backed up through an image-level backup, regardless of what a backup vendor promotes.

Until this is fully available, we will likely continue to need a dual architecture approach to backups of virtualized environments. Image-level backup may very well be used for a large number of virtual machines, but in-guest client software and database agents may be deployed in virtual machines to ensure databases are suitably recoverable.

15.4.3 Recovery Options

If a virtual machine has been backed up via an in-guest agent (the same way a standard physical server of the same operating system type would be), the recovery options available will be exactly those available to the physical version of the host. In short, this means file-level recovery will be the primary recovery method. Some operating systems and products will feature "bare metal recovery" (BMR) options, which allows for a machine to be quickly restored from either a boot-CD or something similar, and such options may be supported for virtualized hosts as well. In particular, where BMR supports booting from a device that can be virtualized (CD, USB),

---

* Mixing incrementals with fulls will partially mitigate this but not solve the problem entirely.

there's a good chance such functions will be supported in a virtual environment as well, if you want to go to that trouble. (Normally switching to image-level backup provides a better BMR option, however.)

When virtual machines have been backed up from their hypervisors at the image level, there are two potential recovery options typically available—image and (sometimes) file.

Image-level recovery is the restoration of the entire virtual machine by recovering its container files (e.g., virtual disks and configuration). This might be done "in place" (overwriting the current instance of the virtual machine) or it might be done to either another hypervisor entirely, or it might simply be done by creating another virtual machine with a new name (e.g., "cerberus" might be recovered on 21 October 2019, as "cerberus-20191021").

Image-level recovery of virtual machines can be particularly efficient when there are a large number of files in the virtual machine, and are perhaps the most efficient form of BMR attainable. After all, instead of building a new host (virtual or physical), booting from a "recovery" system and then performing the recovery, an image-level recovery simply brings back the entire machine in one step from the chosen backup.

Some of the more common traps and challenges associated with image-level backup however include the following:

■ Not efficient when the actual items required for recovery are small (e.g., recovering a 40 GB virtual machine in order to extract 3×100 KB files).
■ The virtual machine will typically be restored with exactly the same configuration. If the virtual machine is recovered as a copy and powered up, it may try to take the same IP address and offer the same services, causing a service disruption or perhaps even data corruption.

With this in mind, more advanced recovery options are becoming more prevalent whereby image-level backup is performed but file-level recovery is an option. This typically requires tighter integration between the backup product and the hypervisor, but provides "the best of both worlds," where backups are fast, and both types of recovery (file and image) are readily available.

Another option available in some products is the utilization of changed block tracking to speed up the recovery. With this option, the same changed block tracking system used for speeding up backups is leveraged to allow for high-speed in-place recovery of virtual machine images: only those blocks that changed between the backup and the current virtual machine state are retrieved from protection storage. For instance, if a 500 GB virtual machine received operating system patches overnight that failed to apply correctly and began crashing on reboot, it's entirely conceivable

that the changes between backups had been 1% or less. At 1% change, just 5 GB of data might need to be recovered in order to complete a full image-level recovery of the virtual machine. Particularly in "emergency recovery" situations, this can drastically reduce the amount of time it may take to recover *hundreds* of virtual machines within a business.

As mentioned earlier, database recoveries from image-level backups are still uncommon. However, even virtual systems with databases running might still receive some form of image-level backup in conjunction with agent-based database backups. This can allow for the rapid restoration of the database server from an image-level backup after a disaster, with the database to be recovered following this via the standard agent-based approach. This is typically tackled in one of two different ways:

1. Periodic (e.g., weekly, or even monthly) image-level backups, with daily in-guest filesystem backups and daily database backups via the in-guest agent
2. Daily image-level backup with daily database backup via the in-guest agent

In the former approach, it may even be deemed acceptable to leave the database running during the periodic image-level backup in order to avoid an outage, and deal with the subsequent inconsistent database state as part of the database recovery process. To avoid considerable "wasted" backups, the latter approach more assumes the database disks are sufficiently independent of the core operating system/application drives for the virtual machine that they can be somehow skipped during the image-level backup process.

A new form of recovery technique becoming available to virtual machines is perhaps best described as "instant access." This requires considerable integration between the hypervisor technology, backup product, and backup target, but allows for extreme flexibility. In this approach, an image-level backup of a virtual machine may be presented back to the hypervisor for copying or power-on without having been recovered. That is, the backup target is presented as a data storage area to the hypervisor, and making use of virtual machine snapshot technology, can be powered up and even written to without overwriting the backup. (Such a technique entirely depends on the backup target storage being random access—disk rather than tape.)

15.4.4 The Long-Term Retention Conundrum

Recall that long-term retention (LTR) backups, otherwise known often as *compliance* backups, are kept in many businesses not just for months, but for years or even decades.

It is reasonable to assume that a traditional, agent-based backup of a filesystem will be recoverable using the same backup product over an extended time. While the versions of the software will change over the years, and the operating systems of the hosts being protected will also change over the years, you would typically expect a Windows NT 4 filesystem backup for instance, to be recoverable into a Windows 2019 server.* However, like complex applications and databases, it is questionable whether a virtual machine image-based backup taken in 2019 would be recoverable in 2029 with any strong guarantee. While the normal considerations apply (e.g., whether the same *backup product* is in use after such a period of time), other key challenges are:

- Will the virtual machine image format be compatible? (e.g., will vSphere 15, assuming it is released at some point in the future, be able to ingest without issue a vSphere 5.5 image-level backup?)
- Will the backup/recovery APIs presented by the hypervisor environment be compatible with older backups?
- Indeed, will the same virtualization stack/vendor be used over such a long period of time?

Businesses that have particularly rigorous compliance requirements will need to keep these considerations in mind when planning long-term retention backups for virtual machine infrastructure, particularly as such infrastructure becomes increasingly prevalent. Depending on the level of rigor placed around compliance recoveries, this may necessitate an approach where the monthly or yearly backups to be kept for an extended time will be performed as agent-based backups. This provides a measure of protection against virtual machine formats changing, hypervisor backup/recovery APIs being altered, the hypervisor *vendor* being altered, *and* the backup/recovery vendor also changing, since in the final scenario it will simplify any conversion or phased retirement process for a replaced product.

15.4.5 *Virtualizing the Backup Infrastructure*

Typically, enterprise backup infrastructure is divided into several different host types:

- *Clients:* The actual servers for the business that are protected by the backup solution.
- *Server:* The "backup service" host that coordinates, controls, and indexes all backups performed, liaising between all the other hosts in the environment.
- *Media server/storage node server:* These hosts are responsible for handling the transport of data from the clients

to the backup targets. The backup server may itself be capable of performing this functionality, though in larger environments that might be kept at a minimum to allow the backup server to run as a "director" for the backup process.

- *Management server:* The host that is used to manage the entire environment. (This is effectively dedicated to communicating with the end-administrator GUI functions.) While the management services might run on the backup server itself (particularly in smaller environments), in order to allow scaling, it's reasonably common to see larger environments offload the management services to another host.

When the primary backup target was tape, virtualization of the backup infrastructure was practically insane. Tape is an anathema to virtualization systems, and those virtualization systems that *do* allow for connection of physical tape to virtual hosts usually place a significant number of caveats on that connection, usually at the point of the hosting hypervisor. (Despite what its name might suggest, even presenting *virtual* tape to virtual backup infrastructure is fraught with challenges.)

As the use of tape as a primary backup target has fallen away for many organizations, the potential to virtualize the backup environment has likewise grown. The backup transport server (which we'll call the storage node from now on) has traditionally needed to be a particularly powerful host within the environment to handle the high-speed throughput requirements for getting data from host A to target B. However, intelligent, random-access backup targets in the form of deduplication storage arrays have reduced the performance requirements for the storage node—environments will find the role of the storage node reduced to a "target facilitator" whereby it arranges access to a particular area on the backup target filesystem to individual clients, then the clients themselves stream the data directly.

There are now eminently practical reasons for the complete or near-complete virtualization of backup infrastructure. As environments scale and deploy larger numbers of hypervisors to handle thousands of virtual machines (or more), the infrastructure requirements for even dedicated hypervisors to host backup host infrastructure represents a minimal cost increase. Where once there had been legitimate fears that backup infrastructure would swamp the performance of hypervisors and impede primary production systems, or that hypervisors would be unable to provide the performance requirements for the backup environment, load balancing, resource provisioning, limiting, and guaranteeing have developed considerably, allowing for a safe mixing of primary production systems and backup/recovery systems within the overall virtualized infrastructure.

Most importantly of all we return to a fundamental architectural requirement of any backup infrastructure: the

---

* We would not expect essential operating system details to still be recoverable—e.g., the Windows "system state" typically needs to be recovered into the same operating system version it was backed up from. Likewise file attributes (permissions, etc.) may not be *as* recoverable over such a long period of time.

backup infrastructure itself must be adequately protected and sufficiently redundant to ensure it doesn't represent a single point of failure for the environment it's deployed to protect. The virtualization techniques and options that allow for advanced data protection for primary production systems are equally applicable to backup and recovery systems themselves. This allows for backup servers (and accompanying hosts) to be readily failed over between sites in the same way regular virtual machines are, increasing the availability of the backup and recovery environment. A fully virtualized backup environment with replicated protection storage could conceivably failover between datacenters in mere minutes. (For example, CDP for virtual systems may enable near-instantaneous failover, failback, and rollback of the server(s) and storage nodes in a fully virtualized environment.)

Such decisions fall squarely into a risk versus cost evaluation. In order to safely guarantee continuity of the underlying virtual infrastructure so that backup and recovery systems can (almost) always be readily available, an organization needs to deploy clustered hypervisors with clustered management systems on replicated storage. Anything less than this and there is too much risk of a catastrophic failure of the virtual infrastructure requiring substantial rebuild prior to building replacement virtual backup infrastructure prior to commencing actual systems recovery. However, for those organizations that are large enough to have a mature, highly redundant virtualization and storage infrastructure, such redundancy will already be built into the base environment, and so adding the backup infrastructure into that protection regime will be entirely logical.

15.5 Containers and Data Protection

Whereas traditional virtualization such as VMware vSphere, Microsoft Hyper-V, and Linux KVM are all centered on virtualizing the entire hardware layer, an emerging form of virtualization (referred to as *containerization*) focuses on virtualizing the operating system. This can allow for a faster, more responsive service running in an emulated or virtualized layer on top of a full stack operating system—for instance, container services tend to start in a trivial amount of time compared to the boot of a full virtual machine.

Containers can run isolated from one another and their parent operating system while sharing resources from the parent—whereas a traditional virtual machine will include a full operating system install, a container may be mounted or executed as an "overlay" filesystem on top of the parent server filesystem. This allows the container to be used read/write, ostensibly writing changes to the filesystem though not affecting the parent operating system—but once it is exited or turned off, the overlay storage is dropped.

While new flavors of container services (e.g., Docker and Kubernetes) are proving to be a popular format for developers, particularly when working on *micro-services*, much of the technology or approach of containers is not new: modern container approaches for instance share much in common with "virtualization" technology from legacy Unix systems, such as Solaris Zones, and AIX workload partitions (WPARs)—though arguably the container architectural approach is designed for much more elastic spin-up and scale-down of resources than traditional Unix virtualization services.

The premise of modern containers is often based around *stateless* processing. Recalling the *overlay* description previously, this is the ideal state for any container: it is started up, performs a series of operations, then is destroyed since no data within the container needs to be kept.

Yet reality is often at odds to the theoretical ideal: temporary databases are spun up in containers, containers generate logs and other data that ideally needs to be kept, and developers find new ways to make use of tools that are outside of the intended design goal. So despite the *preferred* approach of keeping stateful data out of containers, businesses that are starting to develop containerized services are also becoming aware of the need to protect some of the data generated within those containers.

While we might consider image-based backups of virtual machines, containers present their own challenges—there is not necessarily a single "image" file that represents the container; instead, it will comprise of a base template overlaying the host operating system with temporary storage. This then results in the need to consider agent-based data protection techniques—such as embedding a filesystem and/or database agent within the container template so that it might be used in the event of stateful data being generated that must be preserved.

However, just because a backup agent is embedded in the container does not mean it can be immediately used. Backup clients tend to need to be registered with the backup server in order to send data, yet modern containers will be spun up with a random, temporary hostname and a temporary IP address. This may require alternate approaches to backup architecture—backup administrators might need to eschew the notion of hosts being added to the environment via a change control process, and instead allow for container-based hosts to access backup services without going through a registration process. Alternately, deduplication storage platforms may allow containers to connect to them for ad-hoc data protection storage (e.g., a standard filesystem mount operation), though this will require consideration relating to the security of the mounts between different containers, and scalability—after all, a large-scale environment may see hundreds or thousands of containers running.

It might also be noted that businesses taking a firmer approach to "stateless" may seek data protection services for containers that focus on overall environment configuration and template protection, rather than the state of any individual container at any specific point in time.

Containerization though may provide other benefits. Containerization allows for a more "elastic" approach to provisioning services—rapidly scaling up *and* scaling down the resources used to provide a highly responsive and adaptable service. We often think of this elasticity in terms of the primary production benefits: for example, a florist may use elastic cloud services for their online store. Architected properly, the online store may only need a modest amount of services running during normal times of the year, but at peak periods (e.g., mother's day and other major holidays) may increase those services by an order of magnitude or more to cope with increased demand.

It is logical to assume that such scaling might also eventually be applied to data protection services—after all, if the systems run by a business increase by an order of magnitude (or more) during peak seasonal periods, it is unlikely that the data protection services will cope with the increased protection requirements without some change to them. Alternately, sizing the data protection environment to handle the peak loading when it may only happen for 30–50 days a year could be viewed as a wasteful investment.

A first-generation approach to data protection scaling would be to automatically spin up additional backup servers or virtualized deduplication protection storage platforms. However, it is plausible to imagine data protection services actually built around containerization principles where services might be expanded linearly as workloads increase rather than creating new "domains" of protection. What this might mean is that instead of spinning up a new backup environment automatically whenever another 1,000 container clients are added, a containerized backup environment itself might simply continue to scale out its capability by adding more containers for specific functions such as backup scheduling, recovery coordination, backup indexing, and even storage processing. This elastic approach would equally apply in reverse; resources can be spun down and disposed of (while ensuring the actual protected data is kept) when they are not required, minimizing the overall cost to run the service. Such a service approach will have particular merit in public cloud environments where the business must pay regularly for the resources it uses.

15.6 Summary

The layers of integration points virtualization offers a business for data protection are considerable and can deliver substantial rewards. With options to seamlessly snapshot entire hosts, organizations can easily back out of changes or provide added protection prior to upgrades. Those same snapshots also become essential during virtual machine backup and recovery operations, allowing for non-disruptive image-level backup of virtual machines.

Virtual machine replication allows for a new form of high availability, delivering failover previously impossible without clustering. Indeed, when combined with clustering for particularly sensitive systems, replication allows businesses to reach high-nine's availability with far less investment than ever before. Essentially, what was once the kind of availability available only to top-echelon businesses just a decade ago has become the sort of thing even a small or medium enterprise can achieve with relatively minimal effort.

15.7 Self-Reflection

Consider a virtualization environment that averages 20 virtual machines per hypervisor server, with 20 hypervisor servers. Any single hypervisor can access the storage (and therefore the virtual machines) for the entire environment. Each virtual machine has an average of three virtual disks.

There are two different backup approaches that could be used for this environment:

■ Image-based backup
■ Agent-based backup

In an image-based backup process, virtualized proxies run as guests on the hypervisors, and each proxy can simultaneously backup up to 20 virtual disks. The overall hypervisor environment can sustain five fully active proxies at any given point in time.

Using changed block tracking and virtual synthetic full technology, an image-based backup takes approximately 10 minutes to run per virtual machine. The agent-based backup approach however would take on average 45 minutes to complete a full backup. The agent will automatically backup all virtual disks (assuming each virtual disk represents a single filesystem to the guest) simultaneously.

What might you expect the loading of the virtual infrastructure during backups to look like, comparing the image-based backup approach, and the agent-based approach?

Chapter 16

Big Data

16.1 Introduction

> "Space," it says, "is big. Really big. You just won't believe how vastly, hugely, mind-bogglingly big it is. I mean, you may think it's a long way down the road to the chemist, but that's just peanuts to space. Listen …"
>
> —Douglas Adams (The Hitch Hikers Guide to the Galaxy, Pan Books, 1979)

With relatively little modification, one might adapt the iconic description of Space found in *The Hitch Hikers Guide* to the Galaxy to Big Data. Big data, we are assured, represents amounts of data that are at times, barely comprehendible. After all, if we assume an average high-fidelity MP3 takes up 10 MB, you could fit 100,000 songs in just 1 TB. A mere 5 MB will store the text (assuming no images, etc.) for an average novel, so you could store 200,000 such novels in a single TB. If this seems big, think of a NAS server for an enterprise-scale business with say, 4 PB of storage: it could hold 800,000,000 × 5 MB electronic-text novels.

The etymology of the term *big data* is not readily agreed upon, particularly in terms of when it was first used. While its popularity has been growing steadily since the mid-2000s, many researchers suggest that it had been bandied about as early as the mid-1990s.[*]

If big data represents a headache for conventional storage and compute administrators, that's arguably just the tip of the iceberg compared with the challenges faced by those responsible for ensuring said data is adequately protected.

Big data is often characterized by the "3 Vs":

- *Volume*: More data than can be handled by infrastructure for conventional data
- *Velocity*: Usually being generated or requiring interception at high speed
- *Variety*: Largely unstructured, coming from a multitude of sources whose data types have little if no relationship to one another

The closest analogy to big data is data warehousing. While data warehousing is typically an activity associated with enterprise relational databases and therefore operations and analytics on highly *structured* data, big data applies order at the time of analysis to a view of unstructured data (in addition to potentially also dealing with structured data). The value derived from dealing with large amounts of unstructured data is in allowing a freer exploration of the data. Structured systems and databases work by applying the schema or layout of the data on write; big data analysis is so often involved in applying an arbitrary schema to the data as it is being read or processed, allowing the data to be examined from a variety of different viewpoints, and with fewer constraints to how it is selected for review.

In order to be usefully processed, big data is typically analyzed in a massively parallelized environment. A traditional high-performance relational database environment might feature two or more database servers in an all-active cluster, multiple application servers, and perhaps even separate web front ends and administration servers. This allows for the data to be consolidated on potentially just a few LUNs of high-performance SAN storage. A big data analytics service, on the other hand, might feature hundreds or more computational nodes, all working on discrete sections of data.

---

[*] The origins of "big data": An etymological detective story, Steve Lohr, *New York Times*, 1 February 2013, http://bits.blogs.nytimes.com/2013/02/01/the-origins-of-big-data-an-etymological-detective-story

For a long time, CPU manufacturers were focused on one primary concern: making the chips faster and faster: 1, 2, 3 GHz—the goal at each iteration was to make a CPU able to perform more calculations in the same time available. Yet as the number of disparate operations we needed to do at the same time also increased, the net benefits of increasing CPU speed dropped off sharply. If operating systems and applications were designed accordingly, a 4-CPU system running at a lower speed per CPU almost always outperformed a single CPU system with a clock speed higher than the combined 4-CPU system, except in very specific single-threaded circumstances. High-performance computing (HPC) leveraged this by having multiple systems each with multiple CPUs. Over time, CPUs went multicore—effectively providing multiple CPUs on a single die. Instead of trying to develop a 10 GHz CPU, it was easier to develop multi-core CPUs running at lower speed. Thus, today we find ourselves having 4, 8, or even 10 core CPUs just in smart phones—and servers with 20 or more cores now quite common. High-performance computing environments will mix multi-core CPUs *and* massively multicore graphics processor units (GPUs) which may each have *thousands* or more cores.

The problem of scaling *up* was fixed by scaling *out*. It was also fixed as a software function. The "brute-force" approach to software performance is to assume evermore powerful systems for single-threaded problem solving. The smart way of solving performance issues in software is to break the problem up and execute as many parallel streams as there are processors to handle the data.

Figure 16.1 shows how data analytics might work in a conventional environment. The key issue for the conventional approach is a poorly scaling analysis time. A user will come up with an idea of a query or function to perform against the data, which will then be handed over to the database server. The database server will perform the querying process against the entire selected data set (narrowing it down as the query parameters permit) and will eventually provide the answer to the user. Performance here though is limited in several areas, notably:

- Efficiency of the data selection criteria
- Amount of memory and CPU performance within the database server
- Storage speed

If a data set is only small, this processing approach is not normally an issue; however, it becomes time-exhaustive as the amount of data to analyze increases. Logically, this makes sense—if an operation takes 10 seconds to perform against 1,000 complex rows of data for a server, then performing it against 1,000,000 rows of data may very well take 10,000 seconds (approximately 2.8 hours) to complete. As the data continues to increase, the chance of having sufficient memory to hold all data in RAM for the analysis degrades, so the time taken will not even be a linear increase. If each row of data occupies, say, 100 KB, then 1,000 rows of data will require approximately 97.7 MB of RAM. And 1,000,000 rows will require 97,656.25 MB or 95 GB of RAM. Eventually, if RAM is exhausted, virtual memory (i.e., swap files) may be leveraged by the operating system, substantially degrading performance.

Traditionally, such performance limits were resolved by buying or building larger and larger servers with more RAM, more CPU, and putting the data to be analyzed on high-performance storage—what we would call *scale-up*. In-memory database servers such as SAP HANA for instance, might have multiple terabytes of RAM. This however has substantial limitations both in terms of maximum size/performance and the cost associated with building such a server. While it's

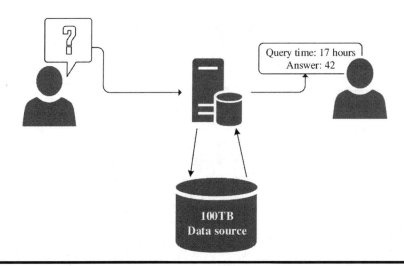

Figure 16.1 Data analytics in a traditional environment.

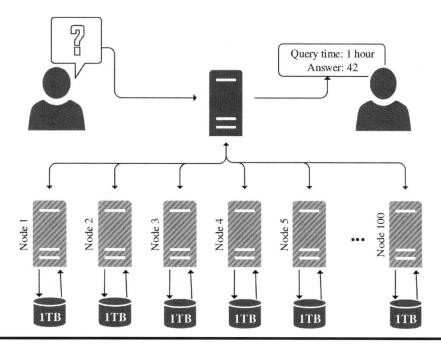

Figure 16.2 A big data approach to data analytics.

possible to configure servers with multiple processors, each with 10 or more cores and even terabytes of memory, there will always be practical or fiscal limits to how far a system can be scaled.

To get around those issues, big data approaches the problem from a *scale-out* perspective. Rather than purchase larger, more powerful, and undoubtedly more expensive stand-alone servers to process the data, big data processing splits the data into much smaller data sets to allow smaller, cheaper servers to digest it and perform processing against it. This might resemble a configuration such as that shown in Figure 16.2.

In such a scenario, the user will develop a query that is sent to the management node of the big data environment. The management node will then coordinate with a potentially large number of nodes, handing each node a small segment of the overall data set. The individual nodes work on their segments of data only, handing the results back to the management node when complete. Once all data sets have been analyzed, the management node collates the results and provides them to the end user. By attacking the analysis in such a distributed fashion, it can be sped up by sometimes orders of magnitude compared to a conventional approach. In essence, big data is about finding new methods other than the classic brute-force approach to data analysis: rather than a few extremely powerful servers trying to crunch through a massive data set, a large number of *adequately* powerful low-end systems each crunch through a comparatively very small data set. (This is not to say that it is trivial to convert any traditional data analysis function to a big data analysis function, though.)

16.2 Protecting within the Big Data Environment

For data protection in a big data environment, the central design requirement will usually come down to whether the "big data" itself needs to be protected or whether it's the *results* that need to be protected. For instance, consider a big data environment populated from a series of other data sources (e.g., web traffic log files, databases, and production filesystems). If each of *those* systems has comprehensive data protection deployed against them, the big data system can conceivably be repopulated in the event of a failure from the original locations—and presumably will be periodically refreshed as well. In these cases, it's usually the results generated by the big data system that need to be protected, and these will typically be orders of magnitude smaller than the actual system itself. So long as those results are written or copied to systems with standard data protection, this may be sufficient.

That being said, there will usually be a degree of primary copy protection used on any data set. For example, the Hadoop Distributed File System (HDFS) achieves storage resiliency by replicating data across multiple hosts. Such filesystems might eschew RAID as the base level of protection by guaranteeing *n* copies of a file, distributed among multiple nodes in the system. (HDFS, for instance, defaults to three copies of the data.) Conceptually, this *n*-way replication might resemble the layout shown in Figure 16.3.

Each node in the big data system will have its own independent filesystem, but to the end user or the accessing APIs this is usually presented as a single logical filesystem. As files are written to or updated on the system, multiple nodes

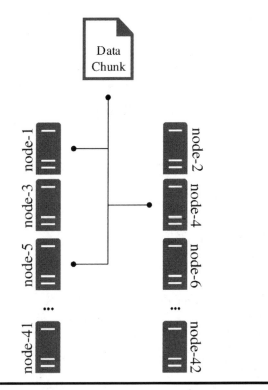

Figure 16.3   Conceptual view of n-way copy protection in a distributed filesystem.

receive and store the content so that the loss of a single node does not cause data loss. Since big data systems are usually built on the basis of large-scale, distributed filesystems can also be node/locality aware—multiple copies of a file may be stored in nodes in the same rack, with an additional copy stored in a node in a physically separate rack.

Such options usually require functionality to rebalance in the event of node failure and to generally avoid "hot spots" of data in the distributed filesystem. Distributed filesystems can still benefit from RAID storage however—read performance can be boosted coming from multiple drives, and administrators might prefer RAID rebuild times within individual nodes rather than having entire node rebalancing operations occur in response to a single disk failure.* In fact, some scale-out NAS systems feature compatibility with big data filesystems such as HDFS, allowing HDFS nodes to make use of the scale-out NAS as their actual data storage platform without the need for the multi-copy replication previously mentioned. This can drive greater storage efficiency while also giving access to the rich data services offered by NAS systems. (New storage systems with higher tiers of performance beyond regular SSD—in the *tens* of millions of input/

output operations per second (IOPS)[†]—have the potential to increase RAID adoption in performance-sensitive big data environments.)

Additional levels of protection can usually be provided in big data processing environments via inter-cluster replication. A business seeking to achieve a degree of data protection for their big data environment will deploy more than one big data processing cluster and use replication. If the primary cluster goes down, the cluster acting as a replication target is able to continue to provide operations against a copy of the data. (Big data inter-cluster replication is often asynchronous however due to the potential for large volumes of data to be flowing into it at high speed—the copy residing in the target cluster may lag behind the content of the source or primary cluster.)

While cluster replication provides protection against cluster failure, it does not necessarily provide protection against more specific data loss—particularly if the filesystem being used across the cluster doesn't implement versioning. An option growing in popularity for big data pools is to be able to trigger an export or a copy of the cluster to an *unrelated* storage system—such as scale-out NAS. This allows large conventional storage systems to be used to provide the services *not* provided by the big data systems—such as days, weeks, or even *months* of snapshots, with replication and even options, where necessary to back up the data to disk-based protection storage.

An added advantage of this type of solution is in having a copy of the data residing on a *different* platform to the original big data system itself, which can suit businesses seeking to limit the potential for data loss originating from a catastrophic platform failure. While this is usually considered to be unlikely, having entirely different systems providing varied layers of protection substantially reduces the risk of cascading failures in a data loss situation. Alternately, big data systems making use of scale-out NAS as their primary storage platform can leave most of these data management functions to the NAS system. Snapshots, replication, and even backup if required can be handled as part of standard NAS data services, allowing the big data environment to focus on analytics.

As the use of integrated data protection appliances (IDPAs) grows within traditional backup environments, these become an alternate option for the protection of big data systems. Designed from the ground up as a specialized protection storage system capable of ingesting and deduplicating large quantities of data as quickly and efficiently as possible, they allow for the transfer of big data content into *true* protection storage. While a traditional copy to or between NAS storage requires a 1:1 copy between data in the big data pool and the target system, copying to an IDPA can

---

* Bearing in mind a RAID reconstruction will affect only one node in the cluster; node rebalancing may affect a large number of nodes in the cluster.

[†] Speed that will undoubtedly continue to scale with performance increases in solid state and memory-like storage.

potentially leverage source-side or distributed deduplication processing, substantially reducing the actual scale of the data that needs to be copied. Such a mechanism might leverage a *client package* integrated with the export options in the big data system or present the IDPA via a specialized filesystem mount that has deduplication assistance drivers built in. In either case, the net result can be to apply traditional deduplication reductions as the data is being read from each node, executing a massively parallel deduplicated data transfer. In the same spirit of reducing the impact of a backup operation on production infrastructure, this could be integrated into a cluster replication target in a big data system, such as in Figure 16.4. Such a configuration allows the primary cluster to continue operations without any additional workload impact while backups are taking place.

Consider the advantage of deduplication integrated into a big data cluster protection scheme. If we assume 100 nodes each with a local storage capacity of 8 TB at 85% utilization, each node has 6.8 TB of stored data. Assuming three-way replication of content (e.g., in the HDFS default configuration), each node theoretically has around 2.27 TB of data that would need to be copied in an export or backup operation (227 TB in total). Even if we assume a lower overall deduplication ratio due to a mix of structured and unstructured data, and inclusion of some data that doesn't deduplicate well, we might be able to achieve an average deduplication ratio of, say, 4:1 on the first transfer. Assuming an even spread across all the nodes,

this would require a first backup transfer of approximately 580 GB per node, occupying approximately 57 TB on the IDPA at the end of the backup (56.75 TB to be precise).

If we consider a 20% growth rate between backups, a 20:1 deduplication ratio against previously backed up data, and an ongoing 4:1 deduplication ratio against *new* data, this could result in ongoing backup sizes as outlined in Table 16.1. (Of course, this assumes commonality between existing backups and new data, but this is quite possible if the deduplication system is also being used for backups from other production systems that the big data system sources its data from.)

Ideally, the number of actual backups that need to be maintained for a big data system should be minimal. This is where we turn to a logical separation between the *data in* and the *information out*. Such backups should be a means of providing short-term levels of operational *or* disaster recovery, not long-term compliance data protection. For the most part, it's the information that comes *out* of big data analysis that will potentially require long-term compliance protection, *not* the data that goes into it.

16.3 Big Data That Isn't Big Data

In the previous discussion, we've mainly focused on the now traditional definition of big data—large sets of data

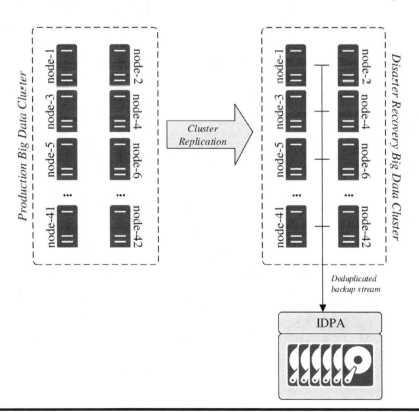

Figure 16.4 Big data protection via clustering and backup to an IDPA.

Table 16.1 Cumulative Deduplicated Protection on Big Data Pool

Backup Instance	Source Size (TB)	Backup Size (TB)	Total Target Consumed (TB)
1	227	56.75	56.75
2	272.4	22.7	79.45
3	326.88	27.24	106.69
4	392.26	32.69	139.38
5	470.71	39.23	178.6
6	564.85	47.07	225.67
7	677.82	56.48	282.16
8	813.38	67.78	349.94
9	976.06	81.34	431.28
10	1,171.27	97.61	528.89
11	1,405.52	117.13	646.01
12	1,686.63	140.55	786.56

combining unstructured and structured data for (primarily) the purposes of analytics, decision support and mass number crunching (or some variant thereof).

Yet there's another type of data that is big but not necessarily thought of as "big data"—truly huge, usually tightly centralized *conventional* data sets that strain data protection resources. For instance, consider scale-out NAS systems that can grow to tens or more petabytes. Even assuming a consistent 30 TB/hour transfer rate,* a conventional *backup* of a 10 PB NAS would take over 14 days to complete. Such systems might be used as general data repositories in very large businesses, or they might be used for specialist purposes: animation studios, special effects companies, TV channels, medical imaging systems, and so on. As our ability to generate larger and more complex data sets grows, so too will these large data sets grow.

Such data sets often require protection mechanisms outside the norm, and more often than not have to more closely leverage the *same* technology for the primary instance as for the secondary copy: that is, replication to another system. For instance, a 10 PB NAS might have regular snapshots taken and also be replicated to a second, perhaps even larger NAS.

Such snapshot and replication protection techniques might see a limited number of short-term snapshots maintained (e.g., 72 × hourly snapshots), followed by retention of less periodic snapshots—4 × weekly snapshots, 12 × monthly snapshots, and so on. This has the potential to introduce two specific risks into a system:

1. *Performance impact*: Depending on the storage technology used and the number of changes made on a system, long-term retention of a potentially large number of snapshots can degrade performance. This requires careful architectural planning to ensure it will not jeopardize system functionality.

2. *Single-platform protection*: Despite there being snapshots and replication, the entire operational protection is provided by the same platform. Since the typical deployment method requires storage arrays from the same vendor as source and target (unless storage virtualization is layered on top), a firmware or software problem—or a deliberate targeted hack—could conceivably result in catastrophic data loss. Even if storage virtualization is being used, we would still consider all protection being sourced from the same platform.

Even in environments with massive amounts of data, it is usually desirable to find a strategy capable of incorporating at least one layer of protection from a different platform or data protection tier. Further, with so few businesses practicing comprehensive data lifecycle management and archiving, long-term compliance retention creates an almost inevitable need for additional steps even in this model.

This usually results in configuring the snapshots and replication options to meet *all* anticipated operational recovery requirements and leveraging backup and recovery systems—not for any SLA-related recovery, but solely for the purposes of satisfying long-term compliance retention. For instance, using our previous example of a 10 PB NAS server, rather than attempt a single, 14-day backup at 30 TB/hour, we

---

* Approximately 8.3 GB/s.

might instead break the data set into a series of 10×1 PB regions and conduct *rolling* backups over the course of an entire month. Assuming an ongoing backup speed of 30 TB/hour, each 1 PB region could be backed up in a little over 34 hours. This would give time for a new backup to be started every 2 days and still have a complete backup executed every month for the content of the NAS system.

Data protection solutions at scale require meticulous planning and evaluation of *all* options and their flexibility, not to mention a more creative approach to meeting business requirements.

16.4 Using Data Protection Storage in a Big Data Environment

A common challenge faced by many organizations making use of big data processing systems is the logistics in populating and refreshing data from a multitude of disparate systems. Advanced analytics and decision support systems, for instance, usually need to leverage data from a large variety of sources within the organization, including everything from unstructured file data, sensor and telemetry content, large log files, production databases, data warehouses, and an almost unlimited number of other enterprise components.

Except in very rare circumstances, data is not static, nor is the data held in analytics systems static. Data that has been populated for processing in a big data system will need to be periodically refreshed in order to ensure up to date information and trends are being gleaned. This regular refreshing allows businesses to do any of the following (and practically anything else):

■ Leverage rapidly changing market conditions to their advantage
■ Offer customers the most likely to succeed bargains based on current buying habits
■ Detect fraudulent activity in near real-time

If we think of all the systems with an environment that might need to have data pulled from them to refresh a big data analytics environment, we might see a small example in Figure 16.5.

While this guarantees access to the most recent data, which sometimes may be an absolute necessity, it can quickly become a logistical nightmare, particularly in larger enterprises. Exporting data from primary production systems *during* production operational hours could have a negative impact on either the performance of the production system or its network link. Application, database, and infrastructure teams directly responsible for production systems may have a plethora of other duties that create delays in copying

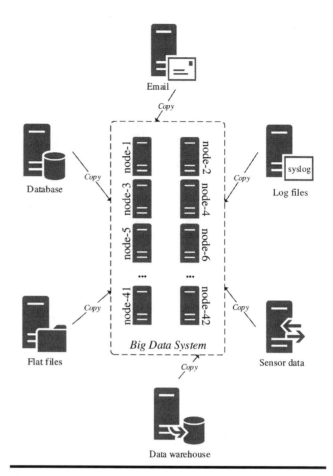

Figure 16.5   Repopulating a big data system from the original sources.

the required data for the big data teams and change freeze windows (sometimes lasting weeks) for some organizations may directly prohibit new data refreshes from occurring. In larger organizations where requests have to be filed through ticketing systems and routed through to various groups, the administrative overheads of repopulating big data systems might in fact reduce that frequency to the point where its potential benefits to the organization are impacted.

Yet if we think about it, this is not the *only* place this data might be found within an organization, and we can take a lesson from database administrators to understand how else these systems might be repopulated.

For as long as there have been databases used in production, there have been development/test databases, and database administrators have needed to periodically refresh these development/test systems from production data. Database administrators who are particularly mindful of potential impact on production systems created by copy operations have traditionally used database copies residing in backup and recovery storage in order to source a recent version of the production database.

Big data terminology often revolves around water: we refer to big data *pools* or *lakes*. Using that terminology, we

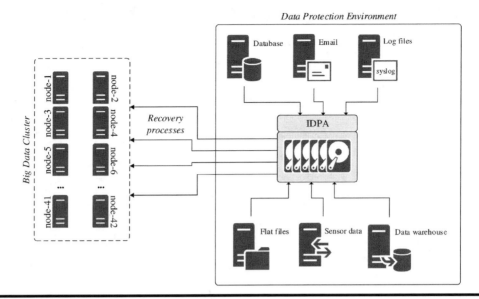

Figure 16.6   Refreshing big data systems from data protection copies

might consider data protection for big data to be symbolic of *wells*. Thus, big data protection storage allows us to plumb the protection well.

With the rise of high-speed, random access centralized protection storage systems, businesses seeking to increase the return on their data protection investment can sidestep many of the challenges of repopulating big data/data analytics systems. By retrieving copies from protection storage rather than the original primary systems, the process can be performed without involving primary production administration and infrastructure teams *and* without risk of performance impact to those same systems. This results in a refresh flow similar to that shown in Figure 16.6.

In Figure 16.6 we note the various data sources used by the big data system all require backups (in this case to an IDPA). Since the data required by the big data system resides on disk and is easily accessible without impact to production systems, the big data teams can refresh *their* systems quickly and efficiently, regardless of what constraints are in place on the primary production teams and systems. (Such techniques must be balanced with the restore speeds available from data protection storage—though the reduction or elimination of primary systems impact by sourcing the data elsewhere may make a recovery more palatable than a direct copy even if it is slower.)

Depending on the mechanism used to protect the original data and the format it is stored in, big data systems might even refer to the copy residing on protection storage directly, without even needing to recover the data. This extends the "instant access" process previously discussed for virtual machines to other data types—databases and filesystems being the most likely requirement. This has all the advantages of being able to access required data without impacting

primary copies *and* reducing the storage footprint required for big data processing. (However, there still can be situations where it is arguably faster in the long run to copy the data from protection storage.)

Of course, snapshots from the data owner on primary storage systems could equally be presented to a big data system for access, but this will inevitably have at least one of two consequences:

1. It has the potential to impact the performance or capacity of the primary storage snapshot regions.
2. In doing so, it has the potential to impact the performance of the actual primary data owner—the original application and so on.

In both cases, sourcing data from actual protection storage mitigates this risk while still providing easy access to the required data. As per copying content from data protection sources, accessing snapshot data directly from data protection sources will depend on the performance characteristics of such storage, and this will likely see higher utility in data protection storage able to at least leverage flash tiers or caches.

Another potential advantage of leveraging data protection sources in a big data system is the option to leverage *earlier* data for combined or comparative analysis. If a big data cluster has been periodically backed up to an IDPA, those backups might be presented as new source data. Assume, for instance, a big data system is backed up to an IDPA once a month, with a 12-month retention on the data. However, to avoid capacity issues within the big data system, data older than 6 months is routinely purged. If the data backed up to the IDPA can be presented via snapshots and network mappings *back* to the big data environment, calculations and comparisons can be run between, say, the data currently in the system and the data held 6 or 12 months ago. As an example, if financial models are being constantly updated and refined, it would allow a business to re-execute those models against old data to see how accurate they are—how closely the results resemble current known details. This process of plumbing the data protection well can conceivably be leveraged for a number of historical, comparative, and innovative analysis techniques, and may enable data scientists and big data analysts to provide new insights and strategic advantages to a business.

It should be noted that in order to be effective, the data protection storage system will usually need to be able to support high-speed random IO operations. This typically rules out tape systems.* For deduplicating systems, such options will require high-performance rehydration options—such as using SSD to hold metadata, or even in some instances, storing deduplicated backups themselves on SSD or other flash storage.

16.5 Summary

In many ways, the problems presented by big data are not necessarily new, but rather are scaled-up variations of existing challenges faced in data protection over the decades. A common problem in IT and computer science as a whole has been that as resources—storage, memory, and computing speeds—have increased, the desire to spend time *optimizing* the use of those resources has declined. Operating systems and applications have grown considerably in functionality, but bloat creeps in as the computers running those applications and operating systems become more powerful. Likewise, data lifecycle management is often seen as a costly and time-consuming process compared to just purchasing and provisioning more storage. Just as big data demonstrates there is a practical limit to how much you can scale *up* the performance of an individual system for data set analysis, big data also demonstrates that there are limits in scaling for conventional data protection approaches as well. The

solution is no longer to throw more capacity or higher-speed networks at the problem and hope it goes away, but to leverage technology more efficiently and perhaps more creatively in order to provide a functional level of protection.

Big data also highlights the importance of choosing *what* data to protect: do you need to protect the source data or just the results? For some environments, you still need to protect the *data*, but for others a more sensible and cost-effective approach may be to protect the *information* generated from the data.

This is still a very new and emerging field, and will continue to present challenges to data protection for some time to come. Yet, data protection potentially offers improvements and scalability to big data environments that might be otherwise difficult to achieve: centralized refresh processes, additional pools of data, and deeper historical analysis.

16.6 Self-Reflection

Big data encompasses more than just unstructured data, of course. You will also find big data in the form of very large relational databases, and a variety of NoSQL databases.

Assume a business has a 100 TB Oracle database that *must* be backed up in under 4 hours to meet the SLAs the business has established.

- How fast (TB/hour, and GB/s) must the backup run in order to meet the 4-hour window?
- What techniques might be used to speed up the backup process?

It's common when there are high throughput requirements for a backup to focus attention on the speed and performance of the backup system, but achieving high-speed streaming for large volumes of data is a shared responsibility. Assume that the data protection environment is more than capable of *receiving* data at the speed you've calculated. What other factors would need to be considered in ensuring the overall environment can achieve meet the backup SLA?

---

* An exception to this might be where a large volume of data needs to be streamed back and processed as it is being read, but this would be more akin to tiered storage such as you might see in Mainframe environments.

Chapter 17

Protecting the Edge

17.1 Introduction

While "the edge" has primarily become used to refer to "internet of things" (IoT) style devices, those that sit at the very edge of a business to gather data via sensors, etc., in this chapter we will be using "edge" to refer to a variety of *edge* systems.

Specifically, in this chapter, we'll deal with the three most common *edge* challenges in data protection, namely:

- Endpoint computing—primarily user desktops and laptops
- Remote/branch office servers
- IoT/edge-based data systems

In each of the above, edge systems represent several common challenges for data protection, including but not limited to:

1. Bandwidth availability
2. Server remoteness
3. Local versus remote storage
4. Environmental hazards
5. Operational hazards
6. Recovery requirements

Bandwidth availability refers to the common problem of systems deployed far from a datacenter—both the bandwidth and latency of the bandwidth may be an anathema to traditional, in-datacenter data protection operations.

Similarly, server remoteness refers to the proximity of the data to the server resources that might direct data protection operations. Within a datacenter, we expect the server to be quite close (physically and/or via network topology) to the systems being protected. As we go to the edge, this expectation diminishes. While the most obvious implication is bandwidth as mentioned above, this does introduce the challenge of latency as well.

The locality of data protection storage can introduce challenges; deploying such storage with the remote system may be convenient for local recoverability, but impractical for portability or deployment costs. Equally, protection storage within a core datacenter might be procured and provisioned more cost-effectively, but be insufficient to provide local recoverability services at the edge.

Server remoteness, bandwidth availability and the local/remote storage issue can all be closely related, though it is worthwhile ensuring they are evaluated as separate considerations, typically on a case-by-case, or at least a function-by-function basis.

We can differentiate between *environmental* and *operational* hazards via simple examples. An environmental hazard might literally refer to the location in which an item is deployed—a user laptop might be highly mobile and taken into dusty, wet, or extremely humid locations. Equally, a sensor system might need to be deployed underwater, or where toxic chemicals routinely pass. On the other hand, operational hazards may refer to the general randomness with which end user devices may be accessed—the conventional process of backing up production systems overnight for instance may be rendered useless in situations where assigned end users could either shut down or remove their equipment overnight.

Finally, recovery requirements speak to the important aspect of data protection: how do we get data back, if it is lost, from our protection system? Within the datacenter this is a question we can usually answer very quickly. At the edge, that changes; time, budget, and bandwidth will likely require a very considered approach to what ideal recovery requirements can be met, and where compromises must be made.

17.2 Laptop and Desktop Protection

Protection of laptop and desktop systems within a business has always been a challenging topic. While many businesses would undoubtedly *desire* to protect laptop and desktop systems, the practical challenges, as well as cost considerations often rules it out. (While *desire* might be overly optimistic, more businesses than not recognize the potential for unique or important data to reside on laptops or desktops, even if they feel they can't do anything practical to protect that data.)

While desktop and laptop users have always been at risk from viruses, the ongoing trend in ransomware and "cryptolocker" style malware significantly exacerbates the challenges business face in preserving important data that staff may need to access. Whereas once a user's computer might have been subverted for use in a "botnet," or a keystroke logger installed to phish for sensitive information, users might now return from a lunch break to find every document on their system encrypted.

Such situations typically result in businesses enacting strict policies that important data is not to be stored locally, and these policies are routinely ignored by end users wherever security permits for the simple expediency of work efficiency. (For instance, systems such as Office365's OneDrive for Business may offer a practical alternative to home-drives, but can result in even slower performance—particularly if IT establish policies to limit individual user bandwidth of uploads and downloads.)

While a business may consume petabytes or more of storage within their primary datacenters, the amount of *potential* data at the laptop and desktop endpoint can be substantial. For instance, a business with 10,000 end users may exhibit the following endpoint storage:

- 2,000 dedicated office workers with desktop PCs that contain on average a 1 TB hard drive or hybrid SSD/ hard drive
- 6,000 mobile users with laptops that contain on average a 512 GB SSD
- 1,500 mobile users requiring additional storage, with laptops that contain 1TB SSD
- 500 users utilizing a virtual desktop interface (VDI) from "dumb" terminals

Excluding the VDI users, who would be using centrally provisioned storage, our example workforce potentially represents a little over 6.5 PB of storage. Without storage policies in place, users with actual desktops or laptops might consume anywhere from 10% to practically 100% of the available local storage, depending on their work function and length of time in the company. Businesses wishing to avoid provisioning or storing laptop/desktop backups for this storage capacity will usually seek to mitigate the overall volume of data to be protected, using methods such as:

- Forced minimal selection of data (e.g., only contents in a user's "Documents" folder)

- Rigorous, administrator-controlled content exclusions (e.g., preventing the backup of multimedia files, temporary files, archive files, and so on)
- Deduplication to minimize the data storage footprint.

Even taking all of these into consideration, there are still several different approaches that businesses might undertake to provide endpoint protection.

17.2.1 Using Enterprise Backup and Recovery Systems

Enterprise backup and recovery systems focused on servers and primary storage often struggle to work with laptop/ desktop protection, and there are several reasons for this, including:

1. *Connectivity*: While traditional datacenter backups are premised around clients being permanently connected to the network, such assumptions can't be made about laptop/desktop clients. For example:
    a. End users may shut down desktops when they leave at the end of the day.
    b. End users may reboot their laptops and desktops during the day without warning.
    c. Laptop users are more likely to be mobile, and may disconnect from the network regularly, taking their laptop with them whenever they leave the office.
    d. Laptop users may plug into an ethernet-cabled dock at their desks, and then switch to WiFi when they unplug—a user attending multiple meetings a day might jump between networks regularly, making it more likely of any in-progress network backup failing.

2. *Scheduling*: Because of the connectivity issues mentioned, backup windows for laptop/desktop systems by necessity will need to run during the workday, when users are most likely to be working and connected to the network. However, particularly with laptop users, there can be no guarantee the end user's system will be connected to the network at the time the backup is scheduled to run, or as noted above, stay connected to the network for the duration of the backup.

3. *Maintenance windows*: If laptop/desktop backups are integrated into the primary backup product, the scheduling differences will drastically reduce available backup windows, since the system will be backing up day and night.

4. *Bandwidth*: Traditional backup systems (particularly those that do not perform source-side deduplication) are likely to consume as much bandwidth as is available

on the client to achieve the backup. For mobile users this may lower the overall end user experience by swamping low-bandwidth connections, and similar impacts may happen for desktop users if connecting over WiFi or 100 MB ethernet.

5. *Higher fault incidents*: Systems that only support central scheduling will encounter higher numbers of backup failures due to systems being powered off, disconnected from the network, or otherwise unavailable during their scheduled backup window.

For these reasons, even if an enterprise backup and recovery system is used for laptop/desktop backups, vendors will usually recommend a separate deployment to handle the laptop/desktop component to that used for central datacenter protection. When an enterprise backup product is used for laptop/desktop backups, it will typically need to exhibit the following traits in order to maximize backup successes while reducing maintenance overheads:

1. *Provide "three strikes" reporting*: That is, it is more likely that individual systems will fail on any given day, so the focus should be on detecting repeated failures. The "three strikes" report favored by some backup and backup reporting products provides details of systems that have missed backups just for a day, for 2 days, or for 3+ days.

2. *Eschew traditional adherence to schedules*: Normally in a backup product, the server (or other designated control host) will expect to start the backup of a host at the designated time, and have that backup data start to flow through soon thereafter. Products that work well with desktop/laptop backups will feature a client "check-in" process, where the backup server will trigger a backup job, but not expect the job to run immediately. Ideally with desktop/laptop configurations, clients should be able to periodically poll the backup server to determine if there are any active work orders, and start whatever process they've been instructed to perform. This prevents backups from failing immediately if a client is not connected: we would then expect warnings to be issued if a work order has not been actioned after a certain length of time (e.g., 48 hours).

3. *Use alternate client identification/verification*: Normally backup products will perform a degree of verification and connectivity via either the client hostname or its IP address. Particularly when we consider laptop clients, hosts being protected in a laptop/desktop situation may have their IP address routinely change as they move around on the network or connect via third-party networks (e.g., users tethering their laptops to a cellular data connection). Registering and authenticating clients via a means other than hostname and/

or IP address, such as shared certificates or keys will be essential to avoid disruption to the backup and recovery process.

4. *Higher tolerance for low bandwidth connectivity*: While a client/server backup will of course need some level of network connectivity, laptop/desktop solutions should have a higher tolerance for lower bandwidth connections (e.g., even potentially supporting Asymmetric Digital Subscriber Line (ADSL), or dial-up) with higher latency. (Focusing on high efficiency deduplication and allowing for more communications pauses/interruptions are essential here.)

5. *Non-direct networking*: Endpoint clients are more likely to be behind one, if not two firewalls on potentially random and overlapping network address spaces. There will need to be greater tolerance for indirect communications paths between the client and the server/storage system for the backup process to succeed regularly.

It's not to say that effective laptop and desktop backups can't be done with traditional datacenter-based enterprise backup and recovery solutions, but there will still be a need for a rigorous architecture process to ensure the solution will work.

17.2.2 Local Systems Protection

There are a plethora of backup and recovery utilities built for laptops and desktops that users could, theoretically, install or use for themselves. Before we consider these options, it's pertinent to first consider one operating system vendor's approach to user backup enablement.

CASE STUDY: MAC OS X TIME MACHINE

In 2007, Apple released Mac OS X 10.5, "Leopard," with a distinctly user-accessible backup and recovery utility: *Time Machine*.

While third-party backup utilities existed to protect Apple Macintosh systems for decades prior to the introduction of Time Machine, and indeed were available for most desktop/laptop operating systems (Linux, Windows, or Apple Macintosh), Time Machine effectively set a new standard in providing user accessible backup and recovery functions *within the operating system itself*. All a user needed was a spare hard drive (external preferred, but Time Machine does not prevent someone from using an internal drive on a multi-drive capable Macintosh).

Once enabled, Time Machine featured several features deemed key to reliable backup systems, including:

1. *Automated execution*: While a user can disable Time Machine, the default process is for it to automatically run a new backup every hour, collecting updated/new files since the last backup.
2. *Backup aging*: Older backups would be automatically pruned, making way for new backups should the selected storage medium become too full.
3. *Retention levels*: Keeping a new backup performed every hour indefinitely would be too capacity-intensive, even with built-in storage efficiency; instead, Time Machine keeps hourly backups for 24 hours, daily backups for a month, and weekly backups for periods older than a month, until the backup volume fills, at which point the oldest weekly backups are removed.
4. *Recovery interface*: A backup tool by itself has relatively little utility if it does not offer a suitable interface for users to conduct recoveries from. While the Time Machine recovery interface was rightly criticized initially for being gaudy and needlessly animated, it did nevertheless provide a way for users to approach data recovery in a relatively straightforward manner. (Recent operating system updates have removed much of the gaudiness in preference to concentrating on the core functionality requirements.)

Time Machine is sufficiently integrated into the operating system that when it has not yet been configured: each new drive that a user plugs in will prompt the user to select whether that drive should be used for backups, and it supports more than the backup and recovery of simple files, with user email and contacts in the default system applications also being accessible for recovery.

Does Time Machine therefore represent a "good" option for protecting at least Apple laptop and desktops computers of end users? In a comparison to no protection at all, the answer is an obvious *yes*, but it is hardly a replacement for enterprise-grade data protection, with a number of distinctly challenging faults, such as:

1. *Backup selection is singular*: While the user can choose what is or is not backed up on a system, if they make use of different hard drives (Time Machine can "rotate" backups between two drives), the same backup selection is used for both drives. There is scope of course to define *what* gets backed up, but that selection applies to all backups. There is no option for instance for laptop users with small portable drives to define a subset of their most mission critical data for backup while "on the road," and have a larger backup drive for their complete data when back in the office.
2. *No mechanism to migrate backups*: If a Time Machine drive becomes full, there is no option within Time Machine itself to migrate the contents to another, larger hard drive to retain older backups. While this can be accomplished through manual intervention, it is nevertheless a shortcoming of the actual utility itself.
3. *Lack of integration points*: Apple have not integrated Time Machine into other obvious "preferred" applications, such as Photos, iCloud Drive, or even their own Calendar application. It seems clear that Apple have focused on backup per se more recently as a silent replication function in their iCloud service, despite the limitations that creates.
4. *Minimal options for backup deletion*: While Time Machine permits the deletion of a folder or a drive from backup, it does not allow for other controls such as pruning a specific backup. Based on the nature of the backup mechanism, the time taken to delete a folder or drive from backup can be considerable.

All of these limitations might in themselves be deemed acceptable if it were enterprise capable in terms of centralized management, reporting, logging, and storage. However, Apple's support forums are littered with examples of people and businesses that have made use of Apple Server functionality to present shared storage for Time Machine storage, only to have the backups abruptly stop working with no apparent reason why. Error codes are inadequately documented and it is not uncommon to see the only "solution" to systemic centralized backup problems using Time Machine to disconnect a client from the backup "drive" and start afresh, effectively losing direct user access to previously completed backups (except, of course, through manual browsing and copying of previous backup content).

Time Machine represents a good example of a consumer marketplace option, but falls flat when it comes to integrating laptop/desktop protection into a broader business context. More recently, Microsoft's Windows 10 has introduced a backup option, which can see user generated content automatically copied to an alternate location whenever modifications are made—though this is effectively limited to files.

Extrapolating beyond Time Machine and Microsoft's more recent foray into local file protection, most desktop and laptop backup products that are designed for consumer-grade use represent problems for business.

These problems include:

1. *Security*: Effectively, these options usually represent a loss of control of a copy of business data. Users might backup to a USB key or portable hard drive, but what happens if it is stolen? Will users have enabled suitably secure encryption? Indeed, it can't be guaranteed that any consumer-grade backup/recovery tool an end user might download and install will even feature encryption. (Even Time Machine, which does support encryption, doesn't enable it by default, for instance.)
2. *Visibility*: The IT organization within the business may be unaware that a backup product has even been installed. This potentially makes it easier for data to leave the company, particularly if an employee departs. While a missing hard drive within a company laptop or desktop should, in theory, be noticed quickly, the business is unlikely to notice the potential for data to have left with the departed employee if they never knew the backup software was installed in the first place.
3. *Management*: Consumer-grade backup and recovery options are usually oriented towards self-management on a per-install basis. This usually puts the onus on status checking onto the end users; the likelihood of users even knowing if there is an error with the backups will be entirely dependent on the diligence of the user and the functionality of the specific backup tool.

With the growing value of data to organizations, and the level of storage accessible to an average end user via portable hard drives and even USB memory keys, it's arguable that consumer-grade local laptop/desktop backup software introduces a much higher risk surface area to the business than they resolve. For this reason, many businesses may explicitly prohibit users from performing locally managed backups as part of their "fair use" IT policies.

17.2.3 Is Cloud Backup the Answer?

Unlike traditional datacenter backup/recovery solutions, cloud backup solutions for endpoint systems such as laptops and desktops are usually designed around flexible scheduling and sporadic network availability.

An example of cloud backup services for laptop/desktop systems can be seen in Figure 17.1.

Performing laptop/desktop backup to the cloud can overcome some of the challenges we noted when considering in-datacenter protection, including:

1. *Connectivity*: Such systems are engineered to accommodate less reliable, lower bandwidth connections with the same client connecting from many potential endpoints.
2. *Reporting*: Increased focus on when the last successful backup was, rather than whether the last backup was successful.
3. *Bandwidth limits*: Cloud backup solutions are more likely to include options to place upper limits on bandwidth utilization, sometimes even with options covering scenarios such as: whether the system is idle or not, whether the system is using ethernet or WiFi, or even if the system is using a metered connection.
4. *Scheduling*: Many of these types of products support continuous backups; rather than the backup only

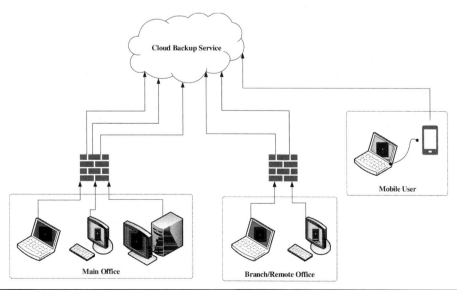

Figure 17.1   Conceptual backup to cloud service.

happening at a specific time, the agent on the laptop/desktop regularly scans for changed content and queues it for backup (e.g., every 15 minutes): the client can automatically backup changes whenever there is a network connection available, rather than the backup taking place at a fixed time, regardless whether the client is available.

Ideally when using a cloud-based backup solution for endpoint systems, businesses can exert control over such functions as outlined below, on top of traditional backup options such as controlling the backup selection, and preventing or at least limiting the potential for end users to change the configuration:

1. *Encryption*: While almost all cloud backup products support in-flight and at-rest encryption, security-conscious organizations will focus on those that allow the default encryption keys/certificate to be replaced with one held only by the business. Thus, even if law enforcement agencies were to somehow "seize" the backup storage (or the backup providers' security be compromised), the backups stored with this level of encryption would theoretically remain inaccessible.
2. *Access*: Allowing the business to limit access to only authorized devices (this may include preventing smart phones and tablets that aren't company-controlled from being able to recover data, and preventing web-based restores).
3. *Compliance*: Beyond being able to query the protection status of any given device, the business should seek products that allow compliance-compatible reporting—exposure levels (due to incomplete or regularly failing backups) and recovery/access reporting.
4. *Sovereignty*: Some cloud backup services even support a business deploying its own private cloud version of the tool, thereby retaining tighter ownership over its data.

However, cloud backup tools do not come without their own challenges. Two key challenges are:

1. *Storage*: While some cloud protection products offer unlimited storage with a simple, fixed fee per client, most charge for the amount of data stored in the cloud (potentially in addition to a subscription fee per client). When costs are accrued based on the amount of storage consumed, this may result in significant monthly fees for the business if not managed carefully. Alternatively, it may result in such restrictions on what can be backed up as to render it ineffective from a user perspective.
2. *Network cost*: Particularly for mobile users, backups and restores may happen over metered connections, resulting in higher mobile data costs. Even if roaming users

have "unlimited data" on their cellular plans, they may find connectivity constrained to low performance links once they've exceeded a particular threshold—which is highly possible with backup and recovery operations added to their activities.
3. *Office link saturation*: Large numbers of clients simultaneously backing up to an external location could easily saturate internet links for offices, even if each individual client has bandwidth limitations placed on it. Additional controls, such as implementing quality of service (QoS) on network switches may be required to prevent cloud backup clients from rendering outgoing internet links inoperable.
4. *WiFi saturation*: Likewise, office WiFi links could easily be overcome with large amounts of endpoint backup traffic. The capabilities of wireless networking within each office will need to be carefully considered when endpoint backup planning takes place.

Cloud backup of laptop and desktop systems can certainly resolve a lot of the challenges faced by traditional enterprise backup products, but comes with its own cost and complexity that is not insubstantial, particularly as the number of systems requiring protection and the amount of data to be protected grows.

17.2.4 Is Cloud Storage the Answer?

There are a number of cloud storage services that masquerade as local folders or drives for users, with arguably the three most popular being DropBox, OneDrive, and Google Drive.

These cloud storage systems are usually designed to automatically provide offline access to the content the user stores. In fact, the user writes content to their local laptop or desktop storage, and then that is replicated to the designated cloud storage when a network connection is available. (This is true at least for the cloud storage systems named.)

To understand whether cloud storage systems such as DropBox, OneDrive, and so on, are suitable for backup of local content, let's consider how they work.

In Figure 17.2, we see a high level view of how cloud drive storage is abstracted and provided to the end user. (Cloud drive storage systems are not actually shared folders presented from a server provider's fileserver, but instead, are usually front-end abstraction layers to object storage.)

Cloud drive systems as outlined in the diagram undoubtedly provide a storage mechanism for the end user, and creates an *off-platform* replica of data which might be accessed remotely (e.g., from another laptop/desktop, a smart phone, or a tablet). In this, it's a data protection mechanism, providing a modicum of redundancy and fault tolerance, but it is by no means something that can be classified as a *backup* solution for end users within the business.

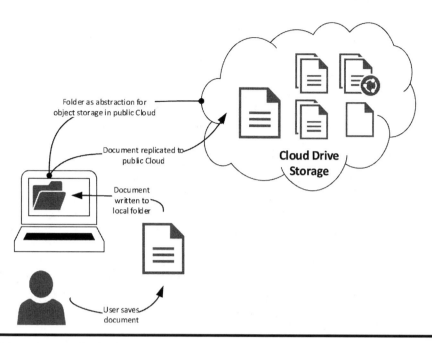

Folder as abstraction for
object storage in public Cloud

Document replicated to
public Cloud

Document
written to
local folder

**Cloud Drive
Storage**

User saves
document

Figure 17.2   Cloud drive storage principles.

If the user writes data directly to the local folder that represents the cloud storage system, that data is immediately copied to the cloud storage system. Deletions, modifications, and new files are updated in cloud storage as soon as they can be synchronized. That effectively represents *asynchronous replication*, not backup.

If the user writes data to other laptop/desktop folders, then copies that data to the local cloud drive folder (thereby triggering a new asynchronous replication), it might be considered that the user has *backed up* the content (for a backup is an off-platform copy), but that does not make the overall cloud drive storage system a *backup system*. For it to be a backup *system*, we would expect to see such functions as:

1. *Automatic execution*: Requiring the user to drag and drop/copy files will result in haphazard or even no protection.
2. *Versioning/retention*: A backup solution that deletes the previous backup prior to making a new backup never provides history. While it is true that many recoveries are for the most recent version, using a cloud storage drive as backup would require the user to manually manage versions of copied files to retain more than the most recent copy.
3. *Reporting and monitoring*: The function of backup does not stop as soon as a copy is made; there must be some level of monitoring and reporting available in order to meet compliance requirements within almost all organizations, regardless of industry vertical.

The saying "if all you have is a hammer, everything looks like a nail" springs to mind when IT departments attempt to

call these systems "backup." They have not been designed for backup, and their data protection focus is minimal. (Other challenges also spring to mind: for instance when using enterprise versions of these products, it is usual to see upload and download speed limits imposed by IT. These may be acceptable in day to day operations, but if a user is forced to "recover" everything—e.g., when replacing a laptop, it may result in a retrieval process that takes *days* or *weeks* to complete.)

All this being said, there *are* backup products that service cloud drive systems. Enterprises can subscribe to or spin up a protection platform that connects using appropriate, authorized API calls, and retrieves *copies* of user content residing in the cloud drive system. This content can then be copied into another cloud, or to an on-premises storage system, thereby representing a *real* backup of the cloud storage system. At this point, *and only at this point* can the cloud storage system be proscribed as a storage point that automatically provides data protection. (Ideally when this is provisioned, recovery should be something that is user self-serviceable.)

17.2.5 Replicating to a Central Server

Some businesses might take the approach of replicating core user data to a central server. The simplest of this might be the use of roaming user profiles, which allows for a user home directory to be automatically stored on a particular server. This allows users to log on to multiple machines while keeping the same profile, desktop and documents data accessible. In the event of a user going out of office, he or she may mark files as being required *offline*.

This only serves as a backup solution if the server the user's content is being stored on is being backed up. Otherwise, at best it represents a replicated copy of the user data. Effectively any replication to a central server will suffer the same challenges as use of a Cloud drive-based system and is usually only effective if the area being replicated to is included in enterprise backup policies.

17.2.6 Summary of Laptop/ Desktop Backup Options

There is no easy answer to the protection of laptop/desktop devices within a corporate environment. Other solutions beyond what we've explored might include providing all users with an external hard drive (portable drive for laptop users, standard USB drive for desktop users), but there are limits and often security concerns with this approach—the most obvious of course being that it's very easy for someone to just pick up and walk off with a copy of business data by taking the external drive.

Protecting laptops and desktops within the business will likely require more compromise than would be seen in a typical datacenter-based data protection model, and out of necessity a variety of different protection options. This might include:

- An option for desktops that differs from laptops (on the basis of them moving around less)
- Tiered protection options, where users who more routinely handle sensitive information backup to corporate housed backup services, and users who handle less sensitive information might backup (encrypted) to public cloud
- An inversion of backup selection criteria; normally we say that *exclusive* backup policies are the best—where something is backed up unless it is explicitly excluded. Given the potential amount of data that could reside on laptops and desktops within an organization, it may become necessary to shift to an *inclusive* based policy: only specific regions on the end user systems are protected.

17.3 Smartphones and Tablets

For some businesses, laptops and desktops have receded from the endpoint/edge; for those businesses, it is the end user's smart phones and tablets that represent the true edge of the user's interaction with the business.

Such devices give superb mobility to end users. Despite all their convenience for instance, laptops are not always practical—tablets and smart phones are significantly more portable for employees who are constantly on the move.

Yet as is so often the case with IT, flexibility, and convenience for one person does not extend to everyone. In particular, navigating the process of ensuring any valuable user data is protected is not always straightforward.

Ideally, for the purposes of company data, smart phones and tablets used should be as stateless as possible: providing a connection and interface to a service hosted either by the business, or in the cloud. For instance, if the majority of mobile users are within sales and *their* primary mobile application is Salesforce, then the data protection planning will switch from an endpoint focus to ensuring that the company's Salesforce instances are properly backed up.

Where this is not the case though, consideration must be given to how and when the data on the device can be protected. The most important thing to keep in mind here is depending on the application or the device, there will be three essential options for syncing or backing up the data on the device, namely:

- Cabled connection (e.g., USB)
- Over WiFi
- Over cellular networking

Cellular networking (e.g., 3/4/5G) presents considerable advantages: the user does not need to be on a specific WiFi network, or connected to a specific computer in order to retrieve the data. However, not all devices may include cellular options (particularly when we consider tablets), and depending on the volume of data and contract options, backups over cellular networking could prove costly. Indeed, it is worth keeping in mind here that many conventional sync or backup options on cellular-connected smart phones and tablets will have various protections in place to prevent excess data consumption: often unless specifically overridden, these will default to only perform backup operations over a WiFi connection.

For users who are constantly on the road, WiFi syncing or backup of data can be just as problematic as USB-only options: users may find themselves without usable WiFi for days at a time, particularly when many "free" WiFi services are either performance or capacity limited, or even don't work with VPN solutions.

As much as it would be done for any internal infrastructure and production applications, data protection specialists within the business will need to work with the teams responsible for smart phones and tablets to determine appropriate data protection patterns based on criteria such as:

- Whether the device is owned by the company, or the end user
- Whether applications can be "contained"—e.g., via tools such as VMware Workspace One, or limited to SaaS/connectivity functionality

■ For applications that generate data, what settings can be made to ensure the data is synced or backed up as soon as is practical

Also, even if the device is backed up, the backup may belong to the user, and be inaccessible to the company—even if they own the device. For instance, if we think of a mobile insurance assessor who takes photos of damaged houses, cars, etc., for case files: if the assessor is using her own cellular telephone for those photos, then while the business may require those photos to be synced/backed up, the photos will likely be backed up to the user's *own* cloud service (Android or iOS). Thus there will be a backup, but it will not be accessible to the business. In order to ensure the data is accessible to the business, a bespoke camera application (or perhaps even an assessment claims application) would need to be used to take the photos, and direct a copy of the photo to the appropriate location for the business.

These sorts of considerations highlight the true challenge of data protection on mobile devices: actually gaining a copy of the data in the first place. Arguably it shifts responsibility for data protection away from the traditional roles (backup administrators and data protection architects) to the development and end user compute teams within the business. For example:

■ If an off-the-shelf application is to be used and provisioned by the end user teams, they must perform due diligence to identify *how* data can be captured from the application, then liaise with the appropriate infrastructure teams to ensure that captured data is protected.
■ If a bespoke application is to be created by in-house or contracted development teams, it is up to the business to require that bespoke application to include appropriate safeguards for data protection—and this should be more than just simply enabling versioning for in-cloud object storage used by the application.

Data protection within cellular devices has significant parallels to cloud native data protection; the explosion of applications pushes a requirement back onto the developers to ensure adequate controls and options are inserted into the application to allow data protection, since the traditional access models no longer apply, and standard data protection patterns that have been developed around in-datacenter infrastructure no longer apply.

17.4 Protecting Internet of Things

The Internet Society[*] defines an IoT device as:[†]

---

[*] www.internetsociety.org
[†] "What is an IoT device?", www.internetsociety.org/iot/

It's a physical object that connects to the Internet. It can be a fitness tracker, a thermostat, a lock or appliance—even a light bulb.

While there is always going to be a degree of overlap, we can often differentiate between *consumer* and *business* IoT devices in terms of whether the device serves a purpose for someone individually, or it contributes to some business function. Thus, while a so-called "smart" light bulb is an IoT device, it is usually something we see in home automation environments as opposed to businesses.

Ironically for consumer IoT devices, the almost singular *data protection* emphasis is security. It is depressingly common for IoT devices to come with little to no security, and consumers regularly install IoT devices within their houses without any consideration that it may open them to all manner of privacy violations and other issues:

Internet of Things devices are notoriously insecure and webcams are among the creepiest targets for hacks. A woman in the Netherlands recently learned just how disturbing these vulnerabilities can be, capturing footage of a home webcam that started tracking her movements and speaking to her in a sinister, unfamiliar voice[‡].

More recently, Amazon admitted of its always-listening "smart speaker:"

It doesn't always delete the stored data that it obtains through voice interactions with the company's Alexa and Echo devices—even after a user chooses to wipe the audio files from their account[§].

Such data protection-as-security implications extend well beyond a voyeuristic hacker watching you get dressed for work in the morning via your web camera, or someone in

---

[‡] Woman's webcam starts following her movements and taunts "hello", Rhett Jones, 6 October 2017, Gizmodo, *www.gizmodo.com .au/2017/10/womans-webcam-starts-following-her-movements-and -taunts-hello/*
[§] Amazon confirms it holds on to Alexa data even if you delete audio files, Makena Kelly and Nick Statt, 3 July 2019, The Verge, *www. theverge.com/2019/7/3/20681423/amazon-alexa-echo-chris-coons- data-transcripts-recording-privacy*

Amazon's datacenter potentially listening to the conversation you had with your dog:

> I WAS DRIVING 70 mph on the edge of downtown St. Louis when the exploit began to take hold.
>
> Though I hadn't touched the dashboard, the vents in the Jeep Cherokee started blasting cold air at the maximum setting, chilling the sweat on my back through the in-seat climate control system. Next the radio switched to the local hip hop station and began blaring Skee-lo at full volume. I spun the control knob left and hit the power button, to no avail. Then the windshield wipers turned on, and wiper fluid blurred the glass[*].

Security experts have long warned that IoT devices, particularly those accessible to consumers, have lax security and are installed by people who don't think about security, leading to situations where hackers can casually drive through a neighborhood or fly a drone past a building and hack lights, speakers, etc., and it is relatively easy to find proof-of-concepts of just this.[†]

Business IoT devices can exhibit all the same security concerns mentioned for consumer-grade IoT devices, but carry additional security concerns (using IoT devices as a gateway to breach internal systems, or leak security details required to access internal networks) and have the potential to generate or transmit data which the business *needs*.

There are practically boundless ways that IoT devices might be used to help businesses gather and process more data including but by no means limited to:

■ Soil sensors in farms (particularly greenhouse style agriculture) placed every 50 centimeters to measure and report moistness, heat, salinity, etc.
■ Water sensors placed every meter within pipes to track flow and help detect blockages for both water and sewerage systems
■ Temperature and humidity sensors throughout a factory
■ Road sensors to detect the number of vehicles using a street, and the weight of the vehicles (which may impact on the surface durability of the road)

■ A variety of physical sensors attached to postal delivery pushbikes, scooters, and motorbikes to allow tracking of bumps and issues in footpaths that could be monetized for pedestrian path repair data
■ Medical trackers on employees who work remotely so the company can fulfill legal duties to maintain a view of staff safety
■ Dashboard cameras for delivery vehicles
■ Voltage, vibration, and other sensors placed every few meters on conveyer belts to track and isolate faults (particularly for conveyer belts that run for kilometers)

With a key focus of 5G cellular network technology to support the billions of anticipated IoT devices all requiring low latency, low power internet access, these sorts of at-edge data gathering systems will undoubtedly explode in both numbers and generated data volume over the coming decades.

Once an IoT device gathers data, it must be processed. There's three effective ways this might happen: leaf, branch, or root. The leaf processing is where the individual IoT device contains sufficient processing power to perform actions based on the data it gathers. For instance, a soil sensor might detect insufficient water moisture in the patch of soil it monitors and triggers a nearby micro-spray to release water.

Branch-based processing is where an "edge" compute device is deployed to aggregate data from multiple nearby IoT devices. This allows decisions and actions to be processed from logically combined data sets—for instance, airflow and heating/cooling decisions might be determined based not just on the temperature at any individual location in an office, but on a per-floor basis, combining sensor data from dozens or more devices on each floor.

Root-based processing is where data from IoT devices is sent to a central datacenter for processing and storage. This might be used by utility providers (power, water, sewerage), etc., to measure the overall health and efficiency of their network and track faults from a 24/7 operations hub.

When determining whether to, or how to protect data generated from IoT devices, the following considerations usually apply:

1. What data needs to be protected: the raw data, or the processed data? (Or both?)
2. What is the combined volume[‡] of the data that needs to be protected?

[*] Hackers remotely kill a jeep on the highway—with me in it, Andy Greenberg, 21 July 2015, Wired, *www.wired.com/2015/07/hackers-remotely-kill-jeep-highway/*

[†] Watch a drone hack a room full of smart lightbulbs from outside the window, Thomas Ricker, 3 November 2016, *The Verge,* www.theverge.com/2016/11/3/13507126/iot-drone-hack; Hacking hue: researchers worm into the internet of things," Max Eddy, 4 August 2016, *PC Magazine,* www.pcmag.com/news/346789/hacking-hue-researchers-worm-into-the-internet-of-things

[‡] Data volume can build up very quickly with IoT devices. For instance, in Fast cars, big data—how streaming data can help formula 1, Carol McDonald describes Formula 1 cars with 150+ sensors generating 2 GB of data per lap, or 3TB in a full race, 11 May 2017, MapR Technologies, https://mapr.com/blog/fast-cars-fast-data-formula1/

3. Does the data require operational retention(days/ weeks), compliance retention (months/years), or both?
4. What is the type of data?

From a simple perspective, these questions are no different from the questions we have to ask of anything that generates data within a business; but whereas a business might have thousands of servers, that same business might have tens or even *hundreds* of thousands of IoT devices accumulating and sending data.

There is no guarantee of course that IoT devices will run conventional operating systems that support existing data protection agents. Indeed, low power architectures such as ARM-based processors abound in the IoT space, and while many devices may run a stripped down version of Linux for instance, there is no guarantee this is the case and since ARM-based systems have (to date) not been present in datacenters, there has been little need for data protection vendors to port their agent software to those processor platforms.

Data protection can then come in several forms:

■ For root and branch processing, where data protection is required it should happen at these locations, rather than the individual IoT devices; branch processing systems for instance are just as likely to be robust, hardened variants of laptop/desktop hardware and more likely to run an agent-accessible operating system. Root processing will see logging data stored in either databases or unstructured data pools, and within the primary datacenters will be more accessible to a variety of data protection options.
■ For leaf-node data protection processing, it should be assumed that conventional agent access will not be possible; instead, systems should rely on a data scooping mechanism—for example, using REST APIs to retrieve relevant/required data.

With increased regulatory focus on information gathering and accumulation coming from many jurisdictions, we are likely to see an increase in data protection requirements for that data (encompassing all three data protection topics: security, privacy and storage). It is important then that architects for IoT projects within businesses ensure the required protection functions are integrated into the system from the ground up, rather than attempting to bolt them on at a later date.

17.5 The Branch Office/Remote Office Conundrum

While we started the chapter referring to "the edge" as IoT and end user systems, there remains a classic "server"-based edge problem that merits discussion, and that is: what are the options for protecting data that resides on branch or remote servers within the business?

Whereas businesses might be able to declare unilaterally that end user systems data will not be protected and users must make reasonable efforts to copy or otherwise sync their data to corporate approved fileservers, any time there is tangible infrastructure in a branch or remote office (and henceforth we'll just use the term *branch office*), there is a more pressing requirement to consider data protection options outside of the datacenters.

Consider for instance that a common systems topology resembles that shown in Figure 17.3. In such an environment, we have:

■ Production and disaster recovery datacenters located at the head office and a "Tier 1" office, respectively.
 – These are connected via dual 10 Gbps links providing high bandwidth data transfers and redundancy between sites.
 – Systems may be failed over, either entirely, or individually, between the production site and the disaster recovery site.
■ Branch offices with computer rooms to provide some local services to the end users at those sites. These services might include:
 – Directory services
 – Local file services
 – Some databases
 – These will be connected over "medium speed" links back to the head office—e.g., 50 Mbps and higher.
■ Remote offices—these may have as few as just one physical server that provides localized directory services, or at most a directory server and a very small file server. These will only support a few local users and have slow speed connections to head office—often 20 Mbps or lower.

While the data protection services for the production and disaster recovery datacenters are expected to be robust and comprehensive, there is less chance of comprehensive data protection services in the smaller offices; usually (though not guaranteed of course), as the number of users and amount of compute services in the remote sites tend to decrease, so too do the data protection services for those remote sites.

What is not guaranteed is the distribution of data at remote/branch offices. There are in fact three typical models for data distribution, viz.:

■ Size of remote site has a tangible bearing on the amount of data there—the more users, the more data at the site

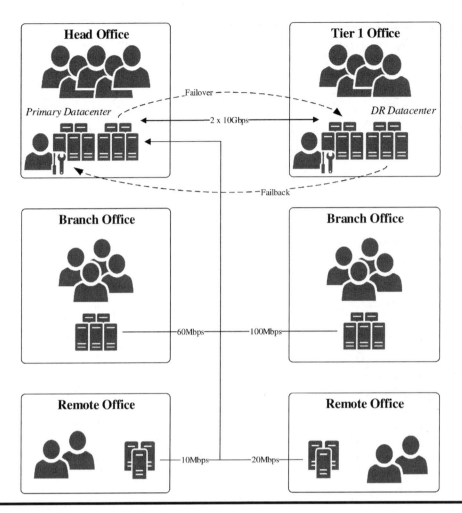

Figure 17.3 Conceptual multi-site systems topology.

- Remote site data is mainly a replicated or cached subset of data residing in the primary datacenters
- Remote sites have large amounts of unique data independently of the primary datacenters (where the combined unique data across all the remote sites equals or even exceeds the unique data in the primary datacenters).

Of course, in some businesses it will not be a "one model only" scenario for remote offices, but two or even all three scenarios.

For the first scenario (where the number of users on-site parallels the amount of data at the site), we will typically see branch data protection options deployed. Ideally these will be "appliance based" that require minimal local administration or physical intervention, since there is a reduced likelihood of there being IT staff permanently on-site.

The second scenario is the most likely scenario to see minimal to no data protection services; at these sites we are likely to see most local systems as static service systems that can be replaced by physically shipping out a replacement server, and any "unique" data is replicated or copied regularly

back a primary datacenter—usually with an expectation that it is acceptable to lose several days of data if replication has fallen behind.

The third scenario presents the most problematic situation for data protection services. Common industry verticals where we expect to see such arrangements include (but are by no means limited to):

- Mining
- Construction and engineering
- Healthcare (hospitals, service providers, etc.)
- Education

In this scenario, individual remote sites may have tens or more TB of data that must be protected, but links from the remote sites to the primary datacenters (or even mid-tier branch offices) are slow. A common architecture to protect these environments focuses on:

- Local data protection services to provide short-term (operational) recoverability—usually in the order of a month, or 4 weeks.

■ Data protection copies are sent off-site for redundancy and fault tolerance against site failure, usually via one of two different methods:
  - For older architectures, by tape
  - For newer architectures, as a deduplicated backup replication, either to the central office, or to public cloud
■ Long-term retention copies are stored effectively exclusively in the off-site location, keeping the remote site data protection focused exclusively on the operational/short-term data protection.

A common desire for businesses in these remote sites (particularly considering that the "computer room" may be something as simple as "a couple of servers under a desk in an air-conditioned office") is to limit the amount of physical infrastructure required. In some cases, this might represent virtualized backup services and protection storage, yet this can create recovery dependencies—in particular, if the backup and protection services reside on the same virtual environment hosting the systems being protected, this creates an "all your eggs in one basket" style risk. (In addition to potential performance and storage capacity implications.) Self-contained appliances may be preferred in these instances as they keep the backup services as physically separate from systems being protected, and will usually be architected for minimum administrative activity.

Of crucial consideration in any scenario is the bandwidth implication on replication. For example, if the remote site is connected via a 50 Mbps link:[*]

■ 10 GB of data would take ~25 minutes to replicate
■ 100 GB of data would take 4.24 hours to replicate
■ 500 GB of data would take 21.19 hours to replicate

Deduplication will become an essential aid in meeting these replication targets—and more specifically, deduplicated replication. That is, only unique, deduplicated data at the remote site should be replicated to the secondary copy location, and only if that data doesn't also exist at the secondary copy location—all without rehydrating the data in the first place.

In this scenario, our example replication times would refer to the post-deduplication replication, rather than the logical (original) backup size. Thus, 100 GB of data (4.24 hours to replicate over 50 Mbps link) might be 100 GB post-deduplication, and actually represent 1 TB per day of logical backups reduced by a 10:1 deduplication ratio. (Of course, in such a situation we are relying on the data being replicated in its deduplicated format—not all backup software and hardware will integrate to this level. Businesses must be

especially cautious when planning remote and branch office data protection that any deduplication process used will apply to replication traffic as much as it does to the remote data protection storage. The usual caveats for deduplication architecture efficiency would apply here, still, since they'd impact not only the amount of storage required at a branch location, but also the amount of data that can be replicated over a poor or minimum bandwidth link.)

When considering branch office protection, it is also worth focusing on whether different links are used for local internet traffic versus a "corporate backbone" network. For instance, it is not uncommon to see branch offices connected to a central datacenter via multiprotocol label switching (MPLS) networks with speeds in the order of 4 Mbps to 100 Mbps, but also have local broadband connectivity at speeds up to 1 Gbit to the internet. In such situations, branch office data protection systems may be better served utilizing Cloud (either as a backup, or replication destination) rather than attempting to squeeze the data through a network pipe orders of magnitude smaller back to a central datacenter. In short: the increased management overhead of having multiple data protection targets within the business will likely be outweighed by the reduced strain on the network backbone.

Despite its utility, deduplication is no silver bullet; should there be a total site failure, recovery scenarios will need to do one of the following:

■ Rebuild the remote backup appliance or solution in the datacenter where there is a replica copy of the data and "pre-seeding" the backup appliance before sending out (effectively, a "sneaker-net" recovery solution),
■ Accept a long replication time as the entirety of the deduplicated datastore is replicated from the secondary copy site back to the remote site, or
■ Accept long recovery times as recoveries are performed from the secondary site to the remote site, with data rehydrated prior to transmission across the Wide Area Network (WAN).

None of these options are necessarily invalid depending on link speed, workload size, and criticality, but they must be considered and the recovery options planned in advance. (It is worth noting that these same considerations apply also to any remote site where there is some data protection service running.)

17.6 Summary

The storage and data explosion we are seeing in business is by no means limited to the datacenter. With focus from governments on data security, privacy, and storage protection growing, it is no longer sufficient for businesses to have a

---

[*] Calculations performed using an online calculation tool at www.calctool.org/CALC/prof/computing/transfer_time

lackadaisical approach to protecting data at the edge of its operating sphere.

Measuring employee satisfaction, too, is an increasing trend within many businesses as they seek to lower costs by hiring the right staff and encouraging them to stay. Providing sub-standard solutions where an employee's files may be easily lost and unrecoverable can directly impact staff satisfaction in addition to productivity. (An employee, expecting to be happy about getting a brand new laptop during a refresh may find the joy significantly degraded as he or she waits almost a month for all data to be synced back from their OneDrive share at a company-enforced 1MB/s download throughput, for instance.)

Since the average user now has more experience with IT functions due to the pervasiveness of consumer technology than they did one or two decades ago, there is the real possibility that users will attempt to use their own form of data protection if the business does not provide something local to them. In the spirit of "just enough to be dangerous," users might know they need to turn on Time Machine or Microsoft File Versioning for instance, but not recognize the need to encrypt their backups, creating a new and serious security/risk vector for the business. Providing a self-service data protection strategy for the end user can help prevent this sort of security risk while reducing the business's overall risk profile.

While there are a variety of data protection services that can be used for remote and branch office environments, it is pertinent to consider that more often than not these will streamline the backup process, but do nothing or little to speed up a recovery process, over smaller bandwidth links.

Finally, when it comes to data protection, IoT is still largely in its infancy. We are seeing increasing adoption of IoT. Gartner predicted 20 billion connected things in 2020, up from 6.4 billion in 2016,[*] and while consumers currently still use more IoT devices than business, it's business that spends the real money on the technology.[†] Businesses deploying IoT systems need to evaluate what the potential impacts to their data protection strategy is or else they are likely to expose themselves to a variety of legal risks.

17.7 Self-Reflection

Find and evaluate at least three different end user-compute backup services (they might be cloud based, appliances, or a traditional software/hardware combination). Be sure to evaluate the following criteria:

■ Do they allow enterprise-controls over encryption and encryption keys?
■ Do they allow for local protection storage (or allow a business to force the deactivation of that)?
■ If they backup to the cloud, what are the costs associated with that? Options may include:
  – Per-user, unlimited data
  – Per-user *and* per MB or GB
  – Per-GB/TB but any number of users
■ Do they feature enhanced options such as deduplication, centralized control and monitoring, etc.?

Consider IoT temperature and humidity sensors that might have REST APIs for retrieving:

■ The current temperature/humidity values
■ The last 24 hours temperature/humidity values measured in 15-minute increments (96 in total)

Assume the sensor is running a closed, inaccessible operating system so there is no option to install backup agents on it. How might you use enterprise backup features discussed in Chapter 11 and a conventional backup client (e.g., a Windows or Linux server) to perform a backup of the 24-hour data scoop from each sensor?

---

[*] The current state of enterprise IoT, *IoT Business News*, 12 April 2019, https://iotbusinessnews.com/2019/04/12/60877-the-current-sta te-of-enterprise-iot/

[†] Ibid.

Chapter 18

Data Storage Fault Tolerance

18.1 Introduction

No discussion about data protection would be complete without a review of the most pervasive form of data protection in use within any datacenter—at-rest data storage protection. The most common type of this style of protection is of course the redundant array of independent disks (RAID). RAID in particular has become so commonplace that unlike almost all other forms of data protection, it's *assumed* to be present. Data storage protection (regardless of what form it takes) is designed to act as the first line of defense against individual hard drive failure (or any similarly used storage technology, such as solid-state disks).

While the undoubted king of data storage protection is RAID, over time as drive sizes have increased the *form* in which RAID is used has altered considerably. What was appropriate for hard drives of 1, 100, or even 500 GB has had to evolve as hard drives increase beyond the 4 TB size range. Each form of data storage protection has its own benefits *and* its own potential downfalls, especially with increased storage capacities and businesses needing to offer 24×7 services with high-performance characteristics. The data protection techniques in this chapter belong to the fault-tolerance aspect of the FARR model.

18.2 Traditional RAID

The December 1987 paper "A case for redundant arrays of inexpensive disks (RAID)"* written by David Patterson, Garth Gibson, and Randy Katz, outlined some of the fundamental principles of RAID that have remained with us over almost 30 years. While the acronym has changed (from "inexpensive" to "independent"), the core concepts have remained at times remarkably similar.

In addition to the potential for higher reliability, RAID was also developed as a mechanism to offer improved storage performance, particularly compared to monolithic disks developed for mainframe computers at the time. This dual promise—of performance and higher reliability—practically created the data storage industry. The précis to the original paper was quite prophetic:

> Increasing performance of CPUs and memories will be squandered if not matched by a similar performance increase in I/O.[†]

There are a number of different RAID levels that we'll discuss. By itself, RAID0 offers no protection—it simply stripes data across all drives included in the RAID set to maximize performance, so we will ignore it until we come to nested RAID levels. We will also ignore RAID levels 2 and 3, which are uncommon to the point of no longer being used.

During the discussion on RAID, keep in mind that RAID serves *only* as data storage protection—it is not a means of protecting against corruption, loss of availability, user error, or deliberate data erasure. The rest of data protection exists for those purposes.

At least within enterprise storage systems (regardless of whether they are for primary, secondary or protection storage systems), you will usually expect to see the presence of one or more *hot spares* within an array. A hot spare is a drive which holds no data, and instead is in the system ready to take the place of a drive that fails. The number of hot spares, and where they can be used in relation to failed drives, is entirely dependent on the architectural decisions made by a

---

* University of California, Berkeley, Technical Report No. USB/CSD-87-391, www.eecs.berkeley.edu/Pubs/TechRpts/1987/5853.html

[†] Ibid.

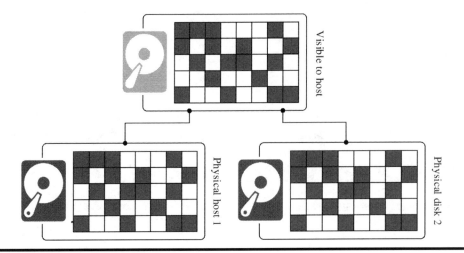

Figure 18.1   Logical representation of RAID-1.

vendor. For instance, some systems may allow one or more hot spares per shelf of drives. Depending on the design of the system, a hot spare might be able to be used to replace any failed drive in the entire storage array (at least, within a particular performance and capacity tier), *or* a hot spare might only be able to replace a failed drive in the same drive shelf.

18.2.1 RAID-1

RAID-1, otherwise known as mirroring, is where two drives are kept 100% in sync with one another. A representation of this is shown in Figure 18.1.

A RAID-1 configuration allows the data to remain accessible and intact in the event of a failure of a single drive. During normal operations (when both drives are present and functional), write operations are doubled as the write must be committed to both physical drives before it is acknowledged back to the host. This is generally described as being the *RAID write penalty*, something that all RAID types other than RAID-0 will suffer in some form or another.

Depending on the RAID implementation, read operations can be staggered across *both* drives, resulting in higher performance than reading from a single drive. (Some cheaper, consumer-oriented RAID-1 implementations might instead preferentially source all reads from a single disk, which will yield no performance benefit over a non-RAID configuration.)

From a capacity perspective, RAID-1 *halves* the physical capacity used to provide data storage. If 2×6 TB hard drives are used in a RAID-1 mirror, the operating system will only be presented with 6 TB of raw capacity.*

Note that RAID sets will usually be constructed by using drives all of the same size, to maximize capacity utilization. Consider, for instance, mirroring a 6 TB drive with a 2 TB drive. In such a case, the only way to provide data protection is to limit the 6 TB drive to 2 TB maximum utilization so that anything written to the 6 TB drive can *also* be written to the 2 TB drive. For the purposes of the standard RAID levels, we will assume in all cases that all the drives in the RAID set are of the same size. (Later in this chapter, we'll discuss other RAID approaches that can mix drive sizes.)

RAID-1, or variants of it (RAID-1 + 0 and RAID-0 + 1, which we'll discuss later), is often used in provisioning storage for mission critical high-performance systems, with a primary reason being the minimized write penalty. Particularly for systems that have a requirement for a high number of IOPS with very little latency, RAID-1 and its variants typically offer the best mix of performance and protection, albeit at a price.

18.2.2 RAID-5

RAID-5 attempts to balance data protection with provided capacity by using the notion of *parity*. The minimum number of drives required for a RAID-5 configuration is 3, but for any *n* drives in a RAID-5 configuration, the total capacity provided will be $(n - 1) \times C$, where *C* is the *smallest* capacity drive in the RAID set. Thus, 3×2 TB drives will yield a 4 TB capacity after data protection, 9×2 TB drives will yield a 16 TB capacity after data protection, and so on. A logical representation of a three-disk RAID-5 configuration is shown in Figure 18.2.

RAID-5 volumes are divided into a series of *stripes*. For a RAID-5 configuration featuring *n* drives, the incoming data is divided into *n* – 1 segments, and the *n*th segment of the stripe is constructed by a parity calculation (usually an "exclusive or" (XOR) process against all the data segments).

---

* For the purposes of simplicity, we will refer to all measurements in TB rather than differentiating between TB and TiB, and we will refer to the raw capacity rather than the expected capacity following formatting, filesystem layout overheads, etc.

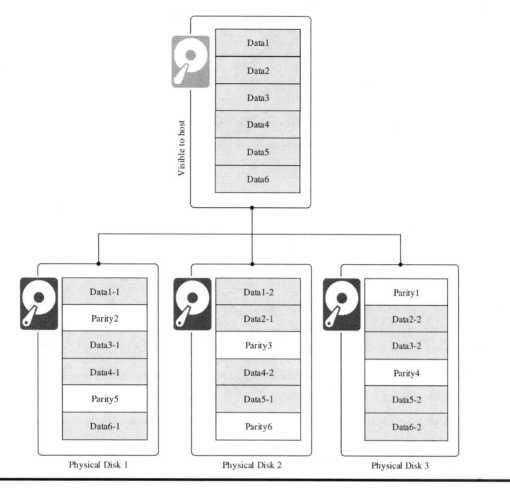

Figure 18.2 Logical representation of RAID-5.

The *n* segments are written as a stripe across all drives in the configuration. Mostly for reasons of performance, stripes are not of bytes but of blocks. (Stripe *size* refers to the size of the data segment written to *each* drive in a RAID configuration.)

RAID-5 volumes can withstand the failure of a single drive; whenever data is to be read, *either* the complete data set will be able to be read or *n* − 2 data segments plus a parity segment will be read, with a data reconstruction calculation performed against the parity segment and retrieved data to construct the entire data set.[*]

While RAID-5 can yield a higher capacity while still providing protection from a single disk failure when compared to RAID-1, this does not come at a cost. In any situation that data is updated on a RAID-5 volume, we must read all the data in each affected stripe *and* calculate a new parity before writing the actual updated data to the disks. Thus, an update to any data in an existing stripe becomes the following sequence of activities:

1. Read all the old data.

2. Read the prior parity value.
3. Calculate the new parity.
4. Write the updated/new data.
5. Write the recalculated parity.

Steps 1, 2, 4, and 5 in this list all represent distinct IO operations that must be performed as part of the single operation. For this reason, RAID-5 is considered to have a write penalty of four—each logical write requires four distinct IO operations to service the request.

Based on the write penalty, RAID-5 is often considered to be unsuitable for any workload that has a high number of writes; conversely, however, RAID-5 yields exceptional performance during large sequential read operations because all drives participate in the read process.

Of late, RAID-5 has begun falling out of favor in enterprise configurations. While still reasonably popular in small- to medium-sized businesses, larger drive capacities have had such a detrimental impact on rebuild times—particularly with the increased risk of a second drive failure during rebuild—that enterprises are increasingly leaning toward RAID-6 for volumes where RAID-1 and its variants are economically unfeasible. (We will cover RAID-6 shortly.)

---

[*] The parity and data reconstruction calculations are beyond the scope of this chapter.

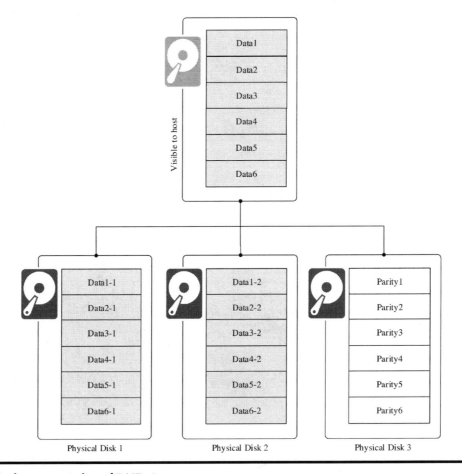

Figure 18.3   Logical representation of RAID-4.

18.2.3 RAID-4

RAID-4 is similar to the behavior of RAID-5, except that the parity disk is dedicated—that is, parity is not striped across all drives in the system. In the event of a single disk failing, data can be read back in one of the two ways:

1. If the parity disk failed, data can be read "as normal" from the original striped data.
2. If one of the disks in the data set failed, the data can be read by reading the remaining segments of the stripes from the working disks *and* the parity details and then subsequently combining the data and the parity information to reconstruct the missing data.

Figure 18.3 shows a logical representation of a three-disk RAID-4 configuration. Note that one disk is dedicated to parity.

RAID-4 is usually avoided for most situations as the dedicated parity disk will experience higher wear than the other drives in the configuration. Like RAID-5, RAID-4 will have a write penalty of four and feature the following sequence of activities whenever any data in an existing stripe is updated:

- Read all the old data.
- Read the prior parity value.

- Calculate the new parity.
- Write the updated/new data.
- Write the recalculated parity.

In a situation where, say, 4 KB of data is updated and the stripe width is 128 KB, there is a reasonably high degree of probability that the updated data will be confined to a single stripe (as opposed to spanning two stripes). In this situation, only two drives will need to have new writes performed to them—the one holding the data to be updated and the one holding the parity data. For a RAID-5 configuration, the disk the parity data belongs to varies per set of stripes; for RAID-4, however, the parity stripes are on a dedicated disk, meaning this disk will *always* be written to whenever new data is added or updated. In environments featuring large numbers of writes and particularly large numbers of *updates*, this can lead to the parity disk wearing out much sooner than the other disks in the RAID set.[*]

---

[*] Some storage systems will attempt to mitigate this by having large, persistent high-performance caches (e.g., in NVRAM) of parity information to stagger writes to the parity drives, or even use mirrored parity drives to mitigate the impact of a parity disk failing. It is usually only with these types of techniques that RAID-4 is considered enterprise suitable.

(There is also a RAID-3 architecture, which is quite similar to RAID-4, except parity and striping is performed at a byte level. RAID-3 is rarely used any longer.)

18.2.4 RAID-6

RAID-6 extends the basic principle of RAID-5 by adding a *second* parity stripe. This means the minimum number of disks in a RAID-6 configuration is *4* (though this minimum is rarely used in practice). Figure 18.4 gives an example of a logical representation of a four-disk RAID-6 configuration.

The advantage of RAID-6 is it offers dual-drive redundancy; up to two drives in a RAID-6 set can fail before data integrity is compromised. This however does mean losing the capacity of two drives to data integrity. Thus, a 4×4 TB RAID-6 set will yield only 8 TB of raw data space. For such a small number of drives, this yields no greater protection than a 2×RAID-1 configuration, but it is rare to see a four-drive RAID-6 set. Instead, RAID-6 yields itself to larger drive numbers—it is not unusual, for instance, to see an entire 15-drive shelf configured in RAID-6. Thus, 15×4 TB drives in RAID-6 will yield 13×4 TB or 52 TB of raw data space with 8 TB of parity protection.

While giving a higher degree of fault tolerance, RAID-6 increases the write penalty from 4 to 6. While there are a variety of algorithms used for RAID-6 parity, the reason the write penalty increases to 6 is that the two parity calculations are executed against *different* data. Thus, an additional data

read, parity calculation, and data write are performed on top of the previously listed IO steps for RAID-5.

Like RAID-5, RAID-6 is suited for scenarios where there is a preponderance of reads over writes, though it should be noted in both cases that the write penalty is only experienced when data is being *updated*. Thus, if writes are primarily the result of new data being written (or entire stripes being overwritten), the penalty can be mitigated. This often makes RAID-6 also ideal for *protection storage* and *integrated data protection* appliances, where the vast amount of writes will be of new data, rather than updates to existing data.

18.3 Nested RAID

Nested RAID refers to two RAID levels combined for greater performance, storage efficiency, or protection. These are normally named in their nesting order (innermost to outermost), and some of the more common options are

■ RAID-0+1
■ RAID-1+0
■ RAID-5+0

(You may sometimes see the "+" removed in the names, shrinking them to 01, 10, and 50, respectively.)

In Figure 18.5, we can see a logical representation of a RAID-0+1 or RAID-01 configuration.

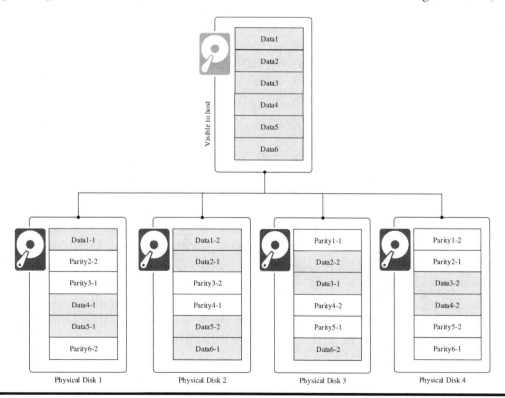

Figure 18.4 Logical representation of RAID-6.

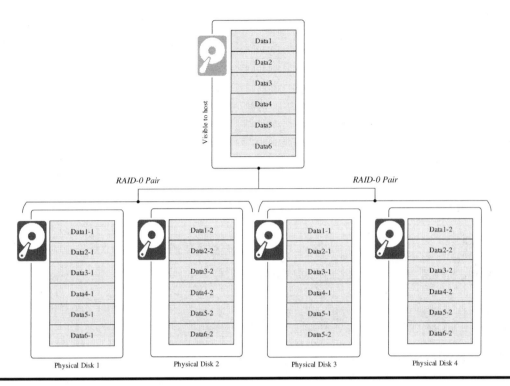

Figure 18.5   Logical representation of RAID-0 + 1.

RAID-0 + 1 sees two sets of striped disks mirrored together. Each pair of RAID-0 stripes offers performance, but no data protection. Data protection is instead achieved by mirroring the two RAID-0 sets. This requires a minimum of four drives and will yield the capacity of half of the drives in the overall presented volume. That is, using 4×4 TB volumes will result in 2×8 TB stripes, mirrored, with a total data capacity of 8 TB. A RAID-0 + 1 configuration can tolerate either the loss of a single drive in RAID-0 pair or the loss of the path to an entire RAID-0 pair.

RAID-1 + 0 is the logical reverse of RAID-0 + 1. Two RAID-1 pairs are assembled, and then a RAID-0 stripe is created using both RAID-1 pairs. This is shown in Figure 18.6. Like its RAID-0 + 1 cousin, RAID-1 + 0 will offer half the capacity of the drives in the overall RAID set. RAID-1 + 0 can tolerate the loss of a disk in *each* of the RAID-1 pairs but, unlike RAID-0 + 1, cannot tolerate the loss of the path to one of the RAID-1 pairs.

RAID-5 + 0 is similar to RAID-1 + 0 except two pairs of RAID-5 sets are striped together, as shown in Figure 18.7. RAID-5 + 0 can withstand the loss of one disk in each RAID-5 pair before data integrity is compromised (though it cannot lose access to the path for either of the RAID-5 sets that data is striped across). If *n* disks are used in *each* RAID-5 set, the total capacity of the RAID-5 + 0 configuration will be $2n - 2$. Thus, a RAID-5 + 0 configuration consisting of RAID-0 striping across 4×4 TB drives in RAID-5 configuration will result in 24 TB of raw data capacity presented to an accessing host.

These are just three of the variants available for nested RAID. (For instance, RAID-5 + 1 might be used in some instances, particularly when continuously available paired storage arrays are used.) In some cases, nested RAID will result in higher performance; in others, it will result in higher performance *and* higher storage capacity, but such levels should be chosen with careful consideration to the broader storage environment. (Both RAID-1 + 0 and RAID-5 + 0, for instance, can offer high-performance improvements, but neither can protect against the loss of connectivity to one stripe in the RAID-0 overlay.)

18.4 Sub-drive RAID

RAID is not necessarily *only* performed at a whole-drive level. Some enterprise storage systems as well as more feature-rich consumer-based RAID may offer sub-drive RAID. This can offer two distinct advantages—optimized capacity versatility and rebuild performance.

18.4.1 Capacity-Optimized Sub-drive RAID

Normally when we consider standard RAID, one of the core expectations is that all drives in a RAID volume are of the same size; otherwise, there will be capacity wastage. Consider, for instance, a RAID-5 set consisting of four drives where two drives are 4 TB and two drives are 2 TB in size. In a standard RAID-5 set, this would result in each

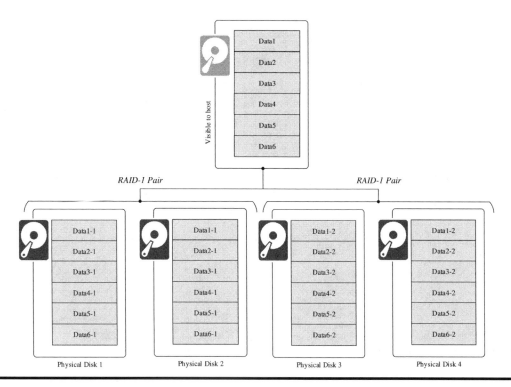

Figure 18.6 Logical representation of RAID-1 + 0.

drive being configured as a 2 TB drive within the RAID set, leaving 2 TB unused and inaccessible in each of the 2 × 4 TB drives. This would resemble a configuration similar to that shown in Figure 18.8.

Sub-drive RAID overcomes this by offering RAID at a level lower than individual drives. This might result in a configuration whereby RAID-5 is performed against the 2 × 2 TB drives *and* the first 2 TB of each of the 4 TB drives, and then RAID-1 is performed against the remaining 2 × 2 TB of each of the 4 TB drives, as shown in Figure 18.9.

This is a particularly common approach in "intelligent" personal/SOHO* RAID storage systems and can be sometimes referred to as "hybrid RAID" due to the mixing of RAID types within individual drives. In such configurations, the total protected storage may be offered as a single volume with the user effectively oblivious to the actual RAID levels being used within the configuration. (Such configurations can be achieved with software RAID generally, using RAID against individual disk partitions rather than whole disks.)

It should be noted that if the individual RAID types created in a sub-drive configuration *are* presented as separate volumes (in the example in Figure 18.9, this would mean a 2 TB RAID-1 volume and a 6 TB RAID-5 volume), this can potentially lead to performance issues. Not only is there the potential for writes to be sent to the same physical drives concurrently, but the different write characteristics of RAID-1 and RAID-5 will add to the performance impact beyond just

a simple scenario of two programs writing to the same physical disk at the same time, given the IO operations involved in writes in *each* RAID type.

18.4.2 Scattered RAID

Another potential advantage of sub-drive RAID comes in the consideration of potential rebuild speeds across large numbers of disks, particularly while still servicing regular IO operations. (This can be known under a variety of terms including *scattered* and *mesh*.) This supposes RAID content has been scattered across a potentially large number of drives. For instance, a RAID-1 configuration might utilize dozens or even *hundreds* of drives, where each data block[†] is mirrored between a *different* pair of drives. In the event of a single drive failing, content can be copied back from multiple drives simultaneously and (more importantly) *to* multiple drives simultaneously. Instead of rebuilding the previous RAID-block pairs, all the participating drives will receive new writes to spare space in order to allow a faster rebuild time.

Consider, for instance, the scattered sub-drive RAID configuration shown in Figure 18.10. In this, just four RAID-1 block pairs are shown for simplicity. In a normal RAID-1 configuration, if one of the drives in the RAID-1 pair failed, the surviving RAID-1 pair member

---

* Small office/home office.

† The actual size of the block will likely depend on the design choices made by any individual vendor that implements this.

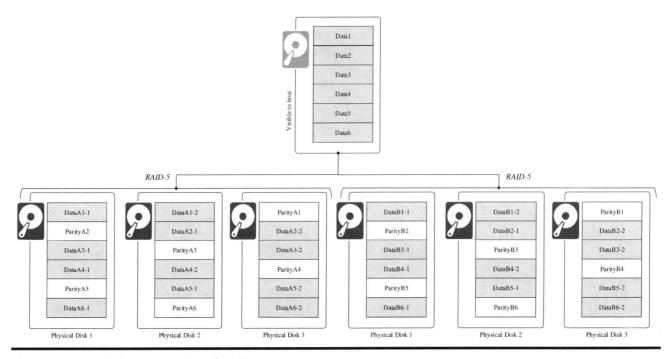

Figure 18.7 **Logical representation of RAID-0+5.**

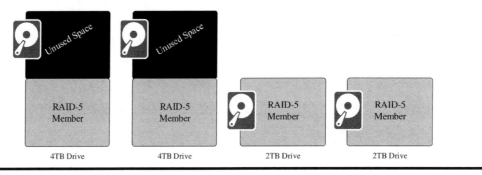

Figure 18.8 **Conventional RAID-5 configuration with mismatched drive sizes.**

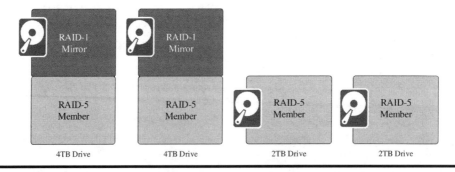

Figure 18.9 **Sub-drive RAID configuration optimizing capacity utilization in varying sized drives.**

will need to be read end to end to copy the contents to another drive in order to re-establish full data protection. This scattered RAID rebuild might resemble that shown in Figure 18.11.

As can be seen in Figure 18.11, each surviving RAID block can be copied to a *different* drive in the overall availability set, which will substantially parallelize the rebuild process. Instead of a single end-to-end read of one disk accompanied by a single end-to-end write of another disk, all disks in the overall protection set are simultaneously used to read the unprotected data and write it to spare drives or drives with spare storage in the set.

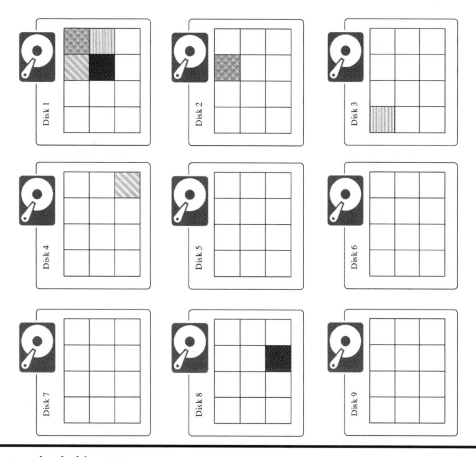

Figure 18.10 Scattered, sub-drive RAID.

It should be noted, however, that this comes with a data protection cost: if during the rebuild process *any* of drives 2–9 fail, the entire data set being rebuilt will effectively be lost. Thus, a sub-drive RAID approach can lead to highly efficient rebuild times, but the failure tolerance of the RAID level remains the same across all the potential drives in the configuration. Usually in this situation, because the rebuild time is so fast (compared to a traditional rebuild) the risks of this happening are very low. Alternatives may see more than two copies of data being stored across the protection set (for example, effectively creating three-way mirroring), or smaller protection sets than the total number of drives deployed to minimize the risk of overall data contamination via cascading failures. (That is, an array with 500 drives might be logically broken up into 10×50 sets. We would typically expect this type of breakdown to create hard limits on the expansion granularity for a system.)

Scattered RAID can be a highly effective solution in all-flash storage systems (i.e., solid-state storage devices) as the space can be more effectively utilized. While a conventional disk solution might need to optimize the data copy process to ensure that no disk being read from is also being written to (or at least minimize the number of disks requiring both), the performance impact of concurrent reads and writes on solid-state storage is so negligible that it usually doesn't

warrant consideration by comparison. Additionally, particularly when using enterprise-grade flash,* the risks of multiple units failing at the same time are substantially reduced compared to conventional hard drives with many parts moving at extremely high speeds.

18.5 Object-Level Protection

Object-based storage, often assumed to be a feature only of cloud storage systems, is an alternative to traditional filesystem-based storage approaches. In fact, object storage had been particularly popular in archive systems for years before cloud storage became available and continues to serve in this function in many solutions. While filesystems are based on potentially deeply nested directories and any number of files in any or all of those directories, object storage is usually based on an exceptionally wide namespace where each

---

* Enterprise-grade flash/SSD is usually classed as such by having a much higher tolerance against degradation caused by repeated rewrites—instead of tolerances in the thousands, enterprise-grade flash will have tolerances in the tens of thousands and will usually have a much higher "spare" storage to fill in should individual memory cells fail.

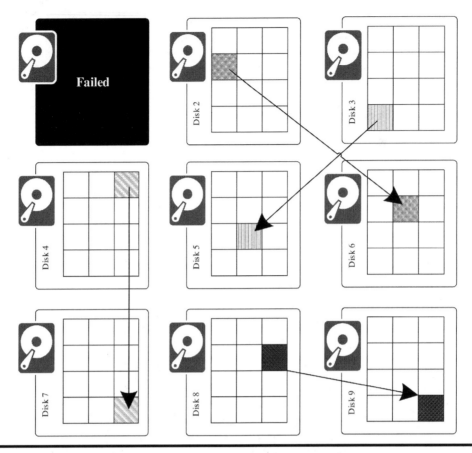

Figure 18.11 Scattered RAID rebuild process.

object (discrete unit of data) contains within its own metadata the globally unique identifier (GUID) that allows it to be individually addressed and referenced, regardless of what end storage system the object is actually located on. While files *may* be encapsulated as objects in object-based storage systems, it should not be assumed there is a 1:1 correlation between objects and files. Object storage systems can be used for practically any type of data, and an object may equally represent a binary large object (BLOB), database, or tuple. Ultimately, the nature of the object is determined by the accessing application.

A single object storage system may be scattered across a massive number of consumer storage systems, bespoke storage arrays, commercial and enterprise storage systems, and anything in between. A key differentiation, however, between object storage systems and enterprise storage systems is *where* data resiliency lays. Enterprise storage systems are typically designed to provide all the resilience within their systems—RAID, snapshots, replication, and so on. Object storage systems are usually designed to provide a particular base level of resiliency (as will be discussed shortly), with additional layers of resiliency usually being an accessing application function. Thus, you will be more likely to see object storage systems focused on commodity or near-commodity hardware rather than being underpinned by classic enterprise storage systems.

Regardless of their type, each component in an object storage system is typically considered to be a node (though the nomenclature is still evolving)—and objects will be distributed across multiple nodes. All this complexity is abstracted from the accessing systems that will typically do one of the following, all accompanied by authorized access keys:

▪ Present a GUID and request the referenced object.
▪ Present an object to be stored and receive a GUID in return.
▪ Present the GUID of an object to be deleted.

While not an exhaustive list, this gives a simple overview of the object storage process. Note this level of abstraction is even higher than we would normally see in, say, a classic filesystem. Within a filesystem in order to access an individual piece of data (i.e., a file), you have to know both the filename *and* the complete path to that file. In an object storage system, you provide the GUID only. (Hence, the common consideration of object storage systems of having a *global* namespace—the GUID—is flat and not hierarchical like a filesystem.)

While being useful for a variety of functions and purposes, one particular advantage offered by an object storage system is scale—while we normally consider classic NAS file servers as scaling to millions, tens of millions, or possibly even a hundred million files or so, object storage systems are usually premised on being able to address *billions* or more objects.

A discussion on the overall nature, benefits, and limitations of object storage is beyond the scope of this book. However, despite the different mechanics of object storage, the fundamental requirement for data storage protection remains the same. Unlike, say, filesystems provided by a NAS server, object storage is *not* typically RAID protected. At the lowest level, the individual disks comprising the object storage pool operate moderately independently, and it is up to the object storage controller layer (which the accessing applications and APIs communicate through) to ensure multiple copies of objects are stored using the appropriate dispersal patterns available. Object storage is typically defined as being protected by erasure coding, either entirely within one location or with geo-distribution. Compared to traditional RAID, erasure coding *can* result in excellent space efficiencies, though this will often depend on architecture of the object storage scheme. (However, remember the rebuild times of RAID systems will grow as the number and size of the drives increase, and while a token or small comparison of RAID vs. object may be more favorable to RAID in terms of storage overhead, as the volume of data grows, the overhead required by RAID will likewise increase as an ever-growing number of LUNs must be presented.)

18.5.1 Geo-Distribution

Geo-distribution, as its name suggests, provides protection from object loss by storing multiple copies of the object in geographically disperse locations. Depending on the object storage system, this might only be offered as an option or it may even be considered to be a key functional requirement/capability. In some object storage models, it might be up to accessing applications to ensure they (1) subscribe to geographically disperse object stores and (2) write copies in each location accordingly. In addition to facilitating object *placement*, geo-distributed object storage can also be used for the purposes of data resiliency. (In this scenario, placement refers to scenarios where users may need to access from either a variety of locations or even anywhere in the world. An object datastore with locations in, say, Melbourne, Austin, and Stockholm, will not only provide each object with geographically disperse protection but *may* also allow users to access the object copy that is closest to them via their network access. This is not necessarily guaranteed, however, and is beyond the scope of the data protection considerations we are currently discussing.)

A common consideration in geo-distributed object storage is how quickly objects are consistent across the different locations. If designed with a global namespace, even if an object is not directly present, it should be accessible (admittedly with a "drag" lag) across locations; object storage systems either might have a high degree of consistency across geographic regions or might offer "eventual" consistency.

Regardless of whether object storage is being deployed in a private or hybrid cloud or being accessed through a public cloud, a subscriber will typically have options to choose between geo-distribution of objects or localized storage only. Geo-distribution is typically considered a more expensive option but offers greater resiliency. In particular, just like traditional IT environments leverage multiple datacenters to avoid putting all the infrastructure eggs in one basket, geo-distribution for object stores avoids a scenario whereby data becomes inaccessible or even lost in the event of a single datacenter failing.

18.5.2 Erasure Coding

At its most basic, you might consider erasure coding to be object-level RAID. This is where an incoming object is split into multiple segments (or *symbols*), with additional segments created such that multiple segments can be lost but the original content can be recreated. Each segment and the encoding segments are then distributed among the disks and nodes in the object storage system to avoid a scenario where the loss of a single node results in unrecoverable data.

There are a variety of erasure coding algorithms, but they usually work along the following lines (see also Figure 18.12):

■ Data object is split into m fragments,
■ The m fragments are re-encoded into n fragments, where $n > m$ (the n-m fragments are usually referred to as the k coding fragments).
■ The n fragments are written.
■ Up to k fragments of the written data can be lost without impacting durability—the remaining fragments can be read and the missing data reconstructed.

While it would be understandable to assume that RAID could do just as useful a job for object protection, we must remember that object storage is typically grown by *scaling out*. Rather than a traditional scale-up storage model with, say, two controllers and a large amount of back-end storage, object storage is grown by adding more nodes into an object storage cluster. This allows object storage systems to potentially grow into hundreds of petabytes or beyond if necessary without the limitations typically imposed on large RAID systems, in terms of both rebuild times and the number of drives assigned to a LUN—an essentially foreign concept to object storage. (If objects are being accessed through public cloud, the additional variability, of course, will be network access speeds—i.e., web speed will not be particularly

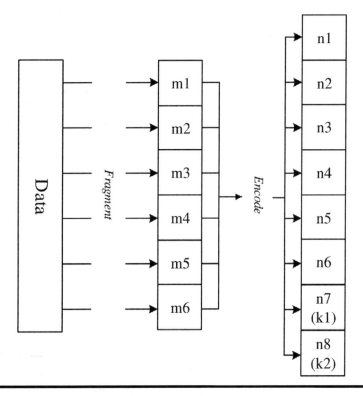

Figure 18.12 **Logical representation of erasure coding process.**

concerned with object storage latencies. While private object storage can be deployed for a greater range of functions, it is not designed to replace, say, Tier-1 enterprise storage in terms of raw access speed, however.)

RAID implementations typically will require all disks in the LUN to be controlled by a single storage processor (or a pair in an active/active configuration); the RAID-*like* nature of object-level storage achieves a similar goal but allows every segment to exist on a different addressable node in an object storage cluster. Location-aware encoding mechanisms increase resiliency by ensuring the loss of a single node does not cause data loss, even though a node may have anywhere between a few drives and dozens of drives. (Indeed, with high-density storage shelves becoming increasingly common, 60 or more drives might be provisioned in a single rack mountable node, with all drives and all nodes contributing to the overall storage pool.) This allows for a configuration designed to "scale out," into up to even the exabyte range, while being highly fault tolerant—particularly when geo-distribution of encoded objects is added to the equation. (Unlike many classic enterprise storage systems, geo-distribution does not really refer to "production" and "disaster recovery" sites but may include many sites—3, 4, or more—all participating in the storage pool.)

Conversely though it is worth noting that the write penalty for erasure encoding results in a storage platform which is not suitable for "Tier 1" workloads—e.g., real-time systems, transactional workloads, and primary file storage, so

both erasure encoding and the more traditional RAID processes have relevance within businesses depending on the workloads to be used.

18.6 Summary

The old mantra "A chain is only as strong as its weakest link" is particularly relevant when we consider at-rest data storage protection. Choosing the *right* data storage protection is the first and most fundamental step on the path toward a full data protection system. By itself it is *not* a data protection solution, but it is extremely rare to find an effective and holistic data protection solution that *doesn't* include at-rest data storage protection.

Each layer of data protection we build into a solution is premised on one simple piece of knowledge: *things* fail. It doesn't matter whether the thing is a storage array, a storage network switch, a filesystem, or an end user making a mistake; *things* fail. A copy-on-write snapshot will not protect against underlying disk failure, and a continuously available system with redundant virtualized arrays is a terrible waste of money if all we need to do is ensure a single disk failure does not result in data loss.

While RAID is practically the standard in data storage protection at the most fundamental layer, as businesses of all sizes move workloads out of traditional storage and into cloud or object storage and we deal with increasingly larger data sets that stretch the capabilities of traditional RAID, we return to this fundamentally *assumed* element of protection and ask the most basic of questions:

- Can it protect the volume of data I need to store?
- Is it even there in the first place?

Ultimately, cloud-scale storage capable of addressing billions or more objects has necessitated new massively scalable architectures and will see continued evolution in data storage over the coming decades.

18.7 Self-Reflection

In our RAID examples, we usually considered the fewest number of drives required to create a RAID set, regardless of whether that was RAID-1, RAID-5, RAID-6, or even the nested RAID types. It is more usual in parity-based RAID systems (e.g., RAID-5 and RAID-6) to see a larger number of drives used.

Consider a situation where you have storage shelves within an array that take 20 disks per shelf. Assume two drives in the shelf can be used as hot spares, leaving 18 drives. Using 4 TB drives, describe at least three different RAID-5 layouts that you could be use, and for each layout, determine:

- The available storage each layout presents to an individual volume
- The total storage available in the configuration for the shelf

In each of the above we refer to the size of the constructed volume, before any filesystem overheads are applied.

Chapter 19

Tape

19.1 Introduction: The Historical Primacy of Tape

There was a time when it was impossible to have a conversation about data protection without tape being a primary focus. Tape has been used in IT practically since its inception, with the UNIVAC* 1 using tape for data storage as early as 1951. Tape initially gained ascendency over punched card and became a common storage format for decades until it in turn was supplanted by magnetic disk for primary storage.

As disk systems were developed, the sequential nature of tape forced it into the realms of backup, hierarchical storage management (HSM) and archive. Simply put, tape could not compete effectively with high-speed random access to active data offered by hard disk systems.

Tape had historically offered advantages disk storage struggled to match, including:

- Scalable capacity at fixed footprint
- Large capacity at low cost
- High-speed *sequential* read and write capabilities
- Portability

In addition to these, more recently, tape has also been seen as a *green* technology—though there are pros and cons of tape from an environmental perspective.

Without fail almost every year someone declares tape to be dead. While this isn't necessarily the case, we must also acknowledge that the role tape plays in the modern datacenter has been changing and reducing. This has been caused by disk-based storage systems and, more recently, alternate storage such as cloud. The disruption of tape use cases in the datacenter are likely to continue for some time to come.

_____
* Universal Automatic Computer.

In order to appreciate the changing role of tape within data protection, we should first examine the primary use cases it had for the last 20 years.

19.2 Hierarchical Storage Management and Archive

HSM is a form of storage tiering pioneered in the mainframe realm where data that is less frequently used is moved out to slower and slower storage until eventually due to economies of access, it is removed from disk entirely and placed on tape. To ensure data can still be retrieved when required, "stubs" are left behind at the filesystem or operating system layer so that when a user or process attempts to access a relocated file, it can be identified by the HSM plug-in to the operating system and be retrieved from tape. To the end user, it would be indistinguishable in access method to data still on disk, albeit as a slower-than-usual access.

While HSM and archive are largely synonymous in terms of data movement functionality, the key difference between them is that HSM is usually seen as a process that deals with data that may still be updated even if it has been moved out to slower storage. (Particularly when tape was used for HSM, this would result in the data being moved *back* to a primary storage tier before modification.) Archive has traditionally differed from HSM in that data once moved is likely to be retained largely for legal or compliance reasons and potentially might even be locked, preventing modification. In this, archive was equally suited to tape because of its write-once read-many (WORM) nature. Since tape does not allow for selective data overwrites, once data is written it is not subject to modification and has therefore been easily deemed to be a "golden," inviolate copy—particularly if additional steps are taken to ensure that tape is not erased/overwritten or otherwise destroyed. Still, the terms have continued to blur, particularly in the non-mainframe IT space.

Typically, HSM and archive systems process files or data based on age and/or access frequency. Particularly when moving data to tape, the goal would always be to ensure that by the time data was relocated from disk to tape, it was old *and* had not been accessed for some time. (In some cases, data might also be moved based on its size and the relative costs of holding it online, regardless of how recently it had been created.)

It was the higher capacity of tape that made it particularly beneficial in archive/HSM environments—particularly when we consider the purpose was to move data that did not require frequent access. Consider, for instance, linear tape open (LTO) Ultrium-1, introduced in 1998 with a capacity of 100 GB. Hard drives, on the other hand, in 1998 had a capacity anywhere between 2.1 and 21 GB. Thus, a single 100 GB cartridge could fit anywhere between 4 and 47 hard drives capacity, a substantial saving for businesses. Even with archival or HSM data written twice (to protect against tape failure), this would still be potentially cheaper than maintaining sufficient hard drives for online storage of all data. Conversely, 100 GB hard drives would not enter commercially availability until approximately 2001.* While each new generation of tape has traditionally started at a high per-unit cost, that cost has inevitably been lower than a comparable capacity in hard drives.

By using even a relatively small tape library for HSM and archive functions, a business could substantially extend its storage capacity at a lower cost and potentially smaller footprint than the disk-only equivalent. Even a basic rack-unit (RU) tape changer with, say, 2 tape drives and 20 slots would offer between 2 and 4 TB (depending on compression) of additional capacity to a business using LTO-1 tape, possibly within a size of approximately 8 RU high or less. Assuming 19 GB drives were used in 3 RU storage shelves with 15 drives per shelf, 106 drives would be required for 2 TB *without* any RAID considerations—occupying as much as 24 RU in space. (Adding configurations such as RAID-5 14 + 1 would result in an increase to approximately 120 drives, but a similar rack size.)

It should be noted that neither HSM nor archive are technically data protection activities, but rather information lifecycle *management* activities. That being said, we reference them here because of their historical impact on tape usage *and* because an effective data protection regime includes policies and processes to delete or otherwise archive data that is

no longer required on primary storage, thereby reducing the overall data protection *and* primary storage costs.

19.3 Backup and Recovery

If HSM and archive seemed like a good value proposition for tape, it was nothing compared to the use case for backup and recovery. Tape ticked almost every box for backup, but most notably it satisfied three very key requirements:

1. Fast
2. Cheap
3. Removable

The backup industry in the 1980s, 1990s, and early 2000s revolved around tape—so much so that when the de facto industry standard (DLT) struggled to evolve beyond the 35 GB backup cartridge, much of the backup and recovery industry stagnated.[†] The LTO consortium breathed new life into the backup industry in 1998 with its first release, a 100 GB cartridge, and the industry accelerated from that point.

Despite sometimes popular opinion, tape offered high-speed backups long before disk-based backup. As early as 1997, backup speeds of 1 TB per hour had been attained using tape, and by 2003 speeds of 10 TB per hour had been achieved. When it came to moving large amounts of data as quickly as possible, tape served the industry well for a long period of time, and this must be acknowledged when considering the history of data protection. Though tape, it might be said, was more fickle in achieving or maintaining that speed when the incoming data stream was variable—and remains so.

Entire backup products were developed with around tape architectures, and it's pertinent to consider several of the key aspects offered by backup vendors to deal with tape-based limitations, since in specific scenarios tape can still offer a valid use case for backup or backup duplication purposes.

19.3.1 Media Spanning

Media spanning refers to a single backup needing to spread across more than one tape. This might happen in situations where the tape is smaller than the backup set (e.g., backing up a 10 TB filesystem to a set of 2 TB tapes) or simply in situations where the remaining capacity on a partially used tape is less than the capacity of the data set being backed up.

While most enterprise backup products supported media spanning, some products, particularly open source products, took a long time to offer this support, which would result in backup and system administrators having to manually

---

* Remember that enterprise storage vendors will usually be slower to support new drive sizes in order to ensure that key requirements such as reliability, stock availability, and maximum compatibility with existing systems have been met. This often means that new hard drive sizes may take some time before they are available in the enterprise storage space.

---

† This is not to suggest DLT was the *only* tape technology at the time. However, it was a critical and highly used technology.

carve up backup sources to allow them to fit on tapes. Such a process is time consuming and error prone (no matter how carefully done) and would inevitably result in media wastage. By allowing backups to span over as many tapes as required to ensure the data is backed up, enterprise products avoided tape wastage and reduced the potential for human error preventing key data from being backed up.

19.3.2 Rapid Data Access

Rapid data access goes hand in hand with both spanning and backup catalogs. Rapid data access refers to whether the backup product is able to identify (via the catalogs) only those pieces of media that are really needed for a recovery, and within those pieces of media, identify as small a portion of data as possible that must be read in order to facilitate a recovery. For example, consider a situation where a backup spanned four tapes, and a single file needs to be recovered, which so happens to be stored on the third tape. Enterprise backup software will first use the catalog to determine that only the third tape is needed for the recovery and then use high-speed tape "seek" operations to jump to a position relatively close to the data required for recovery. Less sophisticated products might need to load the third tape and read from the start, and even more primitive products without a sophisticated catalog might need to start reading the backup set from the very first tape, throwing away the majority of the data read before finally locating the specific file required.

Backup vendors will typically use file and record markers to target with a high degree of granularity the portion of the tape that needed to be accessed. In this case, "file" refers to approximate area on tape, not "file required for recovery."

For instance, regardless of the size of the data being backed up, a backup product might record an end-of-file marker on the tape after, say, every 2 GB of data has been written. If the catalog identifies the data required for recovery is somewhere within the block starting after the 42nd end-of-file marker written to the tape (i.e., somewhere around 86 GB into to the tape), the backup product could load the tape and then issue 42 "forward space file" (FSF) instructions to the tape to do a high-speed fast forward to the starting block of data. Record markers might then be used to provide further granularity in the seek process—for instance, a record marker might be written every 100 MB.

Practically, all tape drives support the following operations:

- *FSF*: seek forward the nominated number of end-of-file markers on the tape
- *Backward space file* (*BSF*): seek backward the nominated number of end-of-file markers on the tape
- *Forward space record* (*FSR*): seek forward the nominated number of records on a tape
- *Backward space record* (*BSR*): seek backward the nominated number of records on a tape

Returning to our example, the backup server's catalog might be able to identify that the required data for recovery is not only in the block of data 42 end-of-file markers through the tape, but within that block starts in the record chunk that is five record markers into the block. This will allow multiple "fast forward" operations to be performed before read operations are initiated, drastically reducing the amount of sequential data reading required to recover the data actually requested by the end user.

OLD DOG TEACHES NEW TRICKS

It's worth noting backup-to-disk benefits from similar levels of catalog data. Despite lay opinion, backup to disk doesn't generate mirror copies of filesystems: the eventual file count over successive backups (especially if deduplication is in use) would render the backup filesystem unusable. So backups tend to be written in large, monolithic files (e.g., one file per filesystem backed up). It would likewise be unfeasible (and wasteful) to read the entire monolithic file for a recovery of a single small file, even with disk access speeds. So even in backup-to-disk environments, catalog data will be maintained to allow quick access to individual files or at least blocks of data in the overall backup file.

19.3.3 Media Multiplexing

Media multiplexing refers to writing multiple backups simultaneously to the same piece of media, and the primary purpose of media multiplexing is to deal with tape streaming performance requirements. While tape drives and tape vendors publish performance guidelines for the speed of their systems (e.g., LTO-1 cited 20 MB/s uncompressed), this performance is entirely dependent on the data flowing from the backup environment to the tape at a *constant* speed. The reduction in backup performance was *not* linear in response to degraded backup throughput. The concept of *shoe-shining*

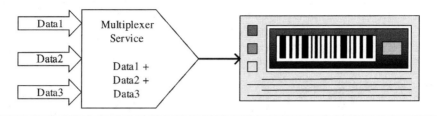

Figure 19.1 Conceptual view of multiplexing.

Figure 19.2 Multiplexed tape segment.

is fairly consistent in most tape technologies—this is where the incoming data speed is lower than the ideal streaming speed of the tape drive. A tape drive will write data at the rated speed of the device (e.g., 20 MB/s), but then due to pauses in the data stream relative to the streaming speed is forced to stop, seek back to the end of the previous data stream on tape before it can continue to write (so as to avoid gaps in the media). Thus, it is entirely conceivable that a tape drive that *streams* at 20 MB/s might, with an incoming data speed of just 18 MB/s, instead write as slow as 10 MB/s once shoe-shining came into play.*

To (partially) work around this, more recent versions of tape technology have included the capability to step down their ideal streaming speed to lower speeds—for example, a drive might be capable of stepping down to 75%, 50%, and 35% of its native streaming speed without needing to shoe-shine.

While the capability to step down streaming speeds helps to smooth performance when writing to tape, it is only a relatively new addition to tape technology, and it still does not provide absolute guarantee against shoe-shining and poor performance when the incoming data stream is slow. The workaround offered by many enterprise backup products is to combine the data streams from several sources into a larger, faster stream going to tape. This is called *multiplexing*.

Figure 19.1 provides a high level conceptual view of multiplexing—rather than individual data streams being sent directly (and 1 by 1) to a tape drive, they are passed through a multiplexer service. The multiplexer service combines the data streams into a single stream that is then sent to the tape drive.

The advantage of multiplexing is that the speed of the backup is no longer directly dependent on the speed of any individual data stream coming from a client—as more data streams are combined, the chances of keeping a tape drive

running at full speed are increased. Slowdowns in data streams from an individual client are compensated for within the multiplexer service by allowing additional data from one or more of the other data streams to be incorporated into the multiplexed stream.

(While in theory there is nothing preventing backup stream multiplexing to disk-based backup devices, it is more usually than not the case that when performing backup to disk, enterprise backup technology will instead write each individual stream as its own backup file or set onto the disk—there are no logical advantages in writing a multiplexed stream as a monolithic data set to disk, given disk does not shoe-shine.)

A segment of multiplexed tape (at the logical level) might resemble that shown in Figure 19.2.

Consider this multiplexed tape as consisting of:

A: Host "orilla," filesystem /Users/pmdg
B: Host "mondas," filesystem /home
C: Host "faraway," filesystem C:\

In the example tape segment, we can see that the tape has been written with three-way multiplexing and filled with data segments as they become available from each of backup jobs A, B, and C. Assuming such levels of multiplexing continued throughout the entire tape, it might be assumed that the hosts "mondas" and "faraway," each providing only 3 of the 11 multiplexed segments, might have been slower clients compared to the host "orilla," which provided 5 of the 11 multiplexed segments in the diagram.

Tape-level multiplexing can be essential to keep tape drives streaming at optimum speed but, depending on the level of multiplexing and the type of recovery that is required, can have a deleterious effect on the most important component of a backup system—the recovery.

Consider again the example of our multiplexed tape. Depending on what size each chunk of data is on the tape, individual file recovery may be relatively unaffected by

---

* This isn't to say that 8 MB/s of data would be lost—just the incoming data stream would likewise need to be reduced to keep up with the slower performing tape drive.

the multiplexing. However, let's examine what would be required to read, say, the entire orilla "/Users/pmdg" filesystem from the tape. Based on the tape segment in Figure 19.2, this would result in the following scenario:

- Read first chunk of A
- Read second chunk of A
- Read over *or* seek past the first chunk of B
- Read the third chunk of A
- Read over *or* seek past the first chunk of C
- Read over *or* seek past the second chunk of C
- Read the fourth chunk of A
- Read over *or* seek past the second chunk of B
- Read over *or* seek past the third chunk of B

- Read the fifth chunk of A

This process would continue until such time as all of the "/Users/pmdg" filesystem for the host "orilla" had been recovered. Depending on the individual chunk sizes and the number of concurrent chunks from backups we're not interested in recovering, the backup software *may* be able to execute an FSR or FSF command to jump areas of the tape that it doesn't need to recover from, but multiplexing is usually performed in reasonably small chunk sizes to reduce the risk of shoe-shining, so potentially a *lot* of redundant data may be read and thrown away by the backup product when doing a complete recovery from a multiplexed tape. The more the tape is multiplexed, the more wasteful this type of recovery becomes.

OPTIMIZING THE WRONG PERFORMANCE

A company wanting to eliminate shoe-shining and keep tape drives streaming at their maximum rated speed tuned their entire backup environment to generate 64-way multiplexing on all their tape-based backups (the maximum supported by a particular product at the time). This seemed to work fine for backups, but shortly after implementing this change they found themselves having to recover an entire filesystem. With the level of multiplexing on the tape, what should have been a 1- or 2-hour recovery at most stretched to over 8 hours. It's a worthwhile reminder that the fastest backup in the world is pointless if it can't be recovered efficiently and quickly.

19.3.4 Twinning/Automated Replication

Larger backup environments that make use of full silos rather than their smaller tape library counterparts sometimes make use of silo-controlled tape replication.

SILO OR TAPE LIBRARY?

You'll note we refer to both *silos* and *tape libraries*. While naming conventions between silos and tape libraries are somewhat vendor dependent, for the purposes of our discussion, we'll refer to a silo as a system that has a separate control host managing partitioning and access control, and more likely to have multiple robotic arms handling tape changing. A tape library, on the other hand, for the purposes of our discussions, is more likely to have a single robot arm handling tape changes and is directly connected to the host(s) using it for backup/recovery purposes. As tape density has increased, this differentiation has blurred, with many tape libraries supporting partitioning.*

While the importance of backup duplication has long been acknowledged, larger businesses have often found it difficult to schedule duplication time when using tape. Silos enable a means of circumventing the time-to-duplicate

problem by effectively performing a form of "RAID-1" on tapes—generating *two* identical tapes. The danger of this approach is usually that the backup product will be unaware of the copies and rely entirely on the silo to ensure that the two copies never become simultaneously visible to the product.

Alternatively, some backup products may perform a software version of this replication approach, simultaneously generating backups to two different tapes. While this has the

* In the context of tape libraries and silos, partitioning (or *hardware* partitioning) refers to presenting one physical unit as multiple smaller units; a 10,000 slot silo might be presented as 10 × 1,000 slot systems, for instance.

advantage of ensuring the backup product is aware of both copies, it introduces a logical challenge to backup administrators—is a backup considered a failure if just one of the two tapes fails (and therefore just one copy of the backup is generated), or is it considered a failure only if *both* tapes failed?

19.3.5 Library/SAN Sharing

While initially tape libraries were SCSI connected, over time this gave way to fiber-channel connectivity, particularly for larger tape libraries, thus enabling SAN sharing of the library. This allows multiple hosts to be zoned in and connected to the tape library simultaneously.

In Figure 19.3, we show a sample SAN shared tape library. In this configuration, there are a variety of standard network connected backup clients, but additionally the tape library is shared over fiber-channel connectivity to both the backup server and a database server. In this scenario, we would assume the database server contains a large amount of data and either can't be efficiently backed up over standard network connections or mustn't be affected by the network impact of such a backup process.

Typically in this scenario, the backup server will maintain control over the robot head that performs tape change operations. One or more tape drives will be zoned into the backup server, and the remaining tape drives will be zoned into the database server.

This style of configuration is often referred to as offering LAN-free backups—for the database server in this example, the backups do *not* traverse the IP network at all, being sent direct via fiber channel to the tapes within the tape library. (Metadata exchanges between the backup server and database server will still typically occur.) Library sharing can also be accommodated via standard SCSI connections—the backup server will typically have control over the robot head and one or more drives, and the remaining drives will have direct SCSI connections directly with the hosts that need dedicated access.

The disadvantage of the basic sharing of tape libraries is *dedicating* tape drives to individual hosts, something overcome with a technique referred to as *dynamic drive sharing* or *SAN drive sharing*, covered in the next topic.

19.3.6 Dynamic Drive Sharing

Referring to Figure 19.3 again, library sharing is where specific tape drives are dedicated to individual hosts within the backup environment, providing maximum resource availability to those hosts. This comes with the risk those tape drives will sit idle for long periods during the backup window once the individual hosts with access have completed their backups.

To make better use of limited tape drive resources, several enterprise backup products developed a technology referred to as SAN sharing or dynamic drive sharing for fiber-channel

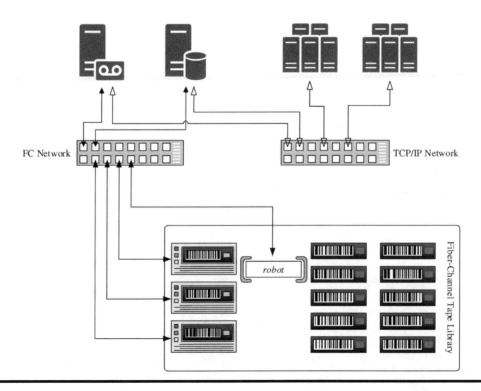

Figure 19.3 Sample SAN shared tape library.

connected libraries. In this situation, individual tape drives would no longer be dedicated to specific hosts, but zoned in such a way that multiple hosts could theoretically access the tape drives. (The robot head would remain controlled by a single host.) The backup server or other nominated host dynamically allocate free tape drives to hosts requiring SAN-level tape drive access during backup or recovery processes, ensuring resources are spread around as required.

This does not come without challenges. Due to multiple hosts having access to individual tape drives, it becomes critical to mask SCSI resets (typically triggered during host reboots or HBA faults). Otherwise, the host *using* a tape drive may find the tape unexpectedly rewinding and ejecting the tape because another host with access to the drive happened to reboot. Additionally, since multiple hosts can access the drives, ensuring a compatible tape block size is used becomes critical, otherwise a tape might be initialized and written to by one host but then loaded *into the same tape drive* by another host (usually of a different operating system) and be completely unusable. Generally speaking, maintenance and hardware faults become considerably more problematic or at least more complex in this style of environment. (In fact, as solutions go, the SAN sharing of tape drives between multiple hosts often introduced more problems than it solved into any but the most rigorously maintained environment.)

19.3.7 Library Partitioning

While originally a feature mainly of silos, a large number of tape libraries now also support partitioning, whereby the library can appear as multiple independent tape libraries (usually each one with a smaller configuration) and thereby be presented to multiple backup servers or storage nodes/media servers.

For instance, a 1,000 slot library/silo with 10 tape drives might be partitioned in such a way that 800 slots and 7 drives are presented to the production environment backup server and 3 tape drives plus 200 slots are presented to a development/test backup server. In such a configuration, the host given access to the large library partition would not have any visibility over the smaller library partition and vice versa—to all intents and purposes, the individual partitions would be seen as entirely separate libraries.

Key reasons for library partitioning for many enterprises includes:

- *Security considerations*: demilitarized zone (DMZ) systems might be configured to use their own backup server, with internal system backups completely inaccessible in another partition.
- *Multiple backup products*: As environments grew and converged, a variety of departments using different backup products might pool resources and share

a single tape library via partitioning. Alternately, a new backup product might be deployed, with the old backup product requiring ongoing access to its media. As the migration progressed more resources could be allocated to the new product, reducing the retired product to minimum access for recoveries only.
- *Mixed library usage*: The workloads of HSM/archive and backup within a tape library are not necessarily complementary, so library partitioning could be used to ensure that sufficient resources were always available to both activities.
- *Mixed media usage*: Particularly when considering older versions, not all backup products have been tolerant to multiple media types within a single tape library. Library partitioning would allow a backup product with such a limitation to access all its media without concern it might try to load, say, an older DLT cartridge into a new LTO tape drive.

For the most part, library partitioning works via the notion of a *control* host for the tape library. When partitioning is performed, no one server using the tape library can have exclusive access to the robot head(s) nor are products designed to service tape load requests for other products (regardless of whether they come from the same vendor or another). In such situations, accessing hosts submit load/unload requests to a library control host, which is the only system with direct access to the robot heads. This host maps the partitioned load/unload request to the physical tape library configuration, performs the operation, and then advises the requesting product that it has been performed.

While library partitioning is now quite a common feature even in relatively small tape libraries, where there are fewer robot arms to service tape movement request than there are partitions (a common enough scenario, since only the largest silos tend to feature more than one robot arm for tape movement), the load and unload times for tapes can be greatly increased—systems can wait several minutes for a robot arm to finish a previous operation for another logical partition before it starts the requested operation. This can require additional consideration on library operation timeouts within software that is accessing the partition.

19.3.8 Physical Media Management

After a tape has been used comes the task of properly storing it and retrieving it when it needs to be accessed again. Tape media and pools will often be written either for designated on-site or off-site retention—the idea being that a copy of each backup resides somewhere other than the datacenter for the duration of its lifetime, and a copy resides either in or *near* the datacenter (e.g., in the same building) for "rapid" day to day operational access.

Multisite businesses may choose to store their off-site copy in alternate datacenters, while other businesses may prefer to use a third-party tape storage and retrieval company. Sending media off-site requires as understanding of the environmental and storage processes, for instance:

- Is the media shipped in sealed boxes or satchels preventing outside humidity or other adverse weather conditions to affect it?
- Is the media tracked individually (e.g., by barcode), or by satchel/box?
- If media is tracked by satchel or box, can it be recalled individually? (If not, it usually requires the business to perform its own mapping between box numbers and contained barcodes/labels.)
- When using a third-party off-site storage provider, is the provider insured, use audited processes, and has appropriate security and document retention credentials?

Since tape media represents a relatively portable copy of production data, strong physical security must be applied to it as well. Businesses with compliance requirements are now required to encrypt data sent to tape and store them securely—either in locked safes or vaults when on-site and not in a library, or with reputable and certified storage companies when off-site.

19.4 Decline of Tape

Tape is still used in many organizations, but many of the use cases, particularly for "average" enterprises, have substantially declined over the past decade or more. In this section, we will discuss where and why tape use cases have been supplanted, and the technology that has replaced them.

While tapes have substantially increased their capacity over the years, so too has their performance, and performance *requirements*. LTO-8, released late 2017, has a native transfer rate of 360 or 900 MB/s based on rated compression ratios. This is like having a jet car on rails: it can go *really* fast, but it can't brake easily, nor can it turn left or right. As the performance of tape scales up, the potential advantages offered by its increased capacity are limited by the streaming performance requirements, reducing its practicality for particular workloads or data set sizes.

Despite the LTO consortium having been formed to prevent the stifling of tape innovation, the road has recently proven to be rocky. LTO-8 has broken convention previously followed within the LTO specification: it was intended that an LTO-*x* drive would be able to write to LTO-*x-1* media, and read from LTO-*x-2* media, but LTO-8 can only read from LTO-7 as part of a technology shift. Of perhaps greater concern was a supply issue caused by patent infringement lawsuits between LTO media suppliers:

> A courtroom showdown over a patent infringement allegation that Fujifilm brought against Sony is crippling supply of LTO-8 tape media stateside and further afield, and a resolution doesn't appear to be imminent.[*]

It was later reported[†] in August 2019 that the lawsuit was resolved, but not before several months had passed where LTO media supplies were constrained in several countries.

19.4.1 HSM and Archive

Consider a standard tape read operation. It will consist of the following activities:

- Load tape
- Seek to location on tape containing the data required
- Read data required
- Rewind tape
- Eject tape

Each of these activities takes tangible periods of time. Even the fastest tape systems typically require 3–5 seconds to load a tape, and *average* tape systems require quite a few more seconds than that. (For example, one vendor[‡] quotes a 7 second load/unload time for its LTO-4 tape drives, and 17 second load/unload time for its LTO-5 tape drives.)

If we assume even just a 60 second seek time for the required data on tape, 5 seconds to read the data required, and then 65 seconds to rewind from that end position, a single access of HSM/archive LTO-5 tape could take as long as 164 seconds to 2.7 minutes.

It is these slow access times that have vastly reduced the use of tape in HSM/archive situations—particularly beyond mainframe use cases. As users and organizations have grown to expect fast access times, a delay of multiple minutes to retrieve data is more likely to have the access request cancelled due to impatience than to actually be completed.

---

[*] LTO-8 tape media patent lawsuit cripples supply as Sony and Fujifilm face off in court, Chris Mellor, 31 May 2019, *The Register*, www.theregister.co.uk/2019/05/31/lto_patent_case_hits_lto8_supply/

[†] Sony, Fujifilm storage patent lawsuit is all taped up: Better LTO-8 than never, right? Chris Mellor, 6 August 2019, *The Register*, www.theregister.co.uk/2019/08/06/sony_fujifilm_storage_patent_lawsuit_settled/

[‡] www.overlandstorage.com/PDFs/LTO_Tape_Media_DS.pdf

Comparing this to HSM/archive stored on lower-speed large-capacity disks, the worst-case access times are likely to be in seconds rather than minutes, and average requests more likely to still be serviced in times of 5 seconds or less, depending on the size of the data being read.

However, disk introduced another efficiency that tape could not match—single instancing and deduplication. Single instancing refers to saving only one copy of any archived data* and works on a similar principle to deduplication, but typically at the file or object level.

Regardless of whether single instancing or deduplication (or both) are used within an archive system, this dramatically decreases the cost of disk compared to tape for storage. Such techniques allow disk systems to hold considerably more than their "raw" capacity with negligible performance impact for data read situations—especially compared to tape access speeds.

(Deduplication in particular is meaningless if tape is being used as the storage medium—read from deduplicated storage consists of many random IOs to reconstruct the data, and such a read from tape would take too long to be of any practical value for a business. Indeed, products that support writing deduplicated data to tape require a large amount of that data to be "staged" back into disk storage to facilitate data access if requested.)

19.4.2 Backup and Recovery

19.4.2.1 Disk-to-Disk-to-Tape

As disk storage became increasingly cheaper, many enterprises started developing disk-to-disk-to-tape backup (D2D2T) solutions. The "disk-to-disk-to-tape" referred to transferring backups from backup client disks to backup server disks and then on to tape. This would allow overnight backups to be written to disk storage on the backup server and/or storage nodes/media servers, and then be "staged" out to tape during the day when backups weren't running.

This had several advantages:

- Tape drive failures would not immediately impact the backup process.
- Shoe-shining during the backup process was eliminated.
- Transfer to tape could happen faster without shoe-shining by being a single sequential read from disk to SCSI or fiberchannel (FC) attached tape on the same host.
- Recoveries executed from backups still on disk were fast.

While initially disk staging areas were often designed to hold only 1 or 2 days' worth of backups, many enterprises found the benefits of being able to service short-term recovery requests from fast-start storage extremely compelling, particularly as environments grew. As such, companies started looking to increase their disk backup environments from relatively small staging areas to larger buckets capable of holding up to and including their smallest backup cycle (e.g., 1 week).

19.4.2.2 Disk-to-Disk-to-Disk

As the recovery utility benefits of keeping backups on disk grew and further influenced backup architecture decisions within organizations, some enterprises began experimenting with completely eliminating tape from their environments, thus disk-to-disk-to-tape became disk-to-disk-to-disk, since the fundamental requirement of ensuring all backups have at least two copies remains regardless of the technology used. (This was sought for reliability as well as cost reduction through elimination of all the manual handling associated with tape.)

Eliminating tape for most organizations is achieved through use of deduplication technology, discussed in detail in Chapter 13. Multiple backups are accommodated on tape by increasing the number of units of media used within the system, but it is not economically feasible to simply continue to write the same data again and again to disk storage, infinitely expanding that disk storage to accommodate the data. That is, disk-to-disk-to-disk requires using disk backup targets intelligently rather than being a like-for-like tape replacement.

As disk targets for backup became more pervasive within businesses, more advanced backup techniques have further driven tape out of backup infrastructure. The SAN infrastructure required to share tape drives out to multiple hosts is expensive and scales poorly, with the number of tape drives always acting as a limiting factor. Intelligent and integrated backup appliances with IP connectivity and client-agents allow for *massively* distributed backup environments, significantly reducing the overall cost of backup services infrastructure by reducing or even entirely eliminating storage nodes/media servers.[†]

At minimum, enterprises will deploy disk-to-disk-to-disk backup solutions with the express intent of cutting tape out of the backup cycle for all but the longest retention backups. For instance, an organization that performs daily incrementals with weekly and monthly fulls, keeping the daily/weekly backups for 6 weeks and the monthlies for 7 years, will typically design a disk-"only" backup solution to ensure

---

* Not including any RAID/storage redundancy.

† Consider that in either tape-based or dumb-disk-based backup environments, storage nodes/media servers are typically high-end servers designed for pushing large amounts of aggregated data through as fast as possible. Such systems often have multiple CPUs, fast backplanes, expensive IO cards, and multiple high-speed network connections.

all daily/weekly backups exist *only* on disk, with only the longer-retention monthly backups *eventually* pushed out to tape. For some businesses, even this has not been a sufficient elimination of tape and they have made use of additional deduplication/compression technology in PBBAs/IDPAs to keep all backups, regardless of their retention time, on disk.

19.4.2.3 Disk-to-Disk-to-Cloud

As discussed in more detail in Chapter 14, we're increasingly seeing a shift to operational expenditure (OpEx) over capital expenditure (CapEx) spending. "Pay as you go" and "pay for what you use" is dominating in an economic landscape where every department in almost every business is required to minimize the amount spent at any given time. Thus, a single up-front purchase of data protection storage requirements for, say, 3 years may be more difficult to arrange for many businesses (particularly in the commercial rather than the enterprise space) than 36 months of operational expenditure, even if the total operational expenditure exceeds the 3-year capital expenditure.

The shrinking cost of cloud storage and increasing bandwidth of internet connectivity is providing these businesses a new avenue of eliminating tape from their environments and we are seeing the start of the disk-to-disk-to-cloud backup strategy. These configurations see short-term retention backups kept on local disk, with longer-term retention backups pushed out to low-cost cloud storage, usually with some form of deduplication involved to reduce the overall cloud storage spend. (Such strategies are based on the economics of a limited number of recoveries from long-term backups* and the generally accepted lower SLA for such recoveries.)

19.5 Do Unmanaged Tapes Provide Protection?

Consider the release dates of common tape formats, as shown in Table 19.1.

If we consider a 7-year retention time in 2016, there is a vast potential for legacy tape formats to still hold data a business is legally required to keep. Counting back from 2016, a business that has updated its tape drives on every new release will have potentially used a large number of tape formats during that time period. Further, tape that is not actively being read is not being checked. While a backup product

may very well be maintained for 7, 10, or 15 years or more within an organization, the number of tape formats that could be cycled through during that period may very well be extensive.

True media management is rarely practiced in organizations. Tapes, once generated, are sent off-site and retrieved *if and only if* a request is made to recover data from them. This isn't real media management.

For organizations using tape, *true* media management must comprise *at least* the following activities:

■ *Migrating all data on old format tapes to new format tapes*: While LTO-*x* guarantees being able to write LTO-*x-1* and *read* LTO-*x-2*, it doesn't read older formats. Before tape drives that read these old formats are decommissioned, the tapes *must* be migrated.†
■ *Periodic recall and testing*: True purpose-built backup appliances will have a rigorous and ongoing consistency check process, performing regular validation of all data written to them *and* avoiding the chance for filesystem corruption (e.g., by only ever deleting or writing new data, never appending to existing data). Tapes sitting on shelves or in storage are *not* being checked, and so must be periodically tested.
■ *Safe storage and transport*: Tapes are actually somewhat delicate, *and* they're also highly portable. *Without correct care and attention*:
■ Tapes have been physically stolen or lost.
■ Tapes have been stored in environments that don't offer suitable temperature and humidity protection.
■ Tapes have been transported so haphazardly as to render them unusable.

If a business *is* going to use tape for data protection, it *must* institute a rigorous, comprehensive tape management regime, or else data protection is just a "check in the box"—premised on luck, designed on false economies, and run by laziness.

Unmanaged tapes do not offer real data protection at all.

19.6 Is Tape a Ransomware Shield?

Proponents of tape will sometimes reference its offline nature as the perfect defense against a destructive ransomware attack. A tape which resides in an off-site storage location can hardly be deleted or encrypted by ransomware, after all.

---

* It is worth noting that as longer-term retention backups become easier and faster to access (something not usually afforded with tape), the chances of more recovery requests being executed against those backups can increase. When calculating the potential costs of retrieval from public cloud, businesses should always assume a higher number of recoveries than might be currently serviced from tape.

† It is not uncommon at all to hear of long-term recovery processes including "buy a second hand tape drive online."

Table 19.1   Release Years of Common Tape Formats

	DLT-IV	LTO-1	LTO-2	LTO-3	LTO-4	LTO-5	LTO-6	LTO-7	LTO-8
Year	1994	2000	2003	2005	2007	2010	2013	2015	2017

There is some truth to this: an offline tape is far less likely to be struck by ransomware than the D:\drive of a Windows server with online, disk-based backups.

Ransomware and other associated types of malware (not to mention hactivism) are evolving, however. It would seem likely that it will only be a matter of time before variants of malware deliberately look for tape drives attached to systems they're infecting, and write random data to any detected tapes in order to increase the likelihood of someone needing to pay a ransom. If this seems unlikely, remember that in 2019 security researchers released details of *tested-in-the-field* malware designed to infect medical imaging systems and add or remove cancerous tumors that were practically impossible to detect by radiologists.* (By comparison, detection of SCSI or fiber-channel connected tape drives seems trivial.)

One might suggest that the erasure of last night's backup tape is not so much of an issue if the previous night's backup is safely offline, and this would, compared to the average impact of a serious ransomware attack be a minor inconvenience.

There are several points that are worth considering on this topic, however:

1. Security protocols on backup servers are often lax.
2. Backup servers do not have to be conventional operating systems.
3. Not all disk backup targets are accessible by conventional servers.
4. Is tape an efficient mass-recovery mechanism?

It is true that there have been several ransomware events where a business has said that the ransomware also attacked their backup server, deleting or encrypting backups. It is an unfortunate fact that in many organizations (particularly ones with less compliance requirements), the security of the backup server is often lax, with security protocols more in line with non-critical development or test servers rather than mission critical servers. Yet, it is arguable that *given* what backup servers do and *given* the types of data that backup servers process, the security assigned to a backup server should be as tight as the security assigned to the most mission critical systems within the business.

Yet at some point, security fails. New versions of ransomware are released regularly, and virus scanners cannot hold all the signatures of all viruses ever released, so it's entirely conceivable that some form of malware might eventually make its way to a backup server.

One might then ask: what is the point of having a backup server on a conventional server at all? In earlier days, backup servers were often repurposed servers, or multi-function servers (e.g., backup and print services), or even just spare PCs. As time went by it became more likely to see dedicated backup servers, but now there are a plethora of backup *appliances* that can be deployed—it's still a server underneath, but it's locked down and rather than being a general-purpose system, it's entirely dedicated: installing third-party software for instance may not be supported at all. Backup appliances provide an additional layer of protection over general-access operating systems. Of course, it's not to say that they are without risk, but a hardened backup appliance is still likely to present fewer attack surfaces than a general-access server installation.

While backup-to-disk storage that is presented as locally attached storage, or network mounted (e.g., NFS or CIFS/SMB†) is vulnerable to ransomware, it is not true that *all* backup-to-disk storage is presented this way. For example, the "Boost" protocol used by Dell EMC Data Domain systems establishes network connectivity between individual clients and the protection storage, but the backup target is not mounted onto the source systems (or backup server), and is therefore not visible to the operating system or third-party applications. Further, a variety of backup-to-disk targets support various forms of *retention lock*—compliance storage options that allow data to be "locked" for a specific retention period once written, preventing deletion of overwrite. (This has led to *cyber-recovery systems* as a means of dealing with ransomware and hactivism, which will be discussed in greater detail in Chapter 24.)

Let's say tape has been used as an offline backup storage platform to protect against cyber-attacks such as ransomware. While tape usually has no problem with single systems restoration, ransomware events often lead to the need to recover many systems within the organization. Yet,

---

* Hospital viruses: Fake cancerous nodes in CT scans, created by malware, trick radiologists, Kim Zetter, 3 April 2019, *Washington Post*, www.washingtonpost.com/technology/2019/04/03/hospital-viruses-fake-cancerous-nodes-ct-scans-created-by-malware-trick-radiologists/

† e.g. Network file share (NFS) or common internet file system (CIFS)/server message block (SMB).

you can only have one tape loaded at a time within a tape drive for recovery purposes, so the recovery speed for the organization is directly impacted by the number of tape drives available to use to read from. Certainly, disk-based backup targets will have limits on the overall throughput they can achieve for recoveries, but so long as this is engineered correctly, it will likely pose less of a challenge than being able to say, only run 4 recoveries at any one time (e.g., if the business only has 4 tape drives). We must remember here that with increased capacity and throughput on modern tape generations (e.g., LTO-7 and LTO-8), businesses have often scaled back the number of tape drives used for backups: whereas once a medium-sized business might have used 700- or 1,000-slot tape libraries with eight or more tape drives in the days of LTO-1 or LTO-2, a 3-drive LTO-8 system with 40 slots might be deemed sufficient for regular operations during a refresh. Consider too that in the event of a destructive ransomware attack, the backup server will likely need rebuilding and its index/catalog found and restored. If multiple tapes must be scanned through to find this information, that could potentially add *days* to the initial recovery time. (Time-to-start, and limited number of concurrent operations might very well lead to situations where businesses believe it is "faster" to pay the ransom than perform recoveries.)

It is inarguably the case that an off-site, unmounted tape will be shielded from the immediate impact of a ransomware attack—but what *is* arguable is to what extent such tapes can be used to provide an effective recovery mechanism for businesses that have been impacted by ransomware. The answer for any particular company might be considered to lay in the following questions:

1. Do you feel that recover-from-tape is a sufficient disaster recovery protocol for the business?
2. How long would it take to recover 20% of business data from tape?
3. How long would it take to recover 50% of business data from tape?
4. How long would it take to recover 100% of business data from tape?

If, and only if all of these questions can be answered in a way that ensures the business can still meet compliance and service requirements might tape be considered an adequate ransomware shield for the business.

19.7 Legal Challenges for Tape

A key selling point in tape, as noted in the previous section, is that tape is a fully *offline* copy. Yet, to what extent

does that *offline* nature of tape potentially expose a business to risk?

First, consider that while backup tapes may be offline, they are also *mobile*, representing an increased data loss surface for a company to deal with:

The Commonwealth Bank has admitted a supplier lost two magnetic tapes in 2016 containing backup data on almost 20 million customers.

The loss, which was first reported by BuzzFeed News, is one of Australia's largest ever privacy lapses.

The bank said in a statement that the tapes "contained customer names, addresses, account numbers and transaction details from 2000 to early 2016."*

The population of Australia in 2016 was estimated at 24.21 million, and there were an estimated 2.2 million businesses operating in the country in that year—a potential 26.41 million customers overall. 19.5 million (an assumption based on *almost 20 million customers*), represented a significant number of customers—effectively, up to 73% of the combined population and businesses within the country were conceivably impacted by the loss of *two* backup tapes.

As an increasing number of legal jurisdictions (state, national, or multi-national) ramp up their efforts to ensure businesses either treat privacy and security seriously, or face commensurate consequences for the failure to do so, the easy mobility of tape does present tangible breach risk to companies. While this can be mitigated with tape encryption, a stolen or lost encrypted tape still represents a risk, and in many countries, a requirement to report a breach to authorities.

More so than the physical loss of backup media, tape can increasingly represent challenges for areas such as legal search, and demonstrable deletion. When a legal discovery operation is performed against disk-based backup media, the data can be scanned and comprehensively indexed without needing to recover the data to (presumably temporary) storage. Full content searches can be built and conducted against data without needing to perform bulk recalls. While in theory this *can* be done against tape, it is more likely to see companies that are required to perform regular legal discovery operations reserve large amounts of secondary tier storage for holding temporary data recoveries. Thus, legal teams might have all of the March 2019 NAS data recovered to a holding area to perform searches, then all of the April 2019 NAS data recovered, then all of the May 2019 NAS data

---

* CBA lost backup tapes with 20m customers' details, Ry Crozier, *3 May 2018, itNews Australia*, www.itnews.com.au/news/cba-lost-bac kup-tapes-with-20m-customers-details-490174

recovered, and so on, until the entire legal discovery period requested has been exhausted. The time difference between the two types of discovery operations is important because there may be limits imposed on the time allowed for a discovery process, without reference to the technical feasibility. It is also important to remember that not all discoveries originate from court orders: the European GDPR legislation for instance allows citizens to request details from businesses of the type and content of data held about them. When this data resides on tape, it is difficult to provide specifics without recalling and recovering data—on disk, it may be checked faster and more efficiently.

The often-contentious *right-to-be-forgotten* likewise poses challenges when tape is used as the backup medium. More often this process is achieved through deletes (or presumably where necessary, anonymization of details) against live data, and *data masking* during recovery processes. This data masking allows filters to be established to prevent the recovery of previously deleted data during a recovery process, though generally the level of integration with backup software is still evolving. That being said, one approach to data masking is through *live-mounting* backup data: accessing the backup copy as if it were a running instance (e.g., of a virtual machine, or database), and performing a copy operation that masks sensitive data. While some data masking software may work against tape, *live-mounting* is not something that can be done against tape—you cannot, for instance, boot a virtual machine from a tape backup. Businesses that are likely to be subject to *right-to-be-forgotten* are being strongly encouraged to look at backup media *other than* tape in order to meet their regulatory requirements.

19.8 Considerations When Migrating Away from Tape

While a large percentage of businesses make use of some disk backup services within their operations, there are still some businesses that are tape focused. It is therefore worth noting a few considerations to keep in mind when either evaluating a move away from tape, or going through with the transition.

19.8.1 Cost-per-GB

The cost-per-GB is likely to appear cheaper for tape—that is, at a quick glance, companies may believe that tape is a cheaper backup medium than disk targets that are under consideration. However, this almost invariably does not take into consideration such factors as the cost of management and migration between tape formats, and the cost-benefit improvements with deduplication. In particular it

is important not to compare the cost of tape to the cost of usable storage from a deduplication platform, but against the expected *logical* capacity. Even in situations where it appears tape is cheaper, remember that tape is more limited in terms of secondary use cases for data, too.

19.8.2 Disk-to-Disk-to-Tape Isn't Always an Efficient Start

"Sticking the toe in the water" is sometimes more expensive than diving in. A common approach is to consider an architecture where backups are performed to deduplication storage, but off-site and/or long-term retention copies are still written to tape. This can be more expensive than transitioning fully away from tape: you will still have all the tape management overheads from before, *and* there will be the challenges of say, rehydrating deduplicated backups to write to tape, or even having to recall backups from tape to disk before being able to do recoveries. (For instance, some recovery types, depending on the product, might *only* be supported when the backup resides on disk.)

Cost-effective backup-to-disk will be more than a staging area. Simply keeping the most recent 5-day backups for instance on disk before pushing backups out to tape can be an inefficient architecture. Deduplication for instance can provide excellent storage efficiency as the number of copies builds up. Retaining only a single copy on disk can destroy the cost-justification of it when deduplication is used, and when deduplication is not used, there may be little room for error (in terms of spare disk capacity) if a copy to tape fails at some point.

19.8.3 Removing Tape Can Remove Complexity

Backup configurations can be simplified. Since tapes don't allow for selective erasure of content, there are multiple architectural approaches that are required for using tape in backup configurations—most notably it is usually essential to ensure that all backups written to a single tape have the same retention period (e.g., not comingling daily and monthly backups), and all backups should be intended for the same location (e.g., not writing on-site and off-site backups to the same tape). This can lead to complex media pool configurations—all of which can increase the management complexity of a backup environment. Moving to disk represents a prime opportunity to revisit a backup configuration and simplify it. (For instance, all backups might be written to a single disk pool, regardless of retention time.)

Operations windows can be adjusted. You cannot simultaneously perform a recovery against a tape that you're currently writing a backup to. Disk-based solutions remove this limitation, which can result in a significant improvement on operational activities and windows—there is nothing stopping the business for instance from having development databases updated with copies from production backups while other backups are still running, for instance.

19.8.4 Disk Will Wait

One of the single most challenging aspects of using tape for backup is the performance implications of the backup data not streaming *fast enough* to tape in order to keep the drive and media streaming. As we've mentioned previously, modern tape drives use *drive stepping* to have a variety of optimal streaming speeds, but the simple fact remains that if you try to backup a remote or slow host where the data can't meet the minimum streaming speed of the tape drive, your backup performance and reliability will be negatively impacted.

Disk on the other hand is not affected by poorly streaming clients. If a host is connected over a 10 Mbit connection and can only send data at 1.25 MB/s, the disk target will have no problems writing data at 1.25 MB/s. A tape drive, on the other hand, will likely head into a shoe-shining situation and end up writing data at half that speed or even slower.

19.8.5 Disk Is Not a Silver Bullet

Disks can't handle infinite numbers of streams either. We usually limit the number of streams going to an individual tape to avoid writing it with too much multiplexing. Multiplexing is not so much an issue with disk, but we must remain mindful of the optimum number of concurrent read and write operations. Trying to run more concurrent streams than a backup-to-disk environment can sustain might result in backup failures, dropped recovery sessions, or abysmally slow operations while the drives are thrashed in an attempt to service all the active sessions concurrently.

19.8.6 Disk Is Online

Disk is online, and that comes with both benefits and risks. With disk backup it is more essential that you have replica copies, and, as we discussed in the ransomware section of this chapter, it becomes extremely important that you apply appropriate security and architectural design to disk backup systems to ensure they are not compromised. This is *by no means* impossible: it merely requires comprehensive consideration and evaluation of options. Techniques that see disk storage used without being mounted by the operating system can be particularly useful to prevent a backup system being compromised by ransomware, for example.

19.8.7 Deduplication Is Not Deduplication Is Not Deduplication

If evaluating the shift from tape to deduplication storage, it is important to keep in mind that deduplication is not a common standard. Each vendor implements deduplication differently, and sometimes even the same vendor will use different deduplication approaches depending on the product. (For example, deduplication algorithms used in primary storage will quite often differ from those used in protection storage systems.) A supplier offering 600 TB of storage with a 6:1 deduplication ratio is not necessarily cheaper than a supplier offering 200 TB of storage with a 30:1 deduplication ratio, even if the former has a lower price on the quote. (600 TB at 6:1 would allow storage of 3.6 PB of logical backups. 200TB of storage with a 30:1 deduplication ratio would allow storage of 6 PB of logical backups.)

Be sure if considering the switch from tape to deduplication storage that you have reviewed the architectural best practices for deduplication as it applies to protection storage, discussed in Chapter 13.

A sure-fire way to ensure an optimal choice is made when migrating from tape to disk, and disk deduplication technology, is to require considered costings or storage footprints and all assumptions. For instance:

■ Daily change rate assumed for each workload.
■ Annual or monthly growth rate assumed for each workload.
■ How many fulls, incrementals, and differentials are performed within the operational window.
■ What the retention size of the operational window is.
■ How long monthlies, yearlies, and other long-term retention backups will be retained for.
■ Where backups are to be migrated to alternate tiers of storage (e.g., object storage), what are the expected monthly consumption rates of that storage over the entire period of interest of the solution?
■ Where possible, you should have a mechanism for reviewing your actual change and growth rates—which comes back to standard capacity management best practices.

19.9 Summary

Tape is not dead. However, the prevalence of considerably cheaper disk storage at high capacities, highly dense storage efficiencies such as deduplication and the benefit of massively distributed backup systems via IDPAs are increasingly pushing tape out to fringe use cases within data protection.

Two key examples of where tape still has relevance within organizations are:

- *Long-term cold storage*: Agencies and businesses that must maintain geological, mapping, or health image data that is rarely if ever accessed *may* still find the economics of tape appealing.
- *Deduplicatability of data*: If data being backed up is already compressed, encrypted, or otherwise does not yield itself to deduplication, tape *can* represent a practical and efficient storage mechanism.

That being said, the ongoing evolution and utility benefits of disk storage for extending and enhancing a data protection environment, as well as the falling costs of cloud storage, will likely continue eroding tape use cases. It can certainly be argued, however, that we've well and truly reached the point where tape use in data protection is by exception rather than by rule.

19.10 Self-Reflection

When working with backup operations, what type of workloads might be *best* suited to tape compared to deduplication storage? What alternatives might be used instead of tape, even if deduplication storage is not an ideal fit?

Chapter 20

Converged Infrastructure

20.1 Introduction

The traditional approach to datacenter components has developed as a series of silos originating out of the individual groups responsible for service delivery. Network administrators procure and build networks, storage administrators procure and build storage systems, and system administrators procure and build hosts that access the storage and the networks. On top of all of this, application administrators, developers, and database administrators request resources and, once they get them, start doing the activities seen by the business. Outside of this, there can be larger business activities where the company assembles authorized personnel from a variety of areas who go off and procure their entire infrastructure stacks for transformative projects that must eventually be integrated into the broader IT environment.

It's almost the proverbial duck on the pond: it looks graceful and effortless (or unmoving and unhurried in particularly process-laden environments) above the water, but if you check under the waterline there's a lot of activity going on.

If we think of standard change and development processes within most enterprises, the start to finish process of allocating a host for a developer or database administrator can be quite a time-consuming one. First, a request is made for an IP address and DNS entry. Then, a request is made for the system as well as a storage request for that host. Assuming the host will be a virtual machine, the host must be provisioned, then the operating system built according to standard processes (unless it's included in the provisioned virtual machine via a template), the storage attached, and so on.

While there are merits to such a formal provisioning process, there are greater merits to being able to step through the process automatically and *quickly*, which is a considerable reason why cloud-based approaches to agility and automation have taken hold in many enterprises.

Converged infrastructure seeks to make this service provisioning and delivery process even faster and easier by tightly coupling network, storage, and compute so their delivery can *all* be automated and available in a self-service manner. This is not, however, something as simple as putting an IP switch, fiber-channel switch, servers, and SAN in the one rack and calling it "converged." An orchestration or management overlay needs to also be present to allow these components to be adroitly handled as a single logical function.

There are in fact two variants of converged infrastructure—converged and *hyper*converged. While there is still a degree of nebulosity for each term and overlap between the two, one generally accepted differentiation is the level of integration; *converged* is deemed to be loosely coupled components, perhaps even following a reference architecture and allowing a prospective business to achieve a degree of modularity in the component types (e.g., replacing storage systems). *Hyper*converged, on the other hand, is generally accepted to be far more tightly coupled through the entire technology layer, with the supplied system almost immediately ready for deployment from the moment it is installed in racks and powered up in the datacenter. Comparing to traditional approaches of infrastructure within the datacenter, the converged and hyperconverged market is about "buy" rather than "build."

Regardless of whether it is converged or hyperconverged, the business imperative of this type of infrastructure is simple: is it the role of IT staff to build infrastructure from the ground up, or build *services* on infrastructure? The old model—much like the "build your own PC" model—is premised on IT departments having sufficient time and resources and skills to build infrastructure. The new model is premised on IT departments providing rapid service creation and presentation to the business on top of modular, scale-out infrastructure ready for production use almost immediately after delivery.

Some will claim that there is a premium to pay for converged or hyperconverged systems, and indeed a dollar for dollar comparison between the cost of the complete infrastructure in its converged/hyperconverged form and the cost of the individual components may seem to back this claim up. Yet such a simple cost comparison fails to take into account all the intangibles in the entire process. Returning again to our analogy about building a PC versus buying one, think of the time and effort required in that build process: determining what parts are going to be compatible with one another, picking the specific parts for each component, and then assembling the entire unit. Compatibility in this sense doesn't just refer to *physical* compatibility, such as whether CPU X will plug into motherboard Y, but whether all the device drivers provided by all the hardware vendors used will not only be supported by the operating system you want to run, but also interoperate with one another without causing system issues. Conversely, someone buying a brand-new PC direct from the manufacturer *should* be confident that the various device drivers and hardware components will be compatible with one another. This is precisely the difference between traditional infrastructure builds and converged or hyperconverged infrastructure—the time taken from the initiation of the project to the point where the equipment is being productively used without fear or concern about compatibility issues. Someone needing to research and buy all the individual PC components and then build the system from the ground up, including OS and application install, will take considerably longer to reach *useful productivity* on the finished system than someone who purchases a complete unit, powers it on, and starts productively using it within, say, 10 minutes.

A complete review of converged infrastructure is outside of the scope of a book about data protection, but as you would well imagine, there *are* data protection implications of utilizing converged infrastructure within a modern IT environment, and this chapter will briefly review those considerations. For the purposes of our discussion, we will consider converged and hyperconverged interchangeably.

20.2 Protecting Converged Systems

Converged infrastructure is almost invariably aligned to 100% virtualization—that is, typically all of the business-consumable systems provided by a converged infrastructure environment are virtualized hosts. The nature of converged infrastructure also tends to result in reasonably *dense* virtualized environments in relation to the rack-space occupied by the physical systems. While converged infrastructure does allow for some level of non-virtualized compute resources ("bare metal"), this is the exception rather than the rule. Hyperconverged, on the other hand, will be 100% virtualized.

The data protection considerations for converged infrastructure will be the same as those used for conventional infrastructure. Storage will still need some form of data storage protection, systems requiring high or continuous availability will require protection from storage system failure, and there will still need to be options for data recoverability in the event of loss.

When deploying converged infrastructure, a key question the business must ask is: "Does the converged infrastructure come with its own data protection solution?"* If the infrastructure *does* come with its own data protection solution, this yields further questions for the business, notably:

■ Is the data protection solution one that allows physical separation of protection data copies and the original data?
■ Are the data protection options available in the in-built solution immutable, or can they be grown and/or changed in response to changing business requirements?
■ Does the company already have a data protection solution?
  – If so:
    • How will management of the two solutions be handled or merged?
    • How will monitoring, reporting, and trending be achieved across the two solutions?
  – If not:
    • Will the protection solution provided within the converged infrastructure be able to provide data protection services for the rest of the business?

If the converged infrastructure is being procured without a complete data protection stack, then the company has to evaluate how to use or extend its existing data protection services to cover the converged infrastructure.

It's fair to say that none of these are new questions: arguably exactly the same total project-life data protection questions asked of any infrastructure must also be asked of converged infrastructure. The list of considerations for a single server relating *just* to backup and recovery outlined in Section 5.3 applies regardless of whether a single server or a thousand servers are being deployed. Even at its most basic, converged infrastructure will very likely deploy a number of servers capable of running a much larger number of virtual machines, and at the extreme end using rack-scale hyperconverged infrastructure may see the deployment of hundreds or thousands of physical nodes capable of running tens of

---

* Ideally a true converged infrastructure, and even more so a true *hyper*converged infrastructure, will have a fully integrated and compatible data protection strategy built into it from the ground up.

thousands of virtual machines. Quite simply: converged infrastructure makes the notion of "dumb luck" serving as a data protection design rule impossible.

20.3 Protection Compatibility

In our virtualization chapter, we noted that there are a variety of ways backup systems might connect to virtualization systems in order to protect them, including:

- Shared SAN access
- Hypervisor agents
- Virtualized proxies
- Simple network transfers

Especially when moving to hyperconverged platforms, the underlying storage will often change from a traditional infrastructure. While a converged platform might still feature a SAN or NAS to provide the underlying storage, hyperconverged systems might instead make use of fully software-defined storage approaches. If the business has traditionally used physical proxies with shared SAN-level access to virtual machine datastores, such an approach will likely not work within a hyperconverged environment at all—requiring a reappraisal of backup and recovery operations.

20.4 What Will Be Protected? (Redux)

In Chapter 8, the question "What will be protected?" was posed. It's very easy to become complacent in IT and think of data protection as only needing to be performed against primary data storage components—servers, SAN systems, and NAS systems, for example. Yet there is a wealth of other systems within your environment that houses data that should be protected—for example, IP switches, SAN switches, and PABX systems. In converged infrastructure, much of this configuration data is hidden from the individual hosts being presented. A set of hyperconverged nodes, for instance, offering a virtualization environment can host a virtual machine that performs backups of all hosted systems, replicating those backups to an offsite location, but what is protecting the hyperconverged data? Is it sufficient to have a multi-node cluster to protect that data, or does the infrastructure management layer of the system require appropriate levels of data protection to mitigate site loss or extreme corruption situations? What guarantees are provided by the converged or hyperconverged vendor that the management systems contained therein are protected—particularly if they are not accessible to customer-deployed data protection services?

Converged and hyperconverged systems can make deployment and management of data protection systems as easy as they make deployment and management of primary production systems, but data protection considerations must be broader than the virtualized infrastructure provided by the said systems. All data points within the infrastructure should support appropriate levels of dump and restore functionality, or be appropriately protected via clustering (local and multisite) and self-healing/self-building capabilities: IP networking, SAN networking, hypervisor management, and orchestration layer databases.

20.5 Converged Staff

As mentioned in Section 4.2.4, the increasing complexity involved in ensuring comprehensive data protection policies are developed and implemented creates a need for *infrastructure administrators*.

Converged infrastructure reinforces this need: trying to keep to traditional, formal deployment processes requiring manual requests and manual intervention at every step along the way completely eliminates the advantages of infrastructure convergence. The management and orchestration layer required for true converged infrastructure allows (or, indeed, *requires*) administrators to become policy coordinators and architects, with the infrastructure's control system handling the mundane, day to day implementation services.

In traditional IT delivery models, there is a reasonable amount of time assigned to each individual group of administrators (virtual, storage, system, application, and database) to contemplate and perhaps even discuss the data protection requirements for a project or service. With converged infrastructure, there is *no* time during the implementation; the data protection options must be baked into the service catalog offerings or they will not be delivered. Properly implemented, the orchestration layer and self-service portals for converged infrastructure will allow subscribers (e.g., developers or technical project managers) to requisition and receive access to their systems within minutes, with no human intervention on the infrastructure side. Data protection will either be performed automatically based on other selections made by the user (or perhaps even the user's profile) *or* will come from a limited set of options available to the user during service provisioning.

Thus, the importance of having broad infrastructure administrators cannot be overstated when using converged infrastructure. The data protection policies made available must be built alongside the rest of the service catalog and be aligned to business requirements. Only administrators and architects who are across all aspects of the converged infrastructure will be able to ensure the service catalog as implemented will maximize data protection capabilities.

20.6 Summary

Once implemented, there's little difference between the data protection requirements for converged or even hyperconverged infrastructure and classic IT infrastructure. Regardless of whether systems are deployed through automated methods or a more traditional, manual approach, systems must be kept available, data must be replicated, snapshots must be generated, and backup and recovery policies must be configured based on the requirements of the business and the type of data, not the infrastructure being used to host it.

In fact, there are usually only two differences between converged/hyperconverged infrastructure and traditional infrastructure when it comes to data protection: scale and automation. As we saw in Chapter 4, the technology used plays only a small part in the successful delivery of a holistic data protection strategy within a business, and this remains the case with converged infrastructure. If anything, converged and hyperconverged infrastructure serves to demonstrate the criticality of planning, processes, and automation in data protection at scale.

Chapter 21

Data Protection Service Catalogs

21.1 Introduction

For a complete understanding of service catalogs, readers are advised to study appropriate disciplines, such as ITIL v3. Completely explaining the entire service catalog approach to business IT systems is beyond the scope of this book, but it is worth understanding some of the critical components of working with service catalogs and data protection.

For many businesses, particularly the small office through to medium enterprise, there has traditionally been a substantial gulf between that which is desirable and that which is achievable for IT systems. This has gradually eroded as virtualization, XaaS, and cloud access have significantly expanded the options available even with relatively limited budgets. Ongoing increases to internet speeds have and undoubtedly will continue to enable greater options, particularly for those that leverage the cloud.

We would consider most businesses now to be reliant on IT (regardless of what form it takes) for operational success. A pharmaceutical company might consider drug manufacturing to be its key operational requirement, but the IT systems that hold and model research data, that control production lines, and that perform inventory, billing, and stock shipping, not to mention payroll and other personnel functions, are *all* significant contributors to the success (or failure) of the company.

While it's usual to consider the cloud model on the basis of user-driven provisioning and elasticity, additional components that are much desired by businesses include rapid turnaround and well-defined service models. At a broad level and focusing on the consumers of the cloud, we can say that there are two key aspects to cloud-like service delivery:

1. Automation
2. Service catalog

The automation is what allows someone to go to a web portal and request a new database server with a particular amount

of storage attached to it. At the back-end, the automation leverages virtualization, REST APIs, highly functional command lines, and DevOps-generated code that takes what used to be days or weeks of disparate provisioning and turns around the request within minutes for the user.

The service catalog becomes the curated menu of options for the consumers. As businesses seek cloud-like service levels within their own operations, a service catalog that clearly defines options available to consumers becomes an imperative—not just for the consumers, but for the teams that automate the process from end to end. Thus, as cloud continues to affect the business attitude toward and requirements of IT, so too will the importance of service catalogs in the business/IT relationship continue to grow.

21.2 Key Requirements for a Service Catalog

In order for a service catalog to actually be useful, it has to meet certain essential criteria. Arguably, the most important criteria (particularly when it comes to data protection) are:

- Utility
- Measurable
- Achievable
- Distinct
- Costed
- Priced
- Repeatable

21.2.1 Utility

There is no point providing a service catalog option that serves no meaningful function. Each service catalog option must be matched to either a business requirement (for internal service catalogs) or a saleable service (for *XaaS* providers). By ensuring all service catalog options have a purpose, we avoid building overly complex and confusing service catalogs.

21.2.2 Measurable

Service catalogs reflect a move toward formalized delivery of IT services, whether they are automated through some DevOps process or merely developed as templates for guaranteed consistency of service. In Chapter 2, we stated:

> If you can't measure something you can't improve it.

Likewise, if you can't measure something, you can't *prove* you're delivering the service the consumer is ordering from you. This can be deemed as critical for any of the following:

- Charging
- Costing
- Continuous improvement
- Monitoring
- Reporting

None of these can be accurately and effectively performed unless the delivery of the service option can be measured.

21.2.3 Achievable

Intimately similar to *service level agreements* (*SLAs*), service catalog options have to be realistically deliverable in terms of the technology, process, automation, and personnel available to the business. Service catalog options should not promise continuous storage availability if the environment can't cater for this; likewise, offering recovery from backup in a disaster to a secondary site in under an hour is meaningless if backups are still performed to tape and it takes 3 hours to ship tapes to the secondary site.

21.2.4 Distinct

Each service catalog option that is listed must effectively be unique. Making the same option available at multiple tiers simply confuses consumers, creates expectations of differing services, *and* likely antagonizes consumers if they could have been paying less for the same option.

From a simple design perspective though, having distinct service catalog options fulfills a basic tenet of IT design, that being

> The system should be as simple as possible, and no simpler.

By introducing nonunique service catalog items, we only serve to make the system more complex than it needs to

be—this in turn has the potential to affect automation, perceived value, utility, measurability, and deliverability. (This is not to say that all aspects of each service catalog tier should be unique. For example, replication might be offered for multiple service catalog tiers, with differentiating features being synchronous versus asynchronous, or more broadly, the lag time between source and target.)

21.2.5 Costed

The business should have an understanding of how much it costs to deliver this service item. This applies to both *XaaS* providers and to businesses offering service catalogs for internal consumption. For *XaaS* providers, the reason is obvious: it allows the business to subsequently *price* the option effectively and avoid scenarios where the cost to the business is higher than the price charged to consumers.

Even for businesses offering the service catalog only for internal consumption this is important, as it allows the business to accurately understand the utility cost of the service catalog, and provides a mechanism to prevent internal consumers from oversubscribing to the highest service catalog options simply because it's a selectable option. Some service catalog options will effectively *share* resources. It could very well be, for instance, that a backup service has both short-term (30 days) backups and longer-term (say, 2 years) written to the same protection storage. The system, and therefore the delivery costs, might be architected on the basis of 75% of subscribers choosing the 30-day retention model and only 25% of subscribers choosing the 2-year retention model. Understanding the cost to deliver a 30-day versus a 730-day retention allows better management of subscriber options and capacity growth.

21.2.6 Priced

In addition to understanding the cost to the business of delivering each service catalog option, the business should understand the price for subscribing to that service, particularly since the price inevitably includes meta-costs outside of IT controls, such as broader staffing considerations, overall business operational costs, etc.

Yet like for the *Costed* option, this applies as equally to the *XaaS* provider models as it does businesses offering service catalogs for internal consumption. For the *XaaS* model, the rationale is simple: the consumer is the customer, and the customer must pay to make use of the service.

For internal service catalog deliveries, there are two (potentially overlapping) reasons why a pricing structure might be developed. For businesses that engage in full cross charging, this might be the mechanism used by the IT department to not only recoup costs of service delivery but also partially fund research and development, or new initiatives. For those businesses that do not engage in cross charging, it is likely the pricing structure will at least match the costing structure to enable per-division or per-subscriber amortization of service provisioning costs.

21.2.7 Repeatable

Behind the service catalog should be appropriate layers of automation that ensure a selected task or option is consistently delivered. There should be no risk that an option selected by the consumer to say, deploy a "bronze protection virtual machine" might end up with different results depending on whether it's deployed on a Monday, Thursday, or Sunday, for instance. This means that once an option is developed and deployed into the service catalog, its execution should be an automated process that does not require human intervention. While service catalogs may go through revisions over time, the broad expectation is that unless there are substantive updates to the service catalog, there should be a consistently repeatable experience for the consumers of the catalog.

21.3 Service Catalog Tiers and Options

Service catalogs tend to be categorized by a few different common naming approaches. The two most common naming approaches are usually aligned to either numbered tiers or precious metals. Thus, options might be "Tier 1," "Tier 2," "Tier 3," and so on, or "platinum," "gold," "silver," and "bronze." There is no right or wrong approach, but the naming standard adopted should be kept consistent to maximize clarity (i.e., you should not have "platinum," "gold," "silver," "bronze," and "Tier 5"). Thus, if a business is concerned they'll need more than four tiers of options for any particular service type, it might be best to avoid using the precious metals naming approach. For the purposes of our discussion, however, we'll use the precious metals approach and stick to just three levels—platinum, gold, and silver.

A service catalog for data protection is not necessarily going to be as straightforward as defining options for "platinum," "gold," "silver," and "bronze," however, and it may not necessarily be the case that all platinum options are created equally, all gold options are created equally, and so on. A few different scenarios that might be leveraged in the classification of service catalog options are outlined next.

21.3.1 Service Catalog Based on Application Type

This strategy focuses on data protection options based on application type. The same service level name might be defined multiple times depending on what applications it is

available for, and the specifics of what is provided by the service level may change based on the suitability for the application. An example breakdown based on this strategy can be found in Table 21.1.

This allows for the presentation of a very simple and straightforward service catalog for data protection, but it does come at the cost of flexibility. What happens, for instance, if a database needs to be placed on continuously available storage (CAS) with 24×7 synchronous replication, *but* has lower performance requirements out of hours and could instead be backed up via a standard database module? In such a scenario, the platinum database service option would need to be used, and this would automatically use the more costly backup option where data is transferred direct from primary storage to data protection storage.

Another potential challenge created by this option is confusing what level of protection is provided *between* applications. Consider the platinum options, for instance: the platinum database option has synchronous replication to the secondary and tertiary site 24×7, whereas the platinum file server option has synchronous replication only to the secondary site, *and* the replication becomes asynchronous out of business hours. While it's perfectly reasonable for a business to require and provide higher service levels for mission critical databases versus file servers, consumers of the service who use *both* options might more readily confuse the service levels provided based on application type.

21.3.2 Service Catalog Independent of Application Type

This model offers the same level of protection irrespective of the application or business function calling for the option, and an example can be seen in Table 21.2.

While this model further simplifies the service catalog and allows subscribers or consumers to more easily choose what they want, it suffers a similar flaw to the previous option—what happens, for instance, if a consumer needs the more advanced storage availability or snapshot options, but doesn't need the more advanced backup options?

21.3.3 Service Catalog Options per Data Protection Activity

This model presents more data protection options for the consumer/subscriber, allowing a higher granularity in the options chosen, as shown in Table 21.3.

While this provides maximum granularity, it can lead to "option overload" to a subscriber—that is, it may be seen as being more complex because of the number of options it provides. There are additional considerations that must be taken into account with this type of service catalog however.

Table 21.1 Data Protection Service Catalog by Application Type

Service Level	Application	Provides
Platinum	Database server	• Continuous storage availability • Synchronous replication of storage systems to secondary and tertiary site • Application-aware snapshots taken every 15 minutes • Snapshots replicated to secondary and tertiary sites • Nightly full backups via direct primary storage to protection storage module
Platinum	File server	• Continuous storage availability • Synchronous replication of storage systems to secondary site during business hours; asynchronous replication with a lag of up to 30 minutes permitted outside of business hours • Snapshots taken every 30 minutes under the backup application and replicated automatically to the secondary site • Snapshots "rolled over" into data protection storage as a backup at midday and midnight
Gold	Database server	• Continuous storage availability • Synchronous replication to secondary site during business hours; asynchronous replication with up to a 15-minute lag permitted out of business hours • Hourly snapshots with replication to secondary site, managed by backup application • Nightly full backups to data protection storage via database module provided by backup software
Gold	File server	• Continuous storage availability • Asynchronous replication to secondary site with no more than a 30-minute lag permitted at any point • Hourly snapshots with replication to secondary site, managed by backup application • 10pm snapshot "rolled over" as the backup into data protection storage each day
Silver	Database server	• Traditional SAN storage • Application journaling and log transport used to keep copy on secondary site up to date asynchronously • Daily snapshots managed by the SAN • Nightly full backups to data protection storage via database module
Silver	File server	• Traditional NAS • Six snapshots generated per day (4-hourly) by storage system policies • Nightly NDMP backups to data protection storage

First, when each service catalog item refers to a single piece of data protection functionality, it is easier for there to be options that are the same for different *levels*. For instance, in Table 21.3 the gold data storage option is listed as "not available (choose platinum or silver)" for the reason that—comparing to previous service catalog examples given—the gold option may be the *same* as the platinum, in this case both would refer to CAS.

This can become less of an issue when a data protection service catalog is also tied to the data storage services as a broader consideration. This might result, for instance, in offerings of

■ Platinum data storage:
  – *Storage tier*: SSD

  – *Storage protection*: continuously available storage
■ Gold data storage:
  – Storage tier: 10,000 RPM SAS, hot spot tiering to SSD (max 10%)
  – Storage protection: continuously available storage

Such offerings may be modified according to the expected technical capabilities of the potential subscriber. For the purposes of clarity, we cite actual storage types earlier; in an actual service catalog provided to subscribers, this might be simplified to state "high performance" and "standard performance" for storage speed, and so on.

Our second consideration with this service catalog is offering this level of granularity requires either careful decoupling of dependencies *between* data protection options

Table 21.2 Data Protection Service Catalog Independent of Application Type

Service Level	Provides
Platinum	• Continuously available storage • Synchronous replication between metro-connected datacenters • Asynchronous replication to tertiary disaster recovery datacenter in an alternate city, maximum half-hour lag • Half-hourly snapshots with replication snapshots between sites • Daily backups using the most appropriate high-performance/minimized impact option for the application or data type • Backups automatically replicated to secondary and tertiary site; backups for secondary and tertiary site kept for the same time as the production site copy
Gold	• Continuously available storage • Asynchronous replication between metro-connected datacenters, maximum half-hour lag • Asynchronous replication to tertiary disaster recovery datacenter in an alternate city, maximum 4-hour lag • Backups automatically replicated to secondary and tertiary site; backup copy at secondary site maintained for same length of time as production site copy; backup copy at tertiary site retained for 7 days only
Silver	• RAID-protected SAN or NAS depending on the data type (RAID-6 for filesystems, RAID-1/RAID-10 for production databases, RAID-6 for non-production databases) • Log shipping as replication between metro-connected datacenters for databases or asynchronous replication with up to 4 hours lag between metro-connected datacenters for file-based data • Daily backups using the most appropriate option for the application or data type • Backups automatically replicated to disaster recovery site only

or logical enforcement of available options to ensure dependencies are always subscribed to. Consider, for instance, a "platinum" backup option that performs backups direct from the primary storage system to the data protection storage system; this might be dependent on a type of primary storage system only available to subscribers of the platinum or gold data storage service catalog options. If a user chooses the platinum backup option but the "silver" data storage option, how would this be reconciled—would the system prevent the platinum backup option being available while the silver data storage option was selected, or would the user be silently "upgraded" (at no extra cost) to the platinum data storage option but not informed?

21.4 Retention Multiplier

For some forms of data protection (e.g., snapshots), it might be acceptable to have the retention time available to the data protection option locked to the service level required. For other forms of data protection, a business may find itself having to offer a variety of retention options for legal or compliance requirements, and this should be understood when working on data protection service catalogs.

Consider snapshots, for instance: if a platinum service level defines that snapshots will be taken every 15 minutes,

that would result in 96 snapshots being generated per day. A silver service level might define snapshots being taken every 8 hours, which would result in three snapshots per day. It might therefore be deemed reasonable to retain only 3 days of platinum snapshots (a total of 288) while retaining 30 days of silver snapshots (a total of 90). Given snapshots in particular can have a detrimental impact on primary storage performance if they're kept too long and the change rate becomes too high, this might be so architected into the solution that there are no variations available to the consumer.

When it comes to backup, it may not be possible or even appropriate to hard-code the retention time into a policy. Some mission critical applications may not require long-term retention of backups, while other applications or systems of lower importance may in fact require the longest retention. A mission critical database, for instance, may have older content automatically copied and/or archived to a data warehouse. As such, a relatively short retention period may be acceptable for backups of the mission critical database itself, while the data warehouse instead might require its less frequent backups (e.g., monthly or yearly) retained for many months, if not years.[*]

---

[*] As mentioned in Chapter 3, a more comprehensive data lifecycle policy should see data deleted if it is no longer required or archived if it has to be retained for an extremely long period of time. However, this is not necessarily well practiced, and many businesses will use backup and recovery software to achieve a simulacrum of archive functionality.

Table 21.3   Data Protection Service Catalog per Data Protection Activity

Service Level	Applies To	Provides
Platinum	Data storage	Continuously available storage
Platinum	Replication	Synchronous replication to secondary and tertiary site
Platinum	Snapshots	Snapshots taken every 15 minutes, snapshots replicated to secondary site, snapshots retained for 7 days
Platinum	Backups	Daily backups via primary storage direct to data protection storage *or* backup application managed snapshot rollover (depending on application applicability). Backups automatically replicated to secondary and tertiary site
Gold	Data storage	*Not available (choose platinum or silver)*
Gold	Replication	Asynchronous replication to secondary and tertiary site, maximum 15-minute lag
Gold	Snapshots	Snapshots taken hourly, snapshots replicated to secondary site. Snapshots retained for 5 days
Gold	Backups	Daily backups via appropriate module or agent, automatically replicated to secondary and tertiary site
Silver	Data storage	Standard SAN or NAS depending on application requirements. RAID-6 for file-based data, RAID-1 or RAID-10 for database data
Silver	Replication	Asynchronous replication to secondary site only, maximum 30-minute lag
Silver	Snapshots	Snapshots taken once per day, not replicated. Snapshots retained for 30 days
Silver	Backup	Daily backups via appropriate module or agent, automatically replicated to tertiary site only

Service providers offering backup and archive as part of an *XaaS* model may not be unduly concerned with any legal retention requirements. For such providers, there is no duty of care, for instance, to confirm that financial accounting data is retained for 7 years: it becomes the responsibility of the subscriber to the service (i.e., the actual legal owner of the data) to ensure the appropriate retention period is offered or the appropriate steps are taken to export/copy the data periodically to meet compliance retention requirements.

When a service catalog is being offered internally though as part of a hybrid or private cloud model or simply for streamlined service access, the line of responsibility is more difficult to draw. Is it the responsibility of the subscriber who is choosing options from the service catalog to confirm the correct retention requirements, will the business just perform the same type of retention per a traditional backup and recovery/archive model, or will the service catalog have retention offerings based on more easily understood options? (For instance, a subscriber might have to choose between whether the data being stored is financial, legal, life sciences, development, or temporary, and each data type has a back-end association with the most appropriate retention policy.)

Regardless of how it is approached, a business should be prepared to have some flexibility for subscribers regarding retention times applied when providing backup and recovery options in a data protection service catalog.

21.5 Including Service Level Agreements in Service Catalogs

Up until now, our focus on the service catalog has been on the level of overall protection provided—frequency of snapshots, level of replication, frequency of backups, etc. However, there's another critical aspect to consider in service catalogs—the SLAs associated with them. In fact, the SLAs effectively dominate the options provided in the service catalog; service offerings of synchronous replication imply a much higher requirement for fault tolerance than, say, asynchronous replication. As we've established throughout this book, a single form of data protection isn't actually enough though—synchronous *or* asynchronous replication will still happily replicate corrupt data, either immediately or with lag. SLAs relating to RPO and RTO in particular will therefore trigger the need to select appropriate forms of data protection at each layer. This might include synchronous replication to allow for automated failover of storage access in the event of an array fault, *and* continuous data protection to allow for application-consistent journaled rollback in the event of a data corruption incident, *and* of course, traditional backup and recovery as well.

Previously, it was desirable to individually consider the SLAs for every single system or business function deployed and customize each SLA precisely. However, the driving goal for agile and automated deployment of infrastructure and applications creates a compromise—the need for reasonably *generic* but sufficiently appropriate tiers of SLAs—again, tied to the *tiers* of actual service levels offered by the catalog.

As mentioned in Table 2.2, a requirement in the modern IT environment is to ensure SLAs are designed around *where* the service may be provisioned from. In Table 2.2, for instance, a gold RTO/RPO was established as dependent on data locality:

- Traditional/private cloud—1 hour
- Hybrid cloud—4 hours
- Public cloud—8 hours

While enterprises with larger budgets or agile businesses with few critical requirements may be able to accommodate the same SLAs regardless of data locality (the former through using like-for-like or similar-enough infrastructure both on premises and in the cloud for data protection, the latter through simply using the worst-case scenario SLA for *all* SLAs), many businesses will have to codify different SLAs depending on data and compute locality. In actual fact, this is merely an analogous extension to the existing requirements of building SLAs based on actual available budget and resources. (That is, a small business might *wish* to have an RPO and RTO of 5 minutes for all systems, but practically this may be unattainable. The "where is the service?" question is merely another consideration along the same lines.)

In businesses not requiring 24×7 services, an additional consideration may need to be made as to whether SLAs for RPO and RTO in particular are the same *inside* operational hours as they are *outside* operational hours. Using a service catalog, the alternate approach however may instead be to limit the highest service levels for rapid RTO and small RPOs to those systems that require 24×7 availability or access, though this would still require business agreement.

The business will also need to carefully define in the context of a service catalog whether SLAs or SLOs are being offered. An SLA defines a hard target that *must* be met, usually at risk of either an internal or external fine being imposed. A service level *objective*, on the other hand, is just that— a desirous option but one that is not necessarily enforced. When a service catalog mixes both SLAs and SLOs, it should be clearly outlined whether an offering is an agreement or an objective, and at no point should SLAs and SLOs be mixed in the *same* option.

21.6 Building a Data Protection Service Catalog

Almost every business will have a slightly different attitude toward service catalog options, and those attitudes will be formed on the basis of the business, its customers, its requirements, and its budget. What might barely be deemed a "silver" data protection option for a multinational enterprise could very easily be classified as "platinum" for a small to medium regional business.

Companies that are unfamiliar with building service catalogs should not shy away from adopting them for data protection. Instead, it can serve as an excellent entry point for formalizing options within the broader IT environment starting with an important yet relatively narrow focus (compared to the whole of IT). Successfully developing and implementing a service catalog for one IT discipline can help provide incentive for the business to expand the discipline to encompass all IT disciplines. (If approaching service catalogs for the first time, businesses are advised to work with consulting companies with experience in service catalog architecture and delivery in IT.)

Except in the smallest of businesses, it is rare for service catalogs to be built end to end by a single individual. Usually, it will be a collaborative project involving both IT and broader business staff. IT staff will include architects, subject matter experts, and the manager who will be responsible for the catalog. The number and type of business staff involved will very much depend on the type of organization and may include any combination of

- Legal counsel
- Financial controllers
- Sales managers
- Key business function managers or their representatives
- Project managers

Indeed, the service catalogs should be discussed in a technology-independent fashion between IT and the business; the business should not need to concern itself with the minutiae of the technology characteristics, but be able to describe availability and protection requirements—and receive service catalogs documented—in business-appropriate language: availability as a percentage, data retention requirements, maximum data loss, etc. It's only when we get to the back-end IT service catalog that the technical details of the service catalog offerings *should* be documented.

Traditionally for many companies, storage systems, virtualization systems, and backup and recovery systems often operate on reasonably different refresh cycles. It's not unusual, for instance, to see backup and recovery software and hardware come up for refresh while there are another 2 or 3 years on a storage system contract, or vice versa.

Ideally if *all* systems are being refreshed simultaneously, it becomes easier to build a complete service catalog based on the most modern options available, rather than, say, having to part-build the service catalog over a series of system refreshes.*

As mentioned previously, for a service catalog to be useful for an organization, each component must:

- Have utility
- Be measurable
- Be achievable
- Be distinct
- Be costed
- Be priced
- Be repeatable

While the technical details of data protection service catalogs will undoubtedly be populated by IT architects, managers, and specialists, the *requirements* for the service catalog ultimately must be provided by the broader business, and this will undoubtedly require negotiations with IT based on what can actually be provided, in the same way that the business and IT must be able to agree to practical limits and capabilities for simple SLAs. This is regardless of whether the service catalog is being developed for internal consumption or whether it will be offered by a *XaaS* provider. In either case, there's no point in offering service catalog options that aren't aligned to either what the business *needs* or what the business is comfortable *selling*.

There will always be *two* versions of a service catalog—the public or consumer-facing version and the business-internal version of the service catalog. Up until now, the service catalog options we've shown have been more representative of consumer-facing catalogs (though the examples have not included pricing). A full internal version of the service catalog provides a complete map to the business and the IT teams of what must be delivered and how much it will cost.

For instance, if we were to consider the platinum options only in Table 21.3, the *internal* details of those options might include details such as the following:

- *Data storage*:
  - *Provides* (*utility*): CAS
  - *Measurable*: 100% agreed uptime, storage allocated on CAS arrays only, monitored by storage reporting system
  - *Costed*: $X per GB per month

---

*This can be a compelling argument for converged and hyperconverged infrastructure: refresh everything at once, deploy highly integrated options, and develop data protection service offerings taking maximum advantage of the hardware/software convergence.

  - *Priced*: $X + y per GB per month
- *Replication*:
  - *Provides* (*utility*): Synchronous replication to secondary and tertiary site
  - *Measurable*: 100% up to date copies at primary, secondary, and tertiary sites, monitored by storage reporting system
  - *Costed*: $X per GB per month
  - *Priced*: $X + y per GB per month

(It could be noted that repeatable should simply qualify based on being demonstrably automated.)

One other factor for consideration is service catalog *versioning*. Almost everything that goes into a service catalog is subject to change—for example:

- Pricing for systems, power, networking, and staffing will fluctuate based on market conditions, conversion rates, and competition
- New technology and functionality becomes available
- Existing technology exits service life or becomes too expensive to maintain due to age
- Maintenance and support contracts may be altered during update cycles

(In more extreme cases, vendors or service providers might exit the market entirely or cease offering services that particular catalog items are designed around.)

Over time, any of these factors (and a variety of others) may cause the service catalog to be updated. Depending on the nature of the change, consumers may either need to have their service options automatically migrated (e.g., if new storage has been purchased and it has new functionality) or the business may need to maintain delivery capabilities for multiple versions of the service catalog until all consumers of previously available options have changed to other options, ceased using the service entirely, or been migrated following contracted period of access to the older options.

21.7 Summary

While there will often be some similarities between service catalogs from different companies, the process of developing a service catalog for data protection is almost entirely dependent on the specific resources (staffing and technical) available to each business, as well as the intended use (internal or external) of that service catalog.

There is a tendency in many IT departments to resist service catalogs due to their perceived formality and binding nature. Yet by formalizing the offerings available, they actually *free* an IT department to more easily provide, monitor, and maintain a well-defined set of services. Rather than every single service being treated and delivered as a wholly bespoke one, services delivered either automatically or via a set of clear templates speed up both provisioning and service delivery, *and* reduce the risk of human error. In the same way that *most* IT departments, particularly within larger enterprises, will have virtual machine templates for common operating systems, database servers, and particular application servers, a clearly defined and readily repeatable set of templates for all facets of data protection services is worth the effort required to develop in order to improve business functionality.

21.8 Self-Reflection

Think of the different systems you might use on a day to day basis. How might you establish standardized data protection service catalog offerings for those systems?

Important things to keep in mind include:

- Online (storage) versus offline (backup) options
- Tiers of service
- How you might measure the various attributes associated with those options (utility, measurable, costed, priced, etc.)

Chapter 22

Holistic Data Protection Strategies

22.1 Introduction

Up until now, we've mostly looked at each type of data protection option or strategy in isolation. While it's important to broadly understand each type of data protection that can be leveraged, implementing a single option is not sufficient for all but the most niche or esoteric of businesses.

As outlined in Section 1.5.3, data protection isn't just one single activity—it's a mix of proactive and reactive steps that you take—or might take—depending on the type of data you're trying to protect, its level of importance to the business, and your business requirements.

The types of data protection we've discussed thus far have included

- Continuous storage availability
- Replication
- Continuous data protection
- Snapshots
- Backup and recovery
- Data storage redundancy

It's fair to say that at-rest data storage redundancy (e.g., RAID, or object storage equivalence) will always feature as part of a complete data storage strategy, enabling data to survive the failure of at least the most fundamental part of the data storage platform, the drives themselves.

As previously shown in Figure 2.1, it's likely that data protection solutions will be both holistically combined and adapted as the data ages or changes priority. The example in Figure 2.1 showed:

- *Data less than 24 hours old*: Use fault tolerance, replication, snapshots
- *High priority active data*: Use fault tolerance, replication, snapshots, and backup

- *Lower priority active data*: Use fault tolerance, replication, backup
- *Long-term storage*: Use fault tolerance and backup
- *Archival storage*: Use fault tolerance and replication

In this chapter, we'll provide some examples of multi-layered data protection approaches based on specific environments. While these are specific examples, they will provide a common baseline to the decision processes and techniques that often go into planning holistic data protection strategies.

22.2 Examples of Holistic Data Protection Strategies

22.2.1 Large NAS Protection

One of the best examples of a multi-layered data protection approach comes from large NAS storage. These systems have always been large, but with the growth of scale-out storage fueling the prevalence of multi-petabyte systems, the data protection challenges posed by NAS are proving to be a common headache for many organizations.[*]

One of the simplest types of protection for NAS systems is to take snapshots of each filesystem, such as that shown in Figure 22.1.

Data protection requirements typically center around the requirements of Recovery Time Objective (RTO) and Recovery Point Objective (RPO). Remember that RTO refers to the maximum amount of time it can take to achieve system recovery, and RPO refers to the maximum amount of data loss that can be achieved. Additional considerations depending on the maturity of the business and the field in which it operates will include business continuity (and

---

[*] While this example is presented from the perspective of NAS storage, similar principles will apply for SAN storage protection options.

313

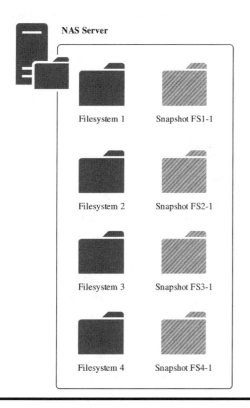

Figure 22.1 Single-level of protection for NAS by taking a snapshot.

specifically, disaster recoverability) and legal compliance requirements.

In response to filesystem corruption or data deletion, a single snapshot is likely to achieve excellent RTO, as the snapshot data can be made available almost instantaneously. The RPO however in such a situation is quite variable, depending on when the snapshot is performed. Therefore, it's more likely to see multiple snapshots performed for active filesystems over the course of a day, such as that shown in Figure 22.2.

The number of snapshots that can be taken per filesystem is usually independent, so the number of snapshots maintained and the regularity of which they are generated will be entirely dependent on the criticality of the data. Some filesystems might be snapped hourly, others even more frequently. Snapshot retention time becomes an important consideration here—unless data is almost entirely static, snapshots *can't* be kept forever. A typical approach is to have time-tiered snapshots offering different levels of retention based on how long ago the snapshot was taken. For example, snapshots might be configured with the following frequencies and retention:

- Hourly snapshots maintained for 24 hours
- Daily snapshots maintained for 7 days
- Weekly snapshots maintained for 14 days
- Monthly snapshots maintained for 3 months

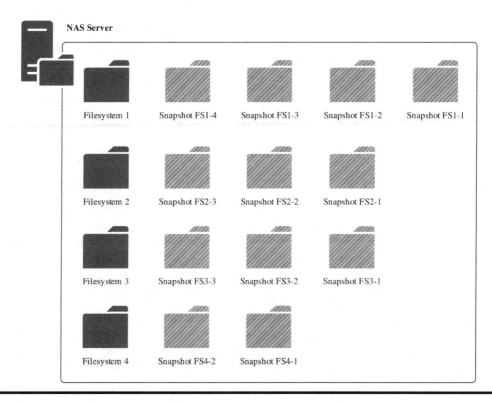

Figure 22.2 NAS system with multiple snapshots.

Typically in these situations the longer-term retention snapshots are designated instances of the more frequently performed snapshots. For instance, the daily snapshot above might simply be the hourly snapshot taken at 6pm, the weekly snapshot might be the Saturday daily snapshot, and the monthly might be the first weekly snapshot of a given month.

Retaining multiple snapshots allow us to address both typical RTO *and* RPO requirements. In the event of data loss or corruption at the filesystem level, the snapshot remains almost instantly available thanks to the nature of its design, and the frequency of the snapshots will conceivably be orchestrated to meet the RPO requirements of the business for the types and criticality of the data held on each NAS filesystem.

However, by their very nature the most common snapshots (CoFW and RoW) are dependent on the original source of the data they are protecting. While they will provide protection against, say, a file being deleted, or even intentional corruption of a filesystem, they offer no protection against catastrophic underlying storage failure—for example, three disks failing in a RAID-6 volume.

Alternately at this point, it might be tempting to consider standard backup services for the NAS server instead. Regular backups of NAS filesystems will offer *a* form of protection that standard snapshots can't, in that the backups are independent of the primary copy and thus can be used to recover the primary copy in the event of a failure.* However, they equally present limitations in large data environments unpalatable to most businesses, namely:

■ The time taken to complete a backup, depending on the size of the data set, may be quite large (most notably in comparison to the amount of time it takes for a snapshot to execute).
■ The time taken to *recover* from a backup may equally be quite large depending on the size of the data set.

Given the less frequent nature of backups (e.g., once a day), it's more usual to see them used for situations where we have an RPO of more than 24 hours, or purely as a disaster recovery option. If the business has data with an RPO measured in hours or even minutes, traditional backups are unlikely to meet these requirements. Equally, needing to stream back the entire backup (in the case of, say, filesystem corruption) may exceed both the RTO *and* RPO.

Each of these examples has effectively only utilized two layers of data protection—an underlying data storage protection (e.g., a RAID-6 LUN allocated per filesystem) and a single higher-level data protection option: snapshots or

---
* We would consider this to be "off-platform" protection, that is, protection that is completely decoupled from the platform the primary data resides on.

backups. For smaller organizations, or even larger businesses looking at protection for test/development systems, this *may* be sufficient. However, other businesses will not stop at this point and have additional RPO, RTO, compliance, or business continuity requirements.

A business that has basic requirements toward providing disaster recovery capabilities of their data might look toward layering snapshots *and* backups, such as that shown in Figure 22.3.

In such a configuration, short-term RTO and RPO requirements can be met by hourly snapshots of the individual NAS filesystems; longer-term RPO/RTO objectives could conceivably be met by the backup and recovery system, as could disaster recovery capabilities. Note that while daily backups have been indicated in the diagram, larger NAS systems might feature less frequent backups—e.g., weekly or monthly. This would usually be coupled with additional protection options outlined following.

We again however return to the specific limitations of each type of data protection here though. Snapshots executed frequently enough will provide excellent RTO and RPO, but are unable to defend against catastrophic storage loss. A backup and recovery system is unlikely to meet stringent RTO and RPO requirements, but offers a layer of protection divorced from the original storage platform and therefore more applicable in a disaster recovery situation.

This three-layer approach to data protection may still not yield sufficient levels of protection for a business depending on its operational needs or regulatory compliance requirements. In particular, so far we've not made any consideration toward the *location* of the data protection. Assuming a business has a requirement to have copies of their data provisioned in a secondary site for disaster recovery requirements, this *might* be met by backing up over a high speed inter-site connection such as dark fiber, effectively yielding a data protection solution such as that shown in Figure 22.4.

By sending backups to a secondary site, a business can both provide local short-term RPO and RTO options while still meeting a level of disaster recovery capabilities, and for some businesses or particular types of data even for larger businesses, this may be entirely sufficient for their requirements.

However, there will be some businesses—either bound by tighter RPO and RTO requirements regardless of whether where data is being accessed from or by compliance requirements where such an arrangement is insufficient. (In the event of a disaster, operational service restoration via a traditional recovery may be deemed to be too slow.)

Ultimately, a comprehensive data protection strategy for a large NAS server might resemble that shown in Figure 22.5.

In such a view, the NAS server is replicated between sites for rapid disaster recovery in the event of a site loss, and the snapshots too are replicated, allowing the same short RTO and low RPO even in the event of that failure. Snapshots locally provide immediate recoverability from regular file or data loss,

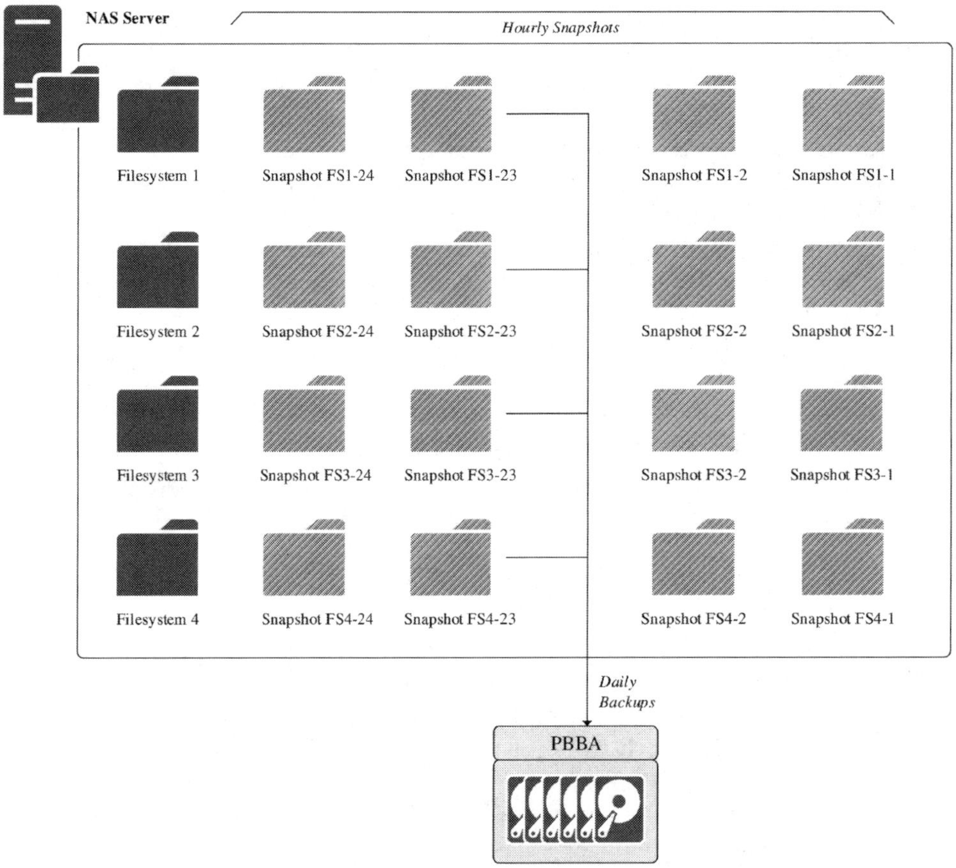

Figure 22.3   NAS snapshots with backup.

and replicated backups provide both the essential off-platform protection *and* longer term, compliance retention copies as well (compliance storage of the backups is not shown). Backups, likewise, are replicated between sites to ensure they are sufficiently protected against failure themselves.

In each configuration we've discussed (and other variants), there are advantages and trade-offs—these map to the limitations for both snapshots, and backup and recovery, discussed in their specific chapters. Part of the build-out of a holistic data protection approach such as we've done here for NAS protection is to evaluate, at each potential level of combined protection, what the remaining risks are. These risks of course are not just "what can still go wrong?"—they will also include "what impact will this configuration have?" The classic scenario to consider for instance is that deciding to eschew backups throughout the configuration options (i.e., using snapshots and replication only) opens the business to risks involving malicious inside actors and vendor lock-in.

22.2.2 Virtual Machine Protection

A common example for most businesses now is the multilayered approach required for comprehensive data protection services in virtual machine environments.

Increasingly virtualization represents a significant and mixed workload/footprint within most organizations. Even the smallest of organizations recognize the cost savings by running multiple independent hosts on a limited number of servers.

This can often lead to a complex mixed workload on these servers; depending on the size or operational requirements of a business, there may be a mix of production and non-production virtual machines running on the same physical servers, and workloads sharing the same physical resources could be file, print, email, terminal services, specific applications, databases, or development platforms—just to name a few.

A holistic approach to virtual machine protection effectively encompasses several (if not all) of the techniques discussed already in Chapter 14, so rather than building a step-by-step sequence as we did for large NAS protection, we can discuss the complete model from the start.

A high level example of multi-layered data protection within a virtualization environment (using VMware) is shown in Figure 22.6, with the numbered segments representing the following activities:

1. The hypervisor clusters running at each location perform cross-site replication for site failover capability.

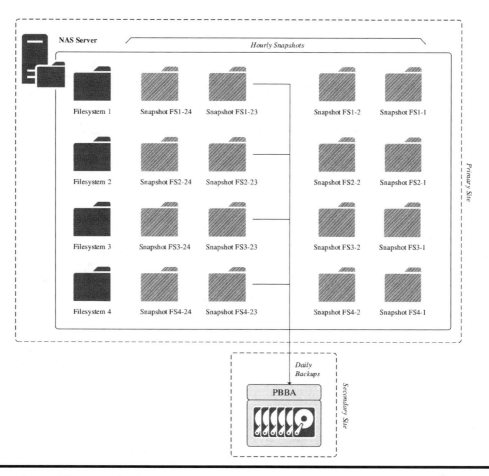

Figure 22.4   Snapshots with remote backups.

2. Critical database or application servers have continuous data protection (CDP) systems deployed against them with application-aware journaling; this provides the facility within the same site to almost instantly roll back a virtual machine to a prior checkpoint in the event of a data corruption issue. The journal system might even be used to trigger an application-consistent clone of the virtual machine for testing purposes. The CDP environment provides both local and remote recoverability at any point in time covered in the IO journal.

3. All virtual machines within the environment, regardless of whether they are production or non-production, receive *image*-level backups via hypervisor plugins to a purpose built backup appliance (PBBA), allowing advanced functionality such as instant-access, and file-level recovery.

4. Traditional, agent-based backups are performed for situations where
   a. A database or complex application resides within a virtual machine and cannot be backed up as an application-integrated image-level backup,[*] *and/or*

   b. Long-term retention of the content of the virtual machine is required and archive systems are not in use.[†]

5. All backups of virtual machines are replicated between sites so that the backup system does not become a single point of failure for the environment.

6. Backups that must be retained for long-term purposes are migrated to a cheap storage tier, such as cloud/object storage.

The architecture described is not the *only* way to provide a multi-layered approach to virtualization systems. Other approaches could more heavily utilize hypervisor-integrated storage snapshot systems, though as per previous discussions of snapshot limitations, this would be limited to short-term retention to avoid performance and/or capacity issues, and the risks associated with having no "off-platform" protection. (Such systems might also limit options for upgrades to the virtualization environment.)

---

[*] In our example you will note there is no agent backup of the virtual database, so we can assume its image-level backup is sufficiently integrated into the database to allow a fully application-consistent backup to take place.

[†] We would typically consider agent-based backups for long-term retention to allow for changes in hypervisor technology or virtual machine container format that might otherwise prevent recovery or use of recovered data after an extended period of time.

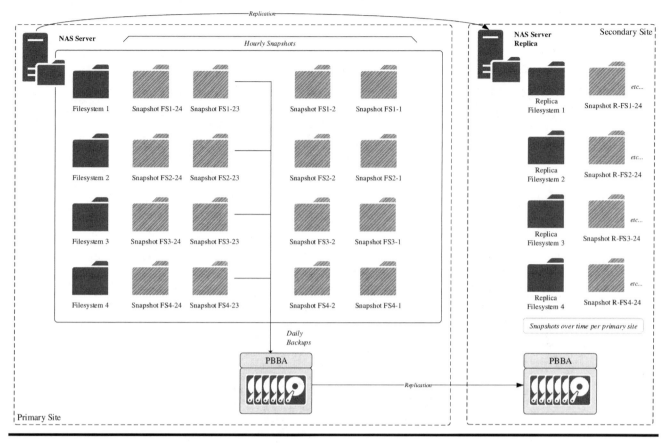

Figure 22.5   Comprehensive protection strategy for NAS.

22.2.3 Mission Critical Database Protection

While it's fair to say the most explosive data growth is occurring in unstructured data, structured data—that is to say, *databases*—still often represent the sources of the most mission critical data within an organization. Core, essential business functions more often than not rely on the application services leveraging specific databases within the organization. For this reason critical database servers will often have an extremely high degree of data protection associated with them, and such data protection will be configured in such a way as to absolutely minimize or even as much as possible completely eliminate any performance impact.

Consider as an example configuration Figure 22.7. Typically, mission critical databases will be clustered affairs, and our example configuration is no different. A cluster of systems is used to provide database services from the production site, with multiple connections per cluster node into the local SAN to achieve resiliency against path failure.* Clusters provide local fault tolerance from individual system

failure—one or more individual servers hosting the database can fail without service lost.

Most database servers feature options for enterprise high availability through some form or another of transaction log transfers. In this, a standby database server, either locally or at another site, is kept up to date with changes performed on the primary database by receiving transaction logs from the primary database as they are closed off. These transaction logs are applied automatically to the standby database, keeping it *mostly* in sync with the production copy.

The transaction log replication (or *shipping*) between sites is useful to allow database controlled rollback to any required point in time in the event of corruption. However, for mission critical systems you may also find SAN level replication as well, allowing for additional recovery models. In such a scenario, transaction log replication might write to the failover copy of the database, and SAN replication might run to alternate LUNs that could be used in other recovery scenarios. For instance, this might allow at least a crash-consistent restart of the database as a fall-back if transaction log shipping fails, or the standby database services are taken offline for maintenance and are therefore unable to receive the shipped logs.

To fulfill the previously stated business requirement of minimized performance impact during backup operations,

---

* For simplicity, the diagram shows direct connections—more correctly though, we would expect to at least see dual, redundant fiber-channel links coming from each server in the cluster, each going to separate fiber-channel switches, with appropriately redundant connectivity from the SAN systems into the fiber-channel fabric, as well.

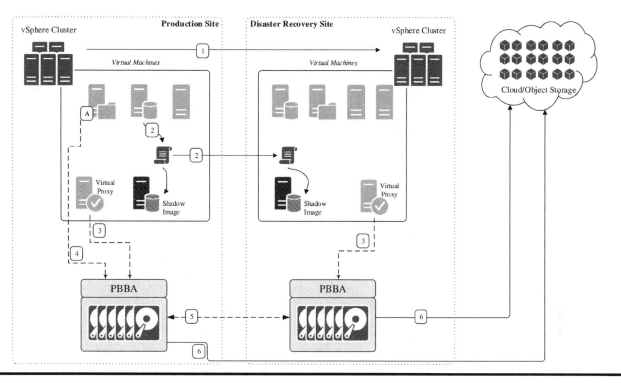

Figure 22.6 Multi-layered approach to data protection within a virtualization environment.

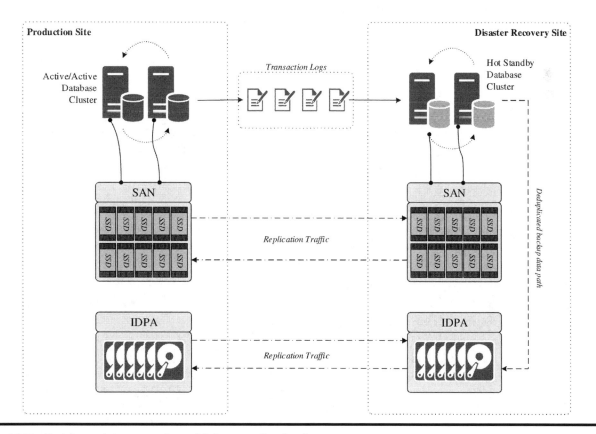

Figure 22.7 Database data protection with hot standby database.

it's quite normal in this type of configuration to have the database backup executed from the disaster recovery site instead—the application of transaction logs from the primary copy is delayed for the time it takes to execute a backup, but this means there is no performance impact on the production database during the backup process. Once the backup has been completed, queued transaction logs on the standby database server are again applied, and in the background the protection storage system on the standby site should replicate a copy of the backup to the production site so the backups as well are protected against site failure.

Such a configuration is not necessarily perfect, however. Database vendors typically charge considerably more for options around standby database servers, which can materially increase the cost of the solution. There are other potential disadvantages as well, including:

- The log holding area on the secondary database server will need to be large enough to hold all the transaction logs that will queue up while the backup is running.
- In the event of a site failover, any performance impact associated with the database backup will be experienced while the standby database server is acting as the production server.
- In normal production site operations, database recoveries from, say, corruption *may* require the recovery

from the "primary" backup, accessible only from the secondary site. This may cause bandwidth constraints on the recovery.
- In a worst-case scenario, it may actually be required to recover the database *into* the secondary database server and then replicate the database back across to the production site.
- Log shipping systems focus on getting updates from the production database to the standby database— they do little, if anything to assist with reversing the process when ready to failback. Such scenarios can require a complete re-seeding of the original production site's system from the failover system.

(While different database servers will support various rollback options to deal with corruption, the level of capability available will be platform dependent.)

Figure 22.8 shows an alternate data protection strategy for a mission critical database system.

The example shown in Figure 22.8 eschews log shipping at the database level and instead integrates application-aware CDP working at the storage array level. CDP typically works by intercepting IO operations and maintaining a journal of write operations performed against the LUN. These are collected into logs such that when they are applied to an alternate system, result in an application-consistent copy.

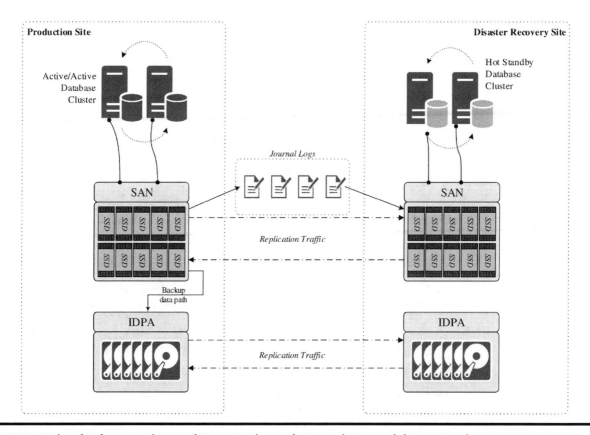

Figure 22.8 Using database continuous data protection and storage integrated data protection.

CDP systems can be used not only to provide application-consistent replication to another host, but can also be used for "rewind" operations against the production system being protected by CDP as well. Thus, in the event of logical corruption to the database it becomes possible to recover quickly and easily by stopping the database, rolling back (at the storage layer) the changes that had been performed, and restarting the database.

While CDP offers excellent RPO and RTO, usually businesses build CDP recoverability only around a limited window—for example, 24 or 48 hours. Longer-term recoverability will still require a more traditional backup process where the data is copied to data protection storage. In the scenario in Figure 22.8, we're showing that the backup could be achieved by leveraging integration between the primary storage system and the IDPA. In such a scenario, we typically see a fiber-channel link between the primary storage system and the IDPA, and the backup process works as follows:

- The database server triggers a backup process.
- If any database tasks need to take place before data transfer can be performed, these are run.
- The primary storage system takes a snapshot of the volume(s) the database resides on.
- If any post-backup tasks need to take place, these are run.
- The primary storage system transfers the snapshot database volume(s) to the IDPA.

Such a backup process frees the database server itself from the need to participate in the data transfer. A traditional database backup will see the database server *read* the data from the storage system and transfer that data to the protection storage system. The net result is the database server itself is the transfer conduit. By removing the database server from this process, the performance impact on the database is removed,* and by halving the amount of paths the data has to take for protection, we substantially increase the backup performance. This might be further improved by leveraging deduplication to reduce transfer requirements. Alternately, leveraging virtual synthetic operations allows the backup to take place by only transferring changed blocks on the LUN since the last backup, with the IDPA logically synthesizing a new full as a set of pointers from these new blocks and prior backups.

There's no such thing as a free lunch, however. While this type of convergent data protection can achieve stellar

performance, the removal of the database server from the workflow of *reading* the data has a logical consequence: there's no *logical* checking performed during the backup process. Elements of the database might be corrupt, and during a normal backup this could be picked up, since the database server will have to successfully read the data.

22.3 Planning Holistic Data Protection Strategies

In essence, the planning of a comprehensive data protection strategy is one which cannot be performed in isolation. This refers as much to the planning of the individual data protection components for a "silo" of business function as much as the view of *all* data protection components for *all* business functions within an organization. Consider, for instance, our three data protection strategies outlined in previous examples: large NAS, virtual machine, and mission critical database protection. While these might be developed and modified independently based on implementation schedules within an organization, a complete data protection strategy must be built with an understanding of the way in which specific solutions might impact on one another. All three strategies, for instance, rely on cross-site replication of:

- Production/mission critical virtual machines
- NAS storage and snapshots
- Backup copies/clones
- Database content

Assuming an organization needed to use both of these data protection techniques, the bandwidth considerations for data protection *can't* be determined in isolation; they will cumulatively consume cross-site bandwidth. If the database protection requires a minimum of 100 MB/s throughput, the virtualization protection requires a minimum of 200 MB/s throughput, and the NAS cross-site protection requires a minimum of 150 MB/s throughput, then a 1 Gbit link is not going to be sufficient[†]—particularly if that link is also shared for standard operational production communications between sites as well. Whenever deduplication is involved, this becomes even more critical a consideration during recovery operations—a link that may be perfectly sufficient for deduplicated *backup* operations may become saturated dealing with the flow of *rehydrated* data during a recovery.

In Chapter 6, we also spoke of the need to accurately track and analyze data protection capacity—in terms of

---

* That is, the SAN will undoubtedly support more than one application accessing it concurrently. When we consider performance impact to mission critical systems during backup, that impact is almost invariably as a result of that mission critical system *participating* in the transfer of its data.

† WAN/MAN (wireless area network/metro area network) link compression techniques can *mitigate* bandwidth requirements to a degree by reducing the amount of data that must be transmitted, but they always have their limits.

both storage requirements *and* performance. In particular, in Section 6.3.2 we discussed the value of reporting for trending in predictive planning, and this becomes even more important in an environment using a mix of data protection techniques. While some data protection techniques will exist largely independently of one another,* others *may* be dependent. Consider the large NAS protection strategy described previously: since the long-term backups are executed from replicated snapshots, then a failure in the snapshot system will likely cause a cascaded failure into the backup and recovery system. So while multi-layered data protection techniques can increase the level and options for data availability and recoverability within an organization, they can introduce additional dependencies that must be understood, tracked, and planned for.

In Chapter 21, we discussed the processes and considerations in building out data protection service catalogs, and in reflection you would note that each tier and option within a data protection service catalog effectively represents a holistic data protection strategy. Table 21.1 for instance had a "Platinum" offering for database servers consisting of:

- Continuous storage availability
- Synchronous replication of storage systems to secondary and tertiary sites
- Application-aware snapshots taken every 15 minutes
- Snapshots replicated to secondary and tertiary sites
- Nightly full backups via convergent data protection (direct from primary to protection storage)

With the likely exception of the lowest-tiered service catalog entries, almost all options in a data protection service catalog will represent a holistic data protection strategy—this synergistic approach is pivotal to building out comprehensive protection for a business.

22.4 Summary

In modern businesses it's practically unheard of to leverage only a *single* data protection strategy. Before host virtualization it was largely possible to merely loosely coordinate data protection strategies: application administrators might generate their own backups or dumps of databases to spare storage, storage administrators would provide specific RAID

protection, and operating system administrators would execute appropriate traditional backups. (As backups grew to be heterogeneous in function, backup administrators became more common to provide a centralized protection option for *all* operating systems within a business.)

Host virtualization and subsequently storage, network, and datacenter virtualization have led to a far more converged level of infrastructure planning (thin provisioning of both storage and virtualization environments, for instance, requires a close working relationship between storage administrators, virtualization administrators, and operating system/application administrators). While businesses may try to keep storage, virtualization, and backup administration as distinct roles, administrators in all three areas must liaise closely and regularly to ensure compatible, holistic data protection strategies are developed and implemented, and these techniques *do not* leave gaps that expose the business to risk. Equally, a holistic approach reduces the number of costly overlapping functions; systems planned in isolation may needlessly duplicate functionality or protection at a direct fiscal cost to the business. Reducing overlap can result in true cost savings. The growing presence of converged infrastructure is demonstrating the need for a new type of administrator: the *infrastructure administrator*, who combines multiple previous siloed roles, and the net benefits are not just for the primary production administration but also the administration of data protection as well. (Arguably, infrastructure administrators add value regardless of whether fully converged infrastructure is used, and in a modern IT environment could be considered essential to developing and maintaining a comprehensive data protection strategy.)

A holistic data protection strategy is no longer something only 24 × 7 and multinational or global businesses require; it is essential for the modern IT environment.

22.5 Self-Reflection

Holistic data protection strategies don't just apply to on-premises or traditional infrastructure.

How might you construct a holistic data protection strategy to enable daily protection of in-cloud databases, with monthly data copies stored in an on-premises environment for long-term retention?

---

* For instance, the type of RAID storage used by a system *usually* does not impact whether or not it can receive traditional backups.

Chapter 23

Making Data Protection Smarter

23.1 Introduction

"Hey Siri, recover the last backup of database C-R-M from D-B-S-R-V-P-R-O-D-16 to a new Gold-Class Postgres server."

While audio interfaces may not be entirely conducive to the ambient noise found in odiously open-plan offices, the idea of being able to request or instruct a data protection system to perform activities—simple or otherwise—in relatively free-form instructions is undoubtedly something we will see more of over time.

The idea of *smarter* data protection has multiple meanings. In this chapter, we'll explore a few of those meanings.

23.2 Secondary Use Cases for Protected Data

While there are still some hold-outs who think data protection can be achieved by buying a few large removable hard drives from the nearest consumer IT equipment store, it's generally accepted in business that data protection as we've been discussing in this book has a tangible price tag associated with it. Enterprise organizations with data in the order of hundreds to thousands of terabytes of data will almost invariably have multi-million-dollar price tags associated with their data protection strategies.

Yet, the primary use case of data protection is insurance, and just like insurance, it's something you *hope* that you don't have to claim on. It would be an odd worldview if at the end of a year, you reflected on not having made any home insurance claim and thought that it would have been better had you been able to.

Where data protection *differs* from insurance though is that insurance generally doesn't have secondary use cases—certainly not for the insured.

Various secondary use cases have been mentioned in previous chapters, including:

- "Instant access" *to copies on data protection storage*: Regardless of whether it's a virtual machine, database, or filesystem, being able to safely access a data protection copy[*] for testing, emergency access, or analysis has a number of benefits, such as:
  - Data is immediately accessible without the time taken to recover.
  - Overlay functions, such as data masking may be performed before the data is copied or recovered, providing additional compliance protection.
  - Primary storage requirements are reduced.
- *Analytics*: Analytics come in many forms, and may include scenarios such as:
  - *Tracking data changes over time*: this might be performed as analysis against data protection metadata (e.g., file sizes, etc.), or it might be targeted against specific datasets by recovering multiple versions of time and analyzing the differences between them.
  - *Legal search*: legal search is usually required as much, if not more across data protection copies as it is across the current data. Making this more easily available against data protection copies *without* having to restore them first can save significant amounts of primary storage space.
  - *Populating data lakes*: Mixing functionality such as instant access, copy access (see below) and even as a transfer function between in-cloud and on-premises systems, data protection can be a powerful way of getting data into data lakes.

---

[*] In situations where the copy is being accessed read/write, it's important that it is accessed via a read/write *snapshot,* or other copy of the copy, since the original data protection copy should be preserved as of the time it was created.

■ *Copy access*: Similar to the instant access approach, but with data recovery, copy access has been a secondary use case for data protection environments for decades, with many organizations choosing to recover data protection copies of production databases as a means of refreshing dev/test and other databases, rather than copying directly from the production environments.

■ *Compliance retention*: While some insist all compliance retention should be achieved through archival storage, practically it is still reasonably common to see data protection systems being used for retention of compliance copies of data—the monthly and yearly backups that may have to be kept for years, if not decades. It's fair to say this use case straddles between primary and secondary use cases for data protection.

It's now increasingly common to see businesses explicitly request that vendors and integrators responding to tenders spell out the various secondary use cases of their proposed products. While this is useful, businesses should also spend time brainstorming options for secondary use cases around their data protection copies, leveraging a variety of groups including business analysts, data protection administrators, and developers.

23.3 Data Protection Overlap

There was a time when the number-one requirement of a backup and recovery system was the ability to integrate into virus scanning technology. While some still seek this, it's often seen as an impediment to data protection performance, and you'll see articles in many vendor knowledge bases about how to exclude at least backup, if not backup and recovery processes from virus scanning.

Yet, there is an essential overlap between the three primary "data protection topics": security, privacy, and storage.

From a security perspective, mature enterprises recognize the intrinsic threat posed by poorly secured data protection environments. Regardless of whether it's storage snapshot and replication, continuous data protection, or backup and recovery services, these systems can grant a savvy attacker access data with minimum effort compared to the original systems security—when security is not approached carefully. (Likewise, ransomware has increasingly attacked poorly secured backup and recovery services as a means of reducing the chances of data access via standard recovery processes.)

It can be argued that the security protocols applied to data protection systems within an enterprise should be comparable to the security protocols applied to the most critical or secure system they are protecting. This is perhaps the most important factor in "smart security" for data protection systems: recognizing the potential for mis-use and taking the appropriate steps to secure them.

Compliance to modern privacy regulations is increasingly impacting on data protection and demanding innovative solutions. Consider the "right to be forgotten"; when successfully, legally invoked, this doesn't apply just to the active, online copy of data, but potentially all copies of data. If the business recovers data sometime *after* a data deletion is performed for a concerned party, and that recovery re-instates the deleted data, the business has placed itself in a legally risky situation.

While one approach to dealing with this technically would be to recover the data, perform the deletion and write it out again, this is entirely impractical in anything but the smallest of environments—and comes with compliance risks: recovering a database from say, 2 years ago, performing a delete and then backing it up again makes it a backup for *today*, not 2 years ago. So instead, it becomes important to be able to apply masking functions during a recovery—or delete the data immediately after it, before the whole data set is released into a "visible" environment. (Legally there may still be a strong distinction between a masked recovery and a *recover-then-delete* scenario.)

Yet data storage protection solutions are not typically designed to perform complex masking operations; this is an entire specialist software field on its own with deep technical experience required. Integration on this front therefore comes more from the data protection software being able to present "instant access" protection copies that can then be accessed by the data masking software to facilitate a controlled recovery with deletes re-applied.

23.4 Automated Processes

> If you have to do something more than once, automate it.

As a new member of the UNIX system administration team in 1996, these instructions were a critical introduction to a team built around automating as much as possible. The flipside of the automation rule was "the best system administrator is a lazy system administrator"—the emphasis being that by keeping operations as automated as possible, one would have the time required to work on projects, and exceptions.

While automation can be used to speed up the implementation of a new data protection solution, the true savings from automation come with applying automation to day to day tasks. Ideally, wherever automation is applied, there should be increased capability relating to:

■ *Consistency*: Each time the task is performed, the result should be the same.
■ *Repeatability*: The task can be repeated as required without any additional intervention.
■ *Reliability*: The process should appropriately handle not only expected results, but unexpected results, also.

There are several key areas of focus within data protection on automation, including but not limited to:

- *Service catalogs*, as discussed in detail in Chapter 21.
- *Compliance auditing*: Many businesses are required to demonstrate recoverability of systems, workloads, and data in order to meet legal compliance requirements. By automating these tasks, compliance obligations can be met with lower staff involvement.
- *Secondary use cases*: Many of the secondary use cases for data protection as previously discussed can become more useful to the business when there is strong automation wrapped around it.

While traditionally the approach to automation has been developing scripts and workflows based on command line interfaces (CLIs), much of the focus more recently has been on RESTful APIs (or REST APIs). REST APIs give two key advantages to developers: first, that they do not require interactive processing (i.e., they are stateless), and second, they do not require execution from the backup server itself. That is, a data protection service running a REST API server will respond via appropriately authenticated HTTP or HTTPS GET, POST, DELETE, etc., commands. For instance, a Dell EMC NetWorker server can be queried via a REST API as follows:

```
https://hostname:9090/nwrestapi
```

Such a query initially will return JSON* output such as the following:

```
{
    "links": [
        {
            "href": "https://orilla.turbamentis.int:9090/nwrestapi/v1",
            "title": "NetWorker REST API v1"
        },
        {
            "href": "https://orilla.turbamentis.int:9090/nwrestapi/v2",
            "title": "NetWorker REST API v2"
        },
        {
            "href": "https://orilla.turbamentis.int:9090/nwrestapi/v3",
            "title": "NetWorker REST API v3"
        }
    ],
    "version": "19.1.0.2.Build.74"
}
```

This indicates that there are three different versions of the REST API available to be queried, as of NetWorker 19.1.0.2. Running a subsequent query against the "v1" URL given in the previous output (https://orilla.turbamentis.int:9090/nwrestapi/v1) yields output as follows:

```
"links": [
    {
        "href": "https://orilla.turbamentis.int:9090/nwrestapi/v1/datazone",
        "title": "Datazone protection"
    },
    {
        "href": "https://orilla.turbamentis.int:9090/nwrestapi/v1/tenants",
        "title": "Restricted data zone protection"
```

---

* JavaScript Object Notation, a data-interchange format that was developed out of the JavaScript language.

```
        },
        {
            "href": "https://orilla.turbamentis.int:9090/nwrestapi/v1/global",
            "title": "Global view of datazone and restricted data zones"
        },
        {

            "href": "https://orilla.turbamentis.int:9090/nwrestapi/v1/schemas/nwrestapi.json",
            "title": "JSON schema for API messages"
        }
    ]
}
```

Based on the way the API works, a developer might query
the configuration for an individual client using the URL:

https://orilla.turbamentis.int:9090/nwrestapi/v1/datazone/clients/46.0.188.30.0.0.0.0.151.199.85.93.192.168.100.4

This might yield the following output:

```
{
    "aliases": [
     "2kpro",
     "2kpro.turbamentis.int"
    ],
    "applicationInformation": [
     "VSS:*=off"
    ],
    "backupType": "Filesystem",
    "blockBasedBackup": false,
    "checkpointEnabled": false,
    "clientId": "6047975c-00000004-5d55ee89-5d55ee88-00055000-9f778f56",
    "hostname": "2kpro.turbamentis.int",
    "indexBackupContent": false,
    "links": [
     {
       "href": "https://orilla.turbamentis.int:9090/nwrestapi/v1/datazone/clients/46.0.188
.30.0.0.0.0.151.199.85.93.192.168.100.4/backups",
       "title": "List of backups"
     },
     {
       "href": "https://orilla.turbamentis.int:9090/nwrestapi/v1/datazone/clients/46.0.188
.30.0.0.0.0.151.199.85.93.192.168.100.4/op/backup",
       "title": "Back up client"
     }
    ],
    "nasDevice": false,
    "ndmp": false,
    "ndmpMultiStreamsEnabled": false,
    "ndmpVendorInformation": [],
    "parallelSaveStreamsPerSaveSet": false,
    "parallelism": 4,
    "protectionGroups": [
     "Adhoc_Legacy"
    ],
    "remoteAccessUsers": [],
```

```
    "resourceId": {
        "id": "46.0.188.30.0.0.0.0.151.199.85.93.192.168.100.4",
        "sequence": 17
    },
    "saveSets": [
    "C:\\"
    ],
    "scheduledBackup": true,
    "tags": []
}
```

REST APIs may be provided in a variety of formats, with different output formats (for instance, XML or HTML output might be received instead of JSON output), but running a few quick queries using the appropriate API instructions, a developer might quickly be able to automate the display of per-client details (based on the drilling down we've done in the example). That might allow a business to integrate data protection functionality into their own business portal—this has the advantage of then being able to make the data protection functionality access independent of the data protection product. (Such an approach is useful in situations where the business might have a number of data protection products performing the same function, either due to acquisitions and mergers, or through a mix of on-premises and cloud-based systems, or even to overcome a lack of prior standardization.)

Vendors can't possibly anticipate every possible way a business might want to use a data protection product. New applications and products appear regularly that might require specific approaches to data protection; few businesses are truly unique in what they do at a macro level, but their processes at a micro level can't possibly be universally predicted. Automation therefore is rarely about a documented process by a vendor, but the *user's* idea of what might make the product work better, and the application of various automation tools provided by the product to get there.

23.5 Adaptive Processes

While we often think of *big data* as a challenge to data protection, the other less visible challenge is *big infrastructure*. That is, how does a business coordinate its data protection activities efficiently and reliably as the overall infrastructure continues to grow?

Consider that within a pair of active/active datacenters, a modern enterprise that's heavily virtualized might have hundreds or even thousands of databases, 20,000 or more virtual machines running within their environment, and hundreds of remaining physical hosts (outside of the virtual machine hypervisors) that still require protection.

Just how does a human being intelligently decide an optimized approach to ensure that all 20,000 virtual machines and, say, 200 physical machines, get snapshots, replication, and backups?

There are some aspects to this that are solved by automation, of course. Virtual machines might be automatically added to dynamic data protection policies based on certain tags or other configuration details they have. This reduces the requirement for manual on-boarding processes, but how does one coordinate the *scheduling* of that many backups?

Yet, to date, the traditional approach is largely a mix of manual configuration and luck, riding the wave of periodic system updates that provide faster performance for the environment. There is little "intelligence" in such systems—the focus is on the administrator(s) thinking of everything that needs to be planned, configured, and scheduled to meet all the SLAs of the environment. This is, at heart, "imperative configuration," where the human has to clearly define everything that must be done.

Yet despite the best efforts of the humans involved in the system, failures still happen—the configuration that works 29 days in a month may struggle at end of month processing, or during other seasonal variations. The reality is that *big infrastructure* needs a smarter approach than an individual administrator somewhere making the decision between whether a collection of 100 virtual machines out of 20,000 or more should start at 19:00 or 19:05.

As machine learning becomes increasingly baked into the innovations seen in other areas of IT, we should likewise expect to see advancements in data protection, focusing on two key aspects:

■ SLA compliance
■ Resource planning

Traditional approaches to SLA compliance within data protection have focused on retention periods for the protection copies (which are usually set within the policies themselves), and basic data movement or tiering functions. Thus, lifecycle management policies might see data retained on high-speed, block-based protection storage for 30 or 60 days, before being tiered to slower storage (traditionally this may have been tape, though object storage continues to gain traction). Smarter approaches to data protection would instead focus on a declarative process, allowing the protection system to enact appropriate governance to achieve a variety of SLA compliance requirements. This might include scenarios such as:

- Preventing premature deletion of protection copies
- Ensuring a sufficient number of protection copies are retained on different tiers of storage
- Relocating data protection to alternate storage platforms to meet performance requirements (e.g., moving from a capacity to performance tier for a mission critical database)
- Prioritizing policies that have previously failed over those that have previously succeeded, in order to reduce exposure from failed protection activities
- Adjusting or recommending adjustments to multiplexing or other forms of concurrent streaming settings in order to better meet protection or recovery objectives

Resource planning might be considered "scheduling on steroids"; within data protection, scheduling tends to be little more than deciding which data protection function runs at which times, and what day(s) of the week. Resource planning, on the other hand, should be seen as a sufficiently comprehensive review of historical data protection activities (i.e., run-times, including seasonal historical information), knowledge of newly introduced activities, *and* ideally, activities *outside* the sphere of data protection that nonetheless affects it. A resource planning approach to data protection for instance should not only take into consideration how fast individual virtual machine backups tend to finish "normally," but also details such as:

- Whether there's any changes to that run-time during say, end of month, end of financial year, or other seasonal variations specific to the business (e.g., during peak enrolment periods for universities)
- If the Windows team has scheduled patching for the server fleet
- If the virtualization team has scheduled downtime for several hypervisors, which will adjust load balancing considerations
- Whether a data protection storage appliance will be offline for scheduled maintenance

Such resource planning should be expected to be revisited daily—in a "smarter" data protection solution we would expect more variance in individual system protection start times, but more regularity in protection success levels and resource utilization across the environment.

SLA compliance and resource planning intelligence would clearly need to act in concert; adjusting the run window for backups without consideration of the SLA requirements might distribute protection workloads, but if that comes at a cost of failing to meet particular protection requirements for critical workloads, it is not a positive outcome for the business.

Just as automation has been an increasing focus in IT infrastructure in recent times, we should expect to see machine learning led adaptive operations begin to gain traction as it becomes easier to anticipate future activities, and build them into daily action profiles based on insights into historical and ongoing operations within a business.

23.6 Summary

Smarter data protection invariably means more cost-effective data protection. That may not always be measured in terms of a cheaper up-front price, but more reflective of being able to amortize the cost of a data protection solution across more aspects of the business, or reduce the staff effort involved in managing the solution.

Just as the primary storage industry stopped measuring storage efficiency in terms of full-time employees per TB managed, data growth likewise requires alternate approaches to managing and evaluating efficiency within data protection services, too. That's not to say it's about removing humans from the process entirely, but it is about reducing the number of decisions they need to make, or processes they need to be involved in so that we can optimize the success of the service, and consumption of available resources.

Smarter management processes to data protection will not come from vendors alone. The industry overall depends on businesses being able to clearly articulate secondary use case requirements, and particularly when we consider automation, it's critical to understand the difference between *providing the tools* and *providing the end-state*. To be sure, vendors need to include CLIs, REST APIs, and other means of programmatically driving their products (i.e., providing "infrastructure as code"), but it is without a doubt up to individual businesses and users of data protection products to address actual runtime automation requirements within their infrastructure.

Machine learning and other branches of information sciences relating to artificial intelligence are only just starting to make their mark in the infrastructure space. We should expect during the decade of the 2020s to see significant changes in the field of adaptive operations—not just within data protection, but across the entire field of infrastructure. An effective end goal is not simply a cloud-like experience (which has a primary focus on *automation* rather than *autonomy*), but an environment which is, as much as possible, self-aware, self-configuring, self-monitoring, and self-healing.

Chapter 24

Data Recovery

24.1 Introduction

Despite all the best proactive steps that can be taken toward data protection—any mix of data storage protection, snapshots, RAID, replication, and continuous storage availability—there is always the chance of *some* data loss situation that requires a form of recovery to be performed.

If we consider data protection to be a form of insurance, then data recovery is what occurs when a business needs to make a claim against its data protection policy: something has happened and data must be retrieved.

Just like a regular insurance policy, a data protection "insurance policy" comes with an *excess fee* when it comes to making claims, and just like insurance, the level of "excess" to claim against the policy—the cost of the recovery—is usually intimately related to whether sufficient financing and planning was invested in the data protection strategy in the first place.

Although recovery operations themselves are product-centric, some common practices and considerations for recoveries exist regardless of what product or technology is being used. These include:

- *System design*: To what level are recovery requirements (and their associated SLAs) a primary consideration when designing a protection system?
- *Best practices*: Procedures and guidelines to follow during recovery and disaster recovery processes.
- Adequacy of recovery testing.

In this chapter, we'll be reviewing various data protection options on the basis of the above key requirements.

24.2 Recovery versus Service Restoration

One of the most important data recovery considerations is one of the most overlooked—the difference between *data recovery* and *service restoration*. Data recovery merely refers to retrieving data from protection storage, but depending on the nature of the failure, storage, and data, there may be considerably more effort involved in achieving service restoration. At its simplest, this might be as rudimentary as starting application services once a recovery process has been completed, but for more complex workloads, this might involve any or all of the following examples:

- Executing recoveries across multiple systems
- Coordinating service starts or restarts across application and database servers
- Adjusting IP addresses and redirecting DNS
- Notifying users or consumers the service is available again

In Chapter 4, we described the elements of a data protection system, with technology only being one element alongside five others (people, training, testing, service level agreements, processes, and documentation). Similarly, we see other components involved in service restoration beyond just transferring data from one source into another or redirecting where we access data from.

Understanding the service restoration activities and times they will take is critical to correctly determining the real service level objectives that can be offered to the business. For instance, merely estimating that a database can be recovered in 8 hours because the backups can be read from protection storage in 8 hours pays no consideration to any consistency activities that may have to be applied post-restore,[*] what services might need to be reset, or what nontechnical post-recovery processes might need to be performed before the business deems the service to be "restored."

---

[*] Consider again for instance that in databases, the nomenclature *restore* versus *recovery* is used. Restore typically refers to pulling data back from protection storage/backup, but *recovery* refers to actually rolling forward transaction logs and other details to reinstate consistency in the database.

24.3 On-Platform versus Off-Platform Recovery

In an optimally designed data protection environment, there will be a mix of on-platform and off-platform protection methods—for example, a NAS share might have a snapshot taken every 4 hours, retained for 14 days, with daily, monthly, and yearly backups taken for longer retention periods.

When a recovery is required, an initial step will be to determine which of the available methods should be used to perform the recovery. This should be a decision made based on:

- Matching the recovery point and recovery time objectives (RPO and RTO, respectively) to the data loss or recovery requirement
- The required granularity of the recovery
- The complexity of the recovery

For example, consider a virtual machine that is protected via continuous data protection (CDP), and image-based backup. The image-based backup can be restored either as an image of the entire virtual machine, an individual virtual machine disk, a rapid-overwrite using changed block tracking, an "instant access," or via file-level recovery.

While a CDP recovery will bring the virtual machine backup to potentially any recent IO (in the order of days), it may not be the most appropriate depending on the type of recovery required. If only a single file has been lost, but the CDP platform requires a virtual machine to be instantiated into an isolated network for access, recovery in this way may take longer and consume more resources than performing a file-level recovery from an image-level backup. On the other hand, if the file had only been created an hour prior to it being accidentally deleted, the granularity of the data loss will likely demand a CDP recovery, as there probably won't have been a backup between the time the file was created and deleted.

There is no single right or wrong answer—rather, in recovery situations (particularly ones that are not *user-self-service*), it's important to consider all recovery options available and make the optimal recovery choice based on the decision criteria previously mentioned: RPO/RTO, granularity, and complexity.* If infrastructure is managed as a holistic stack by a single team, this is a straightforward process—where more planning will be required is in situations where there are separate administrative teams for say, storage (i.e., *on-platform* protection) and backup systems (*off-platform* protection). To avoid having recovery requests re-routed between groups, planning should be done so that help desk teams and enterprise ticketing systems can route requests to the *most likely* team based on information supplied by the user. You might say the aim is to avoid a situation where it takes longer to assign a recovery ticket to the right team than it does to perform a recovery.

24.4 Context Aware Recoveries

You may have an excellent painter working on your house: not a drop splashed, not a line of wall missed, and working at a speed you could never match. But if there's a sudden power surge that leaves half of your house needing to be rewired, would you turn and ask the painter to rewire your house simply because she's the current expert on site?

It's a similar story with data protection. Even with the best backup administrators delivering 100% success rates, is it sensible to have them executing the end-to-end recovery of a complex, mission critical database they're not certified in—just because they're experts at managing the protection infrastructure? In earlier chapters, we mentioned a new form of backup topology—the hybrid approach, with centralized protection storage but the control decentralized and shared between core backup administrators and application administrators. (While referencing backups only, this equally applies to all forms of data protection—just think *storage administrators*[†] and *application administrators*.) The hybrid approach enables greater flexibility in coordinating *backups*, but more importantly it can allow for a more intelligent and efficient approach to coordinating *recoveries*. The backup administrators can coordinate resources at a broader level and assist with recoveries that don't require high degrees of application awareness, without impeding the efforts of application administrators who also need to get mission critical systems back. You might even say that a key principle of centralized protection storage in a hybrid topology approach is to ensure that backup administrators do not become a recovery bottleneck.

24.5 Designing for Recovery

No matter how you look at data protection, one of two fundamental approaches must be taken depending on the RPOs of the data or services involved. These are:

- Design for recovery, *or*
- Design to avoid recovery

If a mission critical system within the organization has an RPO of zero, or near enough to, the primary design principle must be to *avoid* recovery at all practical costs. Such systems

---

* For user-self-service recoveries, it would be expected that the recovery options are very closely aligned to very specific situations, and the user does not have to make any choice between different recovery types.

† Or more broadly, *infrastructure* administrators.

will leverage continuous storage availability, replication, and snapshots to achieve instantaneous or near-instantaneous restoration in the event of a service outage. While traditional backups may still be used for these systems, they are likely to be used for longer-term data retention requirements or reseeding test/dev or even big data systems rather than intended for service restoration. Resorting to traditional backup systems for service restoration in these scenarios is a sign of architected or cascaded failure exceeding operational expectations rather than *by-design*. (However, it's worth pointing out that even when you explicitly design to *avoid*

recovery, that doesn't mean you get to avoid having a recovery plan at all—there is always the risk that something will still go wrong and a recovery may be required.)

For systems with less rigorous SLAs relating to RPOs, RTOs, and service outage times, where traditional backup and recovery systems will be part of their operational recovery strategy, a fundamental design principle must be to ensure that data (and services) can be recovered within the required time frames established by the *business*. (IT alone cannot decide RPOs and RTOs.)

Consider for the moment a backup environment leveraging deduplication. If implemented including source-side deduplication, it can also substantially decrease the amount of data that has to be sent across a network. This has seen an explosion of backup topologies featuring a number of remote office sites backing up to a single central datacenter over relatively small links. For instance, a site with 1,000 GB of data that has high commonality to centrally stored data may comfortably backup across a link that has a maximum sustainable throughput of 10 MB/s, or even less. Backing up 1,000 GB of data at a continuous rate of 10 MB/s would take 28.4 hours without deduplication, but once the first backup is done* assuming a maximum 5% change rate on any given day and a 5:1 deduplication ratio against that changed data, only 50 GB of data would need to be backed up a day, and only 10 GB of new, unique data would need to be sent across the link per day—less than an hour of backup time.

Consider though: what happens if the remote site experiences a catastrophic failure and *all* that data needs to be streamed back from the central site? Deduplication in itself doesn't improve recovery performance, and we've already determined that even maxing out the transfer it would take 28.4 hours to send that data *back*. If this is unacceptable, the system must be designed accordingly—such as installation of a smaller deduplication system in the remote office that acts as a local cache and replicates the backups into the central office; in the event of *many* failure situations, the local cache can be used to facilitate recovery at LAN, rather than WAN speeds.†

Recoverability—or avoiding the recovery in the first place depending on the value of the data to be the business—has to be the primary design requirement of any data protection system; while operationally on a day to day basis the speed at which the protection is executed is important, ultimately the business will be far more concerned with the time required to achieve service restoration in the event of an issue.

24.6 Recovery Facilitation

24.6.1 *Automated versus Manual Recoveries*

As system automation through portals, cloud-like automation and auto-healing storage becomes more commonplace,

automatic recovery processes are likely to enter the datacenter more pervasively. These will gain popularity in highly available storage, continuous data protection and replication systems in the first pass, allowing intelligent storage systems to automatically achieve system restoration in the event of a storage system failure. This is of course not new: RAID systems in particular have long utilized hot-sparing to commence reconstruction of a volume in the event of a single disk failure *without* administrative intervention. Storage virtualization in particular allows for policies to be established more easily and at a higher configuration level by administrators, leaving an automation and orchestration layer in charge to handle the actual actions. While the IT industry has for the most part moved on by considering Full Time Employee (FTE) requirements per TB or even PB, higher levels of automation for provisioning, management, and restoration *do* allow for sometimes even individual administrators to manage large amounts of storage in the tens of petabytes or higher.

Automated recovery can play a part in good system design for backup and recovery environments as well. Products or orchestration layers that support recovery automation can free up application, system, or backup administrators from

---

* Which if timed correctly given the previously stated commonality of centrally stored data may not need to be a full 1,000 GB transfer.
† If service levels permit, an alternate recovery strategy may be "build and ship"—conduct the recovery at the backup destination/central site over a high speed LAN link, and transport the recovered server or data back to the site. This is effectively an evolution of Andrew Tanenbaum's statement: "Never underestimate the bandwidth of a station wagon full of tapes hurtling down the highway."

required but otherwise tedious regular recovery activities such as

- Reseeding development, test, and QA systems from production backups
- Compliance-required regular testing—A catalog of necessary recovery tests might be built and periodically executed to satisfy legal requirements
- Prearranged recovery activities—When a required recovery is known well in advance, building an automated recovery policy to execute the recovery at the required time can free up administrators for other activities

While there will always be scope for manual recoveries, automated recoveries will increase in popularity and use as businesses demand more agility from their data protection products, and third-party orchestration layers become more mature.

24.6.2 Who Performs the Recovery?

There are usually several factors that determine which role will perform a recovery:

- *Data complexity*: Does it require specialist knowledge to perform a particular recovery? As the data or the services reliant on data become more complex or critical, the chances of the recovery requiring specialist knowledge will also increase. Thus, databases tend to be recovered by database administrators rather than, say, help desk staff.
- *System architecture*: Does the data protection system, and the way in which it has been integrated into the environment support the required or desired roles for recovery? A business for instance might *prefer* all end user data to be self-service recoverable, but if the environment has been architected to require administrator-level privileges for any form of recovery, recoveries are likely to require escalation to the IT department.
- *Product architecture and security*: Ensuring that data cannot be recovered by the wrong people can become an active consideration; a product that may allow *any* user to perform a recovery sounds like a good idea until we consider the possibility of an office clerk being able to recover, say, the CFO's sensitive budgetary planning data.
- *User education*: How much training is required for a user before he or she can complete a recovery? Ideally if end users are expected to perform recoveries of at least some of their data (e.g., Office documents or email messages), then the functionality should be integrated such that it appears part of the base product itself, and is completely intuitive. (For example, a SaaS backup product may add a "Recover" option to a user's email toolbar, allowing users to perform self-service recovery without needing to understand the complete backup product.)

Particularly in tape-based environments, recovery functionality is often constrained to a very limited number of users—for example, the backup administrators, application and operating system administrators, and a few help desk staff at most. This reduces the chance of the environment being flooded with recovery requests all waiting on tapes requiring recall, or drives to be freed up.

Businesses are increasingly seeing the benefits of allowing (where possible) user-directed self-service recovery thanks to the growth in disk-based protection storage. "Users" in this scenario may not literally mean end users, but providing self-service recovery access to a broad spectrum of administrators and developers within the organization—application administrators, platform developers, and so on.

True end user self-service recovery is normally seen as a topic reserved almost entirely for files on home drives, and individual email messages. There will still be times where specific types of data will require administrator intervention for recovery, but with cost-cutting (or at least, *operational efficiencies*) a perpetual consideration for IT departments, allowing users to recover their own basic documents and email can substantially free up IT resources for strategic activities. (It is very likely however that businesses shifting to SaaS applications in the cloud will discover more regular opportunities to grant access to self-service recoveries.)

Ensuring the systems deployed can be used by the *right* users at the *right* time is an architectural process and educational challenge, and usually encounters the most challenges where a particular level of self-service or recovery functionality is *assumed* rather than fully investigated. Allowing more users to perform recoveries (be they particular application administrators, help desk staff, or even end users) can have anything from a subtle to a profound improvement over operational efficiencies within a business. Depending on the reason *why* a user needs data recovered, the delay taken to formally request a recovery and wait for a limited number of operational staff (usually with other duties) to complete it may slow down business functions or even effectively cost the business money in lost productivity. Understanding the anticipated load and/or costs associated with self-service recoveries—and being able to track them—is important, too. If there is a tangible cost to the business to perform a recovery (e.g., data restoration from cloud object storage), that cost must be tracked, accounted for, and budgeted the same way as any other.

24.6.3 Frequency of Recovery

The more frequently recoveries are performed, the more the system must be designed to support the recovery workload. When tape was the primary backup and recovery mechanism for instance, this would often mean architecting backup environments to ensure that a sufficient number of tape drives were *always* available to perform recoveries: a tape library with 10 tape drives might be configured such that two drives are permanently configured as "read only," providing greater assurance of their availability to facilitate a recovery.

With disk-based systems being more likely as not to be used as protection storage, the physical limitation between read and write activities found with tape has reduced substantially. However, simply using disk does not create a blank check when it comes to recoveries. Items for consideration include

■ Regardless of storage type used:
  - How many concurrent read streams can the protection storage handle without performance degradation?
  - What impact does the network connectivity to protection storage have to single recovery streams *and* concurrent recovery streams?
■ Are there "housekeeping" activities that must be performed which would reduce the capacity to service recovery requests?
■ If backup data is tiered to slower, longer-term storage (tape or cloud), is the system designed to ensure the most common recovery requests come from online rather than nearline or off-line storage?
■ If data is tiered off to other storage, is it done in such a way as to make access completely transparent to the user?
■ If using deduplication storage:
  - If the deduplication is performed as a "post-process" operation:
    • Are there differences between service capability for deduplicated and non-deduplicated backup data?
  - Post-processing is typically IO intensive—what is the typical duration of post-processing based on average data transfer per day and the impact this might have on a recovery if post-processing is *running* while a recovery is performed?
  - Regardless of inline or post-process deduplication:
    • Has adequate consideration been given to the amount of data that might need to be rehydrated during a recovery process and the time

this takes to complete (regardless of how fast a deduplicated backup can complete)?
  • Does the deduplication service include options to speed up a rehydration recovery—such as compressing data after it is rehydrated but before it is sent over the network to the receiving host?

24.6.4 Recency of Data Protection

Looking at traditional backup and recovery operations in particular, most organizations will want to balance the speed at which a recovery can commence with the recentness of *when* the data was actually backed up in the first place.

For the most part, the more recently something was backed up, the more likely there is of a need to recover—and the faster the recovery should be. For instance, consider an environment with the following basic backups:

■ Daily backups retained for 6 weeks
■ Monthly backups retained for 13 months
■ Yearly backups retained for 7 years

Leaving aside the merits of considering data management and archive operations instead of using backup for long-term retention, the above sort of backup and retention schedule is reasonably common within a lot of businesses. Also common are the chances that the recoveries *most* frequently requested will be for data backed up in the last 24–72 hours. Therefore, the backup system should be designed in such a way that the data backed up most recently can be recovered fastest: it should be online, the product should support an instant start of a recovery when requested.

In architectures where backup to disk is primarily seen as a staging operation—backups land on disk for a relatively short period of time before being moved to tape—the goal should be to support at least 80–90% of the most frequently requested recoveries from the disk backups, and those disk backups should be sized accordingly.

DISK USED JUST FOR STAGING CAN BE RISKY

While backup to disk originated as a "staging" area, ongoing use of disk only for staging does introduce risk into the environment. Since the landing area is normally low in capacity compared to the overall environment being protected, data must be moved quickly to create more room for upcoming backups. A failed tape drive (assuming that's where data is being staged *to*) can quickly result in banked up or even aborted backups as the staging area fills. Also, since staging is an IO intensive process and done *outside* the backup window—usually during production hours—it may potentially impede recovery performance, or perhaps even *block* recoveries until the data has been moved.

Environments where *all* backups are stored on disk (usually leveraging deduplication—or more importantly, *inline* deduplication—to minimize footprint) will rarely need to consider this 80% or 90% rule, since data backed up yesterday will be recoverable at the same speed as data backed

up 3 months, 12 months, or 5 years ago. (It should be noted that deduplication systems performing *post-processing* deduplication can have entirely different performance characteristics depending on whether data can be recovered from the landing tier or the deduplication tier, *and* if the system is IO bound performing deduplication when a recovery request is made, this can substantially impact recovery performance.)

A new data-tiering option gaining traction is moving longer-term backups to cloud-based object storage, regardless of whether that's public, private, or hybrid cloud.* Cloud object storage *can* represent a much cheaper storage mechanism for cold data that is infrequently accessed than near-line storage,† so as an evolution of "disk to disk to tape," "disk to disk to cloud" is entering the data protection field. Cloud object storage typically represents a cheaper storage option at the cost of slower retrieval.‡ It's entirely reasonable after all for the business to maintain different recovery SLAs for operational or "business as usual" recoveries versus long-term compliance recoveries. While operational recoveries need to be geared for speed, recoveries for compliance reasons are usually allowed to take longer. After all, if a business achieves compliance recovery from backup rather than archive platforms, the total capacity required for long-term retention will usually massively exceed the operational recovery capacity.§ This requires cheaper storage, and with it, typically slower storage. Thus, in these situations, cloud object storage as a target for long-term data retention required for compliance only is quite a sensible approach.

24.7 Recovery Procedures and Recommendations

Most of the recommendations in this section are focused on recovery operations from backup; that being said, many will equally apply to any data recovery operation that requires human intervention, regardless of whether it is performed out of a backup product or some other form of protection such as snapshots, CDP, replication, or continuous storage availability.

The purpose of this topic is to move beyond the simple aspects of what can or can't be done for any individual product and discuss the more challenging topic—what *should* or *should not* be done.

---

* This tiering option is usually an attractive *additional* use case for businesses looking to deploy their own multipurpose object storage systems.
† Though the cost of retrieving bulk data from public cloud storage is not always considered, it can have a substantially deleterious effect on budget if unexpected situations occur. (Cloud-tiered storage that can leverage the nearline tier as a cache on long-term recovery requests can be an excellent mitigation technique.)
‡ Remember we previously discussed that tape is often not handled correctly when used for long-term retention, improperly skewing price comparisons.
§ Assume a starting size of 50 TB and no data growth for simplicity. With 4 weeks of daily incremental/weekly full backups and a 3.2% daily change rate, this would generate approximately 240 TB of backups. On the other hand, if 7 years of monthly full backups must be retained for compliance reasons, 84 monthlies will generate 4,200 TB of backups.

24.7.1 Read the Documentation before Starting a Recovery

While this might simply be thought of as "be trained in performing recoveries," there is more to it. While vendor supplied documentation will outline the practical steps involved in performing a recovery *from within the product*, as discussed in Section 24.2, there can be more involved in successfully restoring a function or even basic data than just simply following the recovery instructions in a product manual. This means that staff involved in recoveries should have a grasp of the recovery steps well *before* needing to perform a recovery, and there should be run-books or some other form of instructions customized to the business to handle ancillary details associated with the recovery that occur—or require consideration—outside of the backup product. This might include such details as:

- What processes or authorities need to be consulted to allow a recovery.
- What system activities need to be quiesced (if any) on either the client or the backup server to facilitate the recovery.
- What security requirements must be fulfilled to permit the recovery? Sites with more secure access policies may automatically tie system access or even access permissions with change requests.
- Organization standards or practices for where files and data should be recovered to, and under the various circumstances deemed most likely to occur (e.g., recovery of use files, user mail-boxes, applications, databases).
- How to recall or access backups that are not immediately online, particularly in tape-based environments.
- The procedures or processes to follow at the *end* of the recovery, differentiating particularly between what needs to be done at the end of both successful and *unsuccessful* recoveries.

Of course, this is just a sample list, and the actual list could vary considerably between businesses of different sizes, industry verticals, or maturity—but it does serve to highlight that company-built procedures for recoveries *should* be the norm, not the exception.

24.7.2 Choosing the Correct Recovery Location

It goes without saying that if not handled correctly, a recovery could conceivably result in a loss of even more data than being recovered—or a greater outage. One of the worst ways this can happen is to recover data to the wrong location. If a backup system supports directed recoveries, this can aggravate the problem further. As such it is very important to confirm the recovery location before initiating the recovery, and to understand any limitations that exist on where file(s) or data can be recovered to. Examples of recovery locations include:

- The original host and original location of the data
- The original host but another location for the data
- An alternate host with the same filesystem location/path
- An alternate host with a different filesystem location/path

Each option has different advantages and disadvantages. For instance, being able to perform a recovery to the original host and location is obviously critical when performing disaster recoveries, but can also be important for recovering critical files or system data that has been accidentally deleted or overwritten, as well as recovering partially deleted directory trees.

Recovering to the original host but a different location is typically a useful function for backup administrators, operators, or help desk staff. This is particularly the case if they perform the recoveries for end users who are unsure as to exactly which file(s) they want recovered. In this case, it is not unusual for an entire directory tree to be recovered to an alternate location, with the user asked to winnow through the recovered tree to locate the required file(s) before deleting the remainder of the (unneeded) recovered data.*

When recovering to an alternate host, recovering to an alternate directory path is often useful but may not always be required. For instance, if an environment features a production and a development system configured exactly the same way, the development system could be refreshed periodically with a copy of the production data via a recovery to the same location on a different host. Equally, when end users make recovery requests and can cite the exact files or location of the files to be recovered, many help desk and operations staff will recover those files back to their local machine and then simply email the files back to the end user.

It's recommended when performing recoveries that before the final "go" is executed on the recovery, the person performing the recovery should always ask himself or herself the following questions:

1. Have the correct file(s)/data been selected?
2. Was the correct host logged into prior to running the recovery command?
3. Has the correct recovery location been selected?
4. Is the recovery going to run to the correct destination host?

This typically amounts to 30 seconds or less of checking, but being in the habit of performing these checks can prevent some of the worst types of recovery mistakes that can be made.

THE RECOVERY YOU DON'T WANT

In a former role as both the consulting manager and the backup administrator for a company, a consultant came to me on a Friday afternoon saying he'd patched his Linux laptop but the patching failed. He'd already done some investigation and found that if he rebooted the laptop without recovery, it would likely fail to the point of needing a complete disaster recovery. However, if he could recover the root drive *before* rebooting, it should be OK.

I brought up a terminal window on his system and confirmed a couple of details, but his laptop was experiencing DNS issues, so I ssh'd across to the Solaris backup server to manually tweak some security settings in the backup product to allow connectivity, went back into the command line recovery interface, selected the root filesystem for recovery and hit go. I was keen to get home for the weekend.

The recovery was running for about 5 minutes when someone came in to tell me they couldn't log onto their thin-client desktop—provided by the Solaris backup server. I glanced at the recovery window and saw it was up to the /dev area† ... and realized I'd never logged out of the Solaris backup server before I started the recovery.

I was recovering a Linux root filesystem *over* a Solaris root filesystem, and it was for the actual backup server itself.

Instead of getting home for a relaxing weekend I spent almost all of the weekend in the office fixing a catastrophic mistake.

Since that weekend I have *never* started a recovery, no matter how trivial, without first asking myself those four questions previously mentioned.

---

* These styles of recovery requests might be dealt with alternately in situations where the backup product or an extension to the backup product handles more complex search options. Presented with an imprecise set of requirements from the end user, an administrator or recovery operator might be able to use a web-like search interface to find all matching data/files and execute the recovery directly from the search interface.

† Unix special devices for low-level hardware access, essential for system functionality.

24.7.3 Provide an Estimate of How Long the Recovery Will Take

In a help desk environment recovering standard files, this estimate should be provided effectively by the SLAs: a user should know that files will be recovered within 8 hours of the ticket being assigned, or email will be recovered within a day. But for more complex recoveries, for *infrastructure* recoveries where administrators have to get involved, estimates should be provided of how long the recovery is likely to take.

24.7.4 Provide Updates during Recoveries

In addition to providing an estimate of how long a recovery is likely to take, it's important to periodically provide updates on how the recovery is progressing, even if that update is "still recovering, no problems." Consider for instance a recovery that takes 4 hours and fails toward the end.

If no updates are given, the process might look like the following:

- 09:30—Recovery requested.
- 10:00—Recovery initiated, estimate of 4 hours to complete the recovery given.
- 15:00—User asks for an update because more than 4 hours has passed and the data is still not back.

Told there was an error and the recovery will be reattempted.

Picture yourself as the end user—this will be a frustrating experience, especially if having to *ask* for an update only to be told the clock is going to be reset. However, consider the following:

- 09:30—Recovery requested.
- 10:00—Recovery initiated, estimate of 4 hours to complete the recovery given.
- 12:00—Update indicating the recovery is proceeding OK is given.
- 13:30—Recovery fails. Update given to users saying the recovery will have to be restarted using the off-site copy, and this will take 8 hours to complete.
- 14:00—Users informed the recovery from the off-site copy has been initiated, with a new estimate for the recovery completion being start of business the next morning.

The personnel performing the recoveries are not the only ones under pressure—in some senses the users requesting or *requiring* the data to be recovered are more impacted. As such, keeping them informed of progress is a small but psychologically important task, and can have an excellent impact on business/IT relations.

AVOID SHRAPNEL RECOVERIES

In a former role as a junior system administrator there was one user who would become so panicked at the thought of data loss that he incessantly pestered the team any time he asked for a recovery. He'd be told how long the recovery would take to complete, but would then proceed to contact the team every 5 minutes, or come in and badger the person performing the recovery, even threatening formal complaints if it wasn't recovered "soon."

When we realized his problem was more the "unknown" and started providing regular updates during recoveries, he stopped trying to micromanage the process.

24.7.5 Don't Assume a Recovery Can Be Done If It Hasn't Been Tested

Data protection products should be reliable enough that you do not need to execute tests against 100% of the data being protected on 100% of the systems being protected to guarantee recoveries will work.

However, whenever a *new* system or a *new* application or a *new* set of protection requirements come into the environment, those systems, applications, and protection requirements *should* be thoroughly tested before entering production usage.

Or to put it another way: a business that introduces changes, new types of data or new applications without

appropriate change control and data protection testing is inviting disaster.

24.7.6 Run Recoveries from Sessions That Can Be Disconnected from/Reconnected To

It's the nature of recoveries to take a variable amount of time to complete depending on the amount of data or the complexity of the systems involved. It's frustrating enough having a recovery fail due to a hardware or media failure, but it is particularly time-wasting and frustrating to have a recovery fail simply because the connection was lost between the recovery interface and the backup server. Equally, it's frustrating to be forced to remain in the office until a recovery completes because it's been initiated from a session that can't be disconnected from without interruption.

Keep in mind there are a variety of interfaces that can be used within modern data protection products. These might include:

- Command line interfaces (CLIs)
- REST APIs
- Service portals (e.g., cloud-like portals and automated help desk systems)
- Client-side GUIs
- Modern, web-based GUIs
- Mobile (smartphone/tablet) based GUIs
- Traditional server GUIs (e.g., native applications, or Java based)

Depending on the option chosen, decoupling the initiation of the recovery from the recovery operation may be automatic. Modern, web-based GUIs and many traditional server GUIs for instance (and other interfaces built around

these principles—REST, mobile, etc.) will usually work in this manner. Client-side GUIs and command line tools may not, and may require consideration in advance of starting the recovery to allow the user to disconnect while having the recovery continue to run. For Unix/Linux platforms, this might be achieved via the "screen" utility with a CLI. For Windows recoveries, Microsoft's Remote Desktop software can be used to connect to a system, run a recovery, then disconnect while preserving the session.

24.7.7 Remember Quantum Physics

Monitoring can be useful, but excessive monitoring can result in skewed results if the act of monitoring impacts the performance. Therefore, the level of monitoring should be carefully chosen when performing recoveries. For example, if recovering a few hundred files there may be little impact in seeing a file-by-file listing of what has been recovered. However, if recovering a million files, the display of each file-name may become a limiting factor in the ability to obtain accurate updates of *where* the recovery is up to.

A WATCHED RECOVERY NEVER COMPLETES?

When running a disaster recovery once on a Solaris server via a 9600 baud console, the recovery appeared to take 6 hours to complete. But when the recovery finally "finished" and the server could be accessed again, it was observed the recovery had actually completed in 4 hours—it had simply taken another 2 hours to finish displaying all the files that had been recovered, one at a time.

Recoveries always need to be monitored (if for no other reason to report their completion), but can be frequently monitored through less intrusive mechanisms (even at a loss of some granularity) to see where the recovery is up to. For instance, rather than seeing a file-by-file listing for a large filesystem, periodically checking the *size* of the recovered filesystem, or the amount of data reported as recovered by the backup product may provide a sufficient update on the recovery progress.

24.7.8 Be Patient

Almost everyone would have been told when growing up that "patience is a virtue," usually in response to wanting something faster, sooner, or better. As computers, storage, and data transfer speeds continue to increase patience is sometimes forgotten. This comes down to a "brute force" approach to solving problems—if it isn't fast enough, don't optimize, just throw more memory/CPU/spindles at the problem and hope that it goes away. Yet, big data tells us there is a point at which adding more speed to a single system

becomes either impractical or pointless: sometimes problems have to be optimized, and in fact, sometimes you still just have to wait. This can be particularly true when performing a recovery.

While systems should be designed to ensure recoveries can complete within the required SLAs, there's always a limit to miracles. Recovering 100 GB of data over a link with a maximum usable throughput of 10 MB/s will take at least 2.84 hours no matter how urgently the data is to be recovered. Sometimes aborting a recovery to diagnose why it's "going slow" might result in no performance improvement *and* needing to restart the recovery from scratch. In short: when performing a recovery, there will always be an upper limit on how fast it can be completed, and you should either know or be able to work that out at least approximately.

24.7.9 Document the Current Status of the Recovery

Some recovery scenarios can't be completed in a single work-shift. Particularly in major disaster recovery situations, entire storage systems might need to be rebuilt or re-provisioned, virtual infrastructure may need to be stood up, and *then* a recovery might still need to be performed. A single person may not be able to perform the entire end-to-end recovery, and therefore anyone working on a recovery should be certain to document progress—and any issues encountered to date—so that in the event of someone else having to take over, they have a good understanding of the current progress that has been made.

24.7.10 Note Errors, and What Led to Them

Particularly for mature or compliance-regulated businesses, a root cause analysis (RCA) may be required after a recovery—particularly if there were errors, delays or unexpected results during the process. Alternately, smaller businesses may not need to perform RCAs, but should regardless be desirous of learning from, and making each recovery a more streamlined and simple process.

Either way, if errors are encountered during a recovery, they should be noted, their solution (or workaround) also noted, and this should be documented for the organization. If the errors result in the need for support cases with a vendor, those support case IDs and end solutions should also be noted.

24.7.11 Don't Assume the Recovery Is an Exam

A certification exam usually consists of being locked in a room without any internet access, notes, or communication, and the student is asked to solve a series of problems from memory. This isn't really a real-world situation; it usually demonstrates rote memorization and some problem solving capacity, but it isn't reflective of how we solve problems when we're faced with them in normal situations. During a recovery situation therefore, always remember to leverage any information or access to support that exists, whenever it is needed. Obstinacy does not guarantee results in most cases, nor does getting flustered to the point of not evaluating other options.

It's not uncommon to see people struggling with recoveries for an extended period of time without checking documentation, searching the internet, or contacting vendor support. What starts off as a small problem when there is plenty of time to spare in the recovery window can end up becoming a critical problem when the recovery window has almost expired. Therefore, why exacerbate the problem by treating it like an exam?

24.7.12 Ensure the Recovery Is Performed by Those Trained to Do It

Unless recoveries are designed to be entirely self-service via a cloud-like *X*aaS portal, they should by and large be performed by the *intended* user who has had the *intended* amount of training. While this means an end user might recover their email directly from their email tool by clicking a "Recover" tab (particularly in a SaaS environment), it's equally the case that as the complexity of the recovery increases, the training of the person performing the recovery should also be increased. This is something we've already touched on in Section 21.3—databases and complex applications in particular should be performed by their subject matter experts, not just someone with limited experience in the backup product and no experience in the application.

A corollary to this is to ensure that staff *are* adequately trained, regardless of whether that's formal or informal training. It is still common to encounter managers who are reluctant to train their staff in the administration and operation of low-level infrastructure such as storage and data protection.

24.7.13 Write a Post-Recovery Report

This speaks to maturity and formalization within the environment; application, business function, and system recoveries are *serious* business, and should be documented accordingly. As mentioned earlier, this may be through an RCA, but it may be as simple as an email summary sent to management and the appropriate teams to inform them what was done, what issues were encountered, what lessons were learnt, and, equally importantly, what *worked* properly. (Environments that keep track of support cases or trouble tickets will likely see this report generated as part of ticket closure.)

24.7.14 Update Incorrect Instructions

Documentation is not always updated with the same frequency as changes are made within an environment, however much we'd like them to be in lock-step. Operating systems might be upgraded, backup agents might be upgraded, even applications might be upgraded, and the documentation might be left the same as it was originally written.

So if a recovery is being performed and the steps required to complete the recovery differ with what has been documented, the changes and the circumstances that led to those changes should be included in the documentation. Note that it's preferable to expand documentation with additional use cases rather than simply assuming the scenario encountered is the *only* possible scenario that might be encountered. For instance, while some steps might be determined to be redundant for a particular operating system and database, they may still be essential for an earlier version of either, and such versions may either still be in use or have compliance backups that *might* (one day) need to be recovered from.

24.7.15 Considerations Specific to Tape

While tape is decreasing in use, it still appears in a variety of environments and there are some considerations that are particularly focused on tape:

■ *Acclimatize off-site recovery media*: Tapes are particularly sensitive to changes in humidity and temperature. If tapes are either stored or transported in such a way that their temperature or humidity is different from the computer room in which they'll be used, they should be given up to 24 hours to acclimatize to the new temperature and humidity before being loaded into a drive.* Failing to do this in particularly humid environments can result in tapes being destroyed on access.

■ *Always write-protect tape before starting a recovery*: A customer summed this up perfectly over a decade ago: "if you have to touch a tape, write-protect it." Their policy was a simple one: when removing tapes from their tape library, operators were required to enable the write-protect tab. The write-protect tab would *always* be left in the read-only mode *unless* operators received a specific request to reload the tape *for recycling*.

■ *Patience particularly applies to tape*: Earlier we said you should be patient during recoveries. This particularly applies to tape-based recoveries. Tape loads, unloads, deposit, and withdraw operations all take a particular amount of time and can't be rushed. If your environment still uses tape, you should be particularly cognizant of the amount of time each of these operations take.

■ *Recall all media required before starting a recovery*: If you need to perform a recovery that uses media currently stored off-site, make sure you request *all* required volumes in one go.

■ *If media errors occur, retry elsewhere*: If a tape fails in a particular drive, the error may be with the tape, or it may be with the drive. If the tape gets "chewed up" another copy of the data will be required to recover from, and as much as possible this should be loaded into *another* tape drive to attempt the recovery from in case the fault is with the tape drive rather than the tape.

■ *Preserve the number of copies of backups*: The same number of copies of a backup should exist at the end of a recovery that existed at the start. If a tape fails during

the recovery process and the clone/duplicate tape needs to be used for recovery, then at the end of the recovery a *new* copy should be generated to ensure there are still two copies of the data available.†

■ *Send off-site media back off-site*: If media is recalled from off-site for a recovery, it should be sent back off-site at the end of the recovery, unless it is going to be reused within 24 hours. The media was sent off-site for a reason: for disaster protection. Keeping the media on-site, presumably having *all* copies of the backup on-site, introduces risk to the business.

24.8 Disaster Recovery Considerations

Everything previously mentioned for recoveries will equally apply to disaster recoveries, but there are a few additional recommendations and best practices to apply during a disaster recovery situation as well.

24.8.1 Maintenance Backups

Wherever possible, *before* major maintenance tasks are performed, backups should take place. System patches, core driver changes, major application upgrades, and a plethora of other maintenance operations can cause significant damage if they go awry. Having a backup which is as up to date as possible to recover from can substantially reduce recovery time and amount of data loss in the event of a significant failure.‡ Note that depending on the type of system maintenance being performed, other forms of online data protection such as snapshots may be more desirable before maintenance operations.

Equally, if a major system change is performed (e.g., the operating system is upgraded, or the database is upgraded triggering a data format change), performing a new full backup of the system as soon as possible is equally important. This can dramatically reduce recovery complexity, or even prevent recovery failure, in the event of a failure happening a short period after major system changes.

24.8.2 Avoid Upgrades

Disaster recoveries are not the time or place to perform additional upgrades or changes to the system. The goal should

---

* A customer operating in Darwin, Australia, less than 1,500 km from the equator, would store their "local" tapes in a safe approximately 200 m from their computer room. Even at this short a distance, transporting them from the safe to the computer room would leave the tapes needing acclimatization before being used in a tape drive.

† This is another common example of where best practice tape management is not always performed, and can contribute to complete data loss situations if the same data is requested at a later point in time.

‡ This can be even more critical in virtualized environments. If a product can leverage changed block tracking for *restores* as well as backups, a virtual machine might be recoverable in minutes or less after a failed maintenance cycle.

be to get the system back *as it was* and introduce no further complexity into the process. Indeed, businesses with mature IT processes (e.g., following ITIL) will expressly forbid changes being performed during disaster recovery situations.

IF YOU DO MAKE CHANGES, NOTE THEM WHEN YOU GET INTO TROUBLE

A system administrator was once trying to perform a disaster recovery of a Windows server. When he ran into problems, he logged a support case and the team spent over a day investigating the issue. Every attempt to remediate failed. What should have been a simple Windows 2003 disaster recovery was just running into error after error.

After the customer's IT management demanded on-site assistance to resolve the urgent issue, it was determined that the system that had been backed up was a Windows 2000 server, not a Windows 2003 server. The system administrator had decided to install Windows 2003 as part of the recovery process. As soon as the recovery was reattempted against a Windows 2000 server, it worked first go.

24.8.3 Read the Documentation before Backups Are Performed

Disaster recovery can be a complex task, and may require preparatory steps to be performed as part of the backup process. A "disaster recovery guide" for instance may not only provide steps for performing a disaster recovery, but details of procedures to enact during backups, such as:

- Operating system databases requiring scripted exports
- Operating system or application files that are not backed up by default
- Key files that may not be accessible when in use

All of this information should be known and understood during the backup and, indeed, should be understood as part of the system *architecture* process.

24.8.4 Disaster Recoveries Must Be Run by Administrators

Although standard recoveries can often be handed over to help desk staff or even end users, disaster recovery operations should be considered essential activities of the appropriate administrators relating to the applications, systems, and infrastructure that has failed (see again Section 24.4).

24.8.5 Use Compatible Infrastructure

If recovering physical systems this usually means recovering to the *same* physical systems—the same CPUs, the same adapters, and so on. However, this is not always the case—some backup products support "Physical to Virtual" (PTV) recoveries where a previously physical system is converted into a virtual machine as part of the recovery process. (This may even allow conversion during the recovery between supported hypervisor types.) While PTV recoveries may seem contrary to the previous recommendation to "avoid upgrades," they should be deemed acceptable when (1) required *and* (2) supported by the backup product.

Regardless of whether the recovery is a physical or virtual one, other considerations include:

- Ensuring the same system resources are allocated (CPU, memory, etc.)
- Ensuring the same (or sufficient) storage is allocated
- Ensuring shared infrastructure is not impacted by the recovery—for instance, if a heavy workload virtual server is recovered onto a hypervisor already at its operational limit, this could cause larger problems for the environment

24.8.6 Know the System Dependencies

This combines the need for context aware recoveries, a requirement to understand the difference between data recovery and system restoration *and* the importance of system dependency maps and/or tables, as outlined in Section 4.4.2.2. A system map is critical in disaster recovery situations to ensure that systems are processed in the correct order to ensure business functions are restored as efficiently and quickly as possible. Knowing the system dependencies allows the coordination of multisystem and multifunction recoveries with the appropriate prioritization given to resources and systems.

24.8.7 Keep Accurate System Documentation

This can be reduced to two factors:

1. Deployment of a data protection system should not be seen as an excuse to avoid documenting required system components (e.g., licensing, application configuration).

2. A data protection product can only protect what it is designed to protect—for instance, a backup product can't reconstruct LUNs at the storage level.*

System documentation deemed essential to ensuring overall environment recoverability should be stored both on-site and off-site in a suitably secured location.† Similarly, essential passwords and licenses should be appropriately protected so they are available in a disaster, using corporate and/or regulatory security standards.

24.8.8 Do You Know Where Your Licenses Are at 1am?

Although hinted at in the above point, this deserves special mention: there is more to a disaster recovery than just restoring data. Indeed, if handled correctly, the data restoration component should be the most straightforward and least interactive part of the entire process.

The best-laid disaster recovery plans can come unstuck for the simplest of reasons. What if the data protection software or system won't install or activate required functionality without the licenses? Always ensure the disaster recovery documentation includes *complete* details of all the licenses used by the data protection systems so they can be manually re-keyed or copied/pasted if required.

When recording licensing details, be sure to record all the details associated with the licenses. This includes details such as:

■ The purchase order number used to procure the licenses (in case you need to supply this for a new license activation against your system)
■ Any "anchoring" details of your system—while you may still get licenses in the form of a stand-alone activation key, or a combination of an activation and authorization key, many licenses these days are "locked" to particular details about a host: IP address, hostname, system ID, etc.

Failure to record these additional details may result in licenses which cannot be used in a timely manner during a disaster recovery. Obviously these caveats apply to all systems within your environment, not just the data protection environment itself.

24.8.9 Disaster Recovery Exercises

Disaster recovery exercises are a vital business activity that should be regularly performed to check the health of the data protection environment. There are several approaches to disaster recovery exercises:

■ *Simulated disaster*: A "what if" scenario is posed and the appropriate staff and teams are assembled to map out what would be done to restore business operations.
■ *Readiness tests*: Disaster recovery systems are isolated and their production components (e.g., databases) are started on them to confirm either disaster recovery procedures or functional readiness.
■ *System failover*: Individual hosts or storage systems are failed over from one site to another.
■ *Business function failover*: An entire business function (e.g., invoicing, online shopping/eCommerce) is failed over from one datacenter to another and used in production for a nominated period of time.
■ *Operational failover*: The entire operations are failed over from one datacenter to another and used *as production* for a nominated period of time.

In actual fact, *all* exercises above have their own use within the business. Simulated disasters are an excellent form of planning, readiness tests can be used to validate documented procedures, and each of system, business function, and operational failover actually help the business *prove* that it can successfully migrate functionality from one datacenter to another. Further, each of those exercises (system, business function, operational) provide proof of something equally important: that the disaster recovery environment can in fact run production operations. Many businesses—particularly in the mid-market to low-end enterprise space—will populate their disaster recovery site with equipment that has been phased *out* of their production sites. As production sites grow, this can result in situations where the disaster recovery site may not actually have sufficient compute or storage resources to *run* production. While optimally this should be avoided at an architectural level or discovered at a monitoring level, it is still better to determine it during a disaster recovery exercise when the production site still remains than in a true disaster recovery situation.

For organizations needing to provide compliance-style proof of their disaster recovery readiness, engaging external auditors may be a mandatory function of disaster recovery exercises. For smaller organizations and businesses that are not in heavily regulated industry verticals, external auditors

---

* This is often seen as another advantage of converged or hyperconverged infrastructure and the software defined datacenter. Virtualized and systems running on hyperconverged infrastructure becomes highly mobile and allows infrastructure administrators to execute end-to-end protection processes without regard to the underlying physical infrastructure.
† Remember this documentation is a blueprint to overall environment recovery and practically offers the keys for the environment to an attacker if stolen.

may not be required, but periodic engagement of subject matter experts to supervise and monitor (to "ride shotgun," as it were) the disaster recovery exercise can be essential in providing feedback on the likely reliability and accuracy of the procedures.

24.9 Protecting the Protection Environment

For the most part our discussions have been around the protection of primary data—regardless of whether that's applications, business systems, or core data. Yet, there's another type of data and system within an environment that needs protecting—the protection environment itself. A common mistake is to consider protection systems to be non-production. While they aren't *primary production* in the same way that a database server hosting a mission critical system is, they are true "secondary" production systems in that their availability and reliability is critical to overall infrastructure and systems availability and recoverability within the environment.

Or to put it another way: your protection environment should never represent a single point of failure within the environment. (If, somehow it is, it should only be after the business has signed off against the risks posed by that situation.)

Consider storage replication—this is dependent not only on the availability of the target storage system, but also the link between the two storage systems. A business that seeks to provide synchronous or even small-granularity asynchronous replication between storage systems hosting business-critical functions will find that replication interrupted immediately if the replication link disappears. Thus, a single link between sites may very well represent a single point of failure in data protection to the business. (Indeed, this is one of the most common failure points that businesses will seek to design around.) Having standby links or active/active links that allow data protection replication to survive the failure of a single communications channel isn't about "gold plating" the environment, but about ensuring adequate protection can be provided even in the event of a single failure.

Similarly, when we think of backup and recovery systems, those systems need to include a high degree of redundancy to ensure a cascading failure (e.g., a primary system failure and a protection system failure) does not prevent data recoverability. This includes options such as:

- Ensuring disk-based protection storage uses RAID to survive the failure of one or more disks—protection data loss should not occur as a result of disk failure

- Ensuring deduplication protection storage has self-checking and self-healing mechanisms beyond simple RAID*
- Ensuring backups of production systems are duplicated to another storage system (be it protection storage, cloud, or tape) at another location
- Ensuring the configuration and metadata associated with the backup system—or indeed any protection system—is replicated and recoverable in the event of the protection system itself failing and is retained for the same life span of the protection data being generated

One item often not considered when protecting the protection environment itself is log files—these should be protected (via backup or whatever mechanism is appropriate) for the length of time the data they are protecting is being retained for. The reason is simple: there is a considerable difference between being able to say a failure has occurred and being able to report *why* the failure occurred. Regardless of whether it's snapshots being retained for a fortnight, backups being retained for 7 years, or archives being retained for 70 years, the logging information associated with the protection (or archive) operation performed should be retained for *at least* as long as the data itself is being retained for. This enables far more comprehensive analysis at any point in the retention period if an attempt is made to retrieve the data and it fails. Current logs will allow analysis as to whether the failure has occurred as a result of the retrieval operation, but historical log analysis may allow an administrator or technician to determine if the protection was ever properly performed in the first place. While ideally such failures *should* be captured at the time of the event, short-term log retention against long-term data retention is a reckless space saving approach that blinkers a business during root cause analysis and diagnosis functions.

24.10 Cyber-Recovery

Gone are the days where hacking is primarily seen as a function of corporate espionage. Organized crime and other aggressive malicious hackers are increasingly using tools such as *ransomware* to extort large amounts of sums from individuals *and* businesses. Ransomware might be a payload on top of a normal virus or Trojan which not only infects

---

* For example, regular checksum validation and options around storage evacuation are critical in deduplication systems. While traditional tape-based backups or even regular disk-based backups can potentially survive the loss of a single backup or a single piece of media, deduplication is space-efficient by having multiple copies reference and leverage the *same* stored data, almost in a similar way to snapshots. Without additional checking and healing capabilities a business may be exposing itself to unacceptable risk.

systems, but it *encrypts* systems and refuses to handover the decryption keys until a verified payment is made by the user.

Such an attack on a consumer is bad enough—particularly given end consumers typically have a lackadaisical approach to data protection. Reports of consumers either losing all their data—sometimes years of photos and documents—or being forced to pay hundreds or thousands of dollars to get access to their own data again are becoming a daily occurrence.

Imagine uncontrolled ransomware infecting a corporate fileserver, potentially *petabytes* of data becoming encrypted.* Imagine organized crime deliberately infiltrating via social engineering and other discovery processes an organization enough to not only get ransomware encrypting data, but *also* deleting backups, forcing the payment of millions or more for data access. This is no longer science fiction; it is inevitable. The systematic deletion of backups prior to erasing primary storage data has, in fact, already happened to multiple companies.

This is leading to a new strategy in data protection—cyber-recovery sites (CRSs)—sometimes also known as "Isolated Recovery Sites." These are "dark" sites that business-critical data is written to, typically via protection storage, and architected in such a way that compliance-compatible locking is used to *enforce* data retention and security. This may mean for instance that backups are replicated from the primary or secondary datacenter during a limited window (e.g., the network may only be opened between sites for 4 hours a day), *and* the protection storage is operated in a WORM format—data once written may not be overwritten, changed, or even deleted until the expiration date has passed. Thus, in the event of a significant and destructive intrusion into the IT environment causing complete data loss, the company can resort to a "read only" copy. While such environments may represent a significant spend, the alternative—particularly for businesses seen as key targets of organized crime—of paying orders of magnitude more to gain access to data encrypted by malware is increasingly making the notion of a CRS a *must-have* rather than a *nice-to-have* for major enterprises. Such replication is usually configured as a "pull" replication from the CRS during periodic network connectivity. Most critically, the primary backup system will not be aware of the tertiary, CRS copy. Thus, even if the primary backup environment is compromised, it will not lead to the compromise of the CRS copy.

CRS work best and are architected best in situations where:

- A minimum number of storage, infrastructure, and data protection vendors are used.

- Centralized data protection storage is used.
- Data protection techniques are standardized throughout the business.
- The system is well documented with excellent processes.
- Recovery roles are well understood.

While a CRS can be built and maintained with *none* of the above, each of the above can significantly speed recovery time should the site ever be needed, and can make the ongoing maintenance of the CRS considerably simpler. Critical, of course, is the ability to define "retention locks" against data protection storage that are vendor and compliance certified so that even if a rogue attacker *does* get electronic access to the system, they have insufficient capabilities on their own to cause data deletion or corruption.

It should be noted that a CRS is *not* a disaster recovery site. The typical production/disaster recovery site relationship still exists and remains the same. In Figure 24.1 we can see a basic high level diagram of the relationship between the three sites. For the purposes of simplicity, automated control and test systems residing in the CRS environment have not been shown in the diagram. Control systems will initiate network links and drop them after a predetermined amount of time has elapsed and instruct test systems to validate data. Test systems should be configured within the CRS environment to automatically recover data (including any backup server disaster recovery functions) and verify the integrity of that data. This serves to (a) constantly confirm that recovery in the event of a catastrophic data encryption/deletion is possible and (b) potentially even detect such an event as it is taking place, particularly if it is being executed slowly.

A CRS is not constructed for regular disaster recovery situations—site loss or site destruction—but for one particular scenario, site *erasure*. It assumes the production and/or disaster recovery sites still exist, and still have the equipment required to run the business, *but* have had systems or storage compromised to the point where a large amount of data has either been erased, or *must* be erased in order to restore operational integrity. Thus, the primary infrastructure at the CRS will be whatever retention locked protection storage is required to act as a source for recovery in an erasure emergency, *not* traditional disaster recovery infrastructure including compute, network, and primary storage.

In terms of the amount of content pulled into the CRS, there are two primary schools of thought: the first approach is to focus on the typically 10–20% of data within the business which is most "mission critical." This is often represented as, "If this data ceases to exist, so too does the business." However, this does potentially leave the business exposed: if the other 90–80% of the business data is irretrievably lost due to a significant hactivist/insider attack, there may be significant repercussions, even if the business can stay running, of having lost a significant amount of other data.

---

* Though it would be hoped that such an attack would be noticed before that volume of data was affected.

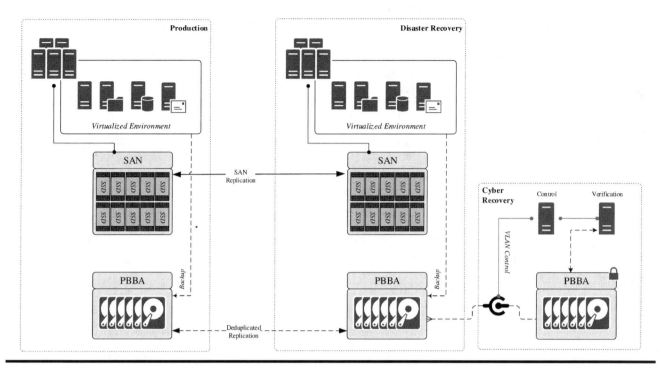

Figure 24.1 Conceptual view of a cyber recovery site.

In a modern, compliance-dominated environment with heavy legal requirements around data retention, an alternate approach is to ensure that *all* data (or at least, all *production* data) is protected by the CRS. The purpose of this approach is to not only get the business back up and running after a significant attack on its internal systems, *but* to also ensure it will continue to meet its legal obligations to governments and the share market(s) it operates in.

24.11 Summary

Data protection is more than just a *proactive* process. A multitude of steps can be taken to avoid the need to recover data, and in cases where mission critical systems must be available 24×7 it's a practical imperative that data *recovery* is never required. Systems with no countenance for data loss and a requirement for instantaneous or near-instantaneous service restoration will require advanced data protection techniques to allow for continuous replication, continuous journaling, continuous availability and the ability to rollback to a prior data point orders of magnitude faster than recovery from a backup or perhaps even recovery from a snapshot. Yet such systems will still usually require backup systems if only for compliance recoveries—and there's still merits in providing

operational recovery services even *if* they should never be called for in normal circumstances.

For most businesses, regardless of their size or their complexity, recovery from backups *is* a typical business process. For smaller businesses this could be an optional recovery technique for almost all systems, and for larger businesses it will apply to a subset of systems for which mission critical 24×7 availability is not required. (Providing "platinum" service levels for *all* systems, even development and test, or noncritical business functions is too costly in an IT world dependent on shrinking budgets and is something few if any Chief Information Officers or company boards would agree to.)

For the foreseeable future, traditional backup systems remain a cornerstone of a data protection environment, and likewise, traditional *recovery* processes remain a cornerstone of a data protection environment.

24.12 Self-Reflection

Consider a situation where a business has focused disaster recovery testing based on "thought exercises," or "dry runs."

What sort of risks would this pose in a real disaster recovery situation?

Chapter 25

Long-Term Retention Considerations

25.1 Introduction

Invariably, long-term retention refers to "compliance" copies of data that we must retain for legal, fiduciary, or other mandatory requirements. Sometimes these requirements may be imposed internally from the business, but more usually they are imposed externally by a government or some other body with authority over the business.

There are two schools of thought in information technology when it comes to long-term retention of data protection copies, and usually more specifically, backups. These are:

- Backups should not be used for long-term retention—all compliance retention should be achieved via archival activities.
- Backups will inevitably be used for long-term retention because it is seen as simpler and easier than an archive-based approach.

While there is real attraction in placing making compliance retention a problem for archival systems, the reality is that this is done rarely—and usually on a workload by workload basis. You are far more likely, for instance, to find email retention compliance being achieved through an archival system than you are say, database retention compliance, or virtual machine retention compliance.

Yet it must be said: businesses that don't perform data classification and lifecycle management as a primary storage activity will inevitably look to backup and recovery systems to solve this problem.

It is relatively common to see confusion around compliance retention of data protection copies. The business might never formally advise the IT department of retention requirements, resulting in a haphazard approach. Or, there might be blanket directives: "keep monthlies forever," that don't consider the cumulative impact on data protection capacity of such approaches.

25.2 Determining Long-term Retention Requirements

Despite common behavior in many businesses, it should not be the responsibility of the IT department to determine the compliance retention requirements, either in terms of frequency *or* longevity. This is the case regardless of whether we are trying to achieve long-term retention via archive, backup, or a mix of the two.

Let us consider the RACI matrix often used in project management, as it is a good model to determine roles when it comes to decisions around long-term retention. RACI is broken down as follows:

- *Responsible*: Who must do the actual task.
- *Accountable*: Who approves or sponsors the work. We might even call this "the buck stops here:" in legal terms, we might consider this to be the most senior person at risk of fine or incarceration of the company fails its duties.
- *Consulted*: Who provides subject expertise on the activity.
- *Informed*: Who is told about the activities.

We can even approach this from two perspectives:

- Determining the retention requirements
- Implementing the retention requirements

Let's consider the process of *determining* the compliance retention requirements for the business. This might see a model such as:

- *Responsible*: Legal
- *Accountable*: Board of directors
- *Consulted*: Business owners and IT
- *Informed*: Business users

When we consider it from the perspective of implementing the required retention policies, the roles shift a little:

- *Responsible*: IT
- *Accountable*: Board of directors
- *Consulted*: Business owners and Legal
- *Informed*: Business users

Indeed, the same RACI lists apply not only to determining and acting on compliance retention, but also equally applies to data classification and data lifecycle management processes, too.

You might note that regardless of whether we're considering the preliminary (and in fact, ongoing) task of *determining* compliance retention requirements, it will (for many jurisdictions) be the board of directors for the company who are ultimately responsible for ensuring the business meets is compliance retention. (Alternately, it may be similarly senior roles, such as CEO, CIO, or CFO. For private companies it may be the managing director.) In short: there should always be a senior executive sponsor of this activity.

Since compliance retention requirements are usually placed on the business from external authorities, the ideal scenario for ensuring those requirements are properly captured comes from legal teams. While they may in turn refer to IT for technical practicalities and to the business owners for an understanding of the data and functions of the business (e.g., confirming what sort of accounting records are kept), it should be the legal counsel for the company that provides appropriately considered recommendations.

A common mistake when considering long-term retention is to focus almost exclusively on financial data—particularly for publicly traded companies. Such data is of course important and forms a part of the compliance retention data, but it is by no means guaranteed to be the *only* compliance retention data—the remainder will often be industry vertical and company product specific.

Ideally those recommendations should include not just retention requirements, but also records *deletion* requirements—guiding the business on best legal compliance practices for when data should be deleted. Without strongly guided recommendations, businesses will usually err on the side of caution and rarely delete data, even though it adds to ongoing management and protection activities—and sometimes without understanding the risk that data kept *beyond* the legally required time can still be discovered or subpoenaed in many jurisdictions.

Effective consideration of long-term retention requirements starts with understanding the legal obligations, and establishing a level of data lifecycle management, as well. There is however another pre-requisite to effectively dealing with long-term retention, however: data classification.

Some would argue that data classification is something that should be handled during data protection activities; this approach might be best described as "locking the barn door after the horse has bolted." Effective data classification is done against primary storage systems, as part of the data lifecycle management process, and *from* this data classification, appropriate data protection policies can be readily established.

25.3 Why Is Archive Challenging?

In a best practices system that utilizes a comprehensive data lifecycle management process (see Figure 3.2), archive is as much as part of the lifecycle as storage, ingestion and deletion. Yet as we discussed in Chapter 3, lifecycle management is the exception, not the norm.

There are two reasons behind this:

- Storage is cheap.
- Archive is hard.

The "storage is cheap" argument is the perennial *kicking-the-can-down-the-road* approach: if it costs $1,000 to develop a data lifecycle policy to manage storage properly, or $200 to expand the storage system to avoid running out of capacity, most businesses will spend the $200 rather than the $1,000. As an initial, up-front investment, implementing data lifecycle management will have a tangible cost to it, but deploying more storage doesn't *solve* the problem, it just *avoids* it for a while. Given IT departments are constantly pressured by businesses to "do more with less," it's perhaps not so very surprising.

The other factor is that archive is not an easy topic. There are decisions that need to be made regarding:

- Does this data have to be kept?
- Can we just delete this data?
- Can we exclude this data from backup?
- How long does this data have to be kept?
- How would we keep this data?

As also discussed earlier, *delete* is an indelicate term for many businesses—not just IT departments. If the business tells the IT department that particular content should be deleted, usually the IT department will comply. However, as stated in 25.2, while the IT department may be responsible for deleting data, it's the business that is *accountable* for deleting the data, and it's often difficult to find someone within the business to accept that accountability. The same goes for archive.

Even after someone has accountability for establishing data lifecycle, the next challenge is picking a product or process that will handle it. Note that this *can* be process driven, particularly in organizations that are project focused. An engineering firm for instance, at the closure of a particular project, might have processes to collect all the data relating to that project and write that data to an archive share on a fileserver in a particular directory structure. This might include designs, customer communications, compliance reports, and even database exports. A magazine company might wrap-up the completion of each month's issue using a similar process, making it easy to get access to previously created content.

Such process driven archive systems have often evolved from removable media days: engineering companies might have generated multiple "archive" tapes prior to deleting data (or scheduling it to be deleted), and magazine companies might have written those issue archives to optical media so they could be still accessed, but removed from primary storage.

Not everything is susceptible to project-based archive processing though. Many areas of document storage, databases and messaging (including, of course, email) will require continuous archive systems. What can be achieved will be dependent on the appetite and budget of the business, and the availability of tools. Herein lays a new challenge: product fragmentation. You can get document archive systems, and you can get database archive systems, and you can get email archive systems—but it's rare to get a single archive system that does all three. Choices, inevitably, have to be made about the number of archive systems that might be used to achieve compliance purposes.

In some cases, these choices might be to *not* use an archive system, and instead fall-back to alternate processes. A business might deploy an email archive system for instance, but when it comes to databases, might elect for regularly scheduled database *exports* so that even if over the course of 20 years, database formats drift, there will be a copy of the database not in binary format, but in a collection of SQL commands. (Such commands may not automatically import into a new database, but they'd be subject for review and adjustment to allow import if necessary—or more likely if nothing else, allow visual review of the data content for an audit/compliance requirement.)

As soon as content goes into an archive system, the business has a new long-term product and data management requirement. Ideally an archive system will require few, if any backups—particularly if done to meet regulatory compliance requirements, archive platforms will be written in WORM format and replicated—thus potentially removing them from backup operations.*

However, archive doesn't mean you can avoid worrying about long-term retention.

ARCHIVE ISN'T JUST "SET AND FORGET"

A business might in 2004 have deployed product A from vendor Y to handle email archive operations. In 2009 the relationship might have changed, and the business switched from product A to product B, sold by vendor Z.

Rather than going through a migration operation involving the re-call and re-archive of email stored by product A, the company might choose to run product A for a year or two before shutting it down, only to be re-started in the event of a legal search being executed.

What happens then, if vendor Y discontinues product A and instead releases product C? That vendor might provide migration services for a year or two between its two products, but eventually drops the migration services after its active install base has been moved across.

Enter 2018, and the company must run a legal search against all archived email. What happens if something prevents product A from working? Maybe it's no longer compatible with the email system in use, maybe it has a corrupt archive index, or maybe someone thought it was OK to move the storage from one share to another, but now that someone attempted to start the archive software when its configuration had been pointing at the old storage, the records are "lost?"

While archive may help to address compliance requirements, it has its own longevity considerations, too.

This isn't just a thought experiment: it happened, causing a legal discovery nightmare.

---

* If replicated, even if WORM-format archives aren't completely removed from backup cycles, their use might be substantially reduced—such as monthly backups retained for 3–6 months. Since data cannot be deleted or modified from the archive, the backup would exist only as a disaster recovery option in the event of a significant cascading failure within the archive platform. Obviously the ideal approach is to design the archive platform to avoid this type of scenario.

25.4 Revisiting Storage Requirements for Long-term Retention

Inevitably, for many businesses, compliance retention will still fall to the backup product. With this in mind, it's worth revisiting *what* sort of storage requirements we need to deal with in these situations. To do this, let's consider an example business that starts with 700 TB of front-end data* with a 20% annual growth rate. We will consider the *logical* (i.e., backed up) data retention requirements, without any consideration of deduplication at this point.

The business has determined that it has a standard 7-year retention requirement and it will achieve this via backups. In such a scenario, we might consider three potential retention policies:

- Retention A: Retain monthly backups for 7 years
- Retention B: Retain monthly backups for 13 months and yearly backups for 7 years (June)
- Retention C: Retain monthly backups for 13 months and six-monthly backups (June and December) for 7 years

(An alternate form to the second two retention profiles might retain monthly backups for only 12 months.)

Let's consider the basics to start with—what does a 20% annual growth rate look like? We will assume the 20% annual growth rate amortizes evenly over the course of every month during the period—i.e., a 1.530947% monthly growth rate. If the monthly backups or yearly backups are always captured at the end of a month, our *first* full backup would be 710.7 TB.

At the end of 7 years, our front-end TB size for the environment will have grown to 2,508.2 TB. If we assume that our operational retention for the environment can be a simple calculation based on the *starting* size for that month plus a 2% daily change rate for the rest of the days, our final set of operational retention backups will be 2,570.4 TB + (30 × 2% of 2,570.4).

Using a short-term (operational recovery) retention of 1 month, our overall storage requirements for each retention scenario are shown in Table 25.1.

These figures give us some perspective over the *size* of long-term retention, and therefore the importance of planning it accordingly—not just for storage, but for the other management aspects of that data:

- Retention option A will see the backup environment managing 124,032.54 TB (124.04 PB) of logical backup data at the end of year 7.

---

* You will recall we use the term "front end TB" to reflect the concept of: *what would a single full backup of the entire protected footprint come to?*

- Actual front-end data would amount to just 2.02% of the logical backup data under management.
- Compliance retention data will be 96.57% of total logical backup data under management.
- Retention option B will see the backup environment managing 43,380.84 TB (43.38 PB) of logical backup data at the end of year 7.
  - Actual front-end data would amount to just 5.78% of the logical backup data under management.
  - Compliance retention data will be 89.64% of total logical backup data under management.
- Retention option C will see the backup environment managing 54,680.14 TB (54.68 PB) of logical backup data at the end of year 7.
  - Actual front-end data would amount to just 4.43% of the logical backup data under management.
  - Compliance retention data will be 91.87% of total logical backup data under management.

We can draw two conclusions from this sort of example:

- Even using different long-term retention models there can be significant differences between the amount of logical data that needs to be retained (the option to retain monthly backups for the full 7 years for instance still generates more than double the amount of the next largest capacity retention option).
- Both the total front-end data footprint and the operational retention footprint pales in comparison to the long-term retention footprint for a backup environment.

One might sum up this review using the adage: "measure twice, cut once." There are significant savings to be made by taking the time to establish retention policies that are tightly aligned to the business requirements.

25.5 Format Considerations

WordStar was a powerful word processor in the 1980s through to the 1990s that for a time had significant market share, and had strong mindshare, too. By the mid-90s, WordStar was still in use, but was losing market share to the likes of WordPerfect, and Microsoft Word. The last release of the software was WordStar 7.0d, in 1999.

While we often think of long-term retention requirements in the order of 7 or 10 years, this is by no means guaranteed. Many medical and medical research organizations need to keep compliance copies of relevant data for the life of the patient, or even the life of the patient plus some additional period. Architecture and engineering/construction companies may have to keep compliance data for the

Table 25.1 Overall Retention Requirements for Sample Data Set over 7 Years

Retention Type	Retention A (TB)	Retention B (TB)	Retention C (TB)
Operational	4,112.64	4,112.64	4,112.64
Monthly compliance	119,919.9	29,814.1	29,814.1
Yearly compliance	0	9,904.1	20,753.4
Total retention	124,032.54	43,380.84	54,680.14

life of the object being constructed—a sports stadium might need records kept for decades, a sky-scraper for fifty or more years, and public infrastructure items such as dams may need records retention for *hundreds* of years.

It is not inconceivable then that there are long-term retention backups in existence that feature WordStar files. Assuming they can be recovered, can they *actually* be read? Various internet resources refer to a free file conversion utility for Microsoft Word able to handle the WordStar format, for instance, yet a search on Microsoft's main site, or their support site, does not yield promising results.

This is the *format* challenge with long-term retention: assuming we can successfully restore data backed up at the start of a compliance retention period at the end of its retention period, how sure can we be that it is usable? This problem is exacerbated by the tendency of many companies to "sweat" assets. The last release of WordStar was in 1999, but conceivably, businesses might have still been using it into the early to mid-00s, perhaps even longer, if it had champions within the company.

The format challenge exists across almost all products used within a business. Can a database backup generated in 2009 be read back by the current version of the database software with the current backup product plugin in 2020, for instance?

As covered briefly in Chapter 15 (Protecting Virtual Infrastructure), the shift to image-based backups equally introduces a format problem for future backup and recovery administrators:

- Will the same hypervisor variant even still be used?
  - If we are, is the version of the hypervisor in 7 years' time able to read the image-based backups taken today?

  - Is the guest operating system going to be compatible for running within the hypervisor in 7 years' time?
- What happens if a different hypervisor is in use?

We see in this a requirement for the architectural bodies within the company to properly understand the data formats in use by the business, *and* similarly a planning process around ensuring those formats can still be read and used in the event of being recovered. (As opposed to trusting "blind luck.")

An absolute minimum must be to ensure that software and operating system installers (and wherever possible, patches) are captured and protected as well. That's only the tip of the iceberg, however. An installer for a software package designed to be run on a Windows 2000 system may be recoverable onto a Windows 2016 server, but can it still be run? Maybe a Windows 2000 ISO can also be recovered, but will it be possible to find hardware (or a compatible virtual environment) to install it on?

The question of compatible formats may drive discussions around alternate data formats, or variants of archive software. Word processor documents for instance might be more recoverable over longer periods of time if a compliance copy is written into Rich Text Format (RTF), or the OpenDocument Format (ODF), which covers a variety of front-end office document types including word processing, spreadsheets and presentation documents. Not all formats are seamlessly interchangeable though; each software package may handle the conversion from one document format to the other a little differently, and this may result in formatting changes within the document. While this may not seem to be too significant an issue, consider the following:

WE USE FORMATTING FOR MEANING AND INTENT IN DOCUMENTS

For instance, a vendor might respond to a request for proposal (RFP) including a software licensing model that's a suite of different packages. Their proposal might list the different packages and note "Product names shown in *italics* are included in the package but will not be deployed as part of the proposal." If formatting such as bold and italics are *lost* in the conversion of the document to a long-term retention format, this may have legal consequences at a later point in time.

In short: the way in which content is formatted can have an impact on the meaning of the content. While legal documents may be written to avoid this, regular proposals and other documents written by people outside of the legal profession may not consider these impacts—which means those who are planning for long-term data recoverability need to.

Overall then formatting considerations don't just apply to the *file* or *data format*, but the structural layout of the content, too.

The net result of this is that attempting format conversion as part of some blanket activity in backup operations (or post-processing of backup operations) is likely a combination of not only foolish, but also legally unwise.

Formats must be dealt with before the backup process. Consider the database export mentioned in Section 25.3—it could very well be that the business will use an approach such as the following:

- Operational retention:
  - Standard backups of the database using database integrated backup tools
- Compliance retention:
  - Standard backup of the database using database integrated backup tools (for ease of recovery wherever possible)
  - Export of database written monthly* as SQL "create and import" commands, backed up as part of a filesystem "sweep" operation

Thus, through an adaptation of processes, an "open format" copy would be generated for capture during the backup.

The level of effort that must go into this ultimately depends on what the compliance retention requirements of the business are. If they're only a few years, much of these formatting considerations can be disregarded. For compliance in the order of 3–10 years, following the approach of ensuring all installers are protected as well for the same duration would be the minimum starting point.

However, make no mistake: if the business really cares about *multi-decade* compliance retention, the *how* must be considered on a workload-by-workload basis, and well before the backup is run. There is no silver bullet.

25.6 Media Considerations

Particularly when we considered tape-based environments, media formats regularly changed. For instance, as mentioned in Chapter 14 (The Cloud), the release years of the various linear tape open (LTO) generations have been as follows:

- LTO-1: 2000
- LTO-2: 2003
- LTO-3: 2005
- LTO-4: 2007
- LTO-5: 2010
- LTO-6: 2012
- LTO-7: 2015
- LTO-8: 2017

Up until LTO-8, LTO formats have featured backwards compatibility for two generations for reading, and backwards compatibility for one generation for writing. That is, an LTO-x tape could read data on an LTO-(x-2), and write data to an LTO-(x-1). This changed with LTO-8, where the LTO consortium limited backwards read compatibility to a single generation.

Prior to LTO there were a variety of competing tape formats—AIT, Exabyte, DDS, StorageTek dual-spool tapes (e.g., the 9840), DLT, SuperDLT, QIC, and a variety of others. Some other tape formats still exist, but particularly when we consider mid-range environments, LTO is the prevailing remaining tape format.

But *which* LTO is the prevailing remaining tape format? As we noted above, just because they share the "LTO" moniker does not make them seamlessly compatible. An LTO-1 tape cannot be loaded into an LTO-5 tape drive and data recovered from it, and more recently now, an LTO-6 tape can't be loaded into an LTO-8 tape drive and read, despite the formats only being released 5 years apart.

While it might seem inconceivable from a common-sense perspective, it is not uncommon to hear of unwritten recovery procedures from long-term retention backups to start with "go to eBay and find a compatible tape drive." Maintaining a hardware inventory of older, defunct tape drives can help, but in a similar vein to our discussions around data formats, just because you've got the old tape drive hardware doesn't guarantee you'll have something to *plug it into*.

One might suggest an appropriate rule of thumb for media considerations with long-term retention is that unless the data is in an online format that can be checked and migrated between underlying storage platforms automatically, long-term retention should trigger migration of backup media every 3–4 years at most. This should in fact go into the planning of migrating between media formats—for example, if the business currently has LTO-6 media and plans to jump to LTO-8 media, it would have to retain some LTO-6 drives to continue to read from the old media. This might be permitted initially, rather than an immediate media migration, but the business should

---

* Since exports may not guarantee consistency, this export might even be done from a database copy, especially created and populated from regular backups for this process.

still plan and budget for an eventual media migration: history has taught us that old media formats become obsolete, and hoping you can still find parts and supplies on eBay, Gumtree or any other auction site is untenable from a risk and compliance perspective.

When using disk-based storage media (be that conventional, deduplicating, or object), a key expectation is that the underlying storage media can be migrated reasonably non-disruptively between successive generations or even platforms, enabling continuity of access. Even if data is to be migrated from say, conventional disk formats to deduplicated storage, the disruption should be relatively minimal (the storage systems will become busier during the migration operation)—but it should be largely a "set and forget" operation.* With some disk-based storage (particularly object storage), if the storage is engineered correctly, it may be possible to even uplift entire hardware generations as a completely background activity without the backup product even being aware of the migration taking place.

When planning media migration operations, a common mistake is to under-estimate the amount of time it will take to complete. Let's consider two examples.

In our first example, consider a situation where a business wants to move all their long-term retention backups stored on LTO-5 media to LTO-8. If they had been using LTO-5 for exactly 3 years and been retaining monthly backups of approximately 400 TB per month, then each month's backup would have consumed approximately 106.67 tapes at a 2.5:1 compression ratio (note that the raw capacity for LTO-5 is 1.5TB, and the compressed capacity is rated at 3TB—a 2:1 compression ratio—we are therefore assuming that we get a slightly higher compression ratio based on the data sets for the business). Since a partial tape can't be sent off-site, we'll assume each month's backup sends 107 tapes off-site.

Over the course of 36×monthly backups, there would be 3,852 tapes generated. Given the performance difference between the two (LTO-5 has a compressed write speed of 400 MB/s, and LTO-8 is 900 MB/s), the business might buy a tape library that only has half the number of tape drives in it

compared to the prior generation. We will assume the LTO-5 tape library had 10 drives, and the new LTO-8 library has 5 drives. While we can read simultaneously from all 10 drives in the old library, we have a couple of considerations here:

■ Running a duplicate or clone operation from one tape to another will often require a single stream read and write; the assumption then is that only one LTO-8 drive can be actively writing for any one LTO-5 drive actively reading.
■ The business still presumably must perform backup and recovery operations using the LTO-8 drives while the migration is taking place.

It takes approximately 3 hours and 10 minutes to perform an uncompressed end-to-end write of an LTO-5 tape. To be favorable to tape, we will assume we can read back the data for any individual tape as a single contiguous read, with no need for shoe-shining or pauses. When we work with compressed data, the data increases but so does the read or write speed, so we'll assume 3 hours 10 minutes for each tape, and for the purposes of practicality, reduce this to a clean 3 hours per tape.

Herein starts our challenge with media migration: if we've generated 107 tapes per month, it would take 11,556 hours for a single continuous single-streamed read operation of all our tapes: 481 days. We could speed this up by working with a planning process such as the following:

■ Assume an 8-hour window each day where only one LTO-8 drive can be used in migration—the other four are being used for backup operations overnight.
■ Assume the remaining 16-hour window each day only 4×LTO-8 drives can be used in migration—1 is kept reserved to perform recoveries.

Since we can't really pause transfer operations, we would ideally aim to only start a media migration if we can finish it before the write drive has to be used for backup purposes. During our 16-hour window with four drives available we can hope to migrate 20 complete tapes; the 8-hour window with a single drive gives us 2.7 tapes ad that 0.7 of a tape could theoretically extend into the 16-hour window, but we'll reduce it to 2 and absorb that remaining time to absorb all tape load, unload, inventory, etc., operations over the course of each day. That means *optimally* we could hope to migrate 22 tapes a day. Assuming no errors, no mistakes, and no drive failures, the migration operation might take *just* 175 days.

Note that in the above we are not considering the practice of giving drives time to cool down: ideally you would allocate at least 2 hours a day when drives are not doing anything.

---

* On the other hand, migrating between tape formats can be quite an exhaustive and interruptive process. Tape failures may become more common when performing large amounts of reading operations (many tape drives are not rated for 24 7 operation), and it may be necessary to ensure the process is executed in a granular way. Rather than say, triggering a mass migration of all LTO-6 media to LTO-8, it might have to be approached in batches: migrate all December 2013 media, migrate all January 2014 media, migrate all February 2014 media, etc. The more discrete migration operations run, the easier it is to deal with the failure of a single tape drive or piece of media, but the more interruptive and manual process it will be for the backup staff. Given end-to-end reads of tape media can take several hours to complete, this is, by and large, tedious.

An alternate migration might be between generations of deduplication appliances. We'll retain our example above: the monthly backups were 400 TB per month, representing a *logical* backup size of $400 \times 36 = 14.4$PB. At a 20:1 deduplication ratio this would have been reduced to 720 TB of used storage. If we were migrating between deduplication vendors, we would have to do a rehydrated read of the 14.4 PB, but if we're able to do a copy of *just* the deduplicated data, we only need to read 720 TB of data. If we're able to read eight concurrent streams, with each stream running at 100 MB/s, this gives us a sustained transfer rate of 800MB/s. Since it's usual for new generations of deduplication appliances to be able to handle increased stream counts, we'll assume that the target system can handle backup and recovery loading simultaneously with the transfer—which gives us a transfer time of approximately 10½ days. Even if we assumed a 50% overhead on this time to account for running it manually (after all, we're more inclined to try to automate something that'll take more than half a year versus something that'll take a few weeks), our migration time would still be well less than a month.

25.7 Data Protection Considerations

It used to be the case that backup software investment was considered "sticky." Once an enterprise committed to a specific backup product, they might stay with it for 10–15 years or even more, upgrading through successive versions.

When a business migrates between data protection products, it usually must consider two key types of data:

- Operational retention data
- Compliance/long-term retention data

For the most part, operational retention data is relatively easy to address. That type of data is typically:

- Short-term backups (e.g., daily backups retained for 30–60 days)
- Replication copies
- Continuous data protection copies
- Recent snapshot data (e.g., hourly snapshots for 24 hours, daily snapshots for 1 month)

Invariably there is a simple process for dealing with operational retention data: allow it to age out. The cost considerations of migrating operational retention data usually significantly outweighs the cost of maintaining the previous data protection product for the relatively short period it takes to age data out. (It is easy to conceive of situations where it takes *longer* to migrate said data than it does to age it out.)

It is long-term retention data that will require a decision when moving between data protection products.

When the business has bought into the notion that "snapshots replace backup," migration is troublesome to the point of impractical in most cases. Using snapshots for long-term retention (e.g., keeping monthly snapshots for 7 years) is perhaps one of the most efficient ways to sign-up for vendor lock-in possible, regardless of whether it's occurring on-premises, or in the public cloud. When snapshots have been used for long-term retention, it's essential to consult legal teams ahead of any migration process—snapshot processes are *not* vendor-independent, and migrating away from the storage platform of vendor A to vendor B while somehow keeping long-term retention copies will require considered legal advice for dealing with the inevitable disconnect it creates when it comes to demonstrably proving a protection copy was generated at a particular point in time. Since this is problematic, it is often the case that the old systems will be retained and gradually phased down over the compliance retention period as data is reclaimed. (As this is a costly endeavor, it further demonstrates the need to avoid this practice wherever possible.)

One might expect that backup products will generate a similar problem as snapshots: after all, backup formats between products are not interchangeable. A backup performed with product A cannot be recovered by product B. This would seem to create a similar impasse then.

One temptation is to simply turn off the old backup product and only launch it when a recovery is required. If you recall our archive example in the introduction you may already envisage the sorts of problems this could entail; if the business ceases paying maintenance for the replaced backup product, they are unlikely to be entitled to updates.

As operating system and application versions continue to advance, it's entirely possible that the old backup product may be able to start and see its catalogs and media but be unable to communicate with newer operating systems and applications. Getting access to a new version of the product may require paying "back maintenance," which would be costly and expensive. Likewise, scaling down the maintenance to be paid to retain the old product for recoveries may be legally challenged by the vendor. For instance, if the company had been using a capacity license (e.g., front end TB) for the prior backup product, just because it's not generating *new* backups does not mean that the previous vendor will see it as no longer protecting the last entitled license volume. This approach can render total cost of ownership calculations, and cost-to-change calculations high enough as to make change difficult to justify, even if the preferred new backup product has significant advantages over the incumbent.

In recent years there have been an increasing number of companies willing to provide recovery services, which can be particularly effective when the business knows it performs few recoveries from long-term retention backups. Such services typically work as follows:

- The recovery service ingests the current product's catalogues, usually into a third-party tool that allows index access without running the backup product, thereby stepping around licensing issues.
- Tapes are handed over to the recovery service to hold.
- Where disk-based backups are used, the recovery service will ingest them (and possibly push them out to deduplicated object storage).
- The business pays a monthly retainer to the recovery service for holding their backups—this will usually be costed based on the amount of data being retained, with the monthly fee decreasing over time as old data ages out and is deleted.
- The business then pays a per-recovery fee for requested data from aged backups.
- The recovery may be "bulk," requiring the business to then manually sift through the data recovered.

There can be variants on the above—for instance, like an insurance policy, there may be a variety of ways to balance the monthly retainer and recovery fee: a business for instance that knows it will conduct recoveries from long-term retention data regularly might negotiate a lower monthly retainer and a lower recovery fee, but have a minimum service charge that must be paid in the event that an insufficient number of recoveries are done in any given month.

The recovery-service approach can have costs constrained by first conducting a data classification and indexing analysis on the actual backup data. As covered earlier in this chapter, it is more likely than not to see blanket long-term retention requirements: "keep all monthlies for 7 years," or "keep all production monthlies for 7 years." Analysis might reveal that as little as 10% of the actual data being stored for long-term retention actually *needs* to be legally retained. Recalling the sheer volume of data that misconfigured long-term retention policies can generate, rationalization and reduction of those long-term copies can result in a far more cost effective migration process between backup products.

In essence, while there is complexity in migrating between data protection products that are used to hold long-term retention or compliance copies of data, with appropriate planning it is a feasible process.

25.8 Summary

It is fair to say that an organization that takes time to consider challenges relating to accessing compliance copies of

data may also find it useful to re-evaluate where archive technology is used within the business.

> Oxford economics historian Avner Offer believes that we're hopelessly myopic. When left to our own devices, we'll choose what's nice for us today over what's best for us tomorrow. In a life of noise and speed, we're constantly making decisions that our future self wouldn't make*.

Perhaps more so than any other area in data protection, it is in the realm of long-term retention that we are most likely to "kick the can down the road," so to speak. This approach makes emotional sense since it relates to data that may never be recovered at all, and if it is recovered, it may happen at a point where we don't even work for the same business. It may even be the preferred approach of the business itself, but if so, that decision needs to be documented as an acceptable risk exposure for the business.

For businesses that like to plan ahead—if only to identify potential challenges for mitigation at a later point in time, long-term/compliance retention copies of data should be discussed and planned for earnestly, given the volumes of data that may be in play. This can lead to strategic and tactical decisions—such as implementing a document management system to hold sufficiently product-neutral versions of data that must be held for extended periods. Equally, it may see the business adopt forms of data warehousing, ensuring that compliance data originating from structured data platforms such as relational databases is captured and stored in a fewer number of databases—resulting in a more manageable long-term retention data layout within the business.

25.9 Self-Reflection

What are examples of document formats from approximately 15 years ago? This might be:

- Multimedia
- Word-processing
- Images

Determine what version(s) of Oracle and Microsoft SQL Server were supported 15 years ago. See if you can find the list of supported operating systems for those versions, and find out whether they are supported by current-day hypervisor technologies such as VMware vSphere, Microsoft Hyper-V, or even KVM.

---

* The freedom of choice, p12, New Philosopher, Issue 6: November 2014–January 2015

Chapter 26

Choosing Protection Infrastructure

26.1 Introduction

As we've established in previous chapters, data protection is rarely, if ever, a one-size-fits-all approach. It's remarkably rare to encounter an individual business where a single data protection product meets all the operational and recoverability requirements. Indeed, as soon as fundamental data storage protection techniques (such as RAID) are considered as part of a holistic data protection approach, a single-product approach is extremely unlikely.

When planning a data protection infrastructure, a simple rule is offered:

> There are old protection environments, and there are bold protection environments, but there are no old, bold protection environments.

Or to put it another way: leading edge is fine for a data protection environment, but bleeding edge could very well cause more trouble than it solves. Always tread carefully when developing a data protection strategy.

26.2 It's Never about the Technology

As we established in Chapter 4, there are multiple components to a data protection *system* for your environment. Reiterating, these are:

- People
- Processes and documentation
- Training
- Service level agreements
- Testing
- Technology

Technology comprises just *one-sixth* of a data protection system. The remaining components—people, processes and documentation, training, service level agreements, and testing—are independent of the technology used, and no technology, no matter how awe inspiringly complete or comprehensive will provide an adequate data protection strategy if the business does not invest in the other five-sixths of the equation.

It's important when reviewing this chapter to keep that equation in mind: one-sixth technology, five-sixths the rest. If unsure, you may wish to take a step back to Chapter 4 and review before continuing this chapter. The simple message is this: investing in the best technology will achieve nothing if the business does not properly *realize* that investment by working through the non-technology components of a data protection strategy.

26.3 It's Always about the Technology

Conversely, choosing a data protection system for your environment is *all* about the technology. It doesn't matter how good the people, processes and documentation, training, service level agreements, and testing are if the *wrong* technology is chosen. If the technology deployed is not fit for purpose, is not compatible with business objectives and requirements, and unable to meet operational needs, then the data protection system will be premised on luck and good fortune rather than an accurate and compatible architecture. The saying "if all you have is a have is a hammer, everything looks like a nail" is often applicable here: shoe-horning processes into poorly fitting data protection solutions usually results in an unsatisfactory experience for users and administrators.

FIT YOUR SOLUTION TO YOUR RECOVERY REQUIREMENTS

In Chapter 24 we discussed the importance of ensuring your data protection solution is optimized for the recoveries you do most often. A business with short term retention requirements only (30 days) elected to *only* perform continuous data protection for their virtual machines between their two production sites. This allowed for rapid virtual machine recovery and disaster recovery operations, but led to tediously slow file level recoveries, since it was required to instantiate a virtual machine from its CDP journal to a server with sufficient resources, edit the virtual machine settings to isolate it from the production network, boot the virtual machine, find the file(s) required for recovery, copy those files onto an FTP server that straddled the isolated and production network, dispose of the instantiated virtual machine, then retrieve the files from the FTP region back onto the required production server. Full recovery of a virtual machine would usually take less than a minute to complete, whereas file level recovery would take half an hour or longer to run through.

This process would have been OK if most recoveries were full virtual machine recoveries—but in actuality, the majority of recoveries required were file level recovery.

It's always best when planning data protection infrastructure to ensure you have more than a single hammer available to you.

Infrastructure choices (regardless of how agile the business is) can be quickly made but *unmaking* them either takes time, costs money, or both. While this is readily understood for *physical*, on-premise infrastructure, the implications in a more abstract and nebulous Cloud-based infrastructure are much less appreciated.

CASE IN POINT

Businesses looking for a "quick win" in a Cloud strategy to satisfy senior executive requirements are frequently looking at moving elements of data protection or data management (i.e., backup or archive) to the Cloud, without a realistic consideration of the potential costs therein. A per month fee of 3c per GB may seem phenomenally cheap compared to purchasing and maintaining centralized backup data storage, but many businesses dive into such arrangements without considering ramifications of needing to perform large-scale data retrievals, or even the costs of returning *all* the data to an on-premises solution. Cloud-based data storage is usually cheap to ingest and cheap to store, but expensive or slow (or both) to retrieve data from.

Some Cloud object storage facilities aimed at archival storage charge seemingly infinitesimal fees for holding the data, but impose serious practical limits on the amount of data that can be retrieved per month without paying hefty egress fees.

In 2016 a widely distributed Medium article* for instance demonstrated this risk, even at a personal level: a user who wanted to do a bulk retrieval from Amazon Glacier ended up paying $2.50 per GB for the retrieval. (Consider extrapolating these sorts of fees out to a company that needs to retrieve 10 TB of archive urgently and had to pay that premium—$25,600.)

This is not to say Cloud object storage *shouldn't* be part of the strategy for a business, but it does serve to remind that there's no such thing as a free lunch: no matter what infrastructure is used, switching will always incur a cost of some sort, and therefore it's imperative to choose wisely and accurately.

---

* How I ended up paying $150 for a single 60 GB download from Amazon Glacier, Marko Karppinen, https://medium.com/@karpp inen/how-i-ended-up-paying-150-for-a-single-60gb-download-fr om-amazon-glacier-6cb77b288c3e

26.4 Coverage

26.4.1 Value Products That Value Protection

In the realm of data protection, it seems odd to suggest the need to value products that actually *value* protection, but there can sometimes be a vast gulf between the operational integrity and reliability of differing data protection products. Sometimes this can be based on product maturity—a v1 product may offer nowhere near the features of a v9 product, but product version numbers are insufficient in themselves to really differentiate degrees of protection. Instead, for each type of data protection being sought, you need to evaluate how true the product is to the data protection you want. Consider for instance the following examples:

- *RAID systems*: There are a variety of high equality consumer grade NAS and DAS RAID systems on the market, and there are equally a large number of "cheap and cheerful" products supposedly in the same market space but usually half to a quarter of the price. Most of the "cheap and cheerful" style consumer products work excellently so long as you're only after RAID-0 for performance. They tend to be far less reliable, and far more likely to struggle or fail under load when using them for actual protection-based RAID, particularly of the parity variety.
- *Backup and recovery*: Some backup and recovery products *still* fail to implement dependency tracking, allowing the product to automatically delete backups outside of a retention window that backups *inside* a retention window rely on for full system recovery.
- *Replication*: A journaling replication system offering bandwidth compression but unable to support cluster mode for the replication appliances (virtual or physical) introduces what many architects would consider to be an unacceptable single point of failure within the data protection framework. If intra-site storage replication can be brought down by a *single* appliance failure at either end, the SLAs offered to the business must be reconsidered.
- *Protection storage*: Deduplicated protection storage that offers no data integrity services beyond standard RAID parity is a risky proposal. Deduplication minimizes the number of data copies (compared to, say, tape), and therefore requires a higher degree of data integrity enforcement than merely protecting against hard drive failure.

A simple rule to follow when evaluating components of a data protection strategy is that no component should introduce a single point of failure. This can be achieved either through the type of product deployed *or* the architecture of the implementation (e.g., ensuring backups are copied to alternate media).

In a marketplace filled with startup companies offering new techniques for data protection we return to the adage "there are old protection environments, and there are bold protection environments, but there are no old, bold protection environments"—a startup may seemingly offer a cheaper or more innovative solution, but will the startup still exist in 1, 2, or 3 years? This is not to disparage startups—by their nature they tend to be industry disruptors, but particularly

in data protection startups exemplify "caveat emptor"—*let the buyer beware.*

26.4.2 Value Frameworks/Modular Composable Functions over Monoliths

Essentially, we should seek products that offer extensibility and customization. A monolithic product focuses on doing everything the designers anticipated or planned for a user to be able to do, but nothing else. A framework product should of course be able to do everything the designers anticipated, but adds a layer of customization and extension. In essence, a monolithic product requires the business to adapt its processes and workflows to suit the limitations of the product, whereas a framework allows the product to be adapted to suit the processes of the business.

It would seem for the most part that framework products have won in enterprise IT. Prospective buyers increasingly look for features such as a rich command line interface or a REST API to allow integration in alternate management, automation, and orchestration tools. Indeed, a framework approach to products is practically essential to deliver an *X*aaS style offering to the business. It should be noted that while REST APIs are favored with almost religious fervor among DevOps and *X*aaS service development teams, a rich CLI can offer equal levels of customizability if the tools being used to access it are flexible enough.

More recently, we are seeing traditional framework products being supplanted by modular composable data protection. If we think of the different data protection functions as "software bricks," this allows different functions to be brought into a solution platform together; instead of a sweeping solution that has framework extensions, it becomes a collection of smaller function-specific components (e.g., "VMware backup module," "filesystem backup module," "Oracle backup module," etc.) each able to be run as loosely or tightly integrated as the business requires.

26.4.3 Don't Assume

It should be common sense, and it should go without saying, but perhaps the most *common* mistake made when planning data protection infrastructure is to *assume* functionality instead of *confirming* it.

At each step in the data protection journey your business should be acting on informed and researched understanding of products rather than assumed knowledge. This applies to the entire data protection spectrum—for example:

- Knowing what operating systems are supported by continuously available storage platforms

Table 26.1 Example List of Feature Support Requirements

Feature	Version in Use	In Planning
Microsoft Windows	2016	2019
Solaris	V10	V11
Oracle	12c R2	18c, 19c
Linux	SLES 12	RHEL 8
SQL Server	2014	2019
IP Networking	Cisco 10Gbit	Dell 40Gbit
FC Networking	Brocade 8Gbit	Brocade 16Gbit
Virtualization	VMware vSphere 6	VMware vSphere 6.7
Cloud—SaaS	Office 365	Office 365, Salesforce
Cloud—IaaS	None	AWS, Azure
Cloud—PaaS	Azure	Azure, AWS

- Determining databases supported by backup and recovery systems
- Understanding application support for CDP-based replication systems
- Confirming storage snapshot support options for virtualization systems

It should actually be a reasonably trivial task for a business to articulate the various operating systems, applications, and databases currently in use as well as any planned upgrades or changes as part of a requirements list. This might be as simple as a table of requirements, such as that shown in Table 26.1.

While business requirements change over time based on a variety of factors, products providing business-critical functions that will rely on an intended data protection service should be particularly probed for current and future compatibility, as well as intended future support.

26.4.4 Functionality Checklist

When planning new protection infrastructure, it's equally important to build a checklist of required product functionality and confirm products supply it. This goes beyond confirming support for in-use products within the business—it's about making sure the product more broadly performs and provides what the business needs.

Table 26.2 provides an example subset of criteria that might be used to evaluate backup and recovery software. In terms of typical tenders, this might be considered to be a baseline for functionality within a product.

DON'T LOCK YOURSELF IN

When calling for a list of requirements (even mandatory ones), be sure to allow for alternative options for non-compliant answers.

For instance, even something as simple as "does your product support incremental backups?" is no longer as straight forward as you might imagine. Some advanced deduplication products actually execute a *full* backup every time, at the cost (time and resources) of an incremental backup, thereby eliminating the need for incremental or differential backups. (This is not so much a "synthetic full" in the classic sense, but an automatically synthesized full, generated at the time of the backup, via efficient data structures.)

In short: Don't eliminate a product from consideration because it provides an architecture not catered for in your questions.

26.4.5 Don't Tie a Legacy Anchor around Your Feet

Many businesses retain "legacy systems," where a "legacy system" is any operating system or application that is so old that the vendor that *made it* no longer supports it.

Legacy systems pose a systemic risk to many businesses. It is not sufficient to say "virtualize it" because legacy systems eventually get so old that even hypervisor vendors refuse to either fully support them, or support them at all.

It's common for businesses with legacy systems to insist on comprehensive support within their data protection environment for those decrepit units. This is often a mistake, as full legacy system support is difficult to achieve without compromising the capability of a new environment. When legacy systems are integrated into a modern data protection environment, they often reduce options for upgrades, or cause the most problems within the data protection environment.

The ideal solution to legacy systems is to properly migrate the workload. The business may see this as costly, but what is the

Table 26.2   Sample Functional Requirements Table for a Backup Product

Functionality	(M)andatory or (O)ptional	Compliant	Alternative
Control and management			
Centralized	M		
Hybrid	O		
Supports remote administration	M		
Supports centralized administration of multiple servers if required	M		
Supports REST API	M		
Supports CLI	M		
Backup levels			
Full	M		
Incremental	M		
Differential	O		
Synthetic Full	O		
Filesystem backup types			
Online	M		
Online via snapshot	M		
Online block based	O		
Retention strategy			
Automatic dependency tracking prevents expired backups from being deleted If unexpired backups rely on them for full system recovery	M		
Media pool support			
Separation for different locations	M		
Separation for different retention	M		
Arbitrary data separation	M		
Virtualization support[?]			
Hypervisor image level	M		
In-guest agent	M		
File-level recovery from image level backup	M		
Database recovery from image level backup	O		
Power on guest from protection storage	O		
Change block tracking during backup	M		

(Continued)

Table 26.2 (Continued)   Sample Functional Requirements Table for a Backup Product

Functionality	(M)andatory or (O)ptional	Compliant	Alternative
Change block tracking during recovery	M		
Cloud support			
Backup to cloud object storage	O		
Duplicate to cloud object storage	O		
Deduplication support			
Source (client) deduplication	M		
Target deduplication	O		
Deduplication embedded in database agent	M		
Compressed recovery of databases	M		
Inline deduplication	M		

cost of potentially maintaining hardware that is 10+ or 20+ years old with unsupported software? What is the cost to the business if such an environment fails and cannot be repaired quickly?

When workload migration can't be done, the next option should be consider stepping down the level of data protection deployed. For instance, rather than trying to get a backup product's Windows client released in January 2020 to install on and protect a Windows NT4 server (released in 1996, last update Service Pack 6a in 2001), consider instead making use of the native NT4 backup functionality to write backup files to shared storage that can then be backed up. It's not as "elegant" a solution, but it will likely save a lot of hassle and ensure the data protection environment is more reliable.

The last fallback position from the above should not be to try to integrate the legacy systems into the primary data protection environment, but to stand up an isolated data protection environment that solely deals with protection for the legacy systems. "Isolated" in this case does not refer to a cyber-recovery site, but rather, an environment that has no shared infrastructure. This allows the primary data protection services to be upgraded as required as the business continues to update its infrastructure, databases, applications, and operating systems without "disturbing" the protection environment for the legacy systems. The protection environment for the legacy systems should, as much as possible, be locked down to prevent any changes or upgrades, since it will likely be finicky in relation to server or protection storage changes.

26.4.6 Plan to Upgrade

"X has not shown innovation" is a common refrain in infrastructure circles, particularly when it applies to data protection. While different products and vendors will update their products according to their own release cycles, just because a vendor updates their product does not mean that the business upgrades to that release.

It is depressingly common to encounter situations where a business deploys a data protection product, expecting it to be used for 3 or 5 years (or longer) and *never updates it.* No maintenance releases, no patches, no major releases—a system budgeted to provide 5 years protection might spend 1,826 days running the same version of firmware and software as deployed on day 1. At this point it is not accurate to say that "X has not shown innovation"—it's far more accurate to suggest that the business has, at best, a lackadaisical approach to systems maintenance. The business, in fact, has failed to show innovation—not the vendor.

If upgrades are performed across the rest of the environment—operating systems, servers, storage firmware, databases and applications, then it stands to reason that the business should also update its data protection solutions as well. Think of the requirements list that might have been drawn up in 2016 for a data protection solution—how much of the business processes and environment might have changed, or even fundamentally shifted by 2021?

26.4.7 Minimize Vendors, Not Products

Given all the different data protection options you may need to consider, product minimization is desirable, but there will always be a lower limit on the number of products you need. (There's not a single backup product on the market for instance that can also double as continuously available storage.) Since there will always be a certain minimum number of products

Table 26.3 Impact of Multiple Data Protection Vendors on Disruption

Event	Percentage of Businesses Impacted	
	One Vendor (%)	Two or More Vendors (%)
Unplanned systems downtime	34	43
Ransomware attack that prevented access to data	17	32
Data loss	21	29
Inability to recover data from the current data protection method/product	21	29
Local disaster which affected access to data for an entire site or group	16	27
No disruption experienced	40	19

Adapted from Dell EMC Global Data Protection Index, 2018.

involved in a data protection strategy, minimization is more something that can be achieved through reducing the number of vendors involved. This allows more strategic relationships to be built between enterprises and their vendors, with increased synergies at different layers of the data protection stack. For instance, if multiple storage vendors provide systems that *all* meet the requirements, but one comes from the same vendor as the backup and recovery software being used, there may be enhanced integration points achievable by picking the same storage vendor as the backup vendor. Recalling the Data Protection Index by Vanson Bourne discussed in Chapter 1, there seems to be a direct correlation between the number of data protection vendors used by a business and the percentage of data loss events, or level of impact.

For instance, the 2018* update for the Data Protection Index interviewed 2,200 businesses and determined that disruptions were more likely when using more than one data protection vendor. Table 26.3 summarizes findings on this topic from the report.

26.4.8 Understand the Costs

There's a wide variety of costs associated with data protection strategies. As mentioned earlier, switching products or strategies is rarely going to be both cheap and easy. This means it's important to understand the various costs associated with new data protection environments, *and* equally to understand the costs associated with a *current* data protection environment.

If a cost comparison is to be made it should be against both the direct and indirect costs. This includes staffing-associated costs—not just the number of staff required to

run a particular service, but also such areas as the training and certification requirements (time and fiscal).

Equally it's important to compare "apples with apples," so to speak. Building a flat rate comparison of cost-per-GB for, say, 100 TB of deduplication storage and 100 TB of standard storage requires understanding of the storage efficiencies achieved via deduplication. (A 100 TB deduplication appliance achieving, say, 8:1 deduplication should be compared to 800 TB of standard storage, not 100 TB of standard storage.†) Likewise, comparing any form of disk protection storage against tape protection storage needs to include details such as:

■ Energy requirements for both the disk system and the tape libraries
■ Per-tile occupancy costs of equipment in a computer room
■ Tape handling fees, including
  – Removing from site
  – Returning to site
  – Storage off-site
  – FTE costs associated with media migration
  – FTE costs associated with media checking
■ Tape duplication times
■ Disk storage replication times, bandwidth requirements, and costs

The high-level costs are usually easy to account for, but as the saying goes— the devil is in the details. Cost comparisons can be tedious, but are truly essential to perform an accurate and complete comparison between different data protection technologies and products.

* https://www.dellemc.com/content/dam/uwaem/production-design-assets/en/gdpi/assets/infographics/dell-gdpi-vb-key-findings-deck.pdf

† Additionally, the bandwidth cost for network replication for a non-deduplicated solution versus a deduplication solution should also factor into the cost comparison.

26.5 You May Be Sizing Your Data Protection Solution Wrong

There are two traditional ways of sizing a data protection solution, and they're both wrong in the modern era.

The first way is to say "we need X TB of data protection storage." This is a broken approach that completely ignores modern approaches to data efficiency. Consider the differences between three solutions: 100 TB of regular storage, 100 TB with 8:1 deduplication, and 100 TB with 20:1 deduplication. The solution with regular storage will store 100 TB of copies. The solution with 8:1 deduplication will be able to store 800 TB of logical copies; the solution with 20:1 deduplication will be able to store 2 PB of logical copies. If you're comparing the cost of each 100 TB of storage, you're not valuing the *outcome*. It's critical that you understand the cost, or the value of the *logical* sizing rather than the *physical* sizing.

The second wrong way is to plan a data protection solution where you lock yourself in to a capital purchase for a 3- or 5-year period. The key mistake businesses make on this approach is to have a rigid, linear growth sizing. Unless your business has demonstrable, extremely linear growth and change rates, any sizing beyond 3 years is likely to lose accuracy by 50% per annum. Think of what a linear growth rate equates to over time: 10% annual growth means that after 5 years your data will have increased by half again. 20% annual growth rate means that after 5 years your data will have *doubled*.

A minor change to the actual overall workload sizes being protected over a 3- or 5-year period can have a significant impact on the data protection solution sizing—consider again Figure 3.3, where we mapped out the proliferation of data protection copies. If a workload uses 1 TB of primary storage, it might use between 20 and 30 TB of protection storage, even with deduplication, once all the copies are factored in. If data growth rates are *assumed* (rather than having strong factual evidence) to be in excess of 10% per annum, it may be warranted more focusing on buying a system which has good expandability than buying a system that has all the *estimated* storage up-front. This allows capacity increases to be planned over time as the impact of deduplication versus the actual data growth and change rates are determined.

Beyond these two sizing considerations, it's equally important to understand projected *incremental* costs. If OpEx storage is to be used in the solution (e.g., public cloud object storage), you need to know how much this is going to cost over time, given you'll pay per month for the consumed storage. It's important *based on the workload sizing details and assumptions*, a full view of the projected object storage requirements over time should be provided and factored into overall solution costing. For example, if you're pushing monthly backups to object storage and keeping them for 7 years, you need to understand the expected cost of that based on the projected growth rates. The business may still elect to go ahead and pay a higher cumulative cost for that storage, but it should go into the decision knowing the projected costs. While projecting these costs over time will obviously still be subject to the same accuracy challenges previously mentioned, when it comes to incrementally building costs, it's important to have at least an *estimate*, and more mature vendors will be able to provide example build-outs of storage requirements so you can make an informed decision. When planning for deduplicated data protection storage, it's also important to keep in mind the phrase, "garbage in, garbage out," which very much applies to sizing considerations for deduplication storage. Not all data sets deduplicate equally: sparsely populated virtual machines and regular filesystem data may deduplicate at a much higher ratio than say, densely populated databases. When requesting suppliers quote for deduplicating protection storage, it's important to provide as accurate and detailed a breakdown on workload sizes as possible.

Data protection solutions will also have infrastructure support costs associated with them. This is most apparent when we review the difference between classic three-tier architectures (server, media server, client) and advanced data-direct architectures where the data path goes direct to protection storage. Using a three-tier architecture, a large-scale data protection solution may require dozens or more media servers to funnel data from the protected hosts to the protection storage, and these systems may not be cheap: after all, their primary design principle is being able to get data transferred as *fast as possible*. It is not uncommon to see physical intermediary servers requiring 32 GB or more of RAM, dual or quad core CPU arrangements, multiple 10 Gbit+ interfaces, and so on. If the business needs 20 of these servers to achieve the data protection SLAs, this will make a tangible impact on the ongoing run cost of the environment, as all these systems will presumably need to have supported hardware and operating systems.

Likewise, as businesses aim for lean infrastructure operations, the resource requirements for any *virtual* support systems should be planned as well. For scalable, adaptive architectures, it may not be possible to determine the exact requirements up-front. (For example, the number of software-defined proxies that need to be deployed to perform virtual machine backups might vary based on the overall number of virtual machines, access to underlying storage by individual hypervisors, and a number of other factors.) Where the solution can be scaled up or down in terms of resource consumption for these options, it still should be possible to capture the atomic granularity required for an individual virtual appliance—and this applies regardless of whether you are providing data protection services on-premises, or in a public cloud environment.

In short, it's easy to get focused on "how much will my data protection storage cost?" when there are significant other factors that go into the sizing and costing for a data protection solution. Businesses with mature processes (or seeking the best possible cost over time for a solution) will aim to factor these costs in, rather than just looking at say, what 100 TB of usable storage costs.

26.6 In Summary

Given the disparate components, data protection is usually mixed over multiple purchase cycles—for example, alternate storage refreshes and backup/recovery refreshes. (Converting to converged infrastructure can substantially simplify planning around data protection, but this is still a relatively new approach for many businesses.)

Further, with growing Cloud (private, hybrid, or public) adoption in many organizations, the borders of data protection for a business are constantly changing.

Few if any businesses are truly unique—for instance, almost every business picking a new data protection product will seek references based on other companies in the same industry vertical. The best approaches therefore in considering data protection infrastructure can be summed up as follows:

■ Don't make assumptions.
■ Don't forget the non-technical aspects of a data protection solution.
■ Do your homework on functional requirements.
■ Understand the costs, both initially and forward looking.
■ Make strategic as well as operational decisions.
■ Be prepared to evaluate strategic or architectural recommendations that don't immediately conform to your idea of a "perfect" strategy (i.e., be prepared to think outside the box).

26.7 Self-Reflection

Many government organizations will provide their tender documentation online. Search for terms like "data protection tender," "backup tender," "backup and archive* RFP." Particularly focus on examples that are 2 or more years old.

Review the sorts of features—functional and non-functional—requested and note the year the tender/RFx was released in. What sort of changes to the ability to deliver those features might you expect to have seen in the time since the document was published?

---

* It's quite common to see the term "archive" lumped into a data protection tender—and usually it actually means *compliance copies*, not archive as we would think of it usually.

Chapter 27

The Impact of Flash on Data Protection

27.1 Introduction

Usually attributed to Benjamin Franklin,[*] "time is money," is probably one of the most recognized adages relating to business. While often used as a caution against wasting time, it can equally be reversed: if you can do something in 20 minutes that your competitors take an hour to do, you have a business advantage that may be able to deliver tangible results. Regardless of whether it's something as simple as billing or stock reconciliation and ordering, or sifting through hundreds of millions of transaction records to detect fraudulent activities, it's generally accepted that the faster you can do something, the more value it can be to business.

In fact, it would be fair to say more generally that the story of information technology is the story of speed. Regardless of whether we're talking about CPU, memory, networking, or storage, we have seen a continual evolution in speed within the datacenter to match ever-increasing requirements for doing more in less time.

27.2 How Does Flash Affect Data Protection?

The first hard drive system was announced in 1956. The IBM 350 disk system had fifty 24-inch platters and a total capacity of 3.75 MB, and it spun at a speed of 1,200 RPM.

To date, the highest performance hard drives operate at 15,000 RPM—a net increase of 13,800 RPM in 60+ years.[†] Over the years, various performance improvements have been made to boost hard drive performance—RAID/striping, caches, improved interfaces, and of course higher rotation speeds. But the actual performance differences between the very first hard drives and the current top of the line hard drives are negligible when we consider the improvements in CPU and memory performance during that same time.

If we consider the transfer rates achievable with hard drives, even 15,000 RPM drives offer sustained transfer rates only of somewhere between 167 and 258 MB/s.

Particularly in enterprise use, a performance characteristic we often focus on with storage is the IOPS—the number of input/output operations per second the drive can process. A 7,200 RPM SATA drive—of the variety commonly used in end-user computers—will provide somewhere between 75 and 100 IOPS, while those high performance 15,000 RPM SAS drives are considered to offer anywhere between 175 and 210 IOPS—which is frequently averaged to around the 190–192 IOPS mark.

Using traditional hard drives, the accepted way to achieve a high number of IOPS was to combine a high number of hard drives working together. This not uncommonly led to storage configurations that were massively over-populated in terms of *capacity* in order to provide sufficient IOPS for the performance requirements of the application. In fact, so common was this technique that the term *short spindling* was coined—referring to the use of a small capacity from a large number of hard drives in order to get the number of combined IOPS increased, even if that led to storage wastage. (More recently, achieving performance in this way can be frowned upon: datacenter space is charged by rack, by energy and cooling consumption, and companies are often measured by their customers and governments based on how environmentally sustainable their operations are.)

---

[*] The accuracy of this attribution is often questioned.

[†] In fact, it took until 2000 for the first 15,000 RPM drive to be released, https://www.pcworld.com/article/127105/article.html

Conversely, when solid state drives started entering the market around 2008, they were already featuring performance ratios of 5,000+ IOPS, and commercially available SSDs are now routinely capable of delivering 50,000–100,000 IOPS per device.* Sustained read and write speeds of 500 MB/s is quite common even just on a SATA-3 interface. PCIe-based flash storage increases these performance options even further, and the emerging trend toward NVMe (non-volatile memory express) has led to dense flash memory storage systems that can deliver sustained performance in the order of 10,000,000 IOPS or greater, with rich data services (snapshots, replication, thin provisioning, compression and/or deduplication) overlaid without any tangible performance impact.

It is no longer the case that SSDs can't match traditional hard drives for capacity—evolutions in hard drive technology such as shingled magnetic recording (SMR) has allowed hard drives to reach capacities of 15 TB as of 2019, and heat-assisted magnetic recording (HAMR) has seen 16 TB drives become available, with 20TB+ drives predicted in 2020. Clearly there is still a capacity future yet in hard drives, yet rarely does a capacity increase result in a significant performance increase.

Yet likewise, flash memory drives have undergone significant capacity expansions over time. While 1–2 TB SSDs have become more cost-efficient for consumer applications, and enterprise flash storage might range from 4 to 16 TB in common configurations, and even significantly larger units in the order of 30† 60,‡ and even 100 TB§ have been announced for various purposes.

While a 15 TB SSD will cost substantially more than a 15 TB hard drive, the performance differences between the two cannot be overstated. There is however a means of increasing the cost benefits of SSD at higher capacity, one which is becoming increasingly common in "flash only" dedicated primary storage systems: deduplication.

As discussed in previous chapters, deduplication works by squeezing out commonality between data, reducing the total storage footprint. Depending on that data commonality, deduplication ratios can become quite high—for instance, consider 100 × Windows Virtual Machines, each built from a standard template and each sized for 100 GB.

At the point where these systems are deployed, they are practically byte-for-byte copies of one another, with only some registry details and basic configuration settings differing. Stored with thick provisioning (i.e., all the required capacity allocated up-front), 100 × 100 GB virtual machines would occupy 10,000 GB of storage—9.76 TB. With global deduplication on the storage array though, that number shrinks dramatically. Assuming the deployed base image achieves even just a mediocre 2:1 deduplication ratio,¶ you might be mistaken for thinking this would result in storage requirements of 4.88 TB. Remember though each of those virtual machines will deduplicate against each other, and the commonality there will be extremely high in a just-deployed scenario. In fact, there might be as much as 99.5% commonality between the virtual machine images; even if the first virtual machine stores in only 50 GB of data, each subsequent virtual machine may require as little as 0.5 GB of additional primary storage initially. The total occupied size then after deduplication for 100 × 100 GB virtual machines would be 99.5 GB. (In fact, this sort of storage has proven to be a common workload for all-flash storage—virtual desktop infrastructure.) Of course, post-deployment they will end up being a potentially large amount of drift between virtual machines as they are used for different functions.

Even with the performance benefits of flash storage, it is unlikely to see a primary storage system achieve the same level of deduplication efficiency as leading protection storage deduplication arrays. This comes down to the performance choices that need to be made—whereas protection storage platforms can focus on storage efficiency and work with variable-sized data segmentation, primary production flash storage utilizing deduplication will typically work with fixed block boundaries—the focus after all must still be on delivering a guaranteed IOPs/mission critical workload performance, with storage efficiency being a secondary consideration.

As all-flash storage becomes increasingly available and leverages deduplication to reach price-parity (or even be cheaper) than traditional disk-based storage systems, we will see a number of shifting dynamics in data protection.

There are several key examples of where flash—and particularly deduplicated flash storage systems—will have marked impacts on data protection: snapshots, replication, continuous data protection, and backup/recovery.

Consider first snapshot technology. In Chapter 11, we described a variety of snapshot techniques, such as Copy on First Write (CoFW), Copy on First Access (CoFA), and Redirect on Write (RoW). Each of these snapshot techniques

---

* Of course, the actual number of IOPS delivered by a stand-alone consumer SSD will depend on overall system performance.
† Samsung 30 TB SSD announced February 2018, www.theverge.com/circuitbreaker/2018/2/20/17031256/worlds-largest-ssd-drive-samsung-30-terabyte-pm1643
‡ Seagate 60 TB SSD, first shown in 2016, https://arstechnica.com/gadgets/2016/08/seagate-unveils-60tb-ssd-the-worlds-largest-hard-drive/
§ Nimbus Data ExaDrive SSD, March 2018, https://thenextweb.com/plugged/2018/03/20/this-100tb-drive-is-the-largest-capacity-ssd-ever-made/

¶ Very unlikely if the virtual machines have been thickly provisioned and are mostly empty. In such a situation the first-round deduplication might be 10:1 or higher, but we have used 2:1 for simplicity and account for a worst-case scenario on the first set of data.

has particular performance implications—CoFW, for instance, is typically geared toward low-write situations, since any write performed against the original filesystem or LUN while the snapshot is active triggers three high level IO operations—a read of the original data, a write of the original data to the snapshot storage pool, and then a write of the new data to the original location.*

In the case of either maintaining active snapshots *or* releasing aged snapshots, there is some form of performance overhead involved, however small. On traditional spinning disk, even a small performance impact for a single snapshot can magnify quickly if a storage system is managing *hundreds* or more snapshots. While some of those performance impacts may logically still exist in an all-flash system, the level of impact given the IO performance of all-flash systems will drop substantially. This will allow more snapshots to be kept without fear of maintenance tasks eating into system performance, and the increased number of IO operations required for writes while snapshots are active (e.g., for CoFW) will not be felt when the overall storage operates orders of magnitude faster than traditional disk systems. Indeed, well-designed systems optimized for flash will likely eschew traditional snapshot options such as CoFW and instead use dynamic pointer tables, allowing ease of access to any snapshot with little or even no performance impact. With deduplication applied to the snapshot storage pool as well, the cost of capacity for maintaining more snapshots will also be reduced.

Likewise, replication will see benefits in an all-flash deduplicated storage environment. As we have observed over the past decade or more with deduplication in backup environments, replicating the deduplicated data substantially reduces the overall bandwidth requirements. One terabyte of data deduplicated down to 100 GB will require far less bandwidth to replicate than one terabyte of data in its original form. Coupled with falling bandwidth costs, this will result in companies being able to replicate more of their data, granting higher availability and fault tolerance for more systems and business functions.

Continuous data protection—journaled replication of data—can enter new realms of utility in all-flash storage systems. With the journals held on flash, and snapshots allowing for access to the journaled data at any time-stamp, some systems may be switched away from backup and recovery for short-term retention, relying almost entirely on CDP. (This of course would be dependent on ensuring the CDP copy is sufficiently "off platform" to provide protection against a failure in the primary storage system.) Note however that CDP systems will still be bound, as much as anything, by

the capacity that can be allocated toward journaling systems: while high capacity journals may be justified for some mission critical data, reserving potentially hundreds of terabytes, or even petabytes of SSD-performance storage for journals will likely be rare based purely on the economy of scale for some time to come (even if the management algorithms support such scale in the first place).

It is in backup and recovery systems that we will see perhaps the biggest *challenges* from flash storage. The transfer speed from flash storage—even factoring rehydrating the data for a read operation—substantially outstrips that of a normal read from hard drive–based storage. Flash storage will likely drive much higher adoption of source/distributed deduplication technology, for two key reasons:

■ As data continues to grow it will be essential to limit the impact of the data on the network; while network performance is increasing, high speed flash based storage systems could still overwhelm a network—for instance, 25 and 40 Gbps networks are becoming increasingly common in datacenters, but 40 Gbps results in only 5 GB/s (18 TB/hour).
■ Even if the network can handle the sustained throughput, in the classic analogy of "pointing a fire-hydrant at a teacup," it matters little if the source system can read at 1 TB per second if the protection storage can only write at 1 TB per minute.

(It might be said that the growth of all-flash hosted data at larger capacities will further highlight the performance differences between source/distributed deduplication backup and other technologies.)

A common assumption would be that a common deduplication mechanism might allow the transfer from source storage platforms to protection storage platforms without the need to rehydrate the data. This is likely to be impractical, at least for some time to come. Recall earlier the comment that the performance requirements of primary storage—even when all flash—typically drives different deduplication approaches to that used for protection storage platforms. Unless the exact same deduplication algorithm is used, and a direct connection is established between the primary storage platform and the protection storage platform, there will be insufficient compatibility to achieve this as a broad function. For example, Dell EMC's *ProtectPoint* software allows for deduplicated backups flowing directly from compatible VMAX3, PowerMax, and XtremIO storage platforms to Data Domain systems, with the Data Domain distributed deduplication Boost algorithm embedded into primary storage (or very close to it). Yet this is not a function that can see the primary storage or protection storage platform swapped out—it creates a hardware-dependent solution. This however may be acceptable given the sorts of performance benefits

---

* Note that *doesn't* include updating pointers for the snapshot or any underlying multi-IO operations required by RAID systems, particularly in sub-block updates.

that can be realized for the backup of databases in excess of 50–100 TB, but has been achieved only because the same vendor develops both the primary storage and the protection storage platforms. An "industry neutral" deduplication standard is unlikely, to say the least.

There are three ways that flash can be expected to appear in protection storage systems:

- Metadata caching
- Tiering and hybrid
- All-flash

Metadata caching refers to using flash storage drives not for the actual deduplicated data, but for the metadata associated with the deduplicated data. It is the metadata, after all, that allows a deduplication appliance to determine which blocks must be combined, and in which order, to rehydrate the logical, original data. Speeding up access to the metadata in this fashion can result in higher speed access to the original data—particularly when that access will be random IOs, such as in "instant access" operations, where data re-use from the protection storage copy is performed.

Tiering systems and hybrid systems can work by mixing SSD and conventional hard drives. Tiering systems might land all data on SSD and migrate deduplicated blocks out to conventional hard drives as the SSD tier fills. Hybrid systems might similarly mix SSDs and conventional hard drives, but with workloads manually directed between the two: administrators for instance might point backups for mission critical databases to the SSD tier, and backups of other systems to a conventional performance tier. This however might result

in different deduplication pools for each protection storage tier. (Note that "hybrid hard drives"—hard drives with small levels of flash storage embedded that perform auto-tiering are unlikely to come into play in these systems, since the tiering mechanism is beyond the control of the protection storage platform and may introduce performance contention or balancing issues.)

All-flash protection storage arrays are emerging to the market in response to the performance requirements of protecting large, mission critical systems on all-flash primary storage. At least for the foreseeable future it will be unlikely that average businesses will adopt all-flash protection storage arrays for *all* the workloads, but it will be increasingly common during the 2020s to see enterprises making strategic use of all-flash protection storage where the performance characteristics of the workload demands it, even if the majority of protection storage continues to be serviced by metadata-caching, tiering, or hybrid protection storage systems.

27.3 In Summary

There is no doubt that flash storage will alter the dynamics of data protection activities—CDP, snapshots, and replication in particular will all benefit. While there will be some challenges faced by backup and recovery services when dealing with all-flash data, new use cases for data protection storage being introduced into the business with flash tiers, delivering additional benefits, will drive down the perceived cost of data protection storage.

Chapter 28

In Closing

Our species has lived through a variety of ages: we speak of the stone age, the bronze age, and the iron age, and each was named after the most prevalently used or important material. Depending on your culture or geographic background, other "ages" are somewhat fluid and may have more elements (e.g., European culture is usually classified as having had a medieval age as well). More recently at around the turn of the eighteenth century, the leap into the Industrial age happened.

While it's commonly said that we're now in the Anthropocene period from the perspective of geological time scales, if we're to name ages of civilization based on the most prevalently used resource, we're now in what could only be defined as the *information age*. This makes data protection a critical activity for any organization: infrastructure can be rebuilt, replaced, or superseded; staff are replaceable, and customers come and go, but the real value of a business is its data. (Look at what happens when a business collapses: any infrastructure is sold off at rock bottom prices, employees leave, and the real horse trading happens over the intellectual property—the *information* of the business.)

A cynic might suggest that the most prevalently used resource now is *money*, but since we're long past counting money in terms of bars of gold bullion stored in a vault, you might equally say that money, too, is merely information.

The core reason for data protection has remained the same for the entire history of the IT industry: bad things happen. Yet in itself this fundamental reason is no longer the *only* driving force behind innovation in data protection. Data protection may be a form of an insurance policy, but businesses seeking to creatively leverage their IT investments and wanting to drive through cost optimization are increasingly looking at data protection as a mechanism to achieve those goals. Thus, data protection is also becoming an *enabler* for new processes around data movement and data processing.

Increasingly, our lives are wrapped up in data. The family photo album has been replaced with digital photos stored in the cloud. Letters between friends have morphed into text messages and snapchats. Banking, insurance, booking a restaurant, finding the nearest coffee shop, and planning a round-the-world trip are done in the palm of the hand using a mobile phone. (Increasingly, for many, the *least* desirable function of a mobile phone is the actual telephone.)

So while we usually consider data protection from a *business perspective*, it's imperative that we never lose sight of the *personal* aspect of the data we're protecting. If you're working in the energy sector, a failure to protect data may result in people losing power—which can have impacts ranging from trivial to life-threatening. In government, failing to protect data may mean that people in need miss their next welfare or pension payment. A data loss in banking may mean people can't access their accounts for 24 hours, and be unable to buy anything. A data loss in the cloud may mean you lose those last photos you'd taken of your father before he passed away. The shift toward an information-centric age of civilization has personalized data in a way we have never experienced before.

Despite the seeming panacea of the cloud, we're learning that it doesn't matter *where* your data is, there's still a high degree of certainty that you have to be actively involved *at some level* in its protection. In the most extreme "as a service" models this will simply mean ensuring you choose the correct protection policy, but for most businesses it will require more involvement for some time to come.

Data protection is not a one-size-fits-all strategy, and it's a topic still continuing to evolve. Options now common were practically unheard of a decade ago, and there is little doubt a peek 10 years into the future would reveal a significantly different landscape again. Machine learning techniques will likely fundamentally shift how data protection is orchestrated and optimized, and modern, agile software development techniques combined with the best service provisioning lessons from public cloud will radically adapt how data protection services scale as they span on-premises and cloud workloads. Once it was envisaged that infrastructure was in a tug-of-war between traditional on-premises solutions and public cloud; this has evolved rapidly in the last 5–10 years. First it was private cloud as a "solution" to public cloud, and then it was hybrid cloud, allowing a merger between the two. More recently, we've seen an increasing emphasis on *multi-cloud*, where the datacenter itself just becomes another cloud in the array of cloud services used by the business.

This shifting infrastructure landscape requires businesses to forget about traditional, rigid approaches to data protection. The notion of buying a solution and making minimal changes to it for a 3- or 5-year investment period seems laughable. The "lowest cost" does not guarantee the "lowest price" over the run period of a data protection solution, even before we consider whether the solution is flexible enough.

A progressive and adaptable data protection environment will be layered, use appropriate tools, enable automation and orchestration, and integrate at the most important layer: reporting and monitoring, such as that shown in Figure 28.1. Ideally, as business requirements change with the system being built as a framework, appropriate products to provide protection should be slotted into the protection layer, and products no longer required should be retired—without disruption to the business or the business functions. The monitoring/reporting and orchestration/automation layers should be the visible aspects of data protection and resemble the proverbial duck on a pond. Truly effective data protection comes from a holistic approach considering the entire data lifecycle and all required SLAs. Data protection is not RAID, is not erasure coding, and nor is it continuous availability, replication, snapshots, or backups—it is *all* of them, combined in a considered and measured approach to meet *all* the requirements of the business. Indeed, with the growing adoption of flash/solid state storage we're seeing new opportunities and challenges for data protection: *challenges*, because on top of cloud, big data, virtualization, and convergence, data protection now needs to keep up with storage systems that are leaping ahead in performance, disrupting a rather long status quo; *opportunities*, because low latencies and the phenomenal access speeds of flash will enable more agile approaches to data protection to emerge—as well as secondary use cases to data residing on protection storage.

A modern approach to data protection requires optimized, appropriate, and integrated technology, but that's only one part to the equation. Virtualization, converged infrastructure, and the cloud are all driving us toward having *infrastructure administrators* who are able to work up the entire infrastructure stack. Big data is driving businesses to find more efficient approaches to moving around and safeguarding data. Through it all, the price of information—the *value* to the business—is going up and up, making the role of a data protection advocate critical to business success.

An agile, integrated approach to data protection based on frameworks, modularity, and extensibility is no longer a luxury, but a necessity.

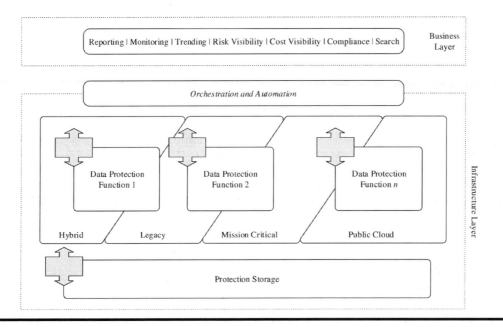

Figure 28.1 Holistic view of a data protection environment.

Appendix A: Glossary of Terms

Term	Description
Asynchronous	In terms of replication and continuous data protection, this refers to a process whereby once a write is issued by a server, it is acknowledged after it has been written to the primary copy, with writes to secondary copies then queued.
CapEx	**Capital Expenditure.** Up-front infrastructure or component investment typically performed on a longer budgetary cycle (e.g., 1–3 years).
Cascading Failure	A series of two or more failures that exceed the architected protection limits and cause a data loss situation (which may be erasure, corruption, or availability). Examples of cascading failure include having the second drive in a mirror fail while the first is being replaced from a previous failure, or all paths in redundant network links going down.
CDP	**Continuous Data Protection.** Refers to a form of replication that occurs concurrently with the actual write stream to a storage target. A writer interceptor or splitter is inserted into the data path and writes that are intended for the target storage system are also committed to an alternate storage system. CDP may be either synchronous or asynchronous. (requiring write-acknowledgement from both the primary and secondary destination before the acknowledgment is sent back to the system that issued the write), or asynchronous (where write-acknowledgment to only the primary destination is required before the acknowledgement is sent back to the system that issued the write—the write to the secondary target can be buffered and issued within
CLI	**Command Line Interface.** Utilities and options that can be executed on a command line (e.g., Windows prompt or PowerShell, Unix shell/terminal).
DevOps	**Development and Operations.** Software development activities designed primarily for automating IT services within an organization. It requires a high level of integration between the developers and the rest of the IT staff (particularly infrastructure staff), and use of deeply functional APIs provided by vendors of the infrastructure used. DevOps originated from Agile development methods that empathize regular incremental release cycles with continuous feedback and improvement rather than large multi-month or multi-year blocks of development.
IOPS	**Input/Output Operations Per Second.** A common measure for determining the performance a storage system can deliver. This can be highly variable depending on the storage system and workload, so key metrics usually include *sustained* and *peak*. While there are other factors, in very broad terms the more IOPS a storage platform can deliver, the faster any storage-related processing can be.

(Continued)

Term	Description
LUN	**Logical Unit Number.** A logical addressable piece of storage presented to an operating system, typically from a SAN. While originally LUN was intended to merely refer to the specific SCSI address of a storage target, it is typically now used to refer to a logical disk presented by a SAN.
NAS	**Network Attached Storage.** Similar in concept to a SAN, with many of the same advanced data protection options and management that is independent of the accessing systems. NAS is focused on *file-based* storage rather than block-based storage.
NDMP	**Network Data Management Protocol.** A standard for allowing backup products to initiate backup and recovery operations for NAS systems.
NVMe	**Non-Volatile Memory Express.** A protocol that allows faster transfer of data between solid state storage and a computer system, typically over a PCIe (Peripheral Component Interconnect Express) bus. Whereas traditional SSD drives are either SAS or SATA connected, NVMe allows higher speed throughput via a much higher performance system bus.
OpEx	**Operational Expenditure.** Short-cycle running costs, such as energy, backup media (when tapes are used), and more recently, unit costs for Cloud computing, typically incurred on a monthly basis.
Parity	A mechanism used to achieve redundancy within storage systems; parity is calculated from the actual data, and both the data and parity are written. Typically associated with RAID.
RAID	**Redundant Array of Independent Disks.** A mechanism used to protect data stored on disks (hard drives or SSD) such that the data can still be read even if one or more drives fail. The number of drives required, the number of drives that can simultaneously fail, and IO penalties depend entirely on the RAID level.
REST API	**Representational State API.** A programming interface that allows stateless interaction between the system being accessed and the application accessing it. This is favored by DevOps and agile development, particularly in infrastructure environments, as it allows a high degree of scaling and extensibility. Unlike command line environments that typically expect a close knowledge of the product in order to automate, REST API environments are designed for iterative query processes that can allow developers who aren't product experts to still integrate automation for that product into a solution.
Retention (Governance) Lock	The option to write data in such a way that it cannot be deleted or modified until a retention time specified at write-time has passed. This is often required for specific government or fiduciary certifications to ensure data is immutable.
ROI	**Return On Investment.** Specific benefits (both tangible/measurable and intangible) achieved as a result of implementing a particular process, operational change, or purchase.
RPO	**Recovery Point Objective.** Refers to the amount of data that can be lost, in time. For example, an RPO of one hour indicates that at most one hour of data can be lost when performing a recovery from the most recent data protection activity.
RTO	**Recovery Time Objective.** The maximum amount of time it can take to perform the nominated recovery. This will vary by organization as to whether the RTO countdown starts at the time the recovery request is *made*, or when it is *actioned*.

(Continued)

Term	Description
SAN	**Storage Area Network.** A disk array that presents logical block storage assembled from a potentially large number of physical devices to a number of hosts. SANs will typically feature advanced data protection in addition to a variety of RAID levels, all of which can be managed independently of a host that has mapped access to the storage.
SAS	**Serial Attached SCSI.** The original form of the SCSI interface (see SCSI, further below) was parallel, meaning multiple devices could be connected together in a chain. While this was useful from a cost perspective, it usually meant performance was always limited to the slowest device in the chain, and a failure of any device in the chain could affect all devices in the chain. SAS was developed as a variation of SATA, allowing each drive in an enclosure to be directly connected to a storage backplane, rather than in sequence.
SATA	**Serial ATA, or Serial AT Attachment.** A commodity/consumer grade storage attachment mechanism common in desktop and laptop PCs and some lower cost storage systems aimed at the mid-market and small office/home office. SATA was the extension of the classic "IDE" connection mechanism, offering considerably higher throughput partly by having each drive connected directly to the backplane of the computer.
SCSI	**Small Compute Systems Interface.** A common connectivity protocol (and sometimes physical interface) typically used for communication between compute resources and storage systems.
SLA	**Service Level Agreement.** A contract between parties for the meeting of specific operational targets. In backup and recovery for instance, SLAs are typically expressed in terms of backup times, failure rates, and RTOs/RPOs.
SLO	**Service Level Objective.** An understanding of preferred operational targets that may not necessarily have contractual obligations.
SSD	**Solid State Disk.** Flash or memory-based storage technology (as opposed to traditional "spinning disk").
Synchronous	In terms of replication and continuous data protection, this refers to a process whereby once a write is issued by a server, it must be written to both the primary copy/storage, *and* to any other configured secondary copy/storage before the write is acknowledged as complete back to the original server.
TCO	**Total Cost of Ownership.** Refers to a comprehensive view of the cost of a purchase. This may either be the total value of the purchase, or an amortized cost representing a value statement. (For example, protection storage with deduplication may be assigned a TCO based either on the up-front cost of purchasing the system, or a per-GB/per-month cost over the investment timeframe and the expected logical storage capacity of the platform.)
WORM	**Write Once, Read Many.** Traditionally representative of tape, WORM refers to appliance compliance grade retention locks on data once it has been written, guaranteeing against modification or deletion prior to a specific timeframe set by the storage, legal, or compliance requirements of the business.
ZLO	**Zero Loss Objective.** A term sometimes applied to systems that have an availability requirement of 100%.

Appendix B: Notes on Self-Reflection

Many of the self-reflection topics in the book are open-ended, and do not have definite answers. This arguably reflects the overall nature of data protection: there are a number of different answers to almost every problem—the importance is often not that you've come up with a particular answer, but that you've at least *considered* the problem.

B.1 Chapter 1: Introduction

B.1.1 Personal Data

It is easy for people to not necessarily think about the data they generate, and likewise easy for people to not think about whether that data is protected. Consider the two dominant smartphone operating systems: iOS and Android. Both of these allow users to sync their key data to the vendor public cloud (Apple and Google respectively). Yet there are often constraints on when and how the data is synchronized, and ideally readers who identify Smartphones will consider these sorts of topics. For instance:

1. Both Android and iOS by default only synchronize photos to the cloud when connected via WiFi.
2. Do users automatically get enough storage space to synchronize all their photos and videos?
3. What happens if a photo or video file is deleted? Does a user get the option to delete it just from the local device, or from all devices?

Email is a very good example of where consumers tend to "assume" their data is protected. Yet, email clients and therefore email services cannot differentiate between a deliberate delete instruction for a single email and an accidental delete instruction for an entire email folder.

Some email clients will offer to backup a user's email system: Apple's default mail application doesn't do this itself as such, but Apple's Time Machine system does integrate to perform mail backup and recovery for the default client. Email backup is a function of some Windows email clients—for instance, "eM Client" has an option, disabled by default, which allows for the creation of periodic email backups, with various hard-coded frequency options (ranging from daily to every 6 months), and the option to keep up to five email backups. There are also some dedicated email backup programs—Horcrux on macOS for instance is not an email client but instead is designed to regularly take backups of a variety of different email accounts including Google Mail, Hotmail, Apple Mail, and other IMAP-style email systems.

Readers should take time to think about the financial, reputational, and emotional costs involved in losing data. It is primarily by understanding the consequences of data loss that we develop the necessary habits around taking appropriate preventative measures. Some examples might be:

- *Financial cost*: A self-employed person might keep a database of clients, suppliers, and outstanding bills. Losing this database would result in a direct financial loss for the person.
- *Reputational cost*: A person who has volunteered to record the video for a sibling's wedding might not be looked upon too favorably if after taking the video accidentally crops and deletes the wedding rather than the first few and last minutes taken to bracket the wedding.
- *Emotional cost*: If you had taken photos and videos of a terminally ill parent on your cellular phone, and subsequent to them passing your phone was stolen but it had not been backed up, the emotional loss might well be considered quite high.

By developing an understanding of and an empathy toward the sort of data we accumulate and could lose, we become more aware of our own personal responsibility toward ensuring that data is adequately protected.

B.1.2 Business Data

Business users (either enterprise or educational) will use a variety of systems on a day to day basis. Some examples include:

- Email
- File shares/services

- Intranet services
- Database services:
  - *In business*: CRM systems, order processing systems, Wikis, customer billing systems, etc.
  - *In education*: Library systems, student records, academic systems, citation services, etc.
- Document management repositories.

Ideally, the reader should have reflected on how much they know about the backend operation of that system. This is not to say that end users should understand infrastructure—in a properly architected environment users should need to understand little to none of the architecture behind the systems they are using, but do they know if there is a process to request data recovery? Is this something they've done previously?

By considering the effects, both personally and to the business of data loss, readers are encouraged to think of how much productivity they might lose should the system either go down, or data is lost. This helps to set an understanding, particularly for those who might at a later date move into management roles, of the importance of adequate data protection and availability.

B.2 Chapter 2: Contextualizing Data Protection

A key aspect of this chapter is data classification, and being able to answer for any data set or workload within the business, the five questions:

- What is the data?
- Where is the data?
- Who uses the data?
- When is the data used?
- How is the data used?

Being able to classify data is a fundamental requirement to the development of appropriate, efficient, and suitably budgeted data protection systems. Without these details, the data protection processes established for any given workload will be determined by a "gut feel." An example of a fleshed-out response here might resemble the following:

- *What data*: Customer Resource Management (CRM) system.
- *Where the data is kept*: In the cloud. (The business might use Salesforce, for instance.)
- *Who would make use of the data*:
  - Sales teams: To track customer contacts and opportunities

- Presales engineering: To track customer opportunities and assets
- Maintenance teams: To track customer assets
- Management: To measure sales performance
- *When would the data be used*:
  - Daily for many teams including sales, presales, maintenance, and management
  - For some teams like business operations, this might be more based around *when* orders are received
  - For financial teams, this could be focused more around end of month processing.
- *How would the data be used*:
  - Tracking customer install base
  - Determining sales productivity
  - Reporting legal compliance (e.g., first point of call in demonstrating you are not selling to interdicted regions)
  - As a system of record in disputes over the start and end periods of maintenance
  - To prove compliance relating to the installed location of equipment and software

The answers will be different of course for just about any business system a reader picks, so the important aspect here is that the reader has identified a *what*, *where*, *who*, *when*, and *how* for each workload or type of business system picked.

B.3 Chapter 3: Data Lifecycle

Self-reflection in Chapter 3 asks the reader to focus on understanding the *age* of data that is stored.

Unix-based operating systems (including Mac OS X and Linux) have the *find* utility, which allows an astute command line user to search for files that have not been accessed since a particular time. While Windows supports this, as of Windows 10, the access time flag has effectively been depreciated; updating the access time is off by default and only turned on if explicitly enabled by the user.

The search capability within macOS also includes the capability to find files based on access date. This would be a search based on:

{Last opened date} is {before} {datestamp}

Where {datestamp} is changed to be a suitably long enough period in the past.

The Windows 10 Explorer search option though focuses on *modified time*. Searching in Explorer, the "Date modified" icon can be clicked on and a variety of hard-coded search options can be selected from: today, yesterday, this week, last week, this month, last month, this year, and last year.

However, searching by modified time is not as useful as searching by access time—modified time tells us when the file was last updated (or created), but a file might be "read only" for most of its life. (For example, PDFs, video training, etc.)

B.4 Chapter 4: Elements of a Protection System

B.4.1 RPO and RTO Reflection

In this chapter a variety of systems in a small business were presented, with the reader encouraged to articulate what the RTO and RPOs might be for systems depending on the number of users in the company (total 100 employees) were affected—a single employee, 20% of employees and 100% of employees.

For the most part the key understanding from this would be prioritizing system recovery more as the number of affected users is increased. However, astute readers might also note that it also depends on the *role* of the user affected. For instance, the business *owner* might require a fast RTO and low RPO for any systems she uses. (Certainly a failure of such systems will get higher visibility when impacting the owner vs the receptionist, for instance.) But there'll also be a dependency on the type of system impacted. Regardless of whether it's a single employee, 20% of employees or 100% of employees impacted, if the payroll database goes down, it might be deemed a critical incident from a RPO/RTO perspective (especially if it's close to or on pay-day.)

B.4.2 Test Scheduling

There are two key aspects the reader should note about the test scheduling based on the requirements, notably:

- Controlled randomness
- Formal rest results register

By "controlled randomness," the goal is that from the collection of tests that may be available to the business, the goal is to randomly pick tests to run at random times, but still ensure the overall test criteria are met. (For example, if twice in a row "recovery from Oracle backup" is randomly selected, the random selection would be repeated to find another, alternate test to run instead.) If the results of the tests are to be reported to the directors, they obviously also need to be noted.

In terms of isolating the test environment, we might expect to see a separate virtual network configured to attach recovered systems into: this would not allow routing out to the primary network (instead, a jump box or some other system would be used to reach *into* the network),

thereby preventing systems from impacting the production environment. Other considerations would be ensuring there are adequate hypervisor resources so that running the test does not impact the performance of the production environment.

B.5 Chapter 5: IT Governance and Data Protection

The reader was encouraged to consider the FARR model of data protection, and note three failure scenarios that the activity would *not* protect against, and which aspects of the FARR model *would* protect against that type of failure.

Examples include:

1. Fault tolerance
    a. *Data deletion or corruption*: Fault tolerance generally won't protect against data deletion or corruption. (It's worth noting however that object storage may be provisioned with *versioning*, which theoretically might provide such protection.) Fixing data deletion is typically a function of recoverability.
    b. *Site loss*: We would normally expect situations such as site loss to be protected via redundancy. (Availability, which is has close relationships to redundancy, will usually protect against system failure within a single location.)

2. Availability
    a. *Data deletion or corruption*: Whenever there is data deletion, or data corruption, we will have to resort to recoverability.
    b. *Link loss*: If the link to the site running the workload goes down, you will need to use redundancy between that site and another site to achieve service restoration/continuance.

3. Redundancy
    a. *Data deletion or corruption*: When asynchronous replication is used between sites, some might arguably suggest redundancy can protect against data deletion/corruption, but this is really focused on a very small window between when the write happens in the primary location, and when it's transmitted to the alternate location. So again, this would require recoverability.
    b. Suitably architected, redundancy can provide protection against fault tolerance and availability failures, though it would generally be considered overkill to failover a workload between entire sites just because of a hard-drive failure or single node in a cluster going down.

4. Recoverability
   a. Suitably architected, recoverability can protect against most failure scenarios within fault tolerance, availability, and redundancy. However, recoverability will be reliant on these other areas for successful operation.
   b. The "reliant on those other areas" will form a significant constraint on recoverability. For instance, in the event of a cluster node failing, you *could* use a recovery function to rebuild the cluster node, but the ideal scenario would be to first *failover* services to the still-working node(s), with recoverability then used to fix the failed cluster node.

A key aspect for the reader to understand from this exercise is that all four aspects of the FARR model are essential for a holistic data protection strategy.

B.6 Chapter 6: Monitoring and Reporting

B.6.1 Backup Job Reporting

The reader was encouraged to think of about the sorts of details they might want to see about backup jobs for databases, virtual machines, and filesystems. The sorts of details you might want to see include:

■ Start time.
■ End time.
■ Whether the job was considered successful, had warnings, or failed.
■ Any other run-times (e.g., time taken to clone or replicate backup data).
■ Number of systems processed.
■ What level the jobs were run at.
■ The size of the jobs.
■ In terms of enumerating the systems the jobs were for, some backup administrators want to see all system names, while others want the focus to be only on those that failed.
■ If a job report is going to database administrators, it's possible they will want to see all databases backed up if they've not been in control of executing the jobs. A similar approach might be used for virtual machine administrators.
■ A common mistake for backup jobs is to assume you want to see a list of all the files backed up. No-one can process this level of detail, and it becomes meaningless: at that low level of detail you have to trust that the backup product will issue warnings if files could not be backed up.

If we then compare the above granular details about dashboards, it's important to note that as an environment scales, your ability to process individual job notification details decreases. It is a much more productive use of time for an administrator to check a dashboard and simply drill into failures, rather than having to review 100, 200, or more overnight backup job emails.

B.6.2 Backup Dashboards

Backup dashboards might include details such as:

■ Backup success ratios over the last 24 hours
■ Clone/replication success ratios over the last 24 hours
■ Recovery success ratios over the last 24 hours
■ The "three strikes report"
■ Additional drill-down options to allow clicking through to see lists of clients/hosts that fit the clicked criteria (e.g., "successful," "failed," "had warnings," etc.)
■ Protection storage capacity—used and free storage for disk-based protection platforms, and available free media for tape-based protection platforms
■ System alerts—components failed or components down (e.g., drives requiring replacing in protection storage, or failed protection storage systems), inability to send health-check data to vendor systems, and so on
■ Percentage of configured clients that have not received protection in the past 24 hours
■ Where the system has hooks into hypervisors and database servers, details on the number of systems that are not protected at all
■ Where the system has hooks into reporting and analysis routines, it may also include details such as adherence to KPIs (recovery success rates, backup success rates, recovery times, etc.), and chargeback or showback details as well

Where we note timeframes of the "last 24 hours," ideally a dashboard will allow customization here—it may be an administrator wants to see the same widget three times: e.g., backup success details for the last hour, 24 hours, and 7 days.

B.7 Chapter 7: Business Continuity

The examples of business functions that a business might perform and their importance to the business will vary industry to industry, and even at times, business to business. Some examples might include:

■ *Consumer bank*:
   – *Mission critical*: Customer account details, ATM/EFTPOS network, fraud detection

- *Critical*: New customer sign-up system
- *Essential*: International money transfer broker system
- *Non-essential*: Individual branch coin-counting machine
- *Hospital*:
  - *Mission critical*: Patient medical records
  - *Critical*: Billing/accounts payable, payroll
  - *Essential*: Stock systems
  - *Non-essential*: Patient ward WiFi systems

Examples such as the above fit neatly into the business continuity profiles (continuity, restoration, triage, and ignore). Consider the hospital example, for instance:

- *Continuity*: Patient medical records database would be clustered, with continuous data protection used to allow rapid rollback in the event of corruption. Would also support failover to an external datacenter in the event of a local site issue.
- *Restoration*: Since none of the cited systems directly affect the ability of the hospital to provide *immediate* medical attention (assuming a universal healthcare situation prevails), billing/accounts payable, and payroll could all be restored from recent backup or online protection copies in the event of a failure. (They might also get continuity options, but here we might see the difference between continuous availability or synchronous replication, and periodic copies/asynchronous replication, etc. These concepts are discussed more in Chapter 10.)
- *Triage*: It may be that the hospital keeps enough supplies stocked to sustain a week or more's outage in the stock replenishment system. In the event of an outage, while systems are being restored the hospital could ask staff to note items retrieved from stocks to assist manual reconciliation later.
- *Ignore*: The hospital may simply advise patients that the WiFi system will not be available until other more critical issues have been addressed.

B.8 Chapter 8: Data Discovery

The reader was encouraged to think of how they might perform backup and recovery operations for appliances such as IP or fiber-channel switches. Some switches will include options for automatically generating configuration exports that can be written to a file-share or read back from a file-share.

Where this isn't possible, we usually have to fall back to programmatic solutions. Newer switches that include REST APIs may have the option to trigger the reading

and writing of configuration details via standard HTTP/HTTPS protocols; this would allow the integration of the backup into the overall backup process—the configuration might be retrieved, and written to a file-share so it can then be backed up.

Even systems that only offer CLI interaction can still be scripted—for instance, The "Expect" programming language (among others) is designed for scripting interactive command line sessions. Thus, it would be possible to use a language like Expect to log onto the switch and run the commands required to dump the configuration, thereby retrieving the content.

B.9 Chapter 9: Security, Privacy, Ethical, and Legal Considerations

For this chapter the reader was encouraged to review security, ethical, legal and privacy considerations for being an infrastructure team leader for "Medical Systems Inc.," a functional healthcare company focusing on imaging, same-day "outpatient" surgical procedures, and pathology testing.

Key details the reader might consider include:

- Required retention time for patient medical data based on their state or country—including results of pathology/imaging versus outpatient data
- How results might be transferred back to requesting doctors/specialists in a way that reduces the risk of a security or privacy breach for the patient
- How traditional medical ethical practices would effectively extend to, or place a similar obligation on those who are *supporting* the medical practices
- Whether there are types of data that can/can't be stored in the cloud
- Whether data needs to be (or should be, regardless of whether there's a legal obligation), encrypted in flight and at rest for data protection

B.10 Chapter 10: Continuous Availability, Replication, and CDP

The reader is encouraged to think of a business or industry vertical they might deal with regularly, and note some IT functions for that business—then note the systems that may require the sort of data protection services discussed in the chapter. Note that other data protection services are likely to be used as well, but the focus is on how the identified systems might be protected using continuous availability, replication, and CDP.

An example collection of systems for a University is provided. This is repeated below, with thoughts on how the chapter's data protection functions might be used:

- *Student records*: Critical information for the University, this could utilize synchronous replication between two nearby campuses, and asynchronous replication to a more remote campus. Both the database server and the web-server could run in clustered configurations.
- *Campus facilities*: This might make use of CDP for file shares, and clustering for the email service.
- *Student file storage*: The file shares for students might be setup with file versioning to allow for self-service recovery of previous document versions for data being actively worked on. Asynchronous replication could be used for disaster recovery.
- *Research storage systems*: Synchronous replication to a nearby campus, and asynchronous replication to a remote campus. Volumes would be created per project, with a mix of CDP and/or file versioning as required. Where specific research compute systems need to be run with high availability, clustering might also be enabled.

This is not to suggest the above are the *only* data protection options that will be considered, but represent examples of where technology discussed in this chapter could be used.

B.11 Chapter 11: Snapshots
B.11.1 Multiple Snapshots

If a copy on first write snapshot is taken at 11am, changes are made, and then another snapshot is taken at 1pm, we would expect changes as follows:

- For the 1pm snapshot, we would expect standard CoFW behavior—i.e., before the data is written to the primary copy, the blocks that will be changed will be written to the snapshot area of the 1pm snapshot.
- If the change affects a region within the 11am snapshot:
  - If that region had *previously* been updated while the 11am snapshot was active, nothing new would be written to the 11am snapshot, since it would have already been copied across.
  - If the region updated had previously *not* been updated in the 11am snapshot, it would be copied across to that snapshot as well prior to the original being updated by the new write.

Depending on the snapshot technology, there may be data sharing between the snapshots for common blocks. This will often depend on the level of storage efficiency built into the

overall platform, and may also be dependent on what performance profile of drives are used within the storage system.

B.11.2 Snapshot Numbers

If a storage system has hourly snapshots kept for a day, daily snapshots kept for 7 days, and weekly snapshots kept for 4 weeks, then we'd expect to see a minimum of 35 snapshots *per* filesystem or storage volume. We'd say "minimum" for that because there may also be ad-hoc snapshots taken by administrators.

B.11.3 Snapshot Storage

The self-reflection also asked: "Assuming an average 2% daily change rate and an original storage size of 50 TB allocated, how much storage capacity would need to be reserved for CoFW snapshots to accommodate the change rate and snapshot schedule?"

It's important to note that merely saying a "2% daily change rate" is not enough to accurately size such a solution. Given CoFW snapshots only generate snapshot data when content is changed, our change rate alone isn't enough to calculate how much storage is needed. For instance, with the 2% daily change rate, how much of the data is repeatedly changed during the day? It might that 2% of *different* data is changed each day, or even though it's only 2% change, the same 2% of data might be updated every *hour* during a day. If we assume simply 2% of randomly distributed content is changed each day:

- 2% of 50 TB is 100 GB.
- Each hourly snapshot might generate *up to* 4.17 GB of data.
- A daily preserved snapshot might use 100 GB of data.
- A weekly preserved snapshot might use 700 GB of data.
- Combined—$24 \times 4.17 + 100 \times 7 + 700 \times 4$, we'd need to assume at least 3.6 TB of snapshot storage required if we assume no data efficiencies are applied.

(It is often the case that a minimum of 10% of the primary occupied storage would be used as a starting point for sizing snapshots—in our example, 5 TB.)

B.12 Chapter 12: Backup and Recovery
B.12.1 Multilevel Differential

A backup schedule was presented as follows:

- Saturday—Full
- Sunday—Incremental
- Monday—Differential Level 5

- Tuesday—Incremental
- Wednesday—Differential Level 7
- Thursday—Incremental
- Friday—Differential Level 3

A backup level diagram for this schedule can be seen in Figure B.1.

B.12.2 Parallelism Review

Assuming standard hard drives, if a client has a two-drive mirror providing the C:\ drive, and a three-drive RAID-5 configuration providing the D:\ drive, then from an IO performance we'd expect to be able to run at least two-way parallelism.

If we increase the RAID-5 configuration to host three filesystems, it would be unwise to increase parallelism beyond three, and it may be that two-way parallelism remains an optimal configuration: with three-way parallelism, we don't have a guarantee that the system will not end up trying to backup the three filesystems residing on the three-drive RAID-5 simultaneously. With only three drives involved in the read, this may result in a sub-optimal backup experience.

B.12.3 Backup Storage Requirements

The reader is asked to calculate three different sets of storage requirements (without deduplication) for protecting a starting size of 500 TB, with 10% annual growth and 2% daily change over a 3-year period. The scenarios are:

- Scenario one:
  - Weekly full backups with daily incrementals, retained for 5 weeks
  - Monthly full backups retained for 7 years (this would be reduced to 36 months in a 3-year review)
- Scenario two:
  - Daily incremental backups retained for 5 weeks
  - Weekly full backups retained for 12 weeks

- Monthly full backups retained for 13 months
- Yearly full backups retained for 7 years
- Scenario three:
  - Daily incremental backups retained for 14 days
  - Weekly full backups retained for 6 weeks
  - Monthly full backups retained for 7 years

Since monthlies are retained for variable time periods, we need to calculate the annual growth as monthly changes. A 10% annual growth amortized monthly gives us a monthly backup size along the lines of Table B.1 (all figures in TB). When calculating storage requirements over three years, use the "end size" of the solution to calculate out what shorter retention backups would require for storage, since this will represent your largest possible size.

Using these figures, at the end of 3 years, each scenario would require storage as follows:

- Scenario one:
  - 5 × Weekly fulls at 660.2 TB per backup = 3,301 TB
  - 30 incrementals, each approximately 13.2 TB = 396 TB
  - All the monthly sizes per the table below = 20,754.6 TB
  - Total size of 24,451.6 TB
- Scenario two:
  - 30 incrementals, each approximately 13.2 TB = 396 TB
  - 12 × Weekly fulls at 660.2 TB per backup = 7,922.4 TB
  - Monthly fulls retained for 13 months—using the last 13 months = 8,187.2 TB
  - 3 × yearly backups—assume the December backup from the table = 1,806.1 TB
  - Total size of 18,381.7 TB
- Scenario three:
  - 12 incrementals, each approximately 13.2 TB = 158.4 TB

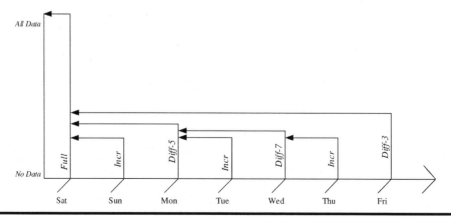

Figure B.1 Backup level diagram for multilevel differential backup.

Table B.1   Monthly Amortized Data Sizes for Growing 500 TB at 10% Per Annum over 3 Years

Year 1											
Jan	Feb	Mar	Apr	May	Jun	Jul	Aug	Sep	Oct	Nov	Dec
500.0	504.0	508.0	512.1	516.1	520.3	524.4	528.6	532.8	537.0	541.3	**545.6**

Year 2											
Jan	Feb	Mar	Apr	May	Jun	Jul	Aug	Sep	Oct	Nov	Dec
550.0	554.4	558.8	563.3	567.8	572.3	576.8	581.4	586.1	590.8	595.5	**600.2**

Year 3											
Jan	Feb	Mar	Apr	May	Jun	Jul	Aug	Sep	Oct	Nov	Dec
605.0	609.8	614.7	619.6	624.5	629.5	634.5	639.6	644.7	649.8	655.0	**660.2**

- 6 × Weekly fulls at 660.2 TB per backup = 3,961.2 TB
- All the monthly sizes per the table below = 20,745.6 TB
- Total size of 24,865.2 TB

(You could increase accuracy by adjusting for the weekly backup sizes changing—i.e., amortize the growth further—but it becomes a case of diminishing gains in terms of the overall storage size projected.)

Scenario three requires the most storage, though only by a relatively small percentage compared to scenario one. You'll note the key factor here is in each case it's the number of full backups that are kept that contribute to the sizing requirements—the incrementals could almost be ignored in each case.

The percentage variances between operational and long-term retention are:

- Scenario one: Operational retention is 15.1% of the storage requirements.
- Scenario two: Operational retention is 45.3% of the storage requirements.
- Scenario three: Operational retention is 16.6% of the storage requirements.

B.13 Chapter 13: Deduplication

B.13.1 *Target versus Source Deduplication*

If we have 100 TB of data that can be backed up over either 1 or 10 Gbit networking, with only a 5% of the data needing to be stored:

- Target-based deduplication:
  - 1 Gbit: The entire 100 TB would need to be transferred; at 1 Gbps, it would take approximately 8.6 days to transfer the content.
  - 10 Gbit: Again, the entire 100 TB would need to be transferred; at 10 Gbps, it would take approximately 20.7 hours to transfer it.
- Source-based deduplication—ignoring any checksum comparisons that need to be sent (a very small percentage of data):
  - 1 Gbit: 5 TB at 1 Gbps would take approximately 10.3 hours.
  - 10 Gbit: 5 TB at 10 Gbps would take just over 1 hour.

B.13.2 *Storage Capacity Comparison*

To calculate the difference between the storage footprint of 2 PB in deduplicated versus non-deduplicated format, first start by working out what the expected occupancy will be after deduplication. In this case, 2 PB getting 15:1 deduplication will require approximately 133.3 TB of storage.

For the deduplication platform, using 4 TB drives in 15-drive shelves, where each shelf is a RAID-6 composite with 1 drive reserved as a hot spare—and needing another 5% overhead for filesystem format and metadata usage, then:

- Each shelf will provide 12 × 4 TB = 48 TB usable—subtract 5% for additional overheads mentioned, therefore approximately 45.6 TB usable for the backup storage.
- If we divide the required storage (133.3 TB) by the storage per shelf, we need 3 shelves of storage (2.9 shelves of storage—i.e., 3) to accommodate the storage. A total 9RU if each shelf is 3RU.

For our non-deduplicating storage, we try to save storage capacity by shifting to RAID-5, while maintaining the hot spare, so:

- Each shelf will provide 14 × 4 TB = 56 TB usable—subtracting 5% for additional overheads, therefore approximately 53.2 TB usable for the backup storage.

▪ 2,000 TB at 53.2 TB per shelf would require 38 (37.6) shelves—114RU.

If we consider traditional 40RU racks, the deduplication solution fits in a single rack, whereas the traditional storage solution would require two full racks, and another 34RU in a third.

In both cases we haven't accounted for additional storage overheads that might be recommended, or controller counts, but you can clearly see a difference between the two in terms of datacenter occupancy.

B.14 Chapter 14: The Cloud

B.14.1 Data Breaches/Loss

Examples of data breaches or data loss situations in public cloud environments should be relatively easy to find even with casual web-searching.

B.14.2 Industry Vertical Storage Requirements

There are some common themes in storage requirements (on-premises vs cloud) for many industry verticals. For instance:

▪ Educational and government environments may allow cloud usage, but require in-country clouds, with no risk of data egress.
▪ Government and research organizations may require higher security requirements than general cloud environments—e.g., US GovCloud style options.
▪ Medical, banking, and government verticals are very likely to require encryption in flight and encryption at rest for backups.

In other areas, data can be allowed in cloud so long as it meets particular requirements, such as encryption at rest, anonymization of data, etc.

B.14.3 AWS Storage Costing

Two key elements should come out of a costing—an understanding of the cost in the local region for storing long-term retention backups in public object storage, both per-month and cumulatively, and as in our examples from Chapter 12, an appreciation that by reducing the number of long-term retention copies we need, we can drastically reduce the storage requirements for a backup solution.

B.15 Chapter 15: Protecting Virtual Infrastructure

When comparing agent-based versus image-based backups, we would usually expect to see significantly lower impacts on the hypervisor environment with the image-based approach.

The example presented for analysis was a hypervisor farm using shared storage, whereby:

▪ There are 20 hypervisor servers.
▪ On average there are 20 virtual machines per hypervisor.
▪ On average there are three virtual disks per virtual machine.
▪ The environment can sustain five proxies for image-based backups, with each proxy able to backup 20 virtual disks simultaneously.
▪ Image-based backups use virtual synthetic fulls and take 10 minutes to complete.
▪ Agent-based backups on average take 45 minutes to complete, and backup all filesystems (one filesystem per virtual disk) simultaneously.

Presumably we have a total of 400 virtual machines. For image-based backups, we can backup 20 virtual disks per proxy simultaneously, and sustain 5 proxies. That means an overall total of $5 \times 20 = 100$ virtual disks receiving simultaneous backups. With 3 virtual disks per virtual machine, it means we can backup (rounding down), 33 virtual machines every 10 minutes.

If we complete a block of 33 virtual machines every 10 minutes, 400 virtual machines will be completed in a little over 120 minutes 2 hours. That would be accommodated via 100 concurrent reads from the environment.

If we tried to start all 400 backups as agent-based backups simultaneously, we'd be running 400×3: 1,200 concurrent reads from the environment. This is the type of challenge that triggered the shift to image-based backups for virtual machines—starting over a thousand concurrent streaming operations simultaneously will very likely stretch the resource requirements of the virtualization solution.

B.16 Chapter 16: Big Data

If a business requires a 100 TB database to be backed up in 4 hours, then the performance requirements would be:

▪ 100 TB = 10,000 GB
▪ 4 hours = 240 minutes
▪ 416 GB per minute, or 6,933 MB per second

Even using 10 Gbps networking, 100 TB would require over 20 hours to transmit. 25 Gbps networking would allow the transfer to take place in 8.28 hours, and even 40 Gbps networking would require 5.17 hours.

Network performance can be aggregated of course—if the data could be streamed consistently and evenly spread over 6×10Gbit ethernet ports, it could be backed up in 3.5 hours.

Sustaining that sort of read or write performance is a significant undertaking though. To achieve this sort of backup throughput, it's likely details such as the following would need to be considered:

■ Source-side deduplication, to reduce the amount of data that needs to be transmitted in the first place

■ Storage integrated data protection, to remove the database server from the data path, allowing the data to be sent directly from the primary storage platform to the protection storage platform.

Even so, with these options included, it's likely to sustain that load there will need to be flash-based storage (e.g., SSD or even NVMe) for the database. When using deduplication, the first backup will always take the longest, as there's more unique data to be sent. But if we assume a 5% daily change to the database, after our "day 1" backup, the average backup size each day will reduce from 100 to 5 TB—far more manageable. A 5 TB daily change backup (which could still generate a daily logical full) would complete in just over an hour using a single 10Gbit interface.

Alternate approaches for protection for a single system this size would be storage snapshots—however, those snapshots would need to be fully integrated with RMAN backup processes to ensure a 100% database-consistent snapshot is generated. Additionally, to avoid needing significant amounts of storage space over time, and ensure there are off-platform protection copies, there would need to be an option to "roll-over," or convert a snapshot copy into a genuine Oracle database backup. (Storage integrated data protection will typically create snapshots as well, providing a "best of both worlds" situation.)

B.17 Chapter 17: Protecting the Edge

B.17.1 End user Backup Services

The reader was encouraged to find and compare at least three different end user compute backup services—either cloud based or traditional hardware/software combinations. Typically cloud software versions can be found by searching for topics such as "best laptop/desktop cloud backup YYYY," substituting the current year.

A variety of enterprise backup systems support end user compute backup options too—it's important when researching these to qualify that the goal is *desktop/laptop* backup. Often different cost models are used for these, compared to server-based backups.

B.17.2 IoT Temperature/Humidity Sensor Backup

This has parallels to the notion of backing up switch configuration data, covered in the review questions for Chapter 8. We might note that while a REST API could be used to "backup" the data from a sensor, the ideal solution would be that if a system is being used to extract those temperature/humidity values regularly, the aggregated data would be protected centrally. This emphasizes the importance of looking at the bigger picture when evaluating *where* to protect data. (However, it's always worthwhile keeping in mind that alternate approaches are available.)

B.18 Chapter 18: Data Storage Fault Tolerance

The question posed was: assuming you can put 20 drives in a disk shelf, and two slots have hot spares, what are at least three different ways you can arrange the remaining 18×4 TB drives in RAID-5 combinations, and what are the capacities associated for the RAID volumes and the shelf in that combination? Assuming we are not going to leave any drives unused, the three combinations are:

	Layout 1	*Layout 2*	*Layout 3*
Format	2+1	5+1	8+1
Means	2×4 TB for capacity, 1×4 TB for parity	5×4 TB for capacity, 1×4 TB for parity	8×4 TB for capacity, 1×4 TB for parity
Number of volumes	6	3	2
Usable size of each volume	8 TB	20 TB	32 TB
Usable size of shelf	6×8 TB=48 TB	3×20 TB=60 TB	2×32 TB=64 TB
Total overhead	24 TB	12 TB	8 TB

The overhead referred to in the table reflects the total amount of capacity *lost* to the RAID configuration. (The hot spares have not been counted toward that capacity as they sit outside any individual RAID configuration.)

Note that depending on the options within the array, a mix of different drive counts could be used. For example, with 18 drives, you could also configure a combination such as:

- 1 × 8 + 1 volume @ 36 TB usable
- 1 × 2 + 1 volume @ 8 TB usable
- 1 × 5 + 1 volume @ 20 TB usable
- Total 64 TB usable

B.19 Chapter 19: Tape

The reader was asked to consider what types of workloads might be best suited for tape in comparison to deduplication storage, and what alternatives could be used rather than tape, even when deduplication is not an ideal solution?

Generally, the types of workloads that are problematic for deduplication are pre-compressed, and pre-encrypted workloads.

Examples of workloads that fall into these categories include:

- Data which is encrypted by an accessing application rather than underlying storage (if encrypted by underlying storage, it's usually assumed that a backup agent reading the data will access the decrypted version of the data)
- Video and photographic data
- Medical imaging (CT scans, Ultrasounds, MRI scans, X-Rays, etc.)
- Geological imaging
- Archive files (zip, tar/gz, tar/bz2, etc.)

Additionally, archive data (e.g., single instance storage of emails or files from fileservers) will yield lower deduplication ratios because much of the redundant data has already been eliminated.

Some workloads may variably affect deduplication: for instance, Oracle databases support columnar compression—shrinking the database by compressing particular columns. If the DBAs are regularly adjusting which columns undergo this compression, it will likely negatively impact deduplication ratios.

One thing that is important to note is that if pre-encrypted or pre-compressed data is backed up to a deduplication appliance, there can still be storage efficiency so long as that data is static. Consider medical imaging: once an X-ray or MRI is taken, it should not ever change. So if it is stored on a fileserver and regularly backed up, then while the first backup will be stored with little efficiency (maybe even a 1:1 deduplication "ratio"), subsequent backups will yield real deduplication benefits.

If the desire is still to avoid tape even when workloads aren't optimal for deduplication, other storage scenarios can include tiered fileserver storage (e.g., writing to a filesystem which subsequently tiers out aged data to object storage), or slow object storage, if the backup access process supports that.

B.20 Chapter 20: Converged Infrastructure

No self-reflection questions were posed for Chapter 20.

B.21 Chapter 21: Data Protection Service Catalogs

Self-reflection for Chapter 21 invited the reader to consider how various systems they use on a daily basis might be standardized into a service catalog for data protection. Key areas of consideration will be:

- Establishing different service tiers based on the criticality of the workload or service
- Ensuring there is a mix of on-platform and off-platform protection
- Have tangible qualities which, when combined, make it a relatively unique service catalog item—aspects of the service catalog definition should be measurable, achievable, distinct, costed and priced, and repeatable as well as provide real utility

B.22 Chapter 22: Holistic Data Protection Strategies

The self-reflection question in this chapter asked about providing a holistic data protection strategy that enables daily protection of in-cloud databases, with monthly data copies stored on-premises for long-term retention.

This can be satisfied via two different techniques:

- IaaS:
  - If the databases are running in IaaS platforms, traditional agent-based backups can be used for both short-term (operational) backups, and long-term compliance retention.
  - Some cloud providers may also provide application-aware snapshot integration—for instance,

AWS snapshots for Windows instances can be integrated with Windows VSS.
■ PaaS:
  – When the database is subscribed to via a PaaS service, the process shifts—there are no agents to install. Day to day protection will usually require whatever the cloud service option is (e.g., database snapshots).
  – Longer-term retention becomes a more challenging topic if the database is to be copied to on-premises storage. Since it is not possible to install agents within a PaaS system, alternative processes are usually required. For instance: many PaaS databases include export/import utilities. These are not necessarily fast, but they do provide the means of egressing data from the PaaS platform. An export can be to a local IaaS compute instance, and that IaaS compute instance backed up and transferred (typically with deduplication to minimize data egress fees) to on-premises data protection storage. If the database is likely to get updates during the export process, additional steps might be inserted to first snapshot the database, do a snapshot recovery to another database in the PaaS service, then perform the export against an unused version of the database.

B.23 Chapter 23: Making Data Protection Smarter

No self-reflection questions were posed for Chapter 23.

B.24 Chapter 24: Data Recovery

The reader was asked to think of what sort of risks might be posed by *only* performing "thought exercises" for disaster recovery testing.

Some real-world examples of issues encountered by businesses that have relied solely on these exercises include:

1. *Failure to understand dependencies*: Over time systems can develop complex and sometimes subtle dependencies on one-another. If disaster recoveries aren't tested in real-world situations, dependencies may go unnoticed, resulting in issues in a real-world DR.
2. *Extrapolating the above issue, functions within datacenters change over time*: If a business is not careful, dependencies will build up *between* datacenters; a datacenter may change over time from being DR to being "DR/NonProd." The addition of standard operational workloads could change what resources are expected within the compute, network, and storage environments within the "DR" datacenter.

3. *Incorrect understanding of timings*: Even experienced infrastructure teams can make inaccurate assumptions about the amount of time specific operations will take to complete—particularly in a disaster when multiple services may be offline.
4. *Insufficient testing against processes*: The planned processes for disaster recovery may be incorrect—the processes may miss steps, get activities out of sequence, or have been developed on the *assumption* that other systems will be available.
5. *Inadequate consideration of "soft" issues*: What happens if senior infrastructure staff are unavailable? What happens if a specific process requires vendor engagement to restart or check a system, and that's outside of the formal support arrangement for that system? Will there be a manager available to approve service fees during a real DR?
6. What are the likely cascading issues that may be experienced? For example, what happens if half-way through an inter-site failover the network link experiences issues?

Thought experiments are a useful way to *plan* for DR exercises, but they should always be supplemented with and evaluated against actual DR exercises.

B.25 Chapter 25: Long-Term Retention

The reader was encouraged to think of software versions that were available/in use from "15 years ago." If we work backward from 2020:

■ Databases:
  – Oracle 10g R2 was released in 2005.
  – Microsoft SQL Server 2005 was released in 2005.
  – PostgreSQL version 8 was released in 2005.
■ Operating systems:
  – Windows 2003 was still the primary Windows server OS.
  – RedHat Linux v4 was introduced in 2005.
  – Mac OS X started the (public) transition from a PowerPC to Intel/X86 architecture in 2005.
■ Office applications:
  – Microsoft Word 2003.
  – Microsoft Excel 2003.
  – (The next version of Office would be 2007).
■ Video formats:
  – Adobe Flash still dominated much of the online streaming/interactive video environment.
  – HD-DVD* was not introduced to the consumer market until 2006.

---

* HD-DVD was abandoned in 2008, losing the high definition format war against BluRay.

VMware publishes an online PDF guide showing virtual machine guest compatibility. As of the time of writing, the 5 September 2019 version of the document could be located at:

> https://www.vmware.com/resources/compati bility/pdf/VMware_GOS_Compatibility_Guid e.pdf

While hypervisor environments will support operating systems as guests for an extended period of time—sometimes longer than new hardware can be obtained to run it natively on, reviewing the compatibility guide should demonstrate that even this has limits.

B.26 Chapter 26: Choosing Protection Infrastructure

The reader is encouraged to search the internet for examples of publicly accessible tenders relating to data protection, and compare (particularly for older tenders), the functionality requests against advancements in data protection.

Common areas to note in older tenders will be:

- A propensity to insist on tape for long-term retention
- Whether deduplication is mentioned at all
- Whether cloud is mentioned (either as a backup target, or something to be backed up)

Index